Practical Bankruptcy Law for Paralegals

THIRD EDITION

The West Legal Studies Series

Your options keep growing with West Legal Studies

Each year our list continues to offer you more options for every area of the law to meet your course or on-the-job reference requirements. We now have over 140 titles from which to choose in the following areas:

Accounting and Financials for the Law Office	Family Law
Administrative Law	Intellectual Property
Alternative Dispute Resolution	Interviewing and Investigation
Bankruptcy	Introduction to Law
Business Organizations/Corporations	Introduction to Paralegalism
Careers and Employment	Law Office Management
Civil Litigation and Procedure	Law Office Procedures
CLA Exam Preparation	Legal Nurse Consulting
Computer Applications in the Law Office	Legal Research, Writing, and Analysis
Contract Law	Legal Terminology
Court Reporting	Paralegal Internships
Criminal Law and Procedure	Product Liability
Document Preparation	Real Estate Law
Elder Law	Reference Materials
Employment Law	Social Security
Environmental Law	Sports Law
Ethics	Torts and Personal Injury Law
Evidence Law	Wills, Trusts, and Estate Administration

You will find unparalleled, practical support

Each book is augmented by instructor and student supplements to ensure the best learning experience possible. We also offer custom publishing and other benefits such as West's Student Achievement Award. In addition, our sales representatives are ready to provide you with dependable service.

We want to hear from you

Our best contributions for improving the quality of our books and instructional materials is feedback from the people who use them. If you have a question, concern, or observation about any of our materials, or you have a product proposal or manuscript, we want to hear from you. Please contact your local representative or write us at the following address:

West Legal Studies, 5 Maxwell Drive, Clifton Park, NY 12065-2919

For additional information point your browser at
www.westlegalstudies.com

THOMSON
—————✦—————™
DELMAR LEARNING

Practical Bankruptcy Law for Paralegals

THIRD EDITION

Pamela K. Webster
Partner, Buchalter, Nemer, Fields & Younger
Los Angeles, California

Richard E. Boyer, J.D.
Wayland Baptist University

David Lauren, M.Ed., J.D.
Hesser College;
New Hampshire Community Technical College

THOMSON

DELMAR LEARNING ™

Australia Canada Mexico Singapore Spain United Kingdom United States

THOMSON
DELMAR LEARNING

WEST LEGAL STUDIES
Practical Bankruptcy Law for Paralegals, Third Edition
by Pamela K. Webster, Richard E. Boyer, and David Lauren

Vice President, Career Education Strategic Business Unit:
Dawn Gerrain

Director of Editorial:
Sherry Gomoll

Acquisitions Editor:
Pamela Fuller

Senior Developmental Editor:
Melissa Riveglia

Editorial Assistant:
Sarah Duncan

Director of Production:
Wendy A. Troeger

Production Manager:
Carolyn Miller

Production Editor:
Matthew J. Williams

Director of Marketing:
Donna J. Lewis

Channel Manager:
Wendy E. Mapstone

Cover Image:
Photodisc

For permission to use material from this text or product, contact us by
Tel   (800) 730-2214
Fax   (800) 730-2215

www.thomsonrights.com

Library of Congress Cataloging-in-Publication Data

Webster, Pamela Kohlman.
  Practical bankruptcy law for paralegals / Pamela K. Webster, Richard E. Boyer, David Lauren.—3rd ed.
    p. cm.
  Includes bibliographical references and index.
  ISBN 0-7668-2856-5
  1. Bankruptcy—United States. I. Boyer, Richard E., J.D.
  II. Lauren, David. III. Title.
  KF1524.W35 2003
  346.7307'8—dc21

NOTICE TO THE READER

Publisher does not warrant or guarantee any of the products described herein or perform any independent analysis in connection with any of the product information contained herein. Publisher does not assume, and expressly disclaims, any obligation to obtain and include information other than that provided to it by the manufacturer.

The reader is notified that this text is an educational tool, not a practice book. Since the law is in constant change, no rule or statement of law in this book should be relied upon for any service to any client. The reader should always refer to standard legal sources for the current rule or law. If legal advice or other expert assistance is required, the services of the appropriate professional should be sought.

The Publisher makes no representation or warranties of any kind, including but not limited to, the warranties of fitness for particular purpose or merchantability, nor are any such representations implied with respect to the material set forth herein, and the publisher takes no responsibility with respect to such material. The publisher shall not be liable for any special, consequential, or exemplary damages resulting, in whole or part, from the readers' use of, or reliance upon, this material.

Contents in Brief

Contents

Preface

BANKRUPTCY IS BIG business in America. Bankruptcy debtors come from every strata of society from unemployed workers and improvident credit card holders to celebrities such as Kim Basinger. Huge multinational corporations such as Enron and MCI/WorldCom as well as thousands of small businesses have sought protection in the bankruptcy courts from their creditors. High-profile bankruptcies such as United Airlines and U.S. Airways are constantly in the news. The number of bankruptcy cases has staggered the bankruptcy courts and often threatens to overwhelm them.

Responding to the deluge of bankruptcy cases, law firms added new bankruptcy lawyers and paralegals to their insolvency departments, and experienced attorneys formed small "boutique" firms specializing in bankruptcy law.

Bankruptcy practice is highly procedural and involves an enormous amount of paperwork for which there is not always enough trained personnel. Many bankruptcy lawyers have far more cases than they can comfortably handle. Further, attorneys' fees in bankruptcy cases are reviewed by the court. Bankruptcy judges today are critical of bills submitted by attorneys for services that can be provided competently by nonlawyers at lower hourly rates. Thus, bankruptcy has become an area of law practice where the need for trained paralegals is critical. Paralegal use is vital in bankruptcy practice to ensure that the many administrative and procedural tasks crucial to the success of a case are completed in a timely and competent manner, and at reasonable rates.

Bankruptcy is a difficult practice to master on the job. It is a convoluted system of federal substantive and procedural law. Hence, a course on the fundamentals of bankruptcy law is a critical first step to the successful practice of bankruptcy law.

This textbook follows a six-level approach to teaching bankruptcy law and procedure for paralegals. First, the student is provided with an overview of the substantive law of bankruptcy. Second, students are provided with some insights as to why the substantive law provides as it does. Third, the book discusses the written and unwritten rules of procedure that guide and often control how the substantive law of bankruptcy is implemented. Fourth, the student is guided through the procedural labyrinth of bankruptcy practice with checklists and analysis aids. Fifth, the student is given hands-on experience in performing bankruptcy tasks that are common in actual practice. Finally, ethical considerations are raised in each chapter.

At the end of each chapter, students are given questions to answer, and research or drafting projects are recommended to reinforce the text discussions. Some of the exercises are quite simple, while others are fairly difficult. Most ask for the application of a statute or procedural rule. Some require the student to contemplate the policy behind a bankruptcy law. Examples of pleadings and other forms are provided in many chapters. Since aspects of bankruptcy practice and procedure differ from court to court, the forms should not be used by the practicing paralegal without first verifying that they meet the formal requirements of local practice. Further, the forms are not always complete for a particular procedure. In many cases, they need to be accompanied by supporting affidavits or declarations and briefs or memoranda of law.

Students tend to come to a course on bankruptcy practice with different levels of knowledge and experience of the subject, and the needs of all of the students must be reasonably met. Hence, this book covers all the basic, underlying concepts of bankruptcy law and the procedural rules governing bankruptcy cases. Each topic is fully developed to the extent necessary for effective use by a beginning paralegal, yet the discussions are of sufficient sophistication to keep the attention of an experienced one. This text also includes treatment of tasks that are typically performed by experienced paralegals and can be used in practice as a continuing reference source.

CHANGES TO THIS EDITION

Not only is the third edition of *Practical Bankruptcy Law for Paralegals* an updated version of the original text; it is also more student and instructor friendly. In revising the text, comments were sought from instructors who have used the text and practicing lawyers and paralegals who appreciate what a student needs to know in order to succeed. These comments were incorporated into the new edition. In addition, chapters were revised and sample forms were updated.

Some of the other more significant changes are:

✦ The text was modified to reflect the many changes to the Bankruptcy Code, the Bankruptcy Rules, and the Official Forms since the second edition was prepared.
✦ A new chapter on electronic filing was added.
✦ A new Ethical Considerations section was added to each chapter.

The Bankruptcy Code and the Federal Rules of Bankruptcy Procedure are not included in this edition. Instead, we suggest the student access the Bankruptcy Code at http://www.access/gpo.gov/uscode/uscmain.html. From here, click on either Title 11 (Bankruptcy Code) or Title 11-A (Appendix—this includes the Bankruptcy Rules).

Supplemental Teaching Materials

✦ The **Instructor's Manual** is available both in print and online at www.westlegalstudies.com in the Instructor's Lounge under Resource. Written by the author of the text, the *Instructor's Manual* contains the following:
  —Lecture outlines
  —Answers to assignments
  —Suggested test questions
✦ **Web Page**—Come visit our website at www.westlegalstudies.com, where you will find valuable information such as hot links and sample materials to download, as well as other West Legal Studies products.
✦ **WESTLAW®**—West's online computerized legal research system offers students "hands-on" experience with a system commonly used in law offices. Qualified adopters can receive 10 free hours of WESTLAW. WESTLAW can be accessed with Macintosh and PCs running Windows. A modem is required.
✦ **Strategies and Tips for Paralegal Educators,** a pamphlet by Anita Tebbe of Johnson County Community College, provides teaching strategies specifically designed for paralegal educators. A copy of this pamphlet is available to each adopter. Quantities for distribution to adjunct instructors are available for purchase at a minimal price. A coupon on the pamphlet provides ordering information.
✦ **Survival Guide for Paralegal Students,** a pamphlet by Kathleen Mercer Reed and Bradene Moore, covers practical and basic information to help

students make the most of their paralegal courses. Topics covered include choosing courses of study and learning note-taking skills.

✦ **West's Paralegal Video Library**—West Legal Studies is pleased to offer the following videos at no charge to qualified adopters:
- *The Drama of the Law II: Paralegal Issues Video*
  ISBN: 0-314-07088-5
- *"I Never Said I Was a Lawyer" Paralegal Ethics Video*
  ISBN: 0-314-08049-x
- *The Making of a Case Video*
  ISBN: 0-314-07300-0
- *ABA Mock Trial Video-Anatomy of a Trial: A Contracts Case*
  ISBN: 0-314-07343-4
- *ABA Mock Trial Video-Product Liability*
  ISBN: 0-314-07342-6
- *Arguments to the United States Supreme Court Video*
  ISBN: 0-314-07070-2

✦ **Court TV Videos**—West Legal Studies is pleased to offer the following videos from Court TV for a minimal fee:
- *New York v. Ferguson—Murder on the 5:33: The Trial of Colin Ferguson*
  ISBN: 0-7668-1098-4
- *Ohio v. Alfieri*
  ISBN: 0-7668-1099-2
- *Flynn v. Goldman Sachs—Fired on Wall Street: A Case of Sex Discrimination?*
  ISBN: 0-7668-1096-8
- *Dodd v. Dodd—Religion and Child Custody in Conflict*
  ISBN: 0-7668-1094-1
- *In Re Custody of Baby Girl Clausen—Child of Mine: The Fight for Baby Jessica*
  ISBN: 0-7668-1097-6
- *Fentress v. Eli Lilly & Co., et al—Prozac on Trial*
  ISBN: 0-7668-1095-x
- *Garcia v. Garcia—Fighting over Jerry's Money*
  ISBN: 0-7668-0264-7
- *Hall v. Hall—Irretrievably Broken—A Divorce Lawyer Goes to Court*
  ISBN: 0-7668-0196-9
- *Maglica v. Maglica—Broken Hearts, Broken Commitments*
  ISBN: 0-7668-0867-x
- *Northside Partners v. Page and New Kids on the Block—New Kids in Court: Is Their Hit Song a Copy?*
  ISBN: 0-7668-9426-7

Please note the internet resources are of a time-sensitive nature, and URL addresses may often change or be deleted.

Contact us at westlegalstudies@delmar.com

ACKNOWLEDGMENTS

Richard E. Boyer and David Lauren, the editors and authors of the revised third edition, would like to thank their families for their understanding and support during the long process of revising the text—in particular, Kathy and our parents. Thanks also go to Karen Cordry, Bankruptcy Counsel of the National Association of Attorneys General, for her advice and willingness to be a resource, and to Kerri M. Kolaities of the Bankruptcy Court, District of New Hampshire. Thanks also to Wayland-Baptist University and Cochise College of Sierra Vista, Arizona, and Hesser College and the New Hampshire Community Technical College of Nashua, New Hampshire, for their support.

Pamela Webster, the original author of the text, thanks John D. Ayer, Frederick Hart, and Theodore Graham, as well as Stephen F. Biegenzahn and all her colleagues and family.

Thanks also go to everyone at West Legal Studies, and in particular Pamela Fuller, Melissa Riveglia, Alexis Ferraro, and Joan Gill. We also want to thank copyeditor Karen Lamoreux for her thoughtful suggestions, and Alex Bilsky.

Finally, thanks are extended to the following reviewers for their contributions to this book:

Michele G. Bradford
Gadsden State Community College
Gadsden, AL

Susan L. Lowe
Myers University
Cleveland, OH

Bob Diotalevi
Florida Gulf Coast University
Fort Myers, FL

Dan Ray
Eastern Michigan University
Ypsilanti, MI

Leslie Sturdivant Ennis
Samford University
Trussville, AL

Barbara Ricker
Andover College
Portland, ME

John Frank
Chippewa Valley Technical College
Eau Claire, WI

Fran Russell
Coastline Community College
Fountain Valley, CA

Jim Hodge
International College
Naples, FL

Paula Sinopoli
Mississippi Gulf Coast Community
College
Gulfport, MS

Jane Kaplan
NYC Technical College
Brooklyn, NY

Judith Sturgill
North Central State College
Mansfield, OH

Cassy Kent
Finger Lakes Community College
Canandaigua, NY

Linda Wimberly
Eastern Kentucky University
Richmond, KY

Penny Lorenzo
Rhodes College
Phoenix, AZ

Introduction

AN OVERVIEW OF BANKRUPTCY

Bankruptcy is society's way of responding to the situations that have made it difficult, if not impossible, for some people who owe money to pay their debts. Bankruptcy law is primarily an application of the basic notions of fairness and common sense.

In the United States, this system is embodied in the federal **Bankruptcy Code,** which attempts to balance two laudable goals: providing relief to debtors from over-burdensome debts, and thus providing them with a "fresh start," and at the same time assuring creditors equitable and fair payment from the debtor's assets. The Bankruptcy Code is found in Title 11 of the United States Code. There are also a few sections in Title 18 (Crimes) that define bankruptcy crimes and in Title 28 (Federal Courts) that regulate procedural matters.

The Bankruptcy Code provides two types of relief: **liquidation** and **reorganization.** In a liquidation, the debtor's property is turned over to a trustee who sells it and distributes the proceeds to the creditors. In a reorganization, the debtor attempts to reorganize its business and reach a mutually acceptable agreement with its creditors for the payment of the debts.

Bankruptcy relief, whether it be liquidation or reorganization, can only be attained through the **bankruptcy courts,** which are specialized federal courts established under the Bankruptcy Code that have exclusive jurisdiction over bankruptcy cases.

To start a bankruptcy case, a debtor, who may be an individual or a business entity such as a partnership or a corporation, files a **petition** with the bankruptcy court. The filing of the petition with the bankruptcy court commences the bankruptcy case in much the same way that a complaint filed in court commences a lawsuit. If the petition is in proper form, the clerk of the bankruptcy court will accept it and assign it a docket number that must appear on all other court papers that are filed in the case. A bankruptcy case is not an adversarial proceeding, however, and there are no plaintiffs or defendants. The case is not titled in the name of the debtor versus the creditors. The debtor is known as the **petitioner,** and the case is titled merely "In re" or "In the matter of" followed by the petitioner's name.

The Bankruptcy Code is divided into chapters. Chapter 7 of the Bankruptcy Code contains the laws for a liquidation type of bankruptcy. This type of bankruptcy is sometimes referred to as "a Chapter 7 case." It provides the kind of remedy most people think of when they hear the word "bankruptcy."

✦ **bankruptcy**
An organized system for creditor payment from a debtor's nonexempt assets.

✦ **Bankruptcy Code**
The bankruptcy law enacted by Congress that became effective on October 1, 1978, as it has been subsequently amended, and that is found primarily in Title 11 of the United States Code.

✦ **liquidation**
A form of bankruptcy in which the debtor's nonexempt property is sold or otherwise disposed of and the proceeds are distributed to creditors.

✦ **reorganization**
A form of bankruptcy in which the debtor's business is preserved and its creditors are paid from the business' earnings.

✦ **bankruptcy courts**
The branch of the federal judicial system that presides over bankruptcy cases and proceedings. Bankruptcy courts are units of the district court.

✦ **petition**
The paper filed with the bankruptcy court that commences a bankruptcy case.

✦ **petitioner**
Another name for the debtor in a voluntary case.

✦ **trustee**
A person appointed to administer the bankruptcy estate. The nature and extent of a trustee's duties differ among Chapters 7, 11, 12, and 13 of the Bankruptcy Code.

✦ **exempt property**
The property that a debtor is allowed to keep and not make subject to creditors' claims.

In a Chapter 7 liquidation, all of the debtor's property is turned over to the **trustee,** who is a neutral third party appointed by the court to sell the property. The trustee will not, however, sell all of the debtor's property. Congress has decided that debtors should keep some of their property so that they can live in a decent fashion. The property that debtors may keep is called **exempt property.** Exempt property includes such things as household goods and clothes, usually a car, and sometimes a house. All other property is sold by the trustee and the proceeds are divided among the creditors. The creditors are rarely paid in full. Creditors typically receive only a small percentage of their claims but may not collect the balance from the debtor. Upon the conclusion of a Chapter 7 case, the debtor obtains a discharge of the unpaid debts so he or she can make a fresh start.

The other type of relief provided by the Bankruptcy Code is a reorganization. In this type of bankruptcy, the creditors are prevented from enforcing their claims against the petitioner while its business or financial affairs are reorganized in the hope that it eventually will be able to pay its debts. The creditors do not always receive full payment of their claims in a reorganization, but they generally recover more of their debt than they would if the petitioner had filed a Chapter 7 bankruptcy.

There are four different types of reorganizations in the Bankruptcy Code, each of which has its own chapter. Chapter 11, which is the best known, is used primarily by businesses, but it may also be used by individuals. Chapter 13 is only for individuals who have a regular source of income and relatively low levels of debt. Chapter 12 is for farmers who may not qualify for Chapter 13 because their incomes are not regular enough or the amount of debt is too high. Finally, Chapter 9 allows for the reorganization of municipalities such as cities, towns, and special districts. Falling revenues, unwise investments, or large personal injury judgments sometimes force these governmental entities into bankruptcy just as they might affect businesses and individuals.

Although the four types of reorganization in the Bankruptcy Code are different in many respects, there are many similarities among them. For example, the debtor may keep all of its property while it tries to reorganize. While the reorganization takes place, the petitioner will, however, be under much greater scrutiny from the bankruptcy court and the creditors. In order to get out of bankruptcy, the petitioner will need to pay creditors more of their claims than the creditors would be paid in a liquidation.

THE HISTORY OF BANKRUPTCY

Bankruptcy is not a recent phenomenon. Ever since people began borrowing goods from one another, there has been a need for debt relief. Societies have usually provided for such debt relief. Indeed, in the time of the Old Testament, debts were discharged in the Jubilee year. Debts were not always simply forgiven, however; sometimes terrible punishment was exacted of the debtor before any relief was available. For example, in ancient Greece and Rome, a bankrupt debtor would be sold into slavery or imprisoned. Harsh as this remedy was, it was better than the alternatives in other societies, which were mutilation and death. Later, Rome developed a more humane system called *cessio bonorum,* which was a procedure not unlike modern bankruptcy: The debtor ceded all of his or her assets for distribution to creditors. Imprisonment for nonpayment of debt returned in the Dark Ages, however.

The word "bankruptcy" is said to be derived from the Italian phrase *banca rotta,* or "broken bench." In fourteenth century Italy, the merchants lined the streets and plazas with their work benches when they performed their crafts. A merchant unable to pay his debts lost his trading place and his bench was smashed by his creditors as a sign to all that the craftsman had become insolvent.

In England, the emphasis also was on punishment. From the thirteenth century, when the first English bankruptcy statute was passed, to beyond the time of Dickens, debt relief was accompanied by confinement in the poorhouse or a debtor's prison, or by involuntary servitude. Many areas of Australia and the original colonies of America were settled by debtors forced out of England. These cruel bankruptcy systems hardly allowed for the rehabilitation of the debtor and almost certainly prevented the creditors from being paid.

Bankruptcy Law in the United States

Introduction Prior to the adoption of the Constitution, several states had bankruptcy laws that were similar to those in Britain and France, with punishment rather than rehabilitation of the debtor as a goal. The Constitution gave Congress the power to write the bankruptcy laws for the United States, but congressional attempts to enact bankruptcy legislation were sporadic and ineffective for over 100 years after the ratification of the Constitution.

The first American bankruptcy statute was the Bankruptcy Act of 1800, but it was not very comprehensive. It dealt almost exclusively with merchants and bankers who were forced into bankruptcy by their creditors. Its aim was to protect creditors rather than to provide any sort of relief for debtors. The law created the office of a commissioner to exercise power over a debtor's estate. The commissioner is the predecessor to the bankruptcy trustee and the bankruptcy judge today. The statute was repealed by Congress in 1803.

Another short-lived bankruptcy statute was passed by Congress in 1841. This legislation gave the district courts exclusive jurisdiction over bankruptcy matters. It also gave the district courts the right to appoint a person called an assignee who had power over the debtor and the right to sell the debtor's property to pay creditors. This law was repealed in 1843, but it was followed in 1867 by an act that gave the district court the power to appoint "registrars" to assist it in the administration of the bankruptcy estate. This act was repealed in 1878.

The Bankruptcy Act of 1898 Finally, Congress passed the **Bankruptcy Act of 1898.** It is usually referred to as the "Bankruptcy Act" or simply the "Act." Many provisions of today's Bankruptcy Code are carried over from the Bankruptcy Act. The Bankruptcy Act allowed for two methods to start a bankruptcy case.

✦ Bankruptcy Act of 1898
The bankruptcy law enacted by Congress in 1898 that was substantially amended in 1938 and repealed in 1978.

1. Voluntarily—in which the debtor begins the bankruptcy case.
2. Involuntarily—in which the creditors commence the proceedings and force the debtor to come into the bankruptcy court.

The Bankruptcy Act also created a comprehensive system for liquidations and reorganizations regardless of whether the bankruptcy case was begun voluntarily or involuntarily. Although the Act was extensively modified in 1938 by the Chandler Act, it continued in existence as the controlling bankruptcy law until 1978, when it was replaced by the Bankruptcy Code.

The Bankruptcy Act called for a bankruptcy referee and a bankruptcy trustee. The trustee was responsible for liquidating or reorganizing debtors. The bankruptcy referee served a dual function under the Act. The bankruptcy referee was given a number of administrative functions that involved the referee in many aspects of the day-to-day operation of the debtor's business until its liquidation or reorganization. At the same time, the referee served as an impartial dispute resolver of those matters impacting the estate. This dual role led to charges of conflict of interest. Further, as the number of bankruptcy filings increased, the burden of administration on the referees became greater and greater.

There were also other problems with the Act. Despite its amendments, the language of the Act was archaic and its provisions were poorly organized. Time exacted its toll; some of the Act became dated because of growth in the economy, and the courts had to interpret and reinterpret other parts frequently to make the Act work efficiently.

The Bankruptcy Reform Act of 1978   In response to growing criticism of the Bankruptcy Act, the Senate Committee on the Judiciary began holding hearings on bankruptcy reform legislation in 1968. In 1970, Congress established a commission made up of practitioners, judges, academicians, and legislators to study and recommend changes in the Act. The commission issued its report in 1973 and proposed new legislation to implement its recommendations, which included a proposal separating the judicial and administrative functions of bankruptcy proceedings and establishing the bankruptcy court. The proposed new legislation was introduced in the same year. Additional legislation was introduced in 1975; it had been proposed by the National Bankruptcy Conference, an organization also made up of prominent persons in the bankruptcy field. Lengthy hearings in the House and Senate were held on both pieces of legislation through the mid-1970s, and what finally emerged from all the congressional wrangling on bankruptcy laws was a compromise that became the Bankruptcy Reform Act of 1978.

The Bankruptcy Reform Act of 1978, usually referred to as the Bankruptcy Code, was more than just a revision of the Bankruptcy Act of 1898. It enacted a total change in the administration of bankruptcy cases. The bankruptcy courts were given expansive jurisdictional powers to determine any dispute involving the debtor as well as authorize acts of the trustee or the debtor.

Although the Code preserved many of the bankruptcy protections that arose under the Act, sometimes they were to be applied differently under the Code. For example, under the Act, there was no **automatic stay** protecting the debtor from enforcement of the creditor's claims. Originally, if the trustee needed to bar creditors from enforcing their claims against the estate, an injunction had to be obtained from the court. The Bankruptcy Code not only provides for such a stay, it is automatic. The instant a bankruptcy petition is filed, all of the debtor's creditors are enjoined from further enforcement of their claims or attempts to take the debtor's property.

Shortly after it was enacted, the Bankruptcy Code's grant of sweeping jurisdiction to the bankruptcy court was criticized. Some of the criticism was based on the Constitution's systems of checks and balances of power between the executive, judicial, and legislative branches of government. Under this system, federal district court judges were given the power to invalidate congressional and presidential acts, but they were protected from retaliation by lifetime appointments to the bench and a prohibition against having their salaries reduced. Bankruptcy court judges were given power in bankruptcy cases comparable to that of district court judges, but they were appointed to 14-year terms and they could have their salaries reduced by congressional action. This problem could only be resolved by cutting back on the power of the bankruptcy court or by granting bankruptcy judges the same privileges as those bestowed on judges of the federal district courts. Neither solution was popular.

Northern Pipeline v. Marathon Oil   It did not take long for a constitutional challenge to the Bankruptcy Code to reach the Supreme Court of the United States. In mid-1982, in the case of *Northern Pipeline Construction Company v. Marathon Oil Company*, the Court ruled that it was unconstitutional for bankruptcy judges to have such broad powers. In an unusual step, however, the Court delayed the effect of its ruling to give Congress a chance to cure the constitutional

✦ **automatic stay**
The injunction that becomes effective upon the filing of a bankruptcy petition (whether voluntarily or involuntarily) and that prevents virtually all actions by creditors to collect their claims, enforce their liens, or exercise control over the debtor's property.

defects. Because of intense lobbying on each side of the issue, Congress could not decide whether the bankruptcy court's power should be limited or whether the bankruptcy court judges should be given lifetime appointments. In 1983, the Supreme Court lost patience with Congress and refused to delay the effective date of its decision any further. Many had predicted that chaos in the bankruptcy system would result. But the courts of appeals responded to the emergency by passing resolutions in each of their circuits that established a system that allowed the bankruptcy courts to continue operating.

The emergency system divided all bankruptcy matters into two categories.

1. **Core matters** were matters that existed only in bankruptcy, such as approving reorganization plans.
2. **Related matters** were matters that could have been decided in other courts but had come under the jurisdiction of the bankruptcy courts because one of the parties had filed a bankruptcy petition. An example of a related matter is a breach of contract claim. Ordinarily, such a claim would be settled in a state or federal trial court; however, if the debtor was in bankruptcy, the claim would have to be tried in the bankruptcy court.

✦ **core matters**
Those matters directly tied to a bankruptcy case and arising under the Bankruptcy Code.

✦ **related matters**
Disputes that would have existed between parties even if one of them was not in a bankruptcy case.

Under the emergency system, the bankruptcy court could hear and determine all core matters. For a related matter, the bankruptcy court could make a binding ruling only if the parties consented. Otherwise, the bankruptcy court would just issue a proposed ruling and send it to the district court where a final determination could be made. While this system was not perfect, it allowed bankruptcy cases to be administered until Congress tried to resolve the conflicting positions over how much judicial power the bankruptcy courts should have.

The 1984 Amendments Finally, in 1984, Congress passed certain amendments to the Bankruptcy Code contained in the Bankruptcy Amendments and Federal Judgeship Act, which are together usually referred to as "BAFJA" or the "1984 Amendments." In the 1984 Amendments, Congress tried to cure the constitutional problem in the Bankruptcy Code by reducing the power of the bankruptcy court rather than giving its judges a lifetime tenure. The amendments established a system similar to that put into place by the courts of appeals in 1983, though far more complicated. It is discussed at some length in Chapter 6 of this book.

While Congress was trying to solve the constitutional dilemma of the Bankruptcy Code, a number of special interest groups took advantage of the delay and lobbied for other changes in the law. As a result, the 1984 Amendments also made a number of substantive changes in the Bankruptcy Code. Among other things, the amendments improved the treatment of real property landlords and institutions who lend money to consumers, made certain prebankruptcy transfers more difficult to unwind, and changed the way that collective bargaining agreements between a debtor and a union were treated in bankruptcy.

The 1986 Amendments Two years after the 1984 Amendments, Congress passed the Bankruptcy Judges, United States Trustees, and Family Farmer Bankruptcy Act of 1986, which is commonly referred to as the "1986 Amendments." This act authorized the appointment of 52 new bankruptcy judges in an effort to reduce the pressure on an overburdened bankruptcy court, which had seen a dramatic increase in filings of bankruptcy petitions since the adoption of the Bankruptcy Code. The 1986 Amendments also made a number of changes in the Bankruptcy Code, including the creation of Chapter 12 that provided reorganizations for family farmers. The most significant amendment, however, was one that institutionalized the office of the **United States trustee.**

✦ **United States trustee**
Charged with monitoring and overseeing the administration of bankruptcy cases.

The United States trustee   During the drafting of the Bankruptcy Reform Act of 1978, Congress sought to eliminate the conflict that plagued the referee system and remove bankruptcy court judges from the day-to-day administration of bankruptcy cases. The result of this congressional study was Chapter 15 of the Bankruptcy Code (which was subsequently removed in the 1986 Amendments and its provisions folded into the other chapters of the Bankruptcy Code). Chapter 15 established the office of the United States trustee as a five-year experimental program operated by the Department of Justice. Chapter 15 gave nonjudicial governmental personnel the responsibility of overseeing and coordinating many of the administrative functions that had been performed by the bankruptcy court. The program was established in 18 districts, including some of the largest and most active districts as well as some of the smaller and less active ones.

The *United States trustee* is a division within the Department of Justice charged with monitoring and overseeing the administration of bankruptcy cases. The division is composed of 21 regions, each with its own United States trustee, appointed by the United States Attorney General. The duties of the United States trustee are set out in Section 586 of Title 28 of the United States Code and include:

1. Establish, maintain, and supervise a panel of private Chapter 7 trustees.
2. Establish, maintain, and supervise a panel of private Chapter 11 trustees.
3. Supervise the administration of cases and trustees in all bankruptcy cases.
4. Deposit and invest money received in Chapter 11 cases.

Also, the United States trustees have the additional and more specific responsibilities as set out in Chapters 7, 9, 11, 12, and 13 of the Bankruptcy Code. In the large reorganizations, the United States trustee monitors the progress of the entire case by supervising the debtor, ensuring that taxes are paid and that appropriate financial reports are filed, organizing a committee of creditors to oversee the debtor's reorganization efforts, and reviewing reorganization plans to ensure that they meet the requirements of the Bankruptcy Code. The only thing that the United States trustee cannot do is to propose a plan of reorganization. The United States trustee also works with law enforcement officials in the detection and prosecution of white-collar crimes related to bankruptcy such as embezzlement, fraud, and concealment of assets.

The 1994 Amendments   In October of 1994, Congress made the most sweeping changes to the Bankruptcy Code yet in the Bankruptcy Reform Act of 1994. The 1994 Amendments made changes in bankruptcy administration, commercial bankruptcy issues, the treatment of consumer debtors and their creditors, and the eligibility of governmental entities to file a bankruptcy case. The 1994 Amendments also have provisions to reduce the number of fraudulent bankruptcy filings by making criminal the improper activities of "bankruptcy petition preparers." These provisions of the amendments will be investigated in Chapter 3 of this book—"The Role of the Paralegal in Bankruptcy Practice."

Finally, the 1994 Amendments establish the National Bankruptcy Review Commission. The purpose of the commission is to study issues and problems related to the Bankruptcy Code. The commission is composed of nine members. Three are appointed by the President, one by the president *pro tempore* of the Senate, one each by the minority leader of the Senate and the House of Representatives, and two by the Chief Justice of the Supreme Court. Distinguished academicians, practitioners, and former legislators or their aides have been appointed.

Additional Amendments   Congress has frequently made additional amendments to the Bankruptcy Code. For example, in 1988, Congress changed the treatment of license agreements for intellectual property, medical benefits for retirees, and eligibility to file a Chapter 9 case. Undoubtedly, further changes will be made to the substantive provisions of the Bankruptcy Code once the Commission has completed its work. Paperback copies of the Bankruptcy Code are published each year by several legal publishers. The lawyer and the paralegal should have the current edition because each session of Congress usually makes changes to the Bankruptcy Code.

ETHICAL CONSIDERATIONS

Ethical considerations have the same significance to the paralegal working as a bankruptcy specialist as they do in all other areas of the law. For example, conflicts are common in bankruptcy cases because they involve so many different parties, each of whom may have competing interests in the debtor's estate. The rules of ethics governing resolution of conflict issues for lawyers are equally applicable to paralegals.

Some of these ethical considerations are found in the Bankruptcy Code and the Bankruptcy Rules. For example, the Bankruptcy Code prohibits fee splitting among attorneys, trustees, and other professionals. This rule does not prevent an attorney from hiring paralegals as employees of a law firm and including compensation for their professional services in an application for approval of fees from the bankruptcy court. This rule does prevent a bankruptcy attorney from associating a freelance paralegal to work in a bankruptcy case and applying for fees to cover the services of the attorney and the paralegal. A paralegal who is not an employee of an attorney or a law firm and who performs services in the bankruptcy case must be employed pursuant to a bankruptcy court order and must file a separate fee application.

SUMMARY

Bankruptcy is a system of federal laws that allows a person who owes money to settle the debts with the creditors. The Constitution of the United States gives Congress the power to make bankruptcy laws, which it has done in a series of bills beginning in 1800. The current bankruptcy law is found in the Bankruptcy Code, Title 11 of the United States Code, which:

1. Establishes specialized courts, called bankruptcy courts.
2. Recognizes the primary parties in bankruptcy proceedings, including debtors, creditors, a bankruptcy trustee, and the United States Trustee.
3. Provides two ways of settling debts, liquidation, and reorganization.

✦ KEY TERMS

automatic stay	bankruptcy courts	petition	trustee
bankruptcy	core matters	petitioner	United States trustee
Bankruptcy Act of 1898	exempt property	related matters	
Bankruptcy Code	liquidation	reorganization	

✦ IMPROVE YOUR UNDERSTANDING

1. List and describe each of the chapters of the Bankruptcy Code.
2. Describe the difference(s) between liquidation and reorganization under the Bankruptcy Code.
3. Describe what is meant by the term automatic stay and how it works in bankruptcy.
4. Describe what is meant by the term core matter.
5. Describe each of the following parties and their role in bankruptcy:
   a. debtor
   b. petitioner
   c. creditor
   d. United States trustee
   e. trustee

The Bankruptcy Code and the Bankruptcy Rules

SUMMARY OF THE BANKRUPTCY CODE

The Format

The Bankruptcy Code is divided into Chapters 1, 3, 5, 7, 9, 11, 12, and 13. All of the chapter designations are odd numbers except for Chapter 12. Each chapter (except Chapter 1) is divided into subchapters that are indicated by Roman numerals. Each subchapter (and Chapter 1) is broken into sections. The first one or two digits of a section number indicate the chapter in which the section appears. For example, Section 701 is in Chapter 7 and Section 1104 is in Chapter 11.

Chapters 1, 3, and 5 contain general provisions and are used in all bankruptcy cases. For example, Section 362 applies in Chapter 7, 9, 11, 12, and 13 cases. These general chapters are followed by the one liquidation chapter (Chapter 7) and the four reorganization chapters (Chapters 9, 11, 12, and 13).

The General Provisions—Chapter 1

Chapter 1 is broadly entitled General Provisions and contains nine sections. Chapter 1, like Chapters 3 and 5, applies in every bankruptcy case. The sections of this chapter are very important in understanding how a bankruptcy case works, since they are the foundation upon which the other chapters are built.

Section 101 contains most of the definitions of words and phrases used throughout the Bankruptcy Code. Some of the definitions merely articulate the popular understanding of a term, but other definitions of apparently common terms are very cleverly written. For example, in Section 101, there is an important distinction between the definitions of "entity" and "person." When Congress wanted governmental units to be included within the scope of a provision, it used **entity,** which was defined to include them. When Congress wanted to exclude government units from the scope of a provision, it used the term **person.** An example of this is found in Section 1102(b)(1), which concerns who may sit on a creditors' committee in a Chapter 11 case.

Other definitions found in Section 101 are important in order to understand the language of the substantive sections of the Bankruptcy Code. For example, the word **claim** is broadly defined to include virtually every possible type of right of payment or right to a remedy. The automatic stay that comes into effect on the commencement of a bankruptcy case applies to any act to collect, assess, or recover a claim. By defining "claim" broadly, Congress made the scope of the automatic stay very broad.

✦ **entity**
A person, estate, trust, governmental unit, or the United States trustee.

✦ **person**
An individual, partnership, or corporation, but not a governmental unit unless it is acting as a receiver or liquidating agent of a person.

✦ **claim**
A right to payment from the debtor, whether or not such right is liquidated, contingent, disputed, or secured.

Section 102 contains special rules of construction for interpreting the Bankruptcy Code. Of these, the explanation of the phrase "after notice and a hearing," which is repeated frequently throughout the Bankruptcy Code, is the most significant. It provides that "after notice and a hearing" or a similar phrase

(A) means after such notice as is appropriate in the particular circumstances, and such opportunity for a hearing as is appropriate in the particular circumstances; but

(B) authorizes an act without an actual hearing if such notice is given properly and if

    (i) such a hearing is not requested timely by a party in interest; or

    (ii) there is insufficient time for a hearing to be commenced before such act must be done, and the court authorizes such act[.]

Therefore, "after notice and a hearing" may mean very limited notice and no hearing at all; it all depends on the circumstances. For example, Section 363 of the Bankruptcy Code allows a trustee to sell the debtor's property "after notice and a hearing." In many instances, the trustee will simply send a notice to the creditors that certain property of the debtor will be sold; and if no creditor objects, the court is deemed to have approved the sale although no hearing was actually conducted. This rule of construction allows for the flexibility needed to administer a bankruptcy case effectively and results in substantial savings of time and money by reducing the amount of time the debtor, the trustee, the creditors, and all of their lawyers spend in court.

Another important provision is Section 109, which establishes the preliminary criteria to file a bankruptcy case and the eligibility for each particular chapter. Section 109 will be examined in detail in Chapter 7 of this book. For now, it is only important to realize that bankruptcy relief is not available to all who want it.

Case Administration—Chapter 3

Chapter 3, entitled Case Administration, has a wealth of information in its 34 sections, including how bankruptcy cases are commenced and how they are administered. Chapter 3 is divided into four subchapters: Commencement of a Case, Officers, Administration, and Administrative Powers.

Commencement of a Case—Sections 301–307 The first subchapter of Chapter 3 covers how bankruptcy cases are commenced (by filing a petition), including cases filed by a husband and a wife, the only two individuals who may file a case together. The subject of an involuntary bankruptcy is also covered. An involuntary bankruptcy is one in which the creditors file a petition with the bankruptcy court and compel the debtor to submit to the bankruptcy proceeding against his or her wishes. This subchapter also covers **abstention** by a bankruptcy court. Abstention is the power of the bankruptcy court to reject a case if the creditors and the debtor would be better served by such a refusal. For example, the bankruptcy court may abstain by dismissing a bankruptcy case that was commenced by the debtor after a receiver had been appointed over the debtor's property by a state court. Finally, Section 307 allows the United States trustee, the arm of the Justice Department charged with supervising bankruptcy case administration, to be heard on any issue arising in a bankruptcy case.

✦ abstention
The refusal of a court to hear and rule with respect to a particular case or proceeding despite the fact that it has jurisdiction to do so.

Officers—Sections 321–331 The second subchapter covers the employment and compensation of "officers of the bankruptcy case." Officers of the bankruptcy case are the trustees and other professional persons, such as attorneys and accountants, employed at the expense of the bankruptcy estate. The qualifications of those eligible to serve as a bankruptcy trustee and the amount of the trustee's compensation are also covered. The subchapter establishes the qualifications of attorneys and other professionals who represent debtors, trustees, or creditors' committees, and addresses the subject of their compensation. The employment and compensation of the officers of the bankruptcy case are discussed in Chapter 9 of this book.

Administration—Sections 341–350   The third subchapter, entitled Administration, contains 10 miscellaneous sections covering a bankruptcy case from its early days to its closing. For the most part, these sections are unrelated, but they are very important. They require the debtor to attend a meeting of creditors soon after the case is filed and to answer any questions the creditors may have. This meeting, the **Section 341(a) meeting,** allows creditors to question the debtor under oath without incurring the expense of a deposition. How these meetings are conducted varies depending not only on the size and complexity of the debtor's finances and assets, but also on the preferences of the trustee or other person conducting the examination. Other provisions of the subchapter on administration set out guidelines that the trustee must follow in investing funds of the debtor's estate, cover certain tax considerations, and deal with the effects of conversion of a case from one chapter to another and dismissal of the bankruptcy case.

✦ **Section 341(a) meeting**
Meeting called by United States trustee that debtor is required to attend to address any creditor questions.

Administrative Powers—Sections 361–366   The six sections in the fourth subchapter on administrative powers are the provisions that are central to a bankruptcy case. Section 361 lists some examples of "adequate protection," a phrase that is used throughout the Bankruptcy Code. One, for example, is the consideration a secured creditor or lessor is entitled to for the trustee's or debtor's use of property in which the secured creditor or the lessor has an interest. Section 362 covers the automatic stay, the injunction that comes into effect when a case is commenced and which stops creditor action. It delineates which acts are stayed, which are not stayed, and how a creditor can obtain relief from its operation. This is perhaps the most important section of the Bankruptcy Code to debtors and creditors and is the reason most bankruptcy cases are started. Chapter 4 of this book discusses the automatic stay. Section 363 explains the debtor's or the trustee's rights to use, sell, or lease property of the bankruptcy estate. Section 364 lists the conditions that must be met if the debtor or the trustee wants to borrow money after the bankruptcy case has been commenced. Section 365 discusses the effect the bankruptcy will have on contracts and leases to which the debtor is a party. Section 365 is very important, and for that reason, it is examined in depth in Chapter 4 of this book. Finally, Section 366 provides the terms and conditions under which a utility service may discontinue service to the debtor.

Creditors, the Debtor, and the Estate—Chapter 5

Chapter 5 of the Bankruptcy Code contains 34 sections divided into three subchapters. They cover such things as how the creditors will get paid and from what source the payments will be made; they specify what exempt property the debtor may keep after the bankruptcy and what debts the debtor will have to pay despite the bankruptcy.

Creditors and Claims—Sections 501–510   Subchapter I is entitled Creditors and Claims, and it covers the filing of a creditor's **proof of claim.** A proof of claim is the form filed by a creditor with the bankruptcy court that states the nature and the amount of the debt owed by the debtor to the creditor. The subchapter also

✦ **proof of claim**
The form a creditor who has a claim against the debtor must file in order to receive a distribution in a bankruptcy case.

covers how claims incurred after the bankruptcy case began are treated, how a secured creditor's claim is determined, and the order in which claims are to be paid.

Debtors, Duties, and Benefits—Sections 521–525 Subchapter II, entitled Debtor's Duties and Benefits, lists the debtor's duties in a bankruptcy case. Principally, the debtor must cooperate with the trustee and file a detailed list of assets and debts. The subchapter also lists some of the benefits to which the debtor is entitled, prohibits discrimination against a debtor by governmental entities and private employers, and enumerates the debtor's **exemptions,** or property that the debtor may keep after the bankruptcy. Also listed in the subchapter are the debtor's **nondischargeable claims,** which are those claims that may be enforced against the debtor after the bankruptcy case.

The Estate—Sections 541–559 Subchapter III is simply titled The Estate. A bankruptcy estate is an artificial entity that is created on the filing of a bankruptcy petition. It owns all of the debtor's property and is subject to all of the debtor's debts. It is used to conceptually distinguish between the prebankruptcy debtor and the postbankruptcy debtor. The common theme of Subchapter III is to enlarge the estate as much as possible by defining property of the debtor very broadly. Thus, these sections provide ways to bring property of the estate that is in the control of the debtor or third parties into the hands of the trustee. They also give the trustee certain powers, called avoiding powers, that allow the trustee to cancel a transfer of the estate property made before or after the commencement of the bankruptcy case and place it in the possession and control of the trustee. The trustee is given the power to cancel transfers that were fraudulent and to recover preferences, which are certain arrangements by which some creditors are treated better than others. Finally, the subchapter deals with **setoff** and **abandonment.** Setoff concerns the ability of a creditor who also owes money to the debtor to apply the debts against each other. Abandonment is the ability of the trustee to decline to administer all or some of the property of the estate.

Liquidation—Chapter 7

The remainder of the Bankruptcy Code's chapters provide for specific types of bankruptcy relief. Chapter 7 is the only one of these chapters that concerns liquidation, sometimes called a straight bankruptcy. It is the simplest form of debt relief and is available for all types of debtors, whether individuals, partnerships, or corporations. Only railroads, insurance companies, governments, and financial institutions such as banks may not be Chapter 7 debtors.

When a bankruptcy petition is filed, an estate is created that consists of all the debtor's property. A Chapter 7 case then proceeds on two tracks. The first track provides the debtor with a fresh start: the debtor will be relieved of the burden of the estate's debts and left with sufficient assets so that a fresh start can be made. The second track is the administration of the estate: collection, liquidation, and distribution to creditors of whatever property is available. Exhibit 2.1 briefly graphs these two tracks.

Administration of the Estate Under Section 701, an interim bankruptcy trustee is appointed by the United States trustee or by the bankruptcy court's administrative personnel. The interim trustee will usually be an individual but may be a company. In virtually every jurisdiction, there is a panel of persons who have applied for and have been selected for appointments as interim trustees.

Generally, trustees have experience in bankruptcy matters and familiarity with selling property. Trustees are often lawyers, but they may be accountants, financial

---

◆ **exemptions**
Those interests in property that a debtor is allowed to keep and not make subject to creditors' claims.

◆ **nondischargeable claims**
Claims that will be enforceable against the debtor despite the discharge.

◆ **setoff**
The application of a debt owed to a person against a debt owed from that same person.

◆ **abandonment**
The release by the bankruptcy trustee or debtor in possession of the estate's rights in property.

EXHIBIT 2.1 ✦ *The Two Tracks of a Chapter 7 Case*

consultants, auctioneers, or other professionals. If the debtor was involved in a particularly complex industry or if the case is of such magnitude that it would be difficult for a panel trustee to administer the estate, the United States trustee or bankruptcy court personnel may select a trustee from the particular industry or other specialist to head the liquidation effort. In addition, if no member of the panel is willing to serve as the trustee, the United States trustee may serve but rarely does.

The interim bankruptcy trustee serves until the meeting of creditors. At that time, creditors who are not affiliated with the debtor and who hold at least 20 percent of the claims may elect a different trustee. If there is no election, which is almost always the case, or if the creditors' candidate does not receive a majority of the votes, the interim bankruptcy trustee becomes the trustee for the remainder of the bankruptcy case.

The trustee's duties are listed in Section 704 of the Bankruptcy Code. They include:

♦ Collecting the property of the estate and reducing it to money.
♦ Investigating the financial affairs of the debtor.
♦ Examining the claims filed by creditors and objecting to improper claims, if applicable.
♦ Opposing the discharge of the debtor, if advisable.
♦ Furnishing information concerning the estate and its administration requested by creditors.
♦ Making a final report and filing with the court a final account of the administration of the estate.

The trustee is compensated by receiving an allowance set by the court. This amount is usually a percentage of the funds that have been disbursed to creditors. The percentages are set out in Section 326.

In administering the estate, the trustee will rely on the general provision sections of Chapter 3 and 5. For example, the trustee will look to Chapter 5 to determine what property is part of the estate and must be administered. The trustee will attempt to increase the size of the estate by recovering preferences, fraudulent conveyances, and improper postbankruptcy transfers. Once the estate has been made as large as possible, the trustee will use the provisions in Chapter 3 to sell the assets for cash. Any property that cannot bring cash to the estate will be abandoned.

Although Chapter 7 involves the sale of a debtor's assets, the court may allow the trustee to operate the debtor's business for a limited period of time if doing so helps the sale of the business. If the debtor was a manufacturing facility in the middle of processing orders when it filed its bankruptcy petition, for example, the business could be continued for a sufficient time to allow worthless raw materials to be processed into valuable finished goods.

When all the assets have been sold, the trustee will be ready to distribute the funds on hand to creditors pursuant to the provisions of Sections 507 and 726 of the Bankruptcy Code. Section 726 establishes a six-tier priority distribution system under which each tier is required to be paid in full before any person on a lower tier receives anything. On the first tier are those creditors who claim a priority, or a right to be paid first, under Section 507 of the Bankruptcy Code. Section 507 in turn has nine tiers of priority claims that are entitled to preferential treatment. They include administrative expenses, such as trustee's and attorneys' fees and costs; wages earned within 90 days before the bankruptcy case was commenced; claims for contributions to employee benefit plans; deposits paid for customer goods not delivered or provided; and certain types of taxes.

If the Section 507 priority claims are paid in full, a distribution is made to the second tier of claims listed in Section 726 for unsecured creditors who filed timely claims against the estate. Late filing creditors are paid next, followed by claims that are for fines, penalties, and punitive damages. If there are still funds left to be distributed, interest is paid to creditors. In the unlikely event that a balance remains, the funds are paid to the debtor. Exhibit 2.2 ranks the various priorities that creditors enjoy and the order in which the funds are disbursed. Once the distribution is made, the trustee will close the estate and the case will be over.

EXHIBIT 2.2 ✦ *Priorities in Distribution*

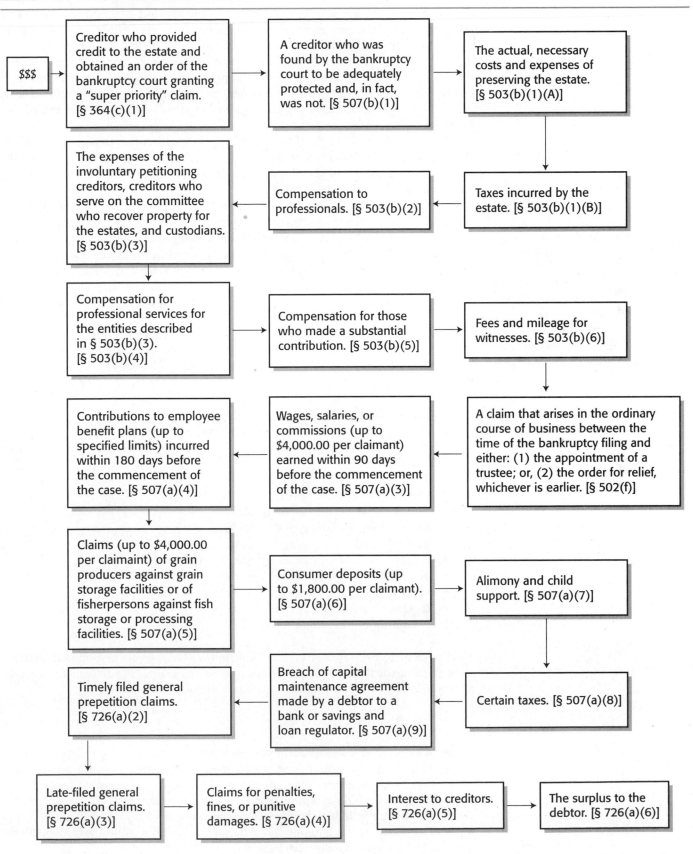

The Fresh Start While the trustee is administering the estate, the debtor should be cooperating with the trustee in collecting and liquidating assets. The debtor will also be acting to preserve the exempt property—those assets Congress has decided a debtor needs in order to make a fresh start. Although all of the debtor's property comes into the bankruptcy estate, the debtor is allowed to keep the property listed in Section 522. Exempt property includes some equity in a house, a car, household goods and furnishings, pension funds, and certain miscellaneous other assets. Exemptions are discussed in greater detail in Chapter 8 of this book.

In many Chapter 7 cases, there are no assets for the trustee to administer, other than those the debtor may claim as exempt. As a result, the trustee will have nothing to liquidate and no funds with which to make a distribution to creditors. These cases are usually called **no-asset cases.**

◆ **no-asset case**
A bankruptcy case in which there are no assets to sell by the trustee. As a result, creditors do not receive a distribution.

◆ **discharge**
The release given to an individual debtor of the difference between the amount of creditor's unsecured claims and the assets distributed to creditors in a bankruptcy case.

As a payment for giving up all nonexempt property to the trustee, the individual debtor will receive a **discharge** or complete forgiveness of most debts. The creditors will never be able to enforce those obligations against the debtor. There is certainly nothing that prevents the debtor from voluntarily repaying creditors, but he or she cannot be compelled to do so. Corporations do not receive a discharge, but since the corporation will no longer have assets after commencing a bankruptcy case (exemptions are only available for individuals), the effect is the same.

For public policy reasons, there are a few types of debts that are not discharged and will be enforceable against the debtor even after the Chapter 7 bankruptcy case is over. These debts are generally referred to as **nondischargeable claims** and are listed in Section 523. They include:

- ◆ Certain taxes and debts incurred to pay those taxes.
- ◆ Money, property, or service obtained through fraud.
- ◆ Luxury goods or credit card cash advances obtained within 60 days prior to bankruptcy.
- ◆ Debts not disclosed during the bankruptcy case.
- ◆ Alimony and child support.
- ◆ Claims for willful and malicious injury.
- ◆ Certain fines, penalties, and forfeitures.
- ◆ Student loans.
- ◆ Claims for damages caused by a drunk driver.
- ◆ Debts not discharged in the debtor's previous bankruptcy case.
- ◆ Fraud or defalcation to a depository institution.
- ◆ Reckless or malicious failure to fulfill a capital maintenance agreement.
- ◆ Condominium association dues.

Pursuant to Section 727 of the Bankruptcy Code, in certain limited circumstances, all of the debtor's claims will be nondischargeable. Those situations nearly always involve the debtor's bad conduct and include:

- ◆ The debtor defrauded creditors or the trustee by transferring or destroying property.
- ◆ Without justification, the debtor transferred or destroyed books and records.
- ◆ The debtor knowingly and fraudulently committed perjury, presented a false claim, tried to obtain an advantage by doing or agreeing to do something (or not do something), or withheld books and records.
- ◆ The debtor failed to satisfactorily explain a loss of assets.
- ◆ The debtor refused to obey an order of the court or improperly invoked the privilege against self-incrimination.

✦ The debtor received a discharge in a bankruptcy case commenced within the last six years.

Stockbrokers and Commodity Brokers   Subchapter III of Chapter 7 has a number of very specialized sections concerning liquidations of the assets of stockbrokers and their spouses. Similarly, Subchapter IV contains provisions for commodity broker liquidations. Since the possibility of widespread investor loss would be a problem in a stockbroker or commodity broker Chapter 7 case, Congress enacted special provisions concerning subordination of insider claims, recovery of voidable transfers, and distributions. The provisions for stockbrokers can be found in Subchapter III of Chapter 7; the provisions for commodity brokers can be found in Subchapter IV.

Reorganization—Chapter 11

Chapter 11 was designed to help business debtors reorganize and continue operations. The benefits flow not only to creditors, who should receive more than they would if the business closed down, but also to the economy that is served by preserving competition and jobs. Chapter 11 cases are usually filed by partnerships and corporations. Individuals can also file a Chapter 11 case. However, individuals are usually better off under Chapter 13, which is less expensive, time consuming, and cumbersome. Because they are heavily regulated by other laws, certain types of individuals and businesses, such as stockbrokers, insurance companies, and banks, cannot be Chapter 11 debtors. There are also special provisions for railroad reorganizations under Chapter 11.

Administration of the Case   A Chapter 11 case may be commenced voluntarily by the debtor or involuntarily by one or more creditors against the debtor. The progress of a typical Chapter 11 case is illustrated in Exhibit 2.3.

The goal of a Chapter 11 case is to have the bankruptcy court approve a **plan of reorganization** that is either voted in by the creditors or found by the court to be in their best interests.

While the plan of reorganization is being developed, the debtor remains in possession and control of the business and its assets and is responsible for administering the estate. For that reason, a Chapter 11 debtor is called the **debtor in possession,** or *DIP.* The debtor will be a debtor in possession unless the bankruptcy court appoints a Chapter 11 trustee, which usually occurs only when the debtor has been guilty of incompetence, gross mismanagement, or some other type of improper and/or illegal act.

The duties of a Chapter 11 trustee are set out in Section 1106 of the Bankruptcy Code. They are similar to those of a Chapter 7 trustee except that, because there will be an effort to reorganize the debtor's business, the Chapter 11 trustee is not required to liquidate the estate's assets.

The duties of the debtor in possession are set out in Section 1107. Generally, the debtor in possession has all of the rights and powers of a trustee and performs most of the functions of a trustee. For example, the debtor in possession may avoid fraudulent conveyances, sell estate property, and reject contracts made by the debtor. Like a trustee, however, the debtor in possession must be accountable for all property received and otherwise act properly.

To ensure that the debtor in possession is behaving properly, it will be required to submit regular reports to the court or the United States trustee showing all receipts and expenditures and whether the estate is losing money. The debtor in possession will also have to pay a fee ranging from $150 to $3,000 each quarter to pay for the United States trustee's monitoring and oversight.

✦ **plan of reorganization**
A document filed in a reorganization case that divides the claims of creditors into classes and provides for their payment or other treatment.

✦ **debtor in possession**
A debtor in a case under Chapters 9 and 13 and a debtor in a case under Chapters 11 and 12 in which no trustee has been appointed.

EXHIBIT 2.3 ✦ *Course of Events in a Chapter 11 Case*

✦ **ordinary course of business**
Transactions made by a business in its day-to-day operations.

Since the goal of a Chapter 11 case is the reorganization of the debtor's business, no specific court order is required for the debtor in possession to continue operations. As long as such actions are in the **ordinary course of business,** the debtor in possession may use, sell, or lease estate property without prior approval of the bankruptcy court. What constitutes the ordinary course of business is not specifically discussed in the Bankruptcy Code. Because of the many different types of businesses that exist, it is virtually impossible to fashion a definition of "ordinary course of business" that would apply in all cases. Generally, the things a business did as part of its day-to-day operations before bankruptcy would be considered as within the ordinary course of business. For example, a grocery store chain buying produce from vendors and selling it to customers would be acting in the ordinary course of business, and no court order would be required to continue that operation. If the grocery store chain wanted to sell one of its stores to another company, however, that would be out of the ordinary course of business; permission would have to be sought from the bankruptcy court for that sale.

Congress envisioned a Chapter 11 plan of reorganization as a cooperative effort between the debtor and the creditors. To facilitate their negotiations, the Bankruptcy Code provides for the appointment of a committee of creditors. The **creditors' committee** ordinarily consists of the seven largest unsecured creditors and is selected by the United States trustee.

In larger cases, more than one creditors' committee will be appointed. If the debtor is a corporation, a committee may be appointed to represent the interests of the shareholders. If the debtor is a limited partnership, there may be a committee of limited partners. These last two types of committees are usually referred to as **equity committees.** Equity committees and creditors' committees have the same functions and duties.

The duties and functions of the committee are listed in Section 1103 and include:

- ✦ Consulting with the debtor in possession concerning the administration of the case.
- ✦ Investigating any matter relevant to the case or the plan of reorganization.
- ✦ Participating in the process of plan formulation and confirmation.
- ✦ Performing any other service that is in the best interest of those the committee represents.

The committee is entitled to appear before the bankruptcy court and be heard on any issue in a Chapter 11 case. Judges are often interested in the opinion of the creditors' committee on any given topic. To assist it in performing its duties and functions, the committee also has the right to employ professionals such as attorneys, accountants, and investment bankers. Fees for these professionals will, as for the professionals employed by the debtor in possession, be paid by the estate.

The Plan of Reorganization The goal in a Chapter 11 case is the confirmation by the court of a plan of reorganization. The debtor may propose a plan of reorganization at any time during the case. During the first 120 days of the case, only the debtor in possession may propose a plan; this is called the period of **plan exclusivity.** The 120-day period can be extended if the court finds that there is a good reason to do so. Once the exclusivity period has expired, any party in interest, other than the United States trustee, may propose a plan of reorganization.

A plan of reorganization divides creditors and equity interest holders into classes and provides a method of treating each class. Unless they consent to a different treatment, each senior class must be paid in full before any junior class can receive a payment under the plan. For example, a simple plan for a corporation would have four classes of creditors as follows:

1. Class 1—Priority creditors.
2. Class 2—Secured creditors.
3. Class 3—All nonpriority unsecured creditors.
4. Class 4—Shareholders.

The plan could provide that Class 1 creditors would be paid in full on the effective date of the plan. Class 2 creditors would retain their liens in the debtor's property and receive the monthly installment payments called for in their contracts with the debtor. Class 3 creditors would receive quarterly payments from the debtor's profits over the next five years and all of the debtor's stock, which should equal 60 percent of the claims. Since Class 3 creditors will not be paid in full, Class 4 creditors will receive nothing under the plan.

✦ **creditors' committee**
A committee composed of two or more of the debtor's creditors, appointed in a Chapter 9 or 11 case by the United States trustee.

✦ **equity committee**
A committee of equity security holders (e.g., stockholders, warrant holders, general or limited partnership interests) appointed in a Chapter 11 case by the United States trustee.

✦ **plan exclusivity**
The fact that for a period of time only the debtor may propose a plan of reorganization.

This example is a very simple, traditional reorganization plan. Most plans either provide for the liquidation of all the debtor's assets and a distribution to creditors or they are a variation on this plan. What the plan actually provides for depends on the debtor's financial situation, the negotiations with the creditors, and the creativity and ingenuity of the **plan proponent.** No two plans are exactly alike, but they must have certain common elements. These include:

✦ **plan proponent**
The entity that proposes a plan of reorganization.

- ✦ The plan must put into classes the various types of claims and interests. The claims in each class must be substantially similar to each other.
- ✦ The plan must identify those classes of creditors that are not impaired under the plan. To be impaired means that the creditors' legal, contractual, or equitable rights are altered. An unsecured creditor is impaired if it will not be paid in full. A secured creditor is impaired if it will not be paid on time, will not be paid in full, or will be receiving substitute collateral under the plan.
- ✦ The plan must state how impaired classes are treated.
- ✦ The plan must treat each member of a class the same.
- ✦ The plan must specifically state how the reorganization will happen.
- ✦ The plan must disclose who will be operating the debtor in the future.

The plan of reorganization may also contain any other provision provided it does not conflict with any of the mandatory provisions. The Bankruptcy Code suggests some optional provisions:

- ✦ The plan may impair the rights of secured and unsecured creditors and equity interest holders.
- ✦ The plan may provide for the assumption or rejection of executory contracts and leases.
- ✦ The plan may provide for the settlement of one or more claims against the estate.
- ✦ The plan may provide for the sale of all or substantially all of the property of the estate.

✦ **disclosure statement**
The document containing adequate information that is distributed with a Chapter 11 plan of reorganization.

The plan of reorganization must be accompanied by a written **disclosure statement** explaining the plan that has been approved by the court. Its purpose is to provide the information that creditors need to intelligently decide whether to vote for or against the plan. The court will approve the disclosure statement only if it contains **adequate information,** which is defined in Section 1125 as:

✦ **adequate information**
Information in sufficient detail that would enable a hypothetical reasonable investor to make an informed decision whether to vote for or against a plan of reorganization.

information of a kind, and in sufficient detail, as far as is reasonably practicable in light of the nature and history of the debtor and the condition of the debtor's books and records, that would enable a hypothetical reasonable investor typical of holders of claims or interests of the relevant class to make an informed judgment about the plan.

The disclosure statement is usually filed with the plan. The court then holds a hearing to determine whether the disclosure statement contains adequate information. If it does, the court sets a date for a hearing to confirm the plan. The plan proponent then mails the plan, the disclosure statement, and a **ballot** to creditors and equity interest holders. Creditors who are impaired under the plan may vote for or against the plan by marking their ballots and returning them to the plan proponent as instructed in the disclosure statement.

✦ **ballot**
The document submitted by holders of impaired claims or interests accepting or rejecting a Chapter 11 plan of reorganization.

At a hearing set by the court, the plan will not be confirmed unless each class of creditors or security holders impaired by the plan has voted to accept it or unless it is **crammed down,** a procedure discussed next. To be accepted, creditors who vote yes must hold at least two-thirds in amount and one-half in number of the claims of those who voted. For example, if there are 10 creditors in an impaired class who vote, at least five must vote for the plan. If each creditor's claim is $10.00, at least seven creditors must vote for the plan to reach the necessary two-thirds in amount.

♦ **cram down**
The approval of a plan of reorganization over the objection or negative votes of creditors.

If one or more classes votes to reject the plan, the plan may still be confirmed if it can be crammed down. In order to have a cram down, the court must find that the plan does not unfairly discriminate and is fair and equitable to the classes who have rejected it. In other words, the nonconsenting class must be paid in full before a junior class receives anything. For a class of secured creditors to be crammed down, the secured creditors must receive roughly the economic benefit of their bargain. For example, a secured creditor who is paid in full but not on time can be crammed down if it receives interest to compensate for the delay in the payment.

A plan that has been accepted by all of the impaired classes will not always be confirmed. A plan cannot be confirmed unless the court specifically finds that the following terms have all been met:

♦ The plan complies with Chapter 11 of the Bankruptcy Code.
♦ The plan proponent has complied with the provisions of Chapter 11 of the Bankruptcy Code.
♦ The plan has been proposed in good faith and not by any means forbidden by law.
♦ All payments made or promised for services and costs in connection with the bankruptcy case or the plan have been disclosed.
♦ The identities of postconfirmation officers and directors have been disclosed.
♦ Any necessary regulatory approval has been obtained.
♦ Unless all creditors and equity security holders agree otherwise, the plan provides more to those parties than they would receive in a Chapter 7 bankruptcy case.
♦ Unless they agree to a different treatment, the priority classes are paid in full on the effective date of the plan.
♦ At least one class has accepted the plan.
♦ The plan can be carried out and will not likely fail thereafter.

If the plan is confirmed, it binds the debtor and all parties to it whether they voted in favor of it or not. Any debts that are not paid or are not paid in full by the plan are no longer enforceable. Unless the plan provides otherwise, the debtor is no longer subject to the scrutiny of the bankruptcy court or the United States trustee; the debtor is charged only with living up to the terms of the plan. The bankruptcy case is closed when the plan has been fully performed.

Small Chapter 11 Cases   As even this brief discussion illustrates, there are a number of time consuming, expensive steps that must be taken in order to successfully complete a Chapter 11 case. Many small businesses that would benefit from a reorganization cannot afford costly legal proceedings, and their financial affairs are not so complicated that all of the plan procedures are necessary.

In response to these issues, some of the bankruptcy judges in the less busy districts began to implement abbreviated Chapter 11 procedures for the smaller cases on their docket. These procedures eliminated or combined hearings and notices and required plans to be proposed shortly after the petition was filed.

As the 1994 Amendments worked their way through Congress, there was considerable pressure to have these procedures or ones like them implemented by all districts in their administration of the smaller Chapter 11 bankruptcy cases in order to reduce the financial burden on debtors in possession and the pressure on the court system. At one stage, Congress even considered enacting a Chapter 10 that would allow small corporate cases to be treated like Chapter 13 consumer reorganizations.

Ultimately, rather than enact an entirely new chapter, Congress changed various sections of Chapter 11 to permit an expedited and less expensive procedure for reorganizing a small business. A small business is defined in Section 101(51)(C) as a person engaged in commercial or business activities (other than solely real estate), with debts of $2,000,000 or less. The changes include not having a creditors' committee; shortening the exclusivity period to 100 days; requiring a plan to be filed within 160 days; and combining the hearing on the disclosure statement and the plan.

✦ **wage earner reorganization**
Chapter 13 cases so designated under the misconception that only employed persons qualify for relief. The statute requires only a regular income that may come from a variety of sources.

✦ **regular income**
A source of income that is fairly stable whether earnings, pension, or other retirement benefits, public assistance benefits, or dividends.

Individual Reorganizations—Chapter 13

Chapter 13 of the Bankruptcy Code was given the title of Adjustment of Debts of an Individual with Regular Income. It is more familiarly known as **wage earner reorganization.** Chapter 13 provides individual debtors and sole proprietors with relief similar to that given to more complex business entities under Chapter 11, with the same goal of achieving a plan to satisfy the claims of the creditors. Chapter 13 is a less expensive and cumbersome vehicle, however. It is also less time consuming: In many cases, Chapter 13 plans can be confirmed in only a few months, as shown in the timeline for Chapter 13 cases found in Exhibit 2.4.

Administration Only individuals are allowed to file Chapter 13 petitions, but not all individuals qualify. An individual must have a **regular income** and

EXHIBIT 2.4 ✦ *Chapter 13 Timeline*

noncontingent, liquidated debts in certain amounts to qualify. The limit on unsecured debts is $250,000, and the limit on secured debts is $750,000. If a debtor had an $800,000 mortgage on a home (secured debt) or was a judgment debtor for $350,000 (unsecured debt), relief would have to be sought under Chapter 7 or Chapter 11. The same debt limits apply to a husband and wife filing jointly under Chapter 13.

Although Chapter 13 is called the wage earner reorganization, the Bankruptcy Code requires only that the debtor have a regular income. Gainful employment is not a prerequisite. Thus, debtors who are on welfare or receive some other form of public assistance, or those living on retirement or investment incomes also may qualify. For a husband and wife filing jointly, only one spouse must have a regular income.

Chapter 13 debtors are also debtors in possession with many of the same rights and duties as Chapter 11 debtors. For example, subject to certain Bankruptcy Code provisions, a Chapter 13 debtor may reject contracts or leases; use, sell, or lease property; and operate a business. Anything out of the ordinary course of business, such as selling or refinancing real property, requires court approval. Like Chapter 7 debtors, Chapter 13 debtors are entitled to claim some assets as exempt, although exemptions are less important because a trustee under Chapter 13 does not administer the debtor's property.

Chapter 13 trustees conduct the first meeting of creditors, examine the debtor's plan of reorganization to ensure compliance with Chapter 13, collect payments from the debtor, and make disbursements to the creditors under the plan. The trustees do not take possession of the debtor's property or control any of the debtor's assets.

Chapter 13 trustees may come from the same panel as the Chapter 7 trustees; however, in most districts, only one or two trustees (called standing trustees) are appointed to serve in all Chapter 13 cases. Only one or two trustees are needed in Chapter 13 cases because their duties are less involved than in Chapter 7 cases.

The Plan   Under Chapter 13, only the debtor may propose a plan of reorganization. The creditors and the trustee may not do so. There is no mandatory form for a Chapter 13 plan, although most districts have forms that are in wide use. No disclosure statement must be filed or approved. Unlike Chapter 11 plans, which can be very complicated, Chapter 13 plans typically are only a few pages long.

Chapter 13 specifies certain common provisions for a plan of reorganization:

✦ The plan must submit to the trustee enough of the debtor's regular income so that the payments called for under the plan can be made.
✦ The plan must provide that priority claims such as the trustee's fee, certain wages, taxes, and consumer deposit claims are paid in full.
✦ The plan must provide for equal treatment of claims in the same class.
✦ The plan must provide that secured creditors receive an amount at least equal to the value of their collateral.
✦ The plan must provide that unsecured creditors receive at least as much as they would have received if the debtor had filed a Chapter 7 case instead.

The Chapter 13 plan may also contain the following optional provisions:

✦ The plan may divide claims into several different classes so long as the claims in each class are substantially similar.
✦ The plan may provide a different treatment for each class.
✦ The plan may modify the rights of secured creditors by extending the due date of the last payment or paying less than the full amount owed if the collateral is not worth the amount owed. The one exception is that a Chapter

13 plan may not modify the claim of the mortgage holder on the debtor's home. All the payments required by the original contract must be paid, although any amount in default when the case began may be paid off in time as part of the plan.

✦ The plan may provide that all creditors be paid concurrently regardless of priority. Priority or secured creditors need not be paid in full first. The plan may provide for the payment of postpetition claims, such as debts the debtor incurred for medical services after the case was filed. All postpetition claims must be paid in full.

Payments to the trustee under the plan may be stretched out for three years. If there is a good reason, the payment plan can be extended to five years. Regardless of the debtor's circumstances, a plan longer than five years cannot be approved.

Once the debtor has proposed a plan of reorganization, the court will hold a confirmation hearing. Unlike under Chapter 11, creditors are not entitled to vote for or against a Chapter 13 plan. They may file objections, but if the plan meets the requirements of Section 1325, it will be confirmed. The creditors do, however, have some leverage. If the plan does not provide full payment for the creditors, they can force the debtor to commit all **disposable income** for payments under the plan merely by filing an objection.

The confirmation hearing is usually held about 45 days after the petition is filed. At the hearing, the court determines the following:

✦ disposable income

Debtor's income not necessary for payment of reasonable expenses for debtor and dependents. If debtor is engaged in business, income not needed for payment of expenses necessary for continuation, preservation, and operation of business.

✦ Does the plan comply with the Bankruptcy Code? (Are the mandatory provisions present?)

✦ Has the debtor paid all fees and charges? This will usually just be the Chapter 13 filing fee.

✦ Has the plan been proposed in good faith and not by any means forbidden by law? Generally, the debtor must have proposed a plan that provides meaningful payments to creditors if at all possible, and performance of the plan must not violate state or federal law. For example, the debtor cannot have a plan confirmed that provides that the payments to creditors will be made from the earnings of the debtor's toxic material disposal service unless the debtor has the proper licenses.

When the debtor has fully performed the plan of reorganization, a discharge of all debts not paid in full will be granted. Unlike Chapter 7, Chapter 13 provides for a discharge of claims based on fraud or the failure to adequately explain loss of assets. In fact, the only types of claims that are not discharged in a Chapter 13 case are obligations for alimony and child support, damages from drunk driving, student loans, and criminal restitution. Even the debtor who is unable to complete the plan of reorganization may obtain a discharge if the court finds that the failure to make the payments was due to circumstances for which the debtor should not be held accountable, that unsecured creditors have already received at least as much as they would have received in a Chapter 7 case, and that a modification of the plan is not practical.

As is true under Chapter 11, once all the plan payments have been made, the case will be closed.

The Family Farmer—Chapter 12

Congress devised Chapter 12 of the Bankruptcy Code in 1986 as emergency debt relief for American farmers. Chapter 12 became a permanent chapter in the code in June 2001. Chapter 12 is a combination of the most favorable parts of Chapters

11 and 13, granting far greater protection to **family farmers** than to other debtors. Chapter 12 is like Chapter 11 because it gives debtors in possession considerable powers to restructure their debts; and it is like Chapter 13 because relief under it is relatively fast and inexpensive. Because Chapter 12 incorporates by reference many of the provisions of Chapters 11 and 13, it is relatively short.

Administration   To qualify for Chapter 12 relief, the debtor, who can be an individual, partnership, joint venture, or corporation, must be a **family farmer with regular income.** A family farmer with a regular income must meet certain criteria, as follows. When it passed Chapter 12, Congress considered that these criteria covered most farming operations.

+ The debtor must have no more than $1,500,000 of secured and unsecured debt. If the debt load exceeds that amount, relief must be sought under Chapter 7 or Chapter 11.
+ At least 80 percent of the debt must have been incurred from farming operations.
+ The debtor must have earned at least 50 percent of the previous year's taxable income from farming.
+ If the debtor is a corporation, at least 50 percent of the outstanding stock must be held by family members engaged in farming. The stock cannot be publicly traded. In addition, at least 80 percent of the corporation's assets must be farm related.

There are a number of benefits of Chapter 12 relief over a Chapter 11 case. They include:

+ Chapter 12 is cheaper. Currently, the filing fee is only $200 compared to $800 to $1,000 in a Chapter 11 case. In addition, Chapter 12 debtors do not have to pay quarterly fees to the United States trustee's office.
+ Payments to secured creditors during the administration of the case may be substantially less in Chapter 12 than in Chapter 11. For example, under Chapter 11, the debtor may be required to make sizable payments to the secured creditors to prevent them from obtaining relief from the stay. Under Chapter 12, however, payments to secured creditors need not exceed the reasonable rental value of the collateral. If there is a glut of available farmland in the area, those payments may be minimal.
+ In Chapter 11, property cannot be sold free of a creditor's valid lien unless the creditor consents or will be paid in full from the sale. Chapter 12 debtors do not need the permission of creditors before selling unnecessary farmland and farm equipment even though the proceeds will be insufficient to pay the secured creditors in full. The sale will, however, require bankruptcy court approval if it is made out of the ordinary course of business.

An individual Chapter 12 debtor will receive a discharge at the end of the case, but this discharge is not as expansive as the one granted to Chapter 13 debtors. In fact, it is very close to the discharge given in Chapter 7 because it also excepts from the discharge the types of claims mentioned in Section 523(a). Like Chapter 13, however, Chapter 12 has a provision that grants a discharge to an individual debtor in certain circumstances even if all of the plan payments have not been made.

A trustee is appointed in all Chapter 12 cases. This trustee is similar to a Chapter 13 trustee who monitors payments under a plan, but the trustee in a Chapter 12 case may have greater duties. The Chapter 12 trustee can appear at any hearing concerning sale of estate property and plan confirmation. The court can

+ **family farmer**
An individual receiving more than 50 percent of income, and incurring debts not exceeding $1,500,000, from farming. Or a corporation or partnership where the majority of stock is held by one family and more than 80 percent of the corporation's assets relate to farming, and debts, arising from farming, do not exceed $1,500,000.

+ **family farmer with regular income**
A family farmer whose annual income is sufficiently stable and regular to allow it to make payments under a Chapter 12 plan.

also order the Chapter 12 trustee to investigate and report on the conduct and financial condition of the debtor and make a determination as to whether the farming operations should continue. Unlike the debtor in Chapter 13, the family farmer in Chapter 12 may be removed for fraud, dishonesty, incompetence, or gross mismanagement, in which case the Chapter 12 trustee may take over responsibility for operating the farm.

The Plan Confirmation of a plan in a Chapter 12 case is designed to be every bit as quick as it is in Chapter 13. A plan must be filed within 90 days unless there is good reason for an extension.

A Chapter 12 plan may be filed only by the debtor. The plan must require the submission of all or a portion of future earnings or other future income to the trustee. It must classify claims and provide for priority creditors to be paid in full. In addition, it must provide for all payments to be made within three years, unless the court approves an extension to five years. As under Chapter 13, all the debtor's disposable income must be used to make payments if a creditor objects to the plan. Unlike Chapter 13, Chapter 12 allows the debtor to modify a residential mortgage.

Chapter 12 plans are not voted on by creditors, and they will be confirmed if they meet the requirements of Section 1225. The hearing on confirmation must be concluded not later than 45 days after the plan is filed. Once all plan payments are made, the Chapter 12 case is closed.

Municipality Reorganizations—Chapter 9

◆ **municipality**
A political subdivision, public agency, or instrumentality of a state.

Chapter 9 provides a means for the adjustment of the debts of certain entities known as **municipalities,** which are political subdivisions, public agencies, or instrumentalities of the states. Generally, Chapter 9 operates similarly to Chapter 11, and many provisions of Chapter 11 are incorporated by reference into Chapter 9. Historically, very few Chapter 9 cases have been filed, and those that were filed were small. In late 1994, Orange County, California and an investment fund it operated filed Chapter 9 petitions, which were the largest cases filed since Chapter 9 was enacted in 1978.

Although Chapter 9 is based on Chapter 11, and the ultimate goal of a Chapter 9 is the confirmation of a plan of reorganization, there are some very meaningful differences that tend to give the municipal debtor much more power than other debtors in possession. For example, because it would be improper for the judicial branch of the federal government to replace elected officials, there is no concept of a trustee in Chapter 9 cases. The court may not interfere with any of the municipality's political or governmental powers or any of its property or revenues. Also, only the municipality may file a plan. Creditors are given the ability to vote to accept or reject the plan, but the only possible remedy if the debtor cannot confirm its plan is dismissal of the case.

Because so few Chapter 9 cases have been filed, it will not be discussed further in this book.

THE RULES GOVERNING BANKRUPTCY PRACTICE AND PROCEDURE

Federal Rules of Bankruptcy Procedure

The Bankruptcy Code establishes the substantive rights, duties, and remedies of debtors, creditors, and trustees. It is the Federal Rules of Bankruptcy Procedure (the "Bankruptcy Rules"), however, that establish the procedures on how the rights are exercised, how the duties are fulfilled, and how the remedies are obtained.

The **Bankruptcy Rules** were formulated by the Supreme Court in 1983 to complement the Bankruptcy Code; they are intended to apply in all bankruptcy cases commenced under the Bankruptcy Code. The Rules are divided into parts by subject matter, and each part applies to all the chapters of the Bankruptcy Code. There are over 200 rules divided into nine parts, as shown in Exhibit 2.5.

Each Bankruptcy Rule is assigned a four-digit number, the first digit of which provides a key to the part in which the rule resides. For example, Rule 6006, which concerns the assumption or rejection of contracts, is in Part VI. Rule 9013, which covers the form and service of motions, is in Part IX.

It would not be particularly helpful to discuss a Bankruptcy Rule without at the same time discussing the section of the Bankruptcy Code the rule was intended to implement. Therefore, this book reviews each Bankruptcy Rule alongside the Bankruptcy Code provision to which it relates.

Federal Rules of Civil Procedure

Part VII of the Bankruptcy Rules concerns adversary proceedings in the bankruptcy court. In bankruptcy practice, **adversary proceeding** is another term for litigation. (See Chapter 6 of this book.) Many of the adversary proceedings in the bankruptcy court are similar to—if not identical to—nonbankruptcy litigation that is conducted in U.S. district courts and to which the Federal Rules of Civil Procedure apply. Therefore, in large part, Part VII of the Bankruptcy Rules merely incorporates provisions of the Federal Rules of Civil Procedure and applies them to adversary proceedings in bankruptcy court.

Each rule in Part VII of the Bankruptcy Rules is numbered in a way that makes it easy to determine which federal rule has been incorporated into the Bankruptcy Rule. The key is in the last two digits of the Bankruptcy Rule. The last two digits of the number of a Bankruptcy Rule in Part VII correspond to the number of the Federal Rule of Civil Procedure it incorporates. Thus, Bankruptcy Rule 7003 incorporates Rule 3 of the Federal Rules of Civil Procedure. Furthermore, the incorporation is usually complete. For example, Bankruptcy Rule 7020, entitled Permissive Joinder of Parties, states in full: "Rule 20 F.R.Civ.P. applies in adversary proceedings." This statement means that the full text of Rule 20 of the Federal Rules of Civil Procedure is used to determine the procedures for the permissive joinder of parties in adversary proceedings conducted before the bankruptcy court. Some of the more common rules of the Federal Rules of Civil Procedure incorporated fully by reference into the Bankruptcy Rules are those relating to third-party practice (Bankruptcy Rule 7015), class actions (Bankruptcy Rule 7023), and discovery (Bankruptcy Rules 7026 through 7037).

✦ Bankruptcy Rules
The rules of practice and procedure governing bankruptcy cases and proceedings drafted by the Judicial Conference of the United States and adopted by the Supreme Court.

✦ adversary proceeding
A type of action that must be commenced by the filing of a complaint.

EXHIBIT 2.5 ✦ *Bankruptcy Rules*

Part	Subject
I	Commencement of case; proceedings related to petition and order for relief
II	Officers and administration; notices; meetings; examinations; elections; attorneys; and accountants
III	Claims and distribution to creditors and equity interest holders; plans
IV	The debtor: duties and benefits
V	Bankruptcy courts and clerks
VI	Collection and liquidation of the estate
VII	Adversary proceedings
VIII	Appeals to district court or bankruptcy appellate panel
IX	General provisions

Not all of the provisions of the Federal Rules of Civil Procedure apply to adversary proceedings in bankruptcy court. In some instances, there have been substantial modifications or revisions to accommodate the special nature of bankruptcy proceedings. For example, Bankruptcy Rule 7003 specifically incorporates most of the provisions of Rule 3 of the Federal Rules of Civil Procedure that apply to the service of a summons and a complaint. Some other parts of Rule 3 are not adopted, however, and Bankruptcy Rule 7003 also sets forth additional methods for serving process in adversary proceedings. Bankruptcy Rule 7012 reflects a similar partial incorporation of provisions from its corresponding Federal Rule of Civil Procedure (Rule 12) that apply to defenses and objections. Provisions governing the time for filing a response to a complaint differ from the federal rule, however, and are specifically provided for in Bankruptcy Rule 7003.

Also, many of the Federal Rules of Appellate Practice have been incorporated in Part VIII of the Bankruptcy Rules, which concerns appeals from bankruptcy court orders. (See Chapter 6 of this book.)

Local Rules

Practice before the bankruptcy court is also governed by local rules that each district has developed to address particular issues or problems left uncovered in the Bankruptcy Rules. Local rules for bankruptcy practice are allowed by Bankruptcy Rule 9029, which states that each district may make whatever rules are needed to govern local practice and procedure. The only limitation is that the local rules cannot be inconsistent with the Bankruptcy Rules.

Local rules often deal with topics such as motion practice, pretrial stipulations and orders, related cases, and the like. Some districts have lengthy local rules, while others do not. Copies of the local rules are usually available through the local legal press or from the clerk of the bankruptcy court. Local rules are also reprinted at the end of some bankruptcy court reporting services and bankruptcy treatises, but these versions are not always kept up to date. Historically, the numbering of local rules was left up to each district. The Judicial Conference of the United States has now asked that each district renumber its rules in the format of the Bankruptcy Rules; many districts have already done so.

The authors of local rules are usually local district judges; having written the rules, they are therefore likely to be very particular about compliance. As a consequence, it is crucial that a paralegal be familiar with all the applicable local rules.

General Orders

Closely related to local rules are general orders. General orders are those issued by one or more of the judges in a particular district concerning specific procedures or other issues impacting cases or appearances before the court. Unfortunately, the distribution of general orders often is not as extensive as it is for local rules, and a good practice is to examine the clerk's bulletin board on a regular basis or ask the clerk whether any new general orders have been made.

In addition to general orders, each bankruptcy judge probably has at least one procedure, idiosyncrasy, or pet peeve that must be observed. These practices may be the most important ones to know from a practical standpoint and are often learned only by trial and error. A good relationship with the court clerk usually helps to avoid transgressing the personal policies of the judge.

Official Forms

To facilitate the processing of paperwork in the bankruptcy administration, 21 official forms have been developed by the Judicial Conference of the United States.

Copies of these official forms are usually published in books and pamphlets containing the text of the Bankruptcy Rules. Some of the official forms are designed for the use of the court clerk. Others are important forms for practitioners; these include petitions, schedules of assets and liabilities, statements of financial affairs, proofs of claim, and ballots for voting on a plan. The more frequently used forms can be generated and filled out using special software programs.

In addition, the Director of the Administrative Office of the United States Courts has created other forms that are used in conjunction with the official forms. These forms are for the use of the courts and the clerk. The Director's Forms, which are not widely published, are available from the clerk's office or from special software programs.

Use of official forms and supplemental forms is obligatory in bankruptcy practice. The rule of substantial compliance applies, however, and Bankruptcy Rule 9009 specifically allows one to alter or combine the forms to fit particular situations.

BANKRUPTCY CRIMES

The Bankruptcy Code offers debtors relief from creditor actions and a fresh start. It does not allow debtors to act without any regard for the rights of others or of the government. In fact, an individual debtor may lose the right to a discharge under Section 727 of the Bankruptcy Code if he or she commits certain improper and/or illegal acts in connection with a bankruptcy case. Also, Section 362(b)(1) lists certain improper and/or illegal acts that are excluded from the scope of the automatic stay.

In addition to state or other federal laws that may punish a company or an individual for illegal acts, Congress has enacted several criminal laws that specifically apply to bankruptcy cases. They are codified in five sections of Title 18 of the United States Code.

Section 152 of Title 18 makes it a crime punishable by a fine of not more than $5,000 or imprisonment for not more than five years, or both, to knowingly and fraudulently perform one of the following acts in connection with a bankruptcy.

- ✦ Conceal property of the estate from anyone charged with the control or custody of property, such as a trustee, or from creditors.
- ✦ Make a false oath or account in or in relation to a bankruptcy case.
- ✦ Present a false declaration, certificate, verification, or statement under penalty of perjury in or in relation to a bankruptcy case.
- ✦ Present or use a false proof of claim.
- ✦ Receive a material amount of property from a debtor after the commencement of a bankruptcy case with the intent to defeat the provisions of the Bankruptcy Code.
- ✦ Give, offer, receive, or attempt to obtain money or property, remuneration, compensation, reward, or advantage for acting or forbearing to act in a bankruptcy case.
- ✦ Transfer or conceal any property before but in contemplation of the commencement of a bankruptcy case with the intent to defeat the provisions of the Bankruptcy Code.
- ✦ Either before or in contemplation of the commencement of a bankruptcy case, conceal, destroy, mutilate, falsify, or make a false entry in any recorded information, including books and records, relating to the financial affairs of a debtor.
- ✦ Withhold from any person entitled to possession recorded information, including books and records, relating to the property or financial affairs of a debtor.

Section 153 makes it a crime punishable by a fine of up to $5,000 or imprisonment for up to five years, or both, for a trustee, custodian, marshal, attorney, or other officer of the court to knowingly and fraudulently appropriate for personal use, embezzle, spend, or transfer any property or secrete or destroy any document belonging to the estate.

Under Section 154, if a trustee, custodian, marshal, or other officer of the court knowingly purchases, directly or indirectly, any property of the estate in which it is involved or refuses to permit a reasonable opportunity for the inspection of documents and accounts relating to the affairs of the estate when directed by the court to do so, he or she is subject to forfeiture of office and a fine of up to $500.

Section 155 makes it a crime for any party in interest, or any attorney for a party in interest, to knowingly and fraudulently enter into an agreement with another party in interest or its attorney for the purpose of fixing the fees or other compensation to be paid for services performed in a bankruptcy case or other insolvency proceeding supervised by a federal court. The punishment is a fine of not more than $5,000 and imprisonment for not more than one year, or both.

Section 156 provides for a fine or imprisonment of up to one year, or both, of a bankruptcy petition preparer who knowingly attempts to disregard the requirement of the Bankruptcy Code or the Bankruptcy Rules. This section was added with the 1994 Amendments. The subject of bankruptcy petition preparers will be discussed in Chapter 3 of this book.

Section 157, also added with the 1994 Amendments, provides for a fine or imprisonment of up to five years, or both, for a person who devises or tries to devise a fraudulent scheme and in the course of that scheme files a bankruptcy petition or other document in a bankruptcy case or makes a false statement or promise before or after the commencement of a bankruptcy case.

Prosecution of bankruptcy crimes is handled by the United States attorney. Investigation assistance is provided by the United States trustee, the Internal Revenue Service, the Federal Bureau of Investigation, and the United States marshal.

ETHICAL CONSIDERATIONS

✦ **ex parte**
A Latin term used to describe an act done without notice to other parties.

Ex parte meetings and communications with the bankruptcy court by parties in interest or their attorneys concerning matters affecting a particular case or proceeding are forbidden by the Bankruptcy Rules. For example, it would be improper to call a bankruptcy judge for the purpose of discussing a pending matter without the participation of adverse parties. It is important to be aware of this rule because paralegals frequently process pleadings through the clerk's office and act as liaisons between the court and the attorney.

SUMMARY

The Bankruptcy Code is divided into odd-numbered chapters, except for Chapter 12. All chapters are further divided into sections. The first one or two digits of a section will tell you in which chapter it is found.

Chapters 1, 3, and 5 contain sections applicable in all bankruptcy cases. Chapter 1 has a number of general provisions including the definitions that are used throughout the Bankruptcy Code. Chapter 3 controls how a case is commenced and administered. Chapter 5 concerns how creditors are paid, what property the debtor may keep, and what claims are enforceable after bankruptcy.

Bankruptcy liquidations are the subject of Chapter 7. In a liquidation, the debtor must deliver all valuable non-exempt property to the bankruptcy trustee.

The bankruptcy trustee will sell the property turned over by the debtor and distribute the proceeds to creditors in the order provided in the bankruptcy case. The debtor will be discharged from most of the unpaid debts except for those that Congress has decided should always be repaid. In addition, the debtor could lose the discharge if he or she commits serious wrongdoing.

Chapter 9 is devoted to reorganizations of municipal entities such as counties, cities, and special districts. Very few Chapter 9 cases have been filed.

Chapter 11 primarily concerns reorganization of businesses, but it can be used by individuals. In a Chapter 11 case, a bankruptcy trustee is not appointed unless the debtor has committed a wrongdoing. The goal of a Chapter 11 case is to confirm a plan of reorganization that provides for a greater payment to creditors than they would receive in a Chapter 7 case. After conducting a confirmation hearing, the bankruptcy court will confirm the plan if it meets the requirements of the Bankruptcy Code.

Chapters 12 and 13 are small-scale reorganizations. Chapter 12 is for farmers and Chapter 13 is for individuals. Each chapter has debt limit and other qualifications for debtors. The goal in these cases is also a plan of reorganization, but a much less complicated one than is found in a Chapter 11 case. Creditors will not vote on the plan, but the bankruptcy court must ensure that the plan complies with the Bankruptcy Code.

The Federal Rules of Bankruptcy Procedure implement the provisions of the Bankruptcy Code. There are more than 200 rules divided into nine parts.

The Judicial Conference of the United States and the Director of the Administrative Office of the United States Courts have developed forms for the more common papers filed in a bankruptcy case. Parties are required to use these forms or ones that substantially resemble them.

✦ KEY TERMS

abandonment	creditors' committee	exemptions	plan exclusivity
abstention	debtor in possession	family farmer	plan of reorganization
adequate information	discharge	family farmer with regular income	plan proponent
adversary proceeding	disclosure statement	municipality	proof of claim
ballot	disposable income	no-asset case	regular income
Bankruptcy Rules	entity	nondischargeable claims	Section 341(a) meeting
claim	equity committee	ordinary course of business	setoff
cram down	ex parte	person	wage earner reorganization

✦ IMPROVE YOUR UNDERSTANDING

1. Determine in which chapter of the Bankruptcy Code and, if applicable, which subchapter, answers to the following questions would likely be found.
   a. What is the deadline for bringing an avoiding power action?
   b. Who may file a claim on behalf of a creditor?
   c. What is the definition of an indenture?
   d. Need a debtor's transaction with his or her attorneys be disclosed?
   e. What happens if the trustee dies?
   f. May the debtor enter into a new lease for its business premises?
   g. When used in the Bankruptcy Code, is the phrase "may not" prohibitive or permissive?

   h. Can the trustee obtain a loan secured by the estate's property?

   i. How many creditors does it take to file an involuntary bankruptcy case?

2. Find the section of Bankruptcy Code concerning the following topics:

   a. How the trustee sells stock belonging to the estate.

   b. The authority of the trustee to operate the debtor's business.

   c. The grounds for dismissal of a Chapter 7 case.

   d. The definition of commodity options dealer.

   e. The role of a creditors' committee in a Chapter 7 case.

   f. The taxable year of the Chapter 7 debtor.

3. Answer the following questions *true* or *false:*

   a. Chapter 7 requires liquidation.

   b. The interim trustee will always serve for the duration of the case.

   c. Claims for fines, penalties, and punitive damages are paid before payment is made to creditors who file late claims.

   d. Alimony and child support claims are nondischargeable.

   e. Trustees must be admitted to practice law in the district in which the bankruptcy court sits.

   f. Trustees are required to object to claims.

   g. The trustee does not need to sell all nonexempt property of the estate.

   h. The debtor is only entitled to keep his or her house to make a fresh start.

   i. The priorities in distribution in a Chapter 7 case are set out in Section 727.

   j. The debtor's refusal to obey an order of the court is a ground to deny discharge.

   k. The debtor's invocation of the Fifth Amendment privilege against self-incrimination will prevent the discharge.

4. Assume Ford Motor Company files a bankruptcy petition and a trustee is appointed. May the trustee purchase a new Ford Motor automobile without violating Title 18?

5. Just before filing a bankruptcy petition, the debtor accidentally sets fire to all his or her books and records. Has a crime been committed?

The Role of the Paralegal in Bankruptcy Practice

THE PARALEGAL'S ROLE IN BANKRUPTCY PRACTICE

Paralegals may participate in virtually every aspect of a bankruptcy case. The paralegal's role in bankruptcy cases is very broad for a number of reasons. First, bankruptcy practice involves a great deal of form work. Courts require certain standardized forms. Practitioners use other widely published forms to convey information to the court. Law school training is rarely required to complete these forms properly; they usually can be filled out by a paralegal under an attorney's supervision.

Second, bankruptcy cases move through the courts rapidly, and clients need attorneys who can get things done quickly. Without paralegals, a busy lawyer could not satisfy the client's needs or the court's timetable.

Third, the use of paralegals enables lawyers to more effectively engage in those activities that only lawyers may perform in bankruptcy court, such as making court appearances.

Fourth, use of paralegals lowers the cost of legal services for clients and for the bankruptcy estate because the billing rate for paralegals is approximately one-half of the rate for attorneys. Lower fees also help a law firm remain competitive. Further, paralegal use is mandatory in many courts where the judges refuse to approve fees for lawyers who perform services that could have been delegated to paralegals.

Community Legal Services

Community legal service agencies or legal aid offices are active in representing low income individuals who have financial problems and who may need to file a bankruptcy case. Paralegals in those offices are often given the responsibility for preparing and managing consumer bankruptcy cases. In a Chapter 7 case, the paralegal may attend, if not conduct, the initial client interview and thereafter may maintain client contact to obtain all the information necessary to prepare and file a petition, the schedules, and all of the other forms necessary. After the petition has been filed with the court, the paralegal may be responsible for notifying the client of the date, time, and place of the Section 341 meeting; preparing the client to answer questions that may be asked at the meeting; attending the Section 341 meeting; drafting reaffirmation agreements; avoiding liens; solving problems such as utility cutoffs, garnishments, repossessions, and foreclosures; and monitoring the case until its end.

In addition to the services just described, the paralegal helping represent a debtor in a Chapter 13 bankruptcy case may draft a plan of reorganization, monitor plan payments, respond to the questions of the client or the creditors, and follow the progress of the case to discharge and closing.

Debtors in consumer bankruptcy cases are very anxious about their financial situations. Paralegals provide a valuable service by being available to answer debtors' questions, and serve as debtors' guides through the often difficult and stressful experience of a bankruptcy case. Often an understanding and supportive tone from a person who quickly returns a phone call is all that is required to reduce a debtor's anxiety. A paralegal will also have to field many calls from creditors providing the case number, the amount for which their claim is scheduled, the date and time of the Section 341 meeting, or other information.

Legal Departments of Corporations, Banking and Lending Institutions, and Government Agencies

The bankruptcy paralegal working with the legal staff of private corporations, public agencies, and lending institutions may be responsible for such tasks as preparing and filing proofs of claims on behalf of the employer, providing documents to support claims, and protecting the employer's interests with respect to unpaid taxes and unexpired leases. The paralegal also may be required to research dischargeability issues, to review bankruptcy notices and pleadings received, and to obtain periodic updates on the progress of the case toward final resolution. In many private companies and public agencies, paralegals have responsibility for drafting various motions that may be used in bankruptcy cases, such as a motion to compel the rejection or assumption of an unexpired lease or a motion to lift the automatic stay.

Law Firms

Most paralegals who are active in bankruptcy matters are employed by law firms. Many law firms concentrate on a particular type of representation—creditors, debtors, committees, or trustees. Other law firm clients may include creditors, debtors, committees and trustees in different cases. Paralegals employed by law firms with a diverse clientele must be versatile and knowledgeable in all areas of bankruptcy practice.

Representing Creditors

Many law firms represent creditors in bankruptcy cases. These clients might be suppliers of goods and services, public utilities, property owners, banks and other secured creditors, or other interested parties. Paralegals working in these firms have responsibilities similar to those of paralegals employed by in-house legal departments of private corporations and public agencies. In addition, the law firm paralegal duties will include keeping the client informed of events in the course of the bankruptcy case. In a firm that has an active creditor practice, a paralegal may be responsible for drafting all relief from stay motions and objections to plans and preparing the attorney for trial.

Representing Debtors

Paralegals working in firms that represent debtors in bankruptcy perform many of the consumer debtor services discussed in this chapter. They also help lawyers commence bankruptcy cases by attending initial meetings with clients, by gathering and reviewing information from the client and the client's representatives, and by preparing drafts of the petition and related documents.

The role of paralegals in representing debtors depends largely on the size and complexity of the case. Usually, a paralegal's functions include establishing filing systems for complex cases, responding to routine questions from creditors and other interested parties, preparing applications for fees of attorneys and other professionals who provide services to the bankruptcy estates, helping with the sale of assets, managing the claims objection process, and assisting counsel in adversary proceedings commenced by or against the estates.

After the commencement of a Chapter 11 case, the paralegal may also establish time frames and responsibilities for filing financial reports, hiring accountants and other professionals, assuming or rejecting leases, collecting accounts receivable, preparing liquidation analyses for the reorganization plan and disclosure statement, preparing pleadings to fix cutoff dates for filing proofs of claim, analyzing claims, filing objections to claims, settling disputed claims, and preparing for the distribution of money and assets to creditors.

Representing Committees

Some law firms regularly represent creditors' or equity holders' committees in Chapter 11 cases. Paralegals in these firms may help their employers gather and analyze information about the debtor's secured and unsecured debt, and they may review monthly financial reports filed by the debtor to chart its financial condition.

A paralegal in one of these firms may also serve as the secretary to the creditors' committee. In this capacity, the paralegal arranges for and attends meetings of the committee, participates in conference calls, takes notes at meetings, prepares and distributes minutes of meetings, and generally keeps the members apprised of developments in the case. The paralegal also tracks developments in the case for the committee by following and summarizing motions filed and orders entered in the bankruptcy court.

Paralegals in firms that represent committees also perform services respecting adversary proceedings by preparing reports on specific issues, researching points of law, assisting the examination and analysis of the debtor's records, and preparing liquidation analyses. The paralegal may also participate in the solicitation of ballots accepting or rejecting a plan of reorganization by organizing mailings, recording results, and filing returned ballots with the court.

Finally, paralegals in firms representing committees help prepare applications to obtain fees for the firm and secure reimbursement of expenses incurred by the members of the committee in attending meetings.

Representing Trustees

Paralegals who work in law firms that represent bankruptcy trustees prepare applications and orders for retaining professionals such as appraisers, auctioneers, and accountants. They also prepare the papers that are used to secure payment for the services provided by these individuals. Paralegals in trustee counsel firms also assist in document production and control in contested matters or adversary proceedings, analyze and prepare objections to claims, prepare applications and orders fixing the final dates for filing administrative claims, and assist in bankruptcy litigation. They also assist their firms in executing on judgments to collect accounts receivable and to recover on preferences and other voidable transfers. Finally, they prepare pleadings and other documents necessary for the sale of assets.

Independent Paralegals

It is increasingly common for paralegals to establish their own firms, providing their services on a contract basis to other legal service providers and, in some instances, directly to consumers of legal services. Indeed, many states are examining the merits of licensing paralegals and allowing them to perform certain types of legal services without attorney supervision. Qualified paralegals can deliver high quality, low cost legal services to people of low to moderate means whose legal needs are not too complicated.

For the most part, bankruptcy is no different than any other area of law in which independent paralegals can play a valuable role in the market. One of the types of legal services being considered which paralegals could be licensed to perform is consumer bankruptcy relief. There is, however, a statutory regulation unique to bankruptcy practice that needs to be considered.

Many districts are experiencing waves of repetitive and abusive filings by individual debtors for the sole purpose of imposing and reimposing the automatic stay in order to stop a foreclosure or an eviction. Most commonly, the debtor intends to do only the minimum amount necessary in order to commence the case and nothing more. For example, the debtor will commence the case by filing only a petition but will never follow up by filing the schedules or a plan. For this reason, the cases are frequently referred to as **face sheet filings.**

In the 1994 Amendments Congress, in an attempt to stem the flood of abusive face sheet filings, added a new Section 110 to the Bankruptcy Code. Section 110 defines a **bankruptcy petition preparer** to be a person, other than an attorney or an employee of an attorney, who prepares a petition or other document to be filed by a debtor in a bankruptcy case for money. Further, Section 110 requires that bankruptcy petition preparers comply with the steps listed in Section 110 in filing the petition.

The bankruptcy petition preparer who fails to do what is required by Section 110 can be fined $500 for each failure. In addition, the court can disallow any fee that is in excess of the value of the services provided. That, however, is not the limit of a bankruptcy petition preparer's liability.

If a bankruptcy case is dismissed because of the negligence or intentional disregard of the Bankruptcy Rules by a bankruptcy petition preparer, if the bankruptcy petition preparer violates Section 110, or if the bankruptcy petition preparer commits any fraudulent, unfair, or deceptive act, the court can order the bankruptcy petition preparer to pay to the debtor the debtor's actual damages, the greater of $2,000 or twice the amount the debtor paid to the bankruptcy petition preparer, and attorneys' fees. If a trustee or creditor brings the bankruptcy petition preparer's conduct to the attention of the court, the bankruptcy petition preparer must also pay the trustee or creditor $1,000 in addition to its attorneys' fees. Section 110 also provides for injunctive relief in addition to damages.

ETHICAL CONSIDERATIONS

The more common ethical problems that paralegals face arise not from contact with the courts or attorneys but with debtor clients. Because the paralegal may have so much interaction with the client, and because the attorney may seem intimidating to the client, the paralegal is often more likely than the attorney to be asked about improper activities. Although there are some gray areas in the application of ethics to bankruptcy practice, there are some absolutes:

1. No information should be knowingly omitted from the schedules that must be filed with the court. For various reasons, clients sometimes say that they do not want a particular debt disclosed. The paralegal must, however, ensure that all assets and debts are properly disclosed.
2. No false information of any kind should be submitted to the court or given to other parties. More often than not, lies in papers filed with the

---

◆ face sheet filings
The commencement of a bankruptcy case by filing only the minimal amount of papers required, usually just the petition, and nothing more to obtain an automatic stay.

◆ bankruptcy petition preparer
A person regulated and defined by Section 110 as a person, other than an attorney or an employee of an attorney, who prepares a petition or other document filed by a debtor in a bankruptcy case for money.

court are discovered, and the ramifications are much more severe than they would be if the correct information was provided initially.

3. Documents should not be backdated. A paralegal should never aid a client in trying to show that an asset was transferred earlier in time than it actually was.

4. Documents should never be modified to disguise or change their original provisions unless all parties to the document agree. A client may say that the document does not express the parties' true intent and should be changed before the bankruptcy filing so that there are no problems later. Changing a document in this manner will almost always lead to greater problems.

5. Documents should be fully completed before they are signed by a client. Never leave blanks that will be filled in later. If the information in such blanks is ever challenged, the client will almost always blame the person who filled in the blanks.

6. Unless approved by the attorney as part of prebankruptcy planning, the debtor's property should not be transferred to another person on the eve of the bankruptcy filing. Even if it is transferred, it should be disclosed in the proper space in the schedules.

7. Any confidential information about the bankruptcy case must remain confidential unless the client allows the information to be shared. Telling any person other than the debtor's attorney information the client provided in confidence violates the attorney–client evidence privilege.

8. Do not become personally involved with the client.

9. Do not hold money or other assets for a client so that they cannot be found by creditors.

10. Ensure the client understands what he or she is signing. Make it a practice to give the client copies of all documents signed.

When in doubt on a particular issue, consult the attorney. Even then, if the attorney asks the paralegal to perform an act that the paralegal believes is inappropriate, he or she should take all reasonable steps to avoid acting improperly.

SUMMARY

Paralegals are particularly valuable in bankruptcy practice. Bankruptcy knowledgeable paralegals are employed by community legal service agencies, inhouse at corporations, banks, and government agencies, as well as law firms. Independent paralegals are increasingly common. Paralegals are active in debtor, creditor, committee, and trustee representation.

In addition to general ethical considerations, special rules govern the use and practice of paralegals in bankruptcy law. Section 110 has detailed rules concerning bankruptcy petition preparers who are not employed by an attorney.

✦ KEY TERMS

bankruptcy petition preparer   face sheet filings

✦ IMPROVE YOUR UNDERSTANDING

1. List the functions that a paralegal could perform for a debtor in a Chapter 7 bankruptcy case.
2. List the functions that a paralegal could perform for a debtor in a Chapter 11 bankruptcy case.
3. List the functions that a paralegal could perform for a creditor in a Chapter 11 bankruptcy.
4. List the types of employers that might employ a paralegal to handle bankruptcy matters.
5. List the steps that Section 110 requires a bankruptcy petition preparer to follow.

The Building Blocks of Bankruptcy Law

THERE ARE TWO important topics in bankruptcy law—the automatic stay and **executory contracts**—that are so important to an understanding of virtually all other bankruptcy topics that they are examined separately in this chapter. In addition, a bankruptcy paralegal will need an understanding of other federal and state law governing how a bankruptcy case functions. This chapter provides an introduction to two such bodies of law—the Uniform Commercial Code and general real estate law.

✦ **executory contract**
A contract that has not yet been fully performed on either side.

AUTOMATIC STAY

In General

The most important benefit a debtor has in a bankruptcy case is the automatic stay. The automatic stay, as mentioned in Chapter 1, is an injunction that prevents anyone from doing anything to interfere with the debtor or the debtor's property once a bankruptcy petition has been filed. This includes repossessions, litigation, foreclosures, or even demand letters. In a reorganization case, for example, the automatic stay gives the debtor some time to reorganize its business, unburdened by the demands of creditors, while in a liquidation case, the automatic stay keeps the creditors at bay while the debtor's assets are liquidated. The automatic stay also reduces the cost of the liquidation or reorganization since the debtor or the trustee will not be compelled to defend litigation in many different locations.

The automatic stay also helps creditors. It prevents a race to the courthouse by stopping all further efforts to collect debts from the debtor. This enables creditors to be treated as equally as is possible.

Automatic Stay Provisions

The Bankruptcy Code lists specific acts that are automatically stayed by the filing of a bankruptcy case; it also lists acts that are not stayed. These are described briefly in the following sections.

Acts That Are Stayed   Section 362(a) lists eight separate acts of creditors that are prohibited. Some of these prohibited acts are against the debtor, some are against the property of the debtor, while others are against the property of the estate, which is not always the same as the property of the debtor. For example, exempt property is property of the debtor but not property of the estate. The prohibitions in Section 362(a) of the Bankruptcy Code appear in the following order:

1. Commencing or continuing legal proceedings of virtually any kind against the debtor.
2. Attempting to collect existing judgments against the debtor or the estate's property.
3. Any act to obtain possession or control of property of the estate.
4. Any act to create, perfect, or enforce liens against property of the estate.
5. Any act to impose or enforce liens on the debtor's property that secure a prebankruptcy claim.
6. Any attempt to collect debts against the debtor created before the filing of the petition.
7. Setoff of any prebankruptcy debts due to the debtor against claims due from the debtor.
8. Proceedings in the United States tax court concerning the debtor.

The eight prohibitions overlap, and more than one provision may apply to a particular act. For example, several provisions of Section 362(a) prevent the debtor from being sued on an old debt. It would be prohibited by provisions 1 and 6 listed above. An attempt to repossess the debtor's car would be precluded by provisions 3 and 4 if the car was not exempt and provision 6 if it was.

Acts That Are Not Stayed   The automatic stay provisions of the Bankruptcy Code do not prevent all creditor activities. In fact, Section 362(b) of the Bankruptcy Code lists 18 specific acts that are not stayed by the filing of a bankruptcy case. The most common exceptions to the automatic stay found in Section 362(b) are:

1. Commencing or continuing criminal proceedings against the debtor. [§ 362(b)(1)]
2. Establishing the right to or collecting alimony, maintenance, or support from property that is not part of the bankruptcy estate. [§ 362(b)(2)]
3. Tax audits. [§ 362(b)(9)(A)]
4. Issuing tax deficiency notices to the debtor by a governmental unit. [§ 362(b)(9)(B)]
5. Eviction of the debtor from commercial real property under a terminated lease. [§ 362(b)(10)]

One previously common exception to the automatic stay was repealed in 1998. The repealed provision [§ 362(b)(5)] provided an exception for actions by governmental units to enforce police or regulatory powers.

Effective Period of the Stay   The automatic stay becomes effective when a bankruptcy petition is filed, regardless of whether the petition is a voluntary petition filed by the debtor or an involuntary petition filed by the creditors. The moment the stay is in place, it is binding on all creditors, even those who have no knowledge of the commencement of the bankruptcy case.

When the automatic stay stops depends on whether the stay is applied to the debtor, the debtor's property, or property of the estate. The stay may terminate against the debtor yet remain in effect against property of the estate. Each element must be analyzed separately. Exhibit 4.1 demonstrates how each element should be viewed separately.

The stay terminates against property of the debtor when the bankruptcy case is closed or dismissed. It terminates against the debtor personally upon the granting or denying of a discharge. Hence, in a Chapter 7 case, the stay terminates against the property and the debtor if and when the trustee abandons all the property and the debtor obtains a discharge.

EXHIBIT 4.1 ✦ *Is the Automatic Stay in Effect?*

	Bankruptcy Petition Filed	Trustee Abandons Property of the Estate	Debtor Exempts Property	Court Gives Bank the Right to Foreclose on Property of the Estate	Debtor Obtains a Discharge	Debtor is Denied a Discharge	Case Closed
Acts Against the Debtor or the Debtor's Property	Yes. The automatic stay will go into effect the instant the case is filed.	Yes. If property is abandoned by the trustee, it becomes property of the debtor.	Yes. Exempt property ceases to be property of the estate and becomes property of the debtor.	Yes. The automatic stay protecting the debtor will still be in place. The creditor can foreclose on the property of the estate but still cannot sue the debtor.	No. Once the debtor has been discharged, he or she no longer has the benefit of the automatic stay. Note though, that if a debt has been discharged, it is no longer enforceable against the debtor.	No. If the debtor is denied a discharge, the automatic stay protecting the debtor and his or her property is no longer in effect.	No. The dismissal or closure of a bankruptcy case ends the automatic stay. Whether or not debts can be pursued depends on whether the debtor received a discharge.
Acts Against Property of the Estate	Yes. The automatic stay will go into effect the instant the case is filed.	No. Once property of the estate is abandoned, it is no longer property of the estate, and the automatic stay will not prevent creditor actions.	No. Once property is exempt, it is no longer property of the estate.	No. The automatic stay is terminated.	Yes. The debtor's discharge will not lift the automatic stay that protects property of the estate.	Yes. Again, the debtor's discharge does not impact the status of the property of the estate.	No. Once a case is closed or dismissed, there no longer is property of the estate.

Secured creditors are seldom content to wait until a case is closed before enforcing their liens against the debtor's property. Typically, secured creditors want the automatic stay lifted as quickly as possible, which can sometimes be accomplished. Section 362(d) of the Bankruptcy Code authorizes the court, on the motion of an interested party and following a hearing, to grant relief from the automatic stay for good cause, such as a lack of adequate protection of the creditor's interest in the property. A creditor may also obtain relief from the automatic stay with respect to an act against property if the debtor does not have equity in such property and if the property is not necessary to an effective reorganization. Typically, creditors seek relief from automatic stays on both grounds. In the 1994 Amendments, Congress made it easier for secured creditors to obtain relief from stay in cases involving real estate. These changes are discussed in Chapter 12 of this book.

✦ **secured creditor**
Person whose money is protected by a mortgage, lien, pledge, or other security interest.

Motions to lift the automatic stay provide the most common type of litigation in bankruptcy court. The practice and procedures involved in such motions are covered in Bankruptcy Code Sections 362(d)–(e) and Chapter 12 of this book.

Scope of the Stay The automatic stay is exclusively for the benefit of the debtor, the debtor's property, and property of the estate. The protection of the automatic stay does not extend to others. If a creditor lends money to two persons and only one of them declares bankruptcy, the creditor may pursue the other party to enforce the debt. Similarly, when a corporate debtor files for bankruptcy protection, the automatic stay does not prohibit the creditors from pursuing any legitimate claims against the corporation's officers and directors. If a partnership files a bankruptcy petition, a creditor can still sue the partners.

There are exceptions to these provisions. In Chapter 13 cases, the automatic stay prevents creditors from enforcing debts not only against the debtor, but also against others who may be liable for the debts. Examples are cosigners and guarantors. On a case-by-case basis, the court may also expand the automatic stay to prohibit acts by creditors that are not specifically covered by the automatic stay.

Violation of the Stay Generally, acts done in violation of an automatic stay are void and of no effect. For example, if a secured creditor forecloses on a parcel of real property after the commencement of a bankruptcy case, the foreclosure is invalid and the debtor still owns the property. If a car is repossessed in violation of the automatic stay, the repossession is invalid and the car must be returned to the debtor. Some courts say that acts in violation of the automatic stay are merely voidable rather than void. In these jurisdictions, the debtor must take some action to undo the effect of a creditor's violation of the automatic stay.

Not every act done in technical violation of an automatic stay is void or voidable. The Bankruptcy Code provides that a transfer of real property in violation of the automatic stay cannot be avoided if it was made to a good faith purchaser who did not know of the bankruptcy case and who paid a fair price, unless, before the transfer, notice of the bankruptcy petition was recorded in the county where the property is located. If less than a fair price was paid for the property, the purchaser may be compelled to return the property, but the purchaser will retain a lien on the property for the value given.

A creditor who willfully violates the automatic stay may be liable for damages to any individual injured by the violation. Creditors who commit innocent violations of the automatic stay are unlikely to be compelled to pay damages.

EXECUTORY CONTRACTS AND UNEXPIRED LEASES

In General

◆ **unexpired lease**
A lease whose term has not been reached prior to its rejection or assumption.

In addition to the automatic stay, Congress provided another tool for the protection of creditors in liquidation cases and for the revitalization of business enterprises in reorganization cases. It is the power to avoid performance under executory contracts and **unexpired leases.** This authority is found in Section 365 of the Bankruptcy Code, which provides that the trustee will not be bound by an executory contract or unexpired lease of the debtor unless it is expressly adopted by the trustee. The other party to the contract or lease may have a claim for damages for breach of the agreement, but the estate will not be forced to perform. A debtor in possession in a reorganization case has the same power to avoid performing under executory contracts and unexpired leases.

The scope of Section 365 includes leases of real and personal property whose terms have not expired and contracts that are executory. An executory contract is not defined in the Bankruptcy Code but is commonly thought of as one in which there is sufficient performance remaining on each side so that if there was a breach by one party, it would excuse the other party from performing. This definition of an executory contract was first suggested by Professor Vern Countryman, and it is known as the Countryman test. The following are some examples of what are and what are not executory contracts:

- A supply contract is an executory contract. An example of a supply contract would be an agreement by a manufacturer to sell to a builder the concrete it requires each month for a set price. If the selling party fails to deliver the concrete, the buyer is excused from paying.
- A management contract is an executory contract. A management contract is an agreement by the owner of property to pay another person or firm to manage the property on the owner's behalf. If the owner failed to pay for the service, the manager would not have to perform further management services. Conversely, if the manager stopped caring for the property, the owner would be relieved of the obligation to make further payments under the contract.
- A promissory note is not an executory contract. A promissory note is evidence of an agreement to repay money already lent. The lender fully performs by lending the money, and there is nothing that could relieve the borrower from paying.

The power to avoid an executory contract or unexpired lease need not be used by the trustee or the debtor in possession. Whether one exercises the option to avoid depends on the circumstances of the particular case. For example, assume the debtor was in the business of buying tomatoes and processing them into tomato sauce. The trustee is operating the debtor's business. If the current market price of the same type of tomatoes that the debtor has agreed to purchase under a supply contract is lower than the contract price, the trustee would want to avoid the contract and purchase tomatoes on the market at the lower price. On the other hand, if the market price for tomatoes is more than the contract price, the trustee would insist on performance of the supply contract by the other party. In the lease context, the debtor may have a long-term lease for warehouse space that was entered into when lease rates were low. The trustee will want to keep that lease. If the lease was entered into when rents were high, the trustee will want to dispose of the lease and the obligation to pay the high rents.

If the trustee or the debtor in possession does not want to be bound by an executory contract or an unexpired lease because it is uneconomical or otherwise burdensome, the contract or lease must be rejected. If the trustee or the debtor in possession wants to be bound by an executory contract or an unexpired lease, the contract or lease must be assumed. The timing and procedural rules for assumption and rejection are very different.

Rejection

The mere fact that a contract is executory or that the term of a lease has not expired does not alone justify rejection of the agreement or lease. The trustee or the debtor in possession is required to exercise good judgment, and there must be a legitimate reason for rejecting the contract or the lease. This is not a difficult test to meet; it is met by proof that the trustee can obtain a better deal elsewhere or that rejection will save the estate money. Application of the test, however, will prevent the trustee or the debtor in possession from rejecting a lease or contract for the purpose of entering into a new, more expensive agreement with an affiliated person.

The **rejection** of an executory contract or an unexpired lease is treated like any other breach of the agreement except that the party entitled to the debtor's performance cannot obtain a court order requiring the debtor to perform as would be true outside of bankruptcy. In order to preserve its damage claim, the other party to the contract or lease must file a proof of claim with the estate. The claim will be treated as if it arose before the commencement of the case and be paid with all the other prebankruptcy claims.

✦ rejection
The means for the estate to rid itself of any ongoing obligations under an executory contract or unexpired lease of the debtor.

Assumption

✦ assumption
The means for the estate to bind itself to an executory contract or unexpired lease of the debtor.

Good judgment is also required for an **assumption;** in fact, the rules for an assumption are much more stringent than they are for rejection. For example, although any lease or executory contract can be rejected, some types of executory contracts can never be assumed unless the other party consents. The following are some examples:

- ✦ Contracts to perform personal services, such as painting a portrait or making a record.
- ✦ Contracts to loan money.
- ✦ Contracts to issue the debtor's stocks or bonds.

These contracts cannot be assumed because of their type. Their inability to be assumed is not caused by the terms of the contract. Some contracts and leases try to prevent an assumption by specifically providing that the agreement terminates on the debtor's insolvency, by the commencement of a bankruptcy case, or on the appointment of a trustee. These provisions are called *ipso facto* **clauses.** Generally, they are not enforceable and will not prevent a trustee or debtor in possession from assuming a contract where there is good reason for doing so.

✦ *ipso facto* clauses
Latin for "by the fact itself" or "by the mere fact that." A provision in a contract or lease that provides that the contract or lease is breached or terminated if one of the parties becomes insolvent or the subject of a bankruptcy case.

If a contract is assumable and the trustee or the debtor in possession wishes to assume it, certain conditions must be fulfilled before the court will allow the contract or lease to be assumed. Those conditions are:

- ✦ All prebankruptcy monetary defaults (other than those created by *ipso facto* clauses) must be cured or adequate assurance given that the defaults will be cured promptly.
- ✦ The other party to the contract or lease must be compensated for any loss incurred by the debtor's breach or must be given adequate assurance that compensation will be paid.
- ✦ The other party must be provided with adequate assurance that the contract or lease will be fully performed in the future.

There are also special requirements for the assumption of a lease of part of a shopping center. They are as follows:

- ✦ The funds generated from the operation of the store must be sufficient to pay the rent.
- ✦ If the lease calls for all or part of the rent to be based on a percentage of the store's receipts, these receipts will not substantially decline in the future.
- ✦ Assumption will not breach any condition of a master lease applicable to all tenants in the shopping center.
- ✦ Assumption will not substantially disrupt any tenant mix or balance in the shopping center.

Assignment If a lease or a contract has value, the trustee or the debtor in possession may find it advantageous to sell or make an **assignment** of rights under the contract or lease to a third party. A lease or contract has value when the property or service to be provided is worth more than the trustee or debtor in possession is obligated to pay under the terms of the agreement. For example, the estate may be entitled to receive under a contract computer equipment it no longer needs. The equipment may have a market value of $10,000 but the contract price is only $8,000. The trustee could sell the estate's rights under the contract to a third party for $1,000, and the third party could obtain the equipment by paying the vendor $8,000. The estate earns $1,000, the buyer saves $1,000 and the vendor has received the benefit of the bargain.

In order to be able to assign a valuable contract or lease, the trustee or debtor in possession must first assume it by complying with the assumption requirements listed earlier. The assumption and the assignment are commonly done at the same time with adequate assurance of future performance given by the third party. Like *ipso facto* clauses, any restriction on assignment in the contract or lease is not enforceable.

Once a contract or lease has been assumed and assigned, the estate has no further liability under it. If there is a breach, no claim can be asserted against the estate.

♦ **assignment**
The transfer of property, rights in property, or money to another person.

Timing

The deadline for assuming or rejecting an executory contract or unexpired lease depends on the chapter in which the case is pending; for leases, a distinction is also made based on whether the lease is for personal property or real property. In a Chapter 7 case, the trustee must assume an executory contract or an unexpired lease within 60 days of the entry of the order for relief, or the agreement is deemed rejected and cannot be revived. In a voluntary case, the order for relief is entered on the same date as the petition is filed; in an involuntary case, it is sometime later.

In a Chapter 11, 12, or 13 case, a lease for nonresidential real property must be assumed within 60 days of the entry of the order for relief, or it, too, will be deemed rejected. The 60-day period for assumption may be extended by the court, however. For all other contracts and leases, the trustee or the debtor in possession may reserve the decision to assume or reject the agreement until any time prior to the confirmation of a reorganization plan. The other party to the contract or the lessor may ask the court to shorten that deadline, however, and the court may in fact order an earlier assumption of the agreement. The creditor's options are discussed in greater detail in Chapter 12 of this book.

Special Situations

In order to avoid prejudice to the nondebtor party and as a result of special interest lobbying, Congress has created four exceptions to the general rules for the treatment of executory contracts. These exceptions apply if the debtor:

1. is a seller of real property or a landlord;
2. is a licensor of a right to intellectual property;
3. has entered into a collective bargaining agreement; or
4. puts at risk the medical, accident, or death benefits of retired employees.

A discussion of each of these special situations follows.

Debtor as Seller of Real Property or Landlord There are special rules for contracts in which the debtor is the seller of real property and for leases in which the debtor is the landlord. Mindful of the detriment that could be suffered by the other parties to those contracts and leases by their rejection, Congress gave them greater protection than other parties.

If the debtor is a landlord and rejects the lease, the tenant may treat the lease as terminated and move out. Alternatively, the tenant can remain in possession for the term of the lease and any renewal. If the tenant remains in possession, any damages suffered on account of the rejection may be offset against the rent that is owing; but the right to sue the debtor for damages is lost, as is the right to enforce a provision in the lease for special services. For example, if the lease obligated the landlord to provide guard services, the tenant who remains in possession may have to make other arrangements for security of the leased premises. The tenant can, however, reduce the rent by the amount it is reasonably required to spend for replacement guards.

If the debtor entered into a contract to sell real property before filing bankruptcy, and the buyer took possession of the property, the buyer may treat the contract as terminated, give up possession, and file a claim for damages upon the rejection of the agreement by the trustee or the debtor in possession. The buyer will also have a lien on the property to secure repayment of any money already paid in performance of the contract. The buyer may also elect to remain in possession of the property, enforce the contract, and setoff any damages against the remaining money due under the agreement. By such election, however, the purchaser waives any claim for damages against the estate. Once the buyer has made all payments due under the contract, the trustee or the debtor in possession must deliver appropriate documents transferring title of the property to the buyer.

There is also a special provision for a buyer of property from the debtor who has not taken possession at the time the bankruptcy case is filed and thus has no right to be in possession after the contract is rejected. That purchaser will have a lien of the property as security for recovery of any payments made as well as a claim for damages.

License Agreements   Special provisions are also made for cases in which the debtor is the licensor of a right to intellectual property, such as computer software, patents, and copyrighted material. Congress was concerned that a licensee who had built a business around the intellectual right would be ruined by the licensor's subsequent bankruptcy and the trustee's rejection of the agreement in order to force a more advantageous contract or license with a third party. Hence, the Bankruptcy Code provides that if the trustee or debtor in possession rejects an executory contract under which the debtor is a licensor of a right to intellectual property, the licensee has an election to treat the contract as terminated or to continue performance of the contract for the duration of the agreement and any extension. If the licensee elects to retain his or her rights under the contract, all royalty payments must be paid and the licensee is deemed to waive any right of setoff and any claim for damages arising from performance of the contract.

Collective Bargaining Agreements   Special requirements also apply to the assumption or rejection of a collective bargaining agreement that was entered into by the debtor before filing for bankruptcy under Chapter 11. The danger Congress sought to address was the likelihood that a person or firm would seek protection under the bankruptcy laws in order to be in a position to reject a union contract, pay lower wages, and offer fewer benefits for the employees. Thus, the Bankruptcy Code requires that the debtor and an agent of the collective bargaining unit attempt to work out an acceptable modification of the agreement. If this cannot be done, the debtor may seek an order authorizing the rejection of the collective bargaining agreement. In order to prevail, however, the debtor must show that the balance of the equities clearly favors the rejection. This is a substantially higher standard than is imposed for the rejection of other contracts.

Retirement Benefits   Congress had similar concerns for retirees who receive medical and other benefits from their former employers who might decide to seek Chapter 11 protection in order to reduce or eliminate those benefits. The Bankruptcy Code provides that the trustee or debtor in possession may not modify the health, accident, or death benefits of retired employees under any program established before the bankruptcy case was commenced in the absence of consent to do so by an authorized representative of the retirees. The court may allow a modification of benefits over the objection of a representative of the retirees, but only if the court first finds that:

1. the trustee has made a modification proposal to the retirees that meets certain criteria;
2. the authorized representative of the retirees has refused to accept the proposal without good cause; and
3. the modification is necessary to permit the reorganization of the debtor and assure that all of the creditors, the debtor, and all of the affected parties are treated equitably.

Procedures

The procedures for obtaining court approval of an assumption or a rejection of an executory contract or an unexpired lease are set forth in Bankruptcy Rule 6006. The court is required to hold a hearing on a motion by the trustee or the debtor in possession, and the creditors must have received notice of the hearing. Court approval is not required for a contract or lease that has been deemed rejected by operation of law because no assumption had been made within the first 60 days and no extension of time was sought or obtained.

Pursuant to 11 USC § 502, there may be some limitations on the amount of a claim for damages that the nondebtor party may assert. If the claimant is the owner of leased property, the claim is limited to the amount that was due at the filing of the case plus future rent for one year or 15 percent of the remaining rent due under the lease for a term not to exceed three years. If the claimant was employed by the debtor under a contract of employment, the amount of the claim is limited to the wages or salary due at the time of the filing of the petition plus wages and salary for one year after termination.

OTHER SUBSTANTIVE LAW IMPORTANT IN BANKRUPTCY PRACTICE

Although the Bankruptcy Code is comprehensive, sometimes it incorporates or refers to other federal or state law. To know how a bankruptcy case functions, it is important to have a basic understanding of a few other bodies of law. This chapter examines the two most significant: the **Uniform Commercial Code,** which governs the sale of personal property and its use as collateral, and general real estate law, including the various forms of ownership and financing mechanisms. This chapter is not an exhaustive discussion of either of these two important areas of the law, but it is designed to give the paralegal an understanding of the issues that might arise in a bankruptcy case.

✦ **Uniform Commercial Code**
A comprehensive set of laws adopted in whole or in part by every state on every major type of business law, including contract law as it applies to the sale of goods, banking, and negotiable instruments.

THE UNIFORM COMMERCIAL CODE

In General

♦ **commercial transaction**
A phrase used to designate dealings of persons engaged in business.

The Uniform Commercial Code, usually referred to as the UCC, was drafted as the set of rules of law to govern **commercial transactions** in the United States. Commercial transactions can include virtually any aspect of business, in part because the definition of commerce is very broad.

The American Law Institute and the National Conference of Commissioners on Uniform State Laws (the two entities responsible for drafting and proposing model and uniform laws to the various states) prepared the UCC in 1949, and it has been modified continually ever since. Unlike the Bankruptcy Code, a federal law enacted by Congress that applies throughout the United States, the UCC is a proposed law for the various states to enact if their legislatures so choose. Each state is free to adopt the UCC in whole or in part or with any variations its legislature finds appropriate. Despite the fact that it need not be enacted, the UCC is now in force in whole or in part in every state.

There are 10 articles (in some states called divisions) in the UCC, as follows:

ARTICLE	TITLE
1	General Provisions
2	Sales
2A	Leases
3	Commercial Paper
4	Bank Deposits and Collections
5	Letters of Credit
6	Bulk Sales
7	Warehouse Receipts, Bills of Lading, and Other Documents of Title
8	Investment Securities
9	Secured Transactions

Each article has a number of sections. As in the Bankruptcy Code, the first digit of the section number indicates which article it is in. For example, Section 2101 is in Article 2; Section 9301 is in Article 9, and so on. Bankruptcy issues may arise in every article of the UCC. The two articles that have the most significance in a bankruptcy case are Sales and Secured Transactions.

Article 2—Sales

♦ **goods**
All things that are movable or are fixtures, but not money, documents, instruments, accounts, chattel paper, general intangibles, or minerals or the like before extraction.

A sale for Article 2 purposes is simply a transaction by which a seller transfers ownership of goods to a buyer for a price. **Goods** are defined as all things that are movable; money and securities are excluded. Article 2 describes the obligations of the seller and the obligations of the buyer and the remedies available to each if either one breaches, or if both of them breach, those obligations. It specifically allows the parties to agree to alter those obligations and remedies set forth in Article 2.

Article 2 is especially important in a bankruptcy case when the buyer becomes the debtor. Article 2 is crucial in order to understand whether a seller has a right to be paid, whether title for the goods has passed to the buyer, or whether the seller has a right to reclaim the goods if title has already passed. Article 2 is also needed to measure damages in order to analyze whether to assume or reject a contract for the sale of goods.

Article 2 also includes a list of contracts that are not enforceable either because they were unacceptably unfair at the time they were made; were not in writing when the law required them to be; or were based on fraud, duress, or mistake. This distinction is important for bankruptcy purposes because under Section 502, any claim that is unenforceable can be allowed in the bankruptcy case.

Obligations Under a Contract   Article 2 sets forth the various obligations of a seller and of a buyer to a contract. To fully perform its side of a contract, the seller must transfer ownership and deliver the goods. In the absence of an agreement between a buyer and a seller as to how the seller will perform its obligations, delivery is to be made at the seller's place of business, within a reasonable time after the contract is made, and the offering of the goods is to be made in a single lot rather than in pieces.

A buyer's obligations are to accept the goods when they are tendered by the seller and to pay the agreed upon price. If the parties fail to specify in their contract how the buyer accepts or pays, Article 2 will fill in the missing terms. Generally, the buyer can accept by signifying that it is accepting, by using the goods, or by failing to reject. A buyer's obligation to pay is usually performed by paying the price as the parties have agreed. If they do not specify when payment is due, it is to be made when the goods are delivered.

Title   Title is the legal recognition of who owns and is responsible for the goods. Under Article 2, the parties may determine by agreement when title to the goods will pass from the seller to the buyer. Obviously, the seller will not want title to pass until the buyer has paid for the goods. The buyer will want title to pass as quickly as possible. Absent an agreement that provides otherwise, the UCC provides that title passes when the seller completes its delivery obligations. When title passes is a very important concept for bankruptcy purposes because it determines whether the seller or the buyer has the right to sell the goods to pay creditors. For a seller, whether title has passed will determine if the seller can take back the goods or the seller will be an unsecured creditor in the buyer's bankruptcy case.

Breaches   Article 2 details how a contract for the sale of goods is breached and describes the aggrieved party's remedies for the breach. A seller can breach by not making any tender of the goods, by making a bad tender by delivering to the wrong place, or by delivering the wrong goods. A buyer breaches by refusing to accept goods properly tendered or by refusing to pay for the goods.

If the seller fails to make any tender, the buyer has two remedies. First, the buyer can force the seller to perform by obtaining a court order requiring the seller to deliver the goods. This remedy is usually only available if the goods are unique or there is some other reason why the buyer will not be satisfied by a money judgment. Second, the buyer may seek damages. The amount of damages the buyer will be entitled to is the difference between the regular price of the goods and the price the buyer agreed to pay. The buyer will be entitled to these damages if it does not buy new goods. If the buyer actually buys replacement goods, the amount of damages will be the difference between what was paid for the replacement goods and the original contract price. The new purchase must be in good faith and without unreasonable delay or upon unreasonable terms. In addition to these damages, the buyer will also be entitled to **incidental damages,** such as the cost of traveling in order to buy the replacement goods, and **consequential damages.** Consequential damages include any loss caused by the breach that the seller knew of and that was not remedied by buying new goods. If, for instance, the buyer was going to use the goods as a component of a part it was selling, and would be financially penalized by its buyer if the part was not delivered on time, the breaching component seller could be liable for the amount of the financial penalty as a consequential damage.

✦ **incidental damages**
Damages incurred as a direct result of the breach of contract.

✦ **consequential damages**
Damages that do not flow directly and immediately from the wrongful act of the party but only from the consequences or results of such act.

If the seller breaches by making a bad tender, the buyer can accept the goods despite the nonconformity or reject them. If the buyer rejects the goods, its remedies are the same as though no tender was made at all. However, the seller may have the right to cure the defect if the time for performance has not expired. If the buyer rejects but has possession of the goods, it must hold the goods for a reasonable period of time to permit the seller to remove them. If the seller does not, the buyer must either store the goods, ship them back to the seller, or sell them on the seller's behalf.

Even if the buyer accepts nonconforming goods, it is still entitled to damages but it must give notice to the seller of the breach within a reasonable period of time after the breach is discovered. If the notice is not given, the buyer is barred from all remedies. If a proper notice is given, the buyer may be able to collect damages for breach of warranty, measured as the difference between the value of the goods without the defects and the value of the goods as delivered. If the breach involved how the tender was made—for example, the delivery was late—the buyer is entitled to recover damages caused by that breach.

If the buyer wrongfully refuses to accept goods properly tendered, the seller can sue for damages, measured by the contract price minus the market price. Alternatively, the seller can sell the goods to a third party and sue for the difference between the contract price and the resale price. If the goods are not salable in the seller's ordinary course of business, the seller can sue for the entire contract price. In all cases, the seller is also entitled to incidental damages, including expenses incurred because of the breach.

If the buyer accepts the goods but then breaches by failing to pay the purchase price, the seller's remedy is to sue to collect the purchase price. However, if after the goods are accepted by the buyer, the seller discovers the buyer's insolvency, the seller may reclaim the goods if the buyer still has them and if a demand is made within 10 to 20 days after the receipt of the goods. Reclamation rights are preserved, indeed made stronger, if the buyer files a bankruptcy case (see Chapter 12 of this book).

Article 9—Secured Transactions

♦ **secured transactions**
A phrase used to describe dealings involving the granting or taking of a security interest.

♦ **personal property**
Property that consists of temporary or movable items.

♦ **security interest**
An interest in personal property or fixtures that secures payment or performance of an obligation. [UCC 1-201 (37)]

♦ **collateral**
Property that is subject to a security interest.

♦ **secured party**
A lender, seller, or other person in whose favor there is a security interest.

The other key article of the UCC for bankruptcy purposes is Article 9. It concerns **secured transactions** involving **personal property** such as goods, bank accounts, and almost any other property that is not real estate. A secured transaction under Article 9 involves a relationship between the debtor and a creditor in which the debtor has given or the creditor has obtained by operation of law an interest in all or some of the debtor's assets to secure repayment of a debt. The assets subject to the interest, which is called a **security interest** or a lien, are labeled **collateral.** The creditor is called the **secured party.** A diagram of a secured transaction is provided in Exhibit 4.2.

EXHIBIT 4.2 ♦ *Diagram of a Secured Transaction*

There are three purposes of a security interest. The first is to make the debt more easily collectible if the debtor will not or cannot pay when the debt is due. The second purpose is to give the secured party a position superior to that of the other creditors of the debtor who might attempt to take the collateral to satisfy their debts. The third purpose is to protect the secured party's rights in the collateral if it is sold by the debtor.

A brief discussion of how a consensual security interest is created follows. Article 9 does not discuss how nonconsensual security interests, which usually arise by operation of law, such as warehouse liens, are created; but it does control the rights of the secured parties as against creditors holding nonconsensual liens.

Article 9 is frequently applied in bankruptcy cases. One of the most common issues is a bankruptcy trustee's ability to defeat a secured party's rights in collateral. A bankruptcy trustee becomes cloaked with all the rights of certain hypothetical persons. If one of these hypothetical persons would prevail over a secured creditor, so will the trustee. If the trustee prevails, the collateral can be sold and the proceeds distributed to all creditors—not just the secured party. This is a very powerful tool for the trustee; the following discussion is key to understanding just how powerful.

Creation of a Security Interest   A consensual security interest can be created in two ways. The first is by a **security agreement.** A security agreement must be in writing, contain a description of the collateral, state that the debtor is granting a security interest in the collateral to the creditor, and must be signed by the debtor. The second method of creating a security interest is by the creditor taking possession of the debtor's property with the intent that the possession is to secure a debt. If the secured party has possession of the collateral, an oral agreement will be sufficient to create the security interest.

A security interest is effective when it has **attached.** In order to have the security interest attach, there must be written or oral agreement, value must have been given by the secured party, and the debtor must have rights in the collateral. Even though there may be a signed security agreement between the debtor and the creditor, the security interest is not valid until the secured party has loaned money to the debtor or given other value. Even if there is a signed security agreement and the secured party has made the loan, there is no security interest until the debtor owns the collateral. For example, suppose the debtor wants to buy a washing machine. The debtor borrows money from a finance company and agrees to grant the finance company a security interest in the washing machine. The debtor then orders the washing machine. At that point, there is an agreement, and the creditor has given value. However, if title has not passed from the seller of the washing machine to the debtor, the secured creditor will not have a security interest in the washing machine because the debtor does not have rights in the collateral. Until all three elements of attachment have occurred, the finance company has no greater rights against the debtor or any of its property than does any other creditor. The final step is the creation of an enforceable security interest or perfection, which will be discussed later in this chapter.

Types of Collateral   There are three types of collateral:

1. goods;
2. **rights evidenced by a writing;** and
3. **intangibles.**

The first type of collateral, goods, includes **fixtures** and everything that is movable. A fixture is a good that becomes so related to a particular parcel of real estate that an interest in it arises under real estate law. A heating system installed in a building is an example of a fixture.

✦ **security agreement**
An agreement that creates or provides for a security interest.

✦ **the process of attachment**
Making a security interest enforceable. Unless explicit agreement postpones the time of attachment, it occurs when: (a) secured party pursuant to agreement possesses collateral, or debtor has signed a security agreement describing collateral; (b) value has been given; (c) debtor has rights in the collateral.

✦ **rights evidenced by a writing**
Instruments, documents of title, and chattel paper.

✦ **intangibles**
Assets that are owned by an ongoing business, such as goodwill, trademarks, copyrights, franchises, and the like.

✦ **fixtures**
Goods that are so related to a particular parcel of real estate that an interest in them arises under real estate law.

Goods can be further broken down into four groups according to how they are primarily used by the debtor. The four groups are:

1. *consumer goods*—those goods used primarily for personal, family, or household purposes;
2. *inventory*—goods sold, leased, or furnished; raw materials to be processed; and materials consumed in a business;
3. *farm products*—crops, livestock, or supplies used or produced in farming operations and products of crops or livestock in their unmanufactured states; and
4. *equipment*—goods used primarily in a business and that are not inventory, farm products, or consumer goods.

If a particular good does not fit in any of the other categories, it is usually labeled as equipment. How a debtor primarily uses a particular good determines the good's category. For example, to a farmer, a tractor is equipment; to a dealer in tractors, a tractor is inventory.

The second category of collateral, rights evidenced by a writing, includes those rights that a person may have that are reduced to a written form. These rights are transferred by transferring the writing. The UCC breaks these rights into three types: *instruments, documents of title,* and *chattel paper.* **Instruments** include promissory notes, stocks and bonds, and any other piece of paper evidencing a right to the payment of money that is, in the ordinary course of business, transferred by delivery of the paper. **Documents of title** are bills of lading, warehouse receipts, delivery orders, and the like. Unlike instruments, which usually represent obligations to pay money, documents of title represent ownership in goods. If you had goods stored in a warehouse and obtained a warehouse receipt, you could transfer ownership of the goods by transferring the warehouse receipt. **Chattel paper** means a writing evidencing both a monetary obligation and a security interest in or a lease of goods. Chattel paper would include security agreements and personal property leases.

The last category of collateral, intangibles, is often evidenced by writings, but the writings have no significance on their own. Under the UCC, there are two types of intangibles: accounts and general intangibles. Accounts are payments due for goods sold or leased or for services performed that are not evidenced by an instrument or chattel paper. A debtor's receivables are usually accounts. The accounts may be evidenced by invoices, but the invoices have no significance other than to show the debt in written form. If the invoice was destroyed, the debt would still be collectible. *General intangibles* is a catchall term for collateral that does not fit into any other category. Examples of general intangibles include copyrights and trademarks.

Purchase Money Security Interests   In many instances, the UCC gives preferential treatment to holders of **purchase money security interests.** A security interest is purchase money to the extent that it is taken or retained by the seller of the collateral to secure all or a part of its price, or taken by a person who gives the money to the debtor to enable the debtor to acquire the collateral. For example, if the debtor bought a washing machine from a dealer who agreed to accept payments over time secured by a lien on the washing machine, the dealer would have a purchase money security interest. If the debtor borrowed the money from a finance company and took that money to the dealer and bought the washing machine for cash, the finance company's lien would be a purchase money security interest.

Secured Party versus Debtor   Remember that secured transactions involve the giving or taking of a lien in a person's property to secure repayment of a debt. If a debtor defaults in repaying its debt to the secured party, the secured party has

✦ **instruments**
Items such as promissory notes, stocks, and bonds that evidence a right to the payment of money.

✦ **documents of title**
A piece of paper normally accepted in business as proof of a right to hold goods.

✦ **chattel paper**
A document that shows both a debt and the fact that the debt is secured by specific personal property.

✦ **purchase money security interest**
A security interest to the extent that it is taken or retained by the seller of the collateral to secure all or part of its price, or taken by a person who gives value in order to enable the debtor to acquire the collateral if such value is in fact so used.

an immediate right to possession of the collateral if it does not already have possession. Outside of bankruptcy, if possession can be accomplished peacefully, then the secured creditor can simply take the collateral. If the secured creditor cannot obtain the collateral without breaking into the debtor's premises or if the debtor resists the creditor's efforts, a court order must be obtained.

Once the secured creditor has obtained the collateral, one of three things will happen.

1. The debtor will take the property back by paying what is owed.
2. The secured party will keep the collateral.
3. The secured party will sell the collateral.

If the secured creditor wishes to keep the collateral, it must give notice of its intention to do so to the debtor and to any other known secured parties. Each of those persons will have 30 days to object. If there is an objection, the secured party must sell the collateral. If there is no objection, the secured party may keep the collateral. If it does, it will be in full satisfaction of the debt.

The secured party's other alternative is to sell the collateral and use the proceeds to satisfy all or a part of the debtor's obligation. The sale may be private (to a particular buyer) or public, such as by auction. In either case, the sale must be conducted reasonably. For example, the secured party could not take highly technical scientific equipment and try to sell it at a garage sale. However, although there must be a reasonable attempt to obtain a fair price, the fact that a better price could have been obtained does not necessarily mean that the sale was unreasonable.

Unless the collateral is perishable, a notice that the secured creditor intends to sell the collateral must be given to the debtor and to all known secured parties within a reasonable time before the sale. What is considered a reasonable time varies from state to state and may be as little as five days.

If the sale of the collateral does not produce enough money to pay the secured party in full, the secured party may bring an action to collect the balance due, which is called the deficiency. If the sale was not conducted by the secured creditor in a reasonable manner, the creditor may have lost the right to collect the deficiency. If the sale produces excess proceeds, those funds belong to the debtor.

Secured Party versus Third Parties   Even though a secured party may have better rights than the debtor to the collateral, it will not necessarily have better rights than others such as other secured creditors, purchasers, or bankruptcy trustees. In order to obtain the best possible rights against these other parties, the secured party must "perfect" its security interest. **Perfection** is similar to recording a mortgage or deed of trust in real property law and the purpose is the same: to put the world on notice of the security interest.

✦ **perfection**
The steps necessary under the Uniform Commercial Code or other law to make a lien effective against a third party and a bankruptcy trustee.

There are two methods of perfection. The first is by taking possession of the collateral. Obviously, if a creditor has possession of the collateral, the world is on notice that the creditor has rights in the collateral. Perfection by possession is the only way to perfect a security interest in instruments. Perfection by possession will not work for intangibles since there is nothing to take possession of. Perfection by possession is also not feasible if the debtor needs the collateral to operate its business. For example, if the collateral is a printing press, if the secured creditor takes possession of the press, the debtor cannot then use the press to make books that could be sold to repay the secured creditor.

The second method of perfection is to file a **financing statement** with either a state or county official. A financing statement is a simple form that contains the name of the debtor and the secured party, describes the collateral, and is signed by the debtor and the secured party. A sample financing statement for a transaction in

✦ **financing statement**
The document typically filed with the secretary of state that contains the name of the debtor, the name of the secured creditor, and a description of the collateral. It is used to perfect a secured interest for most types of collateral.

which a finance company took a security interest in only particular goods is shown in Exhibit 4.3. In most states, financing statements are filed with the secretary of state. A security interest in fixtures is usually perfected by filing a document similar to a financing statement in the local real property records.

The secretary of state or the county recorder will keep a list of all financing statements that have been filed with respect to a particular debtor. The list, usually referred to as a search or a UCC search, can be obtained upon request. In that way, the world and, more particularly those who might care, are on notice of a creditor's security interest.

In one limited situation, the UCC provides that there is a permanent automatic perfection as soon as the security interest attaches and neither possession nor a financing statement is required. That situation is a purchase money security interest in consumer goods.

Usually, perfection takes place immediately upon the occurrence of all of the events that are needed for perfection. When the security interest is purchase money, if the creditor perfects within a period of time set by each state, usually 10 or 20 days after the time the debtor came into possession of the collateral, the date of perfection will then be the date of the debtor's possession.

Priority Problems   A priority problem or dispute occurs when two or more creditors claim rights in the same property and at least one of those creditors is a secured party under Article 9. In determining who wins in a priority dispute, the general rule is that the first-in-time (that is, the first to obtain the security interest or lien) is the first-in-right. In other words, the first to obtain the lien has the first claim to the collateral. There are, however, many exceptions to this rule. Some possible priority problems are presented here.

1. *Secured Party versus General Creditors without Security Interests.* A general creditor is a creditor who does not have a lien on any of the debtor's property. A secured party will prevail against a general creditor, whether or not the secured party has perfected its security interest. However, since many general creditors become judicial lien creditors, perfection should not be ignored.

2. *Secured Party versus Judicial Lien Creditors.* A judicial lien creditor is a general creditor who obtained a judgment against the debtor and completed the act (usually called a **levy**) the state law requires in order to obtain a lien on particular collateral. The levy can consist of having the sheriff take possession of the property, or it can be simply filing a notice. Once the levy is made, the creditor has a lien and becomes a judicial lien creditor. In determining who wins between the secured party and the judicial lien creditor, the first-in-time, first-in-right rule applies. If the judicial lien creditor levies before the secured party perfects its security interest, then the judicial lien creditor wins. If the secured party perfects before the levy, the secured party prevails. Under the Bankruptcy Code, the trustee is given the status of a hypothetical lien creditor. As a result, a trustee will prevail over any unperfected secured creditor.

3. *Secured Party versus Other Secured Parties.* When there are two or more creditors holding security interests in the same collateral, the first to perfect will prevail. If none of the security interests is perfected, the winner will be the first to have attached. There is an exception for purchase money security interests in inventory. If a creditor has such an interest and it perfects before it turns over possession of the inventory to the debtor and if the creditor gives a notice to the other secured creditor of its interest, it will prevail over the other secured party—even if that other party perfected first.

✦ **levy**
The physical or constructive seizure of property in order to enforce a judgment.

EXHIBIT 4.3 ✦ *Uniform Commercial Code—Financing Statement—*
Form UCC–1

INSTRUCTIONS

1. PLEASE TYPE this form. Fold only along perforation for mailing.

2. Remove Secured Party and Debtor copies and send other 3 copies with interleaved carbon paper to the filing officer. Enclose filing fee.

3. If the space provided for any item(s) on the form is inadequate, the item(s) should be continued on additional sheets, preferably 5" × 8" or 8" × 10". Only one copy of such additional sheets need be presented to the filing officer with a set of three copies of the financing statement. Long schedules of collateral, indentures, etc., may be on any size paper that is convenient for the secured party. Indicate the number of additional sheets attached.

4. If collateral is crops or goods which are or are to become fixtures, describe generally the real estate and give the name of the record owner.

5. When a copy of the security agreement is used as a financing statement, it is requested that it be accompanied by a completed but unsigned set of these forms, without extra fee.

6. At the time of the original filing, filing officer should return third copy as acknowledgment. At a later time, the secured party may date and sign the Termination Legend and use the third copy as a Termination Statement.

This FINANCING STATEMENT is presented to a filing officer for filing pursuant to the Uniform Commercial Code:	3. Maturity date (if any):
1. Debtor(s) (Last Name First) and address(es) Videos by Joe, Inc. 18 Hollywood Drive Hollywood, CA 90001 2. Secured Party(ies) and address(es) B & G Finance Company 456 Harass Drive Princeton, N.J. 08890	For Filing Officer (Date, Time, Number and Filing Office)
4. This financing statement covers the following types (or items) of property: Five (5) Sony Model 111N Video Cameras and accessories.	5. Assignee(s) of Secured Party and Address(es)

This statement is filed without the debtor's signature to perfect a security interest in collateral.   (check ☒ if so)

     ☐ already subject to a security interest in another jurisdiction when it was brought into this state.
     ☐ which is proceeds of the original collateral described above in which a security interest was perfected:

Check ☒ if covered: ☒ Proceeds of Collateral are also covered.   ☐ Products of Collateral are also covered. No. of additional sheets presented:

Filed with: California Secretary of State

Videos by Joe, Inc.	B & G Finance Company
By: _____	By: _____
Signature(s) of Debtor(s)	Signature(s) of Debtor(s)

(1) Filing Officer Copy—Alphabetical

STANDARD FORM—FORM UCC-1.

4. *Secured Party versus Transferees.* If there is a conflict between the secured party and buyer of the collateral, the general rule of first-in-time, first-in-right usually applies. A buyer who gives value and takes delivery without actual knowledge of the security interest will win over an unperfected security interest because the buyer did not and could not have known of the secured creditor. The secured creditor could have protected itself simply by perfecting its security interest. On the other hand, if the purchaser takes delivery after the security interest is perfected, the secured party prevails. The purchaser could have ordered a search and discovered the security interest. There are a number of exceptions.

   a. If the secured party gives the debtor permission to sell the collateral, the buyer will take the collateral free of any perfected security interest. If, for instance, the debtor is an appliance dealer, and the secured party who has a lien on the dealer's inventory knows that the dealer is selling washing machines, the buyer can have the washing machine free of the security interest because the secured party implicitly consented to the sale.

   b. A consumer buyer always takes title free and clear of all unfiled security interests even if the secured party was not required to file in order to perfect such as a purchase money security interest in consumer goods. So, a purchase money secured creditor with a lien in consumer goods does not have to file in order to win against another secured creditor, but it will need to file to win against a buyer.

   c. A **buyer in the ordinary course of business** takes title free of all security interests created by the seller even though they are filed or otherwise perfected and even though the buyer had knowledge of the security interest. Under this exception, for example, even if the washing machine dealer had granted a security interest in inventory to a finance company, the washing machine could be bought from the dealer free of the claims of the finance company, unless the buyer knew that the finance company had forbidden the dealer from selling any of the collateral.

✦ **buyer in the ordinary course of business**
A buyer in good faith who buys goods from a person in the business of selling goods of that kind and without knowledge that the sale is in violation of the security interests of others.

Other Applicable UCC Provisions

Articles 2 and 9 of the UCC are the most common UCC articles that a paralegal will encounter in a bankruptcy case. They are not, however, the only ones. Two other articles that the paralegal should be familiar with are Article 2A and Article 6. A short discussion of each of these articles follows.

✦ **lease**
A contract for the use of land or buildings, but not for their ownership.

Article 2A—Leases   In 1986, the National Conference created Article 2A to deal with **leases** of personal property. The term lease means any transfer of the right to possession and use of goods for a period of time in exchange for some consideration. A lease is formed when there is a writing signed by the parties that indicates an intent to enter into a lease, states a term, and identifies the leased goods. Under certain circumstances, such as goods specially manufactured or obtained for the lessee, goods accepted by the lessee, or the admissions of the party, a written lease will not be necessary. Like Article 2, if the parties to a lease have left out important terms, Article 2A will fill those terms in. Also like Article 2, Article 2A addresses such things as how a lease is accepted or rejected, what constitutes a breach by the lessee or the lessor, and each side's remedies.

In a bankruptcy case, it is very important to know the difference between a lease and a security interest because the rights of a secured creditor are very different from the rights of a lessor. Article 2A establishes some rules to help determine the difference in cases where a document may be called a lease but the provisions are similar to those of a security agreement.

Because it is relatively new, Article 2A has not been adopted by all of the states. States that have adopted Article 2A may number it Article 10.

Article 6—Bulk Transfers   The bulk transfers/sales law set forth in Article 6 of the UCC is based on long-existing state law that was designed to protect creditors from a situation in which a debtor sold all or a substantial part of its assets and then absconded with the sale proceeds. Bulk sales law places the responsibility on the buyer to notify all of the seller's creditors that there will be a sale of the debtor's property and gives them the opportunity to file a claim into an escrow. The sale proceeds will be put into the escrow and the claims paid. If the buyer does not make a good faith and reasonable effort to comply with the notice and escrow requirements, it could be liable for the full amount of the creditors' claim even though it had already paid the seller what the goods are worth.

Bulk sales law will not apply to every transaction. In many states, it does not apply if the seller is a restaurant or the sale is for anything other than equipment and inventory. It may not apply if the sale is for less than $10,000 or more than $5,000,000.

While bulk sales law does not apply to a sale by a bankruptcy debtor or trustee, many bankruptcy cases are filed because of bulk sales law. If creditors receive notice of a bulk sale, they may file an involuntary bankruptcy case to stop the sale. A buyer may ask the seller to file a bankruptcy case because it is easier to sell under Section 363 of the Bankruptcy Code than it is to comply with bulk sales law. The seller may decide to sell its assets in a bankruptcy case rather than under Article 6 if the claims submitted by creditors into the escrow are greater than anticipated. Finally, a bankruptcy trustee may seek to assert claims against the buyer who failed to comply with bulk sales law.

> ✦ **bulk transfer**
> *Any transfer of a major part of the transferor's materials, supplies, merchandise, or other inventory not made in the ordinary course of business.*

REAL ESTATE OWNERSHIP AND FINANCING

In many bankruptcy cases, the most valuable asset is the debtor's interest in a parcel of real estate. In some cases, it will be the only asset. Accordingly, it is very important in most bankruptcy cases to know the nature of a debtor's interest in real property and to understand what interests others may have in that same real property. Unfortunately, there is no uniform law on real property interests or financing such as the UCC. However, there are a number of general rules.

Real Property Interests

There are many types of interests (sometimes called estates) in real property. The same parcel of real property may have interests held in it by many different people. These interests are distinguished by their extent and duration. Exhibit 4.4 summarizes the types of interests. Determining the nature and scope of a real property interest is very important in bankruptcy cases because that interest, whatever it is, will be property of the estate.

Fee simple absolute is the greatest interest. An owner of land in fee simple absolute, sometimes referred to as just a *fee interest*, has the right to the surface of the land and to everything above or below it for an endless period of time. The fee owner has the right to dispose of the real property in whole or in part, to possess it, to lease it, and to otherwise use it for any reasonable purpose. It is possible that one person might own a fee interest in everything below the ground and another to own the surface and everything above. It is also possible for one person to own the surface and another to own all the buildings on the surface.

> ✦ **fee simple absolute**
> *An estate in property held by a person and his or her heirs and assigns forever and without limitation.*

EXHIBIT 4.4 ✦ *Common Types of Interests in Real Property*

Rights in Land

Fee Simple Absolute: the right to the surface and to everything permanently situated beneath or above it. Example: "I convey this land to you."

Fee Simple Defeasible: has a special limitation causing the estate to expire automatically upon the occurrence of a stated event. Example: "I convey this land to you in fee simple unless liquor is sold on the premises."

Life Estates: The life tenant has the same right of possession as an owner in fee simple, may make reasonable use of the land, and may receive profits from the land but only for so long as he or she lives. Example: "I convey this land to my husband for so long as he is alive."

Rights in the Land of Another

Easement: An interest in the land of another that entitles the owner of the easement to a limited use or enjoyment of the other's land. Example: "The owners of the adjacent parcel may cross my land to get to the highway."

License: A permission or authority to do an act on land of another. Example: "XYZ company may harvest timber from my land."

Covenants Running with the Land: A promise respecting the use of land. Example: "I will give my neighbors a right of first refusal if my land is ever sold."

Equitable Servitudes: Like a covenant but one that cannot be remedied by money damages. Example: "I will not erect a building on my land so high that it blocks the view from your land."

Leases

Estate for Years: The estate is for a definite period. Example: "I lease this land to you for three years."

Estate at Will: The tenancy has no fixed term and is terminable at the will of either party. Example: "I lease this land to you for so long as you pay rent."

Estate From Period to Period: The tenancy continues for successive period of the same length, unless sooner terminated by notice at the end of one period. Example: "I lease this land to you for one-year periods, which will continue unless I give you notice or you give me notice at the end of any year of termination of the lease."

Estate at Sufferance: The tenant goes into possession lawfully but holds over after the expiration of the lease.

Ownership By Several Persons

Joint Tenancy: A joint interest is one owned by two or more persons in equal shares with the right of survivorship. If one tenant dies, the other tenants take the dead tenant's share.

Tenancy by Entireties: A joint tenancy held by a husband and wife.

Tenancy in Common: A cotenancy without the right of survivorship. The parties can leave to their heirs their interests in the land.

✦ **life estate**
An estate whose duration is limited to the life of the person or of some other person.

✦ **leasehold estate**
An estate in real property held under a lease; an estate for a fixed term.

✦ **deed**
A document conveying an interest in real property other than a leasehold estate.

There are also interests for a limited number of years. One such interest is a **life estate,** which is ownership so long as a person is alive. An interest that carries the right to possession and some use for a period of time is a **leasehold estate.** It does not give the holder the right to dispose of the property.

Real property ownership interests, especially fee interests, are transferred through documents known as **deeds.** To be valid, deeds must be in writing and must contain the seller or the grantor's signature, words of transfer, and a description of the property and the interest transferred. There are a number of different types of deeds. A grant deed is the most common. Under a grant deed, the owner of a real property interest transfers that interest to another, giving a warranty in the deed that it owns the interest being transferred. Another common type of deed is a quitclaim deed. Under a quitclaim deed, the owner transfers its interest to another without giving any warranty as to what is being transferred.

Deeds are filed with the county recorder or other official who keeps track of the transfers of a particular parcel of property. Through those records, it is possible to trace all the deeds from the initial recorded owner to the present. This is known as the **chain of title.** Sometimes leases will also be recorded and will appear of record in the chain of title.

Real Estate Financing

Ever since real estate interests have been recognized, there have been various methods of using those interests to secure repayment of debts or to finance the purchase of property. In most states, the document used when real property is the security is a **mortgage.** It is very similar to a security agreement. If the debtor defaults, the lender takes the property described in the mortgage (called a foreclosure). Although foreclosure usually takes much longer, the process is akin to what a personal property secured creditor follows under the UCC.

Some states use a **deed of trust** rather than a mortgage. In a deed of trust, the owner of the property, called the trustor, deeds the property to a third person known as the trustee who holds the property for the benefit of the lender who is the beneficiary of the deed of trust. If the trustor (debtor) defaults on its obligations to the beneficiary (lender), the beneficiary can instruct the trustee to foreclose and hold a sale of the property.

Mortgages and deeds of trust are more alike than they are different, and both must be recorded to be valid as against third parties. If the mortgage or deed of trust is unrecorded, a buyer of real property without knowledge of the security interest will take title to the property free of it. The general rule of first-in-time, first-in-right will also apply to other secured creditors. The bankruptcy trustee has the status of a purchaser of real property. By using this status or that of a hypothetical lien creditor, the trustee will take the bankruptcy estate's interest in the property free and clear of unrecorded mortgages or deeds of trust.

The mechanics of **foreclosure** and sales by or on behalf of lenders are controlled by state law and vary considerably from state to state. There are two basic types. The first is a **judicial foreclosure** in which a court issues a decree of foreclosure. The sheriff will then sell the property at an auction. The second, and more common in many jurisdictions (especially those that use deeds of trust), is a public auction conducted by the mortgagor or the trustee. These sales do not require an order of the court. Private sales similar to the type authorized by the UCC for personal property are not allowed, although the debtor can give the lender a quitclaim deed.

All foreclosure sales, regardless of type, have a notice period that requires the lender or the trustee to inform the owner of the real property that there is a default in the underlying obligation and that a foreclosure sale will be conducted on or after a certain date. The owner will then be given an opportunity to cure the default or satisfy the obligation and prevent the foreclosure. The owner could also attend the sale and repurchase the property. In some states, even if the property is sold to a third party, the former owner is given an additional period of time to pay off the obligation and take back the property. This is called the debtor's **right of redemption.**

In most states, the mechanics of a foreclosure must be strictly adhered to in terms of timing, extent, and form of notice. If a foreclosure or a sale is improper, the owner may be entitled to damages, to declare the sale a nullity or, if the sale has not yet taken place, to obtain a court order preventing the sale from being conducted.

If there is a sale of real property collateral, the foreclosing lender will receive the proceeds less any prior secured claims and the costs of the sale. If those proceeds are less than the unpaid balance of the secured debt, the lender will suffer a deficiency.

✦ **chain of title**
A list of successive transfers of real property arranged consecutively, from the government or original source of title down to the present holder.

✦ **mortgage**
An agreement that creates or provides for a security interest in real property.

✦ **deed of trust**
A document used in many states that takes the place of a mortgage and by which legal title is placed in a trustee to secure repayment of a loan or performance of an obligation.

✦ **foreclosure**
The enforcement of a security interest, mortgage, or deed of trust in which the secured creditor takes the collateral in partial or full satisfaction of the debt.

✦ **judicial foreclosure**
An action to obtain a court order requiring the sheriff to hold an auction sale of collateral.

✦ **right of redemption**
The right to free property from a foreclosure or other judicial sale or recover the title that passed in a foreclosure by paying what is due.

✦ antideficiency laws
Legislation that prevents a secured creditor from recovering its deficiency (the difference between what is owed and what is received in the liquidation of its collateral) from the debtor.

✦ assignment of rents
An agreement between a lender and a borrower that provides that the rental proceeds from property will be paid to the lender.

✦ land sale contract
An agreement whereby the seller of real property retains title to the property until the full purchase price is paid by the buyer.

In a number of states, if a lender forecloses on its real property collateral, it is not entitled to collect the deficiency. The purpose of such **antideficiency laws** is to deter underbidding at foreclosure sales. There are many variations on the antideficiency rules, and few states have the same rules.

In addition to having the right to foreclose, many mortgages and deeds of trust also grant a lender an **assignment of rents** from the underlying property that serves as collateral for the obligation. This assignment can be a very significant right for the lender to exercise pending a foreclosure sale of an apartment house or office building, especially in the states in which there is a long period of time between the date the lender declares a default and the date the foreclosure sale can take place. If the lender is able to exercise its assignment of rents provision, it will be able to obtain the rent receipts and ultimately will have the property too. In those jurisdictions that have enacted an antideficiency statute, the rents collected before the foreclosure sale may make the difference between the lender being paid in full and suffering a deficiency.

Finally, there is a real property financing tool that is common in some jurisdictions, especially in the sale of single family residences by private parties. It is known as a **land sale contract.** In a land sale contract, the seller will retain ownership of the property until all the payments are made by the buyer. Once the purchase price is paid in full, the seller will give the buyer a grant deed. Usually the buyer will take possession while the installments are being made, will be responsible for the payment of taxes, and may make improvements.

The remedies available upon breach of a land sale contract will depend on which of the parties breaches. An aggrieved seller can regain possession but may have to return to the buyer all amounts in excess of actual damages. An aggrieved buyer can usually obtain specific performance and obtain title or can be awarded damages. Land sale contracts frequently are the subject of bankruptcy court decisions because the seller or the buyer may become a debtor and want to be rid of the obligations required under the contract. These issues were discussed earlier in this chapter in connection with exceptions to the general rules for treatment of executory contracts under the Bankruptcy Code.

ETHICAL CONSIDERATIONS

Ellen is the senior paralegal in the bankruptcy firm of Dead, Broke & Poor. She receives a telephone call one afternoon from a new client who asks the following questions:

1. As the result of a disagreement over a bill, a creditor has sued the client. Will that action be stayed under Section 362 (a) of the Bankruptcy Code?
2. If he conducts a bulk sale in the course of his business, could a creditor force him into involuntary bankruptcy?
3. When is his next appointment with the attorney, and how much of his retainer is still available to be applied to future bills and costs?

What ethical issues, if any, will have an impact on Ellen's ability to answer these questions?

SUMMARY

The automatic stay is the most important protection a bankruptcy debtor has. It prevents virtually all creditor actions against the debtor and its property. The automatic stay becomes effective the instant a bankruptcy case is commenced and lasts against the debtor until he or she receives a discharge. It lasts against the debtor's property until such property is no longer property of the estate. Creditors may be entitled to relief from the automatic stay if they can make certain showings. If they violate the stay without first obtaining relief, they may be liable for damages.

Executory contracts and unexpired leases receive special treatment in the Bankruptcy Code. Executory contracts are ones in which meaningful performance remains on the part of each party to the contract. The Bankruptcy Code allows a debtor or a trustee to reject the contract or lease, which eliminates the need for the debtor to perform under the contract. Alternatively, the debtor or the trustee may assume the contract and agree to be bound by it. An assumed contract or lease can also be assigned to a third party even if the contract or lease prohibits assignment. Real property leases must be assumed or rejected within 60 days unless the court grants an extension of that 60-day period. In a Chapter 7 case, all executory contracts or unexpired leases must be assumed or assigned within 60 days after the case is commenced.

Many questions of law that arise in a bankruptcy case can only be answered by reference to state law. The two most important state law areas are the provisions of the state's application of the Uniform Commercial Code and a state's real estate ownership and financing laws. The UCC governs commercial transactions in every state, although there are some variations among the states. The most widely used portions of the UCC in bankruptcy cases are Article 2, which concerns the sales of goods, and Article 9, which concerns secured transactions. Also very important for a bankruptcy paralegal to know are Articles 2A (leases) and Article 6 (bulk transfers/sales law).

There are a number of different types of real estate ownership, from fee simple absolute to a leasehold estate. An interest in real estate other than a leasehold estate is conveyed by use of a deed. A security interest in real estate will be reflected either in a mortgage or a deed of trust.

In the area of real estate financing, two important concepts are those of foreclosure and the land sale contract. Mechanics of foreclosure are governed by state law, and the paralegal should refer to the individual state code. The land sale contract is distinguished by the fact that the seller retains ownership until the buyer makes all the payments.

✦ KEY TERMS

antideficiency laws	deed	judicial foreclosure	right of redemption
assignment	deed of trust	land sale contract	rights evidenced
assignment of rents	documents of title	lease	by a writing
assumption	executory contract	leasehold estate	secured creditor
attachment	fee simple absolute	levy	secured party
bulk transfer	financing statement	life estate	secured transactions
buyer in the ordinary	fixtures	mortgage	security agreement
course of business	foreclosure	perfection	security interest
chain of title	goods	personal property	unexpired lease
chattel paper	incidental damages	process of attachment	Uniform Commercial
collateral	instruments	purchase money security	Code
commercial transaction	intangibles	interest	
consequential damages	*ipso facto* clauses	rejection	

✦ IMPROVE YOUR UNDERSTANDING

For Exercises 1 through 11, determine whether the acts described are prohibited by the automatic stay.

1. The commencement of a suit against the guarantor when the primary obligor is a debtor.
2. An action by the Environmental Protection Agency to stop the debtor from polluting a nearby lake.
3. The filing of a financing statement to perfect a security interest in the debtor's assets.
4. A demand letter sent to the debtor by an unsecured prepetition creditor.
5. A statement sent to the debtor by an unsecured prepetition creditor.
6. The repossession of the debtor's automobile.
7. A writ of attachment hearing seeking a lien on the debtor's exempt assets for a claim that arose after the petition had been filed.
8. An unlawful detainer action commenced by a landlord on a lease that terminated five days before the petition was filed.
9. The repossession of a Chapter 7 debtor's automobile after the trustee has abandoned all assets and the debtor has received a discharge.
10. The garnishment of the debtor's checking account by the Internal Revenue Service for unpaid payroll taxes.
11. The issuance of a fine against the debtor by the Environmental Protection Agency as a result of pollution caused by seepage from the debtor's underground storage.

Before answering Exercises 12 through 14, review Section 362 of the Bankruptcy Code.

12. For each of the acts described in Exercises 1 through 11 that you determined was prohibited by the automatic stay, state the subsection of the Bankruptcy Code that justifies your answer.
13. For any acts described in Exercises 1 through 11 that you determined were not stayed, state why they were not stayed.
14. If you felt that additional information was needed to accurately determine whether an act would be prohibited, identify the information that was needed.
15. Give two examples of contracts that would be executory under the Countryman test. Give two examples of contracts that would not be executory under the Countryman test.
16. The debtor entered into a 50-year lease for a warehouse at a rent of $1,000 per month. At the beginning of year 10, the debtor was in default for four months' rent. If the debtor filed a Chapter 7 case on January 1 of year 10, when must the trustee assume or reject the lease? If the decision is to assume the lease, what must the trustee do? If the trustee uses the property for one month and then rejects the lease, what claims will the landlord have?
17. List all the ways in which a seller of goods can breach.
18. List all the ways in which a buyer of goods can breach.
19. With a classmate, negotiate a contract for the purchase and sale of a year's supply of strings to be used in the manufacture of a professional model of yo-yos. One person should assume the role of the buyer and the other, the seller. The price of three cents per string has already been agreed on, and the buyer estimates it needs at least 10,000 strings per year with the need evenly spread over the year. All other terms remain to be negotiated.
20. After you have negotiated the contract pursuant to Exercise 19, discuss the rights of the buyer if the seller does not ship or if the strings delivered are too long. Discuss the rights of the seller if the buyer does not accept a proper tender of the strings.
21. Does a seller who refuses to perform a contract because the debtor has commenced a bankruptcy case violate the automatic stay? If the seller commences a bankruptcy case, does a buyer who refuses to pay violate the automatic stay?
22. Construct a chart showing the three types of collateral, including the four categories of goods, and how a security interest is perfected for each type and category.
23. How is a security interest created? What are the steps required for it to attach? What are the steps required for it to be perfected?
24. What must a security agreement contain that is lacking in a financing statement?
25. Determine who prevails in the following situations:
    a. A bankruptcy trustee against a secured party with an unperfected security interest.
    b. A debtor in possession against a secured party with an unperfected security interest.

c. A bankruptcy trustee against a secured party with a security interest in equipment who perfected by taking possession of the equipment before the commencement of the case.

d. A bankruptcy trustee against a creditor with a security interest in promissory notes who perfected before the commencement of the case by filing a financing statement with the secretary of state.

e. A bankruptcy trustee against a seller of washing machines who allows customers to pay for their purchases over time in exchange for a security interest in the washing machines and who does not file a financing statement.

26. Has your state enacted Article 2A of the UCC? If so, briefly summarize sections 2A–401, 2A–501, 2A–508, 2A–509, and 2A–523.

Bankruptcy Legal Research and Writing

MOST PARALEGALS welcome the opportunity to do a legal research and writing assignment. In their most basic form, legal research and writing are merely answering a question and writing the answer.

Of course, it is not that simple. The first step, finding the answer, may require looking at a variety of specialized sources. Those specialized sources for bankruptcy law and procedure are the focus of this chapter. The second step, expressing the answer, can take many forms (a letter, a memorandum, a pleading, or a brief). The answer is usually not a simple yes or no. Learning how to express an answer that is neither black nor white, but shades of gray, while applying the facts of a client's case is the essence of legal analysis. This analysis is at the heart of all well-written letters, memoranda (usually referred to simply as memos), and briefs. While it is beyond the scope of this book to discuss legal writing in depth, we can review the basics.

Let's use a hypothetical situation to examine bankruptcy legal research. An attorney, looking frazzled and obviously short on time, enters your office. The attorney relays the story of the client, a debtor in a Chapter 7 bankruptcy case. Thirty days before she filed the bankruptcy petition, the debtor charged $2,500 on her credit card to purchase that year's edition of major league baseball cards. Now, six months later, the credit card company has filed a lawsuit in the bankruptcy court claiming that the $2,500 debt cannot be discharged in the debtor's bankruptcy case. New to these issues, the attorney wonders whether the debt is dischargeable.

The attorney asks you, the paralegal, two research questions:

1. Is this type of debt dischargeable?
2. Was the credit card company's lawsuit filed on time?

You may not be sure of the answer to either question, but you agree to do the research.

LEGAL RESEARCH

This discussion first presents an overview of the various books and methods the paralegal might use to answer the questions posed. This is followed by a review of computer-aided legal research tools, such as CD-ROMs and online services provided by Westlaw® and LexisNexis™.

Sources

Statutes and Rules   The starting point for an answer to most substantive bankruptcy law questions is the Bankruptcy Code itself. Answers to procedural questions are often found in the Bankruptcy Rules or in the local rules adopted by the courts of each district.

The paralegal can find the Bankruptcy Code in the multivolumed, hardbound set of the *United States Code Annotated*, published by West Publishing Company, or in the *United States Code Service,* published by Bancroft-Whitney Company. The Bankruptcy Code is found in Title 11 of each service.

As discussed earlier in this book, Congress frequently changes the Bankruptcy Code. Rather than republishing all of the Title 11 volumes each year, publishers update the books by the use of **pocket parts,** which are attached to the inside back cover. It is a cardinal rule of legal research to check the pocket part for an amendment to the statute. Without that step, the statute cannot be relied upon.

The *United States Code Annotated* volumes are quite detailed because each Code section is followed by short summaries of cases that interpret the section. The case summaries are a useful research tool. They are discussed in depth later in this chapter. A more succinct version to use is a single-volume softbound edition of the Bankruptcy Code. A number of companies publish such a version each year.

The Bankruptcy Rules can be found either at the end of the *United States Code Annotated* or, more commonly, in a desktop softbound version that is a companion to the Bankruptcy Code softbound volume. The local rules are available from the clerk of the bankruptcy court (often on diskette) or from a local legal publisher. When reviewing any statute, including the Bankruptcy Code, it is often difficult to interpret the intent of a particular section. *Sutherland on Statutory Construction* (published by West Group), a multivolume set of books, is a standard reference that is invaluable in helping the lawyer and paralegal interpret statutory provisions.

Legislative History   Legal research would certainly be easier if all questions were answered in the Bankruptcy Code. Unfortunately, it is impossible for any written law to be so precise. As a result, an important key to legal research is to look at other sources to determine how the Bankruptcy Code should be interpreted and applied to a given set of circumstances.

One source is the record of the passage through Congress of the Bankruptcy Code and its amendments. This record contains the written and oral statements made by various members of Congress and its committees when they were considering the law. The congressional record for the Bankruptcy Code also contains committee recommendations, results of studies, testimonies by academicians and practitioners, and discarded versions of the bill that eventually became the Bankruptcy Code. Needless to say, the opinions and statements made in the record sometimes conflict. Because of this conflict, the legislative history of a particular statute is not binding upon a court, but it will be considered if the law is ambiguous.

Congressional legislative history is found in the *United States Code Congressional and Administrative News,* which is a multivolume set. Another source for this information is Volumes 2 and 3 of the appendix to the 23-volume treatise *Collier on Bankruptcy*®, published by LexisNexis Matthew Bender. Unfortunately, the material is voluminous and relatively unindexed; there are, however, helpful references at the end of each section of the *United States Code Annotated.* If the research must be done quickly, a useful source is the softbound desktop volume of the Bankruptcy Code. Most editions include excerpts from the legislative history after each Bankruptcy Code section.

Case Law   Congress could not have foreseen every possible factual situation that could arise under the Bankruptcy Code. As a consequence, bankruptcy courts

✦ pocket parts
The method of updating bound compilations of decisions, statutes, or digests, consisting of periodically issued paperback editions that are usually attached to the inside back cover of a bound volume.

must apply the law to the facts before them. To do this, they usually look to the decisions of other courts for guidance. Decisions made by higher courts in the same circuit as the bankruptcy court making the decision must be followed. The higher court's ruling is called **precedent,** and the notion that the lower court must follow it is called *stare decisis.* Exhibit 5.1 presents an abbreviated version of the hierarchy of the federal court system.

United States Supreme Court decisions must be followed by all other federal courts. United States court of appeals decisions must be followed by all of the district courts, the Bankruptcy Appellate Panel, and the bankruptcy courts *in that circuit.* For example, a Ninth Circuit Court of Appeals decision is binding upon all lower courts in Arizona, which is in the Ninth Circuit. The same Ninth Circuit decision is not binding on any of the other courts of appeals or on any lower court within other circuits. In other words, the bankruptcy courts in New York, which is in the Second Circuit, are not bound by Ninth Circuit decisions. Bankruptcy court decisions are not binding upon any other bankruptcy court. This does not mean that the decision of another court is not important. The bankruptcy court in Tennessee may find a Maine bankruptcy court's decision to be well-reasoned and may choose to follow it. Likewise, the Hawaiian bankruptcy court, which is in the Ninth Circuit, may find persuasive and follow a nonbinding decision rendered by the bankruptcy court in Texas, which is located in the Fifth Circuit.

In short, while it is important and helpful to find and review all the significant cases that address a given research topic, it is absolutely necessary to find and advise the court of all binding precedent in its circuit and district.

The next question is how to find precedental case law. Unlike other areas of law, no one legal publisher is the official reporter for bankruptcy court decisions. Instead, several publishers report decisions concerning bankruptcy issues regardless of which court issued the decision. Supreme Court and bankruptcy court decisions are contained in the same volume. Exhibit 5.2 presents a list of the more widely used bankruptcy case reporters, arranged by the type of issuing court.

Each publisher has a different method of indexing the cases in its system, yet each method involves the use of **headnotes.** Headnotes are very brief summaries (drafted by the publisher, not by the court) of the issues of law decided in the case. The printed version of the case usually presents a summary of the case

✦ **precedent**
A case or decision considered as authority for an identical or similar case or question of law arising later.

✦ *stare decisis*
The policy of courts to abide by or adhere to precedent.

✦ **headnotes**
Summaries of points of law made in a judicial opinion. They generally precede the text of the opinion.

EXHIBIT 5.1 ✦ *The Bankruptcy Court Within the Federal Court System*

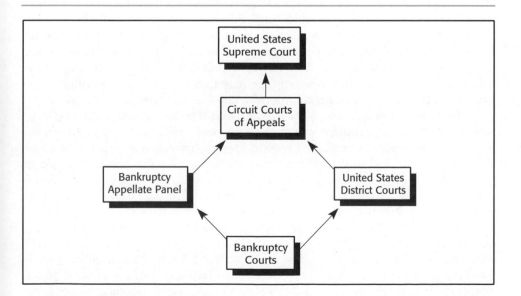

EXHIBIT 5.2 ✦ *Bankruptcy Case Reporters*

Court Issuing Decision	Where to Find the Decision	Publisher
U.S. Supreme Court	*U.S. Reports*	Government Printing Office
	Lawyers Edition, 2d	Bancroft-Whitney
	Supreme Court Reporter	West
Court of appeals	*Federal Reporter*	West
District courts	*Federal Supplement*	West
The above courts, bankruptcy courts, and Bankruptcy Appellate Panels	*Bankruptcy Court Decisions*	L.R.P. Publications (formerly C.R.R.)
	Bankruptcy Law Reporter	Commerce Clearing House
	Bankruptcy Reporter	West
	Collier Bankruptcy Cases	LexisNexis Matthew Bender

or the headnotes after the title of the case and before the actual opinion. The case usually has as many headnotes as it has issues or points of law. The section in this chapter on research approach discusses how to use each publisher's system of headnotes and indexing.

Secondary Sources

Secondary sources are a catchall category of books, articles, outlines, treatises, and other materials that contain general explanations of the law and how it has been applied. These sources are particularly useful when the researcher is unfamiliar with the Bankruptcy Code section and needs a broad overview to help guide the research.

There are many excellent secondary sources that can be used in bankruptcy practice. Most bankruptcy libraries will contain at least one single or multivolume treatise of the law, usually arranged by Bankruptcy Code section. In addition, there are a number of law reviews dedicated to bankruptcy law, such as *The American Bankruptcy Law Journal,* the *Bankruptcy Developments Journal,* the *Journal of Bankruptcy Law and Practice,* and the *California Bankruptcy Journal.* Each of these has insightful articles concerning various bankruptcy issues.

Secondary sources are not binding. They are not pronouncements from courts, and they are sometimes merely statements of the author's opinion. However, if a definitive and binding decision does not exist, it is quite acceptable to quote from secondary sources. The bankruptcy judge may find the logic or reasoning attractive, and it may help to explain an otherwise difficult concept.

There are two general approaches to research. The first assumes that you know only the general topic that the item to be researched falls into, and you are unfamiliar with the specifics, while the second approach involves a situation in which you have been asked to research a particular section of the Bankruptcy Code, or you already know that the answer to a particular legal issue is governed by the interpretation of that particular section of the Code. In the discussion below, we will use the hypothetical given earlier to demonstrate each approach. Exhibit 5.3 may help you visualize the necessary steps for each of the two approaches.

Finding the Law by Topic   When the researcher knows little or nothing about a subject, it is best to start by consulting secondary sources for a general understanding. For example, if the paralegal does not know the general discharge

EXHIBIT 5.3 ✦ *Approaches to Legal Research*

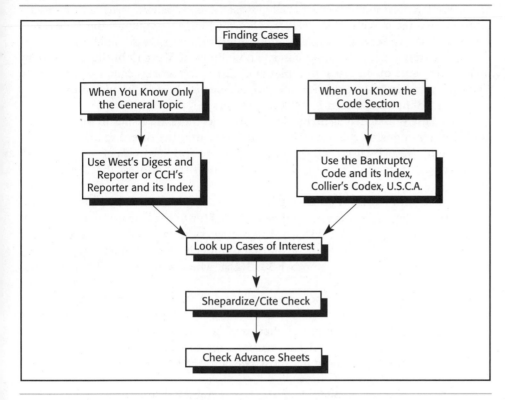

concepts, it would be wise to consult a treatise for a general explanation of how and why a debtor is discharged from debt.

Having learned through secondary sources that there are certain categories of debts that will not be discharged in a Chapter 7 case, the paralegal will be ready to address the question of whether this particular debt can be discharged under the facts given. The first step is to determine whether a particular Bankruptcy Code section is on point. The easiest way to make this determination is to turn to the Bankruptcy Code index. The index shows that Section 523 lists the exceptions to discharge.

Finding Section 523 does not conclude the research. The section states only that consumer debts for "luxury goods and services" owed to a single creditor, aggregating more than $1,150, and incurred within 60 days before the order for relief (the date the voluntary petition was filed) are presumed to be nondischargeable. Section 523(a)(2)(C) does not say whether collectibles are luxury goods. Because a Bankruptcy Code section that applies has been found, it would be appropriate at this point to branch into the second approach of finding the law— by indexes based on a Code section. But, for discussion purposes, the topic approach will be explored a little further.

Sometimes bankruptcy research cannot be accomplished very well or efficiently by use of a Bankruptcy Code section. The research assignment may involve the interrelation of a number of sections, or an issue may not be specifically addressed in the Bankruptcy Code. In those situations, it is more efficient to research by topic.

Although there are many sources that publish cases, the West or Commerce Clearing House (CCH) reporters are best organized for using a topic approach. Of the two, West is the more commonly used.

The West system for locating cases is divided into two parts. The cases are printed in hardbound volumes called West's *Bankruptcy Reporter*. The cases are indexed by topic in West's® *Bankruptcy Digest,* which accompanies the *Bankruptcy Reporter.* The two sets of books are often found side-by-side in the library.

The *Digest* is used to locate cases. The editors of West Publishing Company divide every area of the law into topics and narrow categories called key numbers. Each key number represents one category or issue in the area. Bankruptcy law has been divided into more than 1,000 key numbers.

Each case is assigned as many key numbers as there are issues in the case. The key numbers appear at the beginning of the case, after the title, and are crossreferenced in the *Digest* by topic. Once the correct topic and key number are identified, it is easy to turn to the *Digest* for the list of all cases that address that key number topic.

In the front of each volume of the *Digest* is an outline that lists the key numbers numerically. The outline should be reviewed for relevant words and phrases in the index. For example, the first word that may come to mind in researching the hypothetical is *discharge.* If you consult the outline, a part of which is reprinted in Exhibit 5.4, you will see key number 3353(15), which should lead to all the cases that discuss this subject matter.

After the *Digest* outline, the next stop is the *Digest* itself. Key number 3353 is in Volume 17 of the *Digest.* A page from the *Digest* is reproduced here in Exhibit 5.5. Under the relevant key number, there are short summaries of all the cases that contain the key number. All relevant cases in the topic area can be previewed by reading these summaries; only the most relevant need to be read in their entirety in the *Bankruptcy Reporter* volumes.

In 1988, West reassigned all of the bankruptcy key numbers. A conversion chart is located in the front of the more recent *Digest* volumes. You will need to use the conversion chart if you find a useful topic entry in a pre-1988 opinion.

Key number 3353(15) contains many headnotes, most of which address the issue. The bold abbreviations/initials preceding the headnote indicate the particular court that heard the case (for example, Bkrtcy. is the Bankruptcy Court, C.A. is the abbreviation for one of the Federal Circuit Courts of Appeals, D.C. stands for the United States district court.) In addition, you will find an indication as to the place of origin and date of decision, for example, Bkruptcy.S.D.Fla 1988 stands for Bankruptcy Court, Southern District, Florida, with a decision date of 1988. States small enough to have only one bankruptcy court district will simply be designated as Bkrtcy.LA.1984. (Bankruptcy Court, Louisiana, decision date 1984). This is important for *stare decisis* purposes. The end of the headnote provides a cite to the name of the case, the case reporter volume, and the page on which the case may be found. The reporter abbreviations are explained in the front of the *Digest.* The most common abbreviations are B.R. for West's *Bankruptcy Reporter* and F.2d for West's *Federal Reporter,* second edition. Also, *Id.* is used as a shorthand way to refer to the case cited immediately previous, without having to repeat the long formal citation.

Once you have located the appropriate key number, there are two ways of proceeding. The first is to locate and read the actual cases. The second is to simply write down the cites and move on to the *Digest* of another court, looking for more cases under the same or the updated key number.

It is imperative that the text of any case cited be read in full. The headnotes are not authority; they are merely summaries written by editors who have read the case and attempted to pick out what they thought were the important points. The headnotes can be incomplete.

Once all of the relevant cases have been located, they must be checked to be sure they are up to date. This must be done prior to drafting a memo or other paper

EXHIBIT 5.4 ✦ *West's* Bankruptcy Digest *Outline*

---

17 Bkrptcy D—25   **BANKRUPTCY**

X. DISCHARGE.—Continued.
    (C). DEBTS AND LIABILITIES DISCHARGED.—Continued.
        1. IN GENERAL.—Continued.
            ⇔3353. Debts for goods, services, or credit obtained by fraud, etc.—Continued.
                (14). Reliance; time element.
                (14.5). Reasonableness.
                (14.10). —— Creditor's duty to investigate; sufficiency of investigation.
                (14.15). —— Loss or prejudice.
                (14.20). —— Partial reliance.
                (14.25). —— Particular cases.
                (14.30). —— Banks, cases involving.
                (15). Luxury goods.
        3354. Torts and crimes.
        3355. —— Wilful or malicious injury.
            (1). In general.
            (1.10). Wilful, deliberate, or intentional injury.
            (1.15). Recklessness or negligence.
            (1.20). Knowledge; knowing disregard.
            (1.25). Malice; malicious injury.
            (1.30). Spite, hatred, or ill will.
            (1.35). Just cause or excuse.
            (2). Particular injuries; fraud.
            (3). —— Trover and conversion.
            (4). —— Disposition of or injury to collateral.
            (5). —— Drunk or reckless driving; vehicular homicide.
        3356. —— Larceny or embezzlement.
        3357. —— Fraud or defalcation in fiduciary capacity.
            (1). In general.
            (2). Fiduciaries and fiduciary capacity.
            (3). —— Trustees.
            (4). Defalcation.
            (5). Fraud.
        3358. —— Fines, penalties, and forfeitures; punitive damages.
        3359. —— Probation and conditions; restitution.
        3360. Costs and fees.
        3361. Debts not scheduled or listed.
        3362. Post-petition debts or liabilities.

      2. DETERMINATION OF DISCHARGEABILITY.

        ⇔3381. In general.
        3382. Time for proceedings.
        3383. —— Extension of time.
        3384. Pleading.
        3385. Parties, standing.
        3386. Evidence.
        3387. Hearing and determination; default.
        3388. —— Award on determination of non-dischargeability.

EXHIBIT 5.5 ✦ *West's* Bankruptcy Digest

17 Bkrptcy D—537   **BANKRUPTCY** ☜3353(15)

For collateral, non-bankruptcy questions, see other West Digests

Bkrtcy.D.Utah 1984. Debtor's offhand remarks about campaign debts which he did not expect to be required to pay did not require bank to investigate whether those debts had been reduced to judgment against debtor prior to giving loan to debtor.

In re Harmer, 61 B.R. 1.

Bank acted reasonably within meaning of provision of Bankruptcy Code governing non-dischargeability of debt based upon materially false financial statement in writing, where bank followed its normal business practice of not only procuring debtor's signature on loan application, but also met with debtor and interviewed him, discussing his financial statement and asking for updated version. Bankr.Code, 11 U.S.C.A. § 523(a)(2)(B).

In re Harmer, 61 B.R. 1.

Bkrtcy.Vt. 1983. In order to sustain a claim of nondischargeability, it must be established that debtor made a materially false representation, that representation was made with intent to defraud, and that the bank relied on false misrepresentation; burden of proving each of these elements is upon the party seeking to come within statutory exception to discharge, and this must be proven by clear and convincing evidence. Bankr.Code, 11 U.S.C.A. §§ 523, 523(a)(2).

In re Griffis, 29 B.R. 110.

Bkrtcy.Vt. 1981. Where consolidated loan was made at request of bank's management, debtor was called into bank by loan consultant and was handed both application for loan which was made out by representative of bank and promissory note, there was no attempt by bank's agent to explain necessity of signing accurate statement of then outstanding debts of debtor, and only purpose of consolidation loan was to convert number of delinquent loans into one which was current, there was no intent to deceive on part of debtor and bank could not reasonably have relied on statement which it prepared and was signed by debtor; thus, consolidation loan was not subject to provisions of bankruptcy statute which makes debt nondischargeable on account of false financial statement. Bankr.Act, § 17(a)(2), 11 U.S.C.A. § 35(a)(2); Bankr.Code, 11 U.S.C.A. § 523(a)(2)(B)(i-iv).

In re Bacon, 13 B.R. 559.

Bkrtcy.E.D.Va. 1987. Fact that debtor estimated his annual income in loan application did not render bank's reliance on financial statement unreasonable, for purpose of determining whether debt was dischargeable, where bank took reasonable steps to determine accuracy of estimate and was entitled to rely on information supplied by debtor and third party. Bankr.Code, 11 U.S.C.A. § 523(a)(2)(B)(iii).

In re Dishaw, 78 B.R. 120.

Bkrtcy.Va. 1981. Bank which made its own title search of property and failed to discover existence of deed of trust did not rely on affidavit of seller which did not mention the deed of trust and thus could not avoid discharge of the debtor's debt on the theory that he had acted fraudulently.

In re Hallman, 12 B.R. 502.

Bkrtcy.Wis. 1984. Debtor's debt to bank was not excepted from discharge on basis of debtor's false representations that he had authority to pledge several diamonds as additional security because bank's reliance on the representation was unreasonable and the loan did not remain unpaid as proximate result of debtor's representations. Bankr.Code, 11 U.S.C.A. § 523(a)(2)(A).

Matter of Eaton, 41 B.R. 800.

* Bkrtcy.Tenn. 1979. Bank could not be deemed to have reasonably and justifiably relied on financial statement so as to obtain relief from discharge of its debt on grounds of falsity of the statement, though statement listed certain real estate as being owned by bankrupt when in fact it was owned with his wife as tenants by the entirety, since bank president's actual knowledge that title to the property had been vested in bankrupt and his wife a year and a half earlier was sufficient to put him on inquiry to determine whether there had been the change in title that bankrupt's financial statement indicated. Bankr.Act, § 17(a)(2), 11 U.S.C.A. § 35(a)(2).

In re Yeiser, 2 B.R. 98.

☜3353(15). **Luxury goods.**

Bkrtcy.S.D.Fla. 1988. In order to obtain order denying dischargeability of debt, as having been obtained by false financial statement, creditor must prove by clear and convincing evidence that statement: is "materially false"; that it "reasonably relied" upon statement; in "extension, renewal or refinancing of credit"; and that debtor "caused [the statement] to be made or published with intent to deceive." Bankr.Code, 11 U.S.C.A. § 523(a)(2)(B).

In re Figueredo, 84 B.R. 856.

Bkrtcy.La. 1984. Debtor's use of credit card to go on "spending spree" involving largely luxury, nonnecessary items at time when he was unemployed, hopelessly insolvent, and had discussed bankruptcy with his attorney demonstrated debtor's fraudulent intent sufficient to render resulting debt, including contractually agreed upon interest, attorney fees, and expenses, nondischargeable in bankruptcy. Bankr.Code, 11 U.S.C.A. § 523(a)(2)(A).

In re Kramer, 38 B.R. 80.

Bkrtcy.Minn. 1984. Debt representing credit card purchases of two oriental throw rugs was nondischargeable under Bankruptcy

* denotes cases governed by laws preceding Bankruptcy Code

to be sure that the cases relied upon are not on appeal or, worse yet, overruled. This process of updating, called **Sheparding**® (after *Shepard's*® *Citations,* the publication used), is discussed later in this chapter.

Finding the Law by a Code Section   Starting with the Bankruptcy Code can be a shortcut for bankruptcy research. If there is a Bankruptcy Code section on point, the research can focus on the cases that interpret that section.

Continuing the hypothetical, the best word to look for in the index is *discharge,* which leads to Bankruptcy Code Section 523. As mentioned, this section dictates that certain types of debts, including those for luxury goods and services, can be excepted from the debtor's discharge. The section gives an answer of sorts to the research question, but it is an incomplete answer.

Although the topic approach just explained could be used for further research, there is another method. A LexisNexis Matthew Bender publication, *Collier Bankruptcy Cases,* categorizes cases by the Bankruptcy Code section they interpret. Instead of a digest or key number system, Collier's has a single volume at the end of the bound volumes of cases called the *Codex.* A list of cases that interpret Section 523 appears under Section 523 in the *Codex.* The *Codex* is quite specific; it cites to cases that interpret subparts of subsections of the Bankruptcy Code. *Bankruptcy Code Decisions,* published by L.R.P. Publications, is indexed in the same manner, but each index only covers certain volumes.

Although this statute-specific method is very useful when there is a known Bankruptcy Code section on point, it is not as useful when the task involves integrating a number of different sections or is topical, and not Bankruptcy Code-specific. To be completely thorough, time permitting, it is wise to use both the topic approach and the statute approach. One service may often refer to cases that, for some reason, the other has decided not to report.

A similar statute-specific approach can be used in connection with the *United States Code Annotated* and *United States Code Service.* Although these services cite to every federal code section from criminal law to civil procedure, there are several volumes devoted solely to Title 11. Like the *Codex,* these volumes are arranged numerically by Code section, and the headnotes are arranged under each section. Again, the pocket part in the back of each volume must always be checked because it contains the most recent cases.

Updating Case Law   Once a case on point has been located and will be relied upon in the written analysis, it must be updated to ensure that it is still good law and has not been reconsidered, reversed, or modified. The case also needs to be updated to determine if a higher court affirmed the decision (thereby adding weight to the authority.)

This procedure of updating is referred to by some as **cite checking,** that is, checking to see that the cite in a brief or memo is still good law. Complete cite checking also includes a review of the case cited to be sure it stands for the principle for which it is cited. Frequently, page or volume numbers are mistranscribed: it is only through the cite checking process that such errors are caught.

Shepard's Citations, a publication of LexisNexis Matthew Bender, makes updating fairly easy. Its abbreviations are sometimes confusing, but there is a table of abbreviations in the front few pages of every volume.

All of the services that report cases containing bankruptcy issues are listed in various volumes of *Shepard's Citations.* The bound volumes are divided into sections based upon the name of the reporter. There is a special section for U.S. *Supreme Court Reports,* one for West's *Fed. 2d* series, one for *Collier Bankruptcy Cases,* one for West's *Bankruptcy Reporter,* and another for CCH *Bankruptcy Law Reports,* to name a few. The softbound volumes of Shepard's, which contain the more recent citations, follow the same format.

✦ **Sheparding**
Determining the subsequent history of a case by use of Shepard's Citations.

✦ **cite checking**
The process of reviewing legal writing to ensure that all cases have not been reversed or modified, are correctly cited, and that all quotations are accurate.

The first step in checking a cite is to determine the reporting service and volume in which the case to be checked is found. By way of example, one of the cases located during the dischargeability research was *In re Orecchio* found in Volume 109 of West's *Bankruptcy Reporter* beginning at page 285. In Shepard's *Bankruptcy Citations* (1993) in the West's *Bankruptcy Reporter* section is a page like that shown in Exhibit 5.6. The volume number is listed at the top of the page and is then followed by columns of numbers and letters. The numbers that are in bold and preceded and followed by dashes indicate the first page on which the case may be found in that volume.

Page 285 for Volume 109 is not listed. This could mean several things. In most instances, it will mean that the case is so new that there has been no subsequent history (i.e., no court, or law review for example, has cited the case). It could also mean, however, that there has been an error in transcription, either on the part of the paralegal in the course of his or her research, or on the part of the Shepard's editors. When either of these situations occurs, Shepard's is simply blank.

As with any cite checking, the most recent volumes must always be checked. What was good law when the 1993 edition of Shepard's was published may have since been overruled. Exhibit 5.7 shows the pocket supplement that followed the 1993 bound volume. The *Orecchio* case is reported in this volume. The cite is to one from the Eleventh Circuit decided subsequent to the *Orecchio* case that refers to or mentions *Orecchio*.

Shepard's often gives editorial help by preceding the citation with a letter reference. A small *r, o,* or *c* is crucial since those symbols are used to indicate that the subsequent case **r**eversed, **o**verruled, or **c**riticized the case being shepardized. Other common symbols are *e* for **e**xplained, *d* for **d**istinguished, and *f* for **f**ollowed.

A similarly useful aspect of Shepard's is that when it cites to cases reported in West's publications, it also cites to the headnotes, where appropriate. As you've seen, in West's *Bankruptcy Reporter,* the actual opinion in each case is preceded by a summary of the case and a list of the key numbers found in the case. West's assigns numbers to each headnote and paragraph in the opinion. These assigned numbers correspond to the key numbers. Therefore, if you are interested in only one legal point in a 30-page opinion, you can then turn immediately to that paragraph and point of law rather than reading the entire opinion. Shepard's refers to this paragraph numbering system by use of a small, raised number preceding the page number. Referring to Exhibit 5.6 for a case distinguishing the first headnote of the case found at 109 B.R. 352, Shepard's points to 126 *BRW* at page 39, which discusses only the issue in that headnote.

To properly shepardize, all recent paperback versions of Shepard's must be reviewed. Yet even the most recent Shepard's are sometimes several months old. To be absolutely sure that the case is still valid, the paralegal must also check the advance sheets. Almost every case reporting service publishes a list and short summary, or advance sheet, of the most recent cases on a weekly or biweekly basis.

Researching the Procedural Question   If there is a legal basis for the action a client wants to take, the question of procedure or how the action is implemented must be addressed. This important determination is often left to the paralegal. If the procedure is incorrect or incomplete, the result may range from the papers being "bounced" at the court filing window to complete loss of the client's cause of action.

As is true for legal analysis, a good starting point for procedural analysis is the Bankruptcy Code. Many relevant statutes will give clues as to appropriate procedure. For example, the statute in the hypothetical, Section 523, states in subsection (c)(1) that the debtor will receive the discharge for the debts listed in Section 523(a)(2), which includes the luxury goods exception, unless "on request of the

EXHIBIT 5.6 ♦ *Shepard's* Bankruptcy Citations *(1993)*

BANKRUPTCY REPORTER (WEST) — Vol. 109

Cir. 5	—243—	—283—	132BRW¹	Nebr	—442—	—524—	21BCD1153
134BRW212	a114BRW473	Cir. 7	[1006	457NW⁷801	(19BCD1952)	Cir. 7	22BCD608
Cir. 6	Cir. 6	914F2d³106	Cir. 8		(23CBC2d	f114BRW612	
118BRW524	142BRW162	20BCD1700	927F2d³417	—382—	[354)	f20BCD867	—600—
26CBC2d87	BLD¶74660	BLD¶73622	Cir. 9	Cir. 8		fBLD¶73405	(BLD¶
		23CBC2d	f954F2d572	130BRW299	—445—	f23CBC2d533	[73210)
—197—	—245—	[1161	954F2d574		(20BCD184)		r121BRW140
s92BRW172	Cir. 9		21BCD751	—384—		—527—	r21BCD162
s102BRW71	f116BRW⁴224	—291—	f22BCD846	a131BRW137	—455—	s872F2d496	rBLD¶73729
s117BRW231	Cir. 10	Cir. 6	22BCD847	Cir. 9	(20BCD33)	s684FS319	
Cir. 5	122BRW¹441	140BRW458	BLD¶73991	123BRW878	s75BRW580	26COA295§8	—605—
d914F2d⁵736	122BRW²441	140BRW³459	fBLD¶74539	21BCD553			s936F2d640
d914F2d¹²736	122BRW³441		BLD¶74539		—467—	—534—	s602FS511
113BRW⁵257		—294—	24CBC2d	—392—	(19BCD1937)	Case 1	s603FS370
	—250—	(19BCD1882)	[1532	a940F2d558	85NwL941	Cir. 3	s629FS860
—202—	Cir. 6	Cir. 4	25CBC2d¹			c141BRW¹87	s709FS70
m22BCD1055	125BRW¹179	d128BRW²	[1274	—397—	—478—	Cir. 9	s747FS194
mBLD¶74471	136BRW696	[959	f26CBC2d652	(22CBC2d	s116BRW854	c116BRW¹	N Y
s960F2d1277	Cir. 10		26CBC2d655	[271)		[226	cc121NYA2d
s26CBC2d990	129BRW¹252	—297—	N M	Cir. 4	—481—		[923
Cir. DC	25CBC2d320	(21CBC2d	824P2d358	127BRW⁸365	(20BCD11)	—534—	cc504NYS2d
131BRW¹762		[1431)		Cir. 8	e125BRW¹	Case 2	[646
Cir. 2	—255—		—341—	120BRW²529	[365	Cir. 2	Cir. 2
125BRW⁹777	(20BCD181)	—301—	(19BCD1940)	Cir. 10		130BRW¹401	d113BRW⁴
Cir. 7	Cir. 6	Cir. 2	(22CBC2d	f136BRW873	—484—	cBLD¶74690	[851
137BRW292	115BRW¹584	e142BRW³50	[468)		a127BRW62		d113BRW⁵
22BCD160	20BCD1035	Cir. 6	Cir. 9	—403—	s108BRW799	—541—	[851
BLD¶74262	23CBC2d274	115BRW603	124BRW²804	(22CBC2d	Cir. 2	Cir. 10	d20BCD797
		115BRW³604	124BRW⁴804	[246)	121BRW¹139	138BRW971	dBLD¶73392
—210—	—260—		c124BRW⁴	Cir. 5	Cir. 4	138BRW³973	d22CBC2d
Cir. 2	Cir. 6	—308—	[805	d128BRW155	f141BRW106	Cir. 4	[1733
117BRW¹784	d142BRW⁷	s90BRW344	c21BCD703		26COA773§	cc61BRW349	
117BRW⁵786	[814	Cir. 3	c24CBC2d	—405—	[14	cc75BRW92	—609—
Cir. 5	142BRW⁸814	d124BRW182	[1901	(19BCD1879)			cc77BRW433
125BRW⁵167	dBLD¶74790			(22CBC2d1)	—489—	—550—	Cir. 2
f127BRW⁶793		—315—	—347—	a126BRW822	Cir. 2	Cir. 4	118BRW²236
24CBC2d	—264—	Cir. DC	(19BCD1899)		121BRW139	139BRW²379	119BRW²233
[2120	(BLD¶	d910F2d¹963	Cir. 2	—410—	Cir. 10	BLD¶74614	121BRW¹441
	[73242)		140BRW838	(19BCD1851)	121BRW75		139BRW²796
—214—	s99BRW768	—321—	Cir. 6	(BLD¶	121BRW²77	—557—	Cir. 3
Cir. 5	Cir. DC	Cir. 1	f139BRW³832	[73240)	Cir. 11	Cir. 8	138BRW¹445
e134BRW852	f118BRW¹154	f126BRW⁹417	Cir. 7	(22CBC2d	f142BRW¹518	121BRW³574	
Cir. 3	Cir. 3	Cir. 2	112BRW960	[412)		24CBC2d	—613—
—216—	f135BRW¹501	132BRW⁵7	20BCD598	f142BRW¹518	—492—	[1038	D924F2d480
Cir. 1	f122BRW¹493	Cir. 5	22BCD1555		Cir. 11		s826F2d1177
968F2d²⁵1361	127BRW16	130BRW494	85NwL929	—412—	127BRW²493	—562—	s87BRW779
Cir. 5	Cir. 6	142BRW⁹784		Cir. 5	e132BRW²	(BLD¶	Cir. 2
120BRW80	f131BRW¹814	Cir. 6	—352—	135BRW³815	[466	[73236)	922F2d989
Cir. 7	Cir. 8	118BRW554	(BLD¶	e139BRW²		26COA773§9	922F2d⁸995
133BRW¹⁵	130BRW¹532	Cir. 7	[73195)	[819	—494—		120BRW657
[220	f130BRW¹533	967F2d1154	Cir. 3	Cir. 10	Cir. 1	—569—	120BRW¹⁰
Cir. 8	Cir. 11	f117BRW⁹345	d126BRW¹39	120BRW³576	f113BRW¹112	s103BRW379	[658
126BRW583	f142BRW¹532	c132BRW⁹	dBLD¶73903	20BCD1982	120BRW¹⁵		124BRW⁹642
21BCD861	21BCD1132	[726			f125BRW¹68	—570—	129BRW¹⁰
BLD¶74697	f21BCD1651	133BRW⁶624	—362—	—421—	Cir. 5	(22CBC2d	[843
26COA773§9	f22BCD248	Cir. 9	(19BCD1980)	Cir. 6	134BRW217	[374)	136BRW²926
	f22BCD811	129BRW⁹635	(22CBC2d	115BRW¹95	134BRW¹219	Cir. 2	Cir. 5
—229—	BLD¶73992	Cir. 11	[1316)		Cir. 9	128BRW⁴331	134BRW⁸205
(20BCD109)		125BRW⁹854	Cir. 8	—424—	134BRW10		Cir. 6
Cir. 3	—273—	21BCD1648	112BRW⁴973	Cir. 6	f21BCD828	—575—	142BRW⁹184
127BRW¹350	Cir. 6	fBLD¶73433	Cir. 10	123BRW¹564	22BCD404	Case 1	142BRW185
105ARF568n	133BRW³881	BLD¶74752	123BRW909		d22BCD434	Cir. 1	21BCD180
105ARF579n	133BRW¹882	23CBC2d818	20BCD610	—434—	fBLD¶73893	142BRW¹585	BLD¶73747
	140BRW³457			s109BRW441	26CBC2d108	d142BRW³	BLD¶74030
—238—	140BRW⁴457	—335—	—368—	Cir. 8	26CBC2d109	[586	
Cir. 9	140BRW³888	Cir. 3	Cir. 6	f924F2d²787		Cir. 2	—626—
119BRW³775		141BRW²54	130BRW254	924F2d³791	—497—	133BRW19	s129BRW375
24CBC2d436	—278—	141BRW³54	Cir. 8	947F2d⁴866	s135BRW912	133BRW³22	s25CBC2d237
	Cir. 6	c141BRW55	120BRW⁶526			Cir. 3	Cir. 3
—241—	113BRW398	Cir. 7	Cir. 11	—441—	—506—	119BRW469	137BRW175
Cir. 7	140BRW⁴699	e118BRW²	140BRW⁶587	s109BRW434	(22CBC2d13)	Cir. 8	Cir. 7
130BRW285	140BRW³702	[650	22BCD1625			132BRW³615	129BRW²
21BCD1624		119BRW²644	22BCD1626			Cir. 10	[1009
25CBC2d519		c125BRW972	BLD¶74670			126BRW³103	f134BRW281
101ARF554n		125BRW976	Minn			136BRW⁴873	*Continued*
		c125BRW980	485NW706				

537

EXHIBIT 5.7 ✦ *Shepard's Supplement*

BANKRUPTCY REPORTER (WEST)

Vol. 108

—815— Cir. 1 f151BRW[1]636 Cir. 10 160BRW670 Okla 871P2d425 **—823—** Cir. 8 144BRW[1]850 145BRW[1]298 **—826—** Cir. 5 164BRW545 169BRW626 Cir. 11 157BRW909 29CBC2d856 **—838—** Cir. 11 123BRW[8]121 d162BRW[8] [920 164BRW793 **—854—** s148BRW702 s160BRW404 Cir. 1 147BRW298 153BRW383 164BRW209 164BRW215 Cir. 4 148BRW446 Cir. 9 166BRW923 24BCD231 25BCD995 BLD¶75930 N M 114NM160 836P2d79 **—901—** Case 2 Cir. 2 148BRW[21] [200 28CBC2d63 **—951—** Cir. 2 f165BRW367 Cir. 8 153BRW293 153BRW[4]295 24BCD243 24BCD244 28CBC2d [1179 **—956—** Cir. 3 d148BRW[59] 111ARF457n **—962—** Cir. 2 e131BRW[8] [930 162BRW[1]434 25BCD124	30CBC2d889 c30CBC2d890 **—971—** Cir. DC 148BRW682 Cir. 2 166BRW[1]566 Cir. 3 f141BRW[4]883 144BRW[4]263 e146BRW644 155BRW101 160BRW769 161BRW135 161BRW[1]140 163BRW[5]56 163BRW[6]60 163BRW760 165BRW[12] [567 165BRW[4]570 165BRW[5]571 165BRW[8]575 169BRW[7]109 169BRW[18] [112 Cir. 6 152BRW502 Cir. 8 7F3d131 Cir. 9 166BRW433 Cir. 10 168BRW758 Cir. 11 144BRW[18] [940 160BRW223 163BRW[1]399 168BRW440 e23BCD47 23BCD211 23BCD212 f23BCD213 24BCD611 24BCD1239 24BCD1405 24BCD1562 25BCD1179 BLD¶74986 BLD¶75443 BLD¶75467 BLD¶75901 BLD¶75993 BLD¶75994 q27CBC2d241 27CBC2d568 e27CBC2d [1371 29CBC2d [1587 30CBC2d826 44StnL95 **—998—** Cir. 3 164BRW[11] [902 Cir. 5 148BRW[4]270 148BRW[2]71 f148BRW[10] [271	**—1007—** Cir. 9 157BRW[1]895 24BCD1066 29CBC2d882 **—1009—** Cir. 11 164BRW[1]674 164BRW1007 25BCD637 BLD¶74927 **Vol. 109** **—1—** Cir. 7 f142BRW[1]284 153BRW[1]542 f23BCD149 f27CBC2d711 **—14—** Cir. 1 f149BRW243 f156BRW7 163BRW[1]915 Cir. 3 146BRW944 c23BCD82 23BCD1429 BLD¶75097 **—18—** Cir. 2 145BRW[22] [753 164BRW[22] [819 Cir. 8 168BRW[1]966 **—36—** Cir. 1 150BRW[5]289 156BRW359 Cir. 2 e145BRW793 Cir. 5 151BRW[4]392 Cir. 6 989F2d[1]213 147BRW19 Cir. 7 144BRW[1]82 Cir. 8 c171BRW[2]60 24BCD121 BLD¶75022 BLD¶75169 BLD¶75388 28CBC2d [1122 110ARF179n **—51—** Cir. 2 840FS991 Cir. 9 154BRW313 Cir. 10 q146BRW35 c27CBC2d124 27CBC2d125 78VaL477	**—64—** Cir. 7 c985F2d321 cBLD¶75282 **—74—** Cir. 3 160BRW[7]746 Cir. 8 796FS1242 24BCD1483 30CBC2d181 **—96—** Cir. 9 147BRW243 **—101—** Cir. 2 165BRW366 Cir. 3 145BRW486 27CBC2d [1302 **—107—** Cir. 4 164BRW248 **—113—** Cir. 3 155BRW[13] [925 Cir. 7 166BRW[11] [651 166BRW[4]652 BLD¶75907 28CBC2d419 **—127—** Cir. 3 148BRW781 f148BRW[2]782 d148BRW[3] [782 169BRW[1]562 25BCD1431 **—136—** Cir. 3 151BRW352 155BRW682 **—140—** Cir. 3 22F3d1238 f145BRW[3]498 Cir. 10 154BRW587 f23BCD806 25BCD784 fBLD¶74965 BLD¶75828 **—149—** Cir. 3 167BRW[6]980 167BRW[7]980 **—157—** Cir. 1 c146BRW899 c27CBC2d [1348	**—167—** Cir. 11 169BRW[3] [1022 BLD¶76006 14ARB527n **—179—** Cir. 2 166BRW[4]815 f166BRW816 Cir. 9 d150BRW242 Cir. 11 160BRW248 dBLD¶75200 BLD¶76083 29CBC2d [1374 **—182—** Cir. 7 170BRW379 Cir. 8 156BRW633 BLD¶75394 29CBC2d764 **—195—** Cir. 8 145BRW[3]295 **—197—** Cir. 7 d3F3d[12]1048 dBLD¶75398 25BCD579 f25BCD969 fBLD¶75896 **—210—** Cir. 2 149BRW59 Cir. 3 156BRW939 23BCD1355 BLD¶75393 **—216—** Cir. 2 169BRW839 Cir. 5 f154BRW912 Cir. 6 153BRW482 Cir. 10 990F2d559 990F2d[20]571 Cir. 11 f146BRW306 e154BRW [1021 169BRW[2]233 f23BCD924 f24BCD483 e24BCD580 e24BCD581 25BCD1374 BLD¶75218 BLD¶75220 BLD¶75995 28CBC2d [1001 1992WLR [1002	**—229—** Cir. 6 155BRW461 **—243—** 27CBC2d317 **—245—** 999F2d[3]613 Cir. 11 f150BRW[1]806 150BRW[2]807 **—250—** Cir. 6 e147BRW[2] [413 147BRW[1]414 162BRW[1]750 166BRW[3]321 eBLD¶75001 BLD¶75883 **—255—** Cir. DC 170BRW7 Cir. 5 164BRW942 Cir. 7 e148BRW530 Cir. 11 f166BRW983 e23BCD1276 25BCD579 f25BCD969 fBLD¶75896 **—260—** d27CBC2d352 **—264—** Cir. 3 f135BRW[1]501 146BRW530 148BRW[2]231 148BRW240 Cir. 5 164BRW940 166BRW866 Cir. 7 c145BRW[1] [604 f148BRW[1]310 f148BRW[2]313 152BRW528 c23BCD853 23BCD854 23BCD1159 25BCD578 cBLD¶74966 BLD¶74966 27CBC2d [1284 **—285—** 154BRW768 **—291—** Cir. 6 158BRW952	**—297—** Cir. 6 158BRW[1]975 24BCD1179 **—301—** e27CBC2d410 **—321—** Cir. 2 167BRW19 23BCD299 BLD¶75838 27CBC2d747 **—335—** Cir. 1 152BRW[2]13 Cir. 6 990F2d[2]910 Cir. 7 f149BRW[3]520 c149BRW522 150BRW426 156BRW[2] [1005 d156BRW [1011 167BRW[1]524 167BRW[2]525 Cir. 11 144BRW[3]936 147BRW[3] [1019 q23BCD65 23BCD688 f23BCD1391 c23BCD1393 25BCD1049 BLD¶74936 fBLD¶75105 cBLD¶75105 BLD¶75438 dBLD¶75438 27CBC2d421 q27CBC2d422 27CBC2d [1242 28CBC2d289 28CBC2d [1007 29CBC2d646 d29CBC2d653 La 635So2d714 N M 113NM218 **—341—** j30CBC2d466 **—347—** Cir. 8 e160BRW352 c24BCD1332 e30CBC2d27 **—352—** Cir. 1 164BRW[1]405 BLD¶75736	**—368—** Cir. 2 163BRW[4]696 Cir. 7 150BRW40 Ga 212GaA456 442SE267 **—384—** Cir. 8 149BRW937 **—390—** Cir. 5 157BRW991 **—397—** Cir. 3 19F3d843 Cir. 4 153BRW[6]719 Cir. 8 148BRW[8]562 Cir. 9 171BRW[4]111 25BCD613 25BCD1499 BLD¶75768 30CBC2d [1274 **—412—** Cir. 3 150BRW[2]353 115ARF621n f23BCD1391 c23BCD1393 **—434—** s977F2d1318 **—441—** s977F2d1318 114ARF385n **—455—** Cir. 2 161BRW566 Cir. 3 f160BRW770 25BCD51 BLD¶75664 **—481—** Cir. 7 147BRW[1]472 Cir. 9 f167BRW[2]586 **—484—** Cir. 11 154BRW594 f154BRW[2]596 f154BRW780 d154BRW786 161BRW[1]740 f24BCD144 f24BCD145 d24BCD148 30CBC2d510 **—489—** Cir. 11

Continued

creditor to whom such debt is owed, and after notice and a hearing, the court determines such debt to be excused from discharge. . . ." The procedural requirements are vague as to timing, but they can be interpreted by using the Bankruptcy Rules.

The Bankruptcy Rules, like the Bankruptcy Code, are indexed at the back of the volume. The index lists "Discharge: determination of dischargeability," and in this case points to Rule 4007 (c) for the time for filing a complaint in a Chapter 7 case.

Here, the Bankruptcy Rules do not give the complete procedural answer. They do not state, for example, exactly how the complaint is filed. These matters are instead addressed by local rules.

LEGAL WRITING

The answer to a research question may take a variety of written forms: a letter to the client, a memo to the lawyer, a brief or memorandum of points and authorities. Although each has a different format and a different tone, the essence of good legal writing is the same.

General Rules of Legal Writing

Plain English As a group, lawyers seem to be unable to write plain English. They use six words when one will do and unnecessarily use old, arcane phrases. Their writings are generally wordy, unclear, pompous, and dull. Historically, this could be excused as the result of English law and practice being transplanted to the United States. Now there is no valid excuse.

A paralegal should not fall into the trap of writing like a lawyer because he or she is writing for a lawyer. Even lawyers who are bad writers recognize and appreciate clarity in style and substance. Clarity in substance will be addressed below. The following rules will help develop clarity in style:

1. *Do not use outdated legal jargon.* Wheretofores, heretofores, hereinafters, witnesseth, the party of the first part, and the like have no place in good legal writing. Use definitions rather than "said."
2. *Use familiar words.* There is no reason to write "utilize" if "use" will do fine.
3. *Write short sentences.* The rule of thumb is that no sentence should have more than 25 words, but that may be too many for most writing. Try to have each sentence convey only one thought.
4. *Use the active voice.* When you use the active voice, the subject of your sentence acts. If you use the passive voice, the subject of your sentence is acted upon. An example of the active voice is "The debtor filed the bankruptcy case." An example of the passive voice is "The bankruptcy case was filed by the debtor."

Compare the two paragraphs below. Notice how much easier it is to understand the second paragraph, which uses these four rules for developing clarity in style.

It was ordered, adjudged, and decreed on December 1, 2002 by the United States Bankruptcy Court for the Eastern District of Tennessee that the lease of the real property located on Beale Street, to which theretofore a restaurant had been operated by the debtor, could be abandoned by the trustee. Thereafter, said lease was abandoned by said trustee and the debtor's tenancy terminated by its vacation of the property.

The debtor leased and operated a restaurant on Beale Street (the "Lease"). On December 1, 2002, the Bankruptcy Court for the Eastern District of Tennessee ordered the trustee to abandon the Lease. The trustee abandoned the Lease and the debtor moved out.

Organized Writing   When approaching a legal writing project, the first task, regardless of the type of document to be produced, is to outline its contents. The importance of outlining cannot be overstated; not only does it help the reader follow the argument or points of information, but it also serves as a checklist so that issues and arguments are not omitted.

Outlining is simple. No particular format is needed. It may be that ultimately two outlines will be made: the first listing all the points to be mentioned, in no particular order; and the second, a more refined outline, listing the points in logical sequence with subheadings where appropriate.

Once the outline is done, it is time to write. Whether it is dictated, handwritten, typed, or input in a computer, the strategy is the same. First, state the question or issue raised; second, state the law; third, and this is the most difficult part, analogize or draw comparisons between the actual facts and the case law that leads to the conclusion; and fourth, draw a conclusion. Law students use the mnemonic devise of IRAC to remember this writing form: *I*ssue, *R*ule, *A*nalysis, and *C*onclusion. If the analysis section is long, the writer may want to add a short summary of the conclusion right after the Rule section for the benefit of the reader. A memo following the IRAC method can be found in Exhibit 5.8.

The third step draws comparisons between the actual case and those facts found in the cited cases. The task is to highlight similarities in the facts and the circumstances. Any case that is controlling and decides the issue must be brought to the court's attention, regardless of the harm it may do to the desired conclusion. Failure to do so is an ethical violation in most states. It is, however, acceptable to distinguish the facts or advocate that the case not be followed.

If the suggested organization—issue, citation to the law, comparison and contrast (analysis), and conclusion—is followed and applied to each point in the outline, the result should be a well written and easy to follow piece of legal writing.

Citation Format

Sometimes a particular jurisdiction requires a special format for citation to cases, statutes, and other authorities. In the absence of any rule, the system of citation provided in *The Bluebook: A Uniform System of Citation*, published and distributed by the Harvard Law Review Association on behalf of four prestigious law reviews, can be followed. This is commonly referred to as **Bluebook** citation form.

✦ **Bluebook**
The common name for
The Bluebook: A Uniform
System of Citation, *the standard
most often used for proper
citation format.*

The *Uniform System of Citation* is comprehensive, listing citation form for cases, articles, statutes, legislative history, treatises, and almost every other imaginable source. It does not, however, list in one place citations for commonly used bankruptcy sources. For ease of reference, these citations are compiled in Exhibit 5.9.

Table of Contents and Authorities

A local rule may require that all motions or briefs over a certain length be accompanied by a table of contents and authorities. It is generally a good idea to include the table of contents, regardless of whether it is required, since it gives the reader a quick preview of the arguments.

Sample tables of contents and authorities follow as Exhibits 5.10 and 5.11. There is no special format unless one is required by a local rule.

EXHIBIT 5.8 ✦ *A Sample Memo Answering the Procedural Question Posed Using the IRAC Method*

TO: BANKRUPT C. LAWYER
FROM: L. C. O'PERA
DATE: April 15, 2004
RE: Timing of Dischargeability Complaint

I. Issue

On October 1, 2003, Samuel Pearstein filed a Chapter 7 petition. The meeting of creditors under Section 341(a) of the Bankruptcy Code was first scheduled for November 1, 2003 but, due to the debtor's illness, was continued to February 1, 2004. On that date, it was held and concluded. First City Bank received notice of the first date set for the meeting of creditors.

On March 1, 2004, First City Bank filed a complaint against the debtor under Section 523(a)(2) claiming that the debt due to it was nondischargeable (the "Complaint").

Was the Complaint timely filed?

II. Rule

Federal Rule of Bankruptcy Procedure 4007(c) provides that all complaints seeking to determine the dischargeability of any debt must be filed not later than 60 days following the *first* date set for the meeting of creditors. The court may extend the 60-day deadline, but only upon the motion of a party in interest made before the 60 days has expired.

III. Analysis

The first date set for the meeting of creditors was November 1, 2003. Any complaint to determine dischargeability should have been filed by approximately January 1, 2004.

The fact that the meeting of creditors was not actually held until February 1, 2004 is irrelevant. In *Kelly v. Gordon (In re Gordon)*, 988 F.2d 1000 (9th Cir. 1993), the meeting of creditors was set for March 9, 1990 but not held until March 30, 1990. The creditor filed the dischargeability complaint on May 10, 1990, two days late. The Ninth Circuit rejected the creditors' argument that the 60 days begins to run from the date the meeting takes place rather than the date for which it is first scheduled. The Court stated:

> "The rule makes the deadline 60 days after the 'first date *set*' for the meeting, not the date the hearing is actually held. '[*H*]eld pursuant to [section] 341(a)' simply describes the type of meeting being scheduled."

IV. Conclusion

First City Bank did not file the Complaint until 120 days after the first date set for the meeting of creditors. Since it did not seek an extension of the time period, it untimely filed the Complaint.

COMPUTER-AIDED LEGAL RESEARCH

The increased use of computers has led to a major change in how legal research is conducted. As few as 10 years ago, the primary research tools were hard copies of the various reporters mentioned earlier in this chapter. Today, computer-aided research is the norm rather than the exception.

Computer-aided research includes media such as CD-ROMs, online research services, and internet websites. Both West Group and LexisNexis market CD-ROMs that give lawyers and paralegals a comparatively inexpensive way of accessing bankruptcy case law and statutes via computer. In addition to CD-ROM technology, today's lawyer and paralegal have the option of using online legal research services such as those offered by Westlaw and LexisNexis. Both services have comprehensive bankruptcy databases that accept "plain language" queries.

Each system has the ability to cite check any case or statute. Westlaw uses a proprietary product called KeyCite®, while LexisNexis has an agreement with Shepard's that allows it to offer *Shepard's Citations* online to its customers. Both Westlaw and LexisNexis systems work the same way and use similar symbols. For example, a red flag in KeyCite indicates that the case is no longer "good law" for

EXHIBIT 5.9 ✦ *The Most Commonly Used Bankruptcy Sources and How to Cite Them*

Type of Source	Sample Citation	Additional Information
Statute		
Bankruptcy Reform Act of 1978	11 U.S.C. § 101 et seq. (1994) 11 U.S.C. § 506(c) (1994) 28 U.S.C. § 157(a)(2) (1994)	
Bankruptcy Reform Act of 1898	11 U.S.C. § 101 *et seq.* (repealed 1978)	
Legislative History	S.Rep. No. 989, 95th Cong., 2d Sess. 104 (1977) H.R.Rep. No. 595, 95th Cong., 2d Sess. 390 (1977)	If possible, give a parallel citation to the pertinent edition of the *United States Code Congressional and Administrative News.* For example, S.Rep. No. 989, 95th Cong., 2d Sess. 104, reprinted in 1977 *U.S. Code Cong.Ad.News* 9260.
Rules of Procedure	Fed. R. Bankr. P. 9016 Fed.R. Civ.P. 41(a)	
Cases		
United States Supreme Court	*Cryts v. French (In re Cox Cotton Co.)*, 460 U.S 1072 (1984)	Note that civil actions, such as adversary proceedings, that are brought in bankruptcy court are cited with the name of the bankruptcy case appended parenthetically.
Court of Appeals	*Sulmeyer v. Pacific Suzuki (In re Grand Chevrolet, Inc.)* 25 F.3d 728 (9th Cir. 1994)	
District Court	*In re Battle,* 457 F.Supp. 719 (E.D.Pa.1978)	
Bankruptcy Court and Bankruptcy Appellate Panel Cases		
Bankruptcy Reporter (West):	*Moneymaker v. Bank of America (In re Benning),* 2 B.R. 256 (Bankr.E.D.Ca.1980); or *In re Herskowitz,* 166 B.R. 764 (Bankr. 9th Cir. 1994)	
Bankruptcy Law Reporter (CCH):	*In re Iacovoni,* Bankr. L. Rep. (CCH) ¶ 67444 (Bankr.D.Utah 1980)	
Collier Bankruptcy Cases (Matthew Bender):	*Smith v. Brown (In re Green),* 1 Collier Bank. Cas.2d (MB) 378 (Bankr.M.D.GA.1985)	
Bankruptcy Court Decision (LRP):	*In re Iacovoni,* 5 Bankr.Ct.Dec. (LRP) 1270 (Bankr.D. Utah 1980)	
Treatises, Loose Leaf Services, Books, and Pamphlets	2 L. King, *Collier on Bankruptcy,* § 101.09 (15th ed. 1983) McQueen & Crestol, *Federal Tax Aspects of Bankruptcy,* § 5.03 (1984)	
Periodicals		
Articles	Vix, *Protecting Shopping Centers under the Bankruptcy Code,* 1984 Ann.Surv.Bankr.L. 15. Brown, *U.S. Recognition of Foreign Bankruptcies,* 18 Am.Bankr.L.J. 416 (1980)	
Law Reviews	Note, *Collective Bargaining Agreements and Bildisco,* 45 U.Chi.L. Rev. 255 (1984) Comment, *Arbitration Agreements and the New Bankruptcy Act,* 77 Mich.L.Rev. 363 (1979)	

EXHIBIT 5.10 ✦ *Sample Table of Contents*

TABLE OF CONTENTS

EXHIBIT 5.11 ✦ *Sample Table of Contents*

TABLE OF AUTHORITIES

—CONTINUED

EXHIBIT 5.11 ✦ *Sample Table of Contents* (CONTINUED)

TABLE OF AUTHORITIES

at least one of the points it contains, while Shepard's online uses a red symbol in the shape of a stop sign.

Be sure that your office has the most up-to-date user guides and database compilations for either service. They may be obtained from your sales representative. These materials are quite comprehensive. For example, bankruptcy coverage in the 2002 *Westlaw Database Directory* covers four pages. User guides include specialized material on conducting legal research in the area of bankruptcy.

These online services can be expensive, however. Depending on the particular user plan purchased by a law firm, it might be charged for every minute a paralegal—or anyone—is signed on to the system. In order to help keep expenses down, both Westlaw and LexisNexis offer assistance from reference attorneys who are available via a toll free telephone number. These reference attorneys will assist in the formulation of an appropriate query designed to find the information sought. Paralegals should obtain from their sales representative the telephone number used to access the reference attorneys.

One advantage that Westlaw has over LexisNexis is its capacity to conduct topic and key number searches, thereby reducing a paralegal's research time.

The internet has also greatly increased the research horizons of paralegals. Not only are there numerous websites dedicated to bankruptcy issues (listed at the back of this book), there are also websites of various law schools throughout the nation, which are excellent sources of information. The Franklin Pierce Law Center library (in Concord, New Hampshire) has, for example, developed OLLIE (Online Law Library Internet Edition), which is accessible via its website (http://www.fplc.edu/) or directly (http://www.fplc.edu/library/ollie.htm). OLLIE provides links to sources for both federal and New Hampshire state law, and federal and state agencies. Today's paralegal must be aware of such law school sites in his or her state.

The internet can also streamline the paperwork and filing process for the paralegal. Many of the local bankruptcy courts now have websites from which a paralegal can download local rules and forms. In addition, many states (New Hampshire, for example) are now accepting electronic case filing. This topic is discussed in greater depth in Chapter 14.

ETHICAL CONSIDERATIONS

Pursuant to the Model Rules of Professional Responsibility, attorneys are required to tell any court or tribunal of any laws or court decisions that they know run counter to the interests of their client if opposing counsel has failed to do so. (Model Rules of Professional Conduct, Rule 3.3)

If, in the course of conducting research on a bankruptcy issue, a paralegal comes upon a case that goes against the claims being made on behalf of the firm's client, the paralegal should inform the supervising attorney of the newly discovered case, even though by doing so the firm will be obligated to notify the court of the case should the opposing party overlook it. Upon finding such a case, the paralegal should research other cases that may distinguish the holding. The attorney will then have grounds for arguing that the opposing case, which on the surface is detrimental to the client's interests, can and should be distinguished from the facts of the client's case.

From both an ethical and professional perspective, it is important that a paralegal's research be complete and that the summary and briefing of cases be accurate.

SUMMARY

A bankruptcy legal researcher looks to statutes, procedural rules, legislative history, case law, and secondary sources for information. There are two approaches to bankruptcy research: by topic or by Bankruptcy Code section. To research using the topic method, start with a general discussion in a secondary source and then find an appropriate headnote in West's *Bankruptcy Digest*. Case summaries are arranged by headnote in the *Digest*. To research using the Bankruptcy Code, use the index to find a relevant Bankruptcy Code section. The *Codex* or the *United States Code Annotated* or *United States Code Service* can then be used to find cases concerning a Code section. Always update the cases researched using *Shepard's citations*.

A written report of the research conducted should follow IRAC: issue, rule, analysis, and conclusion. Legal writing should be in plain English. Avoid outdated legal jargon. Use short sentences, the active voice, and familiar words.

Computer-aided legal research has significantly changed the scope of today's legal research. From CD-ROM to the Internet, today's paralegal has many research tools available from the office computer. Online research services such as Westlaw and LexisNexis provide comprehensive research of every conceivable legal issue. The importance of this aspect of legal research is growing in importance as more and more legal resources become available via the internet.

✦ KEY TERMS

Bluebook	headnotes	precedent	*stare decisis*
cite checking	pocket parts	Shepardizing	

✦ IMPROVE YOUR UNDERSTANDING

Correct this citation:

In re Granada, Inc. (*Billings v. Zions First National Bank*), 110 Bankr. 548 (D.Utah Bankr.1990).

✦ RESEARCH PROJECT

The partner in charge of the firm's bankruptcy practice wants to know if the phrase "reasonable compensation" in Section 330(a)(1) of the Bankruptcy Code includes paying interest. Map out a research strategy and perform the research. Write a short memorandum detailing the research steps you took.

Using only the research and hypothetical facts provided to you in this book, draft a memo answering the question of whether the debt incurred for the baseball cards is dischargeable.

Bankruptcy Litigation and Appeals

ONE OF THE purposes of bankruptcy is to resolve all of the disputes between the debtor and its creditors in one place—the bankruptcy court. As a result, bankruptcy practice necessarily includes some litigation. The litigation may involve special bankruptcy issues such as relief from the automatic stay. It may involve state law causes of action such as breach of contract. As shown in this chapter, litigation in the bankruptcy courts is not—or at least should not be—very different from practice in the district courts. An understanding of federal civil procedure and the local rules of practice will almost always suffice.

Since paralegals cannot practice law, they may not appear at trials or hearings on behalf of clients. There are, however, many tasks related to litigation in which their assistance is very helpful. Paralegals may prepare drafts of pleadings, organize documents and other evidence, summarize deposition transcripts, attend the hearings, and take notes. During the tense and often frantic moments of trial, a well-prepared paralegal can help ensure that everything moves like clockwork.

Paralegals can also facilitate bankruptcy litigation by being on cordial terms with court personnel (the courtroom and calendar clerks especially) and by having a thorough understanding of the court system and the functions of the various departments. There will be situations in which the ability to convince a clerk to enter a judgment on the docket immediately will be as important as obtaining the judgment.

To familiarize the paralegal with the process, the following discussion covers the types of litigation that may be held in bankruptcy courts, and how that litigation is started, conducted, and terminated. A short discussion of bankruptcy appellate practice is also included.

JURISDICTION

In General

Jurisdiction is the power of a court to preside over a dispute. Title 28 of the United States Code, not Title 11, governs matters of bankruptcy court jurisdiction and related issues. Under 28 U.S.C. § 1334(b), the district courts have jurisdiction over all civil proceedings arising under the Bankruptcy Code and arising in or related to a case under the Bankruptcy Code. Proceedings are the lawsuits or other procedures within the bankruptcy case that resolve the disputes between the creditors, the trustee, and the debtor.

✦ **jurisdiction**
The power of a court to preside over and decide a dispute between people or property.

So that the district courts will not have to hear all bankruptcy-related disputes, Section 157(a) of Title 28 provides that the district court may refer any or all proceedings in a bankruptcy case to the bankruptcy judges sitting in the district. A blanket reference of all proceedings has been made in every district. At least initially, all litigation involving the debtor or the estate will proceed in the bankruptcy court.

Core and Noncore Proceedings

Even though Section 157(a) provides that the bankruptcy court may preside over all proceedings, it does not mean that the bankruptcy judge will make the final determination of a dispute. Section 157(b)(1) of Title 28 only allows bankruptcy judges to hear, determine, and enter a final order in **core proceedings.** Core proceedings are those matters involving rights or duties created by bankruptcy law. Some examples are objections to claims or exemptions, the request by a trustee for authority to obtain credit, suits to compel turnover of property of the estate or to recover preferences, motions concerning the automatic stay, and determinations as to the dischargeability of a particular debt.

Section 157(b)(2) provides a noninclusive list of core proceedings. This list, shown in Exhibit 6.1, covers general and specific matters.

A noncore, or **related proceeding,** is everything that is not a core proceeding. Usually these are lawsuits pending in the bankruptcy court only because one of the parties commenced a bankruptcy case. If there was no bankruptcy case, the litigation probably would still have been commenced but in a different court. Under Section 157(c) of Title 28, noncore proceedings may be heard by a bankruptcy judge, but unless all parties consent to the bankruptcy judge entering the order, the judge can only propose **findings of fact** and **conclusions of law.** The district court then enters the order or judgment after reviewing any of the bankruptcy judge's findings or conclusions objected to by the losing side.

✦ core proceeding
Those matters directly concerning the bankruptcy case and arising under the Bankruptcy Code.

✦ related proceeding
Those matters concerning a bankruptcy case only because one of the parties to the dispute is a debtor in a bankruptcy case.

✦ findings of fact
Decisions by a fact finder (e.g., judge, jury, hearings officer) about a question of fact.

✦ conclusions of law
Arguments or answers arrived at by not only drawing a conclusion from the facts, but also by applying the law to the facts.

EXHIBIT 6.1 ✦ *Core Proceedings*

General Core Proceedings
1. Matters concerning the administration of the estate.
2. Counterclaims by the estate against creditors who filed proofs of claim.
3. Any other proceeding affecting the liquidation of the estate's assets or creditor claims (other than personal injury or wrongful death claims).

Specific Core Proceedings
4. Objections to claims.
5. Objections to a debtor's claimed exemptions.
6. Estimation of claims (other than personal injury or wrongful death claims).
7. Motions for the debtor or trustee to obtain credit.
8. Turnover disputes.
9. Preference disputes.
10. Motions concerning the automatic stay.
11. Fraudulent conveyance actions.
12. Discharge and dischargeability disputes.
13. Questions of the validity, extent, or priority of liens.
14. Confirmation of plans.
15. Motions approving the use, sale, or lease of property.

Withdrawal of Reference

Even though an action is core under Section 157(a), the bankruptcy court may not be the one to hear and finally decide the dispute. Section 157(d) provides that the district court can always withdraw the reference to the bankruptcy court. Section 157(d) also provides that if the lawsuit involves both bankruptcy law and other federal law, such as questions involving federal securities or pension law, the district court must withdraw the reference if a party makes an appropriate motion in a timely manner.

Abstention

Abstention is a court's ability to avoid hearing a matter that it otherwise has the power to hear. There are two types of abstention that are important in bankruptcy practice. The first type of abstention is described in Section 305 of the Bankruptcy Code; it allows the bankruptcy court to dismiss or abstain from the entire case. If the court abstains, it is as if the bankruptcy case was never commenced. Usually a bankruptcy court will abstain under Section 305 if there is a state or district court receivership proceeding pending and the receiver is doing everything that a bankruptcy trustee would otherwise do. The bankruptcy court will abstain because there simply is no need for a bankruptcy case.

The second type of abstention is much more limited but more widely used. It has two statutory sources. First, Section 1334(c)(1) of Title 28 states that the bankruptcy and district courts *may* abstain from hearing a proceeding in the interest of justice, **comity** for state courts (in deference to them), or out of respect for state law. Under this section, a bankruptcy court could send two parties to state court to have it decide a particular dispute, but still keep the rest of the bankruptcy case alive. Second, Section 1334(c)(2) provides that the courts *must* abstain if a timely motion is made and the proceeding is based on a state law claim, federal court jurisdiction is otherwise unavailable, and the action is commenced and can be timely adjudicated in a state court. For example, if before bankruptcy the debtor had brought a lawsuit for breach of contract in the state courts, the defendant may be able to force the bankruptcy court to abstain. If the bankruptcy court abstains, the matter will be sent back to the state court for a ruling.

✦ **comity**
A willingness to do something official, not as a matter of right, but out of goodwill and tradition.

VENUE

As mentioned, jurisdiction is the power of a federal court to hear a particular matter. **Venue** is the determination of which court is the correct one to hear the matter. Assuming jurisdiction is available, Section 1409 provides that proceedings must usually be commenced in the district in which the bankruptcy case is pending. There are a few exceptions listed in 28 U.S.C. § 1409(b)–(e), including:

✦ **venue**
Where, either geographically or among different types of courts, a case or proceeding is or may be pending.

- ✦ An action to recover a money judgment or property worth less than $1,000 or a consumer debt of less than $5,000 is proper only in the district in which the defendant resides.
- ✦ A claim arising from the postpetition operation of the debtor's business is properly brought only where it would have been had no bankruptcy case been commenced unless the nondebtor party sues, in which case it can also be brought in the district in which the bankruptcy case is pending.

If a proceeding is commenced in the wrong venue, there is no provision that allows the proceeding to remain there even if all parties agree. Technically, the case must be dismissed so that it can be refiled in the proper district.

Even if venue over a particular proceeding is appropriate where the case is commenced, it may not always stay there. Section 1412 of Title 28 allows a court to transfer a proceeding to another district in the interest of justice or for the convenience of the parties. Such changes are usually the result of a creditor making a motion for a change of venue.

REMOVAL

✦ removal

The transfer of an adversary proceeding from the court in which it was commenced to a different type of court.

Section 1452 of Title 28 concerns **removal** of claims related to bankruptcy cases. Removal allows a party to transfer litigation from a state court to the district court where the bankruptcy case is pending, if the district court has jurisdiction. If state court litigation is pending when the case is commenced, the debtor or another party can remove it to the district court and it automatically will be referred to the bankruptcy court. Pursuant to Section 1452(b), the court may **remand** it (send it back) on any equitable ground.

✦ remand

The return of a removed proceeding to the court in which it was originally commenced.

Bankruptcy Rule 9027 gives the mechanics for removing a proceeding. It is very detailed, and the procedure should be followed carefully. Generally, a notice for removal must be filed in the district court. If the lawsuit to be removed is pending at the time of the commencement of the bankruptcy case, the notice must be filed within 90 days after the order for relief, within 30 days after the automatic stay is lifted if the claim or cause of action has been stayed, or within 30 days after appointment of a Chapter 11 trustee. If the action is not pending at the time the bankruptcy case is commenced, the removing party has only 30 days to act. After the application is filed, there are a number of requirements imposed on the party seeking to remove, such as:

- Mandating that the party filing the notice of removal promptly serve a copy of the notice of removal on all parties to the removed claim or cause of action;
- Requiring that the party filing the notice of removal promptly file a copy of the notice of removal with the clerk of the court from which the claim or cause of action is removed. These are two examples of how important it is for paralegals to know the procedural rules, since paralegals are often given the responsibility of making certain that copies of pleadings are sent to the appropriate parties.

TYPE OF PROCEEDING

✦ contested matter

An action in the bankruptcy court seeking relief that is commenced by the filing of a motion.

In General

Separate and distinct from the question of whether an action is a core or a noncore proceeding is the determination of whether it is an *adversary proceeding,* a **contested matter,** or another type of judicial proceeding in the bankruptcy court. That determination will govern the type of pleadings used as well as the procedure and rules to be followed.

✦ complaint

The first main pleading filed in a civil lawsuit. It includes, among other things, a request for specific help from the court and an explanation as to why the court has the power to do what the plaintiff wants.

Adversary proceedings are governed by the 7000 series of the Bankruptcy Rules, which largely adopt the Federal Rules of Civil Procedure (commonly abbreviated as Fed.R.Civ.P.). Adversary proceedings are described in Bankruptcy Rule 7001 and outlined in Exhibit 6.2.

An adversary proceeding is commenced by the filing of a **complaint.** The procedure is almost identical to litigation in other federal courts.

✦ motion

A request that a judge make a ruling or take a particular action.

All controversies that are not specifically listed in Rule 7001 as adversary proceedings are contested matters. They are commenced by a **motion.** Rule 9014 governs the procedure for contested matters, which are discussed later in this chap-

EXHIBIT 6.2 ✦ *Adversary Proceedings Under Bankruptcy Rule 7001*

1. Recover money or property other than a proceeding to:
   a. Compel the debtor to deliver property to the trustee;
   b. Compel the trustee to abandon or otherwise dispose of property;
   c. Recover money from the debtor's attorneys; or
   d. Require a custodian to give an accounting.
2. Determine the validity, priority, or extent of a lien or other interest in property other than an action by a debtor to avoid a lien on exempt property.
3. Obtain the approval for the sale of both the interest of the estate and of a co-owner in property.
4. Object to or revoke a discharge.
5. Revoke an order of confirmation of a Chapter 11, Chapter 12, or Chapter 13 plan.
6. Determine the dischargeability of a debt.
7. Obtain an injunction or other equitable relief.
8. Subordinate any claim or interest unless the subordination is provided for in a plan.
9. Obtain a declaratory judgment with respect to any matter listed in 1–8.
10. Determine a claim or cause of action that has been removed.

Any action not found on this list is a contested matter.

---

ter. The most common contested matters in bankruptcy practice are actions for relief from the automatic stay, motions seeking authority to sell property of the estate, and objections to the claim.

Finally, the general rule that a complaint commences an adversary proceeding and a motion commences a matter is not always true. The following is a list of a very few types of contested matters in which the Bankruptcy Rules require that an application, objection, or other type of paper be filed.

TYPE OF PROCEEDING	TYPE OF PLEADING	BANKRUPTCY RULE NUMBER
Objection to a claim	Objection	3007
Compensation or reimbursement	Application	2016
Opposition to a disclosure statement	Objection	3017(a)
Opposition to a notice of intent to sale, or lease estate property	Objection and request for hearing	6004(b)

A number of the Bankruptcy Rules and certain Bankruptcy Code sections make reference to a request for action by the court. The use of the term "request" does not prescribe a particular form of procedure. Rule 9013 states that a "request for an order, except when an application is authorized by these rules, shall be by written motion. . . ."

Adversary Proceedings

As mentioned, adversary proceedings are commenced by the filing of a complaint (pursuant to Bankruptcy Rule 7003, which cites to Fed. Rule of Civil Procedure 3). There are a few minimum requirements for a complaint: It must identify the parties, establish jurisdiction, and state a cause of action.

The Complaint   The first important party to be identified in the complaint will be the plaintiff, the person starting the lawsuit. Bankruptcy Rule 7017 allows "a

✦ indispensable party
One who, in an adversary proceeding, must be a defendant in order for complete relief to be granted, or who has a significant interest in the subject of the action.

party authorized by statute" to sue without joining the party for whose benefit the action is brought. Bankruptcy Code Section 323 allows a trustee to bring an action on behalf of the creditors of the estate without joining the creditors or the debtor as a party. This allows the trustee to file a complaint on behalf of all creditors.

Pursuant to Bankruptcy Rule 7019, a person must be made a defendant to an adversary proceeding if in its absence complete relief cannot be granted, or if it has a significant interest in the subject of the action. These people are known as **indispensable parties.**

Federal courts are courts of limited jurisdiction and have no power to hear a particular action unless Congress allows them to do so. Pursuant to Bankruptcy Rule 7008(a), a complaint must contain a short and plain statement of the grounds on which the court's jurisdiction depends so the court can determine whether it has the power to entertain the suit. Bankruptcy Rule 7008(a) also requires the jurisdictional allegation to contain a reference to the name, number, and chapter of the bankruptcy case to which the adversary proceeding relates, the district and division where the case is pending, a statement of whether the proceeding is core or noncore and, if noncore, whether the pleader consents to the entry of a final order or judgment by the bankruptcy judge. A sample of an allegation that complies with this requirement in a preference action is shown in Exhibit 6.3.

The rules for pleading the cause of action in an adversary proceeding are set forth in Bankruptcy Rules 7008, 7009, and 7010. Generally, every pleading must contain a caption; allegations must be made in numbered paragraphs; and each claim founded upon a separate transaction or occurrence must be stated in a separate count if it would clarify the facts. Exhibits and earlier statements in a pleading may be incorporated by reference.

A complaint may have one or more claims for relief (sometimes also called causes of action). For example, a complaint filed by a debtor could seek to recover a preference, determine the dischargeability of a debt, and determine the priority of a lien—all from the same person. Typically, the complaint will set out these three different types of relief in separate claims. The complaint should set out each and every element of the claim for relief in addition to the important facts. For example, if a complaint is filed to recover a preferential payment under Section 547, each of the elements of a preferential transfer provided in Section 547(b) should be listed.

Complaints are filed with the bankruptcy court along with the prescribed filing fee. In many districts, along with the complaint and the filing fee, the plaintiff must also file a cover sheet, which sets forth the parties, the attorneys, and the nature of the cause of action. The local rules of each district should be consulted for more particulars on these additional requirements.

EXHIBIT 6.3 ✦ *Sample Allegation Under Bankruptcy Rule 7008(a)*

Jurisdiction and Venue

1. This Court has jurisdiction over this action pursuant to 28 U.S.C. §§ 157 and 1334(a) and the Order of the Chief Judge of the United States District Court, Western District of California, referring bankruptcy cases and proceedings, entered on July 20, 1992. This adversary proceeding is a core matter pursuant to 28 U.S.C. § 157(b)(2)(F) and Plaintiff consents to the entry of a final order or judgment by the Bankruptcy Court.

2. Venue properly resides in the United States Bankruptcy Court for the Western District of California pursuant to 28 U.S.C. § 1409 in that this adversary proceeding is related to In re Videos by Joe, Inc., Bk. No. 95-00001-JF, pending as a Chapter 11 case in the United States Bankruptcy Court for the Western District of California.

Bankruptcy Rule 7004 sets forth the rules regarding service of the **summons** and the complaint. The clerk will issue the summons. It will give the date the response must be filed and the date of the trial or pretrial conference if one is pre-set by the court. The summons must be served with the complaint on the defendant.

Service of the summons and the complaint may be made by personal service, or may be made by first class mail anywhere in the United States. Service by first class mail is not usually allowed in other courts and is one of the benefits of litigating in the bankruptcy court. Service must be made within 10 days after issuance of the summons, or the summons will no longer be valid and a new one will be needed. If service is not made within 120 days after the complaint is filed, the complaint will have to be refiled. Once the complaint and the summons have been served, the person who served the papers must make a proof of service to the court. Usually, this will be done by tendering an affidavit as provided in Bankruptcy Rule 7004(a).

The Response To oppose the claims for relief made in a complaint, the defendant must file an **answer** or some other form of response. Under Fed.R.Civ.P. 8, the answer must state in short and plain terms the defenses to each claim and must either admit or deny the plaintiff's allegations. If the defendant has no knowledge or information regarding the truth of the allegation, it should so state; this will be deemed the same as a denial. If only part of a paragraph is to be denied, the defendant must specify what part is admitted and deny the remainder. Any allegation that is not denied will be deemed admitted.

In addition to merely responding yes or no to the plaintiff's allegations, the defendant may plead other matters known as **affirmative defenses.** Fed.R.Civ.P. 8(c) lists the defenses that constitute affirmative defenses. Under Bankruptcy Rule 7012, certain defenses are waived if not pled prior to or included in the answer, including:

1. lack of jurisdiction over the defendant;
2. improper venue; and
3. insufficiency of service.

Bankruptcy Rule 7012 also requires the defendant to admit or deny the allegation that the proceeding is core or noncore. If the defendant responds that it is noncore, it must say whether it consents to the bankruptcy judge entering the final order or judgment.

The defendant must serve the answer within 30 days after issuance of the summons, unless a different time has been set by the court. If the United States or one of its officers or agencies is a defendant, their answer must be filed within 35 days.

Bankruptcy Rule 7012 details certain motions that may be filed by the defendant instead of an answer. If the complaint is too vague or ambiguous, a party may move for a more definite statement before answering. A party may also move to strike any allegation that is redundant, immaterial, impertinent, or scandalous. In addition, a party may move to dismiss a complaint for any of the following deficiencies:

1. lack of subject matter jurisdiction;
2. lack of jurisdiction over the defendant;
3. improper venue;
4. insufficiency of service of the complaint;
5. failure to state a claim upon which relief can be granted; or
6. failure to join an indispensable party.

A motion to dismiss for failure to state a claim upon which relief can be granted is a very common motion made to delay the filing of an answer. Usually

✦ summons
A document issued by the clerk of the court when a complaint is filed that informs the defendant when it must answer or otherwise respond to the complaint.

✦ answer
The pleading filed by a defendant that admits or denies the allegations in a complaint and asserts any affirmative defenses.

✦ affirmative defenses
Procedural or substantive claims that a defendant may use to defeat the claims made by the plaintiff in a complaint.

the motion asserts that the plaintiff failed to make an important allegation against the defendant. For example, if the lawsuit is based on a preference, the plaintiff may have failed to allege or give the supporting facts to establish that the defendant was a creditor of the debtor at the time the preferential transfer was made. Most of the time, the court will allow the plaintiff to cure any defect by amending the complaint. Then the defendant will have an opportunity to file an answer to the amended complaint or file another motion to dismiss if the defect was not cured or the amended complaint has a new problem.

Most of the grounds for dismissal listed above must be made before an answer is filed, or they will be waived. An objection based on lack of subject matter jurisdiction can be made at any time, even at trial.

Pretrial Procedures   Bankruptcy Rule 7016, which incorporates Fed.R.Civ.P. 16, provides for extensive pretrial procedures so that the court and the parties will focus early on the issues and disputes. Not only does a pretrial procedure force the parties not to put off trial preparation until the last minute, but it often facilitates settlement discussions. The pretrial procedure is discretionary with the court. Usually each district and often each judge will have their own pretrial rules; these rules might vary with the type of proceeding.

Discovery   Rule 7026 contains the general provisions regarding discovery. It fully incorporates Fed.R.Civ.P. 26, which was changed on December 1, 1993 to add controversial sections concerning mandatory disclosure requirements of counsel. Generally, it requires each side to disclose to the other the names and addresses of witnesses, all documents, and computations of damages, without the other side asking for any of the information. Many people claim that these disclosure requirements undermine the adversarial nature of the United States justice system. As a result of the controversy, the Judicial Conference has allowed districts not to adopt the new provisions.

There are other provisions of the Bankruptcy Rules concerning discovery, all of which largely copy the Federal Rules of Civil Procedure. Depositions are covered in Rules 7027 through 7032. Interrogatories are the subject of Rule 7033, and provisions concerning the production of documents are found in Rule 7034. Rules 7035 and 7036 provide for physical and mental examinations and requests for admissions. The subject of failure to make or cooperate in discovery and sanctions is found in Rule 7037.

The Bankruptcy Rules also provide a method of fact finding not available under the Federal Rules of Civil Procedure. Under Bankruptcy Rule 2004, the court may order the examination of any person upon motion of a party in interest. Ordinarily, a Bankruptcy Rule 2004 examination is just like a deposition; however, an adversary proceeding need not be pending. In fact, many courts will not allow a party to an adversary proceeding to examine pursuant to Bankruptcy Rule 2004 and will require adherence to the discovery rules.

A Rule 2004 examination can cover the acts, conduct, liabilities, and financial condition of the debtor and any other matter that may affect the administration of the debtor's estate or the right to a discharge. If the debtor is operating a business, the examination may cover the operation of the business. In a Chapter 12, 13, or 11 case, the examiner may also inquire into matters relevant to a plan of reorganization. A sample motion seeking a Bankruptcy Rule 2004 examination is set forth in Exhibit 6.4.

A Bankruptcy Rule 2004 examination can also involve the production of documentary evidence. The attendance of a person or the production of documents can be compelled by the issuance of a subpoena by the court.

EXHIBIT 6.4 ✦ *Sample Pleadings*

GEORGE G. SNOW
SNOW & WEST
Four Wheel Drive
Los Angeles, California 90017

Attorneys for First City Bank

UNITED STATES BANKRUPTCY COURT
WESTERN DISTRICT OF CALIFORNIA

In re	)	Case No. 03-00001-JF
	)	
VIDEOS BY JOE, INC.	)	Chapter 11
	)	
Debtor.	)	
	)	
Debtor's Address:	)	MOTION FOR ORDER AUTHORIZING EXAMI-
18 Hollywood Drive	)	NATION PURSUANT TO FED.R.BANKR.P.
Los Angeles, CA 90001	)	2004(a); REQUEST FOR PRODUCTION OF DOC-
	)	UMENTS PURSUANT TO FED.R.BANKR.P. 9016
Employer's Tax Id. No. 99-999899	)	
	)	
	)	

TO THE HONORABLE JUSTIN CLAY, UNITED STATES BANKRUPTCY JUDGE:

First City Bank (the "Bank"), through its attorneys, in support of its Motion for Order Authorizing Examination Pursuant to Fed.R.Bankr.P. 2004(a); Request for Production of Documents Pursuant to Fed.R.Bankr.P. 9016, respectfully represents that:

1. The Bank is a creditor in the above-captioned bankruptcy case and is therefore a party in interest within the meaning of 11 U.S.C. § 1109.

2. In connection with this case, it is essential that the Bank undertake certain discovery.

3. Under Fed.R.Bankr.P. 2004, the Bankruptcy Court may order the examination of any person and compel the production of documentary evidence in the matter provided in Fed.R.Bankr.P. 9016.

4. The Bank requests that Joe Businessman, the President of debtor, be compelled to: (a) appear and testify at the office of the attorney for the Bank on November 15, 2003, at 10:00 A.M. to be examined with respect to the acts, conduct, and property of debtor and matters which may affect the administration of this case; and (b) to produce for copying and inspection at the same time and place those documents more particularly described in Exhibit 1 attached hereto.

WHEREFORE, the Bank requests that the Court enter its order compelling the appearance and document production requested in this Motion, and grant such other and further relief as the Court shall deem just and proper.

Dated: October 15, 2003

SNOW & WEST

_____
GEORGE G. SNOW
Attorneys for First City Bank

Default Judgments/Dismissals   A default judgment may be entered when a party has failed to answer or otherwise defend an action. Default judgments are governed by Bankruptcy Rule 7055. Generally, the plaintiff will file a request for the entry of default and lodge an appropriate judgment.

Dismissal is governed by Bankruptcy Rule 7041. A dismissal may be voluntary or involuntary. Except for an action objecting to a discharge, the plaintiff can dismiss an adversary proceeding by merely filing a notice of dismissal anytime prior to the defendant's answer or summary judgment motion. An action may also be dismissed by stipulation signed by all parties who have appeared.

If an adversary proceeding cannot be dismissed as discussed in the previous paragraph, or if it is an action objecting to a discharge, the party that wants the dismissal must make a motion. The proceeding can only be dismissed by order of the court and upon such terms and conditions as the court deems proper.

In addition to a motion to dismiss based on those defenses set out in Bankruptcy Rule 7012, a defendant may move for dismissal for failure of the plaintiff to prosecute, or comply with the rules or an order of the court.

Trials   Trials in bankruptcy court are no different from trials in the district courts. The same rules of evidence and procedure apply. The right to a jury trial in a bankruptcy court, while not clearly delineated, is addressed in both statute and recent case law. Section 1411 of Title 28 states that nothing in the Bankruptcy Code affects any right to trial by jury that an individual otherwise has for personal injury or wrongful death tort claims. However, 28 U.S.C. § 1334(c)(2) requires federal court abstention from these matters if brought by the bankruptcy estate. Claims against the estate are not subject to mandatory abstention but are noncore proceedings that may be tried in district court.

Adding to the confusion regarding this issue is Bankruptcy Rule 9015 concerning jury trials. While the original rule was, according to the Advisory Committee notes, abrogated in 1987 "in light of the clear mandate of 28 USC §2075 that the rules shall not abridge, enlarge, or modify any substantive right," a 1997 amendment to the rule provides criteria that must be met prior to any jury trial occurring in bankruptcy court.

Decisions of the United States Supreme Court provide some guidance in this area. In 1982, in *Northern Pipeline Construction Co. v. Marathon Pipeline Co.* (485 US 50), the Supreme Court drew a clear distinction between Article III judges and bankruptcy judges, finding that the expansion of authority given to bankruptcy judges in 28 USC §1471 et. seq. was unconstitutional.

In *Langenkamp v. Culp, et.al.* (498 US 42 (1991)), the Supreme Court took the opportunity to clarify certain situations where a jury trial is permitted in bankruptcy cases. The Court ruled that if a creditor files a claim in bankruptcy court against the bankruptcy estate, "the creditor's claim and the ensuing preference action by the trustee become integral to the restructuring of the debtor-creditor relationship through the bankruptcy court's equity jurisdiction," thus triggering no Seventh Amendment right to a jury trial. If, on the other hand, "a party does <u>not</u> (emphasis in original) submit a claim against the bankruptcy estate, . . . the trustee can recover . . . only by filing what amounts to a legal action to recover a monetary transfer. In those circumstances, the preference defendant is entitled to a jury trial." In short, if one submits to the jurisdiction of the bankruptcy court by filing a claim with it, no Seventh Amendment right to a jury trial attaches.

Judgments, Findings, and Conclusions   Bankruptcy Rules 7052 and 7054 concern findings of fact, conclusions of law, and judgments. Bankruptcy Rules 9026 and 9027 cover new trials, amendments of judgments, and relief from judgments.

Contested Matters

Actions that are not specifically described in Bankruptcy Rule 7001 are not adversary proceedings. They are contested matters and are governed by certain rules in the 9000 series of the Bankruptcy Rules. Contested matters are far more common than adversary proceedings but are far less discussed in the Bankruptcy Rules.

Unless the Bankruptcy Rules provide otherwise, relief in contested matters must be requested by motion. The motion must be in writing unless made orally during a hearing and must state with particularity its grounds and the order sought. Unless the court directs otherwise, service must be made in the manner directed by Bankruptcy Rule 7004 and upon those whom Bankruptcy Rule 2002 specifies.

In the 1994 Amendments, Congress added Section 342(c), which states that all notices of hearings in contested matters must contain the name, address, and taxpayer identification number of the debtor. However, if this information is not put on the notice, there appears to be no negative result. Section 342(c) specifically states that the failure to follow it will not invalidate the legal effect of the notice.

In March of 1995, the Judicial Conference amended Official Forms 16A and 16C to insert the debtor's address below its name on the caption in order to comply with Section 342(c). Official Forms 16B and 16D do not have this additional information. To be safe, the paralegal may want to use only the Official Form 16A and 16C versions and make the debtor's address and tax identification or social security number part of every pleading in the case. All Sample Pleadings in this book will do so.

Bankruptcy Rule 9014 provides that no response is required to a contested matter unless the court orders otherwise. In almost all jurisdictions, there are local rules that govern motion practice. Many local rules require a response or at least notice that the party intends to oppose the motion.

Bankruptcy Rule 9014 also requires that reasonable notice and opportunity for a hearing must be afforded the person against whom relief is sought. Local rules of practice usually establish the notice period and any procedures for shortening that time.

Finally, Bankruptcy Rule 9014 provides that many of the rules governing adversary proceedings, including the discovery rules, also apply for contested matters. It also allows the court to direct that other Bankruptcy Rules apply in contested matters.

APPEALS

Appeals from orders issued in adversary proceedings and contested matters in bankruptcy cases are not substantially different from appeals from other courts. Under Section 158 of Title 28, an appeal from a final order of a bankruptcy judge is to the district court. A bankruptcy court order can also be appealed to the Bankruptcy Appellate Panel (often called the BAP) if one has been established in a particular district and if all parties consent.

The Bankruptcy Appellate Panel is composed of bankruptcy judges from districts within one or more circuits. The district judges in a circuit must authorize the referrals of appeals to the BAP. Three judges form the panel that will hear a particular appeal. No judge from the district in which the appeal originated may sit on the panel for that appeal.

In noncore proceedings, unless the parties consent to allow the bankruptcy court to do it, the final order is entered by the district court. These appeals are governed by the Federal Rules of Appellate Procedure in the same manner as all other district court judgments and orders. An appeal from the affirmance or reversal by the district court or the BAP is to the court of appeals and proceeds under the Federal Rules of Appellate Procedure.

The mechanics of taking an appeal are governed by the 8000 series of the Bankruptcy Rules and are summarized in Exhibit 6.5. Rule 8001 concerns how an appeal is taken as a matter of right and when leave of the court is required. Generally, appeals are commenced by the filing of a very short and simple notice of appeal. Official Form 17 is a sample notice of appeal.

A notice of appeal is filed with the bankruptcy court; it must be filed within 10 days after the entry of the judgment or order. If it is not timely filed, the appellate court will have no jurisdiction and will be forced to dismiss the appeal. If the party who wants to appeal needs more time, it can seek an order extending the time to appeal, but that order must be entered before the expiration of the initial 10-day period. Any extension cannot be for more than an additional 20 days.

EXHIBIT 6.5 ✦ *Procedures and Deadlines for Appeals*

Timing	Action	Bankruptcy Rule Number	Deadline
Day 1	Notice of appeal filed with bankruptcy court	8001, 8002, 8004	Within 10 days of entry of bankruptcy order
Day 1 or sooner	Order a copy of the docket to use to designate the record.		
Day 10	Designation of items to be included in the record and statement of issues presented.	8006	Within 10 days of notice of appeal
Day 10	Notice of transcript	8006	Within 10 days of notice of appeal
Day 30 or sooner	Reporter files transcript, record is complete. Bankruptcy clerk submits to appellate clerk either the record or a certificate of record.	8007(a)	Approximately 30 days after notice of appeal
	Appellate clerk gives notice to all parties that the record or the certificate has been filed. That date is the date the appeal is considered "entered on appellate docket" for purposes of Bankruptcy Rule 8009.		
Approximately day 45	Appellant must file opening brief. 50-page limit. Copies of all statutes, rules, and regulations cited must be appended to the brief or supplied to the court in pamphlet form.	8009 (a)(1) 8010	15 days after appeal docketed
	Appellant to file appendix to brief if appeal is to Bankruptcy Appellate Panel.	8009(b)	With opening brief
Approximately day 60	Appellee must file brief. 50-page limit. Copies of all statutes, rules, and regulations cited must be appended to the brief or supplied to the court in pamphlet form.	8009(a)(2) 8010	15 days after service of appellant's brief
	Appellee may file an appendix of any material required to be included but omitted by appellant.	8009(b)	15 days after service of appellant's brief
Approximately day 70	Appellant may file reply brief. 25-page limit.	8009(a)(3) 8010(c)	10 days after service of appellee's brief
Anytime thereafter	Court sets matter for oral argument.	8012	

If the order or judgment appealed from allows the prevailing party to do something that is the subject of the appeal, such as sell property, foreclosure on collateral, or the like, the appealing party will need to obtain a stay of the effectiveness of the order or judgment on appeal. If the appealing party does not do so, the appeal may be moot because it is too late for the appellate court to reverse. Stays pending appeal are governed by Bankruptcy Rule 8005 and are usually made to the bankruptcy court. If made to the district court or the Bankruptcy Appellate Panel, the moving party must show why the relief was not obtained from the bankruptcy judge.

Briefs and the appendix are governed by Bankruptcy Rules 8009 and 8010. The appellant's brief usually will be due 15 days after the entry of the appeal of the docket, which is done after the record is complete. The appellee's brief is due 15 days after the brief of the appellant. The appellant may then file a reply brief within 10 days. No further briefs are usually allowed.

LOCAL RULES

As mentioned in Chapter 2 of this text, each of the bankruptcy courts within the United States may develop local rules and forms. A paralegal practicing in the bankruptcy area must be familiar with the local rules and forms in his or her jurisdiction. Many bankruptcy courts have placed their local rules on the court's website, and most compilations of state court rules include the local rules of the bankruptcy court.

ETHICAL CONSIDERATIONS

A paralegal may be tempted to practice delaying tactics while preparing bankruptcy litigation or during the trial. The supervising attorney may not keep a close eye on every case. Model Rule 3.2 of the Model Rules of Professional Responsibility specifies that reasonable efforts should be taken to expedite litigation.

If an attorney has trusted a paralegal to coordinate various trial details with opposing counsel's paralegal, it is unethical for that paralegal to attempt to delay the case without first discussing the matter with his or her supervising attorney. While there may be valid, substantive reasons for delay, it must be attempted only with the approval of the supervising attorney.

SUMMARY

The bankruptcy court derives from the district court jurisdiction to make final rulings in all core proceedings and to make proposed rulings in all related or noncore proceedings in a bankruptcy case. The proceedings can be commenced in the bankruptcy court or removed to it. The bankruptcy court's jurisdiction can be withdrawn by the district court, or the bankruptcy court can abstain from ruling in a particular case or proceeding.

There are two main types of proceedings in a bankruptcy case: adversary proceedings and contested matters. The Bankruptcy Rules determine which type is involved. Adversary proceedings are commenced by the filing of a complaint. They are managed much the same as other federal court litigation. Contested matters are commenced by the filing of a motion.

An appeal from a bankruptcy court order can be made to the district court or, in some jurisdictions, to a bankruptcy appellate panel.

✦ KEY TERMS

affirmative defenses	contested matter	motion	venue
answer	core proceeding	related proceeding	
comity	findings of fact	remand	
complaint	indispensable party	removal	
conclusions of law	jurisdiction	summons	

✦ IMPROVE YOUR UNDERSTANDING

1. Compare Exhibit 6.1 and Exhibit 6.2. To the extent it can be determined by reference only to those tables, which adversary proceedings are core matters and which are not?
2. Who determines whether a matter is core or noncore?
3. If a matter is noncore, under what circumstances can a bankruptcy judge enter the final order or judgment?
4. If a matter is core, under what circumstances would the bankruptcy judge not enter the final order or judgment?
5. Why do you think Section 305 is in Title 11 but Section 1334(c) is in Title 28?
6. What is the primary difference between 28 U.S.C. § 1408 and 28 U.S.C. § 1409?
7. What is the last date for a defendant to plead lack of subject matter jurisdiction? When is the last date for a defendant to plead lack of personal jurisdiction?
8. If the defendant has answered, how can an action be dismissed?
9. List three fact situations in which the losing party would want to obtain a stay pending appeal.

✦ RESEARCH PROJECT

1. Locate a reported decision discussing a motion made pursuant to 28 U.S.C. § 1412. What factors did the court consider in determining whether to change venue?
2. Is there a local rule in your jurisdiction for pretrial meetings or status conferences?
3. What do the local rules in your jurisdiction provide with respect to motion practice?

✦ DRAFTING PROJECT

Review Bankruptcy Rule 9027. Prepare a chart listing the steps required to remove a lawsuit from the state court to the bankruptcy court and the deadlines for performing those steps.

Beginning a Bankruptcy Case

LATER SECTIONS of this book examine a Chapter 7, 11, 12, and 13 case in detail. Very different rules apply to each chapter. At the beginning, however, all bankruptcy cases are subject to the same rules and forms. They are begun with identical petitions, and identical schedules of assets and liabilities need to be filed. So, before examining each type of case separately, we examine the elements common to the beginning of all bankruptcy cases, whether liquidations or reorganizations.

CONSIDERING WHETHER A BANKRUPTCY CASE MAY OR SHOULD BE FILED

Limitations on Filing a Bankruptcy Case

Bankruptcy law provides debtors with extraordinary options that do not otherwise exist, including the ability to compel a creditor to accept less than the full amount owed, to assign contracts not otherwise assignable, and to extend the term of a promissory note. Yet, for a number of reasons, Congress did not want these valuable protections to be available to everyone. As you may recall from Chapter 1, Section 109(a) of the Bankruptcy Code provides that only a person who resides or has a place of business or property in the United States can be a debtor. Person is defined in Section 101(41) to include individuals, partnerships, and corporations— but not governmental units. When governmental units are meant to be included within the scope of a particular section, the Bankruptcy Code uses the word entity, which is defined more broadly in Section 101(15).

In an effort to stem the tide of abusive bankruptcy cases, Congress has determined that there are other persons who, although technically qualified to be debtors under Section 109(a), should not enjoy the protections the Bankruptcy Code has to offer. As Section 109(g) states, an individual or a family farmer cannot file a bankruptcy case if he or she was a debtor in a case that had been pending within the previous 180 days and that was dismissed by the court either because of the debtor's willful failure to abide by the court's orders, or to appear before the court in proper prosecution of the case, or if the debtor voluntarily dismissed the case after a creditor moved for relief from the automatic stay.

Section 109(g), which was added with the 1986 Amendments, requires the court to interpret what constitutes willful failure. The section also has serious problems of enforcement. The court's clerk is unlikely to know whether the debtor was a debtor in a case pending within the previous six months. Even if that fact is known, the clerk is not qualified to determine whether the debtor willfully failed to adhere to a court order. As a result, the petition commencing the second bankruptcy case will be accepted and, at least until a creditor or the United States trustee is able to file a motion to have the case dismissed, the debtor will be able to take advantage of the automatic stay and the other protections of the bankruptcy system.

In addition to the enforcement problems of Section 109(g), it applies only to individuals and family farmers. No similar help is given to creditors from multiple corporate or partnership bankruptcy cases. However, creditors are certainly not without their remedies since they may move to dismiss the second case, claiming it was filed in bad faith as discussed in later chapters of this book.

Choosing the Right Chapter

Assuming eligibility to be a debtor in a bankruptcy case under Sections 109(a) and 109(g), the debtor must decide the chapter of the Bankruptcy Code under which to file. That decision has two inquiries:

1. In which chapters is the debtor eligible? (This is most easily done by eliminating the chapters for which the debtor is *ineligible,* as shown in Exhibit 7.1.)
2. What chapter will best assist in achieving the debtor's goals?

Determining the answer to the first question is simply a matter of applying the statute. The second question involves many different considerations.

Eligibility   Not all persons are eligible to file under every chapter. Section 109 provides that the following persons are ineligible for the chapter indicated.

In short, virtually any entity can be a Chapter 7 debtor, but only a select number qualify for relief under Chapters 9, 12, or 13. Certain entities, such as banks and insurance companies, can never be debtors. Those entities are heavily regulated by Federal laws or by the laws of each state that contain special insolvency proceedings for those types of entities.

Appropriateness   Once one determines under which chapters the debtor *can* file, there remains the decision of under which chapter the debtor *should* file.

EXHIBIT 7.1 ✦ *Ineligible Debtors*

Type of Debtor	Chapters for Which Debtor Is Ineligible
Railroads	All except 11
Insurance companies	All
Banks, savings & loans, and credit unions	All
Stockbrokers or commodity brokers who are not individuals	All except 7
Stockbrokers or commodity brokers who are individuals and who qualify for Chapter 13 relief	All except 7 and 13
All entities other than individuals who have less than $250,000 of liquidated, noncontingent, unsecured debts, $750,000 of noncontingent, liquidated secured debts, and a regular income	Chapter 13
All entities other than "family farmers who have regular annual income" as defined in Section 101(19)	Chapter 12
All entities other than municipalities authorized by the state to be debtors, who are insolvent, and who desire to effect a plan to adjust their debts	Chapter 9

Between Chapter 7, on the one hand, and Chapters 11, 12, or 13 on the other, the question should be simple: Does the debtor want to reorganize and pay creditors over a period of time (Chapters 11, 12, 13), or does the debtor simply want to deliver all nonexempt property to the trustee and allow it to be liquidated (Chapter 7)? For consumer debtors who may be eligible for Chapter 7 and Chapter 13 relief, the answer may be a function of how much they know about the two. The question also becomes more complicated when the issue is between Chapter 11 and Chapter 13 or between Chapter 7 and Chapter 11 when the debtor wants to liquidate but wants to control the liquidation.

When Congress was considering the 1984 Amendments, it was informed that in a large percentage of the no-asset Chapter 7 cases, a debtor could have confirmed a Chapter 13 plan and paid creditors at least a portion of their claims. Congress saw no benefit to the economy in allowing people who could pay at least something to not pay. Yet a person cannot be forced into a Chapter 13 case; that might compel debtors to work to pay off debts, which is prohibited by the Thirteenth Amendment to the Constitution. As a result, the 1984 Amendments included a number of provisions to encourage individuals filing Chapter 7 cases to file Chapter 13 cases instead. This encouragement primarily takes the form of debtor education because Congress believed that most debtors would like to pay their debts and would prefer Chapter 13 if they knew more about it.

One encouragement provision is Section 342(b). It requires the clerk of the court to give written notice to an individual with primarily consumer debts of all the chapters under which that debtor is eligible to file. To comply, the clerk's office will usually insist that when the petition is filed, it is accompanied by Director's Form B 201, which briefly explains Chapters 7, 11, 12, and 13. The form must be signed by the debtor under a statement that the debtor has read the notice.

Another attempt to encourage debtors to file under Chapter 13 is Official Form 1, which is the bankruptcy petition. All individual Chapter 7 debtors who have primarily consumer debts must sign a statement that: they are aware that they may proceed under Chapters 7, 11, 12, or 13 of the Bankruptcy Code; they understand the relief available under each chapter; and they choose to proceed under Chapter 7. In addition, Exhibit B to Official Form 1 requires a consumer debtor's lawyer to sign a declaration stating that the debtor has been informed of the right to proceed under Chapters 7 or 13 and that the relief available under each chapter has been explained to the debtor.

The 1994 Amendments added yet another consumer education provision regarding alternatives to a Chapter 7 case. New Section 341(d) provides that, prior to the conclusion of the Section 341(a) meeting of creditors, the trustee must examine each Chapter 7 debtor (not just those with primarily consumer debts) to ensure that he or she is aware of: (1) the potential consequences of seeking a discharge, including the effects on credit history; (2) the debtor's ability to file a petition under Chapters 11, 12, or 13; (3) the effect of receiving a discharge of debts; and (4) the effect of reaffirming a debt.

Law firms often prepare a form for clients that details the criteria for filing a Chapter 13 case (which is the most common alternative to a consumer debtor's Chapter 7 case) and has a list or chart of the differences and relative merits of the two types of bankruptcy cases. Preparation of that document is an appropriate task for the paralegal. The list or chart should include a brief discussion of the following points:

1. The eligibility criteria for Chapter 13 relief as set out in Section 109(e).
2. Debts that are nondischargeable under Chapter 7 may be dischargeable under Chapter 13 (as discussed in Chapter 8 of this text).
3. There can be no denial of discharge in Chapter 13 as there can be in Chapter 7 cases.

4. A Chapter 13 discharge, unlike a Chapter 7 discharge, can be obtained more than once every six years.
5. The automatic stay also protects some friends and relatives in Chapter/008001/cases.
6. Chapter 13 enables a debtor to stretch out payments to secured creditors; there is no such ability in Chapter 7.
7. Control and use of nonexempt property remains with the debtor in Chapter 13; it must be turned over to the trustee in Chapter 7.
8. Redemption of property can be accomplished through installments in Chapter 13 but only in a lump sum payment in Chapter 7.
9. A Chapter 13 case can be dismissed automatically. A Chapter 7 dismissal requires a hearing before the court.
10. The discharge in Chapter 13 is delayed until plan payments have been made.
11. There is continued supervision in Chapter 13 cases. There is an immediate fresh start in Chapter 7 cases.
12. A Chapter 13 plan will be confirmed only if it meets certain requirements. One such requirement is that, if there is an objection, all disposable income must be used to make plan payments.

The selection of the appropriate chapter for a debtor will not be made by the paralegal. However, the paralegal may help in the education of consumer debtor clients of their right to proceed under either Chapter 7 or Chapter 13 of the Bankruptcy Code.

Substantial Abuse

✦ substantial abuse
A Chapter 7 bankruptcy case of a debtor with primarily consumer debts that offends notions of the proper use of bankruptcy. Typically used to refer to a case in which the debtor could fund a Chapter 13 plan.

In the 1984 Amendments, in partial response to creditors' complaints of abusive and multiple filings, Congress enacted Section 707(b), which provides that after notice and a hearing, the court may dismiss a consumer's Chapter 7 case if it finds that it is a **substantial abuse** for the debtor to be allowed to be in Chapter 7. A substantial abuse case may involve a debtor who files a Chapter 7 case on the eve of signing a large contract so that the contract proceeds become unavailable for creditors. Another example may be a debtor with a $50,000 annual salary and $1,000 per month of disposable income who has only $10,000 in debts.

Section 707(b) reflects a number of congressional compromises. Although Congress considered the creditors' complaints that individuals were taking unfair advantage of Chapter 7's discharge, Congress also heeded warnings that it would be unwise to allow a flood of motions brought by creditors claiming that a consumer's bankruptcy case should be dismissed as a substantial abuse under Section 707(b). At the time the section was enacted, Congress' compromise was that only the court could raise the substantial abuse issue.

Section 707(b) as enacted was an effort to stem a very real problem; nevertheless, it raised many difficult issues. For example, how is a bankruptcy judge to know which cases are a substantial abuse? The judges are too busy to examine every petition and its supporting papers to try to discern which debtors are abusing the system. In addition, if the court dismisses a case as a substantial abuse and the debtor appeals, who will defend the dismissal? There may not be a creditor willing to pay the cost.

The 1986 Amendments remedied these concerns. Section 707(b) now allows the Court on its own motion or the United States trustee to move to dismiss a case as a substantial abuse. Creditors still may not make such a motion.

CASE PREPARATION

Client Relationships

Many papers must be prepared and filed by the debtor in a bankruptcy case. These papers require a substantial amount of information from the debtor. To expedite the case and limit costs, it is likely that the paralegal will gather most of the necessary information. As a result, at the beginning of the case, the paralegal may spend much more time with the debtor than will the attorney.

As commonplace as bankruptcy has become in the United States, it is still an emotional event for individuals, and one that is sometimes frustrating and depressing. The debtor may have undergone a serious illness, the loss of employment, or the failure of the family business. The debtor may be worried about losing the home he or she took years to save for. While bankruptcy will give the debtor a fresh start and relief from distressing financial problems, the emotional problems may not be as easily relieved. The paralegal may frequently have to listen to and reassure the client.

The need to be sympathetic is not limited to bankruptcy cases for individuals. Sometimes the fact that corporations are composed of individuals is overlooked. The stress of a company in trouble falls most heavily on the persons with whom the paralegal will spend the most time—the accountants and bookkeepers. They spend a considerable amount of their time placating and cajoling creditors. When the bankruptcy case approaches, their burdens will be increased by the reporting requirements of the Bankruptcy Code, the Bankruptcy Rules, and the United States trustee. They will become frustrated and often angry. The paralegal may well become the inadvertent target of some of this frustration and anger.

While sympathy may help to alleviate the employees' negative feelings, there are other constructive things the paralegal can do to help. The first is to educate the employees about the bankruptcy system and what the employees can expect over the following months. The second is to inform them how the automatic stay will stop the flood of phone calls that they may be experiencing from angry creditors. Third, if the employees know that once the schedules and statements (the lengthy disclosure documents that we discuss later in this chapter) are filed, their tasks will ease considerably, and they may be more cooperative. Finally, and most importantly, if they know that the paralegal will help them with all the bankruptcy-related tasks that they do not understand and will answer or find answers to their questions, they may be able to approach their jobs more calmly. It is helpful to call a stressed accountant, bookkeeper, or other client contact at least once a week to see if there are any problems and to let them know that their efforts are appreciated.

File Management

In many law firms, paralegals are not responsible for filing paperwork in the office. There are good reasons for this, only one of which is the fact that, since paralegals' time is usually billed to the client, it is unrealistic to expect a client to pay for office filing. Although paralegals may not be responsible for doing the day–to–day filing in all firms, they still may be required to determine which files and subfiles should be created. Because a bankruptcy case has so many facets, and counsel for the debtor must be integrally involved with the debtor's business, the files may be voluminous and need careful indexing and organization. There will also be matters that defy the categorizations often used in filing systems.

The particular files that will be created in a case will depend on the size of the case, the nature of the debtor, and the chapter under which the filing is being made. The filing for an individual's Chapter 7 case in which there is no litigation over dischargeability or other issues may be contained in a single folder. The filing for a large Chapter 11 business reorganization may occupy an entire room.

Each law firm has its own filing system for litigation matters and transactional work. Bankruptcy is really both, and neither system will be exactly right. The paralegal must develop some variations or refinements to the traditional filing approaches to accommodate the bankruptcy process. The sample system discussed here, which is set up for a medium-sized Chapter 11 business case, may be helpful.

General Organization   Like a litigation file, there should be folders for correspondence, notes, documents, and pleadings. There should also be a separate folder for single subject matters. The first folder for each type of file should be numbered 1. When it is full, a new folder should be created and numbered 2, and so on.

Whatever the numbering system, a log or index should be kept and continually updated so that a person looking for a particular piece of correspondence can check the index and then go directly to the correct file rather than needing to first search through the folders. If, for example, you were searching for a letter that was written in November of 1995, you could look in the index and see that correspondence file 4 has all correspondence from October to December of 1995. It is also very helpful if, as soon as a folder is full, a sheet is attached to the top indicating that the next folder in order should be consulted for later material.

Pleadings   In a bankruptcy case there will be at least two types of pleadings or papers filed with the court. The first type consists of pleadings concerning the administration of the estate. The second type is pleadings filed in adversary proceedings in the case. At least one file should be created for the general administrative pleadings; these documents should be placed in the file in chronological order. Separate folders should be created for each adversary proceeding and everything filed with the court in that proceeding should be in the separate pleading file. The pleading files should be numbered 1, 2, 3, and so on as they are filled. Some law firms also put adversary proceeding papers in the general administrative file so that a particular paper can be located in at least two places.

In addition to adversary proceedings, separate pleadings folders may be created for fee applications and their related notices and orders. Even if a particular dispute being waged on paper and before the court is not an adversary matter and the papers would otherwise be filed in the general pleading file, a separate pleading file might be advisable simply for ease in finding a particular paper. For example, if there is a contested motion to appoint a trustee, a separate pleading file for that motion and its response may be appropriate. In addition, because they will be frequently referred to during the pendency of the bankruptcy case, the petition and its supporting documents and the schedules and statements should also be in separate files. At the appropriate time in the case, separate files can be made for the plan of reorganization and the disclosure statement.

Again, a well-maintained log or index will prevent time-wasting rummaging and dog-eared files. It will also help a user know if any files are missing.

Subfiles   Listed here in alphabetical order are some suggested subfile topics. Their need and ultimate size will depend on the facts of each case.

Agendas from Meetings	Legal Research
Appraisals	Mailing Lists—Master
Ballots	Mailing Lists—Special Notice
Bids	Newspaper Releases and Articles
Creditors—Bulletins	Operating Reports
Creditors—Committee	Pension Issues

Creditors—List of

Creditors—Proofs of Claim

Equity Security Holders—List of

Executory Contracts

Fee Application Back-Up

Financial Statements

Insurance

Inventory

Leases

Personal Property

Real Property

Plan Back-Up

Preference Analysis

Priority Claims

Returned Mail

Sale Documents

SEC Matters

Secured Creditor Documents

Special Notice List

Tax Issues

United States Trustee Compliance

Utilities

Gathering Information

A great deal of information will need to be gathered from the debtor prior to commencing the bankruptcy case so that all the court documents can be completed. Since the paralegal can prepare at least the first draft of those documents and may be the one in the office most familiar with what they require, it is efficient for the paralegal to gather the information.

The first contact with the client will likely be by telephone. During that call, the paralegal should try to determine the existence of any conflicts, whether the debtor is qualified to file a bankruptcy case, whether the debtor can afford to hire counsel to help file the bankruptcy case, and whether a bankruptcy case makes the most sense for the debtor. If the indications are that the debtor wants to and should file a bankruptcy case, a more detailed interview should be scheduled.

For consumer cases, the debtor can be told during the telephone call what additional information is needed and can bring it to the first meeting with the attorney. In other cases, at the first meeting, the client can be given a list of the information needed and then return to its business or home to assemble all the information. In any case, a follow-up letter should be sent to the client confirming the material needed at the next meeting. Frequently, the debtor's response to being asked to compile information will be to bring in a paper bag full of correspondence, records, invoices, and cancelled checks; the paralegal will have to make sense of the information provided.

Whether the information is to be obtained at the first client meeting or later, the paralegal should not rely on the client's memory to provide all that is needed. Two detailed, comprehensive lists of what is needed should be made, one for individual cases and one for business cases. If the individual debtor is in business, the two lists can be combined. As with all other lists made, they should be updated frequently.

A simple sample list for an individual consumer might resemble the one that follows. Since there are very short time deadlines in cases under Chapters 7, 12, and 13, virtually all the documents need to be received and the questions answered before the case can be commenced.

1. The debtor's full name and all other names used in the past six years.
2. The debtor's social security number.
3. The debtor's current address and all addresses used in the past six years.
4. The debtor's occupation, employer, pay rate, and all other sources of income.
5. Name, relationship, and age of all dependents.
6. Description of all property.
7. Description of all litigation involving the debtor.
8. Description of all property sold or given away in the last year.

9. List of all property lost to theft or to fire, flood, earthquake, or other disaster. All insurance claims, satisfied and unsatisfied, connected with such losses.

10. For federal, state, and city, if applicable, copies of tax returns and whether tax due was paid or whether refunds were received in the past two years.

11. All creditors, including the amounts of their claims and any collateral.

12. Details as to any prior bankruptcy cases.

13. All monthly expenses including mortgage or rent payments; utilities, food, clothing; medical, dental, and insurance costs; taxes; car or other transportation payments; dues; recreation; education; and so on.

14. Value of car, household goods, home (if owned), jewelry, tools of the trade, and cash surrender value of life insurance contracts. Any social security, unemployment, or other public benefits; veteran's benefits; disability, illness, or unemployment benefits; alimony or child support; or payments under a pension plan. Any right to receive funds under a crime victim's reparation law; benefits under an insurance policy owned by an individual of whom the debtor was a dependent; payments on account of personal injury, pain and suffering, and loss of future earnings.

15. Description of all the debtor's secured property.

A sample list for a corporation intending to file under Chapter 11 might resemble the following. Those items marked with an asterisk(*) must be received before the case is commenced. The other items can follow shortly thereafter.

*1. The debtor's full name and all tradename and division names.

*2. The state of incorporation.

*3. The number of classes of stock.

*4. For each class of stock, the number of shares authorized and the number of shares issued.

*5. The names of all shareholders and the number of shares each holds.

*6. A list of all corporations in which the debtor holds stock, and the percentage of ownership.

*7. The names and addresses of all the debtor's creditors, including all creditors with disputed and contingent claims.

*8. All pending lawsuits involving the debtor.

*9. Identification of the debtor's 20 largest unsecured creditors who are not insiders or governmental units. For each, include the name and address, telephone number, name of person familiar with the debt, and the amount owed.

10. A list of all taxing agencies (federal, state, and local) to which the debtor makes payments.

11. A description of all real and personal property leases.

12. A description of all employment agreements, supply or production agreements, pension, profit sharing or health benefit plans, and any other contracts that have not expired.

*13. Copies of the debtor's articles of incorporation and bylaws.

*14. The names of all the debtor's officers and any director or shareholder employed by the debtor.

15. A short (two or three pages) summary of the history of the debtor, the size and extent of operations, a discussion of product lines and customer bases, and an explanation of current financial problems.

*16. As of a given date, the total dollar amount of assets and liabilities; these should be identified and broken down as secured and unsecured.

CASE COMMENCEMENT

The Checklist

Once all the preliminary information has been gathered, the bankruptcy case will be ready to start. The rules and procedures for starting a voluntary bankruptcy case are generally the same whatever the chapter. There are several critical documents that must be filed to commence the case. If one of them is omitted, the clerk may refuse to accept the other documents, and the start of the bankruptcy case could be delayed. That could be a disaster for the debtor, especially if the automatic stay is needed to prevent a foreclosure sale of property.

The days immediately preceding and following the filing of a bankruptcy petition are frequently chaotic. To prevent the chance of a document being inadvertently omitted in this hectic period, a detailed list should be made that includes a description of every document or item that is needed and every task that needs to be done as soon as the case is commenced or shortly thereafter.

The list should include those documents and items required by the Bankruptcy Rules and everything required by the local rules and by the United States trustee. The list should be updated every time a new or amended rule or procedure is implemented.

A good idea is to make the list into a checklist. Next to each item could be space for the insertion of the name or initials of the person responsible for preparing the document or doing the task. When the document is ready or the task is done, that person could place his or her initials next to the item. All professionals assigned to coordinate the preparation of documents and completion of tasks should have a copy, and one person should keep a master list.

Exhibit 7.2 presents a sample checklist that incorporates many of the items discussed in the balance of this chapter and other portions of this book. The checklist is a good *starting* point. Bear in mind that since it does not reflect local requirements, it must be supplemented to be complete.

The Petition and Supporting Documents

Section 301 of the Bankruptcy Code provides that a bankruptcy case is commenced by the filing of a petition. Slightly more information is provided in Bankruptcy Rule 1002, which states that the petition is filed with the bankruptcy court and must conform substantially with Official Form 1. In 1997, the format of the form was simplified, eliminating the Latin phrase "in re" and reducing the amount of information requested in the "Type of Debts" and "Nature of Debts" boxes. These simplifications have followed through to the present form.

Official Form 1's size and simplicity hides its importance since the filing of the petition will have a tremendous impact on the debtor's financial affairs. The petition consists of just one, two-sided sheet with two exhibits that are mutually exclusive. If a corporation is the debtor, a short Exhibit "A" must be added to the petition. A sample petition for a corporate debtor is presented in Exhibit 7.3; this includes an "Exhibit A." A sample petition for a debtor with consumer debts is presented in Exhibit 7.4.

Official Form 1 consists of a series of boxes, each requesting different information. Preprinted form petitions are widely available. A number of companies market computer software for the creation of petitions and other documents needed in a bankruptcy case.

There are nine parts to the petition: the caption, location of the debtor, information regarding the debtor, statistical and administrative information, related case information, the certification, Exhibit A, the alternative relief advisement that includes Exhibit B, and Exhibit C.

EXHIBIT 7.2 ✦ *Sample Checklist for Bankruptcy Filing*

In re _____, a _____ [individual, corporation, or partnership]

Document or Task	Responsible Person	Date Completed
Prefiling		
1. Filing Fee (28 U.S.C. §1930)		
a. Chapter 7 $155.00	_____	_____
b. Chapter 11 $800.00		
c. Chapter 12 $200.00		
d. Chapter 13 $155.00		
2. Administrative Fee		
All Chapters $30.00		
3. Petition		
Official Form 1	_____	_____
4. Exhibits		
Corporations—A		
Individuals—B	_____	_____
5. Notice to individual consumer debtor		
Director's Form B 201	_____	_____
6. Disclosure of compensation		
Director's Form B 203	_____	_____
7. Corporate resolution and minutes authorizing the bankruptcy case	_____	_____
8. List of 20 largest unsecured creditors (Chapter 11 only)		
Official Form 4	_____	_____
9. List of all creditors (if petition not accompanied by schedules)	_____	_____
10. Master mailing list (paper or diskette)	_____	_____
Shortly after Filing		
11. List of equity security holders	_____	_____
12. Statement of intentions (individuals only)		
Official Form 8	_____	_____

—CONTINUED

The Caption   The caption is required to be on all pleadings and other papers filed with the court. Its contents are listed in Bankruptcy Rule 1005. The first requirement, located in the upper left-hand box of Official Form 1, is the name of the court, such as the United States Bankruptcy Court, Middle District of Tennessee. The second part of the caption is the title of the document. In the case of Official Form 1, the title "Voluntary Petition" is found on the upper-right hand box.

The third item for the caption is the title of the case. The title of the case includes the name of the debtor, followed by all names used by the debtor during the six years before filing the petition. Aliases, fictitious business names, tradenames, maiden names, married names, and the like should be included. They are to be on all papers so that creditors can identify the debtor when they receive notices and orders concerning the bankruptcy case. The title of the case must also include the debtor's social security number if the debtor is an individual or its tax identification number if the debtor is a partnership or corporation. All of the information concerning the title of the case is found in the six boxes directly below the name of the court and the name of the document. If the case is filed by a husband and wife, the information will be given separately with one person identified on the left and the other (joint debtor) on the right. Obviously, if only one person is filing, the right side boxes will be left blank.

EXHIBIT 7.2 ✦ *Sample Checklist for Bankruptcy Filing* (CONTINUED)

In re _____, a _____ [individual, corporation, or partnership]

Document or Task	Responsible Person	Date Completed
13. Schedule of assets and liabilities		
Official Form 6	_____	_____
a. Schedule A Real Property		
b. Schedule B Personal Property		
c. Schedule C Property Claimed as Exempt		
d. Schedule D Creditors Holding Secured Claims		
e. Schedule E Creditors Holding Unsecured Priority Claims		
f. Schedule F Creditors Holding Unsecured Nonpriority Claims		
g. Schedule G Statement of Executory Contracts		
h. Schedule H Codebtors		
i. Schedule I Current Income of Debtor		
j. Schedule J Current Expenditures of Debtor		
14. Statement of financial affairs		
Official Form 7	_____	_____
15. Motion for extension to file 13 and 14	_____	_____
16. Schedule meeting with United States trustee	_____	_____
17. Application to employ attorneys for debtor	_____	_____
18. Application to employ accountants for debtor	_____	_____
19. Motion to pay prepetition wages	_____	_____
20. Application to employ insiders	_____	_____
21. Motion to extend time to assume or reject real property leases	_____	_____
22. Notice of removal	_____	_____
23. Record petition in county where real property is located	_____	_____
24. Distribute notice of commencement of case and the automatic stay	_____	_____
25. Letters to employees	_____	_____
26. Letters to vendors	_____	_____

For every pleading other than the petition, the caption will also include the docket or case number. Every jurisdiction has its own method for numbering cases. The clerk will assign a docket number to the case when the petition is filed. On a petition, the case number will now be inserted in the open space in the lower-right area of the front page. Local practice dictates where the case number will appear on other pleadings.

Location of the Debtor Just below the boxes requesting the debtor and joint debtor's Social Security or Tax I.D. No. are seven boxes requesting information that makes it possible to determine where the debtor and joint debtor can be found. These boxes ask for the street address (including city, state, and ZIP Code) of the debtor and joint debtor, their county or residence or the principal place of business, the debtor and joint debtor's mailing address (if different from the street address), and the location of principal assets in the case of a business debtor, if the location differs from the addresses provided earlier.

Information Regarding the Debtor In the middle of the first page of Official Form 1 and immediately following the box labeled "Location of Principal Assets of Business Debtor" are boxes that request various information relating to the debtor. The first of these boxes is labeled **venue**.

✦ **venue**
The local area where a case may be tried.

EXHIBIT 7.3 ✦ *Sample Pleading for Corporate Debtor*

(Official Form 1) (12/02)

FORM B1	United States Bankruptcy Court	Voluntary Petition
	_____Western_____ **District of** _____California_____	

Name of Debtor (if individual, enter Last, First, Middle): Videos by Joe, Inc.	Name of Joint Debtor (Spouse) (Last, First, Middle):
All Other Names used by the Debtor in the last 6 years (include married, maiden, and trade names):	All Other Names used by the Joint Debtor in the last 6 years (include married, maiden, and trade names):
Soc. Sec./Tax I.D. No. (if more than one, state all): 99-999899	Soc. Sec./Tax I.D. No. (if more than one, state all):
Street Address of Debtor (No. & Street, City, State & Zip Code): 18 Hollywood Dr, Los Angeles, CA 90001	Street Address of Joint Debtor (No. & Street, City, State & Zip Code):
County of Residence or of the Principal Place of Business:　　Los Angeles	County of Residence or of the Principal Place of Business:
Mailing Address of Debtor (if different from street address):	Mailing Address of Joint Debtor (if different from street address):

Location of Principal Assets of Business Debtor   (if different from street address above):

Information Regarding the Debtor (Check the Applicable Boxes)

Venue (Check any applicable box)

☑ Debtor has been domiciled or has had a residence, principal place of business, or principal assets in this District for 180 days immediately preceding the date of this petition or for a longer part of such 180 days than in any other District.

☐ There is a bankruptcy case concerning debtor's affiliate, general partner, or partnership pending in this District.

Type of Debtor (Check all boxes that apply)		**Chapter or Section of Bankruptcy Code Under Which the Petition is Filed** (Check one box)
☐ Individual(s)	☐ Railroad	☐ Chapter 7　　☑ Chapter 11　　☐ Chapter 13
☑ Corporation	☐ Stockbroker	☐ Chapter 9　　☐ Chapter 12
☐ Partnership	☐ Commodity Broker	☐ Sec. 304 - Case ancillary to foreign proceeding
☐ Other_____	☐ Clearing Bank	

Nature of Debts (Check one box)

☐ Consumer/Non-Business　　☑ Business

Chapter 11 Small Business (Check all boxes that apply)

☐ Debtor is a small business as defined in 11 U.S.C. § 101

☐ Debtor is and elects to be considered a small business under 11 U.S.C. § 1121(e) (Optional)

Filing Fee (Check one box)

☑ Full Filing Fee attached

☐ Filing Fee to be paid in installments (Applicable to individuals only) Must attach signed application for the court's consideration certifying that the debtor is unable to pay fee except in installments. Rule 1006(b). See Official Form No. 3.

Statistical/Administrative Information (Estimates only)

☑ Debtor estimates that funds will be available for distribution to unsecured creditors.

☐ Debtor estimates that, after any exempt property is excluded and administrative expenses paid, there will be no funds available for distribution to unsecured creditors.

THIS SPACE IS FOR COURT USE ONLY

Estimated Number of Creditors	1-15 ☑	16-49 ☐	50-99 ☐	100-199 ☐	200-999 ☐	1000-over ☐

Estimated Assets							
$0 to $50,000 ☐	$50,001 to $100,000 ☑	$100,001 to $500,000 ☐	$500,001 to $1 million ☐	$1,000,001 to $10 million ☐	$10,000,001 to $50 million ☐	$50,000,001 to $100 million ☐	More than $100 million ☐

Estimated Debts							
$0 to $50,000 ☐	$50,001 to $100,000 ☑	$100,001 to $500,000 ☐	$500,001 to $1 million ☐	$1,000,001 to $10 million ☐	$10,000,001 to $50 million ☐	$50,000,001 to $100 million ☐	More than $100 million ☐

—CONTINUED

EXHIBIT 7.3 ✦ *Sample Pleading for Corporate Debtor* (CONTINUED)

(Official Form 1)(12/02)   **FORM B1,** Page 2

Voluntary Petition *(This page must be completed and filed in every case)*	Name of Debtor(s): Videos by Joe, Inc.

Prior Bankruptcy Case Filed Within Last 6 Years (If more than one, attach additional sheet)		
Location Where Filed:	Case Number:	Date Filed:

Pending Bankruptcy Case Filed by any Spouse, Partner or Affiliate of this Debtor (If more than one, attach additional sheet)		
Name of Debtor:	Case Number:	Date Filed:
District:	Relationship:	Judge:

Signatures

Signature(s) of Debtor(s)(Individual/Joint)	**Exhibit A**
I declare under penalty of perjury that the information provided in this petition is true and correct. [If petitioner is an individual whose debts are primarily consumer debts and has chosen to file under chapter 7] I am aware that I may proceed under chapter 7, 11, 12 or 13 of title 11, United States Code, understand the relief available under each such chapter, and choose to proceed under chapter 7. I request relief in accordance with the chapter of title 11, United States Code, specified in this petition.	(To be completed if debtor is required to file periodic reports (e.g., forms 10K and 10Q) with the Securities and Exchange Commission pursuant to Section 13 or 15(d) of the Securities Exchange Act of 1934 and is requesting relief under chapter 11) ☐ Exhibit A is attached and made a part of this petition.

Signature of Debtor(s)(Individual/Joint)

I declare under penalty of perjury that the information provided in this petition is true and correct. [If petitioner is an individual whose debts are primarily consumer debts and has chosen to file under chapter 7] I am aware that I may proceed under chapter 7, 11, 12 or 13 of title 11, United States Code, understand the relief available under each such chapter, and choose to proceed under chapter 7.

I request relief in accordance with the chapter of title 11, United States Code, specified in this petition.

X _____
Signature of Debtor

X _____
Signature of Joint Debtor

_____
Telephone Number (If not represented by attorney)

_____
Date

Signature of Attorney

X _____
Signature of Attorney for Debtor(s)
Bankrupt C. Lawyer
Printed Name of Attorney for Debtor(s)
White Charger Legal Clinic
Firm Name
One Learned Way
Address   Los Angeles, CA 90001
213-891-0000
Telephone Number
October 1, 2003
Date

Signature of Debtor (Corporation/Partnership)

I declare under penalty of perjury that the information provided in this petition is true and correct, and that I have been authorized to file this petition on behalf of the debtor.

The debtor requests relief in accordance with the chapter of title 11, United States Code, specified in this petition.

X _____
Signature of Authorized Individual
Joseph Businessman
Printed Name of Authorized Individual
President
Title of Authorized Individual
October 1, 2003
Date

Exhibit A

(To be completed if debtor is required to file periodic reports (e.g., forms 10K and 10Q) with the Securities and Exchange Commission pursuant to Section 13 or 15(d) of the Securities Exchange Act of 1934 and is requesting relief under chapter 11)

☐ Exhibit A is attached and made a part of this petition.

Exhibit B

(To be completed if debtor is an individual whose debts are primarily consumer debts)

I, the attorney for the petitioner named in the foregoing petition, declare that I have informed the petitioner that [he or she] may proceed under chapter 7, 11, 12, or 13 of title 11, United States Code, and have explained the relief available under each such chapter.

X _____
Signature of Attorney for Debtor(s)   Date

Exhibit C

Does the debtor own or have possession of any property that poses a threat of imminent and identifiable harm to public health or safety?

☐ Yes, and Exhibit C is attached and made a part of this petition.
☐ No

Signature of Non-Attorney Petition Preparer

I certify that I am a bankruptcy petition preparer as defined in 11 U.S.C. § 110, that I prepared this document for compensation, and that I have provided the debtor with a copy of this document.

_____
Printed Name of Bankruptcy Petition Preparer

_____
Social Security Number

_____
Address

Names and Social Security numbers of all other individuals who prepared or assisted in preparing this document:

If more than one person prepared this document, attach additional sheets conforming to the appropriate official form for each person.

X _____
Signature of Bankruptcy Petition Preparer

_____
Date

A bankruptcy petition preparer's failure to comply with the provisions of title 11 and the Federal Rules of Bankruptcy Procedure may result in fines or imprisonment or both 11 U.S.C. §110; 18 U.S.C. §156.

—CONTINUED

EXHIBIT 7.3 ✦ *Sample Pleading for Corporate Debtor* (CONTINUED)

Form B1, Exh.A (9/97)

Exhibit "A"

[If debtor is required to file periodic reports (*e.g.*, forms 10K and 10Q) with the Securities and Exchange Commission pursuant to Section 13 or 15(d) of the Securities Exchange Act of 1934 and is requesting relief under chapter 11 of the Bankruptcy Code, this Exhibit "A" shall be completed and attached to the petition.]

[Caption as in Form 16B]

Exhibit "A" to Voluntary Petition

1.   If any of the debtor's securities are registered under Section 12 of the Securities Exchange Act of 1934, the SEC file number is _____.

2.   The following financial data is the latest available information and refers to the debtor's condition on <u>October 1, 2003</u>.

a.   Total assets $ <u>50,000</u>

b.   Total debts (including debts listed in 2.c., below) $ <u>70,000</u>

                                                                                        Approximate number of holders

c.   Debt securities held by more than 500 holders.

     secured / /   unsecured / /   subordinated / / $ _____   _____

     secured / /   unsecured / /   subordinated / / $_____   _____

     secured / /   unsecured / /   subordinated / / $ _____   _____

     secured / /   unsecured / /   subordinated / / $_____   _____

     secured / /   unsecured / /   subordinated / / $_____   _____

d.   Number of shares of preferred stock   _____   _____

e.   Number of shares common stock $10,000 _____   3 _____

     Comments, if any: _____
_____
_____

3.   Brief description of debtor's business: <u>Debtor is in the business of providing videotaping services for</u> <u>social functions and presentations.</u>
_____

4.   List the names of any person who directly or indirectly owns, controls, or holds, with power to vote, 5% or more of the voting securities of debtor:
<u>Joseph Businessman, 40%; Myra Businesswoman, 40%; Maximillion Businessman, 20%</u>
_____
_____

—*CONTINUED*

EXHIBIT 7.3 ✦ *Sample Pleading for Corporate Debtor* (CONTINUED)

WRITTEN CONSENT OF THE BOARD OF DIRECTORS OF
VIDEOS BY JOE, INC. A CALIFORNIA CORPORATION

We, the undersigned Board of Directors as presently constituted of Videos by Joe, Inc., a duly organized California corporation (the "Corporation"), acting pursuant to the provision of Section 307(b) of the California Corporations Code and Section 18 of Article III of the Corporation's bylaws, hereby consent to, approve, and adopt the following resolutions and the actions and proceedings contemplated therein:

WHEREAS, the Corporation has determined that it would be in its best interest to immediately file a voluntary petition (the "Petition") under Chapter 11 of Title 11, United States Code (the "Bankruptcy Code") in the Western District of California.

NOW, THEREFORE, BE IT RESOLVED, that the Corporation hereby authorizes the preparation and filing of the petition and such additional documentation as required by the Bankruptcy Code or otherwise to allow the Corporation to avail itself of the relief available under the Bankruptcy Code; and it is

RESOLVED FURTHER, that the President of the Corporation is authorized, empowered, and directed to execute the petition and any further actions and to execute and deliver all such further instruments and documents in the name and on behalf of the Corporation, and to pay and incur expenses as shall in the President's judgment be necessary or appropriate to carry out the purpose and intent of each and every one of the resolutions set forth herein; and RESOLVED FINALLY, that the Corporation is authorized to retain the services of White Charger Legal Clinic (the "Firm") as its insolvency counsel and to pay to the Firm the sum of $10,000 prior to the filing of the petition as a retainer with the Firm's compensation to be paid in conformity with the Bankruptcy Code.

DATED: October 1, 2003

_____

Joseph Businessman

_____

Myra Businesswoman

_____

Maximillion Businessman

Here the debtor must indicate which of two bases exist for the bankruptcy case to be filed in the particular district. The venue conclusion is now done simply by making one of the elections in that box.

Where a bankruptcy petition should be filed is governed by Section 1408 of Title 28 of the United States Code. Under Section 1408, the debtor cannot file the petition anywhere it chooses. Instead, it may only commence the case in one of the following locations:

✦ where the debtor is domiciled.
✦ where the debtor resides;
✦ where the debtor has its principal place of business; or
✦ where the debtor has its principal assets.

Domicile is where the debtor resides and intends to remain. The debtor's domicile and residence are usually the same location.

✦ **domicile**
The principal place of residence in which the debtor intends to remain.

EXHIBIT 7.4 ✦ *Sample Pleading for Consumer Debtor*

(Official Form 1) (12/02)

FORM B1	**United States Bankruptcy Court**	**Voluntary Petition**
	Western _____ **District of** _____ California	

Name of Debtor (if individual, enter Last, First, Middle): Joseph Consumer	Name of Joint Debtor (Spouse) (Last, First, Middle):
All Other Names used by the Debtor in the last 6 years (include married, maiden, and trade names):	All Other Names used by the Joint Debtor in the last 6 years (include married, maiden, and trade names):
Soc. Sec./Tax I.D. No. (if more than one, state all): 558-15-0001	Soc. Sec./Tax I.D. No. (if more than one, state all):
Street Address of Debtor (No. & Street, City, State & Zip Code): 18 Hollywood Dr, Los Angeles, CA 90001	Street Address of Joint Debtor (No. & Street, City, State & Zip Code):
County of Residence or of the Principal Place of Business: Los Angeles	County of Residence or of the Principal Place of Business:
Mailing Address of Debtor (if different from street address):	Mailing Address of Joint Debtor (if different from street address):

Location of Principal Assets of Business Debtor
(if different from street address above):

Information Regarding the Debtor (Check the Applicable Boxes)

Venue (Check any applicable box)

☑ Debtor has been domiciled or has had a residence, principal place of business, or principal assets in this District for 180 days immediately preceding the date of this petition or for a longer part of such 180 days than in any other District.

☐ There is a bankruptcy case concerning debtor's affiliate, general partner, or partnership pending in this District.

Type of Debtor (Check all boxes that apply)		**Chapter or Section of Bankruptcy Code Under Which the Petition is Filed** (Check one box)
☑ Individual(s) ☐ Railroad		☑ Chapter 7 ☐ Chapter 11 ☐ Chapter 13
☐ Corporation ☐ Stockbroker		☐ Chapter 9 ☐ Chapter 12
☐ Partnership ☐ Commodity Broker		☐ Sec. 304 - Case ancillary to foreign proceeding
☐ Other _____ ☐ Clearing Bank		

Nature of Debts (Check one box)
☑ Consumer/Non-Business   ☐ Business

Filing Fee (Check one box)
☑ Full Filing Fee attached
☐ Filing Fee to be paid in installments (Applicable to individuals only) Must attach signed application for the court's consideration certifying that the debtor is unable to pay fee except in installments. Rule 1006(b). See Official Form No. 3.

Chapter 11 Small Business (Check all boxes that apply)
☐ Debtor is a small business as defined in 11 U.S.C. § 101
☐ Debtor is and elects to be considered a small business under 11 U.S.C. § 1121(e) (Optional)

Statistical/Administrative Information (Estimates only)

☐ Debtor estimates that funds will be available for distribution to unsecured creditors.

☑ Debtor estimates that, after any exempt property is excluded and administrative expenses paid, there will be no funds available for distribution to unsecured creditors.

THIS SPACE IS FOR COURT USE ONLY

Estimated Number of Creditors	1-15	16-49	50-99	100-199	200-999	1000-over
	☑	☐	☐	☐	☐	☐

Estimated Assets

$0 to $50,000	$50,001 to $100,000	$100,001 to $500,000	$500,001 to $1 million	$1,000,001 to $10 million	$10,000,001 to $50 million	$50,000,001 to $100 million	More than $100 million
☑	☐	☐	☐	☐	☐	☐	☐

Estimated Debts

$0 to $50,000	$50,001 to $100,000	$100,001 to $500,000	$500,001 to $1 million	$1,000,001 to $10 million	$10,000,001 to $50 million	$50,000,001 to $100 million	More than $100 million
☐	☑	☐	☐	☐	☐	☐	☐

EXHIBIT 7.4 ✦ *Sample Pleading for Consumer Debtor* (CONTINUED)

(Official Form 1) (12/02)

FORM B1, Page 2

Voluntary Petition *(This page must be completed and filed in every case)*	Name of Debtor(s): Joseph Consumer

Prior Bankruptcy Case Filed Within Last 6 Years (If more than one, attach additional sheet)		
Location Where Filed:	Case Number:	Date Filed:

Pending Bankruptcy Case Filed by any Spouse, Partner or Affiliate of this Debtor (If more than one, attach additional sheet)		
Name of Debtor:	Case Number:	Date Filed:
District:	Relationship:	Judge:

Signatures

Signature(s) of Debtor(s) (Individual/Joint)

I declare under penalty of perjury that the information provided in this petition is true and correct.
[If petitioner is an individual whose debts are primarily consumer debts and has chosen to file under chapter 7] I am aware that I may proceed under chapter 7, 11, 12 or 13 of title 11, United States Code, understand the relief available under each such chapter, and choose to proceed under chapter 7.
I request relief in accordance with the chapter of title 11, United States Code, specified in this petition.

X   Joseph Consumer
‾‾‾‾‾‾‾‾‾‾‾‾‾‾‾‾‾‾‾‾‾‾‾‾‾‾‾
Signature of Debtor

X
‾‾‾‾‾‾‾‾‾‾‾‾‾‾‾‾‾‾‾‾‾‾‾‾‾‾‾
Signature of Joint Debtor

‾‾‾‾‾‾‾‾‾‾‾‾‾‾‾‾‾‾‾‾‾‾‾‾‾‾‾
Telephone Number (If not represented by attorney)
October 1, 2003
‾‾‾‾‾‾‾‾‾‾‾‾‾‾‾‾‾‾‾‾‾‾‾‾‾‾‾
Date

Signature of Attorney

X
‾‾‾‾‾‾‾‾‾‾‾‾‾‾‾‾‾‾‾‾‾‾‾‾‾‾‾
Signature of Attorney for Debtor(s)
Bankrupt C. Lawyer
‾‾‾‾‾‾‾‾‾‾‾‾‾‾‾‾‾‾‾‾‾‾‾‾‾‾‾
Printed Name of Attorney for Debtor(s)
White Charger Legal Clinic
‾‾‾‾‾‾‾‾‾‾‾‾‾‾‾‾‾‾‾‾‾‾‾‾‾‾‾
Firm Name
One Learned Way
‾‾‾‾‾‾‾‾‾‾‾‾‾‾‾‾‾‾‾‾‾‾‾‾‾‾‾
Address Los Angeles, CA 90001

213-891-0000
‾‾‾‾‾‾‾‾‾‾‾‾‾‾‾‾‾‾‾‾‾‾‾‾‾‾‾
Telephone Number
October 1, 2003
‾‾‾‾‾‾‾‾‾‾‾‾‾‾‾‾‾‾‾‾‾‾‾‾‾‾‾
Date

Signature of Debtor (Corporation/Partnership)

I declare under penalty of perjury that the information provided in this petition is true and correct, and that I have been authorized to file this petition on behalf of the debtor.

The debtor requests relief in accordance with the chapter of title 11, United States Code, specified in this petition.

X
‾‾‾‾‾‾‾‾‾‾‾‾‾‾‾‾‾‾‾‾‾‾‾‾‾‾‾
Signature of Authorized Individual

‾‾‾‾‾‾‾‾‾‾‾‾‾‾‾‾‾‾‾‾‾‾‾‾‾‾‾
Printed Name of Authorized Individual

‾‾‾‾‾‾‾‾‾‾‾‾‾‾‾‾‾‾‾‾‾‾‾‾‾‾‾
Title of Authorized Individual

‾‾‾‾‾‾‾‾‾‾‾‾‾‾‾‾‾‾‾‾‾‾‾‾‾‾‾
Date

Exhibit A

(To be completed if debtor is required to file periodic reports (e.g., forms 10K and 10Q) with the Securities and Exchange Commission pursuant to Section 13 or 15(d) of the Securities Exchange Act of 1934 and is requesting relief under chapter 11)

☐ Exhibit A is attached and made a part of this petition.

Exhibit B

(To be completed if debtor is an individual whose debts are primarily consumer debts)

I, the attorney for the petitioner named in the foregoing petition, declare that I have informed the petitioner that [he or she] may proceed under chapter 7, 11, 12, or 13 of title 11, United States Code, and have explained the relief available under each such chapter.

X Bankrupt C. Lawyer   October 1, 2003
‾‾‾‾‾‾‾‾‾‾‾‾‾‾‾‾‾‾‾‾‾‾‾‾‾‾‾‾‾‾‾‾‾‾‾‾
Signature of Attorney for Debtor(s)   Date

Exhibit C

Does the debtor own or have possession of any property that poses a threat of imminent and identifiable harm to public health or safety?

☐ Yes, and Exhibit C is attached and made a part of this petition.
☑ No

Signature of Non-Attorney Petition Preparer

I certify that I am a bankruptcy petition preparer as defined in 11 U.S.C. § 110, that I prepared this document for compensation, and that I have provided the debtor with a copy of this document.

‾‾‾‾‾‾‾‾‾‾‾‾‾‾‾‾‾‾‾‾‾‾‾‾‾‾‾
Printed Name of Bankruptcy Petition Preparer

‾‾‾‾‾‾‾‾‾‾‾‾‾‾‾‾‾‾‾‾‾‾‾‾‾‾‾
Social Security Number

‾‾‾‾‾‾‾‾‾‾‾‾‾‾‾‾‾‾‾‾‾‾‾‾‾‾‾
Address

Names and Social Security numbers of all other individuals who prepared or assisted in preparing this document:

If more than one person prepared this document, attach additional sheets conforming to the appropriate official form for each person.

X
‾‾‾‾‾‾‾‾‾‾‾‾‾‾‾‾‾‾‾‾‾‾‾‾‾‾‾
Signature of Bankruptcy Petition Preparer

‾‾‾‾‾‾‾‾‾‾‾‾‾‾‾‾‾‾‾‾‾‾‾‾‾‾‾
Date

A bankruptcy petition preparer's failure to comply with the provisions of title 11 and the Federal Rules of Bankruptcy Procedure may result in fines or imprisonment or both 11 U.S.C. §110; 18 U.S.C. §156.

In addition, as the second option in the venue box indicates, the debtor may file a petition in the district where there is already a pending bankruptcy case concerning the debtor's **affiliate**, which is defined in Section 101(2). If the debtor has moved its domicile, residence, or the location of its principal place of business or principal assets during the 180 days prior to the filing of the petition, venue is proper where the debtor or its business or its assets were for the greater part of the 180 days.

Immediately following the venue box are five boxes—three on the left side of the page, and two on the right. The first one on the left-hand side is titled "Type of Debtor." Here, the debtor needs to indicate whether it is an individual, corporation, partnership, railroad, stockbroker, commodity broker, clearing bank, or "other." Below that is a box asking that the nature of the debt be specified, i.e., whether it is a consumer/non-business debt or a business debt. Following this box is one that asks whether the debtor is a small business as defined under 11 U.S.C. § 101 or the debtor is and elects to be considered a small business under 11 U.S.C. § 1121(e). The small business election is discussed later in this book. On the right-hand side of the page, next to the three boxes just mentioned, Official Form 1 asks the debtor to indicate in which chapter of the bankruptcy code the case is to be filed. Immediately below this box is one titled "Filing Fee." Here, the debtor is to indicate whether it is paying the filing fee with the petition or whether the debtor wishes to pay the filing fee in installments. Only individuals who have not paid an attorney to represent them may file in installments.

Statistical and Administrative Information   The last four boxes on the first page of Official Form 1 ask for certain statistical and administrative information. The information is beneficial to the Administrative Office of the United States Courts that uses it to monitor the size, type, and number of cases each district has pending. There are four types of information asked for in this section. First, the debtor is asked to estimate whether or not there will be funds available to distribute to unsecured creditors. For most consumer debtors, there will not be. If an undersecured creditor has a lien on all the business debtor's assets, there will not be funds to distribute either. It then asks the debtor to estimate, within the ranges provided, the number of creditors, the value of assets, and the amount of liabilities. The bankruptcy case will not be impacted if these amounts cannot be estimated or are estimated inaccurately.

Related Case Information   The second and third boxes on page 2 of Official Form 1 require certain information concerning the debtor's prior bankruptcy cases in the past six years and the pending bankruptcy cases of a spouse, partner, or affiliate. This information was formerly required by most local bankruptcy rules.

Signatures and Exhibits   Under the related case information boxes are four signature boxes and three "exhibit" boxes. Two of the four signature boxes (one for an individual/joint debtor and another for a corporation/partnership) require the signature of the debtor or authorized individual in the case of a corporation or partnership, and their certification under penalty of perjury that the information provided in the petition is true and correct. In addition, the first signature box asks the debtor to certify that it is aware of the option of proceeding under a chapter of the Bankruptcy Code other than Chapter 7. This signature box is discussed more fully below in the "Consumer Relief Alternatives and Exhibit B" section.

The other two signature boxes on this page must be signed by the debtor's attorney or non-attorney bankruptcy petition preparer, if the debtor is using either. As discussed in Chapter 3 of this book, Section 110 of the Bankruptcy Code, which was added with the 1994 Amendments, requires bankruptcy petition preparers to sign all documents they prepare, and print their name, address, and the social security number of the responsible individual on all documents they prepare. The last box on the right side of page 2 of Official Form 1 has space for all the information required of bankruptcy petition preparers.

Exhibit A, B, & C Boxes   The final three boxes in the right-hand column of Form 1's second page have the headers "Exhibit A," "Exhibit B" and "Exhibit C." The Exhibit A box informs the filer that Exhibit A must be filed "if the debtor is required to file periodic reports (e.g., form 10K and 10Q) with the Securities and Exchange Commission pursuant to Section 13 or 15 (d) of the Securities Exchange Act of 1934 and is requesting relief under Chapter 11." Following this explanation is a box that must be checked if Exhibit A is attached.

The Exhibit B box is to be signed and dated by the attorney for a debtor who is an individual and whose debts are primarily consumer debts. By signing, the attorney is declaring that he or she has informed the petitioner that the petitioner may proceed under Chapter 7, 11, 12, or 13 of the Bankruptcy Code, and that the attorney has explained the relief available under each chapter.

Exhibit C asks the debtor to declare if he or she possesses property that poses or is alleged to pose a threat of imminent and identifiable harm to the public health or safety.

We will now look at Exhibits A, B, and C in greater detail.

Exhibit A   If the debtor is a corporation, Exhibit A must be completed and attached to the petition as provided in the corporate or partnership debtor certification box. The 1997 amendment to Exhibit A simplified the form. Exhibit A requires the debtor to give the following information:

- The debtor's Securities and Exchange Commission file number if any of its securities are registered.
- Certain financial information, including the amount of
  - assets;
  - debts, including debt securities held by more than 500 holders;
- The number of shares of the debtor's preferred and common stock.
- A brief description of the debtor's business.
- The name of any person who directly or indirectly owns, controls, or holds with power to vote 5% or more of the voting securities of the debtor.

Some local rules require a resolution or minutes of a meeting of the board of directors authorizing the commencement of the bankruptcy case to be attached to the petition of a corporate debtor. A sample corporate resolution authorizing the filing of a petition is included as part of Exhibit 7.3.

Consumer Relief Alternatives and Exhibit B   The first box in the Signature section on page 2 of Official Form 1 is a statement by the debtor that the debtor is aware that he or she may proceed under Chapter 7, 11, 12, or 13 of the Bankruptcy Code, knows the difference between them, and still chooses to file the petition under Chapter 7. As discussed earlier, in order for debtors to make an intelligent choice, Section 342(b) requires the clerk of the court to give written notice to the debtor of the differences between the chapters. The clerk's office will use a notice similar to Director's Form B 201, which briefly describes the various chapters. Exhibit B, on the right side of the form, must be included in the petition. Exhibit B is merely a one-sentence statement that the debtor's attorney has informed the debtor that the debtor may proceed under the various chapters and has explained the relief available under each chapter. It must be dated and signed by the attorney.

Exhibit C In 2001, Official Form 1 was amended so that the debtor is now required to disclose whether or not it owns or has possession of property that poses or is alleged to pose any threat of imminent and identifiable harm to the public health or safety. Exhibit C must be filed with Official Form 1 if such property exists. Exhibit C requires the debtor to describe the property, provide its location, along with the potential danger it poses. Exhibit C's intent is to alert the United States trustee and any person selected as trustee that immediate precautionary action might be required.

Supporting Documents The Bankruptcy Rules require that a number of documents and other items be filed with the petition or shortly thereafter. Several of the items, including the schedules and statements, the filing fee, and the master mailing list, are discussed later in this chapter. Other documents include:

- *List of all creditors.* Unless the petition is accompanied by the schedule of liabilities described later, Bankruptcy Rule 1007(a)(1) requires that a list containing the name and address of each creditor be filed with the petition. There is no official form for this list. A simple caption page attaching the list will suffice.
- *List of all equity security holders.* In Chapter 11 cases of corporations and partnerships, Bankruptcy Rule 1007(a)(3) requires the debtor to file a list of its equity security holders of each class showing the number and kind of interests registered in the name of each holder and the last known address or place of business of each holder. This list must be filed within 15 days of the filing of the petition.
- *List of the 20 largest unsecured creditors.* In Chapter 9 municipality cases or in Chapter 11 cases, along with the list of all creditors, Bankruptcy Rule 1007(d) requires the debtor to separately file with the petition a list containing the names, addresses, and amount of claims of the 20 largest noninsider unsecured creditors. Official Form 4 has been drafted for use in complying with this rule. Official Form 4 adds certain information to be inserted in the list. This information, including the phone number and the name of the employee or agent of the creditor who has the most knowledge of the claim, is not required by Bankruptcy Rule 1007. The form also asks for the nature of the debt, such as trade debt, bank loan, judgment, and so on. The purpose of the list is to give the United States trustee the names of the persons who should be solicited to serve on the creditors' committee. The description of the nature of the debt will help the trustee select a committee representative of the varying interests in the case.
- *Statement of intentions.* If a Chapter 7 debtor is an individual with consumer secured debts, Section 521(2)(A) of the Bankruptcy Code requires that, within 30 days after the filing of the petition or at the meeting of creditors held pursuant to Section 341(a), whichever is earlier, the debtor file a statement of intentions specifying whether the debtor intends to retain or surrender the secured property, whether the property is exempt, and whether the debtor intends to redeem the property or reaffirm the debt secured by the property. The statement of intentions is Official Form 8. All of the options it concerns are discussed later in this book.
- *Attorney's statement.* Bankruptcy Rule 2016(b) requires every attorney for a debtor to file a statement of compensation paid or agreed to be paid in connection with the bankruptcy case and the source of that compensation. This statement must be filed with the court within 15 days after the order for relief. Procedural Form B 203 is to be used for this statement. A sample follows in Exhibit 7.5.

EXHIBIT 7.5 ✦ *Disclosure of Attorney Compensation*

UNITED STATES BANKRUPTCY COURT
WESTERN DISTRICT OF CALIFORNIA

In re Videos By Joe, Inc.,   Case No. 03-00001-JF

Debtor. _____

DISCLOSURE OF COMPENSATION OF ATTORNEY FOR DEBTOR

1. Pursuant to 11 U.S.C. § 329(a) and Bankruptcy Rule 2016(b), I certify that I am the attorney for the above debtor(s) and that compensation paid to me within one year before the filing of the petition in bankruptcy, or to be paid to me, for services rendered or to be rendered on behalf of the debtor(s) in contemplation of or in connection with the bankruptcy case is as follows:

   For legal services, I have agreed to accept $10,000.00

   Prior to the filing of this statement, I have received $10,000.00

   Balance Due   -0-

2. The source of compensation paid to me was:

   ☒ Debtor   ☐ Other (specify)

3. The source of compensation to be paid to me is:

   ☒ Debtor   ☐ Other (specify)

4. ☒ I have not agreed to share the above-disclosed compensation with any other person unless they are members and associates of my law firm.

   ☐ I have agreed to share the above-disclosed compensation with a person or persons who are not members and associates of my law firm. A copy of the agreement, together with a list of the names of the people sharing the compensation, is attached.

5. In return for the above-disclosed fee, I have agreed to render legal service for all aspects of the bankruptcy including:
   a. Analysis of the debtor's financial situation, and rendering advice to the debtor in determining whether to file the petition in bankruptcy;
   b. Preparation and filing of any petition, schedules, statement of affairs, and plan which may be required;
   c. Representation of the debtor at the meeting of creditors and confirmation hearing any and adjourned hearing thereof;
   d. Representation of the debtor in adversary proceedings and other contested bankruptcy matters;
   e. [Other provisions as needed].

6. By agreement with the debtor(s), the above-disclosed fee does not include the following services:

   Any non-bankruptcy related legal services.

CERTIFICATION

I certify that the foregoing is a complete statement of any agreement or arrangement for payment to me for representation of the debtor(s) in this bankruptcy proceeding.

October 1, 2003   Bankrupt C. Lawyer
_____   _____
                                             Signature of Attorney

                                             White Charger Legal Clinic
                                             _____
                                             Name of Law Firm

✦ *Bankruptcy Petition Preparers' Statement.* Section 110 requires every bankruptcy petition preparer to file within 10 days of filing the petition a declaration disclosing any compensation received from or on behalf of the debtor within 12 months prior to filing the case and an unpaid fee due. Procedural Form B 280 (see Exhibit 7.6) has been developed for this required disclosure.

The number of copies of the petition and the supporting documents that are required to be filed are governed by local rules. The former Bankruptcy Rule on the subject has been deleted.

The Filing Fee

Bankruptcy Rule 1006(a) provides that a filing fee must accompany the petition. The amounts are set in Section 1930 of Title 28. Currently, the amounts are

Chapter 7	$155.00
Chapter 9	$800.00
Chapter 11	$800.00
Chapter 11 (railroad)	$1,000.00
Chapter 12	$200.00
Chapter 13	$155.00

In addition, in all cases filed under Title 11, the debtor must pay a $30.00 "administrative fee." Cases filed under Chapter 11 of the Bankruptcy Code are also subject to quarterly fees based on the dollar amount of any disbursements made in the quarter. These fees, set out in 28 U.S.C. § 1930(6) range from $250 per quarter in quarters where the dollar value of disbursements is less than $15,000 up to $10,000 for each quarter where disbursements reach the level of $5,000,000 or more per quarter.

If a case is converted to Chapter 11 or 12 from Chapter 7 or 13, the difference in the filing fee must be paid upon the conversion. The clerk will usually not accept the debtor's check for the filing fee.

No matter how poor the debtor may be, it must pay the filing fee and the administrative fee. How much is paid is strictly a function of the chapter of the bankruptcy case. The debtor's wealth or poverty is irrelevant. There is no bankruptcy law or rule equivalent to *in forma pauperis* or other status that allows for the waiver of filing and other fees as exists in other federal and state courts. The reason that has been given is that although access to the civil courts is critical if an individual is to remedy wrongs or defend other actions, access to the bankruptcy court is not as critical. If a debtor wanted to restructure its debts, it could do so by negotiating with creditors and without calling upon the bankruptcy court for assistance. Whether that reasoning makes sense in light of economic and practical reality is of some dispute.

Although there cannot be a waiver of the filing fee or the administrative fee when the petition is filed, in certain circumstances, an individual debtor may be able to pay the filing fee and the administrative fee in installments. Bankruptcy Rule 1006(a) states that if an individual debtor cannot afford the fees, the debtor may propose to pay them in up to four installments, the last of which must be paid no later than 120 days after the case is commenced. However, the court must first approve the installment payments, and no attorney may be paid by the debtor until the entire filing fee is paid. Official Form 3 is the approved form of a combined application for permission to pay the filing fee in installments.

EXHIBIT 7.6 ✦ *Disclosure of Compensation for Bankruptcy Petition Preparer*

Disclosure of Compensation - (12/94)   1998 USBC, District of New Hampshire

UNITED STATES BANKRUPTCY COURT
DISTRICT OF New Hampshire

Attorney or Party Name, Address and Telephone Number	FOR COURT USE ONLY

In re	CASE NO.:
	CHAPTER:
	Debtor Address:
Debtor.	

Social Security Number: _____	Employer's Tax I.D. Number:

DISCLOSURE OF COMPENSATION OF BANKRUPTCY PETITION PREPARER

1. Under 11 U.S.C. § 110(h), I declare under penalty of perjury that I am not an attorney or employee of an attorney, that I prepared or caused to be prepared one or more documents for filing by the above-named debtor(s) in connection with this bankruptcy case, and that compensation paid to me within one year before the filing of the bankruptcy petition, or agreed to be paid to me, for services rendered on behalf of the debtor(s) in contemplation of or in connection with the bankruptcy case is as follows:

    For document preparations services, I have agreed to accept . . . . $_____

    Prior to the filing of this statement I have received . . . . $_____

    Balance Due . . . . $_____

2. I have prepared or caused to be prepared the following documents (itemize):

    and provided the following services (itemize):

3. The source of the compensation paid to me was:

    ❏ debtor   ❏ Other (specify):

4. The source of compensation to be paid to me is:

    ❏ debtor   ❏ Other (specify):

5. The foregoing is a complete statement of any agreement or arrangement for payment to me for preparation of the petition filed by the debtor(s) in this banruptcy case.

6. To my knowledge no other person has prepared for compensation a document for filing in connection with this bankruptcy case except as listed below:

NAME: _____   SSN: _____

—CONTINUED

EXHIBIT 7.6 ✦ *Disclosure of Compensation for Bankruptcy Petition Preparer* (CONTINUED)

Disclosure of Compensation Page Two - (12/94)   1998 USBC, District of New Hampshire

In re	Case No.:
Debtor.	(If known)

DECLARATION OF BANKRUPTCY PETITION PREPARER

I declare under penalty of perjury that the foregoing is true and correct to the best of my knowledge, information, and belief.

X _____   _____   _____
                    Signature   Social Security Number   Date

Name (Print): _____

Address: _____

_____

A bankruptcy petition preparer's failure to comply with the provisions of title 11 and the Federal Rules of Bankruptcy Procedure may result in fines or imprisonment or both. 11 U.S.C. § 110; 18 U.S.C. § 156.

✦ schedules
The document filed by a debtor that discloses all of its property and debts and other pertinent information.

The Schedules

In General   In all cases, the debtor is required to file with the court a detailed schedule of assets, liabilities, and various other types of information as well as a simple budget. This information is designed to give a snapshot of the debtor's financial condition on the date the bankruptcy case was commenced.

Bankruptcy Rules 1007(b) and (c) provide that in a voluntary case, these schedules must be filed with the petition. However, if the petition is accompanied by a list of the names and addresses of the debtor's creditors, the debtor may have an additional 15 days to file the schedules. Bankruptcy Rule 1007 allows the court to grant an extension of the 15-day deadline if the debtor makes a motion; if the debtor gives notice to any committee, trustee, examiner, or other party as the court may direct; and if cause is shown. Preparation of the schedules in even a medium-sized case is a monumental undertaking, and extensions are frequently sought and granted. Exhibit 7.7 is a sample motion to obtain an extension of the 15-day deadline.

The schedules are found in Official Form 6. Preprinted forms are readily available and are commonly used. In addition, a number of software companies market these forms. Not only is a customized form more pleasing to the eye, but it is easier to make corrections. If preprinted forms are going to be used, it is practical to

EXHIBIT 7.7 ✦ *Sample Motion for Extension*

BANKRUPT C. LAWYER
WHITE CHARGER LEGAL CLINIC
One Learned Way
Los Angeles, California 90001

Attorneys for Debtor

UNITED STATES BANKRUPTCY COURT
WESTERN DISTRICT OF CALIFORNIA

In re	)	Case No. 03-00001-JF
	)	
VIDEOS BY JOE, INC.	)	Chapter 11
	)	
Debtor.	)	
	)	
Debtor's Address:	)	MOTION FOR ORDER GRANTING AN EX-
18 Hollywood Drive	)	TENSION OF TIME TO FILE SCHEDULES AND
Los Angeles, CA 90001	)	STATEMENTS
	)	
Employer's Tax Id. No. 99-999899	)	
	)	

TO THE HONORABLE JUSTIN CLAY, UNITED STATES BANKRUPTCY JUDGE:

Videos by Joe, Inc. (the "Debtor"), through its attorneys, in support of its Motion for Order Granting an Extension of Time to File Schedules and Statements, respectfully represents as follows:

1. Debtor is the debtor in possession in the above-captioned case having filed a petition for relief under Chapter 11 of Title 11, United States Code, on October 1, 2003.

2. Debtor's petition was accompanied by a list of all Debtor's creditors. Pursuant to Bankruptcy Rule 1007(c), Debtor is allowed fifteen (15) days in which to file its schedules and its statement of financial affairs (collectively, the "Schedules").

3. As evidenced by the declaration of Joseph Businessman filed concurrently, Debtor has approximately 300 creditors, operates in six states, and has 17 business premises. The analysis and compilation of the information necessary to complete the schedules will require more than 15 days given the size of Debtor's operations, the urgency of other demands created by the filing of the petition, the need to maintain continuity in Debtor's business, and the reduced number of qualified staff to perform and oversee all of the above.

WHERETOFORE, pursuant to Bankruptcy Rule 1007(c), Debtor requests that the Court enter its Order granting Debtor an additional 30 days, up to and including November 15, 2003, within which to file the schedules.

Dated: October 3, 2003

WHITE CHARGER LEGAL CLINIC

_____

BANKRUPT C. LAWYER
Attorneys for Debtor

first write out a rough draft on a copy before having the information typed onto the form. Some of the preprinted forms even come with an extra copy for making a draft.

If the preprinted forms are used, it is unlikely that there will be enough room to include all the information required in the space allotted. In those instances, insert "See Attachment Number _____" or similar language on the schedule and include the information on a separate attachment.

There should never be a blank space in the schedules. If the debtor has no assets or liabilities of the type described in a particular part of the schedules, insert "none" in the space provided.

The number of copies of the schedules that are to be filed with the court is the same as the number of copies of the petition required by the local rules. Since the schedules are papers filed with the court, they will have the same caption as the petition as described in Bankruptcy Rule 1005.

If mistakes are found after the schedules are filed, the schedules can be amended by following Bankruptcy Rule 1009. The clerk will usually charge a small fee for the filing of an amendment to the schedules even though there is no fee for filing the schedules themselves.

The schedules consist of the following parts:

OFFICIAL FORM 6—SUMMARY OF SCHEDULES

Schedule A—Real Property
Schedule B—Personal Property
Schedule C—Property Claimed as Exempt
Schedule D—Creditors Holding Secured Claims
Schedule E—Creditors Holding Unsecured Priority Claims
Schedule F—Creditors Holding Unsecured Nonpriority Claims
Schedule G—Executory Contracts and Unexpired Leases
Schedule H—Codebtors
Schedule I—Current Income of Individual Debtor(s)
Schedule J—Current Expenditures of Individual Debtor(s)
Unsworn Declaration under Penalty of Perjury

Each schedule will be examined separately. Even though the Summary is the first page in the schedule package, it will be completed last.

Schedule A   Schedule A is the list of the debtor's real property. A sample is shown in Exhibit 7.8. Schedule A requires the following information for each parcel of real estate in which the debtor has an interest: its description and location; the nature of the debtor's interest; whether it is owned by the husband, wife, jointly, or as community property; the current market value of the debtor's interest in the property; and the amount of any secured claim.

The property to be listed in Schedule A includes all real property in which the debtor has any legal, equitable, or future interest, including property in which the debtor only holds a partial interest. It will not include leased property.

The description and location should be the street address and a more specific legal description if possible. An attachment will usually be needed for the legal description. If the debtor does not own real estate interests, "none" should be inserted into Schedule A.

The different types of interests that a debtor may have were discussed in Chapter 4 of this text. Whatever interest it is will be set forth in the second column.

If the debtor is married, he or she must state in the third column who owns the property. If the answer is both, the debtor must state whether it is held in joint tenancy or as community property. The differences between those two types of

EXHIBIT 7.8 ✦ *Schedule A*

In re Joe Consumer, Debtor.   Case No. 03-00002-JF

Schedule A—Real Property

Description and Location of Property	Nature of Debtor's Interest in Property	H W J C	Current Market Value of Debtor's Interest in Property, Without Deducting Any Secured Claim or Exemption	Amount of Second Claim
Debtor's single family residence: 18 Hollywood Drive Los Angeles, California 90001	Fee simple absolute	C	$240,000.00	$225,000.00
	Total ➤		$240,000.00	

interests in property were also discussed in Chapter 4. If the debtor is not an individual or is not married, this column should be left blank.

The next column asks for the current market value of the debtor's interest in the property. This will sometimes be difficult to set. Market value is a very broad term and could mean the price received by waiting for the highest offer or it could mean setting the property at an auction. The money received at those two types of sales could be very different. The debtor may have a recent appraisal or another good indication of the value of its interest. Alternatively, the debtor can insert the **book value** of the property. Book value is the value of the property on the debtor's books and records. That number is usually the property's cost less depreciation. Book value is not a good indicator of value because it does not take into account property that is appreciating in value rather than depreciating. Often the best that can be done is to insert "unknown" as the current market value. If book value is used, it should be labeled as such. The bottom of the column of Schedule A should be totalled and the sum placed in the Summary.

The final column in Schedule A is for the amount of any claim secured by this parcel of real property. This information will also be inserted into Schedule D (Secured Claims). By putting in the amount of the secured debt next to the current market value, a reader of Schedule A can make a quick determination if the debtor has any equity in the property available for unsecured creditors.

✦ **book value**
The value of an asset as carried in the owner's books and records. Typically, cost less accumulated depreciation.

Schedule B   Schedule B is a list of the debtor's personal property contained on three pages. Schedule B gives 33 categories of personal property. A sample is shown in Exhibit 7.9. Schedule B asks for the following information for each type of personal property: the description and location of the property; whether it is owned by the husband, wife, jointly, or as community property; and the current market value of the debtor's interest.

Most of the categories are self-explanatory. The paralegal should understand where each type of personal property is inserted and how it should be described. There are a few nuances involved in completing Schedule B, which are shown in Exhibit 7.10.

If the debtor does not have a particular category of personal property, and it is extremely rare for any debtor to have them all, the "None" box should be checked. If all or most of the property is located in one place, it is better to simply state at the beginning of Schedule B that "All the property is located at [list address

Exhibit 7.9 ✦ *Schedule B*

In re Joe Consumer, Debtor.   Case No. 03-00002-JF

Schedule B—Personal Property

Type of Property	N O N E	Description and Location of Property	H W J C	Current Market Value of Debtor's Interest in Property, Without Deducting Any Secured Claim or Exemption
		All property is located at 18 Hollywood Drive, Los Angeles, California 90001 unless otherwise indicated		
1. Cash on hand.			C	$250.00
2. Checking, savings or other financial accounts, certificates of deposit, or shares in banks, savings and loan, thrift, building and loan, and homestead associations or credit brokerage houses or cooperatives. ★ ★ ★		Checking Acct. No. 99 34005 First City Bank Hollywood Branch Los Angeles, California	C	$3,000.00
4. Household goods and furnishings, including audio, video and computer equipment. ★ ★ ★		Miscellaneous home furniture and supplies; one IBM personal computer with monitor and laser printer	C	$4,500.00
6. Wearing apparel. ★ ★ ★		Miscellaneous family clothing	C	$500.00
12. Stock and interests in incorporated and unincorporated business. Itemize. ★ ★ ★		100% ownership of Videos By Joe, Inc., a California corporation	C	0
23. Automobiles, trucks, trailers, and other vehicles and accessories. ★ ★ ★		1992 Dodge Caravan	C	$5,000.00
33. Other personal property of any kind not already listed. Itemize.	X			

_____ continuation sheets attached

Total ➤ $13,250.00

here] unless otherwise indicated." If the debtor's property is being held by someone else, that person's name and address should be provided in the third column.

The market value of the debtor's interest in each particular category of personal property is also required. For liquid assets such as cash, this is easy. For most other categories, it is not. If the debtor knows the market value, it can be used. Otherwise, it is better to use book value or simply state "unknown."

The last page of Schedule B should be totalled and the number inserted into the Summary.

Schedule C   The individual debtor uses Schedule C to claim the exemptions that are discussed in Chapter 8 of this book. A sample of Schedule C is shown in

EXHIBIT 7.10 ✦ *Additional Information Concerning Schedule B*

Question	Property	Comments
1.	Cash on hand	For nonindividual debtors, this should be petty cash only. Individual debtors will disclose the cash they actually have in their possession. Any amounts in bank accounts should be in question 2.
9.	Interests in insurance policies	Often companies will purchase key-person life insurance for its senior executives. The cash surrender value of those policies or any other life insurance policies in which the debtor has an interest should be listed here by the type of insurance, the owner, the beneficiary, the name and address of the carrier, and the surrender value of the policies.
12.	Stocks and interests in incorporated and unincorporated companies	The debtor's stock holdings by company, number of shares, and if publicly traded, their market value must be itemized. If the debtor is a corporation, any subsidiaries and their value should be listed here. Although this question calls for interests in unincorporated companies, the assets of any sole proprietorship and interests in partnerships would be reflected in other places in the schedules.
13.	Interests in partnerships or joint ventures	For each partnership in which the debtor has an interest, the name and type of partnership (general, limited, joint venture) and the percentage of the debtor's holding should be inserted.
17.	Other liquidated debts owing debtor	This section will include employee advances, judgments obtained in debtor's favor, and the like. This is only undisputed tax refunds.
20.	Contingent and unliquidated claims	These are claims owing to the debtor that either are uncertain to arise or have not been fixed as to amount. An example of a contingent claim is a contract awarded to the debtor to construct a building. Upon satisfaction of the contingency—that is, completion of the building—the claim will arise. An example of an unliquidated claim in the favor of the debtor is a lawsuit that the debtor has brought as a plaintiff where the amount has not been fixed.
23.	Automobiles, trucks, trailers, and other vehicles	All vehicles should be itemized by make, model, and year.
28.	Inventory	Inventory should be itemized by type (such as raw materials, work in progress, or finished goods).

that chapter. Because nonindividual debtors are not entitled to exemptions, in a case commenced by a corporation or partnership, Schedule C is left blank.

Schedule C requires that the debtor give the following information:

✦ A description of property claimed as exempt, such as a residence, household furnishings, and automobile. This usually will be as described in the statute giving rise to the right for the exemption.
✦ The specific law creating the exemption, including the subsection. This will be either a citation to a subsection of Section 522 of the Bankruptcy Code or a state law.
✦ The value claimed as exempt.
✦ Current market value of the property.

Schedule D   As seen, there were three schedules (A, B, and C) that covered the debtor's assets. There are also three schedules (D, E, and F) that cover the debtor's liabilities. Schedule D is the list of all secured claims, Schedule E is the list of all creditors holding unsecured Priority claims, and Schedule F is the list of all unsecured, nonpriority creditors.

A secured creditor is one who holds a judgment lien, garnishment, statutory lien, mortgage, deed of trust, or any other type of security interest. Schedule D requests the following information for each secured creditor:

✦ The name and address of the creditor and the account number.
✦ Whether there is a codebtor; i.e., anyone else also liable for the debt (other than the spouse in a joint case).
✦ Whether the debt is owed by the husband, wife, jointly, or as a community debt.
✦ When the claim was incurred, the nature of the lien, a description of the collateral, and the market value of the collateral.
✦ Whether the claim is contingent, unliquidated, or disputed.
✦ The amount of the claim.
✦ The unsecured portion, if any.

Exhibit 7.11 shows how Schedule D can be completed for three different types of secured creditors. If practical, list the creditors in alphabetical order. As is true for all of the schedules listing liabilities, if the creditor is represented by an attorney or has involved a collection agent, the name and address of the attorney and the collection agency should also be listed.

EXHIBIT 7.11 ✦ *Schedule D*

In re Joe Consumer, Debtor.   Case No. 03-00002-JF

Schedule D—Creditors Holding Secured Claims

Creditor's Name and Mailing Address (Including ZIP Code)	CODEBT	HWJC	Date Claim Was Incurred, Nature of Lien, and Description and Market Value of Property Subject to Lien	CONT	UNLIQ	DISP	Amount of Claim Without Deducting Value of Collateral	Unsecured Portion If Any
ACCOUNT NO. 14357495 ABC CORPORATION 123 "M" Street Los Angeles, CA 90017	C	C	October 30, 1988 Voluntary security interest Lien on all personal property Value: $10,000.00				$6,000.00	
ACCOUNT NO. 59475341 ICM Corporation P.O. Box 1 Denver, CO 80808		H	June 7, 2002 Voluntary security interest Lien on personal computer Value: $1,000.00				$2,000.00	$1,000.00
ACCOUNT NO. None. P. Powers c/o J. Barrister, Esq. 124 Main Street Los Angeles, CA 90001		H	September 15, 2003 Judgment lien Debtor's residence located at 18 Hollywood Drive, Los Angeles, California 90001 Value: $240,000			X	$15,000.00	
						Subtotal ➤	$23,000.00	
						Total ➤	$23,000.00	

As was true for preparing Schedules A and B, the greatest difficulty in preparing Schedule D is stating the market value of the collateral. Again, "unknown" may be the best choice.

The terms **contingent, unliquidated,** and **disputed** are not defined in the Bankruptcy Code. Generally, a contingent claim is one that is awaiting the occurrence of an event, which may never occur, to make the underlying debt due. For example, if the debtor guaranteed a loan made by the bank to a relative, the liability would arise only if the relative defaulted on repayment of the loan. The debtor's liability under the guaranty would give rise to a contingent claim. An unliquidated claim is one in which the dollar amount due has not been fixed. If the debtor was at fault in an automobile accident and, because of ongoing medical treatment, the victim's damages have not been finally determined, the liability of the debtor is unliquidated. A disputed claim is just that. The debtor disputes the existence of the creditor's claim or disputes the dollar amount claimed to be owing.

Since the purpose of all of the liability schedules is to give as accurate as possible a statement of the debtor's liabilities, contingent, unliquidated, and disputed claims should be listed regardless of how farfetched the debtor believes the claim to be. Over-inclusion is the rule because under-inclusion may cause problems in the areas of discharge and binding the provisions of a plan on dissident creditors. It is crucial that if a claim is contingent, unliquidated, or disputed, that it be so marked. "Unknown" should be inserted in the column for the amount of the claim if it is contingent or unliquidated or if the entire claim is disputed.

The final column for Schedule D is the unsecured portion of the secured claim. This will be the amount by which the amount of the secured creditor's claim exceeds the value of its collateral. In all of the schedules, a creditor's claim need only be inserted once. Even if a secured creditor has an unsecured deficiency claim, it only need be listed in Schedule D instead of placing the secured portion of the claim in Schedule D and the unsecured portion in Schedule F. If the value of the collateral is more than the amount of the claim, the unsecured portion is zero. If either the value of the collateral or the value of the claim is unknown, the unsecured portion of the claim will also be unknown.

Finally, each page of Schedule D should have a subtotal, and the final page a total, of the amount of the secured claims. The total should also be added to the Summary Page.

Schedule E   Schedule E is for unsecured creditors who hold priority claims. As discussed in Chapter 1 of this book, there are eight different types of prepetition debts listed in Section 507(a) of the Bankruptcy Code that Congress has decided to treat better than others. These claims are placed in Schedule E. They should be segregated by type, with each new type starting a new page, and then in alphabetical order per type.

For each priority claim, Schedule E requires:

+ The name and address of the creditor and the account number.
+ Whether there is a codebtor (other than the spouse in a joint case).
+ Whether the debt is owed by the husband, wife, jointly, or as a community debt.
+ When the claim was incurred and the consideration for the claim.
+ Whether the claim is contingent, unliquidated, or disputed.
+ The total amount of the claim.
+ The amount entitled to priority.

As mentioned earlier, in all of the schedules, a creditor's claim need only be inserted once. Even if a creditor's claim is only entitled to a priority in payment in

+ **contingent claim**
A debt for which liability is dependent on a future event that may or may not occur.

+ **unliquidated claim**
A debt that has not been fixed as to amount.

+ **disputed claim**
A debt of which the debtor objects to the amount or allowability.

part, it only need be listed in Schedule E instead of placing the priority portion of the claim in Schedule E and the nonpriority portion in Schedule F. The first type of priority claim is for any unpaid claims arising after an involuntary case was filed against a debtor but prior to the entry of the order for relief. These claims are entitled to be paid just after all administrative claims are paid pursuant to Section 507(a)(2). There is no limit on the dollar amount of these types of priority claims.

The second type are priority claims under Section 507(a)(3) of the Bankruptcy Code. Congress has given employees a priority in treatment for unpaid wages, salaries, and commissions, including vacation, severance, and sick-leave pay earned within 90 days before the filing of the petition or the cessation of the debtor's business, whichever happened first. This priority is limited to $4,650 per employee. A paralegal should be aware that, pursuant to Title 11, Section 104, on April 1, 1998, and every three years thereafter, dollar amounts within sections 109(e), 303(b), 507(a), 522(a), and 523(a)(2)(c) of Title 11 "shall be adjusted ... to reflect the change in the consumer price index." It is critical for the paralegal to remember that certain dollar amounts may change pursuant to Section 104, and that Section 104 should be consulted whenever the applicable sections are being utilized, in order to ensure that the current dollar amounts are being used.

To complete Schedule E for these priority claims, insert—either in the space provided or on an attachment—the name and address of each employee with a Section 507(a)(3) claim.

For the consideration column, indicate whether the claim is for wages, salaries, or commissions. Employees are not entitled to this priority for expense reimbursement. If they have such a claim, it should be listed in Schedule F with the unsecured creditors without priority. The time period in which the claim was incurred must also be shown. If the claim is contingent, unliquidated, or disputed, the schedule should so state. An employee's claim may be disputed if, for example, the employee also owes the employer money. The total amount of the claim must be inserted in the next-to-last column. The final insertion is the amount entitled to priority, not to exceed $4,650. This amount should be the employee's portion of the wages due. Amounts that the debtor must pay in connection with the wages, such as the debtor's portion of payroll taxes, should be included elsewhere.

A sample insert for an employee's wage priority on Schedule E appears in Exhibit 7.12.

The third type of priority is in Section 507(a)(4). It is for unpaid contributions to an employee benefit plan for services performed within 180 days of the filing of the petition or the cessation of the debtor's business, whichever first occurred. The type of plans with which this priority is concerned are such plans as health insurance. These priority claims are limited to the number of the employees covered by the plan multiplied by $4,650, less the aggregate amount listed in Schedule E for priority wage claims, plus the amount paid by the estate on behalf of the same employees to any other employee benefit plan.

The insertions for these priority claims should include the name of the plan, the plan administrator, the time periods involved, and the amount.

The next two possible inclusions for Schedule E relate to the special priorities granted to people in farming and fishing in the 1986 Amendments after the failure of a number of fish and grain storage companies. Section 507(a)(5)(A) gives a priority to persons engaged in the production or raising of grain with unsecured claims against a debtor who owns or operates a grain storage facility. Similarly, Section 507(a)(5)(B) gives a priority to claims of United States residents engaged in fishing against a debtor who has acquired fish or fish produce through a sale or conversion and who is engaged in operating a fish produce storage or processing facility. The priority of the claim under both Section 507(a)(5)(A) and Section 507(a)(5)(B) is limited to $4,650.

EXHIBIT 7.12 ✦ *Schedule E Pursuant to Section 507(a)(3)*

In re Videos by Joe, Inc., Debtor.   Case No. 03-00002-JF

Schedule E—Creditors Holding Unsecured Priority Claims

Section 507(a)(3)
TYPE OF PRIORITY

Creditor's Name and Mailing Address (Including ZIP Code)	C O D E B T	H W J C	Date Claim Was Incurred and Consideration for Claim	C O N T	U N L I Q	D I S P	Total Amount of Claim	Amount Entitled to Priority
ACCOUNT NO. None. Myra Doe 123 Main Street San Francisco, CA 94628			September 1, 1995 through September 30, 2003 Wages				$6,000.00	$4,000.00

Sheet no. 1 of 3 sheets
Schedule of Creditors Holding
Priority Claims

Subtotal ➤ $6,000.00

Total ➤

Schedule E may also include claims described in Section 507(a)(6), which are unsecured claims of the individuals arising from the deposit of money in connection with the purchase, lease, or rental of consumer property or the purchase of services that were not delivered or provided. This claim priority is limited to $2,100 per individual. Any claim that does not meet the criteria of Section 507(a)(6), such as deposits made by companies rather than individuals or deposits for nonconsumer goods, should be listed in Schedule F. Two different types of inserts for the deposit priority are shown in Exhibit 7.13.

The next priority provided in Section 507(a) is claims for debts to a spouse, former spouse, or child for alimony to, maintenance for, or support of such spouse or child in connection with a separation agreement, divorce decree, or other order or law unless the debt was assigned to another entity. This priority, which was added with the 1994 Amendments, does not have a dollar limit.

The next type of claims for Schedule E is for the unsecured claims of governmental units that are granted a priority under Section 507(a)(8). There are seven types of governmental claims that are afforded this priority. They are primarily taxes, but they also include some penalties and custom duties. These claims are discussed in Chapter 13 of this book. If the debtor is liable for any of these taxes, they should be listed on a separate page of Schedule E, broken down by type of tax (F.I.C.A., personal property tax, and so on) and taxing agency. Claims owing to the United States should be listed first, followed by those owing to any state, and finally those owing to any other taxing authority such as city, county, or special district. A sample Schedule E for a debtor's tax claims is shown in Exhibit 7.14.

The final type of priority claim properly listed on Schedule E is described in Section 507(a)(9). Added with the 1990 Amendments, it is for claims based on a commitment by the debtor to a federal depository institution's regulatory agency (such as the Federal Deposit Insurance Corporation) to maintain the capital of a bank or savings and loan. This priority applies in only a very few cases.

EXHIBIT 7.13 ✦ *Schedule E Pursuant to Section 507(a)(6)*

In re Videos by Joe, Inc., Debtor.   Case No. 03-00002-JF

Schedule E—Creditors Holding Unsecured Priority Claims

Section 507(a)(6)
TYPE OF PRIORITY

Creditor's Name and Mailing Address (Including ZIP Code)	C O D E B T	H W J C	Date Claim Was Incurred and Consideration for Claim	C O N T	U N L I Q	D I S P	Total Amount of Claim	Amount Entitled to Priority
ACCOUNT NO. None. Myra Doe 123 Main Street San Francisco, CA 94126			September 1, 2003 Layaway deposit				$100.00	$100.00
ACCOUNT NO. None. Zane Grey 987 "A" Street San Francisco, CA 94567			September 15, 2003 Deposit on custom order				$2,000.00	$1,800.00

Sheet no. 2 of 3 sheets
Schedule of Creditors Holding
Priority Claims

Subtotal ➤ $2,100.00

Total ➤

EXHIBIT 7.14 ✦ *Schedule E Pursuant to Section 507(a)(8)*

In re Videos By Joe, Inc., Debtor.   Case No. 03-00001-JF

Schedule E—Creditors Holding Unsecured Priority Claims

Section 507(a)(8)
TYPE OF PRIORITY

Creditor's Name and Mailing Address (Including ZIP Code)	C O D E B T	H W J C	Date Claim Was Incurred and Consideration for Claim	C O N T	U N L I Q	D I S P	Total Amount of Claim	Amount Entitled to Priority
ACCOUNT NO. 99-999899 Internal Revenue Service P.O. Box 1 Fresno, CA 94126			Income Taxes due for 2002				$66,000.00	$66,000.00
ACCOUNT NO. 99-999899 Franchise Tax Board P.O. Box 2 Sacramento, CA 96000			Sales taxes collected June 1, 1995 to September 30, 2003				$13,500.00	$13,500.00

Sheet no. 3 of 3 sheets
Schedule of Creditors Holding
Priority Claims

Subtotal ➤ $79,500.00

Total ➤ $87,600.00

The only task remaining to complete Schedule E is to subtotal each page, total all pages, and insert that number at the bottom of the last page and on the summary page. If the schedule has included claims for which the amount is unknown, it is helpful to put an asterisk next to the total and indicate (at a convenient spot in the schedule) that the total does not include claims that were listed on the schedule with an unknown amount.

Schedule F   Since most of the claims against a debtor will be on account of unsecured debts, Schedule F, Creditors Holding Unsecured Nonpriority Claims, will probably be the largest part of the schedules, even though it requires the least amount of information. In order to complete Schedule F, only the following information need be listed for each claim:

- ✦ The name and address of the creditor.
- ✦ Whether there is a codebtor (other than the spouse in a joint case).
- ✦ Whether the debt is owed by the husband, wife, jointly, or as a community debt.
- ✦ The date the claim was incurred, the consideration for the claim, and whether the claim is subject to setoff.
- ✦ Whether the claim is contingent, unliquidated, or disputed.
- ✦ The amount of the claim.

If there are quite a few claims, rather than having the list prepared on Schedule F, it may be possible to attach the debtor's accounts payable register. This is especially convenient if the debtor has the information on its computer system and the printout can be reformatted to give the information in the manner called for in Schedule F. In addition, it will save a considerable amount of time later if the listings for Schedule F are in alphabetical order. Names of attorneys and collection agencies should be included if known. The total of all Schedule F claims should be filled in at the bottom of the last page of the Schedule and transferred to the Summary Page.

Schedule G   Bankruptcy Rules 1007(b) and (c) generally require the debtor to file a statement of executory contracts and unexpired leases with the petition in a voluntary case, or, if the petition is accompanied by a list of all the debtor's creditors and their addresses, within 15 days of the commencement of the case. A description of executory contracts and unexpired leases was given in Chapter 4 of this book. Generally, the contents of this statement will include all real and personal property leases including timeshares, employment contracts, insurance agreements, purchase or supply contracts, pension and medical benefit plans, and collective bargaining agreements to which the debtor was a party.

Schedule G to Official Form 6 is the statement required. For each executory contract and unexpired lease, Schedule G requires:

- ✦ The name and address of the other party to the lease or contract.
- ✦ A description of the contract or lease, including the nature of the debtor's interest (e.g., lessor, lessee, agent), whether the lease is for nonresidential real property, and the contract number of any government contract.

By identifying in Schedule G which leases are for nonresidential real property, a trustee can quickly see which leases must be assumed within 60 days or be deemed rejected under Section 365(d) of the Bankruptcy Code.

These parties listed in Schedule G will also have secured or unsecured claims against the debtor if for no other reason than they have contingent claims based on a possible default by the debtor. Hence, all of the parties listed in Schedule G should also appear in Schedules D, E, or F.

Schedule H   Schedule H is the schedule of codebtors. This schedule only requires the name of each codebtor and the name of each creditor that can look to the codebtor. As stated earlier, a codebtor is anyone else who is liable on a debt with the debtor, such as a guarantor or cosigner, but does not include a spouse if the case was filed jointly by a husband and a wife. If the case was not filed by both the husband and wife, and the husband and wife live in a community property state, include in Schedule H the nonfiling spouse's name and all names used in the previous six years.

Schedules I and J   Section 521(1) of the Bankruptcy Code requires all debtors to file a statement of current income and expenditures. The statement is also required by Bankruptcy Rule 1007(b). The purpose of this requirement is to determine if the debtor projects that it will lose money in bankruptcy or if it believes it will at least break even on a cash basis. For individual debtors, it will also help determine what the debtor's disposable income is.

Schedule I of Official Form 6 is a statement of current income, and Schedule J of Official Form 6 is a statement of current expenditures. Curiously, they are only for individuals to use. For corporate or partnership debtors, a simple sources and uses of cash statement can be attached to a page containing the caption and labeled "Statement of Current Income and Expenditures."

Schedules I and J are simple to use and largely self-explanatory.

Summary Page   After Schedules A–J have been completed, it is time to go back and fill in the first page of the schedules package, the Summary of Schedules. A sample summary page is shown in Exhibit 7.15. Next to the left column listing each schedule, indicate with a "yes" or "no" answer whether each particular schedule is attached and, if so, the number of pages of each schedule. The number of pages should be totaled at the bottom of the page. The dollar amounts that have been placed at the bottom of each page of Schedules A, B, D, E, F, I, and J are carried to this page and inserted into the appropriate box in the three right columns. If the totals have been annotated in any way (for example, if there were a large number of claims listed as unknown in amount), these legends should also be indicated on the summary page. There should be no blanks. If the debtor had no entries on a particular schedule, a zero dollar amount should be indicated on the summary page.

Declaration   The schedules should be followed by a declaration that they are true and correct and signed by the debtor or, if the debtor is a partnership or corporation, by an appropriate person. The last page of Official Form 6 gives both forms of this declaration. The total number of pages, which will be the number on the summary page plus one (for the summary page), should be inserted into the applicable declaration. In 1995, this page was amended to add an appropriate certification for a bankruptcy petition preparer as required by Section 110. The form continues to carry a date of 12/94.

The Statement of Financial Affairs

◆ **statement of financial affairs**
The document filed by a debtor that discloses all information not found in the schedules that a trustee would need to effectively administer the estate.

In addition to the schedules, in order to give interested parties a complete picture of the debtor's financial condition on the date the petition was filed, the Bankruptcy Rules require every debtor to file a **statement of financial affairs,** which is Official Form 7. A sample Official Form 7 is shown as Exhibit 7.16. The time limits for filing the statement and the number of copies needed are identical to those of the schedules.

Like the schedules, there are preprinted statement forms. They should be compared to the official form before being used, to confirm that they are the most

EXHIBIT 7.15 ✦ *Summary of Schedules*

In re Videos By Joe, Inc., Debtor.   Case No. 03-00001-JF

Summary of Schedules

			Amounts Scheduled		
Name of Schedule	Attached (Yes/No)	No. of Sheets	Assets	Liabilities	Other
A. Real Property					
B. Personal Property					
C. Property Claimed As Exempt					
D. Creditors Holding Secured Claims					
E. Creditors Holding Unsecured Priority Claims					
F. Creditors Holding Unsecured Nonpriority Claims					
G. Executory Contracts and Unexpired Leases					
H. Codebtors					
I. Current Income of Individual Debtor(s)					
J. Current Expenditures of Individual Debtor(s)					
Total Number of Sheets in ALL Schedules					
Total Assets					
Total Liabilities					

current version. If there is insufficient room to respond completely on the form, attachments can be used.

There are 25 inquiries in the statement, some of which have multiple parts. Each inquiry must either be answered or the failure to answer explained. If the inquiry is not applicable or if the answer is "none," the box or blank next to the question should be checked. There should be no blanks.

Questions 1–18 of Official Form 7 must be completed by all debtors. Debtors who are or have been in business must also complete questions 19–25. A debtor is "in business" if it is: (a) a corporation, (b) a partnership, or (c) an individual who

EXHIBIT 7.16 ✦ *Official Form 7*

Form 7
(9/00)

FORM 7. STATEMENT OF FINANCIAL AFFAIRS

UNITED STATES BANKRUPTCY COURT

_____ DISTRICT OF _____

In re: _____ ,   Case No. _____
          (Name)   (if known)
                    Debtor

STATEMENT OF FINANCIAL AFFAIRS

This statement is to be completed by every debtor. Spouses filing a joint petition may file a single statement on which the information for both spouses is combined. If the case is filed under chapter 12 or chapter 13, a married debtor must furnish information for both spouses whether or not a joint petition is filed, unless the spouses are separated and a joint petition is not filed. An individual debtor engaged in business as a sole proprietor, partner, family farmer, or self-employed professional, should provide the information requested on this statement concerning all such activities as well as the individual's personal affairs.

Questions 1 - 18 are to be completed by all debtors. Debtors that are or have been in business, as defined below, also must complete Questions 19 - 25. **If the answer to an applicable question is "None," mark the box labeled "None."** If additional space is needed for the answer to any question, use and attach a separate sheet properly identified with the case name, case number (if known), and the number of the question.

DEFINITIONS

"In business." A debtor is "in business" for the purpose of this form if the debtor is a corporation or partnership. An individual debtor is "in business" for the purpose of this form if the debtor is or has been, within the six years immediately preceding the filing of this bankruptcy case, any of the following: an officer, director, managing executive, or owner of 5 percent or more of the voting or equity securities of a corporation; a partner, other than a limited partner, of a partnership; a sole proprietor or self-employed.

"Insider." The term "insider" includes but is not limited to: relatives of the debtor; general partners of the debtor and their relatives; corporations of which the debtor is an officer, director, or person in control; officers, directors, and any owner of 5 percent or more of the voting or equity securities of a corporate debtor and their relatives; affiliates of the debtor and insiders of such affiliates; any managing agent of the debtor. 11 U.S.C. § 101.

---

1. **Income from employment or operation of business**

None
☐
State the gross amount of income the debtor has received from employment, trade, or profession, or from operation of the debtor's business from the beginning of this calendar year to the date this case was commenced. State also the gross amounts received during the **two years** immediately preceding this calendar year. (A debtor that maintains, or has maintained, financial records on the basis of a fiscal rather than a calendar year may report fiscal year income. Identify the beginning and ending dates of the debtor's fiscal year.) If a joint petition is filed, state income for each spouse separately. (Married debtors filing under chapter 12 or chapter 13 must state income of both spouses whether or not a joint petition is filed, unless the spouses are separated and a joint petition is not filed.)

AMOUNT   SOURCE (if more than one)

—*CONTINUED*

EXHIBIT 7.16 ✦ *Official Form 7* (CONTINUED)

2.   Income other than from employment or operation of business

None ☐   State the amount of income received by the debtor other than from employment, trade, profession, or operation of the debtor's business during the **two years** immediately preceding the commencement of this case. Give particulars. If a joint petition is filed, state income for each spouse separately. (Married debtors filing under chapter 12 or chapter 13 must state income for each spouse whether or not a joint petition is filed, unless the spouses are separated and a joint petition is not filed.)

AMOUNT   SOURCE

---

3.   Payments to creditors

None ☐   a.   List all payments on loans, installment purchases of goods or services, and other debts, aggregating more than $600 to any creditor, made within **90 days** immediately preceding the commencement of this case. (Married debtors filing under chapter 12 or chapter 13 must include payments by either or both spouses whether or not a joint petition is filed, unless the spouses are separated and a joint petition is not filed.)

NAME AND ADDRESS OF CREDITOR	DATES OF PAYMENTS	AMOUNT PAID	AMOUNT STILL OWING

None ☐   b.   List all payments made within **one year** immediately preceding the commencement of this case to or for the benefit of creditors who are or were insiders. (Married debtors filing under chapter 12 or chapter 13 must include payments by either or both spouses whether or not a joint petition is filed, unless the spouses are separated and a joint petition is not filed.)

NAME AND ADDRESS OF CREDITOR AND RELATIONSHIP TO DEBTOR	DATE OF PAYMENT	AMOUNT PAID	AMOUNT STILL OWING

---

4.   Suits and administrative proceedings, executions, garnishments and attachments

None ☐   a.   List all suits and administrative proceedings to which the debtor is or was a party within **one year** immediately preceding the filing of this bankruptcy case. (Married debtors filing under chapter 12 or chapter 13 must include information concerning either or both spouses whether or not a joint petition is filed, unless the spouses are separated and a joint petition is not filed.)

CAPTION OF SUIT AND CASE NUMBER	NATURE OF PROCEEDING	COURT OR AGENCY AND LOCATION	STATUS OR DISPOSITION

—CONTINUED

EXHIBIT 7.16 ✦ *Official Form 7* (CONTINUED)

None ☐ b. Describe all property that has been attached, garnished or seized under any legal or equitable process within **one year** immediately preceding the commencement of this case: (Married debtors filing under chapter 12 or chapter 13 must include information concerning property of either or both spouses whether or not a joint petition is filed, unless the spouses are separated and a joint petition is not filed.)

NAME AND ADDRESS OF PERSON FOR WHOSE BENEFIT PROPERTY WAS SEIZED	DATE OF SEIZURE	DESCRIPTION AND VALUE OF PROPERTY

---

5. Repossessions, foreclosures and returns

None ☐ List all property that has been repossessed by a creditor, sold at a foreclosure sale, transferred through a deed in lieu of foreclosure or returned to the seller, within **one year** immediately preceding the commencement of this case. (Married debtors filing under chapter 12 or chapter 13 must include information concerning property of either or both spouses whether or not a joint petition is filed, unless the spouses are separated and a joint petition is not filed.)

NAME AND ADDRESS OF CREDITOR OR SELLER	DATE OF REPOSSESSION, FORECLOSURE SALE, TRANSFER OR RETURN	DESCRIPTION AND VALUE OF PROPERTY

---

6. Assignments and receiverships

None ☐ a. Describe any assignment of property for the benefit of creditors made within **120 days** immediately preceding the commencement of this case. (Married debtors filing under chapter 12 or chapter 13 must include any assignment by either or both spouses whether or not a joint petition is filed, unless the spouses are separated and a joint petition is not filed.)

NAME AND ADDRESS OF ASSIGNEE	DATE OF ASSIGNMENT	TERMS OF ASSIGNMENT OR SETTLEMENT

None ☐ b. List all property which has been in the hands of a custodian, receiver, or court-appointed official within **one year** immediately preceding the commencement of this case. (Married debtors filing under chapter 12 or chapter 13 must include information concerning property of either or both spouses whether or not a joint petition is filed, unless the spouses are separated and a joint petition is not filed.)

NAME AND ADDRESS OF CUSTODIAN	NAME AND LOCATION OF COURT CASE TITLE & NUMBER	DATE OF ORDER	DESCRIPTION AND VALUE OF PROPERTY

—CONTINUED

EXHIBIT 7.16 ✦ *Official Form 7* (CONTINUED)

7. Gifts

None ☐ List all gifts or charitable contributions made within **one year** immediately preceding the commencement of this case except ordinary and usual gifts to family members aggregating less than $200 in value per individual family member and charitable contributions aggregating less than $100 per recipient. (Married debtors filing under chapter 12 or chapter 13 must include gifts or contributions by either or both spouses whether or not a joint petition is filed, unless the spouses are separated and a joint petition is not filed.)

NAME AND ADDRESS OF PERSON OR ORGANIZATION	RELATIONSHIP TO DEBTOR, IF ANY	DATE OF GIFT	DESCRIPTION AND VALUE OF GIFT

8. Losses

None ☐ List all losses from fire, theft, other casualty or gambling within **one year** immediately preceding the commencement of this case **or since the commencement of this case.** (Married debtors filing under chapter 12 or chapter 13 must include losses by either or both spouses whether or not a joint petition is filed, unless the spouses are separated and a joint petition is not filed.)

DESCRIPTION AND VALUE OF PROPERTY	DESCRIPTION OF CIRCUMSTANCES AND, IF LOSS WAS COVERED IN WHOLE OR IN PART BY INSURANCE, GIVE PARTICULARS	DATE OF LOSS

9. Payments related to debt counseling or bankruptcy

None ☐ List all payments made or property transferred by or on behalf of the debtor to any persons, including attorneys, for consultation concerning debt consolidation, relief under the bankruptcy law or preparation of a petition in bankruptcy within **one year** immediately preceding the commencement of this case.

NAME AND ADDRESS OF PAYEE	DATE OF PAYMENT, NAME OF PAYOR IF OTHER THAN DEBTOR	AMOUNT OF MONEY OR DESCRIPTION AND VALUE OF PROPERTY

10. Other transfers

None ☐ List all other property, other than property transferred in the ordinary course of the business or financial affairs of the debtor, transferred either absolutely or as security within **one year** immediately preceding the commencement of this case. (Married debtors filing under chapter 12 or chapter 13 must include transfers by either or both spouses whether or not a joint petition is filed, unless the spouses are separated and a joint petition is not filed.)

NAME AND ADDRESS OF TRANSFEREE, RELATIONSHIP TO DEBTOR	DATE	DESCRIBE PROPERTY TRANSFERRED AND VALUE RECEIVED

—CONTINUED

Exhibit 7.16 ✦ *Official Form 7* (CONTINUED)

11. Closed financial accounts

None ☐ List all financial accounts and instruments held in the name of the debtor or for the benefit of the debtor which were closed, sold, or otherwise transferred within **one year** immediately preceding the commencement of this case. Include checking, savings, or other financial accounts, certificates of deposit, or other instruments; shares and share accounts held in banks, credit unions, pension funds, cooperatives, associations, brokerage houses and other financial institutions. (Married debtors filing under chapter 12 or chapter 13 must include information concerning accounts or instruments held by or for either or both spouses whether or not a joint petition is filed, unless the spouses are separated and a joint petition is not filed.)

NAME AND ADDRESS OF INSTITUTION	TYPE AND NUMBER OF ACCOUNT AND AMOUNT OF FINAL BALANCE	AMOUNT AND DATE OF SALE OR CLOSING

12. Safe deposit boxes

None ☐ List each safe deposit or other box or depository in which the debtor has or had securities, cash, or other valuables within **one year** immediately preceding the commencement of this case. (Married debtors filing under chapter 12 or chapter 13 must include boxes or depositories of either or both spouses whether or not a joint petition is filed, unless the spouses are separated and a joint petition is not filed.)

NAME AND ADDRESS OF BANK OR OTHER DEPOSITORY	NAMES AND ADDRESSES OF THOSE WITH ACCESS TO BOX OR DEPOSITORY	DESCRIPTION OF CONTENTS	DATE OF TRANSFER OR SURRENDER, IF ANY

13. Setoffs

None ☐ List all setoffs made by any creditor, including a bank, against a debt or deposit of the debtor within **90 days** preceding the commencement of this case. (Married debtors filing under chapter 12 or chapter 13 must include information concerning either or both spouses whether or not a joint petition is filed, unless the spouses are separated and a joint petition is not filed.)

NAME AND ADDRESS OF CREDITOR	DATE OF SETOFF	AMOUNT OF SETOFF

14. Property held for another person

None ☐ List all property owned by another person that the debtor holds or controls.

NAME AND ADDRESS OF OWNER	DESCRIPTION AND VALUE OF PROPERTY	LOCATION OF PROPERTY

—*CONTINUED*

EXHIBIT 7.16 ✦ *Official Form 7* (CONTINUED)

15. Prior address of debtor

None ☐

If the debtor has moved within the **two years** immediately preceding the commencement of this case, list all premises which the debtor occupied during that period and vacated prior to the commencement of this case. If a joint petition is filed, report also any separate address of either spouse.

ADDRESS	NAME USED	DATES OF OCCUPANCY

16. Spouses and Former Spouses

None ☐

If the debtor resides or resided in a community property state, commonwealth, or territory (including Alaska, Arizona, California, Idaho, Louisiana, Nevada, New Mexico, Puerto Rico, Texas, Washington, or Wisconsin) within the **six-year period** immediately preceding the commencement of the case, identify the name of the debtor's spouse and of any former spouse who resides or resided with the debtor in the community property state.

NAME

17. Environmental Information.

For the purpose of this question, the following definitions apply:

"Environmental Law" means any federal, state, or local statute or regulation regulating pollution, contamination, releases of hazardous or toxic substances, wastes or material into the air, land, soil, surface water, groundwater, or other medium, including, but not limited to, statutes or regulations regulating the cleanup of these substances, wastes, or material.

"Site" means any location, facility, or property as defined under any Environmental Law, whether or not presently or formerly owned or operated by the debtor, including, but not limited to, disposal sites.

"Hazardous Material" means anything defined as a hazardous waste, hazardous substance, toxic substance, hazardous material, pollutant, or contaminant or similar term under an Environmental Law

None ☐

a. List the name and address of every site for which the debtor has received notice in writing by a governmental unit that it may be liable or potentially liable under or in violation of an Environmental Law. Indicate the governmental unit, the date of the notice, and, if known, the Environmental Law:

SITE NAME AND ADDRESS	NAME AND ADDRESS OF GOVERNMENTAL UNIT	DATE OF NOTICE	ENVIRONMENTAL LAW

None ☐

b. List the name and address of every site for which the debtor provided notice to a governmental unit of a release of Hazardous Material. Indicate the governmental unit to which the notice was sent and the date of the notice.

—CONTINUED

Exhibit 7.16 ✦ *Official Form 7* (CONTINUED)

| SITE NAME | NAME AND ADDRESS | DATE OF | ENVIRONMENTAL |
| AND ADDRESS | OF GOVERNMENTAL UNIT | NOTICE | LAW |

None ☐   c. List all judicial or administrative proceedings, including settlements or orders, under any Environmental Law with respect to which the debtor is or was a party. Indicate the name and address of the governmental unit that is or was a party to the proceeding, and the docket number.

| NAME AND ADDRESS | DOCKET NUMBER | STATUS OR |
| OF GOVERNMENTAL UNIT | | DISPOSITION |

18 . Nature, location and name of business

None ☐   a. If the debtor is an individual, list the names, addresses, taxpayer identification numbers, nature of the businesses, and beginning and ending dates of all businesses in which the debtor was an officer, director, partner, or managing executive of a corporation, partnership, sole proprietorship, or was a self-employed professional within the **six years** immediately preceding the commencement of this case, or in which the debtor owned 5 percent or more of the voting or equity securities within the **six years** immediately preceding the commencement of this case.

   If the debtor is a partnership, list the names, addresses, taxpayer identification numbers, nature of the businesses, and beginning and ending dates of all businesses in which the debtor was a partner or owned 5 percent or more of the voting or equity securities, within the **six years** immediately preceding the commencement of this case.

   If the debtor is a corporation, list the names, addresses, taxpayer identification numbers, nature of the businesses, and beginning and ending dates of all businesses in which the debtor was a partner or owned 5 percent or more of the voting or equity securities within the **six years** immediately preceding the commencement of this case.

| NAME | TAXPAYER I.D. NUMBER | ADDRESS | NATURE OF BUSINESS | BEGINNING AND ENDING DATES |

None ☐   b. Identify any business listed in response to subdivision a., above, that is "single asset real estate" as defined in 11 U.S.C. § 101.

| NAME | ADDRESS |

The following questions are to be completed by every debtor that is a corporation or partnership and by any individual debtor who is or has been, within the **six years** immediately preceding the commencement of this case, any of the following: an officer, director, managing executive, or owner of more than 5 percent of the voting or equity securities of a corporation; a partner, other than a limited partner, of a partnership; a sole proprietor or otherwise self-employed.

   *(An individual or joint debtor should complete this portion of the statement **only** if the debtor is or has been in business, as defined above, within the six years immediately preceding the commencement of this case. A debtor who has not been in business within those six years should go directly to the signature page.)*

—CONTINUED

EXHIBIT 7.16 ✦ *Official Form 7* (CONTINUED)

19. Books, records and financial statements

None ☐   a.   List all bookkeepers and accountants who within the **two years** immediately preceding the filing of this bankruptcy case kept or supervised the keeping of books of account and records of the debtor.

NAME AND ADDRESS   DATES SERVICES RENDERED

None ☐   b.   List all firms or individuals who within the **two years** immediately preceding the filing of this bankruptcy case have audited the books of account and records, or prepared a financial statement of the debtor.

NAME   ADDRESS   DATES SERVICES RENDERED

None ☐   c.   List all firms or individuals who at the time of the commencement of this case were in possession of the books of account and records of the debtor. If any of the books of account and records are not available, explain.

NAME   ADDRESS

None ☐   d.   List all financial institutions, creditors and other parties, including mercantile and trade agencies, to whom a financial statement was issued within the **two years** immediately preceding the commencement of this case by the debtor.

NAME AND ADDRESS   DATE ISSUED

---

20. Inventories

None ☐   a.   List the dates of the last two inventories taken of your property, the name of the person who supervised the taking of each inventory, and the dollar amount and basis of each inventory.

DATE OF INVENTORY   INVENTORY SUPERVISOR   DOLLAR AMOUNT OF INVENTORY (Specify cost, market or other basis)

None ☐   b.   List the name and address of the person having possession of the records of each of the two inventories reported in a., above.

DATE OF INVENTORY   NAME AND ADDRESSES OF CUSTODIAN OF INVENTORY RECORDS

—CONTINUED

EXHIBIT 7.16 ✦ *Official Form 7* (CONTINUED)

21 . Current Partners, Officers, Directors and Shareholders

None ☐
a. If the debtor is a partnership, list the nature and percentage of partnership interest of each member of the partnership.

NAME AND ADDRESS	NATURE OF INTEREST	PERCENTAGE OF INTEREST

None ☐
b. If the debtor is a corporation, list all officers and directors of the corporation, and each stockholder who directly or indirectly owns, controls, or holds 5 percent or more of the voting or equity securities of the corporation.

NAME AND ADDRESS	TITLE	NATURE AND PERCENTAGE OF STOCK OWNERSHIP

22 . Former partners, officers, directors and shareholders

None ☐
a. If the debtor is a partnership, list each member who withdrew from the partnership within **one year** immediately preceding the commencement of this case.

NAME	ADDRESS	DATE OF WITHDRAWAL

None ☐
b. If the debtor is a corporation, list all officers, or directors whose relationship with the corporation terminated within **one year** immediately preceding the commencement of this case.

NAME AND ADDRESS	TITLE	DATE OF TERMINATION

23 . Withdrawals from a partnership or distributions by a corporation

None ☐
If the debtor is a partnership or corporation, list all withdrawals or distributions credited or given to an insider, including compensation in any form, bonuses, loans, stock redemptions, options exercised and any other perquisite during **one year** immediately preceding the commencement of this case.

NAME & ADDRESS OF RECIPIENT, RELATIONSHIP TO DEBTOR	DATE AND PURPOSE OF WITHDRAWAL	AMOUNT OF MONEY OR DESCRIPTION AND VALUE OF PROPERTY

—CONTINUED

EXHIBIT 7.16 ✦ *Official Form 7* (CONTINUED)

24. Tax Consolidation Group.

None
☐

If the debtor is a corporation, list the name and federal taxpayer identification number of the parent corporation of any consolidated group for tax purposes of which the debtor has been a member at any time within the **six-year period** immediately preceding the commencement of the case.

NAME OF PARENT CORPORATION   TAXPAYER IDENTIFICATION NUMBER

25. Pension Funds.

None
☐

If the debtor is not an individual, list the name and federal taxpayer identification number of any pension fund to which the debtor, as an employer, has been responsible for contributing at any time within the **six-year period** immediately preceding the commencement of the case.

NAME OF PENSION FUND   TAXPAYER IDENTIFICATION NUMBER

* * * * * *

—CONTINUED

EXHIBIT 7.16 ✦ *Official Form 7* (CONTINUED)

[If completed by an individual or individual and spouse]

I declare under penalty of perjury that I have read the answers contained in the foregoing statement of financial affairs and any attachments thereto and that they are true and correct.

Date _____   Signature _____
                                     of Debtor

Date _____   Signature _____
                                     of Joint Debtor
                                     (if any)

_____

[If completed on behalf of a partnership or corporation]

I, declare under penalty of perjury that I have read the answers contained in the foregoing statement of financial affairs and any attachments thereto and that they are true and correct to the best of my knowledge, information and belief.

Date _____   Signature _____

                                     _____
                                     Print Name and Title

[An individual signing on behalf of a partnership or corporation must indicate position or relationship to debtor.]

_____ continuation sheets attached

Penalty for making a false statement: Fine of up to $500,000 or imprisonment for up to 5 years, or both. 18 U.S.C. § 152 and 3571

CERTIFICATION AND SIGNATURE OF NON-ATTORNEY BANKRUPTCY PETITION PREPARER (See 11 U.S.C. § 110)

I certify that I am a bankruptcy petition preparer as defined in 11 U.S.C. § 110, that I prepared this document for compensation, and that I have provided the debtor with a copy of this document.

_____   _____
Printed or Typed Name of Bankruptcy Petition Preparer   Social Security No.

_____

Address

Names and Social Security numbers of all other individuals who prepared or assisted in preparing this document:

If more than one person prepared this document, attach additional signed sheets conforming to the appropriate Official Form for each person.

X _____   _____
Signature of Bankruptcy Petition Preparer   Date

A bankruptcy petition preparer's failure to comply with the provisions of title 11 and the Federal Rules of Bankruptcy Procedure may result in fines or imprisonment or both. 18 U.S.C. § 156.

is, or has been within the previous two years, (i) an officer, director, managing executive, or person in control of a corporation, (ii) a general partner, (iii) a sole proprietor, or (iv) self-employed.

Question 1   This question requires the debtor to disclose the gross amount and source of its income derived from its employment, trade, or profession, or from operation of its business, during the current calendar year and the two previous years.

Question 2   This question requires the debtor to disclose the gross amount and source of its income other than that derived from its employment, trade, or profession, or from operation of its business, during the current calendar year and the two previous years. This income may be dividends or other earnings on investments, interest on savings, or rental income.

Question 3   There are two subparts to this question, each of which is designed to elicit the information necessary to determine whether the debtor made any preferential transfers prior to the commencement of the bankruptcy case. Subpart (a) asks for a list of all payments made to creditors of more than $600 made within 90 days preceding the filing of the bankruptcy petition. The response is to be given in a four-column matrix with the following information:

- ✦ Name and address of creditor.
- ✦ Dates of payment.
- ✦ Amount paid.
- ✦ Amount still owing.

For a business, the answer to this question could require a stack of paper. In those situations, it is reasonable to exclude payments to trade creditors and employees that are made in the ordinary course of business and according to ordinary terms. The response should mention that those transactions are not included and that anyone who desires the additional information may request it from the debtor's attorney.

Subpart (b) of question 3 asks for the same information for payments made to or for the benefit of insiders and expands the payments to any made within one year prior to the commencement of the case. The specific information requested is the same as in subpart (a), but the debtor must also provide the creditor's relationship to the debtor, such as officer or relative.

Question 4   Question 4 also has two subparts. Subpart (a) concerns lawsuits in which the debtor was involved at the time or within one year before the commencement of the bankruptcy case even if those lawsuits have been terminated. It does not matter whether the debtor was a plaintiff or a defendant. To answer subpart (a), provide the following information:

1. Caption of the suit and the case number.
2. The nature of the proceeding.
3. Name of the court and its location.
4. The present status of the case or the disposition.

If the debtor has widespread operations, the information needed to complete this part may be difficult to gather. If the debtor does not have in-house counsel monitoring all litigation, as soon as the petition is filed, the paralegal should contact all the law firms the debtor has employed or paid in the previous year and ask for a case status report. The information in those case status reports can then be arranged as part of the response to this inquiry.

Subpart (b) of question 4 requires a description of all property that has been attached, garnished, or seized under any legal or equitable process within the previous year. The needed information is:

+ The name and address of the person for whose benefit the property was seized.
+ The date of the seizure.
+ A description and the value of the property.

Question 5 Question 5 requires the debtor to detail any property that has been repossessed or foreclosed by, or returned to, the secured creditor or seller during the previous year. If there have been any such transfers—whether voluntary or involuntary—the details, including the name and address of the creditor, the date of repossession, foreclosure sale, transfer or return, and a description and value of the property, should be given.

Question 6 Question 6 has two subparts. Subpart (a) requires the debtor to describe any property assigned for the benefit of creditors within 120 days before the commencement of the case by providing the name and address of the assignee, the date of the assignment, and the terms of the assignment or settlement. An **assignment for the benefit of creditors** is a proceeding created by state law. Under this proceeding, the debtor turns over all nonexempt assets to someone called the assignee, who acts very much like a Chapter 7 trustee. The assignee liquidates the assets and distributes the proceeds of the liquidation to creditors. Assignments for the benefit of creditors are no longer common, but they do still occur, especially in the fabric and garment industries.

Subpart (b) requires the debtor to list all property that has been in the hands of a custodian, receiver, or other court-appointed official within one year prior to the commencement of the case. For example, as part of its foreclosure proceedings on an apartment house owned and operated by the debtor, a secured creditor may have a receiver installed to collect the rents. If there has been such an appointment, subpart (b) requires the name and address of the custodian or receiver, the name and location of the court, the case title and the case number in which the custodian or receiver was appointed, the date of the order, and a description of the property, including its value.

Question 7 This question and question 10 are designed to discover whether the debtor made any prepetition fraudulent conveyances. In question 7, the debtor must disclose all gifts and charitable contributions within one year before the commencement of the case other than ordinary and usual gifts to family members aggregating less than $200 per individual family member and charitable contributions of less than $100 per recipient. If there were any such gifts or contributions, question 7 requires the name and address of the person or organization, the relationship to the debtor (if any), the date of the gift or contribution, and a description and value of the gift.

Question 8 Question 8 concerns losses. If the debtor has suffered any losses from fire, theft, other casualty, or from gambling in the year prior to the commencement of the case, it must provide the following information:

+ A description of the property and its value.
+ A description of the circumstances of the loss.

+ **assignment for the benefit of creditors**
A nonbankruptcy proceeding that is similar to a Chapter 7 case, in which the debtor turns over all of its nonexempt property to a third party for liquidation and distribution of the proceeds to creditors.

+ Whether the loss was covered in whole or in part by insurance.
+ The date of the loss.

Question 9   Question 9 deals with payments or other transfers to any persons, including attorneys, for debt counseling or bankruptcy services within one year before the commencement of the bankruptcy case. This includes payments to the attorney or bankruptcy petition preparer who drafted and filed the petition. For each such person, the debtor must list the person's name and address, the date of payment, the name of the person making the payment if other than the debtor, and the amount paid or a description of the property transferred and its value.

Question 10   Question 10 is also designed to discover whether the debtor made any prepetition fraudulent conveyances. In question 10, the debtor must disclose any other transfers of its property not disclosed in earlier responses to questions in Official Form 7 that were out of the ordinary course of the debtor's business or financial affairs and were made within the past year. Transfer is broadly defined in Section 101 of the Bankruptcy Code and includes the granting of a security interest or statutory or judicial lien as well as absolute transfers such as a sale. If there were any such transfers, the debtor must list the name and address of the transferee, its relationship to the debtor if any, the date of the transfer, and a description of the property transferred and its value.

Question 11   Question 11 asks the debtor to list all bank and other financial accounts and instruments (such as certificates of deposit) held by or for the benefit of the debtor and that were closed, sold, or otherwise transferred within the year before the commencement of the bankruptcy case. For each such event, the debtor must provide the name and address of the financial institution, the type of account, the account number, the balance in the account when it was closed or sold, and the date of the sale or closing.

Question 12   If the debtor has or had within the past year any safe deposit boxes in which it had securities, cash, or other valuables, question 12 requires the debtor to provide the name and address of the bank, the names and addresses of all persons who had access to the box, a description of its contents, and, if the box has been transferred or surrendered, the date the transfer or surrender occurred.

Question 13   Question 13 concerns setoffs, which are the application of a debt owed to the debtor against a debt owed by the debtor. Setoffs have the potential of being preferences. As a result, question 13 asks that any setoffs made by a creditor against a debt or deposit of the debtor within 90 days before the commencement of the bankruptcy case be listed by name and address of creditor, date of setoff, and amount of setoff. Married debtors filing under Chapter 12 or 13 must include information concerning either or both spouses, whether or not a joint petition is filed, unless the spouses are separated and a joint petition is not filed.

Question 14   When liquidating the property of the estate, the trustee will want to ensure that nothing is sold that does not belong to the estate. To help guard against this, question 14 requires a listing of all property the debtor holds for another person. These may be goods that were sold but not yet delivered, items stored at the debtor's business premises, and the like. To respond to question 14, the debtor must identify the name and address of the owner, a description of the goods and their value, and the location of the goods.

Question 15   If the debtor has moved within the past two years, all former addresses and dates of occupancy should be listed in question 15.

Question 16   Question 16 calls for a debtor who resides, or has resided, in a community property state, commonwealth, or territory within the six-year period immediately preceding the commencement of the case, to give the name of the debtor's spouse and any former spouse who resides or resided with the debtor in the community property state.

Question 17   Question 17 is a three-part question asking the debtor for environmental information. Subpart (a) asks for the name and address of every site for which the debtor received a notice in writing of potential liability or violation of environmental law. The debtor must provide the site name and address, the name and address of the governmental unit providing the notice, the date of the notice, and the environmental law being cited.

Subpart (b) asks for the name and address of every site the debtor provided notice to a governmental unit of a release of hazardous material. The debtor must provide the site name and location, the name and address of the governmental unit to whom notice was given, along with the date of the notice, and the environmental law impacted.

Subpart (c) asks for all judicial or administrative proceedings, including settlements or orders, under any environmental law, to which the debtor was a party. The debtor must provide the name and address of the governmental unit that was a party to the proceeding, the docket number, along with the status or disposition of the case.

Question 18   Question 18 requires a listing of the nature, location, and name of the debtor's business, including all names used in the past two years. Other required information includes the dates the business commenced and terminated, if it has in fact been terminated.

Question 19   The four subparts of question 19 focus on who has kept the debtor's books and records. The first subpart asks for a list of all bookkeepers and accountants who within the previous two years kept or supervised the keeping of the debtor's books and records. Names, addresses, and pertinent periods of time should be provided for such in-house personnel. Subpart (b) asks for the identity of any persons who audited the books and records or prepared a financial statement during the previous two years. This may be an outside accountant. If no audits have been performed, check none. If there have been audits, the dates of the audits are required. For subpart (c), the current location of the books and records should be indicated. Also, if any portion of the books and records is unavailable, an explanation (such as that they have been destroyed) should be inserted.

The last subpart concerns the debtor's financial statements issued within the previous two years. If any financial statements have been issued in that period, the dates they were issued and the names and addresses of those to whom they were issued must be listed. Typically, the debtor will issue financial statements to secured creditors, Dunn & Bradstreet, trade associations, prospective investors, and others.

Question 20   Question 20 is a two-part question involving inventories. In subpart (a), the debtor must describe the past two physical counts of its goods, name the person who supervised the counts, if any such counts have been performed, and disclose the dollar amount and basis of each inventory. In subpart (b), the debtor must give the name and address of the person having possession of the records of each of the two inventories reported, and the date of each inventory.

Questions 21–25   Questions 21–25 request certain information from debtors who are partnerships or corporations. Question 21(a) asks partnership debtors to list the nature and percentage of partnership interest of each member of the partnership. Specifically, the debtor must provide the name and address of each partner, the nature of their interest, and the percentage of their interest.

Subpart (b) applies to debtors that are corporations. The debtor must provide the name, address, title, and percentage of stockholders who directly or indirectly own, control, or hold five percent or more of the voting or equity securities of the corporation.

Question 22 requires the identification, along with address and date of withdrawal or termination, of any partner, officer, or director whose relationship with the partnership or corporation ended within one year immediately preceding the commencement of the case.

Question 23 requires disclosures of all withdrawals and/or distributions created or given to an insider during the year immediately preceding the commencement of the case. Such withdrawals or distributions include compensation in any form, bonuses, loans, and stock redemptions.

Question 24 calls for a corporate debtor to give the name and federal taxpayer ID number of the parent corporation of any consolidated group of which the debtor has been a member within the six-year period immediately preceding the commencement of the case.

Finally, Question 25 asks any non-individual debtor to list the name and federal taxpayer ID number of any pension fund to which the debtor, as an employer, contributed at any time within the six-year period immediately preceding the commencement of the case.

The statement of financial affairs concludes with a declaration that is virtually identical to the declaration at the end of the schedules.

The Master Mailing List

Bankruptcy Code Section 342 and Bankruptcy Rule 2002(f) require the clerk of the bankruptcy court to give notice of the order for relief to all creditors and the **indenture trustee** (typically a financial institution that is the trustee for holders of bonds or notes issued by the debtor). Bankruptcy Rule 2002(f) also requires that the notice be sent to the debtor although, except in an involuntary case, notice to the debtor that it has commenced a bankruptcy case would seem unnecessary. There are other parties who should receive notice of the pendency of a bankruptcy case even though they are not creditors. For example, even if the debtor is current in paying taxes, the taxing agencies should be notified. All regulatory agencies, such as the Securities and Exchange Commission, if the debtor is a corporation, or the Federal Aviation Agency, if the debtor is an airline, should be notified. How is the clerk of the court to provide such notice?

Bankruptcy Rule 1007 requires the debtor to accompany the petition with a list of creditors unless the petition is accompanied by the schedules. The clerk could then make a mailing from the list of creditors or the schedules; however, there are two problems with the clerk doing so. First, as just discussed, a list of creditors would leave out some parties who should get notice. Second, although using the list of creditors may be acceptable in a small case, for the clerk to prepare mailing labels from a creditor list in a large case would be very labor intensive, time consuming, and simply too unreasonable to expect. The solution that has been developed is to require the debtor to submit along with the petition a list of parties who should receive notice. This list must be in a form that the clerk can use to make mailing labels. In many jurisdictions, this list is called the master mailing list and is a matrix of 33 squares, with one name and address to be typed into each square. A sample matrix form is shown in Exhibit 7.17. In other jurisdictions, local rules may require the debtor to file coded cards, a computer-readable tape or

✦ indenture trustee
A trustee appointed under a mortgage, deed or trust, or other document under which there is a debt against or interest in the debtor.

Exhibit 7.17 ✦ *Sample Matrix for Master Mailing List*

ABE'S OFFICE SUPPLY 19640 7th Street Santa Monica, CA 91202	ACE TRUCKING 58 W. Post Road St. Paul, MN 55164	B & O FINANCE COMPANY 456 Harass Drive Princeton, NJ 08890
BEN'S MAINTENANCE 6123 Hollywood Blvd. Hollywood, CA 90027	BIG BANK 4 Wheel Drive Los Angeles, CA 90017	JOSEPH BUSINESSMAN 12462 Highland Street Beverly Hills, CA 90033
CALIFORNIA STATE BOARD OF EQUALIZATION 12 Hill Street Sacramento, CA 95606	GERALD CAMERAMAN 1901 Exposition Blvd. Los Angeles, CA 90044	DIAMOND RADIATOR P.O. Box 70005 Chino, CA 92113
G & P HONEYMOONERS P.O. Box 482 Lake Isabella, CA 90068	GIGGIE, INC. 1643 Ocean Blvd. Miami, FL 06067	GREAT FILM, INC. 84 Steel Plate Drive City of Industry, CA 90002
IMPERIAL PROCESSING 1000 Milan Way Denver, CO 60606	INTERNAL REVENUE SERVICE 300 N. Los Angeles St. Los Angeles, CA 90015	JUNE FILM CO. 1223 Via Beach Blvd. San Diego, CA 90666
BANKRUPT C. LAWYER, ESQ. White Charger Legal Clinic One Learned Way Los Angeles, CA 90001	M & M GAS COMPANY 155 Flower St. West Covina, CA 98002	VIDEOS BY JOE, INC. 1223 Hollywood Blvd. Hollywood, CA 90027

diskette in a particular format, or mailing labels of some sort. The local rules of each jurisdiction must be consulted for the precise requirements. Whatever the format, a copy should be kept for the debtor's use in mailing notices.

It is helpful to alphabetize the names of at least the unsecured creditors. It will then be much easier to check later to confirm that these creditors received notice. It is also a good idea to leave the three squares along the top blank. Since the matrix may be placed in a file folder with a two-hole top clip, the holes might destroy some of the entries.

ETHICAL CONSIDERATIONS

As you learned in the beginning of this chapter, there are certain limitations on filing a bankruptcy case. Congress has placed limitations on cases it views as abusing the bankruptcy process. Some persons, while technically qualified to be debtors under Section 109(a), are precluded from seeking the protection it offers.

If a client seeks bankruptcy protection but falls within the preclusions specified by Congress, bringing the case to bankruptcy court may well be viewed as bringing a frivolous claim. If, while filling out bankruptcy forms on behalf of a client, a paralegal comes to believe that the client falls within this precluded class of claimants, the paralegal has a responsibility to inform the supervising attorney.

SUMMARY

The first step in beginning a bankruptcy case is determining under which chapters the debtor is eligible. Not all persons can file each type of reorganization, and some companies cannot file bankruptcy cases at all. The debtor must also elect the most appropriate chapter among those for which it may be eligible. There is an emphasis to steer consumer debtors toward a Chapter 13 reorganization and away from a Chapter 7 liquidation. Attorneys must certify that they have explained the different bankruptcy chapters to a debtor, and that the debtor understands the options available to it. If a Chapter 7 case is filed that is a "substantial abuse," the court may dismiss the case.

There is a great amount of information that must be obtained from the debtor before a bankruptcy case is filed and the first few weeks after it is filed. A list of the needed information should be made. Another list of all of the documents that must be prepared should also be made.

The pleading that commences a bankruptcy case is called a petition. It is a two-sided document that asks very basic information about the debtor. If the debtor is a corporation, Exhibit A must be attached to the petition. If the debtor is a consumer, Exhibit B to the petition must be completed. Schedule C is filed if the debtor has possession of property that poses or is alleged to pose a threat of imminent and identifiable harm to the public health or safety. In most cases, the following documents must be filed with the petition or within a short time period: a list of all creditors; a list of all equity interest holders, an attorney's statement, and a bankruptcy petition preparer's statement. The debtor in a Chapter 9 municipality case or in a Chapter 11 case must also file a list of the 20 largest unsecured creditors. A Chapter 7 debtor who is an individual with consumer secured debts must file a Statement of Intentions.

Each debtor must file, within 15 days after the petition, schedules showing various information including its assets and liabilities. These schedules are Official Form 6 and are numbered Schedule A through J plus a summary page. Schedules A and B are for the debtor's real and personal property. Schedule C is the claimed exemptions. Schedules D, E, and F show the debtor's secured, unsecured priority, and unsecured nonpriority debts, respectively. Schedule G is a list of the debtor's executory contracts and unexpired leases. Schedule H is a list of the debtor's obligations in which someone else is also liable. Schedule I is information on the debtor's current income, and Schedule J is information on the debtor's current expenditures.

Each debtor must also file a statement of financial affairs, which is Official Form 7. There are 25 questions in the statement. The first 18 must be answered by all debtors. The last seven need only be answered by debtors who are or have been engaged in business. The questions require a wide range of information, including details on past income, possible preferential and fraudulent transfers, location of assets and bank accounts, and the identity of the debtor's officers, directors, and shareholders.

Local rules also require the debtor to submit a mailing list to be used to send notices to creditors. The form of the list will vary based on local practice.

✦ KEY TERMS

affiliate	contingent claim	schedules	unliquidated claim
assignment for the benefit of creditors	disputed claim	statement of financial affairs	venue
book value	domicile	substantial abuse	
	indenture trustee		

✦ IMPROVE YOUR UNDERSTANDING

1. Answer the following questions true or false.
    a. Joe Conway, a citizen of the Philippines, now lives in Houston, Texas. Joe owns real estate in Manila and in Houston. Joe is ineligible to file a bankruptcy case in Texas.
    b. Joe Conway filed a Chapter 13 bankruptcy case on October 1, 2003. First City Bank, who had a secured lien on Joe's car, immediately filed a motion for relief from the automatic stay. Prior to the hearing on the motion, Joe dismissed the Chapter 13 case. Because the bank's motion was never heard, Joe is eligible to immediately file another Chapter 13 case.
    c. Joe Conway filed a Chapter 7 bankruptcy case on October 1, 2003. When his friend told him that the trustee would be asking for the turnover of his extensive stamp collection, he did not attend the first meeting of creditors or file any of the required papers. The trustee successfully moved to dismiss the case. Since it was the trustee—and not Joe—who moved to dismiss, Joe may immediately file another bankruptcy case.
    d. Banks may file Chapter 7 cases.
    e. Joe Conway owes $800,000 to First City Bank; this loan is secured by a mortgage on his house. He also owes $100,000 to his other creditors, none of whom is secured. Joe is eligible for relief under Chapter 13 of the Bankruptcy Code.
    f. Stockbrokers are never eligible for Chapter 11 relief.
    g. Orange County, California could not have filed a Chapter 7 case.
    h. A Chapter 7 trustee may move to dismiss a case as a substantial abuse.
2. List all the additional documents and portions of the petition that must be included if the debtor is an individual with primarily consumer debts.
3. Joe's Videos Inc., a company with its headquarters at 1643 Ocean Boulevard, Miami, Dade County, Florida 06067, wants to file a Chapter 7 case. It is represented by your employer, Bankrupt C. Lawyer, who instructs you to prepare the petition. Draft as much of the petition as you can. Also draft a letter to the company requesting the additional information you need.

Use the following fact situation in answering Exercises 4 and 5.

Wildcat River Partners, a limited partnership organized under the laws of the state of Texas, has as its sole asset an apartment complex in Detroit, Michigan. Its office is located with its general partner in Los Angeles, California.

4. Could Wildcat River Partners file its bankruptcy case in Texas, Michigan, or California?
5. Sixteen other limited partnerships with the same general partner as Wildcat River Partners have bankruptcy cases pending in Los Angeles. List the benefits and detriments to Wildcat and its creditors in having the case pending in the various possible locations.
6. If a secured creditor's collateral is worth less than the amount owed, could the secured creditor be included on the list of the 20 largest unsecured creditors?
7. Can a partnership pay a filing fee in installments?
8. When must the schedules be filed?
9. If, two weeks after the case was commenced, the debtor inherited $100,000, would the money be disclosed in the schedules? What if the debtor immediately spent it?
10. Give two examples (other than the ones in this book) of contingent claims and unliquidated claims.
11. Brad Stockman is owed the following from his employer, who filed a Chapter 11 petition on October 1, 2003.

Commissions: May 2003	$500
Commissions: July, August, and September 2003	$2,500
Wages: March 2003	$2,500
Expense Reimbursement: September 2003	$200

    In addition, Brad owes his employer for an advance he received at Christmas, 2002, of $1,000.00. Where and in what amounts should Brad and his employer's claims be scheduled in the bankruptcy case of the employer?
12. Is a business owner entitled to a priority claim for prepaid pest control services?
13. If a secured creditor did not perfect its security interest prior to the filing of the bankruptcy petition, should it be included in Schedule D or Schedule F?
14. Where on Schedule B should the following assets be disclosed?
    a. Savings bonds.
    b. Interests in a mutual fund.
    c. Antique gun collection.
    d. Computers that are used by the debtor in its business.
    e. Computers that are sold by a business.
    f. Insurance proceeds for a building that burned down.
    g. The value of the debtor's franchise rights.
    h. A kayak.

✦ DRAFTING PROJECT

1. Prepare a fact sheet that could be given to consumer debtors who are trying to decide between Chapter 7 or Chapter 13. Organize it by benefits of Chapter 7 and benefits of Chapter 13.
2. Prepare a list of information needed to commence a case for a potential debtor, a limited partnership engaged in raising cattle.
3. The debtor informs you that it has litigation pending against it in another state. The debtor is not sure of the status of that litigation. Draft a letter to the attorney representing the debtor in that litigation asking for the information required by question 4(a) of Official Form 7.

Chapter 7: The Debtor's Perspective

DISCHARGE

Discharge in General

For most consumers, the primary reason for commencing a Chapter 7 bankruptcy case is to take advantage of the discharge of debts provision of Section 727. Generally speaking, a discharge bars any collection action against the debtor for debts incurred prepetition. Although a theme of bankruptcy law is to fiercely protect the right to a discharge, in certain circumstances, the debtor will lose the discharge, all debts will remain enforceable, and the benefits of the Chapter 7 case will vanish. How a debtor could lose the right to a discharge is the subject of this section.

Even if the debtor preserves the right to a discharge, not all of the debtor's debts will vanish. Certain types of obligations are always enforceable despite the completion of a bankruptcy case. For other debts, if the creditor can prove certain things, that creditor's debt will remain enforceable. Those instances are discussed in the next section.

Loss of a Discharge

The discharge is the payoff the debtor receives for turning over all nonexempt assets to the trustee and living up to other duties and responsibilities. By engaging in what can be described as improper and/or illegal acts, the debtor may be denied that payoff and not receive a discharge. Bankruptcy Code Section 727 lists the following improper and/or illegal acts of the debtor that may result in the loss of a discharge:

- ✦ The debtor transferred, destroyed, or concealed property within one year prepetition or property of the estate postpetition with the intent to defraud a creditor or the trustee.
- ✦ The debtor unjustifiably concealed, destroyed, falsified, or failed to keep or preserve the books and records necessary to determine the debtor's financial condition or business transactions.
- ✦ In connection with the bankruptcy case, the debtor knowingly and fraudulently made a false oath; presented a false claim; gave, offered, received, or attempted to obtain money, property or advantage for acting or forebearing to act; or withheld from the trustee books and records related to the debtor's property or financial affairs.
- ✦ The debtor failed to satisfactorily explain any loss of assets.
- ✦ The debtor refused to obey an order of the court.

This loss of discharge may even result from improper and/or illegal acts committed in connection with another case, before the debtor's case was ever filed. If the debtor commits such acts within one year before or after the bankruptcy case of an insider such as a relative or a controlled company, this may be cause for preventing the debtor from receiving a discharge. For example, suppose that before filing for bankruptcy, the debtor was the sole shareholder of a corporation, and that in that corporation's bankruptcy case, the debtor falsely informs the trustee that the corporation has no assets. The debtor may lose the right to a discharge in his or her own bankruptcy case.

Other ways a debtor can be deprived of a discharge that do not relate to the commission of an improper and/or illegal act are also set out in Section 727. The first way is if the debtor is not an individual. As a matter of bankruptcy law, only individuals are entitled to a discharge. As a practical matter, however, if a corporation filed a Chapter 7 petition and the trustee liquidates and distributes all the assets, there is nothing left for creditors to look to for payment of their nondischarged claims. A debtor is also not entitled to a discharge if the debtor received a discharge in a Chapter 7 or Chapter 11 case commenced within six years of the pending case or was the debtor in a Chapter 13 case commenced within six years of the pending case in which the unsecured creditors were not paid in full or did not receive at least 70 percent and that payment was the debtor's best efforts. In other words, a debtor is entitled to a discharge only once every six years.

Procedure

Before a debtor will lose the discharge, there must be a court hearing commenced by the trustee, a creditor, or the United States trustee. Among the duties of the trustee listed in Section 704 of the Bankruptcy Code is the duty to oppose the discharge of the debtor if advisable. If a creditor does not want to go to the trouble or expense of bringing a discharge action, the creditor can request that the court order the trustee to determine whether a ground exists for denying the debtor a discharge.

Although Bankruptcy Code Section 727(c)(1) refers to an objection, Bankruptcy Rule 4004 dictates that opposition to a debtor's discharge must be done by the filing of a complaint no later than 60 days after the Section 341(a) meeting of creditors. This is a very important deadline, and a creditor should schedule the meeting as soon as the creditor learns of the case. The 60-day time period may be extended, but cause must be shown and the extension must be obtained before the 60-day period runs. A proceeding commenced by the filing of a complaint objecting to a discharge (see Exhibit 8.1) is governed by Part VII of the Bankruptcy Rules; it is an adversary proceeding. The procedures for adversary proceedings were discussed in Chapter 6 of this book.

Revocation of a Discharge Already Granted

The debtor may have obtained a discharge prior to the commitment of improper and/or illegal acts or before those acts were discovered. Bankruptcy Code Section 727(d) allows a creditor, the trustee, or the United States trustee to seek to revoke a discharge if one of the following occurred:

- ✦ The discharge was obtained through the fraud of the debtor—the creditor or the trustee did not know of the fraud at the time the discharge was granted.
- ✦ The debtor acquired, or became entitled to acquire, property of the estate and knowingly and fraudulently failed to report it or deliver the property to the trustee.

EXHIBIT 8.1 ✦ *Sample Pleading*

GEORGE G. PORTER
Four Wheel Drive
Los Angeles, California 90017

Attorneys for First City Bank

**UNITED STATES BANKRUPTCY COURT
WESTERN DISTRICT OF CALIFORNIA**

In re	)	Case No. 03-00003-JF
	)	
JOSEPH BUSINESSMAN,	)	Chapter 7
	)	
Debtor's Address:	)	
18 Hollywood Drive	)	
Los Angeles, CA 90001	)	
	)	
Debtor's S.S. No. 559-15-1402	)	
_____	)	
	)	
FIRST CITY BANK,	)	Adv. No. 03-00003-JF
	)	
Plaintiff,	)	COMPLAINT OBJECTING TO
	)	DISCHARGE OF DEBTOR
v.	)	
	)	
JOSEPH BUSINESSMAN,	)	
	)	
Defendant,	)	
_____	)	

First City Bank (the "Bank") complains and alleges as follows:

PARTIES

1. Defendant Joseph Businessman ("Debtor") is the debtor in the above-captioned case having filed a petition for relief under Chapter 7 of Title 11, United States Code (the "Bankruptcy Code") on October 1, 2003.

2. The Bank is the holder of an unsecured claim against Debtor in the amount of $50,000.00.

JURISDICTION AND VENUE

3. This action objecting to Debtor's discharge is an adversary proceeding over which this Court has jurisdiction pursuant to 28 U.S.C. §§ 157 and 1334 and the Order of the Chief Judge of the United States District Court, Western District of California, referring bankruptcy cases and proceedings, entered on July 20, 1992. This adversary proceeding is a core matter pursuant to 28 U.S.C. § 157(b)(2)(J), and the Bank consents to the entry of a final order or judgment by the Bankruptcy Court.

4. Venue over this adversary proceeding properly resides in the United States Bankruptcy Court for the Western District of California pursuant to 28 U.S.C. § 1409(a) in that this adversary proceeding is related to *In re Joseph Businessman*, Case No. 95-00003-JF, pending as a Chapter 7 case in the United States Bankruptcy Court for the Western District of California.

—*CONTINUED*

✦ The debtor committed one of the improper and/or illegal acts described in the previous section after the discharge was granted.

The request for revocation, which is done by the filing of a complaint, must be brought before the later of one year after the granting of the discharge or the date

EXHIBIT 8.1 ✦ *Sample Pleading* (CONTINUED)

FACTUAL ALLEGATIONS

5. Since in or about 1997 until on or about September 1, 2003, Debtor operated a videotape store under the name of Videos by Joe. On or about September 1, 2003 Debtor transferred the assets of Videos by Joe to Videos by Joe, Inc., a newly formed corporation, the President and sole shareholder of which is Maximillion Businessman, Debtor's six-year-old son.

6. The transfer described in the immediately proceeding paragraph was for less than reasonably equivalent value.

FIRST CLAIM FOR RELIEF

7. The Bank incorporates by this reference the allegations contained in paragraph 5 and 6.

8. The transfer described in paragraph 5 was made with the intent to hinder, delay, or defraud the Bank and constitutes a transfer of Debtor's property within one year before the date of the filing of the petition.

SECOND CLAIM FOR RELIEF

9. The Bank incorporates by this reference the allegations contained in paragraphs 5 and 6.

10. Debtor knowingly and fraudulently made a false oath or account in connection with his bankruptcy case by failing to reveal the transfer of property described in paragraph 5 in his Statement of Financial Affairs filed on October 15, 1995.

THIRD CLAIM FOR RELIEF

11. The Bank incorporates by this reference the allegations contained in paragraph 5 and 6.

12. Debtor concealed, destroyed, mutilated, falsified, or failed to keep or preserve any recorded information, including books, documents, records, and papers, from which the transfer described in paragraph 5 might be ascertained.

WHEREFORE the Bank requests that the Court enter judgment as follows:

1. That Debtor be denied a discharge;

2. For the Bank's cost incurred in this suit and reasonable attorneys' fees;

3. For such other and further relief to which the Bank may be entitled.

DATED: October 15, 2003

PORTER & PORTER

_____

GEORGE G. PORTER
Attorneys for First City Bank

the case is closed, unless the discharge was obtained by fraud, in which case the complaint must be filed within one year after the discharge was granted.

Dismissal of a Discharge Action

Bankruptcy Rule 4005 provides that the burden of proof of an objection to discharge is on the plaintiff (the nondebtor party). Because these types of actions should not be brought lightly, Bankruptcy Rule 7041 provides that a complaint objecting to discharge may not be dismissed on the plaintiff's request alone. There must be notice, and it may be dismissed only on terms and conditions that the court deems proper. A condition may be the payment of the debtor's attorneys' fees in defending the complaint.

DISCHARGEABILITY

It is very hard to deprive a debtor of a discharge. There are, however, times when a creditor can achieve the same result or an even better result by just having that creditor's particular claim declared *nondischargeable*. The creditor then will receive a distribution on its claim from the trustee from the proceeds of liquidation of the estate's assets and will be free to pursue the debtor for the balance from new or exempt assets after the bankruptcy case is closed.

There are two types of nondischargeable claims. The first are those claims Congress has determined should always be binding obligations notwithstanding the filing of a bankruptcy case. The second are those claims that stem from acts that are not as severe as the ones listed in Section 727. For the first type—those claims that are always nondischargeable—the creditor need do nothing to preserve its rights. For the claims based on improper and/or illegal acts, the creditor must seek a bankruptcy court judgment declaring the debt nondischargeable. How that declaration is obtained will be discussed shortly.

Claims That Are Always Nondischargeable

Section 523 of the Bankruptcy Code provides that the following types of claims will survive and be binding on a Chapter 7 debtor despite a discharge:

- ✦ Taxes or custom duties recently incurred or with respect to which the debtor made a fraudulent return or willfully attempted to evade or defeat the tax.
- ✦ Unscheduled debts where the creditor did not have actual knowledge of the bankruptcy case in time to file a proof of claim or an action to contest the dischargeability of the debt.
- ✦ Alimony, maintenance, and child support.
- ✦ Student loans unless it would be an undue hardship on the debtor and the debtor's dependents to exempt the debt from discharge.
- ✦ Fines, penalties, or forfeitures payable to the government.
- ✦ Debts arising as a result of the debtor's drunk driving.
- ✦ Debts that were not discharged in a prior bankruptcy case of the debtor.
- ✦ Debts for fraud or defalcation to a depository institution (a bank, savings and loan, or credit union).
- ✦ Debts for reckless or malicious failure to fulfill a capital maintenance agreement to a depository institution.
- ✦ Debts for money borrowed to pay a nondischargeable tax.
- ✦ Debts for postpetition condominium fees or assessments for a condominium in which the debtor resided or rented to a paying tenant.

The creditor with one of these types of claims need not take action to preserve the nondischargeable nature of its claim. If the creditor is not completely confident that its claim is of the type listed, it may want to obtain a declaration from the court that the claim fits within the list. In addition, the debtor may want to start an action to declare a particular debt not within the scope of the exempted claims.

Claims That May Be Nondischargeable

For public policy reasons, Congress also wanted to make claims arising from the debtor's improper and/or illegal acts nondischargeable. As discussed, improper and/or illegal acts directed to creditors as a group will destroy the debtor's right to a discharge. Because those acts usually rest on factual issues, a hearing must be held to resolve any factual dispute concerning the acts. The types of claims that may be nondischargeable arise from the following improper and/or illegal acts:

✦ The debtor obtained money, property, services, or an extension, renewal, or refinancing of credit by fraud.

✦ The debtor used a materially false financial statement with the intent to deceive and upon which the creditor reasonably relied.

✦ The debtor incurred a debt to a single creditor of more than $1000 for "luxury goods or services" within 60 days of the commencement of the bankruptcy case.

✦ The debtor obtained cash advances of more than $1,150 under a consumer credit plan, such as a credit card, on or within 60 days before the commencement of the bankruptcy case.

✦ The debtor committed fraud or defalcation while acting in a fiduciary capacity, or committed embezzlement or larceny.

✦ The debtor willfully and maliciously injured another or the property of another.

✦ The debtor incurred debt in the course of a divorce or separation other than alimony and support (which are always nondischargeable) unless the debtor has no ability to pay the debts and discharging the debt would outweigh any detriment to a spouse, former spouse, or child of the debtor.

Procedures

In order to obtain a court determination of nondischargeability for the types of debts cited in Section 523, Bankruptcy Rule 4007 provides that a request must be brought by the filing of a complaint within 60 days following the first date set for the Section 341(a) meeting of creditors. (See Exhibit 8.2.) The courts are very strict about the 60-day time limit and will extend this limit only if the extension is obtained before the end of the 60-day period. The litigation commenced by the filing of the complaint is governed by Part VII of the Bankruptcy Rules, which concerns adversary proceedings. They have already been covered in Chapter 6 of this book.

In order to discourage baseless dischargeability litigation that a debtor may not be able to afford to defend, if a creditor seeks to have certain consumer debts held dischargeable (such as debts allegedly incurred through fraud or procured on the eve of bankruptcy), and the creditor loses that lawsuit, under Section 523(d) the court must grant the debtor reimbursement of costs and attorneys' fees from the creditor if the court finds the creditor's position was not substantially justified. The court may make an exception if special circumstances would make such an award unjust.

REAFFIRMATIONS

As discussed, once a debtor has been granted a discharge, unsecured prepetition debts and any deficiency suffered by a secured creditor do not have to be paid. However, Bankruptcy Code Section 524(f) provides that a debtor may voluntarily repay one or more of those debts even if a discharge has already been granted. A debtor may want to repay a debt out of a moral obligation, or because a secured creditor may seek relief from the stay and repossess its collateral otherwise, or for many other reasons. Yet a debtor's repayment of a discharged debt is enforceable only when the debtor has made an official **reaffirmation** of the debt. For example, Joe Consumer may decide to repay a prepetition loan of $10 from his friend Al even though Joe has received his discharge. This does not mean that Al may now

✦ **reaffirmation**
The act of agreeing to remain liable on a claim despite a discharge.

EXHIBIT 8.2 ✦ *Sample Pleading*

GEORGE G. PORTER
PORTER & PORTER
Four Wheel Drive
Los Angeles, California 90017

Attorneys for First City Bank

**UNITED STATES BANKRUPTCY COURT
WESTERN DISTRICT OF CALIFORNIA**

In re	)	Case No. 03-00003-JF
	)	
JOSEPH BUSINESSMAN,	)	Chapter 7
	)	
Debtor's Address:	)	
18 Hollywood Drive	)	
Los Angeles, CA 90001	)	
	)	
Debtor's S.S. No. 559-15-1402	)	
_____	)	
	)	
FIRST CITY BANK,	)	Adv. No. 03-00003-JF
	)	
Plaintiff,	)	COMPLAINT TO DETERMINE
	)	DISCHARGEABILITY FOR:
v.	)	1. FALSE PRETENSES, FALSE
	)	REPRESENTATIONS, AND
JOSEPH BUSINESSMAN,	)	ACTUAL FRAUD; AND
	)	
Defendants.	)	2. FALSE STATEMENT RESPECTING
	)	FINANCIAL CONDITION
_____	)	

First City Bank (the "Bank") complains and alleges as follows:

PARTIES

1. Defendant Joseph Businessman ("Debtor") is the debtor in the above-captioned case having filed a petition for relief under Chapter 7 of Title 11, United States Code (the "Bankruptcy Code") on October 1, 2003.

2. The Bank is the holder of an unsecured claim against Debtor in the amount of $50,000.00.

JURISDICTION AND VENUE

3. This action to determine the dischargeability of the Bank's claim is an adversary proceeding over which this Court has jurisdiction pursuant to 28 U.S.C. §§ 157 and 1334 and the Order of the Chief Judge of the United States District Court, Western District of California, referring bankruptcy cases and proceedings, entered on July 20, 1984. This adversary proceeding is a core matter pursuant to 28 U.S.C. § 157(b)(2)(I), and the Bank consents to the entry of a final order or judgment by the Bankruptcy Court.

4. Venue over this adversary proceeding properly resides in the United States Bankruptcy Court for the Western District of California pursuant to 28 U.S.C. § 1409(a) in that this adversary proceeding is related to *In re Joseph Businessman*, Case No. 03-00003-JF, pending as a Chapter 7 case in the United States Bankruptcy Court for the Western District of California.

—*CONTINUED*

EXHIBIT 8.2 ✦ *Sample Pleading* (CONTINUED)

FACTUAL ALLEGATIONS

5. On or about September 1, 2002, the Bank and Debtor executed a Security Agreement, a complete and accurate copy of which is attached hereto as Exhibit 1 and incorporated herein by this reference. Under the provisions of the Security Agreement, the Bank lent to Debtor $50,000 (the "Loan").

6. In order to secure repayment of the Loan, Debtor executed three (3) deeds of trust on parcels of real property (the "Property") with the Bank as beneficiary.

7. As of October 1, 2003, Debtor was indebted to the Bank in the sum of $50,000.00 as a result of the Loan. No portion of the Loan has been paid.

FIRST CLAIM FOR RELIEF
[11 U.S.C. § 523(a)(2)(A)]

8. The Bank incorporates by reference the allegations set forth in paragraphs 5 through 7.

9. The Bank made the Loan to Debtor based upon the value of the Property.

10. During 2002, Debtor orally, falsely, and fraudulently overstated to the Bank the value of the Property.

11. Debtor's representations were false and they were then and thereafter known by Debtor to be false. In fact and truth, Debtor did not own the Property as Debtor represented.

12. The Bank believed and relied on Debtor's representations; based upon Debtor's representations, the Bank made the Loan to Debtor.

SECOND CLAIM FOR RELIEF
[11 U.S.C. § 523(a)(2)(B)]

13. The Bank incorporates by reference the allegations set forth in paragraphs 5 through 7.

14. The Loan to Debtor was obtained by use of written statements respecting the Debtor's financial condition (the "Statements") which Debtor delivered to the Bank with the intent to deceive.

15. The Statements were materially false in that Debtor represented to the Bank that the Property was owned by Debtor, thereby overstating Debtor's value.

16. Debtor made the Statements for the purpose of inducing the Bank to make the Loan to Debtor.

17. Debtor knew the Statements were false when they were made and made the Statements with the intent to cause reliance by the Bank and to induce the Bank to make the Loan.

18. The Bank was unaware of the falsity of the information provided by Debtor, believed and relied on the Statements, and was thereby induced to make the Loan to Debtor. The Bank's reliance on the Statements was justified due to Debtor's superior knowledge of the Property. If not for the Statements by Debtor, the Bank would not have made the Loan.

WHEREFORE, the Bank requests that the Court enter judgment as follows:

1. That the Court determine that the Bank's claim in the amount of $50,000.00 is nondischargeable;

2. That the Bank have judgment against Debtor for the sum of $50,000.00, together with interest as provided for in the Security Agreement;

3. For the Bank's costs including reasonable attorney's fees incurred in this suit; and

4. For such other and further relief to which the Bank may be entitled.

DATED: October 15, 2003

PORTER & PORTER

_____
GEORGE G. PORTER
Attorneys for First City Bank

automatically go to court and force Joe to pay. Al and Joe must have first fully complied with the steps provided in Bankruptcy Code Sections 524(c) and (d) and Bankruptcy Rule 4008.

Bankruptcy Code Section 524(c) and Bankruptcy Rule 4008 state that to reaffirm a prepetition debt, the debtor and the creditor must enter into a written agreement in which the debtor reaffirms the debt. (See Exhibit 8.3.) The debtor must also make a motion seeking the agreement's approval and file it with the court before receiving a discharge.

If the debtor has been represented by an attorney while negotiating the reaffirmation agreement, the attorney must file a declaration or affidavit stating that the debtor is fully informed of the consequences and legal effect of the reaffirmation, that it is voluntarily done, and that it will not impose an undue hardship on the debtor or his or her dependents. The attorney will want to explain the consequences of the reaffirmation agreement very carefully to the debtor, ensure that the creditor has not coerced the debtor in any way, and inquire whether the debtor's income is sufficient to repay the reaffirmed debt.

If the debtor was not represented by a lawyer during the negotiation of the reaffirmation agreement, the court must find that the agreement does not impose an undue hardship and is in the debtor's best interest before approving it. The court will also inform the debtor at the discharge hearing of the legal consequences of entering into the reaffirmation agreement.

Even if the debtor successfully performs all the steps necessary to reaffirm and the agreement is approved by the court, the debtor may rescind the agreement at any time within 60 days of the discharge or the filing of the reaffirmation agreement, whichever was earlier. The Bankruptcy Code requires the reaffirmation agreement to contain a "clear and conspicuous" statement to this effect. "Clear" means stated in plain, easily understandable language. "Conspicuous" means capital or bold letters, underlining, or the like. To rescind, the debtor merely gives notice to the creditor.

As a practical matter, creditors with a large volume of consumer customers will frequently send debtors a reaffirmation agreement upon receiving notice of the bankruptcy case. The creditor may have developed a form agreement and motion with blanks for the pertinent information. Procedural Form B 240, which is a combination reaffirmation agreement, attorney's and debtor's declaration, motion for approval of the agreement, and order can also be used.

EXEMPTIONS

As mentioned earlier, one of the purposes of bankruptcy is to allow an individual debtor a fresh start, a chance to put financial problems in the past. Congress and the state governments have always determined that in order to make that fresh start, an individual debtor needs to retain certain ordinary possessions. Weighing between what was fair for a debtor to keep and what would be unfair to creditors, Congress and the state legislatures developed a list of *exemptions:* categories and limits on assets a debtor will be able to retain despite being in bankruptcy. The congressionally created exemptions are listed in Section 522(d) of the Bankruptcy Code and are highlighted in Exhibit 8.4.

Congress created the exemptions listed in Exhibit 8.4 by balancing the different interests of creditors and debtors. They reflect nationwide values. Yet the purpose behind a particular exemption may not be served if the amount allowed for an exemption is too low in a particular state. For example, the federal homestead exemption is designed to ensure that the debtor has a place to live. A $17,425 exemption of the debtor's interest in a residence may be more than sufficient to

---

EXHIBIT 8.3 ✦ *Sample Pleading*

BANKRUPT C. LAWYER
WHITE CHARGER LEGAL CLINIC
One Learned Way
Los Angeles, California 90001

Attorneys for Debtor

**UNITED STATES BANKRUPTCY COURT
WESTERN DISTRICT OF CALIFORNIA**

In re	)	Case No. 03-00003-JF
	)	
JOSEPH CONSUMER,	)	Chapter 7
	)	
Debtor's Address:	)	
18 Hollywood Drive	)	MOTION FOR APPROVAL OF
Los Angeles, CA 90001	)	REAFFIRMATION AGREEMENT;
	)	DECLARATION OF BANKRUPT C.
Debtor's S.S. No. 559-15-1402	)	LAWYER IN SUPPORT THEREOF
	)	

TO THE HONORABLE JUSTIN FAIR, UNITED STATES BANKRUPTCY JUDGE:

Joseph Consumer ("Debtor"), through his attorney, in support of this Motion for Approval of Reaffirmation Agreement, respectfully represents as follows:

1. Debtor and B & B Stereo Company, a creditor of Debtor ("Creditor"), have entered into a Reaffirmation Agreement, a complete and accurate copy of which is attached to this Motion (the "Agreement").

2. The Agreement does not impose any undue hardship on Debtor or the dependents of Debtor and is in the best interest of Debtor.

WHEREFORE, Debtor requests that the Court enter its Order approving the Agreement.

DATED: November 15, 2003

WHITE CHARGER LEGAL CLINIC

BANKRUPT C. LAWYER
Attorneys for Debtor

Reaffirmation Agreement

This Agreement is entered into by and between Joseph Consumer ("Debtor") and B & B Stereo Company ("Creditor") as of November 15, 2003, and is based on the following facts:

1. On or about February 1, 2003, Debtor made, executed and delivered his written Promissory Note to Creditor in the original principal sum of $5,000 (the "Note").

2. Payment of the Note was guaranteed by Flora Consumer.

3. On October 1, 2003, Debtor filed a voluntary petition under Chapter 7 of Title 11, United States Code [11 U.S.C. § 101 *et seq.*]

4. At the time Debtor commenced his bankruptcy case, there remained the sum of $4,000 due and owing under the Note.

—CONTINUED

EXHIBIT 8.3 ✦ *Sample Pleading* (CONTINUED)

In consideration of Debtor's obligations under the Note and in order to induce Creditor to forbear from any legal action on the guarantee of the Note, it is mutually agreed, subject to Court approval of this Reaffirmation Agreement, that:

1. Debtor hereby unconditionally promises to pay Creditor the remaining principal amount of the Note plus any accrued interest and other charges properly payable under the Note by paying the sum of $100.00 per month to Creditor commencing on January 1, 2004 and continuing on the first day of every month thereafter until the Note and all other obligations of Debtor to Creditor are paid in full.

2. Debtor hereby agrees that, except as modified by this Reaffirmation Agreement, the Note and the guarantee shall remain in full force and effect; provided, however, so long as Debtor performs pursuant to the preceding paragraph, Creditor shall take no action to enforce the guarantee.

3. Debtor and Creditor hereby acknowledge and understand that this Reaffirmation Agreement will become enforceable against Debtor at the time of his discharge hearing if he is granted a discharge at that time.

4. DEBTOR UNDERSTANDS AND ACKNOWLEDGES THAT THIS REAFFIRMATION AGREEMENT IS NOT REQUIRED BY THE BANKRUPTCY CODE, NONBANKRUPTCY LAW, OR UNDER ANY AGREEMENT NOT IN ACCORDANCE WITH SECTION 524 (C) OF THE BANKRUPTCY CODE.

5. DEBTOR AND CREDITOR ACKNOWLEDGE THAT DEBTOR MAY CANCEL AND RESCIND THIS REAFFIRMATION AGREEMENT AT ANY TIME UP TO SIXTY (60) DAYS AFTER THIS REAFFIRMATION AGREEMENT IS FILED WITH THE COURT OR THE GRANTING OF ANY DISCHARGE, WHICHEVER IS LATER.

6. DEBTOR UNDERSTANDS AND ACKNOWLEDGES THAT IF HE DOES NOT CANCEL OR RESCIND THIS REAFFIRMATION AGREEMENT BEFORE THE END OF THE ABOVE-REFERENCED PERIODS, HE WILL BE BOUND BY THIS REAFFIRMATION AGREEMENT AND THE TERMS AND CONDITIONS OF THE NOTE.

7. Any cancellation or rescission of this Agreement by Debtor as set forth in paragraphs 5 and 6 hereinabove shall be in writing and delivered to Creditor at 100 Highhanded Drive, Los Angeles, California 90001.

DATED: November 15, 2003

_____

JOSEPH CONSUMER

DATED: November 15, 2003

B & B STEREO COMPANY

_____

Harlan Band
Credit Manager

Declaration of Bankrupt C. Lawyer

I, Bankrupt C. Lawyer, declare as follows:

1. I am an attorney licensed by the state of California and admitted to practice before the United States Bankruptcy Court for the Western District of California.

2. I am the attorney for Joseph Consumer, the above-captioned debtor ("Debtor"). I submit the Declaration in support of Debtor's Motion for Approval of Reaffirmation Agreement and the words defined in the Motion are used in this Declaration with the same meaning.

3. I represented Debtor during the course of negotiating the Agreement with Creditor.

—*CONTINUED*

EXHIBIT 8.3 ✦ *Sample Pleading* (CONTINUED)

4. I have fully advised Debtor of the legal effect and the consequences of the Agreement and of any default of his under the Agreement.

5. To the best of my knowledge, information, and belief, the Agreement represents a fully informed and voluntary agreement by Debtor.

6. After due inquiry, and to the best of my knowledge, information, and belief, the Agreement does not impose an undue hardship on Debtor or a dependent of Debtor.

7. I declare under penalty of perjury that the foregoing is true and correct, is of my own personal knowledge, and if called as a witness, I could and would testify competently.

Executed on November 15, 2003 at Los Angeles, California.

BANKRUPT C. LAWYER

EXHIBIT 8.4 ✦ *Exemptions under Bankruptcy Code Section 522(d)*

Exemption	Explanation
Homestead	Up to $17,425 of value in real or personal property (such as a mobile home) that the debtor or a dependent uses as a residence or intends to use as a burial plot.
Car	One motor vehicle up to $2,775 in value.
Personal effects	$450 per item up to $9,300 in total of household furnishings, households goods, clothes, animals, books, crops, and musical instruments for the personal, family, or household use of the debtor or a dependent.
Jewelry	Up to $1,150 in jewelry held primarily for the personal, family, or household use of the debtor or a dependent.
General exemption	$925 in any item plus up to $8,725 of any unused portion of the residence exemption in any property. If the debtor rents, the exemption will be $9,650 ($925 + $8725) in any asset or group of assets. This is frequently referred to as the grubstake exemption.
Tools of the trade	Up to $1,750 in implements, professional books, or tools of the trade of the debtor or a dependent.
Life insurance	An unmatured life insurance contract owned by the debtor.
Loan value of life insurance contract	Up to $9,300 in any accrued dividend, interest under, or loan value of any unmatured life insurance contract if the insured is the debtor or an individual on whom the debtor is dependent.
Health aids	Professionally prescribed health aids for the debtor or a dependent.
Benefits akin to earnings	Social Security, unemployment, public assistance, veteran's benefits, disability, or illness benefits; alimony and support to extent necessary; payments on account of disability, death, age, or length or service to the extent necessary for support.
Compensation for losses	Reparation awards to crime victims; wrongful death awards for an individual to whom the debtor was a dependent to the extent necessary for support; insurance payments for an individual to whom the debtor is a dependent to the extent necessary for support; up to $17,425 for personal bodily injury, other than pain and suffering, and actual pecuniary loss awarded to debtor or an individual on whom debtor is a dependent; and payment for loss of future earnings to the extent necessary for support.

allow a debtor who is residing in an area where land is inexpensive. A $17,425 exemption for a resident of New York City, where property values and replacement costs are very high, probably will not allow the debtor to retain the residence or purchase replacement housing. Along these same lines, some state legislatures might find it important that a debtor have 20 acres of land, regardless of whether the debtor's interest is worth $5,000 or $500,000.

So that each state might reflect what is necessary for a fresh start in that state, in Section 522(b), Congress provided that a debtor could use either state-law-created exemptions or the congressionally created exemptions unless the state had specifically provided that a debtor could not use the federal exemptions. In other words, each state could decree that a debtor filing in its state could use only the state-created exemptions. This section was commonly referred to as the **opting out** provision and has been invoked by the majority of the states.

If a husband and wife file a joint case, they are each entitled to claim a set of exemptions, but they must each choose the same set. In a state that has not opted out, one spouse cannot elect the state law exemptions while the other elects those provided in Section 522. They must both elect either the federal or the state exemptions. If they cannot agree, they will be deemed to have elected the federal exemptions.

The procedure for claiming exemptions is relatively simple. The debtor merely lists the property on Schedule C of Official Form 6. Also listed will be the statutory basis for the exemption and the value of the exempt property. A sample Schedule C is shown in Exhibit 8.5. This exhibit shows how a debtor can combine exemptions in order to maximize exemptions. The debtor's 1996 Buick Century

◆ opting out
An option granted to the states allowing them to require their residents to use the state statutory exemptions rather than those in the Bankruptcy Code.

EXHIBIT 8.5 ◆ *Schedule C*

In re Joe Consumer, Debtor.   Case No. 03-00002-JF

SCHEDULE C—PROPERTY CLAIMED AS EXEMPT

Debtor elects the exemptions to which debtor is entitled under:
(Check one box)

[×] 11 U.S.C. § 522(b)(1): Exemptions provided in 11 U.S.C. § 522(d). Note: These exemptions are available only in certain states.

[ ] 11 U.S.C. § 522(b)(2): Exemptions available under applicable nonbankruptcy federal laws, state or local law where the debtor's domicile has been located for the 180 days immediately preceding the filing of the petition, or for a longer portion of the 180-day period than in any other place, and the debtor's interest as a tenant by the entirety or joint tenant to the extent of the interest is exempt from process under applicable nonbankruptcy law.

Description of Property	Specify Law Providing Each Exemption	Value of Claimed Exemption	Current Market Value of Property Without Deducting Exemption
Debtor's Residence: 18 Hollywood Drive Los Angeles, CA 90001	11 U.S.C. § 522(d)(1)	$17,425	$240,000
1996 Buick Century	11 U.S.C. § 522(d)(2) and (5)	$3,650	$5,000
Household goods and furnishings, including audio, video and computer equipment	11 U.S.C. § 522(d)(3)	$4,500	$4,500 (No one item more than $450 in value)
Gold ring with one carat diamond inset	11 U.S.C. § 522(d)(4) and (5)	$1,150	$1,200

has a current market value of $5000. Using only the exemption in Section 522(d)(2), the debtor could claim only $2775 as an exemption. The debtor's gold ring has a value of $1200. Using only the exemption in Section 522(d)(4), the debtor can only exempt $1150 of its value.

By using the $925 general exemption of Section 522(d)(5), however, the debtor can exempt $3650 of the car's value ($2775 + $875) and the entire value of the ring ($1,150 + $50). The $925 in Section 522 (d)(5) is the only amount available under that section because the debtor is using the entire homestead exemption of Section 522 (d)(1). If the debtor were renting, however, and had no use for the homestead exemption, it could be used to completely exempt the value of the car. Schedule C, like all of the schedules, must be filed no later than 15 days after the case is commenced and can be amended later if necessary. The debtor may want to amend the schedule to include an omitted item or exclude an asset later returned to a secured creditor in order to take advantage of the exemption for a different item.

If no objection is filed to the exemptions, they are allowed. A creditor or the Chapter 7 trustee might object; for an example, see Exhibit 8.6. The property may

---

EXHIBIT 8.6 ✦ *Sample Pleading*

MILDRED PIERCE
700 Flower Street
Los Angeles, California 90001

Trustee

UNITED STATES BANKRUPTCY COURT
WESTERN DISTRICT OF CALIFORNIA

In re)	Case No. 03-00003-JF
)	
JOSEPH BUSINESSMAN and MYRA)	Chapter 7
BUSINESSWOMAN,)	
)	
Debtor's Address:)	OBJECTION TO CLAIM OF
18 Hollywood Drive)	EXEMPTIONS AND REQUEST FOR
Los Angeles, CA 90001)	HEARING
)	
Debtor's S.S. No. 559-15-1402 and)	
743-47-8459)	
)	

Mildred Pierce, the duly appointed, qualified, and acting Chapter 7 trustee in the above-captioned case (the "Trustee"), pursuant to Section 522(1) of the Bankruptcy Code and Bankruptcy Rule 4003(b), objects to the debtors' claim of exemptions and in support of this objection states as follows:

1. Debtors have claimed as exempt pursuant to Bankruptcy Code Section 522(d)(6), an antique blackboard eraser collection (the "Collection").

2. The Collection is not implements, professional books, or tools of the trade for either of the debtors or any of their dependents.

3. The Trustee requests that the Court set a hearing on this objection and notify the Trustee and the debtors as to the date and time of the hearing.

DATED: November 15, 2003

MILDRED PIERCE
Trustee

be worth substantially more than what the debtor claimed, or the amount exempted from a pension plan may be more than is necessary for the debtor's support. If a creditor or the trustee wishes to oppose a claimed exemption, Bankruptcy Rule 4003 provides that an objection must be filed no later than 30 days after the first meeting of creditors held pursuant to Section 341(a) or after the filing of any amendment to Schedule C. How the hearing will be scheduled differs from jurisdiction to jurisdiction. In some, the objecting party must call the court and obtain a date first. In others, the court will set the hearing after review of the objection. No matter how the hearing is set, the objecting party will have the burden of proving that the exemption was not properly claimed.

Even if a particular exemption is allowed, the property may still be sold by the trustee. Usually what is protected is not the property but a dollar amount of the debtor's interest. For example, if the debtor owns property used as a residence that has a fair market value of $100,000 and was subject to a mortgage in favor of a bank with a balance owing of $60,000, the debtor's interest in the property is the amount of the equity, or $40,000. If the debtor chose the federal exemptions, all that is exempt is $17,425 of the $40,000. The Chapter 7 trustee could sell the residence for $100,000, pay the bank $60,000, pay the debtor $17,425, and distribute $22,575 to the debtor's creditors. The debtor could use the $17,425 as a down payment on a new house for the fresh start. As a practical matter, unless the house is worth at least 10 percent more than the secured debt and the amount of the debtor's exemption, the trustee will not bother to sell it since the broker's fees and other costs of the sale could easily deplete the funds available to the unsecured creditors.

LIEN AVOIDANCE

Because of the public policy of allowing a debtor to keep certain ordinary property for a fresh start, Bankruptcy Code Section 522(e) provides that a prepetition waiver of those exemptions in favor of an unsecured creditor is not enforceable. Similarly, in certain circumstances, the Bankruptcy Code allows a debtor to avoid a lien of a secured creditor on the debtor's exempt property so that the debtor will be able to keep the property for a fresh start.

Bankruptcy Code Section 522(f) allows two types of liens to be avoided if they impair an exemption; these liens are:

1. A judicial lien other than one that secures payment of alimony, maintenance, or support.
2. A nonpossessory, nonpurchase money security interest in the types of assets exempt under:
   - Sections 522(d)(3) and (4)—household furnishings, household goods, wearing apparel, appliances, books, animals, crops, musical instruments, and jewelry held primarily for the personal, family, or household use of the debtor or the debtor's dependent;
   - Section 522(d)(5)—implements, professional books, or tools of the trade of the debtor or the debtor's dependent; and
   - Section 522(d)(9)—professionally prescribed health aids of the debtor or the debtor's dependents.

A **judicial lien** is defined in Section 101(36) as a lien obtained by judgment, levy, sequestration, or other legal or equitable process or proceeding. It does not include statutory liens such as tax liens or material or service liens created by any nonbankruptcy statute. A judicial lien other than one that secures payment of

♦ **judicial lien**
A lien obtained by judgment, levy, or other legal or equitable process or proceeding.

alimony, maintenance, or support is avoidable on every type of property or interest that the debtor may claim as exempt. The avoidance of a nonpossessory, nonpurchase money security interest, on the other hand, is limited to those liens on types of property specified. Thus, an impairing consensual lien given on the debtor's residence, even though nonpossessory and nonpurchase money, could not be avoided using Section 522(f) because the homestead is not one of the covered exemptions. A consensual lien on all of the debtor's household goods could be avoided unless the lien was created to secure repayment of the money borrowed to purchase those same household goods.

A lien can be avoided only to the extent it impairs an exemption. If a $5,000 judgment lien is attached to the debtor's jewelry that has a value of $7,000, the lien cannot be avoided because the exemption is only $1,150 and there is $2,000 available after satisfaction of the judgment lien. If the judgment was in the amount of $5,000 and the jewelry is worth $5,000, only $1,150 of the judgment lien could be avoided because that is the extent it impairs the exemption. In other words, if, after deducting the total amount of the lien from the value of the item(s), the total is less than the exemption amount, the debtor can avoid the lien up to the amount of the exemption.

Section 522(f)(3) was added in the 1994 Amendments. It provides that in those cases where the debtor may be or is required to take state exemptions (as opposed to the federal exemptions in Section 522(d)), and state law either: (1) provides an exemption of unlimited amount or (2) prohibits avoidance of consensual liens on property otherwise eligible to be claimed as exempt, then the debtor may not use Section 522(f) to avoid a nonpossessory, nonpurchase money security interest in implements, tools of the trade, farm animals, or crops to the extent the value of those assets exceeds $5,000. Also, the 1994 Amendments provide that if there are two liens on the same piece of property, one of them can be avoided to the extent that when their amounts are added together, the exemption is impaired.

There is no stated time limit, other than when the case is closed, to seek to avoid a lien. Bankruptcy Rule 4003(d) states that a proceeding by the debtor to avoid a lien under Section 522(f) is initiated by the filing of a motion in accordance with Bankruptcy Rule 9014, which governs contested matters generally. (See Exhibit 8.7.) Because lien avoidance motions are frequently brought and rarely contested, even jurisdictions that require hearings on all motions will commonly provide that all the debtor must do is file and serve the motion. If no objection is made by the secured creditor, the court will enter an order avoiding the lien.

Section 522(f) was new with the enactment of the Bankruptcy Code in 1978. Many companies in the business of lending to consumers in return for security interests in the types of goods described in Section 522(d)(3) complained that it violated due process of law in violation of the Fifth Amendment to the United States Constitution. The courts have generally agreed; as a result, any lien created before the enactment of the Bankruptcy Code (November 6, 1978) cannot be avoided under Section 522(f).

REDEMPTIONS

+ redemption
The payment to a secured party of the value of its collateral in exchange for the release of the security interest.

The Bankruptcy Code provides another mechanism for protecting a consumer debtor's exemptions in addition to lien avoidance. It is called **redemption.** Redemption allows the debtor to extinguish a security interest in certain property by paying the creditor only what the property is worth rather than the full amount due. Typically, a debtor will want to redeem when the property is worth less than what is owed, but avoidance under Section 522(f) is not available because the secured creditor has a purchase money security interest.

Exhibit 8.7 ✦ *Sample Pleading*

BANKRUPT C. LAWYER
WHITE CHARGER LEGAL CLINIC
One Learned Way
Los Angeles, California 90001

Attorneys for Debtor

UNITED STATES BANKRUPTCY COURT
WESTERN DISTRICT OF CALIFORNIA

In re	)	Case No. 03-00002-JF
	)	
JOSEPH CONSUMER	)	Chapter 7
	)	
Debtor's Address:	)	
18 Hollywood Drive	)	MOTION FOR ORDER AVOIDING
Los Angeles, CA 90001	)	LIEN ON EXEMPT PROPERTY;
	)	DECLARATION OF JOSEPH
Debtor's S.S. No. 524-47-7448	)	CONSUMER IN SUPPORT THEREOF
	)	

TO THE HONORABLE JUSTIN FAIR, UNITED STATES BANKRUPTCY JUDGE:

Joseph Consumer ("Debtor"), through his attorneys, in support of his Motion for Order Avoiding Lien on Exempt Property, respectfully represents as follows:

1. On January 1, 2002, Debtor borrowed $500.00 (the "Loan") from Consumer Finance Company ("CFC").

2. In order to secure repayment of the Loan, Debtor granted to CFC a security interest in all debtor's household goods (the "Lien").

3. The Lien is nonpossessory, nonpurchase money and impairs the exemption to which Debtor is entitled and has claimed under Sections 522(b) and (d)(3) of the Bankruptcy Code.

4. The Lien is avoidable pursuant to Section 522(f) of the Bankruptcy Code.

WHEREFORE, Debtor requests that the Court enter its Order avoiding the Lien and granting such other and further relief to which Debtor may be entitled.

DATED: November 15, 2003

WHITE CHARGER LEGAL CLINIC

BANKRUPT C. LAWYER
Attorneys for Debtor

Declaration of Bankrupt C. Lawyer

I, Joseph Consumer, declare as follows:

1. I am the debtor in the above captioned case ("Debtor"). I submit this Declaration in support of my Motion for Order Avoiding Lien on Exempt Property, and the words defined in the Motion are used in this Declaration with the same meaning.

—*CONTINUED*

EXHIBIT 8.7 ✦ *Sample Pleading* (CONTINUED)

2. On January 1, 2002, I borrowed the Loan from CFC and granted the Lien to CFC. As of the date I commenced my Chapter 7 bankruptcy case, I owed CFC $400.00.

3. I have claimed as exempt all my household furnishings. No individual item exceeds $400.00 in value, and the aggregate value of all my household furnishings does not exceed $8,000.00.

4. I declare under penalty of perjury that the foregoing is true and correct, is of my own personal knowledge, and if called as a witness, I could and would testify competently.

Executed on November 15, 2003 at Los Angeles, California.

JOSEPH CONSUMER

Section 722 of the Bankruptcy Code governs redemption and provides that an individual debtor may redeem tangible personal property intended primarily for personal, family, or household use from a lien securing a dischargeable consumer debt, if such property is exempt or has been abandoned by the trustee. In other words, to redeem, each of the following facts must exist:

✦ The debtor is an individual.
✦ A creditor has a lien on tangible personal property.
✦ The property is intended to be used primarily for personal, family, or household use.
✦ The property has either been declared as exempt or abandoned by the Chapter 7 trustee.
✦ The creditor's claim is a dischargeable consumer debt.

If any one of these elements is missing, the debtor will not be able to use Section 722 and must reaffirm the entire debt in order to keep the property. If all the elements exist, the debtor must pay the creditor the allowed secured claim, which Section 506(a) of the Bankruptcy Code defines as the value of the creditor's interest in the estate's interest in the property. The difference between the creditor's claim and the amount paid to redeem will be an unsecured claim and discharged. If the creditor is owed $50 but the collateral is only worth $35, the creditor has an allowed secured claim of $35 and an unsecured claim of $15. If the creditor is owed $50 and the collateral is worth $60, the allowed secured claim is $50. Although the Bankruptcy Code is silent on the point, most courts have required debtors who wish to redeem to make a lump sum payment to the creditor. Installment payments usually will not be allowed.

Bankruptcy Rule 6008 implements Section 722 and provides that redemption is accomplished by the filing of a motion (see Exhibit 8.8) and having a hearing on such notice as the court may direct. At a minimum, the debtor would want to ensure that the secured creditor receives notice so that any objection can be made. Notice should also be sent to the Chapter 7 trustee.

For several reasons, redemption is not a remedy frequently used by debtors. First, there are only limited circumstances where it is available. Second, few debtors have the money to redeem or the credit worthiness to borrow in order to redeem.

EXHIBIT 8.8 ✦ *Sample Pleading*

BANKRUPT C. LAWYER
WHITE CHARGER LEGAL CLINIC
One Learned Way
Los Angeles, California 90001

Attorneys for Debtor

UNITED STATES BANKRUPTCY COURT
WESTERN DISTRICT OF CALIFORNIA

In re	)	Case No. 03-00002-JF
	)	
JOSEPH CONSUMER,	)	Chapter 7
	)	
Debtor's Address:	)	
18 Hollywood Drive	)	MOTION FOR ORDER
Los Angeles, CA 90001	)	AUTHORIZING REDEMPTION;
	)	DECLARATION OF JOSEPH
Debtor's S.S. No. 524-47-7448	)	CONSUMER IN SUPPORT THEREOF
	)	

TO THE HONORABLE JUSTIN FAIR, UNITED STATES BANKRUPTCY JUDGE:

Joseph Consumer ("Debtor"), through his attorneys, in support of this Motion for Order Authorizing Redemption, respectfully represents as follows:

1. On January 1, 2002, Debtor purchased a Sony Video Camera Model 111N (the "Camera") from B & B Stereo Company ("Creditor"). As part of the same transaction, Creditor retained a security interest in the Camera and duly perfected its security interest by filing a financing statement with the Secretary of State for the State of California.
2. Debtor purchased the Camera primarily for personal use.
3. Debtor has claimed the Camera as exempt pursuant to 11 U.S.C. § 522(d)(5).
4. At the time he commenced his Chapter 7 bankruptcy case, Debtor owed Creditor $100.00 on account of his purchase of the Camera.
5. The fair market value of the Camera is $50.00.
6. Debtor is ready, willing, and able to pay Creditor $50.00 in order to redeem the Camera from Creditor's lien.

WHEREFORE, Debtor requests that the Court enter its Order authorizing Debtor to redeem the Camera from Creditor's lien upon the payment to Creditor of $50.00 and granting such other and further relief to which Debtor may be entitled.

DATED: November 15, 2003

WHITE CHARGER LEGAL CLINIC

_____

BANKRUPT C. LAWYER
Attorneys for Debtor

Declaration of Joseph Consumer

I, Joseph Consumer, declare as follows:

—CONTINUED

EXHIBIT 8.8 ✦ *Sample Pleading* (CONTINUED)

1. I am the debtor in the above-captioned case. I submit this Declaration in support of my Motion for Order Authorizing Redemption, and the words defined in the Motion are used in this Declaration with the same meaning.
2. On January 1, 2002, I purchased the Camera from B & B and granted B & B a security interest in the Camera.
3. I filed a Chapter 7 bankruptcy case on October 1, 2003 and have claimed the Camera as exempt.
4. I owe B & B $100.00 for the Camera.
5. I asked Al Garza, the manager of B & B, what the fair market value of the Camera was, and he told me $50.00.

I declare under penalty of perjury that the foregoing is true and correct, is of my own personal knowledge, and if called as a witness, I could and would testify competently.

Executed on November 15, 2003 at Los Angeles, California.

JOSEPH CONSUMER

CONVERTING OR DISMISSING THE CASE

Changing Chapters

Regardless of how much thought went into the decision of which chapter the debtor should file under, during the pendency of the case, the question may arise again. The debtor and the creditors may question whether the case should have been originally filed under a different chapter or whether the case should proceed in the future under a different chapter. In most instances, the case can proceed in a different chapter. The act of changing the chapter under which a case is pending is called **conversion.** The rules governing conversion vary from chapter to chapter.

The one general rule is that a case cannot be converted to a chapter if the debtor was ineligible to begin in that chapter. For example, a debtor with $500,000 in unsecured debts could not convert a Chapter 11 case to a case under Chapter 13 because the debtor does not meet the eligibility requirements for Chapter 13 set out in Section 109 of the Bankruptcy Code. Similarly, a stockbroker could not convert a Chapter 7 case to a case under Chapter 11 because stockbrokers are ineligible for Chapter 11 relief.

To further the congressional goal of encouraging debtors to reorganize rather than liquidate, Section 706(a) of the Bankruptcy Code provides that the eligible debtor may convert a Chapter 7 case to a case under Chapter 11, 12, or 13 at any time as a matter of right. No hearing or court approval is required. All the debtor must do is file the appropriate motion. Although no order is required, it is wise to prepare and file one and provide it to creditors so that they will not be confused as to the chapter under which the case is proceeding.

An exception to the debtor's absolute right to convert to a reorganization case is if the case was previously converted to Chapter 7 from a different chapter. If the debtor commenced the case in Chapter 11 and then converted or had it converted to Chapter 7, the debtor cannot as a matter of right convert it back to Chapter 11. In those situations, court approval after a hearing on notice of creditors must be obtained.

The debtor is not the only one who is entitled to convert a Chapter 7 case. Section 706(b) states that at the request of a party in interest, which could include the Chapter 7 trustee, and after notice and a hearing, the court may convert a Chapter 7 case to a case under Chapter 11. Section 706(c) contains a flat prohibition against a conversion from Chapter 7 to Chapter 12 or 13 unless the debtor requests the conversion. Since Chapter 12 cases frequently involve individuals and Chapter 13 cases always do, and the cases usually provide for a payment to creditors out of

✦ **conversion**
The voluntary or involuntary transfer of a bankruptcy case from one chapter of the Bankruptcy Code to a different chapter.

future earnings, for the court to require the debtor to be in Chapter 12 or 13 would likely violate the Thirteenth Amendment of the United States Constitution's prohibition against slavery.

The procedure for the nondebtor to convert a Chapter 7 case to Chapter 11 is to file a motion as provided in Bankruptcy Rule 9014. Twenty days' notice to creditors is required by Bankruptcy Rule 2002(a).

Dismissing a Bankruptcy Case

An alternative to converting a bankruptcy case is to dismiss it. The Chapter 7 debtor may want the case dismissed because it no longer has any need for the protections bankruptcy affords or may have thought that bankruptcy could accomplish more than it does.

Although converting from a Chapter 7 case is granted to debtors as a matter of right, dismissing a case is not as easy. Section 707(a) allows the court to dismiss a Chapter 7 case only after notice and a hearing and only for cause. Court approval is necessary regardless of whether it is the debtor, the trustee, or the creditors making the motion. Section 707(a) gives examples of cause for dismissal, including unreasonable prejudicial delay, nonpayment of fees and costs required to be paid, and the failure to file the statement of intentions. Like the other sections of the Bankruptcy Code that attempt to explain cause, the list in Section 707(a) is not exhaustive. A common ground for dismissal is that the debtor is now in a position to pay all of its creditors in full.

The procedure for dismissing a Chapter 7 case is governed by Bankruptcy Rule 1017(a). The effect of the dismissal of a bankruptcy case is set out in Section 349 of the Bankruptcy Code. Section 349(b) provides that unless the court orders otherwise, dismissal reinstates any proceeding or custodianship superseded by the bankruptcy filing and any avoided transfer or lien. It also vacates any order concerning turnover, liability of a transferee of an avoided transfer, and setoff. Property of the estate will be revested in the entity in which such property was vested immediately before the commencement of the bankruptcy case.

Unless the debtor is prohibited from filing a new bankruptcy case for 180 days under Section 109(g), upon dismissal, the debtor may refile a new bankruptcy case and obtain a discharge in the new case unless the court finds cause to order otherwise.

ETHICAL CONSIDERATIONS

Due to concerns raised by various bankruptcy courts, Congress has imposed numerous new regulations on independently operating non-attorneys who prepare bankruptcy petitions without attorney supervision. Pursuant to 11 U.S.C. § 110, these non-attorneys are now required to use the title Bankruptcy Petition Preparer (BPP). The intent is to reduce confusion in the public's mind between a paralegal (or similar preparer) and an attorney.

Independent paralegals providing bankruptcy services to clients are also prohibited from using the word "legal" in any advertisement for its services. Any document prepared by a BPP must include his or her name, address, and social security number.

The BPP must disclose any fee paid by the debtor by filing a declaration within 10 days of the filing of the petition. Paralegals and other non-attorneys who violate the provisions of 11 U.S.C. § 110 face fines and damages. The statute provides for fines of $500 for the violation of any of several subsections, and damages of $1,000 plus reasonable attorneys' fees if the trustee or creditor moves for damages on behalf of the debtor.

SUMMARY

For most debtors who are individuals, the primary reason for filing a Chapter 7 case is to obtain a discharge. A discharge releases the debtor from his or her obligation to pay unsecured debts. In certain circumstances, the debtor can lose the right to a discharge. Those circumstances almost always involve fraud or other serious wrongdoing by the debtor to creditors. An example is the hiding of assets from the trustee. The creditor or the trustee must file a complaint to prevent the debtor from obtaining a discharge.

There are also some types of debt that are nondischargeable; they can be enforced against the debtor even after the discharge is granted. These types of debts include student loans, taxes, alimony and child support, and debts incurred by fraud or the use of a false financial statement. Some debts are automatically dischargeable; others will be discharged unless the creditor commences an adversary proceeding and prevails.

Even though a debt may be discharged, the debtor can agree to pay it. For that agreement to be enforceable, the debtor must reaffirm the debt by having the reaffirmation agreement properly approved by the bankruptcy court.

The Bankruptcy Code does not require an individual debtor to turn over all of his or her assets to the trustee. The property the debtor may keep is called exempt property. Exempt property includes some equity in a residence, a car, personal effects, and tools needed by the debtor in his or her trade. In some states, a debtor may use the exemptions provided either in the Bankruptcy Code or in the state's statutes. In other states, the debtor may only use the exemptions provided by state law. Exemptions are claimed by listing them in Schedule C.

If the debtor is entitled to an exemption but the property is subject to a lien, the debtor may be able to avoid the lien to the extent it impairs the exemption. Lien avoidance is only available for certain types of property and against only certain types of liens.

If the debtor cannot avoid a lien, he or she may be able to redeem the property from the lien by paying the creditor the lesser of the value of the property or the amount of the creditor's claim. This is beneficial to the debtor if the creditor is owed much more than the property is worth.

A Chapter 7 debtor has the right to convert its case to a reorganization chapter at any time unless it was previously in a reorganization chapter. An individual's Chapter 7 case cannot be converted to a reorganization chapter against his or her will, but a corporation's or partnership's case can. A Chapter 7 case can be dismissed only after notice to parties in interest and upon the bankruptcy court's order.

✦ KEY TERMS

conversion   opting out   reaffirmation   redemption
judicial lien

✦ IMPROVE YOUR UNDERSTANDING

1. Read Bankruptcy Code Sections 727 and 523. Then, for each of the factual situations presented in exercises a. through j., indicate if there are grounds sufficient to hold a claim nondischargeable, deny a discharge, both, or neither. If not enough information is provided, list the additional facts needed.

a. Shortly before filing his bankruptcy case, the debtor told a creditor that he would pay him soon.

b. The bankruptcy court ordered the debtor to turn over to a secured creditor all the rents from an apartment building the debtor owned. The debtor did not do so.

c. The debtor hired an arsonist who set fire to the business premises of debtor's corporation, destroying all the books and records.

d. The debtor transferred his home to his mother. She had made the down payment, all subsequent payments, and had always thought the home was hers.

e. The debtor's obligations include monthly child support of $500.00.

f. The debtor under-reported the number of employees he had and thereby paid less in payrol! taxes than was actually required. When the under-reporting was discovered, the taxing agency imposed a penalty of 100 percent (100%).

g. The debtor gave a creditor a false financial statement after the creditor had lent money to the debtor.

h. The debtor gave the bank a financial statement that showed that the debtor owned 100 shares in a corporation with a value of $100 per share. The bank knew that the corporation was insolvent and the shares valueless, but it lent the debtor the money anyway.

i. The debtor owes $10,000 for student loans. After graduation, the debtor is stricken by a disease from which he is not expected to recover.

j. The debtor is arrested and convicted of drunk driving. As part of his sentence, he is ordered to pay a fine of $500.00.

2. The debtor has income of $25,000 per year. A creditor who holds what she believes to be a nondischargeable claim for $50,000 believes that the debtor failed to disclose $1,000,000 in assets to the trustee. The debtor has $5,000,000 worth of debts. What should the creditor do?

3. Read Bankruptcy Code Sections 524(c), (d), (e), and (f) and Bankruptcy Rule 4008. Then answer Exercises a. through f. based upon the following factual situation:

Consumer bought a video camera from B & B Stereo Company; it was to be paid for over time. Joe's mother Flora, a pensioner on a limited salary, guaranteed to B & B that if Joe did not pay, she would. Joe filed a Chapter 7 petition when he still owed B & B $100. His discharge hcaring is set for December 1. Joe does not want B & B pursuing Flora for the $100.

a. If Joe receives a discharge, will Flora's obligation also be discharged?

b. Joe decides to reaffirm his debt to B & B. To be enforceable by B & B, when is the last day the reaffirmation agreement must be filed?

c. What else must Joe file with the reaffirmation agreement?

d. If Joe is represented by a lawyer during the course of negotiating the reaffirmation agreement, what must the lawyer file and what must it contain?

e. If Joe is not represented by a lawyer, what types of questions will the judge ask Joe at the hearing on the reaffirmation agreement?

f. Joe filed the reaffirmation agreement on November 15. Flora filed her own Chapter 7 bankruptcy case on December 15 and received a discharge on her guaranty obligation to B & B. Since the threat of B & B pursuing Flora was the only reason Joe reaffirmed, he has decided to rescind. When is the last day Joe may do so?

4. List three reasons other than to prevent enforcement of a guaranty why a debtor might want to reaffirm a debt.

5. Do your local rules have any provisions concerning reaffirmations?

6. Read Section 522(f) of the Bankruptcy Code carefully. Then, for each of the following fact patterns, determine whether the lien can be avoided under Section 522(f) and, if so, whether the basis is Section 522(f)(1) or 522(f)(2).

a. The applicable state law creates a lien on all assets in favor of unpaid seed suppliers to farmers. Joe, a farmer, claims as exempt his tractor, which is worth $700.

b. Joe owns a set of antique dueling pistols worth $2,000, which he has claimed as exempt. Consumer Finance Company ("CFC") lent Joe $6,000 so that he could build a swimming pool and took a security interest in all of his assets of every description.

c. Assume the same facts as Exercise b., except that CFC was an unsecured creditor who obtained a judgment against Joe and levied on all of his personal property.

d. The applicable state law creates a lien in favor of an unpaid car mechanic and allows the mechanic to retain the car until paid. Joe's car is being held by Bill's Service Station because Joe cannot pay Bill the $1,000 he owes for repairs to the car. Joe files a Chapter 7 bankruptcy case and claims the automobile as exempt.

7. For each of the fact patterns given in this exercise, decide whether redemption is available to the debtor; if so, decide whether the debtor should redeem.

    a. In order to capture the first steps his child took, Joe Consumer purchased a video camera from B & B Stereo Company on an installment plan with B & B retaining a security interest in the camera. At the time Joe commenced his Chapter 7 case, he owed B & B $100 and the camera was worth $50. Joe used part of his general exemption under Section 522(d)(5) to exempt the camera.

    b. Same fact pattern as Exercise 7.a., but Joe purchased the camera for his business of videotaping weddings.

    c. Same fact pattern as Exercise 7.b., but the camera was purchased by the Chapter 7 debtor, Videos by Joe, Inc.

    d. Same fact pattern as Exercise 7.a., but the camera is worth $150.

    e. A month after Joe purchased a video camera, he borrowed $100 from Consumer Finance Company ("CFC") and granted CFC a security interest in the camera. Joe still owes CFC $100 and the camera, claimed as exempt under Section 522(d)(5), is worth $50.

    f. Joe borrowed $500 from his mother Flora and gave her a lien on his as-yet uncollected judgment of $400 for bodily injury against a motorist who rear-ended him. Joe claimed the judgment as exempt under Section 522(d)(11)(D).

8. Same fact pattern as Exercise 7.a. B & B objects to Joe's motion for redemption, claiming the camera is worth $200. What are two ways Joe can prove the camera's value?

9. Bankruptcy Rule 6008 provides that a trustee may bring a motion seeking redemption. Can you think of a set of facts that would compel a trustee to bring such a motion?

✦ RESEARCH PROJECTS

1. Has the state in which you work opted out?

2. Are there any local rules in your jurisdiction governing lien avoidance procedure?

3. Cite one case for each of the following holdings:

    a. A debtor may reopen a case to avoid a lien under Section 522(f).

    b. Section 522(f) is applicable in Chapter 13 cases.

    c. Section 522(f) is inapplicable in Chapter 13 cases.

    d. A lien on an automobile cannot be avoided under Section 522(f)(2).

4. Locate two reported decisions in which the courts have held that redemption under Section 722 must be made in a lump sum payment and not on an installment basis.

✦ DRAFTING PROJECTS

1. Draft a complaint, based on facts you create, objecting to a discharge based on Section 727(a)(4) or Section 727(a)(9) of the Bankruptcy Code.

2. Draft a complaint, based on facts you create, to determine whether a debt is nondischargeable based on Section 523(a)(4) or Section 523(a)(6) of the Bankruptcy Code.

3. When B & B sold the stereo to Joe, it retained a security interest in the stereo to secure payment of the note. Revise the sample Reaffirmation Agreement (included as part of Exhibit 8.3) to provide for this new fact.

4. B & B had filed a complaint to determine dischargeability of Joe's debt under Bankruptcy Code Section 523(a)(2)(B). The Reaffirmation Agreement (included as part of Exhibit 8.3) moots that action, and it should be dismissed. Revise the sample Reaffirmation Agreement to provide for this new fact.

5. Use the following set of facts to draft a Schedule C maximizing the exemptions. Assume there are no state-created exemptions.

    Joe Businessman and his wife Myra, a schoolteacher, are the shareholders of Videos by Joe, Inc. All three are Chapter 7 debtors, and Joe and Myra filed a joint case. Joe owns free and clear a 1978 Ford Pinto that is worth $1,000. Myra drives a 1987 BMW 318i that is worth $8,000 but on which she still owes $6,000. Myra and Joe jointly own a house with an equity of $21,500. Their other personal property is modest, although they do own a piano with a value of $600, Myra's engagement ring is worth $1,000, and Myra's prized blackboard eraser collection is worth $1,000. Joe owns one video camera and their company owns two, each worth $700. The value of the stock of Videos by Joe, Inc. is $2,000.

6. Prepare a table comparing the exemptions provided in Section 522(d) of the Bankruptcy Code with the exemptions enacted by your state.

Chapter 7: The Trustee's Perspective

THE PREVIOUS chapter examined Chapter 7 from the debtor's perspective. That perspective is only half of the story. While the debtor is busy obtaining a discharge, claiming exemptions, avoiding liens, and redeeming collateral, the nonexempt assets of the estate will be sold or otherwise liquidated and creditor claims will be paid. Those latter tasks will be performed by the trustee rather than the debtor. This chapter will focus on the role of the trustee.

COLLECTING THE ESTATE

Section 541 of the Bankruptcy Code provides that the commencement of a bankruptcy case creates an estate that consists of all the debtor's legal and equitable interests as of the date the petition is filed. The interests become property of the estate wherever they are located and by whomever they are held. The estate will also include property recovered by the trustee on account of fraudulent conveyances, unenforceable statutory liens, preferences, authorized postpetition transfers, and improper setoffs. As Exhibit 9.1 shows, in a Chapter 7 case, the trustee has the duty of assembling all of the property of the estate, liquidating it, and then distributing the proceeds to creditors.

Locating Property of the Estate

It is very important for the trustee to identify, locate, and obtain all of the property of the estate in order to maximize the distributions to creditors. Usually the trustee will make an initial identification as to what constitutes property of the estate by reviewing the schedule of assets and reviewing the statement of financial affairs. The trustee will also question the debtor at the meeting of creditors held pursuant to Section 341(a) or earlier about the existence and location of other assets.

In a larger case, if the debtor is uncooperative or if the trustee suspects that the debtor may have hidden assets, the trustee will examine the debtor's books and records to see if there are missing assets. The trustee may also question the debtor's employees about property held by third parties or transfers made prepetition. A search in the debtor's name of the county recorder's office or the Department of Motor Vehicles may also yield information about unscheduled assets. Creditors, who have an interest in making the estate as large as possible, will sometimes come forward to advise the trustee about the location of assets.

EXHIBIT 9.1 ✦ *Duties of the Chapter 7 Trustee*

Duties of the Chapter 7 Trustee

- Take into Possession and Control Property of the Estate
  - Identify Property
  - Locate Property
  - Possess and Control Property
    - Lock Up What Debtor Possesses
    - Obtain Turnover of Debtor's Property in Third Party's Hands
    - Notify Post Office, Banks, and Taxing Agencies
  - Safeguard Property
- Account for All Property Received
- Liquidate Property
  - Personal Property
  - Real Property
  - Claims for Relief
    - Preferences
    - Fraudulent Conveyances
  - Abandon Property of No or Minimum Value
- Ensure Performance with Debtor's Statement of Intentions
- Furnish Information to Parties in Interest
- Investigate Debtor's Financial Affairs
- Examine and Object to Proofs of Claims
- Oppose Debtor's Discharge
- Final Report and Account

Once the trustee identifies property of the estate, it still must be located and obtained. Movable property may be very difficult to locate and, even once located, the holder may not be willing to give it to the trustee.

The trustee should obtain the debtor's mail that was delivered after the case commenced. The post office should be notified to divert all future mail to the trustee. Similarly, all bank accounts in the name of the debtor should be discovered as soon as possible and closed. Any funds in those accounts should be transferred to new accounts the trustee will open. All taxing agencies should be notified to send any refunds due the debtor to the trustee.

The trustee should try to discover if any of the debtor's property is in the hands of a third party, whether because it is on consignment, leased, or for some other reason. If the arrangement is profitable or if it saves storage fees, the trustee may elect to keep the property where it is for the time being. If the trustee would like to sell the property, the trustee should make immediate demand for its possession. If the third party refuses, the trustee will have to bring a **turnover** action, which is discussed later in this chapter.

✦ **turnover**
The act of delivering possession or control of property of the estate to the trustee.

Safeguarding Business Assets

In an ideal Chapter 7 business bankruptcy case, the debtor would wind the business down as best it could before filing; deliver all customer orders; turn all raw inventory and work in process into finished goods; pay all employees before termination; deliver the books, records, and keys to its attorney; and notify all creditors that it would be filing a Chapter 7 case. Unfortunately, the ideal is rarely seen. More commonly, the trustee will be appointed in an estate where customers are clamoring for their goods, the employees are confused and bitter, the principals are disinterested, and no one is quite sure where the keys are.

The first task the trustee and the trustee's agents will want to undertake is to make some order out of the chaos. Perhaps the trustee or the trustee's administrator will try to meet with the former owners to obtain their ideas on the best way to maximize the value of the assets. The trustee might discover that it makes good business sense for the operations to continue for a short period of time so that raw material inventory can be converted to finished goods, which can then be shipped to customers to create valuable accounts receivable. Bankruptcy Code Section 721 allows the trustee to operate the debtor's business for a limited period if it is in the best interest of the estate, consistent with the orderly liquidation of the assets, and if the court approves. The trustee might hire a few employees in the areas of production, sales, and accounting to help run the operations for this short period of time.

Whether the business is operated or not, the trustee will want to ensure that the debtor's assets are protected so that they can be liquidated for their maximum value. What this preservation will mean varies from case to case. For real property, it may mean that needed repairs are made to the roof. For equipment, it may mean hiring someone to service it on a regular basis so that it does not become dysfunctional. For assets that are easily portable, the trustee may need to have the locks on the debtor's business premises changed and arrange for guard service. The books and records will be very valuable for the administration of the estate since they will be needed to collect accounts receivable and object to proofs of claim. It is usually better that all books and records be put in storage or kept at the trustee's office. If the debtor's books and records are on computer tape or disk, copies should be made to protect them from loss of power or damage.

If the debtor's insurance has lapsed, the trustee should obtain coverage for all real and personal property to safeguard against loss and damage. If the debtor's insurance policies are still in effect, the trustee should maintain them and have his or her name added as an insured.

The trustee must also pay immediate attention to the debtor's leased business premises. The trustee should discover as quickly as possible whether there is any value in the lease. The lease may be valuable if the rent payments are less than the current market rate. If so, someone may be willing to pay the trustee to take an assignment of the lease. If the lease is not valuable, the trustee must evaluate whether it makes sense to stay in the premises while liquidating or whether the assets should be moved to a different location and stored at a lesser cost. For every month the trustee remains in the leased premises, an administrative expense that could be very substantial is incurred.

Turnover

Once the trustee has located all estate property, the property must be collected so that it can be sold. The debtor has a duty to deliver all nonexempt property of the estate to the trustee upon the trustee's appointment. Sometimes property of the estate may be in the hands of the debtor or third parties who will not voluntarily turn it over. In those circumstances, the Bankruptcy Code gives the trustee several weapons to use to recover the property.

Section 542 The first of these weapons is Section 542. It provides (with some exceptions) that someone in possession, custody, or control of property of the estate must account for and deliver such property or its value to the trustee. If there is someone who owes a debt to the estate, Section 542 also requires that the debt be paid to the trustee unless and only to the extent that the person may have a right to offset claims it has against the debt. In addition, subject to any applicable privilege, an attorney, accountant, or other person who holds books and records relating to the debtor's property or financial affairs must turn the information over to the trustee. If the professional does not do so voluntarily, the trustee is authorized (under Section 542) to compel turnover in the bankruptcy court. The trustee may also want to include a cause of action for conversion (theft) under applicable state law. An action to compel turnover against anyone but the debtor is listed in Bankruptcy Rule 7001 as an adversary proceeding that is commenced by the filing of a complaint. (See Exhibit 9.2) An action to compel the debtor's turnover is commenced by the filing of a motion.

The exceptions to Section 542 are:

✦ If the property is of inconsequential value or benefit to the estate, it need not be turned over.
✦ If an entity does not have actual notice or knowledge of the commencement of the case, it may transfer property of the estate or pay a debt owing to the debtor in good faith to an entity other than the trustee.
✦ A life insurance company may transfer property of the estate it holds to itself to pay the premium on a life insurance contract that is property of the estate.
✦ If a custodian is in control of property of the estate, it need not be turned over under Section 542. Instead, Section 543 will apply. Section 543 is discussed next.

✦ **receiver**
A person usually appointed in a nonbankruptcy case by a state court whose duties are similar to those of a bankruptcy trustee.

✦ **assignee for the benefit of creditors**
The person who acts like a bankruptcy trustee in an assignment for the benefit of creditors.

Section 543   The rules for turnover by a custodian are set forth in Section 543. A custodian is defined in Section 101(11) as a **receiver** or trustee appointed in a nonbankruptcy case, an **assignee for the benefit of creditors,** or a trustee, receiver, or agent appointed by contract or applicable law. Section 543(a) states that if a custodian has knowledge of the commencement of the case, the custodian may not make disbursements or take action with respect to property of the estate in his or her control unless the expenditures or actions are necessary to preserve the property.

Section 543(b) requires the custodian to deliver the property of the estate in his or her control to the trustee when the custodian has knowledge of the case. The custodian must also file an accounting of his or her administration. Bankruptcy Rule 6002 requires that the accounting be filed promptly. Upon the filing of the accounting and after an examination has been made into the custodian's administration, the bankruptcy court will determine the propriety of the custodian's actions, including all the disbursements. The examination may be initiated on motion of the custodian for approval of the accounting, on motion (or objection to the accounting) by the trustee or other party in interest, or even at the court's own initiative. At the hearing, the court can protect all entities with whom the custodian became indebted (presumably by authorizing the trustee to pay them or otherwise allow their claim) and may set compensation for the custodian. The court can also surcharge the custodian for improper or excessive disbursement unless it had been made pursuant to law or approved by a court.

Under certain circumstances, it makes sense for the custodian to remain in control of the property of the estate. Perhaps the state court appointed a receiver over a large construction project that the debtor was mismanaging. The receiver has specialized knowledge in the area and, since having been appointed, has become very familiar with the project. The debtor subsequently files the Chapter 7 petition because the custodian refuses to employ an affiliate. There is a serious question in those circumstances whether the creditors are better served by the appointment of a trustee or whether the receiver should stay. Section 543(d) allows the court to excuse turnover by a custodian if the interests of the creditors and the

EXHIBIT 9.2 ✦ *Sample Pleading*

MILDRED PIERCE
700 Flower Street
Los Angeles, California 90001

Trustee

UNITED STATES BANKRUPTCY COURT
WESTERN DISTRICT OF CALIFORNIA

In re)	Case No. 03-00001-JF
)	
VIDEOS BY JOE, INC.,)	Chapter 7
)	
Debtor.)	
)	
Debtor's Address:)	
18 Hollywood Drive)	
Los Angeles, CA 90001)	
)	
Debtor's Tax Id. No. 99-9999899)	
———————————————————)	
)	
MILDRED PIERCE, Trustee)	Adv. No. 03-00002-JF
)	
Plaintiff,)	COMPLAINT FOR TURNOVER OF
)	PROPERTY OF THE ESTATE
v.)	
)	
SUZANNE's WEDDING)	
PHOTOGRAPHY,)	
)	
Defendant,)	
)	
———————————————————)	

Mildred Pierce (the "Trustee") complains and alleges as follows:

THE PARTIES

1. The Trustee is the duly appointed, qualified, and acting Chapter 7 trustee in the above-captioned case.

2. The Trustee is informed that Suzanne's Wedding Photography ("Defendant") is a Delaware corporation authorized to and operating its business in the state of California.

JURISDICTION AND VENUE

3. This action for the turnover of property of the estate is an adversary proceeding over which this court has jurisdiction pursuant to 28 U.S.C. §§ 157 and 1334 and the Order of the Chief Judge of the United States District Court, Western District of California, referring bankruptcy cases and proceedings, entered on July 20, 1992. This adversary proceeding is a core matter pursuant to 28 U.S.C. § 157(b)(2)(E), and the Trustee consents to the entry of a final order or judgment by the Bankruptcy Court.

4. Venue over this adversary proceeding properly resides in the Western District of California pursuant to 28 U.S.C. § 1409(a) in that this adversary proceeding is related to *In re Videos by Joe, Inc.*, Case No. 03-00001-JF pending as a Chapter 7 case in the United States Bankruptcy Court for the Western District of California.

—CONTINUED

EXHIBIT 9.2 ✦ *Sample Pleading* (CONTINUED)

FACTUAL ALLEGATIONS AND CLAIM FOR RELIEF

5. Among the assets of the estate are five (5) Sony Model 111N Video Cameras and related equipment (the "Cameras"). The Cameras are property that the Trustee may use, sell, or lease pursuant to 11 U.S.C. § 363(b).

6. The Cameras are in the possession and under the control of Defendant.

7. Despite demand, Defendant has refused to turn over the Cameras to the Trustee.

8. The Cameras have a fair market value of $5,000.00.

WHEREFORE, the Trustee requests that the Court enter judgment against Defendant ordering it to surrender and deliver possession of the Cameras to the Trustee or, in the alternative, in the amount of $5,000.00 together with costs of suit, and for such other and further relief as the Court deems just and proper.

DATED: November 1, 2003

_____

MILDRED PIERCE
Trustee

---

equity security holders would be better served. Such an order would be obtained by filing a motion. If it is important that the custodian's administration not be disturbed because it is effective or if the property should not be turned over to an untrustworthy debtor in possession, the motion may need to be made on an emergency basis immediately after the filing of the petition.

Finally, under Section 543(d)(2), if the custodian is an assignee for the benefit of creditors and was appointed or took possession more than 120 days before the filing of the petition, the court must let the assignee remain in possession or control of the property unless fraud or injustice would result.

✦ **postpetition transfers**
A transfer made after the commencement of a bankruptcy case that may be avoidable.

Improper Postpetition Transfers

Sometimes unscrupulous debtors abscond with or sell property of the estate after the bankruptcy case is commenced. In addition, creditors sometimes violate the automatic stay and foreclose on their collateral without a bankruptcy court order allowing them to do so. Finally, in an involuntary case, the debtor may make some unwise transfers before the order for relief and the appointment of the trustee.

The trustee is not helpless in the face of these acts that deplete the estate and reduce the distribution to the other creditors. In addition to the remedies given to the trustee in the Bankruptcy Code sections concerning violation of the automatic stay, turnover, preferences, and fraudulent conveyances, Section 549 allows the trustee to avoid a transfer of property of the estate made after the commencement of the case that was not authorized by the Bankruptcy Code or by the bankruptcy court. Section 549 also allows the trustee to recover postpetition transfers if their only authorization was Section 303(f), which allows a debtor in an involuntary case to continue to use or dispose of property pending the entry of an order for relief as if no involuntary case had been commenced.

The trustee may also recover postpetition transfers that were only authorized under Section 542(c) or Section 303(f). Section 542(c) protects someone who owed money to the debtor and who paid the debt to other than the trustee because it did not have notice or knowledge of the bankruptcy case. The transferor will still be protected because Section 549 is directed at avoiding the transfer and recovering the property from the transferee. Section 303(f) provides that "to the extent the

Court orders otherwise," the debtor's business can continue operation and can continue to use, acquire, and dispose of property as if an involuntary case had not been initiated.

There are some exceptions to the recovery of postpetition transfers. Section 549(b) provides that in an involuntary case, the trustee cannot avoid a transfer to the extent of any value, including services but excluding satisfaction or securing of a prepetition debt, given in exchange for the transfer. Section 549(c) prohibits the avoidance of a transfer of real property to a good faith purchaser without knowledge of the commencement of the case and who paid fair value unless a copy of the petition was recorded with the county recorder before the transfer of the real property is recorded.

Section 549 gives the trustee the cause of action to avoid a postpetition transfer. That is really only half a remedy if there has been a physical transfer of the property because the trustee must also either recover the property or the property's value so that the estate can be made whole. This second half of the remedy is given in Section 550, which provides that if a transfer is avoided under Section 549, or a number of other sections discussed later, the trustee is also entitled to recover the property or, if the court so orders, its value. (See Exhibit 9.3.) An action under Section 549 should always be coupled with an action under Section 550 and perhaps a claim for state law conversion as well as damages for violation of the automatic stay.

An action to avoid a postpetition transfer and recover the property or its value is an adversary proceeding commenced by the filing of a complaint, and it is governed by the procedures in the 7000 series of the Bankruptcy Rules. Section 549(d) states that the action must be brought within the earlier of two years after the transfer or the time the bankruptcy case is closed or dismissed. Pursuant to Bankruptcy Rule 6001, the party who asserts the validity of any postpetition transfer under Section 549 has the burden of proof in establishing that the transfer was valid.

Preferences

In General   To ensure a fair distribution to all unsecured creditors, Section 547 of the Bankruptcy Code authorizes the trustee to avoid many transfers that were made within 90 days of the filing of the bankruptcy case, if those transfers benefit one or more creditors at the expense of others. The transfers that may be avoided are called **preferences.**

Section 547(b) establishes six elements of a preferential transfer, all of which must be present. If even one out of the six is absent, the transfer cannot be recovered by the trustee. The six elements are:

1. A transfer of property of the debtor must be made.
2. This transfer must be to or for the benefit of a creditor.
3. It must be on account of an **antecedent debt** owed by the debtor.
4. It must be made while the debtor was insolvent.
5. It must be made within 90 days before the date of the filing of the petition or within one year of the filing if the transferee was an insider.
6. It must have enabled the transferee to receive more than it would have received in a Chapter 7 case had the transfer not been made.

Transfer is broadly defined in Section 101(54) and encompasses virtually every conceivable mode, voluntary or involuntary, of disposing of an interest in property. A typical preferential transfer is the payment of money, but it also could be the granting of a security interest, the attachment of a judgment lien, or the levy of a garnishment order.

✦ **preferences**
A transfer of the debtor's property to a creditor in satisfaction of an existing debt made during the 90 days (or one year if the transfer was made to an insider) before the bankruptcy case was commenced and which enables the creditor to receive more than other creditors.

✦ **antecedent debt**
A debt that predates another transaction.

Exhibit 9.3 ✦ *Sample Pleading*

MILDRED PIERCE
700 Flower Street
Los Angeles, California 90001

Trustee

UNITED STATES BANKRUPTCY COURT
WESTERN DISTRICT OF CALIFORNIA

In re	)	Case No. 03-00001-JF
	)	
VIDEOS BY JOE, INC.,	)	Chapter 7
	)	
Debtor.	)	
	)	
Debtor's Address:	)	
18 Hollywood Drive	)	
Los Angeles, CA 90001	)	
	)	
Debtor's Tax Id. No. 99-9999899	)	
	)	
	)	
MILDRED PIERCE, Trustee	)	Adv. No. 03-00003-JF
	)	
Plaintiff,	)	COMPLAINT TO:
	)	
v.	)	(1) AVOID POSTPETITION
	)	TRANSFER; AND
PERFECT PROCESSING, INC.	)	
	)	(2) RECOVER PROPERTY OR ITS
Defendant,	)	VALUE
	)	
	)	

Mildred Pierce (the "Trustee") complains and alleges as follows:

PARTIES

1. The Trustee is the duly appointed, qualified, and acting Chapter 7 trustee in the above-captioned case.

2. The Trustee is informed that Perfect Processing, Inc. ("Defendant") is a corporation organized and doing business in the state of California.

JURISDICTION AND VENUE

3. This action to avoid a postpetition transfer and recover property or the value thereof is an adversary proceeding over which this Court has jurisdiction pursuant to 28 U.S.C. §§ 157 and 1334 and the Order of the Chief Judge of the United States District Court, Western District of California, referring bankruptcy cases and proceedings, entered on July 20, 1984. This adversary proceeding is a core matter pursuant to 28 U.S.C. § 157(b)(28)(D), and the Trustee consents to the entry of a final order or judgment by the Bankruptcy Court.

4. Venue over this adversary proceeding properly resides in the Western District of California pursuant to 28 U.S.C. § 1409(a) in that this adversary proceeding is related to *In re Videos by Joe, Inc.*, Case No. 03-00001-JF pending as a Chapter 7 case in the United States Bankruptcy Court for the Western District of California.

—CONTINUED

EXHIBIT 9.3 ✦ *Sample Pleading* (CONTINUED)

FACTUAL ALLEGATIONS

5. Prior to the commencement of Debtor's bankruptcy case, Defendant was a creditor of Debtor with a claim in the amount of $5,000.00 (the "Claim").

6. On October 1, 2003, Debtor filed a petition for relief under Chapter 7 of Title 11, United States Code.

7. At the time of the commencement of Debtor's bankruptcy case, it had in its deposit account at First City Bank in excess of $10,000 (the "Account").

8. On October 2, 2003 Debtor's president withdrew the sum of $5,000.00 from the Account and paid such sums to Defendant in satisfaction of the Claim (the "Transfer").

FIRST CLAIM FOR RELIEF
[11 U.S.C. § 549]

9. The Trustee incorporates by this reference the allegations contained in paragraphs 5 through 8 above.

10. The Transfer was made after the commencement of Debtor's bankruptcy case and was not authorized by the Court or by Title 11 of the United States Code.

11. The Trustee is entitled to avoid the Transfer pursuant to 11 U.S.C. § 549.

SECOND CLAIM FOR RELIEF
[11 U.S.C. § 550]

12. The Trustee incorporates by this reference the allegations contained in paragraph 5 through 8 and 10 through 11 above.

13. The trustee is entitled to recover the Transfer from Defendant pursuant to the provisions of 11 U.S.C. § 550.

WHEREFORE, the Trustee requests that the Court enter judgment against Defendant as follows:

1. On the First Claim for Relief, that the Court avoid the Transfer.

2. On the Second Claim for Relief, that the Trustee have judgment against Defendant in the amount of $5,000.00 plus interest thereon as provided by law;

3. On all Claims for Relief, for the Trustee's reasonable attorneys' fees and costs incurred in this action; and

4. For such other and further relief as the Court may deem just and proper.

DATED: October 15, 2003

MILDRED PIERCE
Trustee

The transfer must be of the debtor's property. If a third party pays a creditor, there is no preference because there is no transfer of the debtor's property. If the third party gives the money to the debtor who then pays the creditor, there may be a preference.

Usually, the element of "to or for the benefit of a creditor" is easily met. Most transfers are simply payments made by the debtor to its suppliers of goods or services.

A payment to a creditor is not a preference unless it is for or on account of an antecedent debt owed by the debtor. An antecedent debt merely means one that previously existed. Under this element, a prepayment or a payment at the same time as the delivery of goods or services would not be on account of an antecedent debt and would not be a preference. Also, as mentioned earlier, the transfer must be to or for the benefit of a creditor. If the debtor prepaid for goods, the supplier would not be a creditor.

Section 547 requires the debtor to have been insolvent at the time the transfer was made for it to be preferential. Insolvent is defined in Section 101(32) to mean that the value of the debtor's assets is less than the debtor's liabilities. This is sometimes called **balance sheet insolvency.** Although a debtor need not be insolvent to file a petition, most bankruptcy debtors are. In order to prevent lengthy and needless hearings on the issue, pursuant to Section 547(f), the debtor is presumed to have been insolvent on and during the 90 days immediately preceding the date of the filing of the petition. Insolvency is only presumed, and the creditor may attempt to rebut the presumption; in such cases, insolvency will need to be proved by the trustee.

In most cases, a preference must have been made during the 90 days preceding the filing of the petition. When the transfer is to an **insider,** a term defined in Section 101(31), the preference period is one year. If the trustee is trying to recover a preferential transfer to an insider made more than 90 days before the case was filed, there is no presumption of insolvency; the trustee will have to prove it.

Section 547(e)(2) governs when a transfer is deemed to have been made. It is usually the date the transfer takes effect between the parties. If the transfer was a payment in cash, it is the date the cash was turned over. A payment by check is made when the check clears. If the transfer involves the perfection of a security interest, the transfer is made when the interest is perfected, but if the interest is perfected within 10 days after the transfer took effect between the parties, it relates back to the date the transfer took effect.

The transfer must improve the return to the creditor. It will not be preferential unless it enables the creditor to receive more than it would have received in a hypothetical Chapter 7 case had the transfer not been made. If all creditors are being paid in full or if the transferee is a secured or priority creditor, there can be no preference since the transferee is not being treated better. For example, suppose the debtor's total debts were $100,000, and within 90 days before the petition was filed, it paid a creditor it owed $10,000 in full, leaving only $90,000 in debt. If the trustee was able to accumulate only $50,000, the creditor recovered a preference because it was paid in full while other creditors were not. If the trustee had $90,000 to distribute to the remaining creditors, there would be no preference because all creditors would be paid in full.

Exceptions   A common theme running through the Bankruptcy Code is to lay down a general rule and then make a number of exceptions. Section 547 is a prime example of this theme. Section 547(b) lists the elements of a preference. Section 547(c) identifies eight types of transfers that, although they meet all of the preference requirements, nevertheless may not be avoided by the trustee. The exceptions are:

1. A contemporaneous exchange for new value.
2. A payment made and received in the ordinary course of business.
3. A security interest given to a lender whose loan enabled the debtor to obtain the collateral and which was perfected within 20 days.
4. Transfers where the transferee subsequently gave new value to the debtor.
5. A transfer to an account receivable or inventory financier who did not improve in position during the preference period.
6. Any statutory lien that cannot be successfully attacked under Section 545.
7. Transfers to a former spouse or child for alimony, maintenance, or support under a separation agreement, divorce decree, or other court order unless the debt was assigned to someone else or is not actually in the nature of alimony, maintenance, or support.
8. A transfer by a consumer debtor that does not exceed $600.

The reason for these exceptions is that the creditor did something good for the debtor by, for example, selling it more goods, dealing with it in the ordinary course, or otherwise increasing the value of the estate. This is conduct that the trustee would want to encourage. If the transfers the creditor did receive had to be paid back, it would discourage creditors from dealing with companies in financial trouble. Next, the four most common exceptions are examined in a bit more detail.

For a successful contemporaneous exchange defense, the transfer must have been intended by the parties as a **substantially contemporaneous exchange for new value,** and it must have been in fact a substantially contemporaneous exchange. Section 547(a)(2) defines new value to mean new money, goods, or services. It does not include the substitution of a new obligation for an old obligation. If there was an existing unsecured debt between the parties, rewriting the note and securing it with collateral would not save the transfer from preference attack as a substantially contemporaneous exchange for new value. What constitutes "substantially" in this context depends on the facts of the transaction. Obviously, if the debtor gave money to a creditor and received the money's worth in goods or services at the same time, there would have been a contemporaneous exchange for new value.

The most commonly used preference exception is for ordinary trade transactions. Prior to 1984, any payment made more than 45 days after it was first due was preferential. In the 1984 Amendments, Congress did away with this hard-and-fast rule in favor of one that is more flexible. Now, to fit within this exception, the debt must have been incurred in the ordinary course of the debtor's business, the payment must have been made in the ordinary course of the debtor and the creditor's business, and the payment must have been made according to ordinary business terms. What is ordinary between the debtor and the creditor will need to be examined for every preference. It may be that a creditor gives only very short credit terms and requires all invoices to be paid within 10 days. Any payment made on the eleventh day could be a recoverable preference. If the creditor gives longer credit terms, that payment may not be recoverable. It will also be important in some instances to know what was ordinary in a particular industry. For example, if in the automobile parts industry, payments to suppliers are usually due in 20 days, but a particular supplier gives 40-day terms, those payments may not be considered ordinary in the industry. As a result, even though the debtor paid the supplier timely pursuant to their agreement, it still might be preferential.

Enabling loans, which are almost identical to purchase money loans, are also exempted from preference attack. A lien will be protected if it is given in exchange for the money to acquire particular property. The money must have been actually used by the debtor to acquire the property, and the security interest must be perfected on or before 20 days after the debtor receives possession of the property.

To encourage creditors who do business with insolvent entities, Congress shielded from preference attack transfers to the extent that, after the transfer, the creditor gave new value to the debtor. The transfer of the new value must have been unsecured and not paid for by the debtor unless the payment can be recovered as a preference. For example, if the creditor sold goods to the debtor and received a preferential payment for them, the preference would not have to be paid back if the creditor later delivered more goods to the debtor.

Procedure to Analyze Preferences   An analysis of the debtor's records to determine what transfers may be preferential could be the task of the paralegal. For most preferences, when the 45-day rule was in effect, it was a simple matter of comparing dates on checks to dates on invoices. Now that the standard is more flexible, the paralegal must do a much more thorough analysis of the payment history between the creditor and the debtor to see if the payment was in the ordinary course of business. Exhibit 9.4 may be helpful in analyzing the payment history to determine whether a transfer is potentially recoverable because it was outside the ordinary course of business and whether there are any new value defenses.

✦ **substantially contemporaneous exchange for new value**
A preference defense that destroys the creditor's liability if the antecedent debt was intentionally created at or about the same time as the otherwise preferential transfer was made.

✦ **enabling loans**
A loan made for the purpose of paying the purchase price of property.

Exhibit 9.4 ✦ *Analysis of Potential Preferential Transfers*

Invoice Date	Invoice Number	Date Due*	Amount	Check Date	Check Number	Check Amount

*There may be two or more dates an invoice is due. The creditor may allow a discount of a certain percentage if the invoice is promptly paid. This discount is usually reflected by the shorthand "2/10, n/30," which translates to a two-percent discount if the invoice is paid in 10 days with the full amount ("net") amount due in 30 days. For preference purposes, the net date is the appropriate date to use.

Procedure to Recover Preferences   Typically, the trustee will first send demand letters to those who have received preferences requesting that the preferences be repaid. Not only does this lessen litigation costs to the estate, but most courts will allow the estate to collect interest from the transferee from the date of the demand. A sample demand letter is shown in Exhibit 9.5.

An action to set aside a preference should be joined with an action under Section 550 to recover the transferred property or its value. Such an action is an adversary proceeding and, under Bankruptcy Rule 7001, commenced by the filing of a complaint. (See Exhibit 9.6.)

If the bankruptcy case was commenced prior to the effective date of the 1994 Amendments (October 22, 1994), under Section 546(a) of the Bankruptcy Code, the trustee would have two years after his or her appointment to sue to set aside the preference unless the case were closed or dismissed before those two years are up. In a case commenced after the effective date of the 1994 Amendments, the trustee will have two years after the case was commenced (which in a Chapter 7 case may be a few days before the appointment unless the case is closed or dismissed earlier).

At trial on the preference lawsuit, the trustee has the burden of proving all of the elements of the transfer under Section 547(b) except insolvency, which will be presumed although the presumption is rebuttable. The preference recipient has the burden of proving that one more of the exceptions applies.

Finally, a creditor who is forced to repay a preference to the estate will have a general unsecured claim for the amount repaid and will be entitled to share in the proceeds of the estate.

EXHIBIT 9.5 ✦ *Sample Pleading*

Mildred Pierce, Trustee
700 Flower Street
Los Angeles, California, 90001

December 1, 2003

Perfect Processing, Inc.
444 Main Street
San Francisco, CA 94041

Re: In re Videos by Joe, Inc.,
    Case No. 03-00001-JF

Dear Sir or Madam:

The undersigned is the duly appointed, qualified, and acting Chapter 7 trustee in the above-referenced bankruptcy case that was commenced on October 1, 2003.

The debtor's records reflect that on or about September 1, 2003, you received a payment of $1,000.00 from the debtor on account of a preexisting debt that was overdue for payment. It is my opinion that this transfer constitutes an avoidable preference, which I am entitled to avoid and recover pursuant to Sections 547 and 550 of the Bankruptcy Code.

I would like to resolve this matter without the need for litigation. Therefore, I request that you immediately send me the sum of $1,000.00. Alternatively, if you are of the opinion that the payment was not a preference, kindly immediately provide me with whatever information you have to support your assertion.

Very truly yours,

Mildred Pierce,
Trustee

Statutory Liens

Statutory liens are defined in Section 101(53) of the Bankruptcy Code as liens created by a state or federal law concerning very specific circumstances or conditions or a lien arising on the nonpayment of rent because of a provision in a statute or in a lease. Some statutory liens are referred to as **secret liens** because they will not appear of record in the county recorder's or the secretary of state's office. A creditor trying to locate any evidence of the lien could not find it. An example of a statutory lien would be if state law provided that if an electrician did work on a house and was not paid for those services, without further act, the electrician would have a lien on the house. Statutory liens do not include security interests consensually granted. They also do not include liens arising from the enforcement of a judgment even though those liens may be provided for by a statute.

Section 545 of the Bankruptcy Code states that the trustee may avoid a statutory lien to the extent that the lien becomes effective at the following times:

✦ At the commencement of the bankruptcy case or other insolvency proceeding.
✦ When a custodian is appointed.
✦ When the debtor becomes insolvent or fails to meet a particular financial standard.
✦ When another party levies on the debtor's property.

✦ **statutory liens**
A lien arising under a state or federal statute solely due to specified circumstances or conditions.

✦ **secret liens**
A lien, usually created by statute, the existence of which cannot be discovered through a search of the applicable public records.

EXHIBIT 9.6 ✦ *Sample Pleading*

MILDRED PIERCE
700 Flower Street
Los Angeles, California 90001

Trustee

UNITED STATES BANKRUPTCY COURT
WESTERN DISTRICT OF CALIFORNIA

In re	)	Case No. 03-00001-JF
	)	
VIDEOS BY JOE, INC.,	)	Chapter 7
	)	
Debtor.	)	
	)	
Debtor's Address:	)	
18 Hollywood Drive	)	
Los Angeles, CA 90001	)	
	)	
Debtor's Tax Id. No. 99-9999899	)	
————————————————	)	
	)	
MILDRED PIERCE, Trustee	)	Adv. No. 03-00004-JF
	)	COMPLAINT:
Plaintiff,	)	
	)	(1) TO AVOID PREFERENTIAL
v.	)	TRANSFER; AND
	)	
PERFECT PROCESSING, INC.	)	(2) TO RECOVER PROPERTY OR
	)	THE VALUE THEREOF
Defendant,	)	
	)	
————————————————	)	

Mildred Pierce (the "Trustee") complains and alleges as follows:

PARTIES

1. The Trustee is the duly appointed, qualified, and acting Chapter 7 trustee in the above-captioned bankruptcy case.

2. The Trustee is informed that Perfect Processing Inc. (the "Defendant") is a California corporation organized and authorized to do business in the state of California.

JURISDICTION AND VENUE

3. This Court has jurisdiction over this action pursuant to 28 U.S.C. §§ 157 and 1334(a) and the Order of the Chief Judge of the United States District Court, Western District of California, referring bankruptcy cases and proceedings, entered on July 20, 1984. This adversary proceeding is a core matter pursuant to 28 U.S.C. § 157(b)(2)(F), and the Trustee consents to the entry of a final order or judgment by the Bankruptcy Court.

4. Venue properly resides in the United States Bankruptcy Court for the Western District of California pursuant to 28 U.S.C. § 1409 in that this adversary proceeding is related to *In re Videos by Joe, Inc.*, Case No. 95-00001-JF pending as a Chapter 7 case in the United States Bankruptcy Court for the Western District of California.

—CONTINUED

EXHIBIT 9.6 ✦ *Sample Pleading* (CONTINUED)

FACTUAL ALLEGATIONS

5. At all times relevant herein, Defendant was a creditor of Debtor within the meaning of 11 U.S.C. § 547.

6. Debtor filed a petition for relief under Chapter 7 of Title 11 United States Code on October 1, 2003 (the "Petition").

7. Defendant received a transfer of monies from debtor in the amount of $5,000.00 (the "Transfer"):
   (a) for or on account of antecedent debt;
   (b) within ninety (90) days before the date of filing of the Petition; and
   (c) which enabled Defendant to receive more than Defendant would receive if:
      (i) The case were a case under Chapter 7 of Title 11 of the United States Code;
      (ii) The transfer had not been made; and
      (iii) Defendant received payment of its debts to the extent provided by the provisions of Title 11 of the United States Code.

FIRST CLAIM FOR RELIEF
[11 U.S.C. § 547]

8. The Trustee hereby incorporates by reference the allegations contained in paragraphs 5 through 7 above.

9. The Trustee is entitled to avoid the Transfer pursuant to 11 U.S.C. § 547(b).

SECOND CLAIM FOR RELIEF
[11 U.S.C. § 550]

10. The Trustee hereby incorporates by reference the allegations contained in paragraphs 5 through 7 above.

11. The trustee is entitled to recover the Transfer from Defendant pursuant to the provisions of 11 U.S.C. § 550.

WHEREFORE, the Trustee requests the Court to enter judgment against Defendant as follows:

1. On the First Claim for Relief, that the Court avoid the Transfer.

2. On the Second Claim for Relief, that the Trustee have judgment against Defendant in the amount of $5,000.00 plus interest thereon from the date of demand;

3. On all Claims for Relief, for the Trustee's reasonable attorneys' fees and costs incurred in this action; and

4. For such other and further relief as the Court may deem just and proper.

DATED: October 15, 2003

_____

MILDRED PIERCE
Trustee

A statutory lien is also avoidable if a good faith purchaser of the property could buy the property free and clear of the lien. In addition, all liens for rent are avoidable.

Like postpetition transfers, statutory liens are avoided by the filing of a complaint and commencing of an adversary proceeding. Such a complaint is presented in Exhibit 9.7. The claim for relief to avoid the lien should be coupled with a claim under Section 550 of the Bankruptcy Code to recover the property transferred or its value.

The limitation period for bringing an action to avoid a statutory lien is in Section 546. As was true for preferences, if the bankruptcy case was commenced prior to the effective date of the 1994 Amendments, the trustee will have two years after his or her appointment, or until the time the case is closed or dismissed if that occurs first, to sue to set aside the statutory lien. In a case commenced after the

EXHIBIT 9.7 ✦ *Sample Pleading*

MILDRED PIERCE
700 Flower Street
Los Angeles, California 90001

Trustee

UNITED STATES BANKRUPTCY COURT
WESTERN DISTRICT OF CALIFORNIA

In re	)	Case No. 03-00001-JF
	)	
VIDEOS BY JOE, INC.,	)	Chapter 7
	)	
Debtor.	)	
	)	
Debtor's Address:	)	
18 Hollywood Drive	)	
Los Angeles, CA 90001	)	
	)	
Debtor's Tax Id. No. 99-9999899	)	
_____	)	
	)	
MILDRED PIERCE, Trustee	)	Adv. No. 03-00005-JF
	)	COMPLAINT:
Plaintiff,	)	
	)	(1) AVOID STATUTORY LIEN; AND
v.	)	
	)	(2) RECOVER PROPERTY OR ITS
LLOYD PROPERTIES,	)	VALUE
	)	
Defendant.	)	
	)	
_____	)	

Mildred Pierce (the "Trustee") complains and alleges as follows:

THE PARTIES

1. The Trustee is the duly appointed, qualified, and acting Chapter 7 trustee in the above-captioned case.

2. The Trustee is informed that Lloyd Properties ("Landlord") is a corporation organized and doing business under the laws of the state of California.

JURISDICTION AND VENUE

3. This action to avoid a statutory lien and recover property or its value is an adversary proceeding over which this Court has jurisdiction pursuant to 28 U.S.C. §§ 157 and 1334 and the Order of the Chief Judge of the United States District Court, Western District of California, referring bankruptcy cases and proceedings, entered on July 20, 1992. This adversary proceeding is a core matter pursuant to 28 U.S.C. § 157(b)(2)(E), and the Trustee consents to the entry of a final order or judgment by the Bankruptcy Court.

4. Venue over this adversary proceeding properly resides in the Western District of California pursuant to 28 U.S.C. § 1409(a) in that this adversary proceeding is related to *In re Videos by Joe, Inc.,* Case No. 95-00001-JF pending as a Chapter 7 case in the United States Bankruptcy Court for the Western District of California.

—*CONTINUED*

EXHIBIT 9.7 ✦ *Sample Pleading* (CONTINUED)

FACTUAL ALLEGATIONS

5. Debtor leased from Landlord improved real property located at 18 Hollywood Boulevard, Los Angeles, California (the "Premises").

6. At the time of the commencement of Debtor's bankruptcy case, Debtor was indebted to Landlord for the sum of $5,000.00 on account of Debtor's lease of the Premises (the "Debt").

7. At the time of the commencement of the Debtor's bankruptcy case, the Debtor owned five (5) Sony Model 111N Video Cameras, which were stored in the Premises (the "Cameras").

8. The Cameras are property of the estate with a value of $5,000.00.

9. Pursuant to the laws of the state of California codified in Civil Code Section 3406.47, a statutory lien in the Cameras is asserted by Landlord to secure repayment of the Debt.

10. Despite demand, Landlord has refused to deliver the Cameras to the Trustee.

FIRST CLAIM FOR RELIEF
[11 U.S.C. § 545]

11. The Trustee incorporates by this reference the allegations contained in paragraphs 5 through 9 above.

12. The Trustee is entitled to avoid the lien asserted by Landlord pursuant to 11 U.S.C. § 545.

SECOND CLAIM FOR RELIEF
[11 U.S.C. § 550]

13. The Trustee incorporates by this reference the allegations contained in paragraphs 5 through 9 and 12 above.

14. The Trustee is entitled to recover the Cameras or their value from Landlord pursuant to 11 U.S.C. § 550.

WHEREFORE, the Trustee requests that this Court enter judgment against Landlord as follows:

1. On the First Claim for Relief, that the Court void the lien on the Cameras asserted by Landlord;

2. On the Second Claim for Relief, that the Trustee have judgment against Landlord in the amount of $5,000.00 plus interest thereon or that Landlord immediately surrender the Cameras to the Trustee;

3. On all Claims for Relief, for the Trustee's reasonable attorneys' fees; and

4. For such other and further relief as the Court deems just and proper.

DATED: October 15, 2003

_____

MILDRED PIERCE
Trustee

---

effective date of the 1994 Amendments, the trustee will have two years after the entry of the order for relief or until the case is closed or dismissed.

Fraudulent Transfers or Obligations

Under state law, creditors are sometimes allowed to undo the debtor's transfers or debts if they were fraudulently made or incurred. A transfer or debt may be fraudulent because it was intentionally made to prevent creditors from being paid, which is actual fraud, or because the debtor received less than the property was worth, which is constructive fraud.

✦ **fraudulent conveyances**
The transfer of the debtor's property with an actual intent to defraud creditors or for less than reasonably equivalent value while the debtor was insolvent or became insolvent as a result.

This right of creditors is now given to the trustee as a representative of all the creditors. It is yet another way for the trustee to increase the size of the estate (or decrease the amount of claims) and maximize the distribution to creditors. The Bankruptcy Code has two sections that give fraudulent transfer or debt avoidance rights to trustees: Section 544(b) and Section 548.

Section 544(b) permits the trustee to avoid a transfer of property or the incurrence of a debt by the debtor if it is voidable under applicable nonbankruptcy law by an unsecured creditor with an allowable claim. In other words, if the state or other federal law would allow a creditor to undo a transfer or the incurring of an obligation, the trustee may step into the shoes of that creditor. But there must actually be an unsecured creditor who could otherwise sue. This is rarely a problem since all that is needed is a creditor who was owed money at the time of the transfer or the incurring of the debt. Even if that is not possible because all those creditors were subsequently paid, some state fraudulent conveyance laws grant standing to creditors who became creditors after the transfer.

Section 548 is the Bankruptcy Code's own fraudulent transfer or obligation law. It allows the trustee to recover property that was fraudulently transferred and to disallow obligations that were fraudulently incurred within one year before the filing of the petition. There are two types of transfers or debts that can be set aside under Section 548.

The first type of transfer or obligation avoidable under Section 548 is one in which there was an actual intent to hinder, delay, or defraud an existing or future creditor. An example would be a doctor transferring all personal assets to a professional corporation to prevent judgment creditors from levying on those assets. If the doctor's motivation can be proved, the transfer can be undone as a transfer made with the intent to defraud creditors. It is rare for actual intent to be proved since the transferor is usually unwilling to admit that intent. Sometimes the court will infer actual fraud if the circumstances indicate that there could be no other motivation.

The second type of avoidable transfer or obligation under Section 548 does not require fraudulent intent. It merely requires that the debtor received less than reasonably equivalent value in exchange for the transfer or obligation, and one of the following conditions is met:

✦ The debtor was insolvent when the transfer was made or the obligation was incurred, or the debtor became insolvent as a result of the transfer or obligation.

✦ The transfer or obligation left the debtor with an unreasonably small amount of money to run its business or financial transactions.

✦ The debtor intended to incur or believed it would incur debts beyond its ability to pay.

Obviously, proving that reasonably equivalent value did not change hands is very important. Value is defined in Section 548(d)(2) as property or the satisfaction or securing of a debt. It does not include an unperformed promise to furnish support to the debtor or to a relative of the debtor. Thus, if a debtor transferred all of his assets to a nursing home in exchange for the nursing home's pledge to support his mother when she became infirm, no value was given to the debtor and the transaction could be set aside. The Bankruptcy Code is silent as to what exactly constitutes reasonably equivalent value, preferring instead to let the court make that determination in each case.

The trustee may use Section 548 only when the transfer was made or the obligation was incurred within the year preceding the commencement of the bankruptcy case. If it took place earlier, only a Section 544(b) action would be available.

As is true for other avoiding power actions, a suit to avoid a fraudulent transfer that is not a lien or a fraudulent debt is typically joined with an action to recover the property or its value under Section 550 and is commenced by the filing of a complaint. If the trustee is trying to avoid a lien or a debt under Section 544(b) or 548, it is not necessary to include a claim to recover property or its value. The parties must follow the rules governing adversary proceedings in the 7000 series of the Bankruptcy Rules.

The deadline for a trustee bringing a fraudulent conveyance action under either Section 544(a) or Section 548 will either be two years after the trustee was appointed (in a case commenced prior to the enactment of the 1994 Amendments) or two years after the case was commenced (in a case commenced after the enactment of the 1994 Amendments). In either event, if the case is closed or dismissed prior to the two-year period, the closure or dismissal date will be the deadline.

Other Avoiding Powers

Suits to avoid preferences, statutory liens, and fraudulent conveyances are not the only tools a trustee has to bring property into the estate. Section 544(a) gives a trustee three other ways to maximize the estate by avoiding transactions. It does so by giving the trustee the status of three different types of creditors. These creditors are hypothetical. Unlike the creditor needed under Section 544(b), the creditors need not actually exist for the trustee to exercise their rights. Section 544(a) is sometimes known as the "strong arm clause"; it brings into play many of the provisions of the Uniform Commercial Code and state real property law discussed in Chapter 4 of this book.

The first status given to the trustee in Section 544(a) is that of a creditor who extended credit to the debtor when the case was commenced and who received at that time a judicial lien on all property. Under this provision, if there are unperfected secured creditors, their security interest will be subordinate to the trustee's hypothetical judicial lien.

The second type of creditor is one who extended credit to the debtor when the case commenced and who obtained at that time an execution that was returned unsatisfied. Some states may provide certain remedies to creditors in those circumstances that are not available to the holder of a judicial lien. If so, the trustee would be able to take advantage of those remedies.

Finally, the trustee is given the status of a buyer of real property who purchased the property from the debtor when the case was commenced. If there is any interest a buyer of real property would take free and clear under applicable state or federal law, such as an unrecorded mortgage or an easement, the trustee will also take that interest free and clear. Remember that the trustee's status in these situations is hypothetical. The trustee's actual knowledge is immaterial. If the trustee knows of the mortgage or easement, the trustee may still use the strong arm clause to avoid the interest because a hypothetical buyer could.

If the trustee can take advantage of any of these hypothetical statuses to increase the extent of property of the estate, the correct procedure is to commence an adversary proceeding by filing a complaint. (See Exhibit 9.8.) The deadline for bringing an action under the strong arm powers of Section 544(a) is identical to the limitation for preferences, statutory liens, and fraudulent conveyances.

LIQUIDATING THE ESTATE

Abandonment

After all of the property of the estate has been gathered into the trustee's control, the trustee will need to liquidate it to cash. Yet not all property of the estate will

EXHIBIT 9.8 ✦ *Sample Pleading*

MILDRED PIERCE
700 Flower Street
Los Angeles, California 90001

Trustee

UNITED STATES BANKRUPTCY COURT
WESTERN DISTRICT OF CALIFORNIA

In re	)	Case No. 03-00001-JF
	)	
VIDEOS BY JOE, INC.,	)	Chapter 7
	)	
Debtor's Address:	)	
18 Hollywood Drive	)	TRUSTEE'S APPLICATION TO
Los Angeles, CA 90001	)	EMPLOY COUNSEL; DECLARATION
	)	OF IRWIN SULLY IN
Debtor's Tax Id. No. 99-999899	)	SUPPORT THEREOF
_____	)	
	)	
MILDRED PIERCE, Trustee	)	Adv. No. 03-00006-JF
	)	
Plaintiff,	)	COMPLAINT TO AVOID
	)	UNPERFECTED SECURITY INTEREST
v.	)	
	)	
FIRST CITY BANK,	)	
	)	
Defendant.	)	
	)	
_____	)	

Mildred Pierce (the "Trustee") complains and alleges as follows:

PARTIES

1. The Trustee is the duly appointed, qualified, and acting Chapter 7 trustee in the above-captioned bankruptcy case.

2. The Trustee is informed that First City Bank is a financial institution chartered and doing business in the state of California (the "Bank").

JURISDICTION AND VENUE

3. This Court has jurisdiction over this action to avoid an unperfected security interest pursuant to 28 U.S.C. § 157 and 1334(a) and the Order of the Chief Judge of the United States District Court, Western District of California, referring bankruptcy cases and proceedings, entered on July 20, 1992. This adversary proceeding is a core matter pursuant to 28 U.S.C. § 157(b)(2)(K), and the Trustee consents to the entry of a final order or judgment by the Bankruptcy Court.

4. Venue properly resides in the United States Bankruptcy Court for the Western District of California pursuant to 28 U.S.C. § 1409 in that this adversary proceeding is related to *In re Videos by Joe, Inc.*, Case No. 03-00001-JF pending as a Chapter 7 case in the United States Bankruptcy Court for the Western District of California.

—CONTINUED

EXHIBIT 9.8 ✦ *Sample Pleading* (CONTINUED)

FACTUAL ALLEGATIONS AND CLAIM FOR RELIEF

5. Prior to the commencement of Debtor's bankruptcy case, Debtor executed and delivered to the Bank a written security agreement whereby Debtor granted a security interest in all of Debtor's inventory to the Bank (the "Security Interest").

6. The Bank did not perfect the Security Interest.

7. The Trustee is entitled to avoid the Security Interest pursuant to the provisions of 11 U.S.C. § 544(a)(1).

WHEREFORE, the Trustee requests that the Court enter judgment against the Bank as follows:

1. Avoiding the Security Interest;

2. For the Trustee's reasonable attorneys' fees and costs incurred in this action; and

3. For such other and further relief the Court may deem just and proper.

DATED: October 15, 2003

_____

MILDRED PIERCE
Trustee

---

have value, and sometimes the cost of preserving and selling an asset will be more than the asset is worth. In situations where the property is burdensome or is of inconsequential value to the estate, Bankruptcy Code Section 554(a) authorizes the trustee to abandon the property. *Abandonment* is common when the property has more liens against it than it is worth or the costs of sale would eat up what little equity there may be.

Abandonment may result from a bankruptcy court order or through neglect. Section 554(c) provides that if the trustee does not affirmatively abandon property, and it is not otherwise administered during the course of the case, it will be deemed abandoned when the case is closed if it was listed in the debtor's schedule of assets. Nonscheduled property will remain property of the estate and will not be deemed abandoned.

Court authorization for the abandonment of property may be obtained on the trustee's notice or on the motion of a party in interest. The procedure for both is found in Bankruptcy Rule 6007. Bankruptcy Rule 6007(a) provides that the trustee must give notice of a proposed abandonment or other disposition of property to all creditors, indenture trustees, and any committees in the case. (See Exhibit 9.9.) They then have 15 days after the mailing of the notice to file and serve an objection. A party might object if it believes the property has value and should be liquidated for the benefit of the creditors. Alternatively, a party in interest might believe that the property is unsafe and should be dealt with rather than abandoned to a debtor who may not be around. If an objection is made, the trustee or the objecting party must set a hearing and give notice of the hearing to the other party. If no objection is filed and served, no hearing need be held, no order authorizing the abandonment will be required, and there will be no inquiry as to the propriety of the abandonment.

Bankruptcy Rule 6007(b) briefly discusses a motion to compel abandonment. It merely states that a party in interest may file and serve a motion requiring the trustee to abandon property and the court shall set a hearing on notice to such entities as it shall direct. Assuming the motion is granted, the order will compel the trustee to abandon the property. The abandonment is not automatic, and the trustee will still have to send out the required notice.

EXHIBIT 9.9 ✦ *Sample Pleading*

MILDRED PIERCE
700 Flower Street
Los Angeles, California 90001

Trustee

UNITED STATES BANKRUPTCY COURT
WESTERN DISTRICT OF CALIFORNIA

In re	)	Case No. 03-00001-JF
	)	
VIDEOS BY JOE, INC.,	)	Chapter 7
	)	
Debtor.	)	
	)	
Debtor's Address:	)	NOTICE OF INTENT TO ABANDON
18 Hollywood Drive	)	PROPERTY
Los Angeles, CA 90001	)	
	)	
Debtor's Tax Id. No. 99-9999899	)	
	)	

TO THE DEBTOR, CREDITORS, AND OTHER PARTIES IN INTEREST:

NOTICE IS HEREBY GIVEN that pursuant to 11 U.S.C. § 554(a), Mildred Pierce, the duly appointed, qualified, and acting Chapter 7 trustee in the above-captioned estate (the "Trustee"), intends to and will abandon all uncollected accounts receivable of the debtor as burdensome and of inconsequential value to the estate unless, within fifteen (15) days from the date of service of this Notice, a party in interest files a written objection and request for hearing with the Bankruptcy Court and serves a copy of such objection on the Trustee and the United States Trustee. Any objection not timely filed and served may be deemed waived.

DATED: December 1, 2003

_____

MILDRED PIERCE
Trustee

If property is abandoned, it is released to whomever is entitled to it. All liens and other interests remain attached to the property. For example, if the trustee abandoned the debtor's residence, the debtor would be revested with possession and ownership. If the house was subject to a mortgage, the debtor's rights in the house would still be subject to that mortgage, and if the mortgagee obtained relief from the automatic stay, it could foreclose.

Sale of Assets

In General   As soon as possible, the trustee will begin liquidating property of the estate. The trustee may negotiate a sale for all the assets to one purchaser, may sell the property piecemeal to a number of different buyers, or may hold an auction. If the trustee requires assistance to complete any of these types of sales, the trustee will seek bankruptcy court authority to employ attorneys, brokers, auctioneers, and other professionals as discussed later in this chapter.

Section 363(b) of the Bankruptcy Code governs sales of property of the estate in and out of the ordinary course of business. Unless the trustee is operating the debtor's business pursuant to a court order, all sales in a Chapter 7 case are out of the ordinary course of business. Section 363(b) authorizes the trustee to sell property of the estate out of the ordinary course of business after notice and a hearing. Bankruptcy Rule 6004(a) is more informative, and it dictates that 20 days notice of a proposed sale must be given to the debtor, all creditors, any committee, and all indenture trustees.

The content of the notice is described in Bankruptcy Rule 2002(c)(1). The notice must include the time and place of any public sale, the terms and conditions of any private sale, and the time fixed for filing objections. It must also describe the property to be sold, although it is sufficient if it does so generally. (See Exhibit 9.10.) If a camera is to be sold, the make and model will suffice without reference to the serial number. A notice of an intended sale of real property need not contain the legal description.

A party in interest may oppose the sale for any legitimate reason including that the purchase price is inadequate. Any objection to the proposed sale must be filed and served not less than five business days before the date set for the proposed action. Bankruptcy Rule 6004(b) states that an objection is governed by Bankruptcy Rule 9014, which means that it is a contested matter. If there is no objection, the court is deemed to have authorized the sale, and no separate order is required.

If an objection is made, Bankruptcy Rule 6004(e) provides that the date of the hearing may be set out in the original notice of the intended sale. Yet, since no hearing is required, if there is no objection, it would be unusual for the notice to set the hearing on an objection that has not yet been made. The more common method of providing notice of a hearing on the objection is for the objecting party to obtain a date and time from the court and state it on the objection.

If all of the nonexempt property of the estate has a value of less than $2,500, the trustee may merely give a general notice of intent to sell such property without having offers or auction dates chosen. The notice must still be provided to all creditors, indenture trustees, committees, the U.S. trustee, and other persons as the court may direct. Any objection must be filed and served by a party in interest within 15 days of the mailing of the notice.

Conduct of the Sales Pursuant to Bankruptcy Rule 6004(f), unless it is impracticable, an itemized statement of the property sold, the name of each purchaser, and the price received must be filed with the clerk of the bankruptcy court. If the property is sold by an auctioneer, the auctioneer must file the statement and furnish a copy to the trustee.

Sales Free and Clear Commonly, property of the estate will be subject to liens or security interests. The trustee may want to sell the property free and clear of those liens and security interests because buyers typically pay a higher price for unencumbered property. Section 363(f) allows the trustee to sell property free and clear only if one of the following is true:

- ✦ Applicable nonbankruptcy law allows it.
- ✦ The lien holder consents to a sale free and clear of its interests, which it might do if its lien will attach to the proceeds of the sale. Any such consent should be in writing.
- ✦ The purchase price is greater than the amount of all the liens.
- ✦ There is a bona fide dispute about the lien. For example, the trustee might allege that the granting of the lien was a preference.
- ✦ The lien holder could be compelled by law to accept a money satisfaction of its claim.

EXHIBIT 9.10 ✦ *Sample Pleading*

MILDRED PIERCE
700 Flower Street
Los Angeles, California 90001

Trustee

UNITED STATES BANKRUPTCY COURT
WESTERN DISTRICT OF CALIFORNIA

In re	)	Case No. 03-00001-JF
	)	
VIDEOS BY JOE, INC.,	)	Chapter 7
	)	
Debtor.	)	
	)	
Debtor's Address:	)	NOTICE OF INTENT TO SELL REAL
18 Hollywood Drive	)	PROPERTY
Los Angeles, CA 90001	)	
	)	
Debtor's Tax Id. No. 99-9999899	)	
	)	
	)	

TO THE DEBTOR, CREDITORS, AND OTHER PARTIES IN INTEREST:

NOTICE IS HEREBY GIVEN that Mildred Pierce, the duly appointed, qualified, and acting trustee in the above-captioned case (the "Trustee") intends to sell to Bountiful Buyer all the estate's right, title, and interest in and to improved real property commonly known as 18 Hollywood Drive, Los Angeles, California (the "Property") on or after January 1, 2004.

NOTICE IS FURTHER GIVEN that the purchase price for the Property is $100,000.00 to be paid at closing in cash or certified funds (the "Purchase Price"). The Trustee has reserved the right to accept offers for the Property received prior to January 1, 2004 in excess of the Purchase Price.

NOTICE IS FINALLY GIVEN that any objection to the sale of the Property for the Purchase Price must be in writing, filed with the Bankruptcy Court, and served on the Trustee and the United States Trustee no later than December 22, 2003. Any objection not timely filed and served may be deemed waived.

DATED: December 1, 2003

_____

MILDRED PIERCE
Trustee

The procedure to sell free and clear of liens is provided in Bankruptcy Rule 6004(c), which states that a motion must be filed for authority to sell free and clear, and it must be served on the parties who have liens or other interests in the property to be sold. As a practical matter, the motion for authority to sell free and clear (see Exhibit 9.11) will be noticed with the intent to sell (see Exhibit 9.10) and served on all creditors. All secured creditors have a right to bid at any auction sale of their collateral pursuant to Section 363(c). They may deduct from the purchase price the amount of their claim and merely pay the balance to the trustee.

Sale of Co-owner's Interest   Often the debtor owns property with another who is not a debtor in a bankruptcy case. The debtor may be a tenant in common

EXHIBIT 9.11 ✦ *Sample Pleading*

MILDRED PIERCE
700 Flower Street
Los Angeles, California 90001

Trustee

UNITED STATES BANKRUPTCY COURT
WESTERN DISTRICT OF CALIFORNIA

In re	)	Case No. 03-00001-JF
	)	
VIDEOS BY JOE, INC.,	)	Chapter 7
	)	
Debtor.	)	
	)	
Debtor's Address:	)	MOTION TO SELL PROPERTY FREE
18 Hollywood Drive	)	AND CLEAR OF LIENS
Los Angeles, CA 90001	)	
	)	
Debtor's Tax Id. No. 99-9999899	)	
	)	

TO THE HONORABLE JUSTIN FAIR, UNITED STATES BANKRUPTCY JUDGE:

Mildred Pierce, the duly appointed, qualified, and acting trustee in the above-captioned case (the "Trustee"), for and in support of her Motion to Sell Property Free and Clear of Liens, respectfully represents as follows:

1. Among the assets of the estate is certain improved real property commonly known as 18 Hollywood Drive, Los Angeles, California (the "Property").

2. The Trustee is informed that the Property is subject to the following encumbrances:
   (a) A lien in favor of the County of Los Angeles for 2003 real property taxes (the "Tax Lien").
   (b) A mortgage in favor of First City Bank securing a promissory note with a remaining principal balance of $80,000.00 (the "First Lien").
   (c) A mortgage in favor of B & B Finance Company securing an obligation of $20,000.00 (the "Second Lien").
   (d) A judgment lien in favor of Perfect Processing, Inc. securing a judgment in the amount of $5,000.00 (the "Third Lien").

3. The Trustee has negotiated a sale of the Property free and clear of the First Lien, the Second Lien, and the Third Lien, and all other encumbrances other than the Tax Lien, to Bountiful Buyer for a purchase price of $100,000.00 to be paid in cash at closing (the "Sale"). Bountiful Buyer has agreed to purchase the Property subject to the Tax Lien. The Trustee is of the opinion that the sale of the Property to Bountiful Buyer is for terms that are fair and reasonable and the best that may be obtained under the circumstances.

4. The Trustee requests that this Court authorize the sale free and clear of the First Lien, the Second Lien, and the Third Lien pursuant to 11 U.S.C. § 363(f) on the following bases:
   (a) The Second Lien is in bona fide dispute in that the Second Lien is not of record and may be avoided by the Trustee pursuant to 11 U.S.C. § 544(a)(3). The Trustee has filed her Complaint to Avoid Lien against B & B Finance Company concurrently with this Motion.
   (b) The Third Lien attached within 90 days prior to the filing of the petition that commenced the above-captioned case and meets all the other elements of a preference and may be avoided by the Trustee pursuant to 11 U.S.C. § 547. The Trustee has filed her Complaint to Avoid Preference against Perfect Processing, Inc. concurrently with this Motion.

—CONTINUED

EXHIBIT 9.11 ✦ *Sample Pleading* (CONTINUED)

(c)   First City Bank has consented to the Sale provided the First Lien attaches to the proceeds of the Sale in the same extent, priority, and validity as it attached to the Property.

WHEREFORE, the Trustee requests that the Court enter its Order authorizing the Sale free and clear of the First Lien, the Second Lien, and the Third Lien with only the First Lien to attach to the proceeds of the Sale.

DATED: December 1, 2003

_____

MILDRED PIERCE
Trustee

---

or a joint tenant. The trustee can sell just the debtor's interests, but there may not be a market for a one-half interest in a piece of property. For that reason, in certain limited circumstances, Section 363(h) of the Bankruptcy Code authorizes the trustee to sell the entire property, including the nondebtor's interest, even if the nondebtor owner objects. The circumstances under which this may occur are as follows:

✦ Partition of the property among the various co-owners is impracticable.
✦ The sale of the debtor's interest alone would yield substantially less than the proceeds due to that interest after a sale of the entire property.
✦ The benefit to the estate outweighs any detriment to the co-owners.
✦ The property is not being used for public utility purposes.

All four of these elements must be shown.

Co-owners are not without their remedies if the trustee seeks to sell their interest in property over their objection. Not only can they dispute that the trustee has met all of the elements of Section 363(h), but they also have certain explicit protections. For example, the co-owner has a right of first refusal. If the trustee has negotiated a sale of the property to a third party, the co-owner has a right to buy the property for the same amount. If the co-owner opts to buy the property itself, it can credit bid the value of its share and pay to the trustee only the value of the debtor's share. The co-owner will also not have to pay from its share any of the trustee's compensation, although it is liable for a share of the sale costs and expenses.

Unlike ordinary sales or sales free and clear of lien interests, authority to sell a co-owner's interest requires the filing of a complaint and the commencement of an adversary proceeding under the 7000 series of the Bankruptcy Rules.

Financing the Liquidation

In General   While performing Section 704 duties, the trustee will incur expenses. There will be costs for appraisers, security, rent, utilities, accountants and attorneys, and numerous other items that are necessary to maximize the value of the assets and the return to creditors. If the estate has a lot of cash, the trustee will be able to satisfy the estate's obligations as they are incurred or allowed by the court. Rarely will the trustee initially have enough cash to pay those expenses. To meet the shortfall until property is sold, Section 364(b) allows the trustee to incur unsecured debt and borrow funds out of the ordinary course of business provided there is prior court approval. Even though potential lenders would be entitled to an administrative expense priority for repayment, not many creditors are willing to extend credit or otherwise lend money on an unsecured basis to a bankruptcy estate.

Recognizing the problems trustees would have in obtaining unsecured credit, the Bankruptcy Code allows the trustee to use two different methods to attempt to obtain the cash required to finance a liquidation. The first method is the use of a secured creditor's **cash collateral.** The second method allows the trustee to obtain new financing by borrowing funds on a secured or on a super priority unsecured basis.

Cash Collateral   The term cash collateral is used frequently in the Bankruptcy Code. It is defined in Section 363(a) to be "cash, negotiable instruments, documents of title, securities, deposit accounts, or other cash equivalents whenever acquired in which the estate and an entity other than the estate have an interest." Cash collateral also includes the proceeds of property subject to a security interest. If a creditor has a lien on the debtor's accounts receivable, the cash or checks that are the proceeds of the accounts are cash collateral. If a creditor has a lien on the debtor's bank account, the content of that account is cash collateral.

The Bankruptcy Code states that the trustee cannot use cash collateral unless the other party with an interest in the cash collateral consents or unless the court, after notice and a hearing, authorizes its use. If a secured creditor has a lien on the debtor's accounts receivable, as the payments come in, the trustee will not be able to use any of those payments to pay expenses unless the secured creditor first authorizes the cash collateral to be used or until the court gives its authorization. Pending the authorization, the trustee must put the cash collateral in a separate account and must provide an accounting. This prohibition against use applies even if the secured creditor allowed the debtor to use all or a portion of the proceeds before the case was commenced.

If the secured creditor and the trustee come to an agreement allowing the use of cash collateral, the agreement must be reduced to writing. Bankruptcy Rule 4001(d) provides that a notice and a motion for approval of such a written agreement must be served on the debtor and whomever the court directs. A copy of the agreement must accompany the motion. Sample pleadings involving cash collateral agreements for debtors in possession that can be readily adapted for trustees are found in Chapter 11 of this book.

If any party in interest objects to the agreement between the trustee and the secured creditor, that party must file and serve an objection within 15 days of the date of the notice. If no objection is filed, the court can approve or disapprove of the agreement without a hearing. If there is an objection or if the court wants to hold a hearing, the hearing will be held. The debtor, the objecting party, those who received the motion, and anyone else the court requires must receive at least five days notice of the hearing.

If an agreement cannot be reached, the trustee will have to make a motion for authority to use cash collateral. Bankruptcy Rule 4001(b) provides that such a motion must be served on any creditor that has an interest in the cash collateral, the debtor, and any other person the court may direct. The hearing must be held no earlier than 15 days after the motion is served. If the trustee has an immediate need for the use of cash collateral, the court can hold a preliminary hearing before the expiration of the 15-day period but may authorize the use of only that amount of cash collateral as is necessary to avoid immediate and irreparable harm to the estate pending a final hearing.

At any contested hearing concerning use of cash collateral, the trustee will have the burden of showing that he or she should be allowed to use the secured creditor's cash collateral because the creditor is adequately protected or, in other words, that the estate's use of cash collateral will not harm the creditor. Section 361 establishes three nonexclusive means by which adequate protection may be provided, including:

✦ cash collateral
Property of the estate that is cash, negotiable instruments, deposit accounts, and other cash equivalents in which a creditor has an interest.

1. periodic payments to the secured creditor to compensate for any cash collateral used;
2. additional collateral; and
3. any other method that gives the creditor the equivalent of the cash collateral used.

For example, the trustee may argue that, in consideration for the use of the proceeds of the accounts receivable, he or she will grant the secured creditor a lien on all new accounts created. Alternatively, the trustee may argue that the **equity cushion,** the difference between the value of the collateral and the amount of the loan, is so large that it alone is sufficient to provide adequate protection. Whether the facts and the trustee's offer point to adequate protection will be for the court to decide.

✦ equity cushion
The difference between the value of the collateral and the amount of the loan.

Section 364 Financing   In some cases, the trustee will need the use of more than cash collateral alone. In such instances, the trustee will need to borrow new funds rather than only use cash collateral as it comes in.

As mentioned, the trustee may borrow funds on an unsecured basis in the ordinary course of business without notice, a hearing, or a court order. Section 364(b) also authorizes the trustee to borrow funds on an unsecured basis other than in the ordinary course of business with repayment entitled to an administrative expense priority. The trustee, however, must first obtain an order allowing the loan. Bankruptcy Rule 4001(c) governs the procedure for obtaining an order authorizing borrowing. It is virtually identical to Bankruptcy Rule 4001(b), which concerns motions for orders authorizing the use of cash collateral.

Although lenders can be repaid as administrative expense claimants, most lenders will not be willing to make new funds available on this basis because they will share pro rata with all other Chapter 7 administrative claims if there are not enough funds to pay all administrative claims in full. Section 364(c) provides that if the trustee is unable to obtain unsecured credit otherwise, he or she may incur debt with priority over all other administrative expenses (which gives the creditor a super priority claim), secured by a lien on property of the estate that is not otherwise subject to a lien, or secured by a junior lien on property that is already subject to a lien. For example, the creditor might agree to lend the trustee $10,000 to pay immediate expenses secured by a second in priority mortgage on the debtor's office building.

In the event that even those protections for a lender are insufficient, the trustee may obtain financing secured by a senior or equal lien on property of the estate that is already encumbered. In the example just given, the creditor's lien on the office building would be first in priority, and the existing mortgage holder would drop down to a second priority position. This is typically referred to as a **priming lien.** It is available only if the trustee can prove that sufficient funds are not otherwise available and the creditor with the former priority lien is adequately protected.

✦ priming lien
A new lien that is made senior in priority to existing liens.

Unlike cash collateral use, financing cannot be compelled by the court. The lender can only make funds available to the trustee voluntarily. As a result, lenders often request substantial protections as the price of their cooperation. Among the terms they may insist on in any agreement for Section 364 financing other than a super priority claim and a lien on all the assets of the estate are:

✦ cross-collateralization
The securing of prepetition claims with assets acquired postpetition or the securing of postpetition claims with prepetition assets.

✦ An acknowledgment of the validity, perfection, and enforceability of any prepetition claim and liens.
✦ A ruling that the prepetition loans are secured by the liens obtained for the postpetition financing and the postpetition loans are secured by the prepetition liens. This is known as **cross-collateralization.**

✦ A prohibition against any equal or senior liens or a surcharge for the costs of administration of the Chapter 7 case.

✦ A lifting of the automatic stay to allow the secured creditor to exercise its rights and remedies in the event of default and to setoff all proceeds received against the debt.

✦ A provision that the new liens and security interests are perfected without further act.

Bankruptcy Rules 4001(c) and (d) deal with the notice and procedure for obtaining court approval of secured debt financing. The procedure is the same as obtaining approval of cash collateral use.

Surcharge   The trustee may take advantage of two other sections of the Bankruptcy Code to find the funds needed to pay the estate's expenses. The first is Section 506(c), which states that the trustee may recover from property securing an allowed claim the reasonable, necessary cost of preserving or disposing of such property to the extent of any benefit to the creditor. This ability to recover the expenses from the property is commonly known as **surcharge.**

Section 506(c) is very controversial, and the courts seem to be having difficulty in determining what is reasonable and necessary, what constitutes preservation or disposal, and how benefit is measured. Section 506(c) will usually be invoked only if the Chapter 7 estate is insolvent, which means that the trustee incurred more in expenses than he or she received in proceeds from the liquidation of all of the unencumbered assets. In those situations, the secured creditor probably was not paid in full from the sale of its collateral. Predictably, when a secured creditor has suffered a deficiency, it will not want to voluntarily pay over money to the trustee so that administrative creditors can be paid. As a result, surcharge actions are almost always hotly contested.

One instance of when surcharge might be allowed would be, for example, when the trustee conducts an auction of the debtor's printing press, which occupied a substantial portion of the debtor's premises. The trustee hires the auctioneer, pays for the advertising and, during the period before the auction, pays for rent, guard service, utilities, and a worker to lubricate the press once a day to keep it from becoming unusable. During this time, the secured creditor knew of the trustee's efforts and made no effort to obtain relief from the automatic stay. Assuming the expenses were reasonable, the court might well allow the surcharge and force the secured creditor to pay the trustee's expenses from the auction proceeds. The trustee's expenses are the same ones the secured creditor would have to pay if it sold its collateral, and its benefit is directly related to the trustee's costs. In addition, it could be argued that the secured creditor agreed to pay the expenses since it knew that the trustee was incurring them, and it made no effort to obtain the right to conduct its own liquidation.

Another section the trustee may be able to use is Section 552(b), which provides that if the creditor had a prepetition security agreement that granted it a lien in particular collateral and the proceeds of that collateral, the commencement of the bankruptcy case will not interfere with its lien in the proceeds unless the court orders otherwise based on the equities of the case. Using the example just given, the trustee could argue that because it incurred all those expenses that served the interest of the secured creditor, equity dictates that the creditor's lien not extend to the proceeds of the sale to the extent of the trustee's costs.

Surcharge actions under Section 506(c) and actions under Section 552(b) are adversary proceedings controlled by the 7000 series of the Bankruptcy Rules and are commenced by the filing of a complaint (see Exhibit 9.12).

✦ **surcharge**
The payment of administrative expenses from the proceeds of collateral because the expenses benefited the secured party.

EXHIBIT 9.12 ✦ *Sample Pleading*

MILDRED PIERCE
700 Flower Street
Los Angeles, California 90001

Trustee

UNITED STATES BANKRUPTCY COURT
WESTERN DISTRICT OF CALIFORNIA

In re	)	Case No. 03-00001-JF
	)	
VIDEOS BY JOE, INC.,	)	Chapter 7
	)	
Debtor.	)	
	)	
Debtor's Address:	)	
18 Hollywood Drive	)	
Los Angeles, CA 90001	)	
	)	
Debtor's Tax Id. No. 99-9999899	)	
———————————————	)	
	)	
MILDRED PIERCE, Trustee	)	Adv. No. 03-00007-JF
	)	
Plaintiff,	)	COMPLAINT FOR REIMBURSEMENT
	)	OF EXPENSES OF PRESERVING AND
v.	)	DISPOSING OF COLLATERAL
	)	
FIRST CITY BANK	)	
	)	
Defendant.	)	
	)	
———————————————	)	

Mildred Pierce (the "Trustee") complains and alleges as follows:

PARTIES

1. The Trustee is the duly appointed, qualified, and acting Chapter 7 trustee in the above-captioned case.

2. Defendant First City Bank (the "Bank") is a creditor of debtor.

JURISDICTION AND VENUE

3. This action seeking reimbursement for the cost of preserving and disposing of collateral is an adversary proceeding over which this Court has jurisdiction pursuant to 28 U.S.C. § 157 and 1334 and the Order of the Chief Judge of the United States District Court, Western District of California, referring bankruptcy cases and proceedings, entered on July 20, 1984. This adversary proceeding is a core matter pursuant to 28 U.S.C. § 157(b)(2)(O), and the Trustee consents to the entry of a final order or judgment by the Bankruptcy Court.

4. Venue properly resides in the United States Bankruptcy Court for the Western District of California pursuant to 28 U.S.C. § 1409 in that this adversary proceeding is related to *In re Videos by Joe, Inc.,* Case No. 03-00001-JF pending as a Chapter 7 case in the United States Bankruptcy Court for the Western District of California.

—CONTINUED

EXHIBIT 9.12 ✦ *Sample Pleading* (CONTINUED)

FACTUAL STATEMENT AND CLAIM FOR RELIEF

5. Upon appointment, the Trustee took possession of certain machinery and equipment that was property of the estate (the "Equipment").

6. At the time the Trustee took possession of the Equipment, it was located in a warehouse pursuant to a written lease agreement between the debtor and the landlord that had expired by its own terms prior to the commencement of the debtor's bankruptcy case.

7. The Trustee caused the Equipment to be moved to a storage facility where it remained until it was sold by the Trustee for the sum of $5,000.00.

8. In connection with the relocation and sale of the Equipment, the Trustee incurred the following expenses (the "Expenses"):

Moving	$250.00
Rent	$150.00
Advertising	$100.00
Total	$500.00

9. The Trustee determined that the Equipment was subject to a perfected security interest in favor of the Bank to secure an indebtedness of $10,000.00. All proceeds from the sale of the Equipment were turned over to the Bank by the Trustee.

10. Despite demand by the Trustee, the Bank has refused to reimburse the Trustee for the Expenses.

11. The Trustee is entitled to recover the Expenses from the Equipment pursuant to 11 U.S.C. § 506(c).

WHEREFORE, the Trustee requests that the Court enter judgment in favor of the Trustee and against the Bank in the amount of $500.00, for attorney's fees and costs incurred by the Trustee in this action, and for such other and further relief as this Court deems just and proper.

DATED: December 1, 2003

MILDRED PIERCE
Trustee

EMPLOYMENT AND COMPENSATION OF PROFESSIONALS

Employment of Professionals

In General   In a large case, or a case involving litigation, it will be difficult for a trustee to perform all the required duties without professional assistance. For this reason, Section 327 of the Bankruptcy Code provides that the trustee may employ attorneys, accountants, appraisers, auctioneers, or other professional persons to represent the trustee or assist in the duties listed in the Bankruptcy Code.

Conflicts of Interest   Whether a professional can accept employment from the trustee is subject to very strict rules in the Bankruptcy Code. Section 327(a) allows a person to be employed only if they "do not hold or represent an interest adverse to the estate, and are disinterested." A "disinterested person" is defined in Section 101(14). It excludes a creditor, an equity interest holder, and an insider. Accordingly, creditors, stockholders, and insiders are disqualified from representing the estate.

Bankruptcy Rule 5002 sets forth further restrictions. It prohibits the employment of a trustee or professional related to the bankruptcy judge approving the employment. It also provides that if the individual is ineligible for appointment, so is the individual's firm, partnership, corporation, and any other form of business association or relationship, and all members, associates, and professional employees thereof. If the case judge's daughter is a lawyer, the daughter and her entire law firm are disqualified from being employed at the expense of the estate. Even if the trustee, examiner, or professional is not a relative of the judge, Bankruptcy Rule 5002(b) prohibits the appointment or employment if the person is or has been so connected with the judge to render the appointment or employment improper. Typically, however, it is the judge who will disqualify himself or herself and have the case reassigned to a judge who is not related or closely connected to the professionals.

There are exceptions that reflect the difficulty of finding competent professionals to accept employment in a particular case or the cost savings in employing a professional already knowledgeable about the facts of a particular case. For example, Section 327(c) provides that a professional will not automatically be disqualified for employment simply by virtue of having once been employed by a creditor unless the United States trustee or a creditor expressly objects. If either objects, the court must disapprove the employment if an actual conflict of interest exists.

Similarly, Section 327(e) allows the trustee to employ an attorney who has represented the debtor for a specified special purpose if it is in the best interest of the estate and if the attorney does not represent or hold any interest adverse to the debtor or the estate with respect to the matter on which the attorney is to be employed. This helps solve the problem of litigation pending at the time of the appointment of the trustee. The cause of action now belongs to the estate, and the trustee steps into the shoes of the debtor as plaintiff or defendant. Section 327(e) allows the debtor's counsel to continue in the litigation as the trustee's special counsel for that limited purpose.

Requirement of Court Approval   As indicated earlier, all professionals who will be performing services to the trustee and who want to be compensated for those services must have their employment first approved by the court. When approval has not been obtained before the services are performed, it may be possible to obtain an order approving employment retroactively. Most courts disfavor retroactive employment, and it should be relied on only as a last resort.

Procedures   Bankruptcy Rule 2014 gives the procedure for obtaining approval of employment. First, there must be an application of the trustee. This is one of the few times in bankruptcy practice that relief is properly sought by application. The application must state the following:

✦ Specific facts showing the necessity for the employment.
✦ The name of the professional to be employed.
✦ The reason for the selection of that professional. A resume or statement of past experience is the best method for meeting this requirement.
✦ The professional services to be performed.
✦ The proposed arrangement for compensation. This would include any retainer and the current hourly rate or the percentage of recovery to be received in a contingent fee arrangement.
✦ All of the professional's connections with the debtor, creditors, any other party in interest, and their attorneys.

If more than one of a particular type of professional is to be employed, the application should detail the need for multiple professionals, the services to be performed by each, and an affirmative statement that there will be no duplication of services.

Generally, a separate application is required for each professional. If the trustee needs counsel in many jurisdictions, it may be possible to prepare and have approved one application for all of these assorted professionals.

Although the Bankruptcy Rules do not require it, it is good practice, and it may be required by the United States trustee or local rules, for an employment application to be accompanied by the declaration or affidavit of the person sought to be employed. (See Exhibit 9.13). The declaration or affidavit can put into evidence any connection the professional has with the debtor, creditors, or any other party in interest.

Because of the general disfavor shown to retroactive orders, court approval should be obtained immediately. The United States trustee may require that the application be presented first for its review. Unless there is an objection to the application, it will usually be approved without a hearing.

A well-stocked form book should contain an application and accompanying order for employment of attorneys and accountants by the trustee. A form application for employment of an auctioneer and an appraiser should also be prepared. (See Exhibit 9.14.)

Compensation of Professionals

The preceding section discussed employment of professionals by the estate and described the various steps that must be taken before a professional can be employed. There is always the possibility that the employment will not be authorized. Even if the professional has successfully cleared the employment hurdle, there is still the risk that he or she will not be paid for the services performed. Professionals employed at the expense of the estate must apply to the court for approval of their compensation, and Section 328(a) provides that the court may allow different compensation from that which was agreed to earlier and approved by the same court "if such terms . . . prove to have been improvident in light of developments not capable of being anticipated . . ." when the original terms and conditions were fixed. In other words, the Court may authorize a lesser or greater amount of compensation than originally agreed to. Fortunately for professionals, this section is infrequently invoked since most contingencies can be anticipated at the time the employment is negotiated.

Section 328(c) allows the court to deny compensation and reimbursement of expenses altogether if at any time during the bankruptcy case, the professional loses his or her status as a disinterested person or represents or holds an interest adverse to the estate. If, for example, after an attorney was approved as special litigation counsel to the trustee for the purpose of collecting a fraudulent transfer from XYZ Corporation, the attorney was appointed to XYZ's board of directors, all compensation could be denied.

Finally, Section 330 provides that professionals are entitled only to *reasonable* compensation for actual and necessary services based on the nature, the extent, and the value of such services; the time spent; and the cost of comparable services in nonbankruptcy cases. The subject of professional fees in bankruptcy cases has generated tremendous controversy. Congress expressed outrage at the compensation paid in the larger cases and sought in the 1994 Amendments to limit fees. In the past, courts have always had substantial discretion in this area.

One of the things Congress did was extensively modify Section 330 in the 1994 Amendments. Section 330(a)(2) now specifies that the court may, on its own motion or on motion by a party in interest, award less compensation than that requested. In determining the reasonable amount of compensation, as required by subsection (a), Section 330(a)(3) states that the court must consider the following relevant factors:

- ✦ The time spent.
- ✦ The rates charged.

EXHIBIT 9.13 ✦ *Sample Pleading*

MILDRED PIERCE
700 Flower Street
Los Angeles, California 90001

Trustee

UNITED STATES BANKRUPTCY COURT
WESTERN DISTRICT OF CALIFORNIA

In re	)	Case No. 03-00001-JF
	)	
VIDEOS BY JOE, INC.,	)	Chapter 7
	)	
Debtor.	)	TRUSTEE'S APPLICATION TO
	)	EMPLOY COUNSEL; DECLARATION
Debtor's Address:	)	OF IRWIN SULLY IN
18 Hollywood Drive	)	SUPPORT THEREOF
Los Angeles, CA 90001	)	
	)	
Debtor's Tax Id. No. 99-999899	)	
	)	

Mildred Pierce, the duly appointed, qualified, and acting Chapter 7 trustee in the above-captioned case (the "Trustee"), in support of this Application to Employ Counsel, respectfully represents that:

1. The petition commencing this case was filed on October 1, 2003. The Trustee was appointed on October 2, 2003, accepted the appointment, and qualified on October 4, 2003.

2. To perform her duties as trustee, the Trustee requires the services of attorneys for the following purposes:
   (a) To advise and consult with the trustee regarding questions arising in the case and concerning the rights and remedies of the Trustee with regard to property of the estate, including rights in property that may have been the subject of voidable transfers prior to the filing of debtor's petition, and in regard to any secured, priority, or unsecured creditors of the estate;
   (b) To appear in, prosecute, and defend suits and proceedings concerning property of the estate;
   (c) To take all necessary steps in other matters involving or connected with the affairs of the estate;
   (d) To prepare or assist in preparing necessary applications, answers, orders, reports, and other papers, if any, required to be filed in the case; and
   (e) To perform all other legal services for the Trustee that may be necessary and appropriate in the case or to ensure the retention of such special counsel as may be necessary and proper for such services.

3. The Trustee desires to employ the law firm of Sully, Cooper and Rausch (the "Firm") for the purposes set forth in Paragraph 2. The attorneys of the Firm who will appear in the case are duly admitted to practice before this court. The Trustee has selected the Firm because it has considerable experience in matters of this character.

4. Based upon the foregoing, pursuant to the provisions of 11 U.S.C. § 327 and Rule 2014(a) of the Bankruptcy Rules, the Trustee requests this Court's approval of the employment of the Firm.

5. The Firm proposes to charge fees based upon its prevailing hourly guideline rates, which currently range between $80 for the most junior associates to $250 for certain of the more senior partners. The Firm intends to apply to this Court in conformity with 11 U.S.C. § 330 and 331 for interim compensation and reimbursement for costs advanced.

—CONTINUED

EXHIBIT 9.13 ✦ *Sample Pleading* (CONTINUED)

6. At the conclusion of the case, the Firm will file an appropriate application seeking allowance of all fees and costs, regardless of whether interim compensation has been paid. Upon allowance of such fees and costs, the Trustee will pay to the Firm the difference between the amounts allowed and any interim compensation paid.

7. The Firm understands and agrees that the proposed compensation arrangement shall be subject to 11 U.S.C. [section] 328, which authorizes this Court to allow compensation different from what is provided here if the fee arrangement appears, in retrospect, to have been improvident in light of developments unanticipated at the outset. The Firm understands and agrees that if aggregate interim payments exceed the amount that is ultimately allowed, the Firm will be required to and will promptly repay the difference to the estate.

8. Except as disclosed in the accompanying Declaration of Irwin Sully, the Trustee is informed and believes that the Firm is not connected with debtor, its attorneys, accountants, or creditors. The Trustee is further informed that the Firm represents no other party in interest and that it neither represents nor holds any interest adverse to the estate and that the employment of the Firm would be in the best interest of the estate.

WHEREFORE, the Trustee requests that she be authorized to employ the Firm at the expense of the estate upon the terms set forth above.

DATED: October 10, 2003

_____

MILDRED PIERCE
Trustee

Declaration of Irwin Sully

I, Irwin Sully, declare that:

1. I am an attorney at law duly admitted to practice in the State of California and before the United States Bankruptcy Court for the Western District of California.

2. I am a partner of Sully, Cooper and Rausch, the attorneys whom Mildred Pierce (the "Trustee") wishes to have represent her in the bankruptcy case of Videos by Joe, Inc. (the "Firm").

3. I know of no reason why, if the Firm is appointed as the Trustee's counsel, it cannot fairly and efficiently discharge all duties required of the Firm to be performed in this case.

4. To the best of my knowledge, information, and belief, and except as stated below, the Firm has no connection with debtor, its attorneys, accountants, creditors, or any other party in interest; moreover, the Firm neither represents nor holds any interest adverse to the estate in the matters upon which it is to be engaged. It is possible that the Firm may have represented from time to time one or more creditors of debtor in matters unrelated to this case; however, I am not aware of any conflict that would exist and moreover, I warrant that the Firm will not represent any creditor or other party in interest in this case, nor will it hereafter represent any person in connection with this case other than the Trustee.

5. No agreement exists in violation of the prohibitions of 11 U.S.C. § 504(a) or Rule 2016(b) of the Bankruptcy Rules for a division or sharing of any fees that may be awarded in this case.

I declare under penalty of perjury that the foregoing is true and correct, is based upon personal knowledge except for those matters stated to be on information and belief, and if called as a witness, I could and would testify competently thereto.

Executed at Los Angeles, California, on October 10, 2003.

_____

IRWIN SULLY

EXHIBIT 9.14 ✦ *Sample Pleading*

MILDRED PIERCE
700 Flower Street
Los Angeles, California 90001

Trustee

UNITED STATES BANKRUPTCY COURT
WESTERN DISTRICT OF CALIFORNIA

In re	)	Case No. 03-00001-JF
	)	
VIDEOS BY JOE, INC.,	)	Chapter 7
	)	
Debtor.	)	
	)	
Debtor's Address:	)	
18 Hollywood Drive	)	TRUSTEE'S APPLICATION TO
Los Angeles, CA 90001	)	EMPLOY AUCTIONEERS
	)	
Debtor's Tax Id. No. 99-999899	)	
	)	

Mildred Pierce, the duly appointed, qualified, and acting Chapter 7 trustee in the above-captioned case (the "Trustee"), in support of her Application to Employ Auctioneers respectfully represents that:

1. Among the assets of the above-captioned estate are eighteen (18) Sony Model 111N Video Cameras (the "Property"). The Trustee has attempted to sell the Property without third-party involvement, but is of the considered opinion that a well advertised, well conducted auction sale will generate the highest net return to the estate.

2. Going, Going & Gone, licensed auctioneers (the "Auctioneers"), have agreed, subject to Court approval, to conduct an auction sale of the Property. The terms of the understanding are set forth in a written Auction Agreement, a complete and accurate copy of which is attached hereto (the "Agreement").

3. The Agreement provides, *inter alia,* that Auctioneers will be paid their actual costs, up to a maximum of $500.00, and ten percent (10%) of the gross sales price for the Property. The Auctioneers will file a fee application upon the completion of their services and understand that the Court may modify the compensation arrangement at that time.

4. The compensation to be paid the Auctioneers is competitive with other bids the Trustee received.

5. As indicated in the Declaration of B. B. Going filed concurrently, the Auctioneers have no connection with debtor or its creditors and are a "disinterested party" as the phrase is used in 11 U.S.C. § 327.

WHEREFORE, the Trustee requests that she be authorized to employ the Auctioneers at the expense of the estate on the terms set forth above.

DATE: December 1, 2003.

MILDRED PIERCE
Trustee

✦ Whether the services were necessary to the administration of the case or beneficial toward the completion of the case at the time at which the service was rendered.
✦ Whether the services were performed within a reasonable amount of time commensurate with the complexity, importance, and nature of the problem, issue, or task addressed.

✦ Whether the compensation is reasonable based on the customary compensation charged by comparably skilled practitioners in nonbankruptcy cases.

Pursuant to Section 330(a)(4), no compensation can be awarded for unnecessary duplication or services that were not reasonably likely to benefit the debtor's estate or were not necessary to the administration of the case. Any compensation paid for the preparation of the fee application must be based on the level and skill reasonably required to prepare the application. Section 330(4)(b) does provide an exception for cases in the consumer context by providing for "reasonable compensation to the debtor's attorney for representing the interests of the debtor . . . based on a consideration of the benefit and necessity of such services to the debtor . . . ."

The issue of the reasonableness of compensation and expense reimbursement is brought before the court by the filing of a fee application. Typically, professionals seek court approval for their requested compensation and reimbursement of expenses at the end of a Chapter 7 case. The Bankruptcy Code does not, however, require that a professional wait to be paid until the end of a case. Section 331 of the Bankruptcy Code states that a professional may apply to the court not more than once every 120 days after the order for relief, or more often if the court permits, for compensation and reimbursement of expenses. This is called **interim compensation,** and the applications are **interim fee applications.** Circumstances that would warrant bringing an interim application usually involve cases where the work is very extensive.

Sometimes the court will not allow all of a professional's requested compensation to be paid on an interim application. The court may authorize only 75 percent or so to be disbursed with a 25 percent holdback to be received at the end of the case. Even if the court authorizes the disbursement of the entire amount, the award is only interim, and the court can always reconsider its interim allowance, reduce it, and force the professional to pay back the excess amount.

Whether it is interim or final, an application for approval of compensation and expense reimbursement (see Exhibit 9.15) must contain the information required by Bankruptcy Rule 2016. That rule requires a written application, setting forth:

✦ A detailed statement of the services rendered, the time expended, the expenses incurred, and the amounts requested.
✦ A statement of payments previously received or promised to the applicant for services rendered or to be rendered in any capacity whatsoever in connection with the case.
✦ The source of any compensation paid or promised.
✦ Whether any compensation previously received has been shared.
✦ Whether an agreement or understanding exists between the applicant and any other person for the sharing of compensation received or to be received for services performed in or in connection with the bankruptcy case.
✦ For the particulars of any sharing of compensation or agreement or understanding for the sharing of compensation.

Much of the information required by Rule 2016 will be provided in all applications, which may be prepared by the paralegal. With respect to the detailed statement of the services performed and the time spent, the best method is to attach the pertinent time records for the professionals as an exhibit to the application. Since reading the time records will give the court and parties in interest a lot of detail but not the flavor of the case and the professionals' involvement, a narrative in the body of the application highlighting the professionals' services is always well received. It will also supplement time records that are not explicit.

One of the more common objections to a professional's fee application is that the hourly rate charged is too high. It is helpful to include a short biography in the

✦ **interim compensation**
Postpetition payments made to professionals employed at the expense of the estate prior to the end of the bankruptcy case.

✦ **interim fee application**
The document filed with the court by which professionals seek interim compensation.

EXHIBIT 9.15 ✦ *Sample Pleading*

IRWIN SULLY
Sully, Cooper and Rausch
633 Hill Lane
Los Angeles, California 90001

Attorneys for the Trustee

UNITED STATES BANKRUPTCY COURT
WESTERN DISTRICT OF CALIFORNIA

In re	)	Case No. 03-00001-JF
	)	
VIDEOS BY JOE, INC.,	)	Chapter 7
	)	
Debtor.	)	
	)	
Debtor's Address:	)	
18 Hollywood Drive	)	APPLICATION FOR APPROVAL OF
Los Angeles, CA 90001	)	COMPENSATION AND
	)	REIMBURSEMENT OF EXPENSES
Debtor's Tax Id. No. 99-999899	)	
	)	

TO THE HONORABLE JUSTIN FAIR, UNITED STATES BANKRUPTCY JUDGE

Sully, Cooper and Rausch (the "Firm"), in support of its Application for Approval of Compensation and Reimbursement of Expenses, respectfully represents that:

1. The Firm was retained by Mildred Pierce, the Chapter 7 trustee (the "Trustee") of Video's By Joe, Inc. (the "Debtor") to serve as her bankruptcy counsel in connection with Debtor's bankruptcy case. On October 15, 2003, the Court issued its order authorizing the employment of the Firm by the Trustee.

2. For the period from October 15, 2003 through and including this date, the Firm has provided legal services to the Trustee in connection with Debtor's bankruptcy case. Those services, together with all costs incurred in connection with those services, are particularly described in Exhibit A to the Declaration of Irwin G. Sully, which is filed concurrently (the "Declaration"). Exhibit A also identifies the professional who performed the services.

3. A review of Exhibit A indicates the following initials, which reflect that time was expended by the following attorney and paralegal:

Initials	Identity
IGS	Irwin G. Sully
JAM	Julius A. Murray

4. Irwin G. Sully is, and at all relevant times has been, a member of the Firm. He graduated from the University of California School of Law at Berkeley (Boalt Hall) in 1970 and has practiced law in the insolvency area for almost 25 years. Mr. Sully's billing rate is $200.00 per hour. As set forth in Exhibit A, Mr. Sully performed 40 hours of professional services to the Trustee since the Firm was retained. During that time, Mr. Sully's services ensured that the Trustee was fully, fairly, and adequately represented.

5. The Firm proposes to charge fees based upon its prevailing hourly guideline rates, which currently range between $80 for the most junior associates to $250 for certain of the more senior partners. The Firm intends to apply to this Court in conformity with 11 U.S.C. § 330 and 331 for interim compensation and reimbursement for costs advanced.

—CONTINUED

EXHIBIT 9.15 ✦ *Sample Pleading* (CONTINUED)

6. The billing rates set forth in paragraphs 4 and 5 are identical to the rates charged all the Firm's clients for whom the referenced individuals performed services during the same period.

7. Billed at the Firm's ordinary hourly rates, fees total $10,000.00.

8. All of the services for which compensation is requested were performed by the Firm for and on behalf of the Trustee, and not on behalf of the Debtor, any creditor, or any other person.

9. No agreement exists in violation of the prohibitions of 11 U.S.C. § 504(a) or Bankruptcy Rule 2016 for the division or sharing of any fees that may be allowed pursuant to this Application or any future Application.

10. Also attached to the Declaration is a list of all disbursements made by the Firm in connection with its representation of the Trustee. Total costs are $750.00.

11. The firm believes and represents that the services performed have been beneficial to the estate, and that fees of $10,000.00 and costs of $750.00 are fair and reasonable, represent services or costs actually performed or incurred, and were necessary.

12. This Application seeks allowance of a claim for $10,750.00; the Firm also requests at this time authorization for the Trustee to pay the allowed amount. The Trustee has ample funds on hand to pay the balance of the amount allowed.

WHEREFORE, the Firm requests that this Court enter its Order:

1. Approving compensation and reimbursement of expenses for the Firm as follows:

Fees:	$10,000.00
Expense Reimbursement:	$ 750.00
Total:	$10,750.00

2. Authorizing the Trustee to disburse the sum of $10,750.00 to the Firm; and
3. Granting such other and further relief as the Court deems just and proper.

DATED: February 1, 2004
SULLY, COOPER and RAUSCH

_____

IRWIN G. SULLY
Attorneys for the Trustee

---

fee application of each professional involved. The biography could include length of practice, educational background, major cases involved in, publications, and other information to justify the hourly rate charged in comparison to other professionals.

Bankruptcy Rule 2002 requires 20 days notice to all creditors and other parties in interest of any hearing on an application for compensation or reimbursement of expenses totalling in excess of $1000. Typically, in a case where a number of professionals are employed, such as attorneys and accountants for the debtor in possession and the creditors' committee, the parties will confer before the hearing is set, and one of the attorneys will prepare and serve the notice of the hearing for all professionals.

DISTRIBUTING THE ESTATE

Objections to Claims

Once the trustee has reduced all of the estate's assets to cash, the next step is to distribute the funds to the creditors in the order of priority. Naturally, before making any distributions, the trustee will need to know the dollar amount of all the allowed claims to ensure that there are sufficient funds to make such a distribution.

The trustee has the duty under Section 704(5) to examine the proofs of claims that have been filed and make objections to improper claims if a purpose would be served. Obviously, if it was a no asset case and there were no funds in the estate to distribute to unsecured creditors, no purpose would be served by objecting to claims.

◆ **claims register**
A list prepared by the clerk of the bankruptcy court of all proofs of claim filed in the bankruptcy case.

If the trustee will have funds to distribute, the first step in determining the amount of allowed claims is to order a **claims register** from the clerk of the court. This will list all the proofs of claims filed and their dollar amount if the creditor specified one. The claims register will also indicate those creditors who asserted that their claim was secured or entitled to a priority of some sort. The clerk will assign each claim a number, usually in the order it was received. The trustee must then compare the claims listed in the register with the debtor's schedules or the debtor's books and records to see if the amounts correspond. If they do not, the trustee will want to examine the proof of claim on file with the court. Alternatively, the trustee can send a form letter to the claimant asking it to send a copy of the proof of claim to the trustee.

Sometimes the debtor's books and records will be wrong and the proof of claim correct. Other times, the proof of claim will be invalid for a number of reasons, most of which are listed in Section 502(b) of the Bankruptcy Code. The most common reason to object to a claim is that it is a duplicate of another proof of claim. Creditors often file two or more claims in a particular case because they have forgotten that they already filed one or in an abundance of caution to ensure that they receive a distribution.

Other reasons the claim would be invalid in whole or in part are:

◆ The claim is unenforceable against the debtor or its property under any agreement or applicable law. For example, the claim could be based on a contract entered into by the debtor under duress.
◆ The claim is for interest that was not earned by the creditor as of the date of the filing of the petition.
◆ The claim is for taxes against the property, and the taxes are more than the property is worth.
◆ The claim is made by an insider or the debtor's attorney, and the amount of the claim is unreasonable.
◆ The claim is for postpetition alimony or child support. These amounts are not dischargeable, and the claimant should seek to be paid from the debtor rather than from the estate.
◆ The claim is for damages due to the rejection of a lease of real property, and the amount claimed is more than the amount due at the commencement of the case and either one year's rent or 15 percent of the remaining term of the lease as long as it is no more than three years.
◆ The claim is for damages due to rejection or an employment agreement, and the amount claimed is more than one year's salary plus any actual amounts due.
◆ The claim results from a reduction due to late payment of a credit available to the debtor in connection with an employment tax on wages, salaries, or commissions earned from the debtor.

In addition, if the estate has a claim against an entity for turnover; improper postpetition transaction; improper setoff; a voidable lien that impairs an exemption; a fraudulent conveyance, statutory lien, or preference; or if the claimant has a lien that secures payment of a claim for punitive damages or a fine, the court can disallow the claim until the entity or transferee had paid the amount, released the lien, or turned over any property. Finally, if the claim was filed late, it should be objected to as untimely. Creating a table like the one in Exhibit 9.16 may be helpful in reviewing the claims and preparing a large number of objections.

Pursuant to Section 502(a), any party in interest has standing to object to claims. The procedure is discussed in Bankruptcy Rule 3007. It requires the objection to be in writing and filed with the court. A copy of the objection with a notice of the hearing must be mailed to the claimant, the debtor, and the trustee at least 30 days prior to the hearing. If, in addition to objecting to the claim, the trustee asks for affirmative relief of some sort (such as to recover the preference), the objection process is turned into an adversary proceeding and, as required by Bankruptcy Rule 7001, a complaint must be filed.

There are many different ways of preparing the appropriate pleading for objections to claims. Two different methods are shown in Exhibits 9.17 and 9.18. If there are only a few objections, a separate pleading may be made for each one. If there are many, the trustee may prepare one notice and attach as a schedule a list of all the claims to which objections are being interposed. In some jurisdictions, the local rules dictate the form of objections.

Sometimes the trustee will first write letters to the claimants explaining why their claims are invalid. At that point, a claimant may simply withdraw its claim by filing a notice of withdrawal as authorized by Bankruptcy Rule 3006. If the trustee has already filed the objection, a complaint has been filed against that creditor, or the creditor has significantly participated in the case, the claimant must obtain court approval of the claim withdrawal.

If a claim is allowed or disallowed, Bankruptcy Rule 3008 specifically authorizes a party in interest to move for reconsideration at any time before the case is closed. Notice and a hearing are required.

Payment of Claims

Once the trustee has reduced all of the estate's assets to cash and objected to all improper claims, the next step is to pay the proceeds to the creditors. Bankruptcy Rule 3009 states that "In a Chapter 7 case, dividends to creditors shall be paid as promptly as practicable." Despite this requirement, it is the unusual case in which any distributions are made before the case is ready to close. The reasons for this are many. Objections to claims are often among the last tasks done in a case, and it may not be until the case is ready to close that the trustee knows the total dollar amount of the claims. Similarly, until the case is ready to close, the trustee will not know the full amount of the administrative liabilities, thereby leaving the amount of the dividend to nonpriority creditors in question. This is not to suggest that interim distributions are never made to creditors. It is possible that the trustee could set aside sufficient reserves for anticipated future administrative expenses and disputed claims that might later be allowed, pay the priority creditors, and make a partial distribution to the general unsecured claimants.

The mechanics of making the payments are set by the Bankruptcy Rules. Bankruptcy Rule 3009 requires the payments to be made by check. Many financial institutions offer a free service of preparing the distribution check for trustees who have deposits of estate funds at that institution. The trustee need only supply the institution with the name and address of the claimant and the amount of the claim, and the bank will figure the exact amount of each check. The checks will then be issued by computer with the name of the trustee, the debtor, the bankruptcy case number, the full amount of the allowed claim, and the percentage distribution that the check reflects stated on the check. The trustee will also receive a register with the check number, claimant, amount of claim, and amount of distribution listed. This will be important for preparation of the final report and

EXHIBIT 9.16 ✦ *Analysis of Potential Preferential Transfers*

Claim Number	Claimant	Claim Amount	Wrongly Filed As Priority/ Secured	Duplicate of Claim #	Late-Date Filed	Estate Has Claim Against Claimant	Other Basis for Objection

EXHIBIT 9.17 ✦ *Sample Pleading*

MILDRED PIERCE·
700 Flower Street
Los Angeles, California 90001

Trustee

UNITED STATES BANKRUPTCY COURT
WESTERN DISTRICT OF CALIFORNIA

In re	)	Case No. 03-00001-JF
	)	
VIDEOS BY JOE, INC.,	)	Chapter 7
	)	
Debtor.	)	
	)	
Debtor's Address:	)	NOTICE OF HEARING ON
18 Hollywood Drive	)	OBJECTION AND OBJECTION TO
Los Angeles, CA 90001	)	CLAIM NUMBER 11
	)	
Debtor's Tax Id. No. 99-9999899	)	
	)	

TO DIAMOND RADIATOR AND ITS ATTORNEY OF RECORD:

NOTICE IS HEREBY GIVEN that Mildred Pierce, the duly appointed, qualified, and acting Chapter 7 trustee in the above-captioned case (the "Trustee"), hereby objects to claim number 11 in the amount of $3,666.25 filed by Diamond Radiator on November 1, 2003 on the ground that debtor's records reflect that only $1,479.36 is owing.

NOTICE IS FURTHER GIVEN that a hearing on this Objection will be held on January 1, 2004, at 10:00 A.M., or as soon thereafter as the parties may be heard by the Honorable Justin Fair, United States Bankruptcy Judge, sitting in his courtroom located in the United States Courthouse, 312 North Spring Street, Los Angeles, California.

NOTICE IS FURTHER GIVEN that if you wish to oppose this Objection, you must file a written response with the Court and serve it upon the Trustee not less than eleven (11) days prior to the hearing on the Objection.

NOTICE IS FINALLY GIVEN that should you fail to oppose this Objection, the Trustee will request that the Court enter its Order sustaining the Objection.

DATED: December 1, 2003

_____

MILDRED PIERCE
Trustee

---

account. If the trustee does not have access to such a service, suitable software for preparing the checks and the register can be used. Alternatively, the checks can be manually prepared, but that is a labor intensive and expensive task in a large case.

Since most Chapter 7 cases are no-asset cases in which the creditors do not receive distribution, it is not surprising that even in many asset cases, the dividend to creditors is quite small. In order to reduce the costs as well as the inconvenience of making dividends, Bankruptcy Rule 3010 provides that no dividend can be made to a creditor in an amount less than $5.00 unless authorized by a local rule or approved by the court. If any dividend is not distributed to a creditor because it is too small, the funds are paid into the court.

Exhibit 9.18 ✦ *Sample Pleading*

MILDRED PIERCE
700 Flower Street
Los Angeles, California 90001

Trustee

UNITED STATES BANKRUPTCY COURT
WESTERN DISTRICT OF CALIFORNIA

In re	)	Case No. 03-00001-JF
	)	
VIDEOS BY JOE, INC.,	)	Chapter 7
	)	
Debtor.	)	
	)	
Debtor's Address:	)	NOTICE OF HEARING ON
18 Hollywood Drive	)	OBJECTION AND OBJECTION TO
Los Angeles, CA 90001	)	CLAIMS
	)	
Debtor's Tax Id. No. 99-9999899	)	
	)	

TO THE CLAIMANTS LISTED IN EXHIBIT 1 ATTACHED HERETO:

NOTICE IS HEREBY GIVEN that Mildred Pierce, the duly appointed, qualified, and acting Chapter 7 trustee appointed in the above-captioned case (the "Trustee"), hereby objects to your claim for the reason set forth in Exhibit A to this objection. Hearing on these objections will be held before the Honorable Justin Fair, United States Bankruptcy Judge, sitting in his courtroom located in the United States Courthouse, 312 North Spring Street, Los Angeles, California on January 1, 2004 at 9:00 A.M. or as soon thereafter as the Trustee may be heard.

NOTICE IS FURTHER GIVEN that if you wish to contest the Trustee's objection, you must file and serve upon the Trustee a written response not less than eleven (11) days prior to the date of the hearing on the objection. Any ground for opposition to the relief requested by the Trustee not timely and properly filed and served will be deemed waived.

DATED: December 1, 2003

_____

MILDRED PIERCE
Trustee

Exhibit A

Claim No.	Claimant	Amount of Claim	Reason for Objection
4	Giggie, Inc.	$7,000.00	This claim is a duplicate of claim no. 14. This claim should be disallowed in its entirety.
10	Joseph Businessman	$20,000.00	Debtor's records do not reflect that it is indebted to this claimant in any amount. This claim should be disallowed in its entirety.
12	Diamond Radiator	$3,666.25	Claimant filed its claim in the amount of $3,666.25. Debtor's records reflect that only $1,479.36 is owing. This claim should be allowed in the amount of $1,479.36 only.

Dividend checks are mailed to the claimant unless a power of attorney, substantially in the form of Official Form 11A (the general power of attorney form) or Official Form 11B (the special power of attorney form) has been filed. If a power of attorney form has been filed, the dividend check is to be made payable to the creditor and the other person and mailed to the other person. Any power of attorney form received by the trustee should be noted on the claims register or other place where it will be handy when it is time to prepare the distribution checks.

CLOSING THE CASE

Once an estate is fully administered, the case will be ready to close. How a case is closed is primarily a matter of local practice, although the clerks have imposed some standardization. Generally, the trustee will file what is referred to as a **final report and account** concerning all of the estate's activities, including what assets were located and what they sold for; what expenses were incurred in the administration of the estate; and the total amount of allowed secured, priority, and general unsecured claims. The final report may also seek authority to pay dividends to creditors and seek the discharge of the trustee. A sample final report is presented as Exhibit 9.19. In some jurisdictions, the trustee will be required to give the clerk 90 days notice of his or her intent to file a final report so that the asset closing section of the clerk's office can perform the tasks it needs to do before the case can be closed.

♦ **final report and account**
The document filed by the trustee at the end of a Chapter 7 case that sets out the receipts, distributions, and allowed claims of the estate as well as any other relevant information.

Several weeks before the trustee is ready to file the final report, the trustee should notify all professionals of his or her intent to file the report. This will put the professionals on notice that they should file their final fee applications so that they can be heard by the court at the same time as the final report. Once the final report is filed, the clerk will prepare a notice of filing final account of trustee, of hearing on application for compensation, and of hearing on abandonment of property by the trustee under Bankruptcy Rule 2002(f). It will summarize much of the information in the final report and the various fee applications filed by the professionals. The notice will be served on the debtor, all creditors, and any indenture trustee if the net proceeds realized by the trustee exceed $1,500.00. Presumably, if the net proceeds do not exceed $1,500.00, no notice need be given.

At the hearing on the final report, the court will either approve or disapprove it, along with any applications by professionals and any request for authority to pay dividends. Assuming all requests are approved, the trustee will make a final distribution in the manner discussed in the previous section. Ninety days after the dividend checks are sent, Bankruptcy Code Section 347(a) requires the trustee to stop payment on any check remaining unpaid. The funds that were on deposit to cover those checks must be paid into the court by turning the funds over to the clerk. Bankruptcy Rule 3011 also requires that the trustee file with the clerk a list of all the names and addresses of the persons entitled to a distribution but who did not cash their checks.

Once the final report is approved, the final distribution made, and all unclaimed funds paid into the court, the case is fully administered, and it will be closed.

ETHICAL CONSIDERATIONS

If a paralegal is working for a firm that represents a trustee in bankruptcy, the trustee may bring to the firm numerous questions regarding the trustee's responsibilities. While the paralegal can never give legal advice, neither can the paralegal ignore a statement from a client that he or she intends to act in a fraudulent manner.

Pursuant to Model Rule of Professional Conduct 1.2(d), an attorney must not advise or assist a client in committing criminal or fraudulent conduct. Should the

EXHIBIT 9.19 ✦ *Sample Pleading*

MILDRED PIERCE
700 Flower Street
Los Angeles, California 90001

Trustee

UNITED STATES BANKRUPTCY COURT
WESTERN DISTRICT OF CALIFORNIA

In re	)	Case No. 03-00001-JF
	)	
VIDEOS BY JOE, INC.,	)	Chapter 7
	)	
Debtor.	)	
	)	
Debtor's Address:	)	FINAL REPORT AND ACCOUNT OF
18 Hollywood Drive	)	CHAPTER 7 TRUSTEE
Los Angeles, CA 90001	)	
	)	
Debtor's Tax Id. No. 99-999899	)	
	)	
_____	)	

TO THE HONORABLE JUSTIN FAIR, UNITED STATES BANKRUPTCY JUDGE:

Mildred Pierce, the duly appointed, qualified, and acting trustee in the above-captioned estate (the "Trustee"), hereby submits to the Court and to the Office of the United States Trustee this Final Report and Account in accordance with 11 U.S.C. § 704, and respectfully represents that:

1. The petition commencing this case was filed on October 1, 2003. The Trustee was appointed on October 2, 2003, accepted the appointment, and qualified on or about October 4, 2003. The Trustee's bond was set in the amount of $5,000.00.

2. At the meeting of creditors held pursuant to 11 U.S.C. § 341(a) on November 10, 2003, the Trustee examined the debtor with respect to its financial affairs and subsequently investigated matters concerning the administration of the estate.

3. To the extent required by 11 U.S.C. § 704, all claims have been examined and all objections have been determined by the Court. The time for filing claims in this case expired on February 10, 2004.

4. The claims filed in this case can be summarized as follows:

Administrative	$ 3,000.00
Priority	$ 1,000.00
Secured	$ —0—
Unsecured	$48,000.00
Total	$52,000.00

5. To the best of the Trustee's knowledge, all professionals employed by the estate have been notified of the Trustee's intent to file this Final Report and Account.

6. The time for filing applications for compensation has expired.

7. All property of the estate was inventoried, collected and liquidated, abandoned, or should be deemed abandoned. The estate is ready to close.

—CONTINUED

EXHIBIT 9.19 ✦ *Sample Pleading* (CONTINUED)

8. The receipts and disbursements made during the administration of the case are summarized below and detailed in Exhibit 1 to this Final Report and Account:

Receipts	$7,000.00
Disbursements	$1,000.00
Interest	$ 500.00
Balance on hand:	$6,500.00

9. The Trustee respectfully requests the statutory fee be allowed in this case in the sum of $405.00, based upon the total disbursements of $7,500.00. The Trustee also requests the further sum of $95.00 for reimbursement of administrative expenses.

10. As of this date, no dividends have been paid to creditors. After the payment of administrative expenses sought to be allowed, the Trustee will have on hand $4,900.00, which she seeks authorization to pay to those creditors in those amounts listed on Exhibit 2.

11. No agreement exists between the Trustee and any other person for sharing of compensation received or to be received for services rendered in connection with the case.

WHEREFORE, the Trustee requests that the Court enter its Order: (1) allowing, approving, and confirming this Final Report and Account; (2) fixing, establishing, and directing paid the fees, allowances, and expenses of administration incurred herein; (3) authorizing the payment of dividends; (4) discharging the Trustee and exonerating the Trustee's bond; and (5) granting such other and further orders as may be necessary or convenient for any orderly termination of the estate.

DATED: March 30, 2004

_____

MILDRED PIERCE
Trustee

Exhibit 1
RECEIPTS AND DISBURSEMENTS

Receipts:

Sale of Personal Property	$4,000.00
Refunds	
Utilities	$ 50.00
Workers Compensation	$ 50.00
Insurance Premiums	$ 50.00
Collection of Accounts Receivable	$2,850.00
Interest	$ 500.00
TOTAL:	$7,500.00

Disbursements:

Administrative Rent	$ 500.00
Utilities	$ 50.00
Auction Commission/Expenses	$ 200.00
Collection Agency	$ 200.00
Storage	$ 50.00
TOTAL:	$1,000.00

—CONTINUED

EXHIBIT 9.19 ✦ *Sample Pleading* (CONTINUED)

Balance on Hand:	$6,500.00
Proposed Trustees' Fees	$ (405.00)
Administrative Expenses	$ (95.00)
Attorneys	$ (750.00)
Accountants	$ (250.00)
Estimated Closing Costs	$ (100.00)
Estimated Balance Available for Creditors:	$4,900.00

Exhibit 2
DIVIDEND REGISTER LEDGER

Claim No.	*Claimant*	*Allowed Amount*	*Amount of Dividend*
1	June Film Co.	$ 5,410.71	$ 552.43
2	Imperial Processing	$ 2,417.54	$ 246.83
3	Ace Trucking	$ 990.00	$ 101.08
5	A-D Motor Freight	$ 6,800.00	$ 649.28
6	J. Businessman	$20,000.00	$2,042.00
7	Ben's Maintenance	$ 100.00	$ 10.26
8	United Parcel Svc.	$ 1,611.58	$ 164.54
9	Abe's Office Supply	$ 61.65	$ 6.29
11	Shell Oil	$ 129.16	$ 13.19
12	Diamond Radiator	$ 1,479.36	$ 151.04
13	XYZ Advertising	$ 2,000.00	$ 204.20
14	Giggie, Inc.	$ 7,000.00	$ 714.70

trustee client indicate to a paralegal that he or she intends to act in a criminal or fraudulent manner in the context of the trusteeship, the paralegal must immediately notify the supervising attorney. The paralegal is not in a position to give legal advice to the client, but the attorney is.

SUMMARY

The trustee's duties in a Chapter 7 case are to collect and liquidate all property of the estate and to distribute the proceeds of the liquidation to creditors. To collect property of the estate, the trustee must first locate and safeguard it. The trustee may need to bring a turnover action to obtain property of the estate in the hands of a third party. The trustee will also try to make the estate as large as possible by recovering any improper postpetition transfers of property of the estate. The trustee may also seek to recover any prepetition transfers of the debtor's property if the transfers acted to prefer one creditor over others, or if the transfers were made fraudulently: either with actual intent to defraud creditors or for too little consideration. The trustee can also avoid various debts and liens that are either improper or give one creditor a benefit over others.

Once the estate is as large as possible, the trustee will reduce the valuable assets to cash. Property that has little value or is burdensome to administer can be abandoned. Other assets will be sold. The Bankruptcy Code allows the trustee to sell assets without bankruptcy court approval in the ordinary course of business. All other sales require notice to creditors and, in most circumstances, a court order.

Under certain circumstances, a trustee can sell assets free and clear of liens or any co-owner's interests.

If the trustee does not have enough cash to finance the liquidation, he or she may borrow the funds on a secured or unsecured basis with court approval. The trustee may also use a secured creditor's cash collateral with the creditor's consent or with court approval, which will require a finding that the creditor is adequately protected. A trustee may also be able to involuntarily surcharge the secured creditor for the trustee's costs in preserving and protecting collateral.

The trustee is entitled to employ attorneys, accountants, auctioneers, and other professionals to assist in the performance of the trustee's duties. Court approval is required for any such employment, and certain procedural and substantive requirements must be met. In addition, the professionals can only be paid by filing fee applications, which must be approved by the court.

After or during the sale or other disposition of property of the estate, the trustee will review the proofs of claims filed by creditors and will object to the claims believed improper. Once all the objectionable claims have been resolved and the estate has been otherwise fully administered, the trustee will prepare a report of the administration of the case, pay creditor claims to the extent possible, and close the case.

✦ KEY TERMS

antecedent debt	cross-collateralization	interim compensation	secret liens
assignee for the	enabling loans	interim fee application	statutory liens
benefit of creditors	equity cushion	postpetition transfers	substantially contemporaneous
balance sheet insolvency	final report and account	preferences	exchange for new value
cash collateral	fraudulent conveyances	priming lien	surcharge
claims register	insider	receiver	turnover

✦ IMPROVE YOUR UNDERSTANDING

1. Why would Bankruptcy Rule 7001 exclude from its list of adversary proceedings, actions to compel the debtor to deliver property to the trustee?

2. One example of a situation in which it might be proper for a custodian to remain in possession of the estate's assets was given. Develop two others.

3. Why does the burden concerning allowing a custodian to stay in place shift when the custodian is an assignee for the benefit of creditors?

4. Postpetition, one of the debtor's customers pays the debtor for goods the debtor delivered prepetition. What are the trustee's remedies if the customer did not know that the debtor had commenced a bankruptcy case? What if the customer did know that a case had been commenced?

For each of the following exercises, determine whether the postpetition transfers are invalid under Section 549.

5. The trustee pays for guard service to protect the debtor's business premises.

6. Before the appointment of the trustee, the debtor pays its attorneys for their services in connection with the filing of the bankruptcy case.

7. Same question as above, but the services were performed in contesting an involuntary petition.

8. A secured creditor forecloses on a parcel of real property the day after the petition is filed. The petition was not recorded with the county recorder's office, and the secured creditor had no notice or knowledge of the commencement of the case. A third party who knows of the commencement of the bankruptcy case successfully bids for the property at the foreclosure sale and pays fair equivalent value.

9. An involuntary petition is filed against the debtor on June 10. On June 12, the debtor pays its landlord June's rent. The order for relief is entered on June 30.

In the following hypotheticals, first determine whether any of the transfers are preferences. If so, then determine whether any of the exceptions apply. For each hypothetical, assume the petition was filed on October 1, 2003.

10. On January 1, 2003, Big Bank obtained a judgment against the debtor and immediately filed an abstract of judgment with the county recorder. On August 1, 2003, the debtor sold a parcel of real property to which Big Bank's judgment lien had attached and paid the judgment.

11. On June 1, 2003, the debtor repaid his mother a loan of $1,000.00 made the year previously. On September 1, 2003, the debtor's mother lent him $500.00.

12. The debtor was very delinquent in his payments to the telephone company. On September 1, 2003, he paid the telephone company $500.00 in order to prevent it from terminating service.

Use the following factual situation in answering Exercises 13 through 15.

The debtor and her brother each own an undivided 50 percent interest in a 12-unit apartment building. The apartment building is subject to a mortgage in favor of First City Bank securing a note with a remaining principal balance of $50,000.00. There is also a junior mortgage securing an obligation of $5,000.00 held by B & B Finance Company, but this mortgage was never recorded. Two weeks before the debtor filed her petition, a previously unsecured creditor levied and obtained a judgment lien against the debtor's interest in the property in the amount of $1,000.00.

The debtor's brother has offered to purchase the estate's interest subject only to First City Bank's interest for $5,000.00. The trustee has been informed by a broker that similar properties in the same neighborhood are selling for approximately $75,000.00. Costs of sale would approximate 10 percent of the purchase price.

13. What should the trustee do?
14. If the trustee accepts the brother's offer, what steps must be taken and what papers must be prepared?
15. If the trustee decides to try to sell the entire apartment building, what steps must be taken and what papers must be prepared?
16. List the different types of financing the administration of an estate by how difficult they are to obtain. Next to each type of financing, indicate the showing the debtor must make in order to get the financing approved.
17. Which Bankruptcy Rule concerns motions to use cash collateral? What does it require if the secured creditor does not consent? What does it require if the secured creditor consents?
18. Can you think of any professionals other than those mentioned who would require bankruptcy court approval before they could be employed by the estate?
19. Through the course of a two-year long case, the trustee's counsel files and has approved a series of interim fee applications. Will counsel have to file a final application covering the services that were the subject of the interim applications?
20. Must the attorney for a Chapter 7 debtor file a fee application?
21. If a petition is filed on December 1, 2003, when is the first date that an interim application can be made?

✦ RESEARCH PROJECTS

1. Locate two cases that discuss the meaning of substantially contemporaneous exchange.
2. Locate a case interpreting the ordinary course of business exception. What factors did the court identify as material in determining whether the payment was in or out of the ordinary course of business?
3. Can you discover any statutory liens for the state in which you reside? Would they be avoidable under Section 545?
4. Obtain a copy of the fraudulent transfer statute of the state in which you reside. Compare it to Section 548 and note the similarities and the differences. What is the statute of limitations under the state law?
5. Locate a case under Section 548 in which the plaintiff prevailed on a claim for actual fraud. How was it proved?
6. One issue receiving substantial attention in the area of abandonment is whether the trustee can or should abandon real property that poses a health risk because of prepetition hazardous material storage or disposal. Locate and summarize two published decisions on this issue.
7. Locate a Section 506(c) case in which surcharge was granted and another in which it was denied. Compare the factual differences between the two cases.
8. Locate a case where retroactive employment was denied.
9. Locate another case where retroactive employment was approved.
10. Locate a reported decision that used the "lodestar" approach to determining the reasonableness of attorneys' fees. What is the "lodestar" approach?
11. Are there any local rules in your jurisdiction concerning objections to claims?
12. Are there any local rules in your jurisdiction concerning how a case is closed?

✦ DRAFTING PROJECTS

1. Draft a letter to the debtor's bank on behalf of the trustee effectuating the trustee's rights to the debtor's accounts.
2. Draft a letter to the United States Postal Service on behalf of the trustee effectuating the trustee's rights to the debtor's mail.
3. The debtor is in the business of renting videos. It operates in five locations, all of which are leased. Its other assets consist of five cash registers, 19,000 videocassettes, and some cash. Its liabilities consist almost exclusively of membership fees for which creditors will have refund claims. Prepare a list of tasks the Chapter 7 trustee will need to do to safeguard the assets and preserve their value. Think of some ways in which the trustee may be able to increase the distribution to creditors.
4. The debtor manufactures doorknobs. It buys components and assembles and packages the doorknobs for sale to retailers. It filed its Chapter 7 case suddenly and in the middle of its busiest season. Draft a motion on behalf of the trustee seeking authority to operate the business until all the components have been assembled and shipped to customers. Develop whatever facts are necessary.
5. Draft a complaint under Sections 548(a)(2) and 550 seeking to recover a transfer of a debtor's vacation home to his mother.
6. Draft a motion seeking approval of a Section 364(c) or Section 364(d) financing agreement.

7. Draft a withdrawal of claim notice pursuant to Bankruptcy Rule 3006 containing facts that allow simply a notice to be used.
8. Draft a motion requesting authority to withdraw a claim using facts that require the filing of a motion.

Chapters 12 and 13: Family Farmer and Individual Reorganizations

CHAPTER 7 CASES are the most common type of bankruptcy cases filed in the United States. The second most frequently filed case is a Chapter 13 reorganization for individuals. Chapter 12, the family farmer counterpart to Chapter 13, is just as common—among those who meet its eligibility requirements. In most nonrural jurisdictions, however, few Chapter 12 petitions are filed.

There are many similarities between Chapters 12 and 13. In fact, Chapter 12, which was enacted eight years after Chapter 13, merely copies many of its provisions. For this reason, and the fact that far more Chapter 13 cases are commenced than are Chapter 12 cases, we will consider Chapter 13 first.

CHAPTER 13

Chapter 13 Administration

A Chapter 13 bankruptcy is available generally to individuals with *regular income* and less than $750,000 in secured debt and $250,000 in unsecured debt as provided in Section 109(e) of the Code. It is important to remember that the secured and unsecured debt dollar amount limits for a Chapter 13 bankruptcy are covered by the adjustment of dollar amount limits of Section 104. Although most Chapter 13 debtors are wage earners, there are some small business Chapter 13 cases in which the debtor is self-employed or runs a small sole proprietorship. In those Chapter 13 cases, the business will continue to operate in the ordinary course without trustee or court control. Only transactions out of the ordinary course of business, such as a sale of the business, will require notice and a hearing. In addition, a Chapter 13 business debtor will be required to submit periodic reports concerning the operations of the business to the court or to the Chapter 13 trustee. Exhibit 10.1 shows the report required under the local rules of New Hampshire. This report will be discussed in greater detail later in this chapter.

In virtually all cases, the Chapter 13 trustee serves merely to ensure the debtor's compliance with Chapter 13 rules and make disbursements under the plan. The Chapter 13 trustee has the power to compel turnover of property of the estate in a third party's hands and has all the avoiding powers of a Chapter 7 trustee. These powers, however, are rarely exercised except by the debtor. Further, nothing in the Bankruptcy Code authorizes a Chapter 13 trustee or any other person to operate the debtor's business regardless of how badly the debtor may be doing so.

EXHIBIT 10.1 ✦ *Local Rule Chapter 13 Plan*

LBF 3015-1A

UNITED STATES BANKRUPTCY COURT
DISTRICT OF NEW HAMPSHIRE

In re: Bk. No.
                                                                                       Chapter 13

      Debtors

CHAPTER 13 PLAN DATED _____

This is a _____ month plan.

If this plan is in excess of 36 months, the reason therefor is as follows:

_____

_____

_____.

Debtors: (H)_____   SS #_____-___-_____
            (W)_____   SS #_____-___-_____

Plan Payment: Debtor(s) to pay to trustee monthly: $_____
                Number of months: _____
                Total paid into plan $_____

I. ADMINISTRATIVE:

Trustee's fee pursuant to 11 U.S.C. § 1302 and debtor's attorneys' fees.

A. Trustee's maximum 10% fee: $_____
B. Attorney's fee requested to be paid through the plan: $_____
C. Other: $_____

II. PRIORITY CREDITORS:

Creditor	Total Claim	Monthly Plan Payment

—*CONTINUED*

EXHIBIT 10.1 ✦ *Local Rule Chapter 13 Plan* (CONTINUED)

LBF 3015-1A

III. CREDITORS SECURED BY PRIMARY RESIDENCE:

Regular mortgage payments and arrearage to be paid as follows:

( )　　outside plan – mortgage is current and payable directly by debtor.

( )　　the debtor's estimate of the fair market value of such primary　　　residence is $_____.

( )　　the mortgage is not current and the arrearage only is to be paid　　through the plan as follows:

	Regular Payment	Arrearage	Total Monthly Plan Payment
1st	$_____	$_____	$_____
2nd	$_____	$_____	$_____
3rd	$_____	$_____	$_____

IV. SECURED CREDITOR (OTHER) :

( ) outside plan: current regular payment to be made by debtor.

Collateral	Value	Current Monthly Payment	Arrearage Payment Thru Plan	Total Monthly Plan Payment

V. UNSECURED CREDITORS:

Unsecured creditors' claims total $_____. The percentage to be paid toward these claims will be determined after the bar date for filing claims has passed and will be specified in the proposed order of confirmation. Unsecured creditors will begin receiving payment on a pro rata basis with secured arrearages and priority claims. If all scheduled claims are allowed, the percentage distribution to creditors is estimated at _____%.

Total available monthly for unsecured creditors: $_____
Monthly plan payment: $_____

—CONTINUED

EXHIBIT 10.1 ✦ *Local Rule Chapter 13 Plan* (CONTINUED)

LBF 3015-1A

Liquidation Analysis

In the event of a liquidation under Chapter 7, I/we would claim the state/federal exemptions, based on which unsecured creditors would receive_____%.

I.   REAL ESTATE (located at):_____

		Fair Mkt. Value	Liens	Exemption	Avail. Ch. 7
A.	1st 2nd 3rd				
B.	1st 2nd 3rd				
C.	1st 2nd 3rd				
D.	1st 2nd 3rd				
E.	1st 2nd 3rd				

Net Value Equity: $_____
Basis for exemption_____.
Value determined by_____.

II. TANGIBLE ASSETS:

A. Automobile (describe year, make, model):

Description	Value	Liens	Exemption	Avail. Ch. 7

—CONTINUED

EXHIBIT 10.1 ✦ *Local Rule Chapter 13 Plan* (CONTINUED)

LBF 3015-1A

Net Value Equity: $_____
Basis for exemption_____.
Value determined by_____.

    B. Household Goods:

Description	Value	Exemption	Avail. Ch. 7

Net Value Equity $_____
Basis for exemption_____.
Value determined by_____.

III. INTANGIBLE ASSETS:

    A. Litigation, Personal Injury Claims, etc.
        Please state estimated value and basis for determining same.

        Avail. $_____.

IV. OTHER ASSETS

	Description	Value	Exemption	Avail. Ch. 7
A				
B.				
C.				
D.				
E.				
F.				

Net Value Equity: $_____
Basis for exemption_____.
Value determined by_____.

Total Available in Chapter 7 $_____

—CONTINUED

EXHIBIT 10.1 ◆ *Local Rule Chapter 13 Plan* (CONTINUED)

LBF 3015-1A

<u>OTHER PROVISIONS</u>

If any of the following issues are raised please indicate here and specify the details thereof by an attachment hereto:

(a) Co-debtor matters (11 U.S.C. § 1301)

(b) Cramdown (11 U.S.C. § 1322(b)(5))

(c) Executory contracts & leases

(d) Undersecured claims

(e) Lien avoidance (impairment of exemption or preferential lien)

(f) Unliquidated claims

(g) Liquidating plan — sale of property

(h) Return of secured collateral

(i) Other:

I/We declare under penalty of perjury that the foregoing is true and correct.

Date: _____   _____
                        Debtor

Date: _____   _____
                        Debtor

The Chapter 13 Plan

In General   The unique feature of a Chapter 13 case is the plan, which can be proposed only by the debtor, not by any of the creditors. Although it looks like a relatively simple document, it allows for a substantial restructure of an individual debtor's secured and unsecured debt. As we shall see in the next chapter, unlike Chapter 11 reorganizations, creditors are not given an opportunity to vote to accept or reject the plan. As long as it adheres to the requirements of Chapter 13, the court will confirm it.

Some Chapter 11 cases will drag on for years without a plan being proposed, but a Chapter 13 plan must be filed no later than 15 days after the petition is filed.

Bankruptcy Rule 3015 does allow the 15-day period to be extended by the court, but cause must first be shown. If the plan is not timely filed, the court may dismiss the case or convert it to Chapter 7. Usually, the plan is filed with the petition.

While there is no uniform official form for a Chapter 13 plan, and the only formal requirement in Bankruptcy Rule 3015 is that the form be dated, the local rules of each district may include a suggested form as part of their local bankruptcy forms. In New Hampshire, for example, the local rules include a standard form for a Chapter 13 plan as part of their local bankruptcy forms (see Exhibit 10.1) and require that the plan "shall conform substantially to the form specified . . . with such alterations as may be appropriate to suit the circumstances." As can be seen by reviewing New Hampshire's local form for a Chapter 13 plan, it asks for detailed information on creditors, real estate, tangible assets, and intangible assets.

If the local rules do not specify a prescribed form, a personalized form can be developed and installed on the paralegal's computer. It might be wise to have the Chapter 13 trustee comment on its contents first, as the trustee's review of the plan will be the first hurdle to overcome at confirmation.

The number of copies and the persons to whom service of the plan should be made are controlled by the local rules of each district. Even though Bankruptcy Rule 3015 requires only that the creditors receive a summary of the plan's terms, some districts require that the plan itself be served on all creditors. For example, New Hampshire local rule 3015-1(b) provides that "a copy of the plan or a summary along with the notice of the confirmation hearing" will be served by first class mail "upon the Chapter 13 trustee, all creditors, and other parties in interest."

The Terms of the Plan   Exhibit 10.2 presents a very simple but very common Chapter 13 plan. It provides for the restructure of the debts of an individual who is behind in his house payments and taxes and is proposing to cure the defaults to his mortgage holder, redeem other secured debt, cure all tax obligations over time, and contribute a portion of future earnings to pay all other claims. As you examine the plan and the following discussion of it, you will see how all of these goals are achieved in the plan.

The first part of the plan is its means of implementation or, in other words, how creditors are going to be paid. Section 1306 provides that property of the estate, including earnings of the debtor, shall remain in the possession of the debtor, except as provided in a confirmed plan or order confirming a plan. Taking that into account, Section 1322(a) provides "for the submission of all or such portion of future earnings or other future income of the debtor to the supervision and control of the trustee as is necessary for the execution of the plan." As will be shown, this plan provides that the debtor's monthly mortgage payment of $700 will be made by the trustee. In addition, the debtor will pay $400 of *disposable income* to the trustee each month so that the payments to the other creditors can be made. Thus, in order to implement the plan, the debtor will pay the trustee $1,100 each month for the term of the plan.

The second part of the plan is its duration. Plan payments must be completed within three years. If the debtor can establish good cause, the court can allow the payments to be stretched to up to five years but no longer. The exception to this rule is if the debtor has long-term debt such as car or mortgage payments that have more than three or five years to go. Payments to those creditors must continue after the end of the plan period. In this case, the debtor has proposed a 36-month plan. If the proposed plan was to exceed 36 months, in the second section, the debtor would detail the cause for the extension.

Section 1322(b) of the Bankruptcy Code allows a Chapter 13 debtor to divide the claims of creditors into different classes as long as the claims in each class are substantially similar. Section 1332(b) also allows the debtor to provide a different

EXHIBIT 10.2 ✦ *Sample Pleading*

BANKRUPT C. LAWYER
White Charger Legal Clinic
One Learned Way
Los Angeles, California 90001

Attorneys for Debtor

UNITED STATES BANKRUPTCY COURT
WESTERN DISTRICT OF CALIFORNIA

In re	)	Case No. 03-00002-JF
	)	
JOSEPH CONSUMER,	)	Chapter 13
	)	
Debtor.	)	
	)	
Debtor's Address:	)	CHAPTER 13 PLAN OF REORGANIZATION
18 Hollywood Drive	)	
Los Angeles, CA 90001	)	
	)	
Debtor's S.S. No. 524-47-7448	)	
	)	

Joseph Consumer, the debtor in the above-captioned Chapter 13 case ("Debtor"), hereby proposes this Chapter 13 Plan:

I
Means of Implementing Plan

Debtor will submit future earnings or income of $1,100.00 per month to the Chapter 13 trustee to make the distributions required by this Plan.

II
Term of Plan

Payments under this Plan shall be made over a period of thirty-six (36) months.

III
Classifications and Treatment of Claims

1. Class 1 claims are those entitled to priority in payment under Section 507 of Title 11, United States Code. Class 1 claims will be paid in full, in deferred cash payments with interest, as follows:

	ALLOWED PRIORITY CLAIM	MONTHLY PAYMENT	NUMBER OF PAYMENTS	TOTAL
a. Trustee's charges	$500.00	$56.00	10	$560.00
b. Attorneys' fees	$500.00	$56.00	10	$560.00
c. Internal Revenue Service	$1,000.00	$112.00	10	$1,120.00
d. State of California	$200.00	$22.40	10	$220.40

2. Class 2 consists of the allowed secured claim other than the claim secured solely by an interest in the Debtor's principal residence. It shall be treated as follows:

—CONTINUED

EXHIBIT 10.2 ✦ *Sample Pleading* (CONTINUED)

NAME OF CREDITOR	ALLOWED SECURED CLAIM	MONTHLY PAYMENT	NUMBER OF PAYMENTS	TOTAL
B & B Finance Company	$500.00	$15.00	36	$540.00

3. The Class 3 claim is the allowed secured claim secured by the Debtor's principal residence. It is treated as follows:

NAME OF CREDITOR	AMOUNT IN DEFAULT	MONTHLY PAYMENT	NUMBER OF PAYMENTS
First City Bank			
a. Cure of default	$1,400.00	$53.00	36
b. Maintenance of payments		$700.00	

4. Class 4 claims are allowed unsecured claims not otherwise referred to in the Plan. Class 4 claims shall be paid pro rata seventy percent (70%) of such claims.

5. Class 5 claims are postpetition claims allowed under Section 1305 of Title 11, United States Code. Postpetition claims allowed under Section 1305 shall be paid in full by Debtor when due.

IV

Liquidation Analysis

As of the effective date of the Plan, Debtor owns property which, if a case under Chapter 7 of Title 11, United States Code were commenced, would be a part of the Section 541 estate and which has a fair market value of $20,000.00 Debtor would also be entitled to exempt property having a value of $20,000.00. Debtor would owe claims entitled to priority under Section 507 in the total amount of $1,200.00 and allowed unsecured claims in the total amount of $13,500.00.

As a result, there would be no funds available for distribution to creditors holding allowed unsecured claims under Chapter 7.

DATED: October 1, 2003

_____

JOSEPH CONSUMER
Debtor

_____

treatment for each class, but there must be the same treatment for claims in the same class. In the sample plan, the debtor has divided claims into five classes. They are:

Class 1   Priority Claims
Class 2   General Secured Claims
Class 3   Residential Secured Claim
Class 4   Unsecured, Nonpriority Claims
Class 5   Postpetition Claims

Class 1 claims under the plan are those claims entitled to a priority in payment under Section 507(a) of the Bankruptcy Code. They include administrative expenses, such as the Chapter 13 trustee's fee and the fee charged by the debtor's counsel. They also include the claims of the taxing agencies. Section 1322(a) of the Bankruptcy Code provides that all priority claims must be paid in full for the plan to be confirmed. It does not, however, require that the claims be paid upon confirmation or before payments can be made to nonpriority creditors. Under the sample plan, the debtor has provided that all priority claims will be paid in full over a period of 10 months. The debtor could have chosen fewer or more months to make these payments, but not more than 36 months. The payments are not exactly a simple division of the amount of the claim by the number of months the payments will be made because the debtor has provided that the claimants will receive interest on their claims. Of the payments the debtor sends to the trustee each month, $226.40 will be used to pay the Chapter 13 trustee and the other priority creditors. After the debtor makes 10 months of payments and the priority claims have been paid in full, the debtor will still pay $1,100 per month, but the trustee will use the $226.40 that was previously paid to the priority creditors to make payments to the other creditors.

Class 2 claims are the allowed secured claims against the debtor that are not secured by the debtor's residence. This could include appliances or furniture purchased on credit terms, an automobile, or other personal property secured loans. Class 2 claims could also include real property owned by the debtor that is not used as a principal residence.

For these types of secured claims, Section 1322(b) states that the debtor may modify the creditor's rights by extending the due date of the last payment or paying it less than the full amount that is owed; however, Section 1322(a) states that the secured creditors must receive no less than the value of their collateral. If the creditor is owed $100 and the collateral is only worth $50, its allowed secured claim is $50. The creditor will have an unsecured claim for the deficiency, which in the example would be $50. The deficiency will share in the amounts paid to unsecured creditors and usually will not be paid in full. This is the same result as redemption (discussed in Chapter 8) except that in a Chapter 7 case, the redemption amount must be paid in a lump sum at the time of the redemption. In Chapter 13 cases, the debtor can redeem by making installment payments under the plan.

In the sample plan, there is only one Class 2 claimant. Its allowed secured claim is $500, which the plan proposes to pay in full, and with interest, over 36 months. Of the $1,100 the debtor pays under the plan each month, the Chapter 13 trustee will pay $15 to B & B Finance Company. If B & B's total claim was greater than the $500 of its collateral, the balance would have been a Class 4 claim.

In a separate class from the other secured creditors is the creditor whose claim is secured by the debtor's home. For this type of creditor, Section 1322(b) prohibits a modification of rights. If the debtor wants to keep the house, even if it is only worth a fraction of what is owed against it, the full amount due to the creditor must be paid and the debt must be paid according to its terms. If the underlying note is due in one year, the debtor cannot stretch the amount due to two years. The debtor can stretch out repayment of the prepetition arrearages, but it can only do so for the length of the plan or until the note is due, whichever is shorter.

There are, however, two exceptions added by the 1994 Amendments. First, a Chapter 13 debtor may cure a default on a lien secured by the debtor's principal residence up to the time of the sale at foreclosure. Many states also give the debtor this right. Second, a debtor can now cure defaults within a reasonable time and maintain payments on a residence's mortgage even if the last payment due on the original payment schedule is due before the final payment on the plan. The courts will need to decide what constitutes a reasonable time.

Under the sample plan, the debtor has provided that the two monthly payments missed before the case was commenced will be paid with interest over 36 months. In addition to the arrearage payment, the regular monthly payment of $700 will also be made. In some jurisdictions, the debtor is allowed to make these payments directly rather than making them through the trustee.

Class 4 claims are those of the general unsecured, nonpriority creditors of the estate. Under the plan, they will receive a pro rata share of what is left of the $400 paid by the debtor to the trustee each month that is not needed to make payments to the other creditors. Beginning in the first 10 months, the amount available to these creditors will be $85.60. In month 11, after all the priority creditors are paid in full, the Class 4 creditors will share $332.00. In all, there will be $9,488.00 to be distributed to the unsecured creditors. This will be approximately 70 percent of their claims.

There is no minimum amount or percentage that must be paid to unsecured, nonpriority creditors. However, if the amount is too low in light of the debtor's disposable income, the court may refuse to confirm the plan because the debtor is acting in bad faith. Also, if the creditors will not be paid in full, a creditor can object and force a debtor to contribute all disposable income to the plan.

The final class of creditors under the sample plan is postpetition claims. The debtor will continue to incur various debts after the Chapter 13 case is commenced. All postpetition claims are to be paid in full. These claims can be paid through the Chapter 13 plan or, as is done in the sample plan, by the debtor directly. If postpetition claim payments are to be made by the trustee, the debtor should provide in the first section that, in addition to other amounts required under the plan, the amount paid to the trustee will be increased to whatever is necessary to pay Class 5 claims in full.

Under Section 1325, the bankruptcy court cannot confirm a Chapter 13 plan if the unsecured creditors will receive less under the plan than they would receive if the debtor's assets were liquidated under Chapter 7. In order to satisfy the court that the plan payments are greater than anything the creditors would receive if the debtor had filed a Chapter 7 case, many Chapter 13 plans include a liquidation analysis to compare the difference. In the sample plan, the debtor has shown that there would be no distribution to unsecured creditors in a Chapter 7 case because all assets would be exempt. Since the plan provides for a payment of 70 percent on unsecured claims, the debtor has easily met the Section 1325 requirement.

As mentioned, the sample plan is a fairly simple one. There are other provisions that could be added depending on a debtor's needs and wishes. For example, the plan can provide for the rejection or assumption of executory contracts or leases to which the debtor is a party. A plan can also provide for the sale of some of the debtor's assets with the proceeds distributed to creditors.

Plan Confirmation Once the debtor has proposed a plan and it or a summary has been provided to all creditors, the court will hold a confirmation hearing. Section 1325 of the Bankruptcy Code provides that the plan will be confirmed at that hearing if it meets all the requirements of the Bankruptcy Code, if the debtor has paid all required fees and charges to the court, and if the plan has been proposed in good faith and not by any means forbidden by law. Creditors are not entitled to vote for or against the plan. Their sole remedy if they do not like the plan is to object to confirmation. They will object if the plan has their claim in the wrong amount. For example, in the sample plan, First City Bank may claim that it is owed $1,500 in arrearages, not $1,400. B & B Finance company may assert that its collateral is worth $95 and not $50. Finally, creditors can claim that the plan was proposed in bad faith.

Plan Modifications

After the plan is confirmed, the debtor's situation may change and there may be a need to adjust the payments from what was provided in the plan. For example, the debtor may no longer be able to make the scheduled payments or, alternatively, its financial situations may improve markedly and it may wish to accelerate the payments. Either situation calls for a revision to the plan, which must be approved by the court. To modify the provisions of the plan, the debtor must obtain the court's permission to pursuant to Section 1329, which provides that "at any time after confirmation of the plan but before the completion of payments under such plan, the plan may be modified, upon request of the debtor, the trustee, or the holder of an allowed unsecured claim. . . ."

While the debtor is the only one who can propose a Chapter 13 plan, this is not the case when it comes to modifying the plan. Section 1329 extends this ability to "the trustee, or the holder of an allowed unsecured claim. . . ." Regardless of which party proposes the modification, the content of the modified plan must continue to meet the requirements of Section 1322. This means that the modified plan still may not provide for payments over a period longer than three years, unless the court, for cause, approves a longer period. In no case may the payment period be longer than five years.

In deciding whether to grant a modification, the court is guided by Section 1325, as it was in making a decision on the original plan's confirmation. While the court must confirm the original plan if it meets all the requirements of Section 1325, this is not necessarily the case when it comes to granting a plan modification. Aside from needing to ensure that the plan as modified complies with the requirements of Section 1325, most courts also require that the party seeking the plan's modfication show a substantial, material change in the debtor's financial situation that has occurred after the original plan's confirmation that now justifies the proposed modifications. If the court approves the proposed modifications, the modified plan takes the place of the original plan and has the same force and effect.

Life During the Plan

During the months and/or years that the payments are being made pursuant to the confirmed plan, which will lead to the granting of a discharge, the debtor typically retains the use, possession, and even the right to dispose of the assets. Although Section 1306 provides that upon filing a Chapter 13 petition, the debter's property becomes an asset of the estate, Section 1303, expressly, and Section 1304, impliedly, authorize the debtor to continue to used, sell, or lease the estate property.

Section 1303 applies where the transaction, be it the use, a sale, or a lease, is not in the ordinary course of business. In such cases, Section 1303 provides that the debtor's authority is based on Section 363, which requires that the debtor, like the trustee under Section 363, first obtain court approval for the sale or lease or other type of transaction that is not in the ordinary course of business. For example, if the debtor desires to sell its residence because of the need to relocate due to a job transfer or a new job, then because the residence presumably is not property used in the ordinary course of the debtor's business, the debtor would need to apply to the court for permission to sell the residence.

On the other hand, in the rare case where the debtor is self-employed and the court has allowed the debtor to continue to operate its business, the debtor's use, sale, and lease of business property is governed by Section 1304. While under both Sections 1303 and 1304, the debtor can continue to use, sell, or lease the property, which continue to be an asset of the estate. Under Section 1304, the debtor, who has met the difficult burden of being approved by the court to continue to be self-employed and operate its business, is not required to obtain the court's permission for transactions involving property used and disposed of in the ordinary course of business.

Discharge

In a Chapter 7 case, an individual debtor obtains a discharge of all of its debts except those listed in Section 523(a). To review, the most common nondischargeable debts are:

◆ Most taxes.

- ✦ Debts incurred through fraud or false financial statements.
- ✦ Debts incurred on the eve of bankruptcy for luxury goods or services or cash advances.
- ✦ Claims for fraud or defalcation in a fiduciary capacity, embezzlement, or larceny.
- ✦ Alimony and child support.
- ✦ Fines, penalties, or forfeitures payable to the government.
- ✦ Student loans.
- ✦ Claims arising from drunk driving liability.
- ✦ Debts that were not discharged during a prior bankruptcy case.

The Chapter 7 debtor need do nothing other than comply with its obligations under the Bankruptcy Code to be entitled to a discharge. In a Chapter 13 case, a discharge is also available—but it is much more difficult to obtain. Yet, once received, it is much broader than the discharge granted to a Chapter 7 debtor.

Under Section 1328(a), if a Chapter 13 debtor fully complies with the terms of the confirmed plan, there will be a discharge of all debts except claims for alimony and child support, claims for drunk driving, student loans, criminal restitution obligations, repayment of reenlistment bonuses, and claims on which payments are due after the plan is completed (such as residential mortgages). All other debts, including those that would not be discharged in a Chapter 7 case (such as fraud claims and claims not discharged in an earlier Chapter 7 case), are forgiven. The discharge will be automatic.

In some circumstances, the debtor can obtain a discharge in Chapter 13 even if all payments due under the confirmed plan were not paid. To obtain this discharge, Section 1328(b) requires that the court find that:

- ✦ The debtor's failure to complete the payments is due to circumstances for which the debtor should not be held accountable.
- ✦ Unsecured creditors have already been paid at least as much as they would have received in a Chapter 7 case.
- ✦ Modification of the plan is not practicable.

This is called a **hardship discharge,** and it is more limited than a regular Chapter 13 discharge. It will not discharge those types of debts that would have been nondischargeable in a Chapter 7 case (such as fraud claims). The debtor must make a motion requesting a hardship discharge.

✦ hardship discharge
The discharge granted to a Chapter 12 or 13 debtor who did not complete all plan payments but whose failure to do so was due to circumstances for which the debtor should not justly be held accountable.

Another difference between a Chapter 13 discharge and a Chapter 7 discharge is the frequency in which they can be granted. A Chapter 7 discharge is available only once every six years. There is no bar in the Bankruptcy Code to receiving a Chapter 13 discharge shortly after a Chapter 7 discharge. In fact, some debtors file a Chapter 7 case to discharge most debts and then file a Chapter 13 case to pay the nondischarged debts over time under the plan. These strategies are sometimes referred to as a "Chapter 20." Many courts disapprove strongly of the practice.

According to Section 1328(e), once granted, a Chapter 13 discharge may be revoked only if the debtor obtained the discharge through fraud that is discovered after the discharge is granted. The motion requesting that the discharge be revoked must be made no later than one year after the discharge. Even if the fraud is not discovered until the one-year period has run, the discharge will still stand.

Converting, Dismissing, and Closing the Case

Changing Chapters   As discussed in Chapter 9 of this book, a Chapter 7 case cannot be converted to Chapter 13 against the debtor's will. The reason is that to force the debtor to work to repay creditors violates the Thirteenth Amendment to the U.S. Constitution. For this same reason, a debtor cannot be forced to remain in Chapter 13. The debtor has the absolute right to convert the Chapter 13 case to a Chapter 7 case at any time and for any reason. The procedure is not covered in the Bankruptcy Rules, but since it is an absolute right, and the court has no discretion, no notice to creditors or opportunity for a hearing need be given. A simple motion indicating that the debtor desires to convert to Chapter 7 and a corresponding order for clarity in the file is all that is needed.

The rules for converting a Chapter 13 case to a case under Chapter 11 or 12 are very different. That conversion is entirely within the discretion of the court. It can be done at any time before the Chapter 13 plan is confirmed on request of any party in interest, including the debtor, the Chapter 13 trustee, the United States trustee, or a creditor.

Creditors may also want to convert a Chapter 13 case to Chapter 7. The Chapter 13 trustee may also believe that the case should proceed under Chapter 7 instead of Chapter 13. In such cases, upon request of a party in interest and after notice and a hearing, the court may convert the case to Chapter 7 if "cause" is shown and so long as the debtor is not a farmer. Section 1307(c) lists some examples of cause, including:

✦ The debtor's unreasonable and prejudicial delay.
✦ The debtor's nonpayment of fees and charges assessed by the Bankruptcy Code.
✦ The debtor's failure to timely file a plan or the debtor's failure to commence making timely payments under the plan.
✦ The court's denial of plan confirmation or revocation of a previously confirmed plan.
✦ The occurrence of a material default in the terms of a plan or termination of the plan.

To convert a Chapter 13 case to a case under Chapter 7, the party in interest must make a motion alleging the cause. Bankruptcy Rule 1017(a) concerns the notice and opportunity for a hearing that must be provided on such a motion.

Section 348 of the Bankruptcy Code details the effects of conversion of a case from one chapter to another. As discussed in Chapter 8 of this book, Section 348(a) provides that conversion constitutes an order for relief but, unless specifically stated otherwise, does not effect a change in the date of the commencement of the case, the filing of the petition, or the first order for relief.

Those items where the date of conversion overrides any earlier date are listed in Section 348(b) and (c). They include the debtor's exclusivity period, the end of the debtor's tax year, and the enforceability of any discharge waiver. In addition, the timing requirements of Section 365(d) start anew with the conversion of a case. Dates that had no significance in the prior case, such as the deadline to file a complaint to determine the dischargeability of a debt in the debtor's prior Chapter 13 case, spring in to existence in the converted Chapter 7 case.

To facilitate a smooth transition to a Chapter 7 case and the administration of the Chapter 7 trustee, Bankruptcy Rule 1019 requires that when a Chapter 13 case has been converted to Chapter 7, the following must be done:

✦ If the debtor has not filed the schedules, statements, inventories, or any required list, it must do so.
✦ Within 20 days after entry of the order converting the case, notice of the order must be given to all creditors.
✦ Chapter 13 debtors must turn over to the Chapter 7 trustee all records and property of the estate in their control.

✦ Within 30 days of the conversion, the Chapter 13 debtor must submit to the United States trustee a final report and account.
✦ Within 15 days of the conversion, the debtor must file a schedule of the unpaid debts incurred during the Chapter 13 case.

Dismissing a Chapter 13 Case   An alternative to converting a Chapter 13 case is to dismiss it. Creditors may believe the case was filed in bad faith and may want to proceed with their state law collection remedies. The Chapter 13 trustee may not be receiving sufficient cooperation from the debtor and may dismiss the case because it cannot be administered effectively. The debtor may want the case dismissed because it no longer has a need for the protections bankruptcy affords or may have thought that bankruptcy could accomplish more than it does.

Like conversion, and for the same policy reasons, a Chapter 13 debtor can dismiss the bankruptcy case at any time as a matter of right. A sample request for a case to be dismissed is shown in Exhibit 10.3. The only exception is if the case was originally commenced under a different chapter, in which event court authorization is required. Court approval will not be withheld, but the requirement for notice and a hearing will allow creditors the opportunity to object to the dismissal and request conversion instead.

Creditors and trustees will frequently add to their request for conversion an alternative request for dismissal (or will add conversion to their motion to dismiss as the alternative remedy). The coupling of these two types of relief is natural since the Bankruptcy Code generally provides that the basis for the relief is the same. In fact, Section 1307(c) states that the court may convert or dismiss "whichever is the best interest of the creditors and the estate." The best interest of the debtor is not a consideration. Bankruptcy Rule 1017(a) governs motions seeking the dismissal of Chapter 13 cases.

The effect of the dismissal of a Chapter 13 case is set out in Section 349 of the Bankruptcy Code. Section 349(b) provides that unless the court orders otherwise, dismissal reinstates any proceeding or custodianship superseded by the bankruptcy filing and any avoided transfer or lien. It also vacates any order concerning turnover, liability of a transferee of an avoided transfer, and setoff.

Unless the debtor is prohibited from filing a new bankruptcy case for 180 days under Section 109(g), upon dismissal, the debtor may refile a new bankruptcy case and obtain a discharge in the new case unless the court finds cause to order otherwise.

Closing the Chapter 13 Case   In a Chapter 13 bankruptcy case, the debtor is not required to do anything to close the case. When all the Chapter 13 plan payments have been made, Section 1302(b) requires the Chapter 13 trustee to file with the court and the United States trustee a report that shows all funds received and paid out and a certification that the estate has been fully administered. Under Bankruptcy Rule 5009, if no objection to the report is filed by the United States trustee or a party in interest within 30 days, there will be a presumption that the estate has been fully administered and no order closing the case will be required.

CHAPTER 12

Chapter 12 Administration

A Chapter 12 bankruptcy may be voluntarily commenced by a *family farmer with regular income*. This is a person, which can include an individual and some partnerships and corporations, who:

✦ Is engaged in farming operations.

EXHIBIT 10.3 ✦ *Sample Pleading*

BANKRUPT C. LAWYER
WHITE CHARGER LEGAL CLINIC
One Learned Way
Los Angeles, California 90001

Attorneys for Debtor

UNITED STATES BANKRUPTCY COURT
WESTERN DISTRICT OF CALIFORNIA

In re	)	Case No. 03-00002-JF
	)	
JOSEPH CONSUMER,	)	Chapter 13
	)	
Debtor.	)	REQUEST THAT CASE BE
	)	DISMISSED AND ORDER THEREON
Debtor's Address:	)	
18 Hollywood Drive	)	
Los Angeles, CA 90001	)	
	)	
Debtor's S.S. No. 524-47-7448	)	
	)	

Joseph Consumer, the debtor in the above-captioned Chapter 13 case (the "Case"), pursuant to Section 1307 of Title 11 of the United States Code, requests that the Court dismiss the Case.

DATED: October 30, 2003

_____

JOSEPH CONSUMER

WHITE CHARGER LEGAL CLINIC

_____

BANKRUPT C. LAWYER
Attorneys for Debtor

ORDER

IT IS SO ORDERED.

DATED: October 30, 2003

_____

JUSTIN FAIR
United States Bankruptcy Judge

✦ Has annual income sufficiently stable and regular to fund a Chapter 12 plan.

✦ Has less than $1,500,000 in debts.

✦ Incurred 80 percent or more of its debts in farming operations.

✦ Received 50 percent or more of its gross income in the previous year from farming operations.

✦ If a corporation or a partnership, 80 percent or more of its assets relate to farming operations.

✦ If a corporation, has no publicly traded stock and 50 percent or more of the stock is held by one family.

✦ If a partnership, 50 percent or more of the partnership interests are held by one family.

Upon the filing of the Chapter 12 case, the debtor becomes a debtor in possession. As debtor in possession, the Chapter 12 debtor will remain in control of its farm and will operate it subject to the benefits and restrictions of the Bankruptcy Code. For example, under Section 363, the debtor may use, sell, or lease property in the ordinary course of business without notice and a hearing. This would include cultivating and harvesting its crops or raising its livestock.

The trustee in a Chapter 12 case, like a Chapter 13 trustee, usually only serves to disburse plan payments to creditors. Unlike Chapter 13, however, the debtor can be removed as the debtor in possession. In that event, the Chapter 12 trustee's duties will expand to include management and operation of the debtor's farm. Under Section 1204, a debtor can be removed as debtor in possession only upon the request of a party in interest and after notice and a hearing. The grounds for removal are fraud, dishonesty, incompetence, gross mismanagement, or similar cause.

The Chapter 12 Plan

In General   Only a debtor may file a Chapter 12 plan, even if the debtor has been removed as the debtor in possession. Under Section 1221, the plan must be filed within 90 days of the filing of the petition. The bankruptcy court can extend that 90-day period, but only if it finds that the extension is needed because of circumstances that are not the debtor's fault. Like Chapter 13, in most cases, the Chapter 12 plan is filed with the petition or shortly thereafter.

The Terms of the Plan   Like Chapter 13 plans, most Chapter 12 plans are very similar and relatively simple. Usually they will designate one or more classes of secured claims, one class of unsecured claims, and if the debtor is a partnership or corporation, one class of equity interests. The plan payments to creditors will be funded from the income of the farming operations after the payment of the debtor's operating and living expenses for three or sometimes five years. Priority creditors will be paid in full. Secured creditors will be paid their full allowed claim and unsecured creditors will receive a percentage of this claim, depending on the profit projected. Payments will be made by the debtor to the Chapter 12 trustee who will then distribute the funds to the creditors in the manner and amounts provided in the plan. A typical Chapter 12 plan is shown in Exhibit 10.4.

Section 1222 sets forth the mandatory provisions that must be contained in every Chapter 12 plan. It also lists certain permissible provisions that the debtor may opt to include. The mandatory provisions set out in Section 1222(a) are:

✦ The plan must provide for the submission of the debtor's future income to the Chapter 12 trustee as is necessary under the plan.

✦ The plan must provide for the payment in full of all priority claims listed in Section 507, such as taxes and administrative expenses, unless the priority creditor agrees to different treatment.

Exhibit 10.4 ✦ *Sample Pleading*

BANKRUPT C. LAWYER
White Charger Legal Clinic
One Learned Way
Los Angeles, California 90001

Attorneys for Debtor

UNITED STATES BANKRUPTCY COURT
WESTERN DISTRICT OF CALIFORNIA

In re	)	Case No. 03-00005-JF
	)	
JOSEPH FARMER,	)	Chapter 12
	)	
Debtor.	)	CHAPTER 12 PLAN OF
	)	REORGANIZATION
Debtor's Address:	)	
18 Hollywood Drive	)	
Los Angeles, CA 90001	)	
	)	
Debtor's S.S. No. 524-47-7448	)	
	)	

Joseph Farmer, the debtor in the above-captioned Chapter 12 case ("Debtor"), hereby proposes this Chapter 12 Plan:

I

Means of Implementing Plan

Debtor shall make annual payments to the trustee on October 1st of each year, commencing October 1, 2003, and continuing until October 1, 2006, in the amount of the debtor's excess income for the previous year, but in no event less than $10,000 per year. Excess income shall mean the net income received by Debtor from farming operations during the applicable year less $47,000, which constitutes the debtor's living expenses and $5,000, which the debtor shall retain as a reserve for funding of the next year's crop.

II

Classification and Treatment of Claims

1. Class 1 claims are those entitled to priority in payment under Section 507 of the Bankruptcy Code. The trustee shall receive and retain as the trustee's percentage fee under the Plan an amount equal to five percent (5%) of all payments distributed by the trustee pursuant to the plan from the effective date of the plan up to and including October 1, 1998. All other Class 1 claims shall be paid in cash in full out of the funds received and distributed by the trustee.

2. Class 2 consists of the allowed secured claim of Credit Agribusiness Bank ("CAB"). CAB has a lien on Debtor's real property securing a debt of $100,000. Debtor values the real property at $60,000 and, accordingly, the secured claim of CAB shall be reduced to $60,000. CAB's allowed secured claim shall bear interest at the existing contract rate of ten percent (10%). CAB's allowed secured claim shall be paid directly by Debtor in 120 equal monthly installments of principal of $500 plus accrued interest, on the first day of each month commencing October 1, 2003, and continuing through October 1, 2013. The balance of CAB's claim in excess of $60,000 shall be a Class 3 claim.

3. Class 3—Allowed Unsecured Claims. These claims shall share *pro rata* in the distributions made by Debtor to the trustee after payment in full by the trustee of the Class 1 claim.

—*CONTINUED*

EXHIBIT 10.4 ✦ *Sample Pleading* (CONTINUED)

III

Executory Contracts and Unexpired Leases

All executory contracts and unexpired leases not previously rejected are hereby assumed.

IV

Liquidation Analysis

Based upon its projections of farming income during the term of the Plan, Debtor believes that he will distribute to creditors approximately 50 percent of the allowed amount of their claims. Based upon the values of the Debtor's assets and the amount of secured and unsecured claims as set forth in Debtor's schedules, Debtor believes that the return to general unsecured creditors in a Chapter 7 case would be zero because all of Debtor's assets are encumbered by liens or security interests. Accordingly, Debtor believes that the value, as of the effective date of the plan, of property to be distributed under the plan on account of each allowed unsecured claim is not less than the amount that would be paid on such claim if the estate of Debtor were liquidated under Chapter 7 of the Bankruptcy Code.

DATED: October 1, 2003

_____

JOSEPH FARMER

✦ Each claim within a class must receive the same treatment unless a holder in the class agrees to less favorable treatment.

Section 1222(b) lists the optional provisions of a plan. They include:

✦ The plan may designate various classes of unsecured claims provided the claims in each class are substantially similar and the plan does not discriminate unfairly among the classes. The plan may also create an administrative convenience class consisting of claims that are less than a certain amount. These small claims will usually be paid in full so that very small distributions to these creditors will not have to be paid over time to the creditors.

✦ The rights of holders to secured claims, including home mortgages, can be modified. Payment terms can be reduced, stretched out, or otherwise changed provided the secured creditor is paid the full amount of its allowed claim.

✦ Payments to unsecured creditors can be made at the same time as payments are being made to secured creditors.

✦ Executory contracts and unexpired leases can be assumed or rejected.

✦ The plan can provide for a sale of all or most of the debtor's property.

Section 1222(c) provides that under the plan, payments to unsecured creditors can be made over three years unless the court approves up to five years. The Chapter 12 trustee will receive all payments under the plan for priority and unsecured claims. The trustee may receive payments for secured claims, but Chapter 12 allows those payments to be made directly by the debtor.

Plan Confirmation   The bankruptcy court must finish the Chapter 12 plan confirmation hearing within 45 days after the plan is filed, unless it finds cause to extend that deadline. Bankruptcy Rule 2002(a)(8) requires 20 days notice to the trustee, all creditors, and all equity interest holders of the confirmation hearing date in a Chapter 12 Bankruptcy. Bankruptcy Rule 3015(d) states that a copy of the plan, or a court approved summary of the plan must accompany the notice.

The Bankruptcy Rules do not set a deadline for filing objections to a Chapter 12 plan other than before the plan is confirmed. Because only 20 days notice is provided, a creditor or other objecting party will want to act quickly. A sample objection to a Chapter 12 plan is shown in Exhibit 10.5.

The requirements for confirmation of a Chapter 12 plan are set out in Section 1225. There are five requirements that apply in all Chapter 12 cases and two that sometimes apply. If the plan meets all applicable requirements, it will be confirmed.

The five general requirements are:

✦ The plan complies with Chapter 12 and all other relevant provisions of the Bankruptcy Code.
✦ All required fees and costs have been paid.
✦ The plan was proposed in good faith and not by any means forbidden by law.
✦ Creditors will receive at least as much under the plan as they would under the debtor's Chapter 7 liquidation.
✦ The debtor will be able to make all payments under the plan and to otherwise comply with the plan.

There is a sixth requirement that only applies if the debtor has secured creditors. Unless the secured creditor consents, or unless the debtor returns the creditor's collateral, under Section 1225(a)(5)(B), the plan must satisfy two requirements for each secured creditor. First, the creditor must retain its lien. Second, the creditor must receive under the plan the allowed amount of its claim. The allowed amount is the amount due up to the value of the collateral. If the creditor is due $100 and the collateral is worth $100, the allowed amount of the claim is $100. If the collateral is only worth $50, the allowed amount of the claim is $50.

The debtor is not obligated to pay the creditor all at once. The plan can stretch out the payments to a secured creditor provided the creditor is paid interest. The length of time the payments can be stretched out and the interest rate are not set in the Bankruptcy Code or the Bankruptcy Rules but will depend on the existing contracts of other parties, market conditions, and the type of collateral. Payments to secured creditors can exceed the three-to-five year term of the plan.

The final plan confirmation requirement only applies if the Chapter 12 trustee or an unsecured creditor objects to confirmation. If there is an objection by one of those parties, Section 1225(b)(1) states that the plan can only be confirmed if unsecured creditors are being paid in full or all of the debtor's disposable income is being used to make plan payments. Disposable income is defined in Section 1225(b)(2) as the debtor's income that is not necessary for the maintenance and support of the debtor and his or her dependents or for the continuation, preservation, and operation of the debtor's business.

The provisions of a confirmed plan will bind the debtor and each of the creditors. If the Chapter 12 debtor is a partnership or corporation, confirmation will also bind the partners or shareholders. However, if the debtor does not receive a discharge, the plan will have no binding effect.

Discharge

Once all the plan payments have been made, the debtor is entitled to a discharge of all debts provided for in the plan. The only exceptions under Section 1228 are those payments that extend beyond the plan, such as long-term obligations to secured creditors and those listed in Section 523(a) that would not be discharged in a

EXHIBIT 10.5 ✦ *Sample Pleading*

WARREN PEASE
Pease, Inyore, & Time
1000 Star Boulevard
Los Angeles, California 90001

Attorneys for Credit Agribusiness Bank

UNITED STATES BANKRUPTCY COURT
WESTERN DISTRICT OF CALIFORNIA

In re	)	Case No. 03-00005-JF
	)	
JOSEPH FARMER,	)	Chapter 12
	)	
Debtor.	)	OBJECTION TO CHAPTER 12 PLAN
	)	
Debtor's Address:	)	
18 Hollywood Drive	)	
Los Angeles, CA 90001	)	
	)	
Debtor's S.S. No. 524-47-7448	)	
_____	)	

Credit Agribusiness Bank ("CAB"), the holder of an unsecured and a secured claim against Joseph Farmer, the above-named debtor ("Debtor"), hereby objects to confirmation of Debtor's Chapter 12 plan for the reasons set forth below:

1. Debtor is not eligible to be a Chapter 12 debtor under Section 109(f) because, on the date of the filing of the petition, Debtor received less than 50 percent of his gross income for the taxable year immediately preceding the taxable year in which the case was filed from a farming operation.

2. Debtor is not eligible to be a Chapter 12 debtor under Section 109(f) because Debtor's annual income is not sufficiently stable and regular to enable Debtor to make payments under a Chapter 12 plan.

3. The plan does not meet the confirmation requirements of Section 1225(a)(1) because it does not comply with the provisions of Chapter 12 and with other applicable provisions of the Bankruptcy Code for the following reasons:

   (A) The plan does not provide for submission of sufficient income to the trustee as is necessary for execution of the plan;

   (B) The plan does not provide for full cash payment of all claims entitled to priority under Section 507; and

   (C) The plan discriminates unfairly by placing the claim of CAB in a separate class from other claims that are substantially similar.

4. The plan does not provide for the submission of all of Debtor's disposable income as that term is defined in Section 1225(b)(2) of the Bankruptcy Code.

DATED: October 15, 2003

PEASE, INYORE, & TIME

_____

WARREN PEASE
Attorneys for Credit Agribusiness Bank

Chapter 7 case. The list of claims exempted from discharge under Section 1328(a) was set forth earlier in this chapter in the discussion of a Chapter 13 discharge.

Even if the debtor cannot make all the payments called for in the plan, it can apply for a hardship discharge. The court may grant a family farmer a hardship discharge if:

+ The debtor's failure to make all plan payments is due to circumstances for which the debtor should not justly be held accountable.
+ The creditors received as much under the plan as they would have received if the debtor had commenced a Chapter 7 case.
+ Modification of the plan is not feasible.

The only differences between a typical Chapter 12 discharge and a hardship discharge is that the hardship discharge is not automatic and does not extend to postpetition debts.

Pursuant to Section 1228(d), a discharge can be revoked by the court upon the request of a creditor or other party in interest within one year if the discharge was obtained through fraud and the moving party did not know about it at the time the discharge was granted.

Converting, Dismissing, and Closing the Case

Changing Chapters   As is true for debtors under Chapters 11 and 13, a family farmer has an absolute right under Section 1208(a) to convert its Chapter 12 case to a Chapter 7 case at any time unless the case was previously converted to Chapter 12 from another chapter.

The court may also convert a case to Chapter 7 upon the request of a party in interest. However, the grounds allowing the court to do so are limited solely to fraud on the debtor's part in connection with the bankruptcy case. Even gross mismanagement, dishonesty, and incompetence are not sufficient cause under Section 1208(a) to involuntarily convert a Chapter 12 reorganization to a Chapter 7 liquidation. Accordingly, one of the benefits of filing a Chapter 12 case is that it is very difficult for creditors to force a liquidation against the debtor's wishes. The best the creditors can do is to move to dismiss the case as discussed below. That will still not, however, force a liquidation. Remember that creditors cannot involuntarily commence a Chapter 7 case against a farmer's will.

The effect of the conversion of a Chapter 12 case is the same as it is for a Chapter 13 case discussed earlier in this chapter.

Dismissing a Chapter 12 Case   The family farmer's right to dismiss a Chapter 12 case is identical to that for a Chapter 13 case. The right is absolute unless the case has been previously converted from Chapter 7, 11, or 13. As examined in the discussion of conversions earlier in this chapter, the court's ability to convert a Chapter 12 case against the debtor's will is extremely limited. It can be done only on a finding that the debtor has committed fraud in the bankruptcy case. The ability to dismiss is more expansive. Section 1208(c) provides that on the request of a party in interest, and after notice and a hearing, the court may dismiss a Chapter 12 case for cause including:

+ Unreasonable delay or gross mismanagement by the debtor that is prejudicial to creditors.
+ Nonpayment of fees and costs.
+ Failure to timely file a plan.
+ Failure to timely make payments required by a confirmed plan.
+ Denial of confirmation of a plan.

✦ Material default by the debtor with respect to a term of a confirmed plan.
✦ Revocation of an order of confirmation of a plan.
✦ Termination of a confirmed plan by reason of the occurrence of a condition specified in the plan.
✦ Continuing loss to or diminution of the estate and absence of a reasonable likelihood of rehabilitation.

Bankruptcy Rule 1017(a) also governs the procedural aspects of dismissing Chapter 12 cases. The effect of dismissal is the same as it is for Chapter 13 cases.

Closing the Chapter 12 Case   Upon the completion of all plan payments, the Chapter 12 trustee will file a final report and account as discussed in Bankruptcy Rule 5009. Thirty days later, unless there is an objection, the case will be deemed to be fully administered and closed.

ETHICAL CONSIDERATIONS

Paralegals and other law office staff are required to adhere to the same rules regarding client confidentiality as an attorney. With the advent of cellular phones and other modern technology, the risk of violating that confidentiality increases on a daily basis.

Unlike conversations conducted on traditional land-line telephones, conversations conducted on cellular phones risk being overheard by others with a receiver tuned, accidentally or intentionally, to the particular cellular phone frequency. As a paralegal, it's advisable never to discuss confidential information with a client on a cellular phone. Similarly, paralegals should refrain from discussing confidential details of a case with the supervising attorney who is speaking on a cellular phone while outside the office.

SUMMARY

Chapters 12 and 13 have much in common, although each is designed to assist different types of debtors. Chapter 12 is for family farmers (which can include partnerships and corporations) with stable income. Chapter 13 is only available for individuals with relatively small debts and stable income. Chapter 13 cases are more common.

In a Chapter 13 case, a trustee is appointed, but the trustee's duties are limited to administering the distributions to creditors under the plan of reorganization. The Chapter 13 plan is a simple document that divides creditors into classes and proposes a payment schedule to them. A Chapter 13 plan may only be proposed by the debtor. Creditors will not vote on the plan, but they can file objections. If the plan meets the requirements of the Bankruptcy Code, it will be confirmed. If a Chapter 13 debtor completes the payment schedule in the plan, he or she will receive a discharge that relieves the debtor of the obligation to pay most unsatisfied debts. Even if all plan payments are not made, in some circumstances, the debtor can still receive a discharge. The debtor can dismiss the Chapter 13 case, or convert it to Chapter 7, at any time. Creditors can seek to dismiss a Chapter 13 case or convert it to a Chapter 7 case in some situations.

In a Chapter 12 case, a trustee is appointed, as in a Chapter 13 case. Unlike the Chapter 13 trustee, however, the Chapter 12 trustee can be called upon to manage and operate the debtor's farm—if the debtor after notice and hearing is found to have engaged in serious misconduct. A Chapter 12 plan is similar to a Chapter 13 plan, and the confirmation procedures and results are also similar. The Chapter 12 conversion and dismissal rules are based on the Chapter 13 rules; however, a Chapter 12 case cannot be converted to Chapter 7 without the debtor's consent unless the court finds fraud.

✦ KEY TERMS

hardship discharge

✦ IMPROVE YOUR UNDERSTANDING

1. Can a family farmer file a Chapter 13 case?
2. Who may file a Chapter 12 case but not a Chapter 13 case?
3. Compare Sections 1222(a) and 1322(a). What is the difference? Why?
4. Compare Sections 1222(b) and 1322(b). List the differences.
5. Compare Sections 1225 and 1325. Are there any meaningful differences?
6. How does a Chapter 12 discharge compare to a Chapter 13 discharge?
7. Under what circumstances would a creditor prefer to have a case converted rather than dismissed?
8. Under what circumstances would a creditor prefer to have a case dismissed rather than converted?
9. Compare Sections 1303, 1304, and 1306 and explain what they say regarding the use and disposition of the debtor's property in a Chapter 13 case.
10. What are the requirements of modifying a Chapter 13 plan?

✦ RESEARCH PROJECTS

1. Locate at least one case in which a hardship discharge was sought. What facts did the court consider in granting or denying the discharge?
2. Locate at least one case in which a debtor sought a Chapter 13 discharge after having received a Chapter 7 discharge. Was it granted? Why or why not?

✦ DRAFTING PROJECTS

1. Myra Consumer is trying to decide between filing a Chapter 7 case and starting all over or filing a Chapter 13 case. Given the following facts, outline a possible confirmable Chapter 13 plan for her. Assume that the matter will be handled by a legal aid clinic without charge and that the trustee's fee will be $100. Also assume that it is not necessary to pay interest on any claim or arrearage.
   - Myra owns and operates a dress shop where she creates custom designs for her clientele. She has a steady group of loyal customers who provide her with a disposable monthly income of $200 when she can work. She charges $100 for her custom designs, half of which is paid when the dress is ordered and the other half when the dress is picked up, usually two or three weeks later.
   - Myra lives in a small apartment over her shop in a building she rents.
   - Myra has recently recovered from a lengthy illness. During her illness, she fell behind in her orders and, therefore, behind in paying her rent and other bills.
   - Presently, Myra has orders and deposits for six designs. She owes her landlord $200, the phone company $30, the electric company $30, a number of doctors $1,000, a sales tax agency $50, a fabric and pattern supplier $500, and the store where she bought her industrial-model sewing machine $500. The store has a purchase money security interest in the sewing machine, which is worth $300.
   - The fabric supplier sued Myra in small claims court and obtained a judgment lien that attached to her sewing machine.
2. Using Sections 109, 1322 and 1325, make a checklist of possible objections to a Chapter 13 plan for the case mentioned in project 1 above.

Complex Reorganizations

IN THE PREVIOUS chapter of this book, we examined bankruptcy reorganizations for the consumer and small farmer. The other type of bankruptcy reorganization is designed for larger businesses and individuals who have substantial debt or entangled financial problems. In this chapter, we consider these larger and more complicated reorganizations controlled by Chapter 11 of the Bankruptcy Code. With the collapse of business entities such as Enron and MCI-WorldCom, the issue of complex reorganization in the bankruptcy context has held the attention of many both within and outside the business community. As has been evident from both Enron and MCI-WorldCom, the collapse of such corporate giants impacts the lives of not only the investors and creditors, but also employees who stand to lose their pensions invested in corporate assets.

Such complex reorganizations involve many billable hours on the part of both bankruptcy attorneys and their paralegals. While paralegals working in smaller firms may not have the opportunity to work on a complex reorganization, the ripple effect of such bankruptcies may well impact business clients of smaller law firms. It is, therefore, important for the paralegal to know the process of a complex reorganization in order to better understand the potential ramifications for businesses that supply the bankrupt firms.

THE MANAGEMENT OF A CHAPTER 11 DEBTOR

The Debtor in Possession

In a Chapter 11 bankruptcy, the debtor usually continues to operate its business throughout the case. For this reason, unless the court appoints a trustee, the debtor is known as the *debtor in possession*. Section 1107 of the Bankruptcy Code gives the debtor in possession all the rights and most of the responsibilities of a trustee. Debtors in possession can sue to recover preferences, sell assets, reject leases, and otherwise use all the tools a trustee has available. The only duties the debtor in possession need not perform are to investigate its own operations and make a report to the court as a trustee must do under Sections 1106(a)(3) and (4) of the Bankruptcy Code. In almost all instances in a Chapter 11 case, whenever the word "trustee" appears in the Bankruptcy Code in connection with some right or power the trustee may exercise, the words "debtor in possession" may be substituted.

The Appointment of a Trustee

In General   Although a debtor in possession is usual in Chapter 11, there are some situations in which a trustee should be appointed. Perhaps the debtor's owners believe the business can be reorganized, but they want to be involved and cannot find anyone to take over. In those situations, the debtor will ask the court to appoint a Chapter 11 trustee. More commonly, a trustee is appointed by the court on a motion by the United States trustee or a creditor and over the objection of the debtor in possession. Chapter 11 trustees are not frequently appointed. They are something of a rarity, and a party other than the debtor seeking the appointment of a trustee has a heavy burden to convince the court that one should be involved in the debtor's affairs.

Grounds for the Appointment of a Trustee   Section 1104 of the Bankruptcy Code authorizes the appointment of a trustee at any time prior to confirmation of a plan. The grounds for such an appointment are cause and the best interests of creditors. Obviously, by using such broad concepts, Congress wanted to give the courts substantial flexibility in determining whether a trustee should be appointed. What constitutes cause and what is in the best interests of creditors will be tested on a case-by-case basis.

Congress has not, however, left the courts without guidance. Examples of cause are set out in Section 1104. They include fraud, dishonesty, gross mismanagement, and similar acts or omissions either before or after the commencement of the bankruptcy case. The mismanagement required is gross mismanagement; simply poor management is not enough. In fact, some mismanagement is usually expected in companies that have been forced to seek the protections of Chapter 11.

The second ground for the appointment of a trustee, the best-interests-of-creditors test, is designed for those situations that fall outside the scope of cause but where there is still the need for a trustee. For example, there may be so much dislike between the debtor in possession and the creditor body that attempts to negotiate a plan have been stymied. Appointing a neutral trustee might move the case along toward confirmation. Alternatively, the debtor in possession may be guilty of only poor management. Although insufficient to constitute cause, poor management may be enough for a trustee to be appointed as in the best interests of creditors. Typically, whatever the basis for the appointment of a trustee, the moving party will allege both grounds so that if the court finds insufficient cause, it may still determine that the best interests of creditors compel the appointment of a trustee.

Duties of a Chapter 11 Trustee   A Chapter 11 trustee steps into the shoes of the debtor in possession in running the business, filing reports with the United States trustee or the court, and otherwise attempting to reorganize the debtor. The Chapter 11 trustee is also required to investigate the debtor's acts, conduct, assets, liabilities, and business. The trustee must file a written report of the investigation and make recommendations. Subject to court approval, the trustee is authorized to employ accountants and other professionals under Section 327. One significant difference is that while the debtor in possession's management will be paid a salary, the trustee's compensation is limited to a percentage of assets administered.

Procedures   The procedure for the appointment of a trustee is governed by Bankruptcy Rule 2007.1, which requires the filing of a motion in accordance with Bankruptcy Rule 9014. The trustee will be selected by the United States trustee after consultation with the creditors. If the creditors do not like the trustee selected by the United States trustee, they have remedies. The 1994 Amendments provide that on the request of a party in interest made not later than 30 days after the court orders the appointment of a trustee, the United States trustee must convene a creditor's meeting for the purpose of electing a trustee. The Chapter 11 trustee election will be conducted in the same manner as a Chapter 7 trustee election under Section 702 of the Bankruptcy Code.

Termination of Trusteeship　　Once appointed, a trustee usually remains until the case is closed. The trustee will try to have a plan confirmed, will move to have the case converted to Chapter 7, or will move to have it dismissed if it is not feasible to propose a plan. There are exceptions that allow a trustee's appointment to be terminated before the case is over. Bankruptcy Code Section 1105 expressly states that at any time before plan confirmation, after notice and a hearing, the court may terminate the trustee's appointment and restore the debtor in possession. The court may grant such a motion if the debtor demonstrates that it has cured whatever caused the trustee's appointment or if it is shown that the trustee was wrongfully appointed.

Examiners　　In many cases, the appointment of a trustee will be very disruptive to the debtor's business and may herald the demise of the business. Courts are mindful of this disruption and to the expense of the trustee. One alternative the courts and the parties can use to avoid a trustee but still give creditors some comfort that the debtor is not engaged in any wrongdoing is the appointment of an **examiner.**

Section 1104(c) authorizes the court to appoint an examiner to conduct whatever investigation of the debtor the court orders. The investigation can include allegations of fraud, dishonesty, incompetence, misconduct, or mismanagement by the debtor's officers. Under Section 1104(c), the appointment of an examiner may be made if the appointment is in the interests of the creditors, stockholders, or other interested parties, or if the total unsecured debts exceed $5,000,000, excluding debts for goods, services, taxes, or debts owing to insiders.

The role of the examiner is much different than that of a trustee. The examiner does not replace the debtor in possession or in any way control the business operations. The examiner merely makes the investigation ordered and reports back to the court and all parties in interest on the findings. Based on the examiner's report, the court may then proceed to appoint a trustee. To prevent an examiner from too enthusiastically recommending the appointment of a trustee in a case, Section 321(b) specifically prevents the examiner from serving as the trustee.

Unlike the trustee, the compensation paid to an examiner is not limited to a percentage of the assets administered in the estate but is only limited by what is reasonable and comparable for similar services performed in nonbankruptcy cases.

✦ **examiner**
A court-appointed investigator authorized to delve into the financial and business affairs of a debtor in possession in a Chapter 11 case.

The Creditors' Committee

Formation　　As stated earlier, the general rule is that a Chapter 11 debtor will be a debtor in possession and will remain in control of its assets while in bankruptcy. This is not to suggest that it is business as usual. A number of controls prevent the situation from becoming analogous to a fox in the hen house. The first control is the requirement that anything unusual or out of the ordinary course of business first be noticed to creditors and approved by the court. The second is the creation of a *creditors' committee.* A significant role of a creditors' committee is to keep an eye on the debtor in possession and its activities. Another important role is to facilitate representation of the creditors' interests and their communication with the debtor.

As soon as practical after the commencement of a Chapter 11 case, the United States trustee will appoint a committee of unsecured creditors. Sometimes the creditors who serve on the committee will also be secured creditors, but they qualify for appointment on the committee because their collateral is not worth as much as they are owed.

Generally, even if a creditor's claim is disputed by the debtor, the creditor is still eligible to serve on the committee. However, in at least a few cases, creditors who are competitors of the debtor will not be allowed to serve because the committee may be provided with confidential information that could be used against the debtor. Governmental agencies are not usually eligible to serve on the committee.

In most cases, the United States trustee will select the members of the committee from the list of the 20 largest creditors that the debtor filed with the petition. The United States trustee will normally select seven of those from the list willing to serve. If fewer than seven are willing to join the committee, the United States trustee will appoint a smaller committee provided it has more than one or two members. A larger committee may also be chosen.

Often the debtor will have made an attempt at reorganization prior to the filing of the bankruptcy petition. There may have been a committee created in that out-of-court workout to negotiate a payment plan with the debtor. Where a committee has been selected prepetition, rather than create a new committee, the United States trustee may have the existing committee continue. The United States trustee has that option if, as required by Section 1102 of the Bankruptcy Code, the prepetition committee was "fairly chosen and is representative of the different kinds of claims to be represented." Bankruptcy Rule 2007 is more specific. It allows an already formed committee to continue if the following criteria are met:

+ It was selected by a majority in number and amount of unsecured creditors who could and did vote at a meeting in which all unsecured creditors with claims over $1,000 or the 100 largest creditors were invited on at least five days notice. There must be written minutes of the meeting and the voting results.
+ All proxies are filed with the court.
+ The organization of the committee was in all other respects fair and proper.

Usually only one creditors' committee is appointed. If the debtor has a large number of shareholders, there might also be a shareholders' committee formed to represent the equity interests. In large reorganization cases, there might also be a need to have more than one creditors' committee. For example, the debtor may have issued a large amount of bonds whose repayment is subordinated to that of the general trade debt. The bondholders' interests are different from those of the debtor's vendors, and the subordinated debt may require their own committee to make sure that their interests are adequately considered. Section 1102(a)(2) provides that, on request of a party in interest, the court may order the appointment of additional committees of creditors or equity security holders if necessary to ensure their adequate representation. If the motion is granted, the United States trustee will select the new committee's members. The debtor and the existing creditors' committee frequently oppose motions to appoint additional committees because of the added expense.

Once a committee is formed, its size may not remain static. The United States trustee may appoint additional members if the existing members are not as representative as first thought. In addition, the United States trustee may decrease the size of a committee by excusing members who do not participate or attend meetings, thereby making it difficult to obtain a quorum, or who are later found to have a conflict of interest.

Operation   The powers and duties of a creditors' committee are set out in Section 1103(c) of the Bankruptcy Code. They are to:

+ Consult with the debtor in possession concerning the administration of the case.

✦ Investigate the acts, conduct, assets, liabilities, and financial condition of the debtor, the operation of the debtor's business, and the desirability of continuing that business, as well as any other matter relevant to the case or the formulation of a plan.

✦ Participate in the formulation of a plan, advise the creditors of the committee's determination as to the plan, and collect and file with the court acceptances or rejections of a plan.

✦ Request the appointment of a trustee or an examiner.

✦ Perform such other services as are in the interest of the creditors.

The committee's role is generally to advise—not to replace—the debtor. For example, the committee is not given an explicit statutory grant of the right to bring suit or to intervene in an adversary proceeding in which the committee is interested. Most courts, however, will allow the committee to do so if the debtor in possession has unjustifiably refused or has abused its discretion in commencing suit.

To assist the committee in the performance of its duties and the exercise of its powers, Section 1103(a) allows it to select and employ one or more attorneys, accountants, or other agents with the employment subject to the approval of the court. The selections must be made at a scheduled meeting of the committee at which a majority of the members are present.

The committee will also likely choose a chairperson to call or otherwise arrange committee meetings and to be the primary representative of the committee. Depending on the committee's size and the complexity of the debtor's operations and case, one or more subcommittees may be formed. The committee may also appoint or employ a secretary to keep minutes and to ensure that all committee members are informed of events in the case between committee meetings. These tasks might fall to the chairperson of the committee or the committee's counsel. Often, coordination of these matters will be the task of the paralegal to the committee's counsel. Another task that might be delegated to the paralegal in the larger cases is preparation of bylaws for the committee so that there is no confusion as to procedure and authority. A sample set of bylaws is presented as Exhibit 11.1.

Compensation Members of a committee will not be compensated by the estate for their time spent while serving on the committee. Committee members are entitled to be reimbursed for their out-of-pocket expenses such as airfare, hotel costs, and parking as an administrative expense when the expenses are incurred in the performance of their duties. It will generally be the responsibility of the paralegal employed by the committee's counsel to gather all amounts with backup documentation such as receipts from each committee member who has incurred expenses. A motion should then be prepared detailing the reimbursement sought.

ADMINISTERING THE CHAPTER 11 CASE

Joint Administration

The only two entities that may file a bankruptcy petition together, although they may also file separate cases, are a husband and wife. All other entities must file individual bankruptcy petitions, and they will have separate bankruptcy cases each identified by its own docket number.

Many Chapter 11 debtors have affiliates or entities that are otherwise closely related that are also debtors. A parent corporation may have one or more of its subsidiaries in bankruptcy. Limited partnerships controlled by a common general partner may all have filed bankruptcy cases. An individual may be in bankruptcy

EXHIBIT 11.1 ✦ *Sample Pleading*

BYLAWS
OF THE
OFFICIAL COMMITTEE OF CREDITORS
HOLDING UNSECURED CLAIMS

In re Videos by Joe, Inc.

ARTICLE I
NAME

This Committee is the Official Committee of Creditors Holding Unsecured Claims in the Chapter 11 bankruptcy case pertaining to Videos by Joe, Inc., may be referred to as the VBJ Creditors' Committee, and is referred to herein as the "Committee."

ARTICLE II
PURPOSE

The purpose of the Committee is to carry out the functions provided by the Bankruptcy Code.

ARTICLE III
MEMBERSHIP

The membership of the Committee shall consist of those creditors that have been duly appointed by the United States trustee.

ARTICLE IV
OFFICERS

The Officers of the Committee shall be the Chairperson and Vice-Chairperson.

ARTICLE V
DUTIES OF OFFICERS

Section 1. CHAIRPERSON. The Chairperson shall organize the agenda and preside at all meetings of the Committee. The Chairperson may consult with counsel and other professionals to the Committee on all matters, and all such communications may be discussed and reviewed by the Committee at the appropriate Committee meeting. The Chairperson shall have other executive powers, perform such other duties, and be available for such specific assignments as are directed by the Committee.

Section 2. VICE-CHAIRPERSON. The Vice-Chairperson shall perform the duties of the Chairperson when the Chairperson is absent, or as directed by the Chairperson.

Section 3. SECRETARY. The Secretary, although not an officer of the Committee, shall be responsible for arranging meetings of the Committee, recording and distributing minutes of each meeting of the Committee, notifying members of meetings of the Committee, distributing such notices and materials as are directed by the Committee, and for such other matters as are assigned by the Committee. Counsel shall act as secretary to the Committee.

Section 4. TERM. Each officer shall serve until removed, with or without cause, by the vote of a majority of the members of the Committee or until resignation.

ARTICLE VI
SUBCOMMITTEES

If the Committee determines that the work of the Committee would be benefited by the establishment of one or more subcommittees, the Committee may from time to time establish one or more such subcommittee to facilitate and economize the work of the Committee. Subcommittees shall have rights and powers as designated by the Committee.

ARTICLE VII
MEETINGS

Section 1. REGULAR MEETINGS. Regular meetings of the Committee shall be those as established by the vote of the Committee at a duly held meeting of the Committee.

—*CONTINUED*

EXHIBIT 11.1 ✦ *Sample Pleading* (CONTINUED)

Section 2. SPECIAL MEETINGS. Special meetings of the Committee may be called by the Chairperson or Vice-Chairperson, as the case may be, on such notice as is appropriate.

Section 3. NOTICE. Notice of a regular meeting of the Committee shall be given orally or by writing, whichever method is appropriate, to each member at least three (3) days prior to the date of such meeting.

Section 4. PARTICIPATION IN MEETINGS BY CONFERENCE TELEPHONE. If and when such procedure is appropriate, members of the Committee and any subcommittee may participate in a meeting through use of a conference telephone or similar communications equipment, as long as all members participating in such meeting can hear one another. In such case, votes may be taken and certified by the Chairperson or by the Secretary. Participation in such a meeting shall constitute presence at such meeting. The notice provisions of Section 3 above shall apply to such meetings.

Section 5. QUORUM. The presence of a majority of the members of the Committee constitutes a quorum of the Committee for the transaction of business.

Section 6. VOTING. All voting shall be oral or by show of hands. No member may vote except by its representative, alternate representative, or by proxy. The Secretary shall record a Committee member's specific vote, if requested. Every act or decision done or made by a majority of the members present (or through proxy) at a duly held meeting shall be regarded as the act of the Committee.

Section 7. PROXY. A member may vote by proxy, whether oral or written, by providing the proxy to any member of the Committee or counsel.

Section 8. DISSEMINATION OF NOTICES, MINUTES, MATERIALS. Notice of Committee meetings, minutes of such meetings, and copies of all reports and other significant written information generated or obtained by the Committee, or prepared for the Committee by its counsel or accountants, shall be provided by the Secretary to all members.

Section 9. PARTICIPATION BY NONMEMBERS. At the invitation of the Committee, or Officers of the Committee, nonmembers may attend all or any portion of Committee meetings.

ARTICLE VIII
EXPENSES

Reasonable expenses of Committee members incurred in connection with Committee and subcommittee business shall be sought to be reimbursed by the Debtor. Reasonable expenses shall include, at a minimum, travel, hotel, and meal expenses for meetings for one representative or alternate representative of each member; telephone calls; and postage or delivery costs incurred on the Committee's behalf.

ARTICLE IX
AMENDMENTS TO BYLAWS

These Bylaws may be amended by a vote of a majority of the members of the Committee.

ARTICLE X
RATIFICATION UPON CHANGE OF COMPOSITION

Notwithstanding any other provision hereof, if the court or United States trustee orders a change in the composition of the voting members of the Committee, these procedures shall continue only upon the affirmative vote of one-half of the members of the Committee at the meeting of the Committee immediately following the effectiveness of any order mandating such change in Committee membership.

ARTICLE XI
NO LIMITATION ON INDEPENDENT ACTION

Nothing herein and no action taken by the Committee shall be construed or interpreted as binding upon each member of the Committee, or as limiting or restricting action taken by each such member, when acting other than as a member of the Committee.

ARTICLE XII
EXECUTIVE SESSION

The Chairperson may, as may be appropriate, call for an executive session during any meeting wherein one or more members of the Committee or other persons are excused from the meeting and not present for all or a portion of such meeting.

along with his or her wholly owned corporation. The affiliated debtors may be represented by the same attorneys, have cases pending before the same judge, and may have the same trustee. Whatever the nature of the affiliation, there will likely be tasks that need to be done in each case. It makes sense for one motion or other action to accomplish the task in all the cases. For example, if two closely related debtors in possession want to extend the time to assume or reject executory contracts, it is much more efficient for only one motion—rather than two separate motions—to be filed to accomplish that goal.

Bankruptcy Rule 1015(b) provides that if two or more petitions are pending in the same bankruptcy court by or against a husband and wife; a partnership and one or more of its general partners; two or more general partners; or a debtor and its affiliate, the court may order **joint administration** of the estates. Joint administration allows a combining of the estates so that a single docket for the matters occurring in the administration will be kept, only one notice to creditors of the different estates need be sent, and the other purely administrative matters can be handled together to expedite the cases and make the process less costly. Often joint administration will be referred to as **administrative consolidation.** Either label is correct, but they should not be confused with **substantive consolidation,** which is a form of consolidation that actually merges the two or more entities involved into one company. Substantive consolidation is discussed in the next section of this chapter.

It does not make a difference in joint administration whether one case was commenced voluntarily and one was commenced involuntarily. Likewise, although virtually all jointly administered cases are pending in Chapter 11, it does not matter if one is pending under Chapter 7 and one is pending in Chapter 11. This last situation is not common since the purposes of Chapter 11 are very different from Chapter 7, but it may be feasible to administratively consolidate a liquidating Chapter 11 case where a trustee has been appointed and a Chapter 7 case that has the same trustee.

If a trustee has been appointed, Bankruptcy Rule 2009 specifically authorizes one trustee to serve in jointly administered cases unless there is a showing that creditors or equity security holders would be prejudiced by a conflict of interest. Since joint administration does not mean that the estates are merged, if a single trustee is appointed over administratively consolidated estates, there must be separate accounts of all receipts and disbursements.

Under the general procedure outline of Bankruptcy Rule 9014 regarding contested matters, to obtain an order granting joint administration, a motion is filed. One such motion is presented in Exhibit 11.2.

Substantive Consolidation

There are circumstances in which even joint administration of separate debtors will not lead to an effective administration of the estates. An illustration would be two affiliated corporate debtors whose management did not treat them as separate entities, kept only one set of books, and commingled funds. The cost to straighten up the intertwined affairs would cost the estate a substantial amount of money otherwise available to creditors. There are other times when continuing to recognize the separateness of the debtors will lead to unfairness in the treatment of creditors. For example, there may be two corporate debtors that were structured so that one debtor had all the assets and the other had all the debt, the division of which was kept hidden from creditors who relied on the value of the assets in making their credit decision.

In those circumstances, the bankruptcy court may go beyond administrative consolidation and order a substantive consolidation of two or more debtors. The

---

✦ joint administration or administrative consolidation
The merger of two or more bankruptcy cases for the limited purpose of making their administration more convenient.

✦ substantive consolidation
The merger of two or more entities, at least one of which is a debtor, into a single entity under a plan of reorganization or by motion.

EXHIBIT 11.2 ✦ *Sample Pleading*

BANKRUPT C. LAWYER
White Charger Legal Clinic
One Learned Way
Los Angeles, California 90001

Attorneys for Debtors

UNITED STATES BANKRUPTCY COURT
WESTERN DISTRICT OF CALIFORNIA

In re	)	Case No. 03-00001-JF
	)	
VIDEOS BY JOE, INC.,	)	Chapter 11
	)	
Debtor.	)	
	)	
Debtor's Address:	)	
18 Hollywood Drive	)	
Los Angeles, CA 90001	)	
	)	
Debtor's Tax Id. No. 99-9999899	)	
————————————————	)	
	)	
In re	)	Case No. 03-00006-JF
	)	
JOE'S VIDEO, INC.,	)	MOTION FOR ORDER DIRECTING
	)	JOINT ADMINISTRATION OF
Debtor,	)	ESTATES PURSUANT TO
	)	
Debtor's Address:	)	BANKRUPTCY RULE 1015(b)
18 Hollywood Drive	)	
Los Angeles, CA 90001	)	
	)	
Debtor's Tax Id. No. 03-999899	)	
	)	
————————————————	)	

TO THE HONORABLE JUSTIN FAIR, UNITED STATES BANKRUPTCY JUDGE:

Videos by Joe, Inc. ("VBJ") and Joe's Videos, Inc. ("JVI"; collectively "Debtors"), through their attorneys, in support of their Motion for Order Directing Joint Administration of Estates Pursuant to Bankruptcy Rule 1015(b), respectively represent as follows:

1. Debtors are the debtors in possession in the above-captioned separate Chapter 11 cases. VBJ and JVI both filed their petitions on October 1, 2003.

2. JVI is a wholly owned subsidiary of VBJ. Debtors are, therefore, affiliates within the meaning of 11 U.S.C. [section] 101(2) and Federal Rule of Bankruptcy Procedure 1015(b).

3. Debtors believe that unnecessary and expensive duplication can be avoided by jointly administering their cases.

4. Debtors propose that all pleadings relating to one or both of Debtors' Chapter 11 cases contain a consolidated caption in the form of Exhibit 1 to this Motion and that all such pleadings be filed and maintained under Case Number 03-00001-JF. However, each pleading will indicate either that both Debtors are parties to or are affected by the pleading or shall indicate which of Debtors is a party to or is affected by the pleading.

—*CONTINUED*

EXHIBIT 11.2 ✦ *Sample Pleading* (CONTINUED)

5. Nothing contained in this Motion is intended to effect a substantive consolidation of Debtors' respective estates.

WHEREFORE, Debtors request that this Court enter its Order directing the joint administration of the cases of Debtors in the manner set forth in this Motion.

DATED: October 15, 2003

WHITE CHARGER LEGAL CLINIC

_____

BANKRUPT C. LAWYER
Attorneys for Debtors

BANKRUPT C. LAWYER
White Charger Legal Clinic
One Learned Way
Los Angeles, California 90001

Attorneys for Debtors

UNITED STATES BANKRUPTCY COURT
WESTERN DISTRICT OF CALIFORNIA

In re	)	Case No. 03-00001-JF
	)	
VIDEOS BY JOE, INC., and JOE'S VIDEO, INC.,	)	Chapter 11
	)	
Debtors.	)	
	)	(Joint Administration of Case Nos.
Debtors' Address:	)	03-00001-JF and 03-00006-JF)
18 Hollywood Drive	)	
Los Angeles, CA 90001	)	THIS PLEADING AFFECTS [BOTH
	)	DEBTORS] [ONLY _____]
	)	

Exhibit 1

effect of substantive consolidation is to treat the debtors as if there always had been only one entity or as if, before the bankruptcy cases were commenced, the debtors had affected a merger under applicable state law. After substantive consolidation, the cases continue together with a combination of the assets and liabilities of the formerly separate debtors. Again, although substantive consolidation is not limited to Chapter 11 cases, it is more likely to occur in a Chapter 11 case.

The authority for a bankruptcy court to order substantive consolidation is not expressly provided for by statute or rule except through the court's general equity power to enter any order necessary to effectuate the provision of the Bankruptcy Code as provided in Section 105. Substantive consolidation can be accomplished through filing a motion seeking such relief or, in a Chapter 11 case, a joint plan of reorganization can be proposed that calls for substantive consolidation. In either event, the party in interest proposing substantive consolidation must show that there is a necessity for substantive consolidation, or a harm to be avoided, and that the benefits of substantive consolidation outweigh any harm that would be caused to creditors.

Limiting Notice

Bankruptcy Rule 2002 governs the timing and the extent of notice of certain activities in a bankruptcy case. Subpart (a) of Rule 2002 requires that 20 days notice by mail of the following acts be given to the debtor, the trustee, all creditors, and any indenture trustees:

+ The date and time of the Section 341(a) meeting.
+ A proposed use, sale, or lease of property out of the ordinary course of business.
+ A hearing for approval of a compromise or a settlement.
+ The last date to file claims.
+ In a Chapter 7 or Chapter 11 case, a hearing on conversion or dismissal.
+ The time fixed for acceptance or rejection of a proposed plan modification.
+ Hearings on applications for compensation.

Other Bankruptcy Rules set when and to whom certain other notices must be sent. For many matters, these requirements will be established only by local rule.

If the debtor has many creditors, it may be unnecessarily expensive and cumbersome to comply with Bankruptcy Rule 2002(a) and other rules by giving notice of every act to every creditor. Many small creditors may not care every time the debtor or a trustee seeks to sell an asset or obtain approval of a settlement of a dispute concerning an account receivable. This will be especially true in a Chapter 11 case in which an active creditors' committee has hired counsel to assist it in monitoring the debtor's conduct.

Recognizing that complying with Bankruptcy Rule 2002(a) may not be necessary in all cases, Bankruptcy Rule 2002(m) expressly provides that the court may enter orders designating the matters in respect to which, the person to whom, and the form and manner in which notices must be sent. This rule can be used to more effectively and economically administer an estate in two ways.

1. Rule 2002(m) is authority for obtaining an order limiting notice on a particular motion or procedure. For example, the debtor in possession may seek an order limiting notice of an upcoming hearing on applications for compensation to the 20 largest creditors and to the United States trustee.
2. Rule 2002(m) can be used by the debtor or the trustee to obtain an order limiting notice on most motions, applications, and other procedures early in the case. For example, the debtor in possession could seek an order providing that notice of all future compromise motions, applications for compensation, and other regular administrative matters be noticed only to the creditors' committee's counsel, the United States trustee, and any party in interest who has requested special notice. (See Exhibit 11.3.)

If an order limiting notice has been obtained, and the notices will be sent by the debtor in possession or the trustee, a separate mailing list should be created and maintained by the paralegal.

Employees

The successful reorganization of most companies will often depend on maintaining or increasing prepetition production levels. In order to achieve that goal, the employees' cooperation will be essential. Because those employees may not understand bankruptcy and reorganizations and may automatically assume that they are about to be laid off, early communication is needed if the debtor's goodwill with its workers is to be preserved. Management should consider scheduling a meeting

EXHIBIT 11.3 ✦ *Sample Pleading*

BANKRUPT C. LAWYER
White Charger Legal Clinic
One Learned Way
Los Angeles, California 90001

Attorneys for Debtors

UNITED STATES BANKRUPTCY COURT
WESTERN DISTRICT OF CALIFORNIA

In re	)	Case No. 03-00001-JF
	)	
VIDEOS BY JOE, INC.,	)	Chapter 11
	)	
Debtor.	)	
	)	
Debtor's Address:	)	MOTION TO LIMIT EXTENT OF
18 Hollywood Drive	)	NOTICE ON CERTAIN
Los Angeles, CA 90001	)	ADMINISTRATIVE MATTERS
	)	
Debtor's Tax Id. No. 99-999899	)	
	)	
	)	

TO THE HONORABLE JUSTIN FAIR, UNITED STATES BANKRUPTCY JUDGE:

Videos by Joe, Inc. ("Debtor"), through its attorneys, in support of its Motion to Limit Extent of Notice on Certain Administrative Matters, respectfully represents as follows:

1. Debtor is the debtor in possession in the above-captioned case having filed a petition for relief under Chapter 11 of Title 11, United States Code, on October 1, 2003.

2. In the course of its Chapter 11 case, Debtor anticipates undertaking the review of numerous outstanding executory contracts relating to its business of providing videotaped depositions, wills, musical productions, and weddings. Debtor further anticipates numerous hearings with respect to assumption and rejection of such contracts, as well as for other relief pertaining to the administration of its bankruptcy case.

3. Pursuant to Bankruptcy Rule 2002(m) and 9007, this Court is authorized to limit the scope of notice required on matters generally, including those relating to the use, sale, or lease of property other than in the ordinary course of business, hearings on approval or compromises or settlements, and similar administrative matters.

4. Debtor's final creditor list will likely exceed 200 creditors. The claims of the majority of these creditors do not exceed $100.00 each. Debtor submits that it would be unduly burdensome to require it to notice each of these parties in interest with respect to matters that can, under the Bankruptcy Rules, be heard on limited notice.

5. Under the circumstances, Debtor proposes that this Court limit notice on motions to assume or reject executory contracts, on motions to authorize the use, sale, or lease of property, for hearings on employment and compensation, on motions to approve compromises and settlements, and on other similar administrative proceedings, to the following persons:
   (a) the United States trustee;
   (b) debtor's 20 largest unsecured creditors;
   (c) the members of Debtor's creditors' committee;
   (d) all secured creditors; and
   (e) parties in interest who have requested special notice.

—CONTINUED

EXHIBIT 11.3 ✦ *Sample Pleading* (CONTINUED)

6. Debtor believes that notice to the entities referred to above will be representative notice to all major positions in this case. Furthermore, upon analysis of the list of the 20 largest creditors filed by Debtor in this case, all creditors owed more than $100.00 will receive notice. These creditors hold approximately eighty percent (80%) of the dollar amount of claims.

WHEREFORE, Debtor requests that this Court enter its Order limiting notice with respect to administrative matters described in this Motion to the entities listed above.

DATED: October 15, 2003

WHITE CHARGER LEGAL CLINIC

BANKRUPT C. LAWYER
Attorneys for Debtor

---

with the employees in the first few days after a case is commenced, if not before, to give them an honest report of the causes of the bankruptcy filing, the immediate plans for continued operations, and the long-term prospects. Ideally, such a meeting will calm fears, reassure those financially dependent on the next paycheck, and quash the invariably present and usually harmful rumors. If a face-to-face meeting cannot be held or would be impractical, a letter to all employees might be a good substitute if it explains in terms a layperson will understand what bankruptcy is all about and what the employees can expect.

If the employees are also creditors because their last paycheck bounced or was never issued, a meeting or a letter is not likely to cool their anger. Trade creditors, although they may be very insistent that they be paid, are familiar with nonpayment and have probably experienced one of their customers filing a bankruptcy case before. Employees do not usually have such experience and generally are not sympathetic to the debtor's financial problems. The ideal is for the debtor to do enough prepetition planning so that employees do not become creditors. If the debtor has enough cash and the luxury of being able to decide when to file the petition, it should wait until the end of a payroll period to file its petition and pay all the employees in cash just before the filing. As a practical matter, this is difficult; payday usually follows the end of a payroll period by a week, or it takes time to process the payroll and figure the deductions, or there may be three shifts at the debtor's plant and regardless of when the debtor files, there will be employees who are owed wages. Adding to the problem of preventing employees from becoming creditors is the fact that a debtor in possession should be closing all its checking accounts immediately after the bankruptcy case is commenced. No matter how strongly employees are encouraged to cash their payroll checks immediately upon receipt, there will be unpresented checks when the account is closed, leaving those employees as prepetition creditors.

When prepetition planning is not practical, a common solution is to seek, shortly after the case is commenced, court approval to pay outstanding prepetition wages. The debtor may also seek authority to honor vacation and sick leave accrued days and other personnel policies. This relief is almost always granted in a Chapter 11 case. An example of such a motion is shown in Exhibit 11.4.

Finally, as discussed in Chapter 4 of this book, there are special issues concerning rejection of executory contracts when a collective bargaining agreement or retiree medical benefits are involved. Generally, before the debtor can reject those executory contracts, a strong showing of need must be made.

Exhibit 11.4 ✦ *Sample Pleading*

BANKRUPT C. LAWYER
White Charger Legal Clinic
One Learned Way
Los Angeles, California 90001

Attorneys for Debtors

UNITED STATES BANKRUPTCY COURT
WESTERN DISTRICT OF CALIFORNIA

In re	)	Case No. 03-00001-JF
	)	
VIDEOS BY JOE, INC.,	)	Chapter 11
	)	
Debtor.	)	
	)	
Debtor's Address:	)	MOTION FOR ORDER
18 Hollywood Drive	)	AUTHORIZING DEBTOR TO PAY
Los Angeles, CA 90001	)	PREPETITION WAGES AND
	)	HONOR OUTSTANDING PAYROLL
Debtor's Tax Id. No. 99-999899	)	CHECKS, VACATION DAYS, SICK
	)	LEAVE DAYS, AND OTHER
	)	PERSONNEL POLICIES
	)	

TO THE HONORABLE JUSTIN FAIR, UNITED STATES BANKRUPTCY JUDGE:

Videos by Joe, Inc. ("Debtor"), through its attorneys, in support of its Motion for Order Authorizing Debtor to Pay Prepetition Wages and Honor Outstanding Payroll Checks, Vacation Days, Sick Leave Days, and Other Personnel Policies, respectfully represents as follows:

1. Debtor is the debtor in possession in the above-captioned case having filed a petition for relief under Chapter 11 of Title 11, United States Code (the "Bankruptcy Code"), on Monday, October 1, 2003.

2. It is Debtor's policy to pay its employees by check each Friday for services performed through the previous Saturday. Hence, at the time it filed its petition, all 17 of Debtor's employees had performed prepetition services for which wages had accrued but were not yet due. In addition, on the Friday before it filed its petition, Debtor issued payroll checks to all of its employees from its general payroll account. Many of those checks were not cashed prior to the filing of the petition.

3. At the time that it filed its petition, Debtor had certain employment and personnel policies, including allowing each employee one day of paid vacation and one-half day of paid sick leave for each full month that the employee worked.

4. In order to avoid the risk of resignations and of discontent or loss of morale among its employees, and in view of the priority awarded to wage claims, Debtor requests that it be permitted to take whatever steps are necessary to:
    (a) ensure that the uncashed payroll checks of its employees are honored by retaining its present payroll account;
    (b) pay accrued payroll through the date Debtor commenced its bankruptcy case; and
    (c) continue personnel policies and permit employees to use accrued benefits, such as sick leave days and vacation leave, even if earned prior to October 1, 2003.

Debtor believes that obtaining such relief will enable it to retain employees and keep their morale high, all of which is vital to the success of Debtor's bankruptcy case.

—CONTINUED

EXHIBIT 11.4 ✦ *Sample Pleading* (CONTINUED)

5. The amount to be paid to each employee, whether by honoring prepetition issued payroll checks, paying prepetition accrued wages, or allowing use of accrued vacation and sick leave days, will not exceed $4,000.00. Accordingly, the amounts to be paid would have distribution priority under any plan of reorganization of Debtor. Further, this Motion is not intended to apply to any officer of Debtor and is not intended to be an assumption pursuant to Section 365 of the Bankruptcy Code of any employment contract.

WHEREFORE, Debtor requests that this Court enter its Order authorizing Debtor to retain its present payroll account, to permit uncashed payroll checks drawn on the payroll account to be honored, to pay prepetition wages, and to honor existing employee and personnel policies, including vacation day and sick leave commitments to its employees, not to exceed $4,000.00 per individual.

DATED: October 15, 2003

WHITE CHARGER LEGAL CLINIC

_____

BANKRUPT C. LAWYER
Attorneys for Debtor

Relationships with Suppliers

Just as frequent and honest communication is essential for good continued relations with the employees, it is important to keep the suppliers of the debtor's inventory and needed services informed of the debtor's financial condition and of its intentions. Without an ability to obtain inventory and services, the debtor will not have a business to reorganize. If the debtor has not been keeping current on its obligations in the months preceding the filing of the bankruptcy petition, it may have already begun meeting with representatives of its creditors to obtain a moratorium on debt collection or other forms of cooperation. Discussions should continue during the pendency of the bankruptcy case. In fact, the debtor in possession should consider calling a meeting of its suppliers soon after the case is commenced to discuss its financial condition and business plan. The paralegal can assist in that meeting by helping to ensure that notice of the meeting is provided to the creditors; that the information the debtor wishes to distribute to the creditors—such as financial information, a list of creditors, and a business plan—is collated and presented in a useful manner; and that sign-up sheets and name tags are made.

If a meeting cannot be held, the debtor's attorney may ask the paralegal to prepare a letter to suppliers similar to the one presented here as Exhibit 11.5. During the course of the case, the paralegal may be called upon to draft other communications to the creditors to give them status reports on the reorganization effort.

Utilities

Because of the monopolies given by various laws to utilities, such as an electric company, gas supplier, or telephone company, the Bankruptcy Code protects debtors from termination of a utility's services because of unpaid prepetition bills. Section 366(a) of the Bankruptcy Code prevents a utility from altering, refusing, or discontinuing services to, or discriminating against, the trustee or the debtor solely on the basis of the commencement of a bankruptcy case or a debt for prepetition services. If the trustee or the debtor believes that a utility is discriminating or threatening to discontinue services because of unpaid prepetition bills, they may seek an injunction from the bankruptcy court preventing the utility's actions.

EXHIBIT 11.5 ✦ *Sample Pleading*

VIDEOS BY JOE, INC.
18 Hollywood Drive
Los Angeles, California 90001
"Here's Looking At You"
October 2, 2003

Manuel Perez, President
Great Film Inc.,
Steel Plate Road
City of Industry, California 91744

Re: *In re Videos by Joe, Inc.*

Dear Mr. Perez:

This letter is to inform you that Videos by Joe, Inc. filed a petition for reorganization under Chapter 11 of the Bankruptcy Code on October 1, 2003. The Chapter 11 filing was caused by the bankruptcy of our largest customer, who owes us in excess of $100,000.

As you may know, Chapter 11 is designed to enable companies to continue in business under the control and protection of the bankruptcy court while restructuring financial obligations to creditors and taking other actions to enable them to return to profitability. With this in mind, we at Videos by Joe will continue our normal business of selling, producing, and shipping quality products to our customers during the pendency of the Chapter 11 case. We hope to be able to propose a plan of reorganization that provides for meaningful payments to creditors out of future earnings. To this end, we would like to continue to buy video film from you.

Videos by Joe will make prompt payment for the goods and services you supply since the date of the commencement of the bankruptcy case. Our lender, First City Bank, has pledged to work with us and continue to finance our operations while we reorganize.

Unfortunately, we are not permitted by law to make payment on any debt owed to you that arose before October 1, 2003 until such time as we have confirmed a plan of reorganization. We sincerely apologize for any inconvenience or harm this may cause you.

Videos by Joe has valued our past relationship and looks forward to a mutually beneficial future. If you have any questions, please give me a call.

Sincerely,

VIDEOS BY JOE, INC.

_____

JOSEPH BUSINESSMAN
President

Section 366 is not one-sided. It also gives considerable protection to the utilities in exchange for the protection given to trustees and debtors. Section 366(b) provides that utilities may alter, refuse, or discontinue service if the trustee or the debtor does not furnish to the utility "adequate assurance of payment" for postpetition services. The adequate assurance may take the form of an additional deposit or other security and must be made within 20 days after the commencement of the case. Once aware of the petition filing, utilities typically will send a letter asking for a two-month deposit even if the debtor was current in its bills at the time of the commencement of the case.

The bankruptcy court will ultimately decide what constitutes "adequate assurance of payment." If the utility makes a demand that the trustee or debtor in possession believes to be excessive, the court, after a notice and a hearing, may modify the amount of the deposit or other security demanded by the utility. (See Exhibit 11.6.)

EXHIBIT 11.6 ✦ *Sample Pleading*

BANKRUPT C. LAWYER
White Charger Legal Clinic
One Learned Way
Los Angeles, California 90001

Attorneys for Debtors

UNITED STATES BANKRUPTCY COURT
WESTERN DISTRICT OF CALIFORNIA

In re	)	Case No. 03-00001-JF
	)	
VIDEOS BY JOE, INC.,	)	Chapter 11
	)	
Debtor.	)	
	)	
Debtor's Address:	)	MOTION FOR ORDER MODIFYING
18 Hollywood Drive	)	AMOUNT OF DEPOSIT REQUESTED
Los Angeles, CA 90001	)	BY UTILITY COMPANY
	)	
Debtor's Tax Id. No. 99-9999899	)	
	)	
_____	)	

TO THE HONORABLE JUSTIN FAIR, UNITED STATES BANKRUPTCY JUDGE:

Videos by Joe, Inc. ("Debtor"), through its attorneys, in support of its Motion to Modify Amount of Deposit Requested by Utility Company, respectfully represents as follows:

1. Debtor is a debtor in possession having filed a petition for relief under Chapter 11 of Title 11, United States Code (the "Bankruptcy Code") on October 1, 2003.

2. By a letter dated October 5, 2003, M & M Gas Company (the "Gas Company") made a demand on Debtor, under Section 366 of the Bankruptcy Code, for a cash deposit or other security of $10,000.00 as adequate assurance of future payment. The letter also served as notice of the Gas Company's intent to terminate services to Debtor if such deposit was not made within 20 days of the date of the letter.

3. Debtor believes that the demand made by the Gas Company is unreasonable and unnecessary to provide adequate assurance of payment within the meaning of Section 366 of the Bankruptcy Code. Debtor has contracted for services from the Gas Company for more than 10 years. There are no pre- or postpetition payments due to the Gas Company from Debtor. Moreover, the estate is sufficiently liquid to ensure that all administrative claims will be paid in full even in the event that Debtor's case is converted to a case under Chapter 7 of the Bankruptcy Code. In short, adequate assurance of payment in the form of a cash deposit is not necessary under the circumstances of this case.

WHEREFORE, Debtor requests that this Court find that a guarantee of an administrative expense priority for any claim of the Gas Company further supported by Debtor's ability to promptly pay all postpetition obligations is sufficient to constitute adequate assurance of payment for the continuation of the Gas Company's services, and enter its Order that Debtor is not required to post a cash deposit or other security to the Gas Company.

DATED: October 15, 2003

WHITE CHARGER LEGAL CLINIC

_____
BANKRUPT C. LAWYER
Attorneys for Debtor

Financial Reports

The United States trustee in each district will require the debtor in possession to furnish the United States trustee with regular reports of postpetition operations. These reports will allow the United States trustee, and any creditor who may wish to examine the reports, to determine if improper payments are being made, if the debtor is paying its taxes as they become due, and whether the debtor is losing money during its Chapter 11 case.

There are two types of reports. The first is often called an interim statement. It is very similar to a sources and uses of cash statement that some companies prepare in the ordinary course of their operations. It is also akin to a check register. The interim statement shows only actual cash, checks, or other cash equivalents that the debtor has received or has paid out during a particular period. If rent became due during that period but was not paid, the payable due to the landlord would not be reflected on the interim statement. The interim statement allows the reviewers to know whether the debtor is making improper payments and whether it is writing bad checks.

The second report is commonly known as the operating report. Unlike the interim statement, the operating report reflects all accrued income and liabilities in a particular period. For example, it shows all of the debtor's sales even though some of those sales were on credit and have not yet been paid for. All the debtor's liabilities incurred during the same period, whether or not they have been paid, are also reflected. Outside the bankruptcy context, this type of report is frequently known as a profit and loss statement or an income statement. At the bottom of the operating report, the debtor subtracts its accrued liabilities from its income to show whether it earned a profit or lost money for the period of time covered by the operating report.

The United States trustee for a particular district may have developed other required reports. Full compliance with their requirements can be assured only by reviewing any guidelines issued and by speaking with the analysts or paralegal specialists of the office of the United States trustee. Typically, they will require that an interim statement be filed once every two weeks and an operating report monthly. In the larger or smaller cases, this timing can sometimes be modified.

It is not usually the task of the paralegal to prepare the interim statements or the operating reports other than to inform the debtor's bookkeeper or accounting staff about what needs to be done and when they need to be filed. A conscientious paralegal will also check every period to make sure that the reports have not been ignored by a busy debtor.

There is no requirement in the Bankruptcy Code or in the Bankruptcy Rules that the financial reports be filed with the court or served on creditors or other parties in interest. They are usually provided to the secured creditors, whose loan documents may require periodic reports of this type anyway, and to the creditors' committee.

FINANCING AND SALE TRANSACTIONS

Financing Operations

In only the unusual Chapter 11 case will all of the debtor's assets be free from a creditor's security interest or lien. In addition, only rarely will a debtor in possession of a large company be able to continue to operate without some form of financing. Although Section 364(a) of the Bankruptcy Code allows the debtor in possession to incur unsecured debt in the ordinary course of business without bankruptcy court approval, such credit is not always readily available and is often insufficient to meet the debtor's cash needs. Vendors who extended the debtor credit prepetition and were unpaid at the time of commencement of the case may not be willing to extend more credit even if they would be a priority creditor.

Recognizing the problems debtors in possession have in obtaining unsecured credit, and to facilitate reorganizations, the Bankruptcy Code allows the debtor to use the same two methods to obtain the cash required to continue operations as a Chapter 7 trustee may use to finance a liquidation. As discussed in Chapter 9 of this book, the first method is the use of a secured creditor's *cash collateral.* The second method allows the debtor to obtain new financing by borrowing funds on a secured or on a super priority unsecured basis.

Cash Collateral   *Cash collateral* as defined in Section 363(a) of the Bankruptcy Code is "cash, negotiable instruments, documents of title, securities, deposit accounts, or other cash equivalents whenever acquired in which the estate and an entity other than the estate have an interest."

To review the discussion in Chapter 9 of this book, the Bankruptcy Code states that the debtor in possession cannot use cash collateral unless the other party with an interest in the cash collateral consents or unless the court, after notice and a hearing, authorizes its use. If a secured creditor has a lien on the debtor's accounts receivable, as the payments come in, the debtor in possession will not be able to use any of those payments to pay its expenses unless the secured creditor first authorizes the cash collateral to be used or until the court gives its authorization. Pending the authorization, the debtor must put the cash collateral in a separate account and must provide an accounting. This prohibition against uses applies even if the secured creditor allowed the debtor to use all or a portion of the proceeds before the case was commenced.

If an agreement cannot be reached, the debtor in possession must make a motion for authority to use cash collateral. A motion seeking permission to use cash collateral is found in Exhibit 11.7. Bankruptcy Rule 4001(b) provides that such a motion must be served on any creditor that has an interest in the cash collateral, on the committee, or if no committee has been appointed, on the 20 largest unsecured creditors and any other person the court may direct. The hearing must be held no earlier than 15 days after the motion is served. If the debtor has an immediate need for the use of cash collateral, the court can hold a preliminary hearing before the expiration of the 15-day period but may authorize the use of only that amount of cash collateral as is necessary to avoid immediate and irreparable harm to the estate pending the hearing on full notice.

At any contested hearing concerning cash collateral use, the debtor in possession will have the burden of showing that it should be allowed to use the secured creditor's cash collateral because the creditor is adequately protected or, in other words, that the debtor's use of the cash collateral will not harm the creditor. Section 361 establishes three nonexclusive means by which adequate protection may be provided, including:

+ Periodic payments to the secured creditor to compensate for any cash collateral used.
+ Additional collateral.
+ Any other method that gives the creditor the equivalent of the cash collateral used.

For example, the debtor may argue that in consideration for the use of the proceeds of the accounts receivable, it will grant the secured creditor a lien on all new accounts created. Alternatively, the debtor may argue that the *equity cushion,* the difference between the value of the collateral and the amount of the loan, is so

EXHIBIT 11.7 ✦ *Sample Pleading*

BANKRUPT C. LAWYER
White Charger Legal Clinic
One Learned Way
Los Angeles, California 90001

Attorneys for Debtors

UNITED STATES BANKRUPTCY COURT
WESTERN DISTRICT OF CALIFORNIA

In re	)	Case No. 03-00001-JF
	)	
VIDEOS BY JOE, INC.,	)	Chapter 11
	)	
Debtor.	)	
	)	
Debtor's Address:	)	MOTION FOR ORDER
18 Hollywood Drive	)	AUTHORIZING USE OF CASH
Los Angeles, CA 90001	)	COLLATERAL
	)	
Debtor's Tax Id. No. 99-999899	)	
	)	
_____	)	

TO THE HONORABLE JUSTIN FAIR, UNITED STATES BANKRUPTCY JUDGE:

Videos by Joe, Inc. ("Debtor"), through its attorneys, hereby moves for an Order authorizing Debtor to use, in the ordinary course of its business, the income and proceeds received from or on account of its business operations including all cash on hand (the "Cash Collateral"). In support of this Motion, Debtor respectfully represents as follows:

1. Debtor is the debtor in possession. It commenced its case by filing a petition for relief under Chapter 11, Title 11 of the United States Code on October 1, 2003.

2. Debtor was founded in 1990 as a videotaper of weddings, presentations, and other social functions. Today, Debtor is one of the largest independent video filmers in western California, operating from three offices.

3. Debtor employs approximately fifteen people on a daily basis. These employees perform a myriad of services including marketing, filming, processing, shipping, clerical work, and sales.

4. Debtor's major source of funds with which to operate is a $100,000 line of credit with First City Bank ("the Bank"). Under the line of credit, the Bank agreed to lend to Debtor on a formula based on eighty percent (80%) of eligible receivables. As of October 1, 2003, the outstanding balance owed to the Bank, including principal and interest, was approximately $85,000. The Bank asserts a lien on all of Debtor's assets to secure the outstanding balance on the line of credit.

5. As of October 1, 2003, Debtor's major assets had the following approximate value.
   Inventory: $5,000
   Receivables: $110,000
   Equipment: $30,000

6. If Debtor is unable to use the cash balance on hand at the commencement of its case and the proceeds of receivables during this case, Debtor will be forced to terminate its operations immediately. In contrast to the approximately $145,000 in aggregate of going concern value, Debtor's assets would have an aggregate value of only approximately $103,000 on liquidation, broken down as follows:
   Inventory: $3,000
   Receivables: $75,000
   Equipment: $25,000

—CONTINUED

EXHIBIT 11.7 ✦ *Sample Pleading* (CONTINUED)

7. If Debtor is forced to terminate its operations, its employees would be laid off, its relationship with its customers would be impaired, and it could be subject to potential damage claims for breach of contracts, many of which are profitable to Debtor. In short, without immediate use of the Cash Collateral, Debtor's ability to reorganize would be severely adversely affected, and its estate would suffer immediate and irreparable injury within the meaning of Bankruptcy Rule 4001(a)(2).

8. A debtor in possession is authorized to use cash collateral in the ordinary course of its business operations under Sections 363(c)(2) and 1107 of the Bankruptcy Code, provided that upon a request of a party that has an interest in the cash collateral, the Court shall condition such use as is necessary to provide adequate protection of such interest.

9. If the Bank has a perfected lien on Debtor's assets, its lien is adequately protected within the meaning of 11 U.S.C. [section] 363 by an equity cushion that exceeds the loan by approximately seventy percent (70%) on a going concern basis and by approximately twenty percent (20%) on a liquidation basis.

10. In addition, Debtor proposes to provide the Bank, concurrently with this Court's granting the relief requested in this Motion, with replacement liens of the same type as its prepetition liens on all cash, inventory, and accounts receivable acquired by Debtor after the filing of its petition to the extent of the Cash Collateral used. Together with the large existing equity cushion, these replacement liens will more than ensure that the Bank's alleged secured claim is adequately protected.

WHEREFORE, Debtor requests that this Court enter an Order:

1. Authorizing Debtor to use, in the ordinary course of business, the Cash Collateral free and clear of any liens or claims of the Bank;

2. Directing the Bank to turn over to Debtor all the Cash Collateral in its possession or control;

3. Granting the Bank replacement liens of the same type as its prepetition liens on Debtor's postpetition inventory and accounts receivable to the extent of the Cash Collateral use;

4. Decreeing that to the extent the Bank has a valid lien in Debtor's assets, the Bank is adequately protected by the equity cushion in its collateral and the replacement liens; and

5. Granting such other relief as is appropriate.

DATED: October 1, 2003

WHITE CHARGER LEGAL CLINIC

_____

BANKRUPT C. LAWYER
Attorneys for Debtor

---

large that it alone is sufficient to provide adequate protection. Whether the facts and the debtor's offer point to adequate protection will be for the court to decide.

If the secured creditor and the debtor in possession come to an agreement allowing the use of cash collateral, the agreement must be reduced to writing. Bankruptcy Rule 4001(d) provides that a notice and a motion for approval of such a written agreement must be served on the committee or, if no committee has been appointed, on the 20 largest unsecured creditors and whomever else the court directs. (See Exhibits 11.8 and 11.9.) A copy of the agreement must accompany the motion. If any party in interest objects to the agreement between the debtor and the secured creditor, that party must file and serve an objection within 15 days of the date of the notice. If no objection is filed, the court can approve or disapprove of the agreement without a hearing. If there is an objection or if the court wants to hold a hearing, the hearing will be held. The debtor, the objecting party, those who received the motion, and anyone else the court requires must receive at least five days notice of the hearing.

EXHIBIT 11.8 ✦ *Sample Pleading*

BANKRUPT C. LAWYER
White Charger Legal Clinic
One Learned Way
Los Angeles, California 90001

Attorneys for Debtors

UNITED STATES BANKRUPTCY COURT
WESTERN DISTRICT OF CALIFORNIA

In re	)	Case No. 03-00001-JF
	)	
VIDEOS BY JOE, INC.,	)	Chapter 11
	)	
Debtor.	)	
	)	
Debtor's Address:	)	NOTICE OF FILING OF MOTION
18 Hollywood Drive	)	FOR ORDER APPROVING
Los Angeles, CA 90001	)	STIPULATION AND STIPULATION
	)	FOR ORDER AUTHORIZING
Debtor's Tax Id. No. 99-999899	)	USE OF CASH COLLATERAL
	)	
————————————————————————	)	

TO ALL PARTIES ENTITLED TO NOTICE:

NOTICE IS HEREBY GIVEN that on October 3, 2003 Videos by Joe, Inc., the debtor in possession in the above-referenced case ("Debtor"), and First City Bank, a secured creditor of Debtor (the "Bank"), filed with the United States Bankruptcy Court for the Western District of California their Motion for Order Approving Stipulation and Stipulation for Order Authorizing Use of Cash Collateral (the "Motion"). A complete and accurate copy of the Motion is attached to this Notice.

NOTICE IS FURTHER GIVEN that, pursuant to Bankruptcy Rule 4001, if you wish to object to all or any portion of the Motion, within fifteen (15) days of October 3, 2003, you must file your written objection with the Clerk of the Court and serve a copy of such written objection on: (1) Bankrupt C. Lawyer, Esq., White Charger Legal Clinic, One Learned Way, Los Angeles, California 90001; (2) George G. Snow, Esq., Snow & Porter, 4 Wheel Drive, Los Angeles, California 90017; and (3) the United States Trustee, 300 N. Los Angeles St., Room 3101, Los Angeles, California 90012. Any objection not so served and filed may be deemed waived.

NOTICE IS FINALLY GIVEN that if no objections are filed, the Court may enter its Order approving or disapproving of the Motion without conducting a hearing. If an objection is filed or if the Court determines a hearing is appropriate, the Court will hold a hearing on no less than five (5) days notice.

DATED: October 3, 2003

WHITE CHARGER LEGAL CLINIC

—————————————————————
BANKRUPT C. LAWYER
Attorney for Debtor

Section 364 Financing In many cases, the debtor in possession will not be able to survive on cash collateral use alone. It may be that its receivables are slow paying or that it needs to borrow based on its inventory value. In such instances, the debtor will need to borrow new funds rather than only use cash collateral as it comes in.

EXHIBIT 11.9 ✦ *Sample Pleading*

BANKRUPT C. LAWYER
White Charger Legal Clinic
One Learned Way
Los Angeles, California 90001

Attorneys for Debtors

UNITED STATES BANKRUPTCY COURT
WESTERN DISTRICT OF CALIFORNIA

In re	)	Case No. 03-00001-JF
	)	
VIDEOS BY JOE, INC.,	)	Chapter 11
	)	
Debtor.	)	
	)	
Debtor's Address:	)	MOTION FOR ORDER APPROVING
18 Hollywood Drive	)	STIPULATION AND STIPULATION
Los Angeles, CA 90001	)	FOR ORDER AUTHORIZING
	)	USE OF CASH COLLATERAL
Debtor's Tax Id. No. 99-9999899	)	
_____	)	

TO THE HONORABLE JUSTIN FAIR, UNITED STATES BANKRUPTCY JUDGE:

First City Bank (the "Bank") and Videos by Joe, Inc. ("Debtor"), through their respective attorneys, in support of their Motion for Order Approving Stipulation and Stipulation for Order Authorizing Use of Cash Collateral, respectfully represent, and where appropriate stipulate and agree, as set forth in detail below, that Debtor may use the Bank's cash collateral.

In support of this Motion, the parties respectfully represent as follows:

1. In or about July of 1998, the Bank made certain financial accommodations to Debtor for which Debtor was obligated to the Bank, as of October 1, 2003, in the approximate amount of $85,000 (the "Loan").

2. The terms of the Loan are embodied in a Loan and Security Agreement and a Promissory Note (collectively the "Loan Documents"), which are attached to this Motion as Exhibits 1 and 2.

3. As collateral for the Loan, the Bank was granted a security interest in all of Debtor's assets including its inventory and accounts receivable (the "Collateral").

4. The Bank duly perfected its security interests in the Collateral.

5. Certain defaults exist under the Loan Documents.

6. On October 1, 2003 Debtor filed a petition under Chapter 11 of the Bankruptcy Code (thereby commencing the "Case").

7. Debtor desires to use the Bank's cash collateral for general business purposes. The Bank will consent to the use of its cash collateral by Debtor on certain terms and conditions.

Based on the facts set forth above, the Bank and Debtor have and hereby do stipulate and agree, subject to Court approval, as follows:

A. The Bank consents to the use by Debtor of up to sixty percent (60%) of the collections of Debtor's accounts receivable commencing October 5, 2003 provided that the Court approves this Motion and Debtor observes and performs all of its obligations and promises hereunder.

B. As adequate protection for the use of its cash collateral, the Bank is granted liens and security interests in and to all assets of the estate, including all presently existing and hereafter acquired assets, whether real or personal, including but not limited to, the Collateral, general intangibles, causes of action, avoiding powers and the proceeds thereof, equipment and real property owned by or in which Debtor has an interest, and the proceeds therefrom.

—CONTINUED

EXHIBIT 11.9 ✦ *Sample Pleading* (CONTINUED)

C. In the event that the protection provided by the liens and security interests herein granted turns out, in retrospect, to have been inadequate, the Bank shall be entitled to the priority afforded by Section 507(b) of the Bankruptcy Code to the extent of any deficiency.

D. Upon the occurrence of an event of default under this Stipulation, the voluntary or involuntary dismissal of Debtor's bankruptcy case, the appointment of a trustee, the conversion of the case to one under Chapter 7 of the Bankruptcy Code or the entry of an Order confirming a Chapter 11 Plan of Reorganization, the Bank shall have no obligation to allow the further use of its cash collateral by Debtor and Debtor shall not use the Collateral, including the cash collateral, without the Bank's express written consent.

E. The Bank and Debtor have, in accordance with the requirements of Bankruptcy Rule 4001(d), provided notice of this Motion to the 20 largest creditors holding unsecured claims in Debtor's bankruptcy case. Copies of this Motion have also been provided to the United States Trustee. Debtor believes that there are no other entities with an interest in the Collateral.

DATED: October 3, 2003

WHITE CHARGER LEGAL CLINIC

_____

BANKRUPT C. LAWYER
Attorneys for Debtor

DATED: October 3, 2003

SNOW & PORTER

_____

GEORGE G. SNOW
Attorneys for First City Bank

As discussed in Chapter 9 of this book, Section 364(b) authorizes the debtor in possession to borrow funds on an unsecured basis other than in the ordinary course of business with repayment entitled to an administrative expense priority.

The debtor, however, must first obtain an order allowing the loan. Bankruptcy Rule 4001(c) governs the procedure for obtaining an order authorizing borrowing. Under Section 364(c), if the debtor in possession is unable to obtain credit otherwise, it may incur debt with priority over all other administrative expenses (which gives the creditor a super priority claim), secured by a lien on property of the estate that is not otherwise subject to a lien, or secured by a junior lien on property that is already subject to a lien. In the event that even those protections for a lender are insufficient, the debtor in possession may obtain financing secured by a senior or equal lien on property of the estate that is already encumbered.

Bankruptcy Rules 4001(c) and (d) deal with the notice and procedure for obtaining court approval of secured debt financing. The procedure is the same as it is to obtain approval of cash collateral use.

Use, Sale, and Lease of Property

Section 363(c)(1), read together with Section 1107, authorizes the debtor in possession to use, sell, or lease any property of the estate in the ordinary course of business without the need for court approval. Accordingly, the debtor may sell its inventory at its regular prices, use its equipment to manufacture goods, and lease delivery trucks if that is what it commonly does in the scope of its operations. This ability to run the business as usual ceases only if the court revokes authorization to operate or otherwise restricts the use, sale, or lease of the assets. For example, a regulatory agency might bring a motion for an order prohibiting the debtor in possession from selling its inventory because it poses a danger.

The debtor in possession may also use, sell, or lease its property out of the ordinary course of business. To do so, it must first obtain court approval by following the procedures established in Bankruptcy Rule 6004. How property of the estate is sold outside of the ordinary course of business by a Chapter 7 trustee is discussed in Chapter 9 of this book. The section of that chapter on liquidating the estate should be read carefully since it has equal application in a Chapter 11 case. In only rare cases does the debtor in possession not seek to sell or lease a portion of its assets during the administration of its bankruptcy case.

Obviously, the distinction between ordinary course and nonordinary course of business is very important. Some things are clearly outside the ordinary course of business, such as a sale of a division by a manufacturing company or even one piece of machinery for such an operation. Other transactions are not so clearcut. For example, if the debtor was a car rental agency, the lease of its cars to customers would be in the ordinary course of its business and would not require a bankruptcy court order. But, car agencies typically sell their fleets when they are a few years old and replace them with newer models. Would the sale of the older cars require court approval? If there is any doubt as to whether a particular transaction is or is not within the ordinary course of business, it is best to assume that court approval is required.

Another asset sale issue that arises in Chapter 11 cases is whether a debtor in possession can sell all or substantially all of its assets by following the motion procedure of Section 363(b) and Bankruptcy Rule 6004 or whether major asset sales can be accomplished only through confirmation of a plan of reorganization. The concern is how much information the creditors will be provided. If the sale is through a plan, they will receive a disclosure statement. Outside a plan, they will receive only a motion. Under the prior Bankruptcy Act, sales of substantially all of the debtor's assets outside a plan were only allowed if there was an emergency or if the assets were perishable. Under the current Code, the standard is more lax, and such sales will usually be approved if there is a good business reason for doing it in the manner the debtor proposes.

THE PLAN

The ideal culmination of a Chapter 11 case is the confirmation of a plan of reorganization. Unfortunately, although few cases are commenced with the idea that they will fail, a plan is confirmed in only a small percentage of cases.

The path toward confirmation can be very arduous. Negotiation and formulation of plans and disclosure statements is usually extremely complicated. Only in the very rare case will any of the documentation be assigned to the paralegal for preparation. There are, however, many tasks short of actual negotiating or drafting of the plan and disclosure statement that are better done by the paralegal. These tasks are summarized in this section.

Plan Exclusivity

Section 1121 of the Bankruptcy Code provides that in the first 120 days after a Chapter 11 case is commenced, unless a trustee has been appointed, only the debtor may propose a plan. If the debtor proposes a plan within this time period, it is given another 60 days to have the plan confirmed. These time frames are called the debtor's **exclusivity period.** The court may extend the exclusivity period upon the debtor's motion if the debtor demonstrates cause for the extension. Frequently in large cases, the exclusivity period will be extended at least once as a matter of course. A sample motion to extend the exclusivity period is presented in Exhibit 11.10.

If a trustee has been appointed or if the exclusivity period has expired without being extended, any party in interest may propose a plan. This would include any committee that has been appointed in the case or a trustee. Only the United States trustee is expressly prohibited from proposing a plan. Once exclusivity has lapsed, even if the debtor has proposed a plan, a party in interest can file a plan to compete with the debtor's plan as long as it is filed prior to the hearing on the disclosure statement. After that, court approval is required. Competing plans are not common.

The Disclosure Statement

The Bankruptcy Code requires that every plan of reorganization be accompanied by a disclosure statement that contains *adequate information* sufficient to allow a creditor to make an informed judgment whether to accept or reject the plan. In the words of Section 1125(a) of the Bankruptcy Code,

> 'adequate information' means information of a kind, and in sufficient detail, as far as is reasonably practicable in light of the nature and history of the debtor and the condition of the debtor's books and records, that would enable a hypothetical reasonable investor typical of holders of claims or interests of the relevant class to make an informed judgment about the plan. . . .

How much information will be adequate will depend on the facts of each case.

Preparation of a disclosure statement is not something typically assigned to a paralegal. Nevertheless, the paralegal can be instrumental by reviewing drafts of the statement and confirming that nothing significant has been omitted. Although there are few mandatory requirements of what the disclosure statement must contain, most disclosure statements contain the following:

- ✦ A short history of the debtor's business activities.
- ✦ A description of the debtor's capital structure. This includes the type and number of issued and outstanding shares for corporations and the type and percentage of interests for partnerships.
- ✦ A list of all parent and subsidiary corporations.
- ✦ A complete description of the debtor's business, including competitive conditions, principal products and services, dependence on one or more customers, distribution methods, raw material availability, patents, trademarks, licenses, number of employees, foreign operations, governmental regulatory matters, working capital position, and income and profit both historical and projected.
- ✦ A complete list of the debtor's assets.
- ✦ A discussion of the debtor's liability.
- ✦ Information concerning executory contracts and leases.
- ✦ A description of current and anticipated legal proceedings.
- ✦ A description of securities being issued.
- ✦ Information regarding present officers and directors.
- ✦ An analysis showing that the plan provides a better return to creditors than would a liquidation under Chapter 7.

EXHIBIT 11.10 ✦ *Sample Pleading*

BANKRUPT C. LAWYER
White Charger Legal Clinic
One Learned Way
Los Angeles, California 90001

Attorneys for Debtors

UNITED STATES BANKRUPTCY COURT
WESTERN DISTRICT OF CALIFORNIA

In re	)	Case No. 03-00001-JF
	)	
VIDEOS BY JOE, INC.,	)	Chapter 11
	)	
Debtor.	)	
	)	
Debtor's Address:	)	MOTION FOR ORDER EXTENDING
18 Hollywood Drive	)	PERIODS OF PLAN EXCLUSIVITY
Los Angeles, CA 90001	)	
	)	
Debtor's Tax Id. No. 99-999899	)	
	)	

TO THE HONORABLE JUSTIN FAIR, UNITED STATES BANKRUPTCY JUDGE:

Videos by Joe, Inc. ("Debtor"), through its attorneys, for and in support of its Motion for Order Extending Periods of Plan Exclusivity, respectfully represents that:

1. Debtor filed a petition for relief under Chapter 11 of Title 11, United States Code (the "Bankruptcy Code") on October 1, 2003.

2. As debtor in possession, Debtor has through February 1, 2004 the exclusive right to propose a plan of reorganization (the "Plan") and until approximately April 1, 2004 to have the Plan accepted.

3. For reasons delineated in the accompanying Declaration of Joseph Businessman, proposing a viable Plan capable of acceptance and consummation at this stage in the proceeding is not possible.

4. Debtor submits that its bankruptcy case has too brief an operating history to allow it to propound a meaningful Plan. Moreover, the uncertainty in the negotiations of a purchase of Debtor's assets further reinforces the notion that filing a Plan would be inappropriate at this time.

5. Based upon the foregoing, Debtor submits it is reasonable to extend the plan exclusivity and acceptance periods for two months, respectively, subject to further increase for cause shown.

WHEREFORE, Debtor requests that the Court enter an Order granting the Motion and such other and further relief as the Court shall deem just and proper.

DATED: January 1, 2004

WHITE CHARGER LEGAL CLINIC

_____

BANKRUPT C. LAWYER
Attorney for Debtor

The Plan

As is true for the disclosure statement, it is unlikely that the plan of reorganization will be drafted by a paralegal. Yet, as with the disclosure statement, the paralegal can be a tremendous help in ensuring that the plan meets the requirements of the Bankruptcy Code and the Bankruptcy Rules.

There are two basic types of plans. The first and easiest is a plan that contemplates the sale of debtor's assets and the proceeds being pooled together and paid to creditors. This type of plan is called a **liquidating** or **pot plan.** A sample of a very simple plan of this type for an estate that has already sold its assets and has no secured debt is presented as Exhibit 11.11. The sale contemplated can be on a piecemeal basis or the debtor can sell all of its assets to a single buyer.

The other type of plan is sometimes called an **earn-out.** It provides that the debtor will continue to operate and will make periodic distributions to creditors from its earnings over a number of years. Often the plan also provides for creditors to receive shares of stock in the debtor. The disclosure statement will contain projections of what the debtor thinks its revenue and expenses will be over the period of time distributions are to be made. This disclosure is intended to demonstrate to creditors that they should receive more in the earn-out than they would if the debtor immediately liquidated. A plan can combine elements of a pot plan and an earn-out plan by providing for the sale of some of the debtor's assets but also for the continued operation of the debtor's business, thereby making two sources of cash available to pay creditors.

Whatever the type, the plan must have the mandatory provisions set out in Section 1123 of the Bankruptcy Code. That section can be used as a checklist. Among its requirements are:

- ✦ The plan must classify claims and interests.
- ✦ The plan must identify all classes that are unimpaired.
- ✦ The plan must specify the treatment of all classes of claims or interests that are impaired.
- ✦ All claims in the same class must be treated the same.
- ✦ The plan must contain provisions indicating how it will be carried out (that is, whether it is a pot plan or an earn-out plan).
- ✦ The plan must contain provisions to protect the voting rights of shareholders.
- ✦ The plan must disclose the members of the debtor's management after confirmation and how future management will be chosen.

The plan can also contain the optional provisions listed in Section 1123(b). The options include:

- ✦ Providing for the assumption, assignment, or rejection of executory contracts or unexpired leases.
- ✦ Settling any claim belonging to the estate.
- ✦ Selling all or substantially all of the property of the estate.
- ✦ Modifying the rights of secured creditors.

The only prohibition is that any optional provision may not conflict with a mandatory provision.

Approval of the Disclosure Statement

Having the disclosure statement approved by the court is the first step toward plan confirmation. Bankruptcy Rule 3016(b) states that the disclosure statement must be

---

✦ liquidating or pot plan

A plan of reorganization that provides for the sale or other disposition of all of the assets of the estate or distributes the proceeds of a previous sale or other disposition in the plan.

✦ earn-out

A plan of reorganization that provides for distributions to creditors to be made from the debtor's future income.

EXHIBIT 11.11 ✦ *Sample Pleading*

BANKRUPT C. LAWYER
White Charger Legal Clinic
One Learned Way
Los Angeles, California 90001

Attorneys for Debtors

UNITED STATES BANKRUPTCY COURT
WESTERN DISTRICT OF CALIFORNIA

In re	)	Case No. 03-00001-JF
	)	
VIDEOS BY JOE, INC.,	)	Chapter 11
	)	
Debtor.	)	
	)	
Debtor's Address:	)	PLAN OF REORGANIZATION
18 Hollywood Drive	)	March 1, 2004
Los Angeles, CA 90001	)	
	)	
Debtor's Tax Id. No. 99-999899	)	
	)	

Videos by Joe, Inc. ("Debtor") proposes the following Plan of Reorganization:

I
DEFINITIONS

A. The following definitions apply in this Plan:

1. "Bankruptcy Code" means 11 U.S.C. § 101, *et seq.*
2. "Bankruptcy Court" means United States Bankruptcy Court for Western District of California.
3. "Confirmation" means entry of an Order of the Bankruptcy Court confirming the Plan.
4. "Distribution" means the pro rata distribution to holders of allowed general unsecured claims.
5. "Effective Date" means the date the Plan takes effect, as described in Article VII of the Plan.
6. "Estate" means the estate created in the Reorganization Case pursuant to Bankruptcy Code Section 541.
7. "Final Order" means an order of the bankruptcy court as to which any appeal that has been or may be taken has been resolved or as to which the time for appeal has expired.
8. "Petition Date" means October 1, 2003.
9. "Plan" means this Plan of Reorganization, as it may be modified from time to time.
10. "Reorganization Case" means Case No. 03-00001-JF, in the bankruptcy court.

B. Any term used in the Plan that is not specifically defined but that is used in the Bankruptcy Code has the meaning assigned to that term in the Bankruptcy Code.

II
CLASSIFICATION OF CLAIMS AND INTERESTS

A. *Class 1* consists of all allowed claims entitled to expense of administration priority under Section 507(a)(1) of the Bankruptcy Code.

B. *Class 2* consists of all allowed claims against Debtor, if any, allowed under Bankruptcy Code Sections 507(a)(3), 507(a)(4), 507(a)(6), or 507(a)(7).

C. *Class 3* consists of all allowed unsecured claims against Debtor.

D. *Class 4* consists of all allowed interests in Debtor.

—CONTINUED

EXHIBIT 11.11 ✦ *Sample Pleading* (CONTINUED)

III

TREATMENT OF CLASSES OF CLAIMS AND INTERESTS

A. *Pro Rata Distribution.* For any class of claims or interests that the Plan impairs, the property to be distributed to the class under the Plan shall be divided pro rata among the holders of allowed claims or allowed interests of the class, based on the amount of the holders' allowed claims or allowed interests.

B. *Class 1* and *Class 2* are not impaired in that each Class 1 and Class 2 claim that has not already been paid or provided for during the Reorganization Case shall be paid in cash in full on the Effective Date.

C. *Class 3* is impaired. The holders of Class 3 claims will receive a pro rata distribution of the cash available for Distribution after payment of all Class 1 and Class 2 claims.

D. *Class 4* is impaired in that the holders of the Class 4 interests shall receive nothing by reason of their ownership of common stock of Debtor.

IV

EXECUTORY CONTRACTS

Without admitting that any contract or lease is an executory contract or unexpired lease, or that Debtor has any liability under any such contract or lease, all contracts and leases are rejected as of the Effective Date. Any claims arising from the rejection of these executory contracts or unexpired leases shall be classified as Class 3 claims.

V

MEANS OF EXECUTION

A. *Cash Payment to Creditors.* The cash available for the Distribution, after payment of all Class 1 and Class 2 claims, shall be paid pro rata by check mailed to Class 3 creditors within thirty (30) days of the Effective Date or after the last payment to creditors in Classes 1 and 2, whichever occurs later.

B. *Disbursing Agent.* Debtor shall serve as disbursing agent and shall distribute all property to be distributed under the Plan to holders of Class 1, Class 2, and Class 3 claims. In this capacity, Debtor shall serve without bond and shall receive for its services only such fees as the bankruptcy court approves.

C. *Disputed Claims.* Debtor shall withhold from property to be distributed under the Plan a sufficient amount to be distributed on account of the face amount of any claim that is disputed and that has not been allowed by a Final Order as of the date of the Distribution under the Plan. Debtor shall invest funds so withheld and shall retain all interest so earned for distribution to the holders of Class 3 claims. As disputed claims, if any, are allowed by a Final Order, Debtor shall distribute property under the Plan to the holders of such disputed claims as soon as practicable. Property remaining after the termination of all disputed claims shall be distributed pro rata among holders of all allowed claims of Class 3.

D. *Additional Property.* To the extent additional property shall come to Debtor after the Distribution, it shall be distributed pro rata by Debtor to holders of allowed Class 3 claims at such time or times when distribution is practical and/or appropriate.

E. *Unclaimed Property.* Any property to be distributed under the Plan that is not claimed by the entity entitled to it before the later of six (6) months after Confirmation and sixty (60) days after an Order allowing the claim or interest of that entity becomes a Final Order shall be redistributed pro rata to Class 3 creditors who have negotiated their checks.

F. *Directors.* Since Debtor will have no corporate existence postconfirmation, there shall be no change in the current composition of the board of directors; Debtor's directors will continue to be Joe Businessman, Myra Businesswoman, and Maximillion Businessman, who will oversee the dissolution of Debtor.

G. *Officers.* The officers of Debtor at Confirmation shall serve as the officers of Debtor after Confirmation.

VI

BANKRUPTCY COURT JURISDICTION

After Confirmation, the bankruptcy court shall retain such jurisdiction over property of the estate and claims thereto, if any, as is legally permissible.

—CONTINUED

EXHIBIT 11.11 ✦ *Sample Pleading* (CONTINUED)

VII
EFFECTIVE DATE

The Plan takes effect on the eleventh day after Confirmation, but the Plan does not take effect if a stay of the Order confirming the Plan is in effect on the eleventh day after Confirmation.

DATED: March 1, 2004

VIDEOS BY JOE, INC.

_____

JOSEPH BUSINESSMAN
President

_____

filed with the plan or within such time as the court fixes. There will be a hearing after notice to the debtor, all creditors, equity security holders, and other interested parties. Bankruptcy Rule 2002 has proscribed that there must be at least a 25 day notice before the hearing to consider approval of the disclosure statement.

It would be appropriate for the paralegal to prepare the notice of the hearing and see that it is correctly served. Official Form 12, an order and notice for hearing on disclosure statement, can be used. A simple notice will also suffice.

The disclosure statement will not be sent to creditors and the other parties until it has been approved by the court. A copy will be sent to the debtor, the United States trustee, the Securities and Exchange Commission, and the creditors' committee, but otherwise, distribution should be limited. Some creditors will want to review the disclosure statement and will ask for a copy of the plan and disclosure statement before the hearing. If they make a request in writing, as is required by Bankruptcy Rule 3017(a), they should be promptly provided with a copy. A list of those creditors who were provided copies should be kept. The reason is that disclosure statements are frequently amended prior to the date of the hearing. The latest versions should be sent to all who had received the earlier version.

Any party in interest may object to the disclosure statement by alleging that it does not contain adequate information. Unhappy creditors often use the disclosure statement hearing to voice their objections to the plan. While the timing is not correct, it will give the plan proponent forewarning as to possible problems with the plan and an opportunity to either correct any plan defects or prepare for a contested confirmation hearing.

If it contains adequate information, the court will approve the disclosure statement and will also set the date and time of the confirmation hearing on the plan of reorganization, the date by which any objections to confirmation of the plan must be filed, and the date by which the ballots accepting or rejecting the plan must be submitted. The paralegal may prepare such an order. It can be modeled after Official Form 13 (which is entitled Order Approving Disclosure Statement and Fixing Time for Filing Acceptance or Rejections of Plan, Combined with Notice Thereof). It should reflect the disclosure statement approval and the dates set by the court.

As soon as possible after the disclosure statement is approved, a packet of documents must be sent to all creditors, any trustee, all equity security holders, and other parties in interest. The packet must contain:

✦ The plan.
✦ The disclosure statement.

✦ A ballot for recipients to use to vote for or against the plan.
✦ A notice of the date by which objections must be filed and ballots submitted, and the date, time, and place of the confirmation hearing.
✦ Such other information as the court orders.

Often if the debtor is proposing a plan that is a result of successful negotiations with the creditors' committee, the debtor will ask the committee's counsel to prepare a letter to be included in the packet stating that the committee supports the plan and urges creditors to vote for it. Sometimes the packet will also include an addressed and postage-paid envelope for returning the ballot.

The Ballot

Bankruptcy Rule 3017 provides that all creditors and equity security holders entitled to vote for or against a plan are to receive a ballot conforming to Official Form 14. In larger cases, the ballot should be customized for the party to whom it is being sent. The ballot for equity interest holders will be different from the one for creditors since it will speak of number of shares rather than dollar amount of claims. In fact, separate ballots can be drafted for each class provided for in the plan. By doing so, any guesswork as to what class the ballot from a particular creditor or interest holder would fall into is eliminated either because the person was sent only one ballot or because it returned only the ballot from a particular class.

When the ballots are received, they have to be sorted according to class and counted to see if more than two-thirds in amount and one-half in number of the claimants voting accepted the plan. One method to make the counting much easier is to have the ballots coded by having them photocopied onto different colored paper. For example, Class 1 could have blue ballots; Class 2, green; Class 3, pink; and Class 4, yellow. Although color coding the ballots will take time, sorting time will then be substantially shortened.

Typically, after the packages to creditors have been sent out and while the ballots are being returned, the plan proponent will want to know how the votes are running. The paralegal should keep a tally by class. When the deadline for voting has passed, the plan proponent must file a declaration or affidavit with the court detailing how many ballots in each class were received and the number of votes for and against the plan. If the tally has been kept, the counting for the purposes of preparing the declaration will already be done. A sample of such a declaration is included as Exhibit 11.12.

The Confirmation Hearing

On the date set by the court and disclosed in the notice sent with the packets, the court will hold a hearing to consider confirmation of the plan of reorganization. Bankruptcy Rule 3020(b)(2) provides that if there have not been objections and the plan proponent submits evidence that the plan has been accepted by the requisite majority of creditors, the court may enter its order confirming the plan without taking any other evidence. If a party in interest has filed an objection, the court will need to resolve the questions raised in the objection before proceeding to confirmation.

If the plan is confirmed, the court will enter its order substantially in conformance with Official Form 15. Bankruptcy Rule 3020(c) requires the clerk to give notice of the entry of the order confirming the plan to all creditors, the debtor, equity security holders, and all other parties in interest.

EXHIBIT 11.12 ✦ *Sample Pleading*

BANKRUPT C. LAWYER
White Charger Legal Clinic
One Learned Way
Los Angeles, California 90001

Attorneys for Debtors

UNITED STATES BANKRUPTCY COURT
WESTERN DISTRICT OF CALIFORNIA

In re	)	Case No. 03-00001-JF
	)	
VIDEOS BY JOE, INC.,	)	Chapter 11
	)	
Debtor.	)	
	)	
Debtor's Address:	)	DECLARATION OF BANKRUPT C.
18 Hollywood Drive	)	LAWYER RE BALLOTS ACCEPTING
Los Angeles, CA 90001	)	OR REJECTING PLAN OF
	)	REORGANIZATION
Debtor's Tax Id. No. 99-9999899	)	
	)	

I, BANKRUPT C. LAWYER, declare as follows:

1. I am an attorney licensed by the State of California and admitted to practice before, *inter alia,* the United States District Court for the Western District of California.

2. I am a partner in White Charger Legal Clinic, attorneys for Videos by Joe, Inc. ("Debtor"). I am the attorney primarily responsible for representing Debtor in its bankruptcy case.

3. In the course of my representation of Debtor, I supervised the receipt of all ballots accepting or rejecting the Debtor's Plan of Reorganization (the "Plan"), the review of those ballots for compliance with appropriate procedures, and the process of recording the ballots so that this Declaration could be generated reflecting the tabulation of the votes. Although only Classes 3 and 4 were impaired under the Plan, all classes were provided with ballots.

4. Attached hereto collectively as Exhibits 1 through 4 are the original ballots received on or before 5:00 P.M. Pacific Standard Time, May 1, 2004, accepting or rejecting the Plan.

5. As evidenced by Exhibit 1, the holders of Class 1 administrative claims voted as follows:

YES VOTES
    COUNT: 2
    AMOUNT: $10,000.00
NO VOTES
    COUNT: 0
    AMOUNT: $0

6. As evidenced by Exhibit 2, the holders of Class 2 priority claims voted as follows:

YES VOTES
    COUNT: 5
    AMOUNT: $17,500.00
NO VOTES
    COUNT: 1
    AMOUNT: $2,000.00

—CONTINUED

EXHIBIT 11.12 ✦ *Sample Pleading* (CONTINUED)

7. As evidenced by Exhibit 3, the holders of Class 3 general unsecured claims voted as follows:

YES VOTES
     COUNT: 10
     AMOUNT: $39,520.64
NO VOTES
     COUNT: 2
     AMOUNT: $8,476.36

8. As evidenced by Exhibit 4, the members of Class 4 equity interest holders voted as follows:

YES VOTES
     COUNT: 0
     NUMBER OF SHARES: 0
NO VOTES
     COUNT: 3
     NUMBER OF SHARES: 10,000

I declare under penalty of perjury that the foregoing is true and correct, is of my own personal knowledge, and if called as a witness, I would and could testify competently with respect thereto.

Executed at Los Angeles, California, on May 5, 2004.

_____

BANKRUPT C. LAWYER

Postconfirmation Matters

Once the plan has been confirmed, its terms are binding on all parties including the debtor, creditors, and equity security holders, whether or not they voted for the plan. All assets of the estate, unless the plan provides otherwise, are vested (actually revested) in the debtor, and then commonly referred to as the **revested debtor.**

    Sometimes, despite best intentions, the plan will not work. Usually this happens when the debtor fails to meet its projected sales or profits. At that point, the debtor or another party in interest can move to have the case converted to Chapter 7 or dismissed. In the alternative, the plan proponent can move to have the plan modified to make it work under the changed circumstances. Modification can be sought if the plan has not been substantially consummated. The notice and hearing required for any plan modification is governed by the procedures in Bankruptcy Rule 9014.

    Finally, Section 1144 of the Bankruptcy Code allows the court to revoke a confirmation order on a motion by an interested party if confirmation was obtained through fraud. Such a motion must be made within 180 days after the confirmation order is entered.

✦ **revested debtor**
A debtor after confirmation of a plan of reorganization if the plan provides that title to the estate's assets will be vested in the debtor upon confirmation.

SPECIAL RULES FOR SPECIAL CHAPTER 11 CASES

The Single-Asset Real Estate Case

Many Chapter 11 cases involve an artificial debtor, such as a corporation or a partnership, that has an interest in only one asset, which is usually a piece of real estate. Sometimes these cases are clear abuses of the bankruptcy system. For example, in an effort to stop a foreclosure sale on a parcel of real property, a solvent person transfers the parcel to an empty corporation. The corporation then immediately files a bankruptcy petition to take advantage of the automatic stay. The person's other assets are not brought into the case despite the fact that the creditors may have relied on all the assets in making the credit decision. In other situations, the fact that the case involves a single real estate asset is appropriate because the debtor, commonly a limited partnership, was formed for the sole purpose of owning and operating the asset. The creditors relied on only the real property when making their credit decision.

Single-asset real estate cases are much easier to administer than cases in which the debtor is involved in manufacturing or other operations. The central concern, other than a secured creditor seeking relief from the stay, is to ensure that any valuable leases to tenants are assumed, tenant security deposits are protected, a management company is authorized to be employed by the court, and insurance is in place.

The reporting requirements that the court or the United States trustee might otherwise require are often inapplicable in single-asset real estate cases since they may require information about payroll, inventory levels, and other information for a debtor in possession who operates a business. Upon request, the reporting requirements to the United States trustee will usually be modified so that an initial questionnaire about the property and the debtor's intent with respect to it, as well as monthly narratives about the status, will be sufficient.

Creditor groups frequently complained that single-asset real estate cases were improper bankruptcies because they involved simply a two-person (the debtor and the lender) dispute better left for the states to deal with. In partial support of creditor dissatisfaction with single-asset real estate cases, in the 1994 Amendments, Congress singled out small single-asset real estate cases for more stringent treatment than that given to other Chapter 11 cases.

First, the 1994 Amendments added a definition for a single-asset real estate case. In new Section 101(51B), a single-asset real estate case is defined as one involving: (1) real property constituting a single property or project (other than residential real property with less than four units); (2) which generates substantially all of the gross income of a debtor; (3) on which no substantial business is being conducted by the debtor other than the business of operating the real property and incidental activities; and (4) having noncontingent liquidated secured debt of no more than $4 million. If the debt is more than $4 million, the new rules will not apply. The new rules will also not apply if the debtor has multiple projects located at different locations, or has businesses other than the operation of the property. Yet, despite these limitations, Congress believes that most real estate–related bankruptcy cases will fit within the definition.

The consequence of fitting within the definition of a single-asset real estate case is that the secured creditor will be entitled to relief from the automatic stay under Section 362(d)(3) unless within 90 days after the case is commenced either: (1) the debtor files a plan of reorganization that has a reasonable possibility of being confirmed within a reasonable time; or (2) the debtor begins making monthly interest payments to the secured creditors. This consequence will likely not reduce the amount of time the courts and creditors must devote to these cases. For example, the court will need to determine whether the debtor's plan has a reasonable possibility of being confirmed within a reasonable time. Also, the amount of interest to be paid each month in lieu of a plan is required to be at a "current fair market rate." The court will have to determine that rate if the debtor and the lender cannot agree.

The Small Business Case

Many involved in Chapter 11 cases are concerned about how the rules and regulations make Chapter 11 too expensive and time consuming for those small businesses in need of reorganization that do not qualify for relief under Chapter 12 or 13. Some judges had devised time- and cost-saving measures designed to speed small businesses through Chapter 11, which were very effective but of questionable legality. Impressed with those efforts, Congress decided to formalize and implement them nationally in the 1994 Amendments.

First, the 1994 Amendments added Section 101(51C), which is the definition of a small business. According to that definition, a small business means a person engaged in commercial or business activities other than the ownership or operation of real estate whose secured and unsecured debts total less than $2 million. If a debtor fits within the definition of a small business under Section 101(51C), it can voluntarily opt to be treated as a small business under the Bankruptcy Code. If it does, the special rules discussed below will apply. It need not make that election, however, in which case it will be subject to all of the rules and regulations governing non-small business Chapter 11 cases.

One of the consequences of being a small business is that under Section 1102(a)(3), on request of a party in interest (usually the debtor) and for cause, the court may order that a committee of creditors need not be formed. As a result, the debtor will be saved the delay in negotiating the plan with the committee and paying the expenses of the committee as well as the fees and costs of the committee's attorneys and accountants.

In addition, Section 1121(e) has special plan exclusivity rules for those debtors who opt to have their cases treated as small business cases. In those cases, only the debtor may file a plan within the first 100 days, which is down from the 120 days exclusivity given in other Chapter 11 cases. Regardless of who files it, the plan must be filed within the first 160 days. For cause, the Court can reduce either the 100-day or the 160-day period. Conversely, the Court can increase the 100-day period if the debtor shows that its failure to file a plan in the 100-day period was caused by circumstances for which the debtor should not be held accountable. In any event, pressure is added to have the plan filed sooner than would otherwise be true in any other Chapter 11 case.

One of the most helpful consequences of being treated as a small business case is that a court can "conditionally" approve a disclosure statement (presumably without a hearing or notice and presumably without ever seeing it) and then combine the hearing on the disclosure statement with plan confirmation. This should substantially reduce time and costs. To further speed matters up, the conditionally approved disclosure statement need only be mailed 10 days before the confirmation hearing. Official Form 13 is the Order conditionally approving the disclosure statement and the notice for the combined hearing on the disclosure statement and plan. Procedural Form B15S is the order finally approving disclosure statement and confirming plan.

In all other respects, small business Chapter 11 cases are treated as regular Chapter 11 cases although, in the future, the Bankruptcy Rules may be modified to further accelerate the pace of these cases.

EMPLOYMENT AND COMPENSATION OF PROFESSIONALS

Employment of Professionals

In General   As discussed in Chapter 9 of this book, Section 327 of the Bankruptcy Code provides that the trustee, which also includes the debtor in possession under Section 1107, may employ attorneys, accountants, appraisers, auctioneers, or other professional persons to represent the trustee or assist in the duties listed in the Bankruptcy Code. Similarly, Section 1103 of the Bankruptcy Code allows a creditors' committee to employ attorneys, accountants, or other agents to represent or perform services for the committee.

Conflicts of Interest　As also mentioned in Chapter 9 of this book, whether a professional can accept employment for the trustee, the debtor in possession, or the committee is controlled by some strict rules in the Bankruptcy Code. Section 327(a) allows people to be employed only if they "do not hold or represent an interest adverse to the estate, and are disinterested." A "disinterested person" is defined in Section 101(14). It excludes a creditor, an equity interest holder, and an insider. Accordingly, creditors, stockholders, and insiders are disqualified from representing the estate. This creates a problem for debtors in possession when their prepetition lawyers or accountants were not paid at the time of the commencement of the bankruptcy case. These professionals are creditors, are not disinterested, and may be disqualified from continuing to represent the debtor. Some courts have taken a strict approach and have refused to authorize the employment of professionals who are prepetition creditors. Others take a more pragmatic approach, and using their discretionary powers, may allow the employment if it is in the best interest of the estate.

Requirement of Court Approval　As indicated earlier, all professionals who will be performing services to the trustee, the debtor in possession, or the committee and who want to be compensated for those services must have their employment first approved by the court. When approval has not been obtained before the services are performed, it may be possible to obtain an order approving employment retroactively. Most courts disfavor retroactive employment, and it should be relied on only as a last resort.

Procedures　Bankruptcy Rule 2014 gives the procedure for obtaining approval of employment. First, there must be an application of the trustee, the debtor in possession, or the committee. This is one of the few times in bankruptcy practice that relief is properly sought by application. The application should be signed by the person seeking to employ the professional. The other requirements of Rule 2014 were listed in Chapter 9 of this book. Those requirements are shown in Exhibit 11.13, a sample application of a debtor in possession to employ counsel.

　　Court approval of an employment application should be obtained as soon as possible. For the debtor in possession's counsel, the application should be prepared at the same time as the petition so that the employment application can be presented immediately after the case is commenced.

Rule 2016 Statement　Whether or not the attorney ultimately applies for compensation, a debtor's attorney in a case under any chapter of the Bankruptcy Code must file with the court a statement of the compensation paid or agreed to be paid if such payment or agreement was made within one year previous to the date of filing of the petition for services rendered or to be rendered in contemplation of or in connection with the case by the attorney. The source of the compensation must also be disclosed. This is required by Bankruptcy Rule 2016; Procedural Form B203 can be used.

Compensation of Professionals　The discussion in Chapter 9 of this book regarding professional compensation is equally applicable in Chapter 11 cases. A sample fee application of a debtor in possession's attorneys is shown in Exhibit 11.14. Compare it to Exhibit 9.15 in Chapter 9.

EXHIBIT 11.13 ✦ *Sample Pleading*

BANKRUPT C. LAWYER
White Charger Legal Clinic
One Learned Way
Los Angeles, California 90001

[Proposed] Attorneys for Debtor

UNITED STATES BANKRUPTCY COURT
WESTERN DISTRICT OF CALIFORNIA

In re	)	Case No. 03-00001-JF
	)	
VIDEOS BY JOE, INC.,	)	Chapter 11
	)	
Debtor.	)	
	)	
Debtor's Address:	)	DEBTOR'S APPLICATION TO
18 Hollywood Drive	)	EMPLOY COUNSEL; DECLARATION
Los Angeles, CA 90001	)	OF BANKRUPT C. LAWYER IN
	)	SUPPORT THEREOF
Debtor's Tax Id. No. 99-999899	)	
	)	

Videos by Joe, Inc. ("Debtor"), for and in support of its Application to Employ Counsel, respectfully represents that:

1. Debtor filed a voluntary bankruptcy petition on October 1, 2003 and is the debtor in possession in its Chapter 11 case pursuant to 11 U.S.C. §§ 1107 and 1108.

2. Debtor requires the services of counsel to ensure its compliance with applicable provisions of the Bankruptcy Code, the Bankruptcy Rules, and other applicable statutes and procedural constraints, and to maximize the likelihood of a successful reorganization. Debtor desires to employ White Charger Legal Clinic (the "Firm") for these purposes.

3. In addition to the foregoing, the Firm is needed for the purpose of performing the following professional services:
   (a) To advise and consult with Debtor regarding questions arising in its case and concerning the rights and remedies of Debtor with regard to property of the estate, including rights in property that may have been the subject of voidable transfers prior to the filing of Debtor's petition, and in regard to any secured, preferred, or unsecured creditors of the estate;
   (b) To appear in, prosecute, and defend suits and proceedings concerning property of the estate;
   (c) To take all necessary steps in other matters involving or connected with the affairs of the estate;
   (d) To prepare or assist in preparing necessary applications, answers, orders, reports, and other papers, if any, required to be filed in Debtor's case; and
   (e) To perform all other legal services for Debtor that may be necessary and appropriate in Debtor's Chapter 11 case or to ensure the retention of such special counsel as may be necessary and proper for such services.

4. The attorneys of the Firm who will appear in Debtor's case are duly admitted to practice before this Court. Debtor has selected the Firm because it has considerable experience in matters of this character and because the Firm has represented Debtor for over five years and has, during that time, become familiar with Debtor's operations.

5. Based upon the foregoing, pursuant to the provisions of 11 U.S.C. § 327 and Rule 2014(a) of the Bankruptcy Rules, Debtor requests this Court's approval of the employment of the Firm.

—CONTINUED

EXHIBIT 11.13 ✦ *Sample Pleading* (CONTINUED)

6. The Firm proposes to charge fees based upon its prevailing hourly guideline rates, which currently range between $80 for the most junior associates to $250 for certain of the more senior partners. The Firm intends to apply to this Court in conformity with 11 U.S.C. §§ 330 and 331 for interim compensation and reimbursement for costs advanced.

7. At the conclusion of Debtor's case, the Firm will file an appropriate application seeking allowance of all fees and costs, regardless of whether interim compensation has been paid. Upon allowance of such fees and costs, Debtor will pay to the Firm the difference between the amounts allowed and any interim compensation paid.

8. Debtor and the Firm understand and agree that the proposed compensation arrangement shall be subject to 11 U.S.C. § 328, which authorizes this Court to allow compensation different from what is provided here if the fee arrangement appears, in retrospect, to have been improvident in light of developments unanticipated at the outset. The Firm understands and agrees that if aggregate interim payments exceed the amount that is ultimately allowed, the Firm will be required to and will promptly repay the difference to the estate.

9. Except as disclosed in the accompanying Declaration of Bankrupt C. Lawyer, Debtor is informed and believes that the Firm is not connected with Debtor, its other attorneys, accountants, or creditors. Debtor is further informed that the Firm represents no other party in interest and that it neither represents nor holds any interest adverse to Debtor or the estate and that the employment of the Firm would be in the best interest of the estate.

WHEREFORE, Debtor requests that it be authorized to employ the Firm at the expense of the estate upon the terms set forth above.

DATED: October 1, 2003

VIDEOS BY JOE, INC.

_____

JOSEPH BUSINESSMAN
President

DECLARATION OF BANKRUPT C. LAWYER

I, Bankrupt C. Lawyer, declare that:

1. I am an attorney at law duly admitted to practice in the State of California and before the United States Bankruptcy Court for the Western District of California.

2. I am a member of White Charger Legal Clinic, the attorneys whom Videos by Joe, Inc. ("Debtor") wishes to have represent it in its Chapter 11 bankruptcy case (the "Firm").

3. I know of no reason why, if the Firm is appointed as Debtor's bankruptcy counsel, it cannot fairly and efficiently discharge all duties required of the Firm to be performed in this case.

4. To the best of my knowledge, information, and belief, and except as stated below, the Firm has no connection with debtor, its other attorneys, accountants, creditors, or any other party in interest; moreover, the Firm neither represents nor holds any interest adverse to the estate in the matters upon which it is to be engaged. It is possible that the Firm may have represented from time to time one or more creditors of Debtor in matters unrelated to this case; however, I am not aware of any conflict that would exist and moreover, I warrant that the Firm will not represent any creditor or other party in interest in this case, nor will it hereafter represent any person in connection with this case other than Debtor.

5. No agreement exists in violation of the prohibitions of 11 U.S.C. § 504(a) or Rule 2016(b) of the Bankruptcy Rules for a division or sharing of any fees that may be awarded in this case.

6. The Firm has been employed by Debtor in connection with its operations for approximately five years. During that period, the Firm has been paid on a monthly or more often basis. Fees are current through October 1, 2003.

—CONTINUED

EXHIBIT 11.13 ✦ *Sample Pleading* (CONTINUED)

7. The Firm has been paid a retainer of $2,000.00 by Debtor. The retainer will be held pending Orders of the Court under 11 U.S.C. §§ 330 and 331.

I declare under penalty of perjury that the foregoing is true and correct, is based upon personal knowledge except for those matters stated to be on information and belief, and if called as a witness, I could and would testify competently thereto.

Executed at Los Angeles, California, on October 1, 2003.

BANKRUPT C. LAWYER

Employment of Insiders   In most bankruptcy cases, the salaries and benefits enjoyed by the officers, shareholders, directors, and partners of a debtor will be a sensitive issue to the creditors. More than one company has suffered because of excessive insider payments. Although such payments may be tolerated by the creditors when their checks were merely late in coming, they may not be tolerated at all when, because of the bankruptcy, the creditors may be forced to wait years before they receive any distribution.

In accordance with the debtor in possession's duties to its creditors, it should not be making excessive distributions to insiders. Surprisingly, although compensation and employment of professionals are extensively regulated in the Bankruptcy Code and Rules, there is no such regulation for the employment of insiders. Many jurisdictions have filled in this gap by having local rules on the subject. In addition, the United States trustee has developed guidelines in many jurisdictions.

If court, United States trustee, or creditor approval is required, the debtor would want to emphasize at least some of the following points:

*   ✦ The number of years the individual has been associated with the debtor.
*   ✦ The prepetition salary and benefits as compared to the postpetition salary and benefits.
*   ✦ The responsibilities of the individual.
*   ✦ The benefits the debtor derives from the person's services.
*   ✦ The difficulty in replacing the individual.
*   ✦ The added responsibilities caused by the commencement of the bankruptcy case.
*   ✦ The number of hours devoted by the individual to the debtor.
*   ✦ The lack of other income.

CONVERTING, DISMISSING, OR CLOSING THE CHAPTER 11 CASE

Changing Chapters

Regardless of how much thought went into the decision of filing a Chapter 11 case, during the pendency of the case, the question may arise among the debtor and the creditors as to whether the case should have been filed originally under Chapter 7 or whether the case should proceed in the future under Chapter 7. As discussed in Chapter 8 of this book, the act of changing the chapter under which a case is pending is called *conversion*.

According to Section 1112(a) of the Bankruptcy Code, if a Chapter 11 case was commenced voluntarily and no trustee has been appointed, the debtor in

EXHIBIT 11.14 ✦ *Sample Pleading*

BANKRUPT C. LAWYER
White Charger Legal Clinic
One Learned Way
Los Angeles, California 90001

Attorneys for Debtors

UNITED STATES BANKRUPTCY COURT
WESTERN DISTRICT OF CALIFORNIA

In re	)	Case No. 03-00001-JF
	)	
VIDEOS BY JOE, INC.,	)	Chapter 11
	)	
Debtor.	)	
	)	
Debtor's Address:	)	APPLICATION FOR APPROVAL OF
18 Hollywood Drive	)	COMPENSATION AND
Los Angeles, CA 90001	)	REIMBURSEMENT OF EXPENSES
	)	
Debtor's Tax Id. No. 99-999899	)	
	)	

TO THE HONORABLE JUSTIN FAIR, UNITED STATES BANKRUPTCY JUDGE:

White Charge Legal Clinic (the "Firm"), in support of its Application for Approval of Compensation and Reimbursement of Expenses, respectfully represents that:

1. The Firm was retained by Videos By Joe, Inc. (the "Debtor") to serve as its bankruptcy counsel in preparation for, and during the pendency of, its bankruptcy case. On October 1, 2003, the Firm filed a Chapter 11 petition for the Debtor and on October 5, 2003, the Court issued its order authorizing the employment of the Firm by the Debtor.

2. For the period from October 1, 2003 through and including this date, the Firm has provided legal services to the Debtor in connection with its bankruptcy case. Those services, together with all costs incurred in connection with those services, are particularly described in Exhibit A to the Declaration of Bankrupt C. Lawyer, which is filed concurrently (the "Declaration"). Exhibit A identifies the professional who performed the services.

3. A review of Exhibit A indicates the following initials, which reflect that time was expended by the following attorney and paralegal:

Initials	Identity
BCL	Bankrupt C. Lawyer
JAM	Julius A. Murray

4. Bankrupt C. Lawyer is, and at all relevant times has been, a member of the Firm. He graduated from the University of California School of Law at Berkeley (Boalt Hall) in 1980 and has practiced law in the insolvency area for almost 15 years. Mr. Lawyer's billing rate is $200.00 per hour. As set forth in Exhibit A, Mr. Lawyer performed 40 hours of professional services to the Debtor since the Firm was retained. During that time, Mr. Lawyer's services ensured that the Debtor was fully, fairly, and adequately represented.

5. Julius A. Murray is an insolvency paralegal whose billing rate is $50.00 per hour. Mr. Murray holds a paralegal certificate from the University of Santa Clara Institute for Paralegal Studies and is experienced and capable in bankruptcy procedure, case management, and administrative matters. Mr. Murray also spent 40 hours on the Debtor's case.

—CONTINUED

EXHIBIT 11.14 ✦ *Sample Pleading* (CONTINUED)

6. The billing rates set forth in paragraphs 4 and 5 are identical to the rates charged all the Firm's clients for whom the referenced individuals performed services during the same period.

7. Billed at the Firm's normal hourly rates, fees total $10,000.00.

8. All of the services for which compensation is requested were performed by the Firm for and on behalf of the Debtor, and not on behalf of any committee, creditor, or any other person.

9. No agreement exists in violation of the prohibitions of 11 U.S.C. § 504(a) or Bankruptcy Rule 2016 for the division or sharing of any fees that may be allowed pursuant to this Application or any future Application.

10. Also attached to the Declaration is a list of all disbursements made by the Firm in connection with its representation of the Debtor. Total costs are $750.00.

11. The Firm believes and represents that the services performed have been beneficial to the estate, and that fees of $10,000.00 and costs of $750.00 are fair and reasonable, represent services or costs actually performed or incurred, and were necessary.

12. As stated in the Debtor's Application to Employ Attorney previously filed, the Firm was paid a $2,000.00 retainer from the Debtor. The retainer has since been residing in the Firm's trust account. No withdrawals have been made.

13. This Application seeks allowance of a claim for $10,750.00; the Firm also requests at this time authorization for the Debtor to pay the allowed amount less the amount of the retainer. The Debtor has ample funds on hand to pay the balance of the amount allowed.

14. The Firm has served a copy of this Application together with the Declaration and its Exhibits upon the Office of the United States Trustee and the Official Creditors' Committee, through counsel.

WHEREFORE, the Firm requests that this Court enter its Order:

1. Approving compensation and reimbursement of expenses for the Firm as follows:
   Fees: $10,000.00
   Expense Reimbursement: $ 750.00
   Total: $10,750.00

2. Authorizing and directing the Debtor to disburse the sum of $8,750.00 to the Firm; and

3. Granting such other and further relief as the Court deems just and proper.

DATED: February 1, 2004

WHITE CHARGER LEGAL CLINIC

_____

BANKRUPT C. LAWYER

---

possession may convert to a case under Chapters 7, 12, or 13 without interference by the court or any of the creditors. If the case was commenced involuntarily, or was originally other than a Chapter 11 case and was then converted upon the request of a person other than the debtor, or if a trustee has been appointed, this absolute right of the debtor to convert would not exist.

Sometimes the creditors and other parties in interest would prefer the case not remain in Chapter 11 and would just as soon see the estate's assets liquidated. To facilitate those wishes, Section 1112(b) provides that upon request of any party in interest, if cause is shown, the court may convert a Chapter 11 reorganization to a liquidation case under Chapter 7. (See Exhibit 11.15.) A number of examples of cause are given in Section 1112(b) including:

✦ Continuing losses or diminution of the estate, and absence of a reasonable likelihood of rehabilitation.

EXHIBIT 11.15 ✦ *Sample Pleading*

BANKRUPT C. LAWYER
White Charger Legal Clinic
One Learned Way
Los Angeles, California 90001

Attorneys for Debtors

UNITED STATES BANKRUPTCY COURT
WESTERN DISTRICT OF CALIFORNIA

In re	)	Case No. 03-00001-JF
	)	
VIDEOS BY JOE, INC.,	)	Chapter 11
	)	
Debtor.	)	
	)	
Debtor's Address:	)	MOTION TO CONVERT CASE TO
18 Hollywood Drive	)	CHAPTER 7 OR, IN THE
Los Angeles, CA 90001	)	ALTERNATIVE, TO APPOINT A
	)	CHAPTER 11 TRUSTEE
Debtor's Tax Id. No. 99-999899	)	
_____	)	

TO THE HONORABLE JUSTIN FAIR, UNITED STATES BANKRUPTCY JUDGE:

First City Bank, a creditor in the above-captioned case (the "Bank"), through its attorneys, hereby moves the Court for an Order converting the above-captioned case from Chapter 11 of the Bankruptcy Code to Chapter 7 of the Bankruptcy Code or, in the alternative, that the Court appoint a Chapter 11 trustee. In support of this Motion, the Bank respectfully represents as follows:

1. Videos by Joe, Inc. ("Debtor") filed a voluntary petition under Chapter 11 of the Bankruptcy Code on October 1, 2003. As shown by the Operating Reports and the Interim Statements Debtor has filed with the Office of the United States Trustee, copies of which are attached to this Motion as Exhibits 1 through 10, Debtor has lost money in each month since the commencement of its case.

2. Debtor's continuing losses operate to the detriment of the creditors by diminishing any value in the estate.

3. In part because of the continuing losses, Debtor has not been able to effectuate a plan of reorganization.

THEREFORE, the Bank respectfully requests that the Court enter its Order converting Debtor's Chapter 11 case to a case under Chapter 7 of the Bankruptcy Code or, in the alternative, appointing a Chapter 11 trustee.

DATED: June 1, 2004

SNOW & PORTER

_____

GEORGE G. SNOW
Attorneys for First City Bank

- ✦ Inability to effectuate a plan of reorganization.
- ✦ Unreasonable, prejudicial delay to creditors.
- ✦ The debtor's failure to propose a plan.
- ✦ The court's denial or revocation of confirmation of a plan.
- ✦ The debtor's inability to substantially consummate the plan or the debtor's material default under the terms of the plan.
- ✦ Termination of the plan because of a failure to meet a specific condition of the plan.

Creditors are not limited to just those acts or omissions mentioned in Section 1112(b) as cause to convert the case to Chapter 7. For example, fraud or gross mismanagement on the part of the debtor could also be grounds for conversion.

Creditors will frequently add to their conversion requests the alternative that the court appoint a trustee. The coupling of these two types of relief is natural because the Bankruptcy Code provides that the court must make the same general findings for each.

Bankruptcy Rule 2002(a)(4) requires that all creditors be given 20 days notice by mail of a hearing on a motion to convert a Chapter 11 case to a case under any other chapter.

Section 348 of the Bankruptcy Code details the effects of conversion of a Chapter 11 case to another chapter. As discussed in Chapters 8 and 10 of this book, Section 348(a) provides that conversion constitutes an order for relief but, unless specifically stated otherwise, does not effect a change in the date of the commencement of the case, the filing of the petition, or the first order for relief. The fact that these dates do not change is important for such actions as preferences and fraudulent transfers that require the transfer to take place within a set period of time prior to the bankruptcy case being commenced. If the date of conversion was the deciding factor, then most preferences would have taken place more than 90 days prior to the conversion and would not be recoverable for the benefit of the estate. Those items where the date of conversion controls over any earlier date are listed in Section 348(b) and (c). Dates that had no significance in the prior case, such as the deadline to file a complaint to determine the dischargeability of a debt in a debtor's Chapter 11 case, would spring to existence in the converted Chapter 7 case.

Upon conversion, the services of any trustee or examiner previously appointed are terminated. Unless creditors have an administrative claim, their claims incurred during the pendency of the earlier case will be treated as prepetition claims. Administrative claims incurred during the earlier case are still entitled to a priority in distribution but will now be paid after the administrative expenses of the case under its new chapter.

In order to facilitate a smooth transition to a Chapter 7 case and the administration of the Chapter 7 trustee, Bankruptcy Rule 1019 requires that when a Chapter 11 case has been converted to Chapter 7, the following must be done:

✦ If the debtor has not filed the schedules, statements, inventories, or any required list, it must do so.
✦ Within 20 days after entry of the order converting the case, notice of the order must be given to all creditors.
✦ Either the debtor in possession or the trustee appointed in the former case must turn over to the Chapter 7 trustee all records and property of the estate in their control.
✦ Within 30 days of the conversion, either the debtor in possession or the trustee appointed in the former case must file with the court a final report and account.
✦ A schedule of the debtor's unpaid debts incurred during the previous chapter must be filed within 15 days of the conversion.

Any proofs of claims filed by creditors in the previous case are deemed filed in the superseding Chapter 7 case. In a Chapter 11 case, if the creditor is listed in the debtor's schedules and is not scheduled as having a claim that is disputed, contingent, or unliquidated, it need not file a proof of claim. That will not be true upon conversion. Even if the creditor is listed in the correct amount in the debtor's schedules, in most jurisdictions upon conversion, the creditor must file a proof of claim to share in any distribution.

Dismissing a Chapter 11 Case

The debtor in a Chapter 11 case does not have the absolute right to dismiss its bankruptcy case that Chapters 12 and 13 debtors enjoy. Under Section 1112, the debtor or any creditor who wants the case dismissed must make a motion to the court and establish cause for the dismissal. The types of cause discussed for conversion apply equally to dismissal, and the court is charged with finding whichever is in the best interests of the creditors and the estate. If the debtor is ineligible for involuntary Chapter 7 relief because it is a farmer or a charitable organization, when a creditor makes a motion to convert or dismiss, the court's only alternative is to dismiss unless the debtor consents to the conversion.

Bankruptcy Rule 1017(a) governs the procedural aspects of dismissing Chapter 11 cases. The effect of dismissal was discussed in Chapters 8 and 10 of the book, which is equally applicable in Chapter 11 cases.

Closing a Bankruptcy Case

In a Chapter 11 case, where there is a debtor in possession, it will be responsible for seeing that the case is closed. After an estate is fully administered, which usually means that most of the plan payments have been made and all adversary proceedings and contested matters have been completed, the debtor in possession should file a motion with the court stating that the plan has been complied with and the case should be closed. In that motion, the debtor should summarize how the debtor consummated the plan, what claims were allowed in full, what claims were disallowed, what claims were allowed in a reduced amount, and what amounts were paid to creditors. The order closing the case is called a final decree. A sample motion for a final decree is shown in Exhibit 11.16.

ETHICAL CONSIDERATIONS

As a new paralegal, one of your tasks is to set up appointments for prospective clients when they call into the office. One day, a prospective client calls in and tells you that she wants to set up a meeting with an attorney to discuss suing the XYZ Widget Company. Unknown to you, your firm represented the XYZ Widget Company two years previously during the time it underwent bankruptcy reorganization.

This situation accentuates the importance of performing a conflict check whenever a prospective client contacts the firm. The Model Rules of Professional Responsibility prohibit an attorney from creating a situation where a former client is an adversary, unless the former client gives its express consent.

Every law firm should have in place a method for checking conflicts. If you go to work for one that doesn't, you should discuss developing one with your supervising attorney. Within the conflict database should be the names of all past and present clients, past and present adverse parties, and prospective clients who have had an appointment with one of your firm's attorneys, whether or not they retained the firm. It is important to realize that a prospective client, even though he or she may not have retained the firm, may have disclosed much confidential information within the context of the initial meeting. Such disclosures can serve to disqualify the firm from representing the adverse party, even though your firm was never retained following the meeting with the other side. Before an appointment is set up with any prospective client, this database should be consulted.

If you find that you are "conflicted out," you should tell the caller that the firm is not in a position to represent him or her. Nothing more should be said. To even say "We have already met with the opposing party" may disclose information that should remain confidential. In a marital matter, for instance, by telling a husband

EXHIBIT 11.16 ✦ *Sample Pleading*

BANKRUPT C. LAWYER
White Charger Legal Clinic
One Learned Way
Los Angeles, California 90001

Attorneys for Debtors

UNITED STATES BANKRUPTCY COURT
WESTERN DISTRICT OF CALIFORNIA

In re	)	Case No. 03-00001-JF
	)	
VIDEOS BY JOE, INC.,	)	Chapter 11
	)	
Debtor.	)	
	)	
Debtor's Address:	)	MOTION FOR ENTRY OF
18 Hollywood Drive	)	FINAL DECREE
Los Angeles, CA 90001	)	
	)	
Debtor's Tax Id. No. 99-999899	)	
	)	

TO THE HONORABLE JUSTIN FAIR, UNITED STATES BANKRUPTCY JUDGE:

Videos by Joe, Inc., the debtor in possession in the above-captioned case ("Debtor"), through its attorneys, respectfully requests an order of this Court entering the final decree thereby closing Debtor's Chapter 11 case.

I
BACKGROUND AND SUMMARY

On October 1, 2003, Debtor filed a voluntary petition under Chapter 11 of Title 11 of the United States Code. Debtor's plan of reorganization (the "Plan") was confirmed by an order of the court entered on January 31, 2004. Pursuant to the terms of the Plan, Debtor sold all of its assets to Videos by George, Inc.

The Plan sets forth four classes of claims against Debtor and the proposed treatment of those classes, including the allocation of funds to each class from the proceeds of the sale. Class 1 claims are claims entitled to a priority in payment pursuant to Section 507 of the Bankruptcy Code. Class 2 claims are claims of secured creditors up to the value of their collateral. Class 3 claims are the claims of the prepetition unsecured creditors. Class 4 is the class of interest holders in Debtor.

II
DISTRIBUTIONS

Schedule 1 to this Motion is a list of all of the Class 1 claims and the allowed amount of their claims. Class 1 claim holders received the full amount of their claim on the effective date of the Plan or upon the entry of an Order of the Court allowing their claim.

Schedule 2 to this Motion is a list of all the Class 2 claims and the amount of the value of each secured creditor's collateral. To the extent that a secured creditor's collateral was worth less than the amount of that creditor's claim, the secured creditor also has a Class 3 claim.

Schedule 3 to this Motion is a list of all the Class 3 claims and the allowed amount of those claims. Each holder of a Class 3 claim received a fifty-three percent (53%) distribution on the allowed amount of its claim. The dollar amount of the distribution to each Class 3 claimant is also set forth in Schedule 3.

The names of the interest holders in Debtor are set forth in Schedule 4. No distribution will be made on claims of interest holders.

Claims disallowed in their entirety pursuant to Orders of the Court are set forth on Schedule 5. No payment will be made on these claims.

—CONTINUED

EXHIBIT 11.16 ✦ *Sample Pleading* (CONTINUED)

III

CONCLUSION

Based on the foregoing, Debtor requests that the Court enter its Final Decree closing Debtor's Chapter 11 case.

DATED: March 30, 2004

WHITE CHARGER LEGAL CLINIC

_____

BANKRUPT C. LAWYER
Attorneys for Debtor

SCHEDULE 1

Claimant	Amount of Claim
The Internal Revenue Service	$10,000.00
Board of Equalization	$ 3,000.00
Joseph Businessman	$ 2,000.00
Gerald Cameraman	$ 2,000.00
George and Pamela Wreckers	$ 500.00

SCHEDULE 2

Claimant	Value of Collateral
First City Bank	$75,000.00
B & B Finance Company	$ 9,000.00

SCHEDULE 3

Claim No.	Claimant	Allowed Claim	Distribution
1	June Film Co.	$ 5,410.71	$ 2,867.68
2	Imperial Processing	$ 2,417.54	$ 1,281.30
3	Ace Trucking	$ 990.00	$ 524.70
5	A–D Motor Freight	$ 6,800.00	$ 3,604.00
6	First City Bank	$20,000.00	$10,600.00
7	Ben's Maintenance	$ 100.00	$ 53.00
8	United Parcel Ser.	$ 1,611.58	$ 854.14
9	Abe's Office Supply	$ 61.65	$ 32.68
11	Shell Oil	$ 149.30	$ 79.13
12	Diamond Radiator	$ 1,479.36	$ 784.06
13	XYZ Advertising	$ 2,000.00	$ 1,060.00
14	Giggie, Inc.	$ 7,000.00	$ 3,710.00

SCHEDULE 4

Interest Holders	Number of Shares
Joseph Businessman	5,000 shares
Myra Businesswoman	3,000 shares
Maximillion Businessman	2,000 shares

SCHEDULE 5

Claim No.	Claimant	Proof of Claim Amount
4	Giggie, Inc.	$ 7,000.00
10	Joseph Businessman	$10,000.00
12	Diamond Radiator	$ 3,666.25

that there is a conflict because his wife already called you can disclose confidential information if the parties have not yet indicated to each other that they were seeking legal counsel. Especially in an abusive relationship, such a breach of confidentiality could have deadly effects.

SUMMARY

A debtor will continue to hold and operate its assets in a Chapter 11 case unless it is unable or unqualified to do so. For this reason, a Chapter 11 debtor in a case in which no trustee has been appointed is called a debtor in possession. A debtor in possession has all the rights and powers of a trustee. These rights and powers include the ability to use cash collateral, obtain financing, employ and compensate professionals, and sell or lease property.

Although a trustee may be appointed to replace the debtor in possession in certain circumstances, such an appointment is rare. Sometimes, an examiner rather than a trustee will be appointed to investigate the debtor's conduct or its business. Also, a creditors' committee, usually composed of the largest unsecured creditors willing to serve, will be appointed to represent the interests of the creditors in the case and to review the debtor's performance. Creditor committee members are not paid for their services, although they may employ professionals at the expense of the estate. As a further check, the debtor in possession will be required to submit regular financial statements to the United States trustee for review.

There are several techniques to make a Chapter 11 case proceed more smoothly. These techniques include joint administration or substantive consolidation of related debtors, limiting notice of most proceedings before the bankruptcy court, and keeping employees and vendors apprised of developments. Special rules have been implemented to make small Chapter 11 business and real estate cases more efficient and economical. Special rules for the treatment of utilities, such as the power or telephone company, have been created.

The goal of a Chapter 11 case is to confirm a plan of reorganization. For the first four months after a case is commenced, the debtor in possession has the exclusive right to propose a plan, although this time period can be shortened or lengthened by the court. After the period of exclusivity has lapsed, any party in interest other than the United States trustee may propose a plan.

A disclosure statement must accompany a proposed plan of reorganization. The disclosure statement must provide information about the debtor, explain the plan, and give other information that creditors need to decide whether to support the plan. Except in small Chapter 11 cases, before the plan is distributed to creditors, the court will review the disclosure statement to ensure that it contains the necessary information.

The plan of reorganization will divide creditors into classes and describe their treatment. A plan can provide that the debtor will pay creditors over time from future earnings, provide that creditors will be paid from sale proceeds, or a combination of the two. Once the bankruptcy court has approved the disclosure statement, a copy of it, the plan, and a ballot will be sent to creditors. A class of creditors will have accepted the plan if a super majority in each class votes to accept the plan. If all classes accept the plan, it will be confirmed provided all other requirements have been met.

Sometimes a confirmed plan will fail. In other cases, the debtor will be unable to confirm a plan. In those instances, the debtor or the creditors may wish to convert the case to Chapter 7 or dismiss it. The debtor can convert to Chapter 7 at any time, but a dismissal or an involuntary conversion requires court approval.

If a plan is confirmed and there is no need for further bankruptcy court involvement, the Chapter 11 case can be closed. This is accomplished by the court's entry of a final decree.

✦ KEY TERMS

earn-out	joint administration or	revested debtor
examiner	administrative consolidation	substantive consolidation
exclusivity period	liquidating or pot plan	

✦ IMPROVE YOUR UNDERSTANDING

1. At a duly held meeting, a majority of the creditors' committee votes to require the debtor to sell certain assets. Must the debtor do so?

2. The United States trustee finds only one creditor willing to serve on a committee. Can a committee of one be appointed? Should there be a committee of one?

3. Can a creditor have its attorney serve on a committee on its behalf? If the attorney serves, is the creditor entitled to reimbursement of attorneys' fees?

4. Which of the professionals listed in Section 327(a) is the committee most likely to employ? Why?

For Exercises 5 and 6, assume that the debtor pays its employees on Monday for work through the previous Friday and that the business is closed over the weekends.

5. When should the debtor file its petition?

6. How should the debtor pay the employees to prevent them from being creditors?

7. Does the Bankruptcy Code contain a definition of "utility"?

8. Does Section 366 authorize a utility to take action to collect any prepetition obligation owing from the debtor?

Use the following information in responding to Exercises 9 through 11. XYZ Corporation has a wholly owned subsidiary, Baby XYZ Corporation. Baby XYZ owes $50,000 to XYZ as its share of corporate overhead for their joint headquarters.

9. A partner in a law firm owns stock in XYZ Corporation. Can that law firm represent XYZ in its Chapter 11 case?

10. Can (and if so, should) the same law firm represent XYZ and Baby XYZ? If your answer is yes, give reasons why the same law firm should represent both corporations. If your answer is no, explain why not.

11. Assume that only Baby XYZ will be filing a Chapter 11 case and the law firm's retainer will be paid by XYZ because Baby XYZ is suffering a severe cash flow problem. Must the retainer be disclosed in the firm's employment application?

12. Is there a requirement in the Bankruptcy Code or in the Bankruptcy Rules that retainers must be applied to interim awards?

13. Prepare a table like the example shown here. After reviewing the conversion sections in Chapters 8, 10, and 11 of this book, fill in the boxes with the information necessary to convert (as a matter of right or within the court's discretion, whether a party in interest can move to convert and other pertinent facts) from one chapter (on the vertical axis) to the other (on the horizontal axis).

	CHAPTER 7	CHAPTER 11	CHAPTER 12	CHAPTER 13
CHAPTER 7	x			
CHAPTER 11		x		
CHAPTER 12			x	
CHAPTER 13				x

14. Prepare a table along the lines of the example shown next. After reviewing the dismissal sections in Chapters 8, 10, and 11 of this book, fill in the boxes with the information necessary to dismiss.

	Hearing Required	*Notice Required*	*Grounds*	*Also Move to Convert*
CHAPTER 7				
CHAPTER 11				
CHAPTER 12				
CHAPTER 13				

✦ RESEARCH PROJECTS

1. Locate a reported opinion in which a Chapter 1 trustee was appointed and another in which an examiner was appointed. What facts did the courts find important in making their decisions?
2. Find and read at least two decisions of bankruptcy courts discussing substantive consolidation. List the factors the courts considered in support of or in opposition to substantive consolidation.
3. What financial reports are required by the court or the United States trustee in the district in which you live?
4. Locate a reported decision that approved a sale by the debtor in possession of all or substantially all of its assets outside a plan. What factors did the court consider in making its decision?
5. Locate a reported decision that disapproved of the act given in Research Project 4. What factors did the court consider in making its decision?
6. Does Section 1121 discuss how many extensions of the exclusivity period a debtor can obtain?
7. Do any reported decisions discuss how many extensions of the exclusivity period a debtor can obtain?

✦ DRAFTING PROJECTS

1. Draft a motion to limit the notice to be provided on a sale of the debtor's East Coast operations. Develop whatever facts are desired.
2. Draft a letter to a fictional creditor explaining in layperson terms the priority its claim will receive pursuant to Section 503(b)(1) of the Bankruptcy Code if the creditor ships goods or provides services to the debtor in possession.
3. If you did not perform Drafting Project 6 in Chapter 9, go back and do it now for a Chapter 11 debtor in possession.
4. After consulting the materials in Chapter 9 on how a trustee sells assets, Section 363(b), and Bankruptcy Rule 6004, prepare the papers necessary to obtain the bankruptcy court's approval for a debtor in possession to lease new office space.
5. Create a timeline for plan confirmation that includes the exclusivity period, the disclosure statement hearing, and confirmation.
6. Compare the sample plan presented in Exhibit 11.11 to Section 1123 of the Bankruptcy Code. For each requirement of Section 1123, indicate where it is satisfied, if at all, in the sample plan.
7. Draft a ballot for Class 4 interest holders to use for the sample plan presented in Exhibit 11.11.
8. Presume that the local rules require that before insiders receive compensation from the estate, the compensation must be preapproved by the United States trustee. Draft a letter to the United States trustee asking for approval of $5,000 per month compensation for Joe Businessman, the President of Videos by Joe, Inc., a debtor in possession. Create whatever facts you think are necessary.
9. Prepare an application on behalf of a committee to employ counsel.

The Creditor's Perspective

SO FAR, WE HAVE focused on the representation of the debtor or the trustee. The rights and remedies of creditors have not been discussed except as they are impacted by the debtor's or the trustee's exercise of his or her rights in the case. This chapter examines different bankruptcy scenarios from the viewpoint of the creditor, secured and unsecured, priority and non-priority.

THE UNSECURED CREDITOR

Involuntary Cases

In General   Most but not all bankruptcy cases are commenced by the debtor filing a petition. Section 303 of the Bankruptcy Code provides a method for creditors to force a debtor into bankruptcy. Creditors may want to do so if the company or person is making preferential transfers to other creditors or insiders, if the debtor is selling off assets and not using the funds to pay creditors, if the debtor has abandoned the business and someone is needed to liquidate the assets, or for a myriad of other reasons.

The eligibility for involuntary relief is more limited than in voluntary cases. First, an **involuntary case** cannot be commenced against anyone who is ineligible to be a voluntary debtor. For example, an involuntary petition could not be filed against an insurance company because insurance companies cannot file voluntary petitions. Second, involuntary cases cannot be commenced against a farmer, defined in Section 101(20) as a person who derived more than 80 percent of its gross income from farming operations in the year before the petition was filed. Finally, any corporation that is not a moneyed business or commercial corporation, which is generally thought to mean not-for-profit corporations, cannot have an involuntary petition filed against it.

✦ **involuntary case**
A bankruptcy case commenced by one or more creditors against a debtor.

Involuntary cases can be filed only under Chapter 7 or Chapter 11. Chapter 12 cases involve farmers, who cannot be forced into bankruptcy. Since Chapter 13 generally involves wage earners, forcing someone into Chapter 13 would usually mean forcing that person to work. As we have seen, this is thought to violate the prohibition against slavery established in the Thirteenth Amendment to the United States Constitution.

Grounds   A debtor cannot be put into bankruptcy simply on the whim of one of its creditors. If the debtor has 12 or more creditors, at least three must join in the involuntary petition. If the debtor has fewer than 12 creditors, one creditor will suffice. Employees, insiders, and those who hold avoidable transfers of the debtor's property are excluded in determining the number of creditors. If there is a danger that one of the creditors will be ineligible, others can join in the petition to cure the numerical defect. Whether one or three or more, the petitioning creditors must hold claims that aggregate at least $11,625 in unsecured or undersecured, non-contingent claims that are not subject to bona fide dispute by the debtor. The exclusion of claims in bona fide disputes added by the 1984 Amendments is designed to prevent creditors who are in litigation with the debtor from compelling a bankruptcy case to obtain an advantage in that litigation.

In order to succeed on their involuntary petition, the petitioning creditors must show that the debtor is generally not paying its debts as they become due or that a custodian has been appointed or has taken possession of substantially all of the debtor's property within 120 days before the filing of the petition. There is no requirement that the debtor be insolvent before it can be the subject of an involuntary case. As long as a debtor is not generally paying its debts as they become due, it is subject to an involuntary case no matter how high its net worth. In contrast, a very insolvent company cannot be forced into bankruptcy if no custodian has been appointed or taken possession of substantially all the assets and if it is paying its bills on a current basis. Since creditors do not usually force a bankruptcy when the debtor is timely paying its debts, meeting this requirement is seldom a problem. But, if the petitioning creditors are wrong, and the involuntary case should never have been brought, the debtor could obtain substantial damages against the petitioning creditors.

Procedure   Bankruptcy Rules 1010, 1011, and 1013 contain the procedures for the commencement and prosecution of involuntary cases. Like voluntary cases, involuntary cases are commenced by the filing of a petition, although the petition has different information. Official Form 5 is the involuntary petition. A sample is shown in Exhibit 12.1. The petition is filed with the court along with the appropriate filing fee. The clerk of the court will issue a summons, which then must be served on the debtor with a copy of the involuntary petition.

Once the summons and involuntary petition are served, the debtor has 20 days to file an answer or to otherwise respond. If the debtor wishes to contest being in a bankruptcy case, it may deny that it is not generally paying its debts as they become due or may assert that one or more of the creditors who joined in the petition is ineligible because the claim is in bona fide dispute or is contingent. Of course, if more than three creditors filed the petition or if other creditors joined in it after it was filed, one creditor's ineligibility will not prevent the petition from being effective.

The debtor may be willing to be in a bankruptcy case or may realize that fighting it would be senseless. In that case, the debtor may file a notice with the court that it consents to the entry of the order for relief. Such a consent is given in Exhibit 12.2. Alternatively, the debtor will do nothing, and upon lapse of 20 days time, the court will take the debtor's default. In either event, the court will enter an order for relief. From then on, the case will continue as if it had been commenced voluntarily. If it is a Chapter 7 case, a trustee will be appointed. If it is a Chapter 11 case, the debtor will become the debtor in possession.

If the petition was filed in Chapter 7, the debtor in its notice of consent may elect to convert the case to Chapter 11 or 13 if the debtor is eligible for relief under those chapters. If the creditors want a liquidation, they will then need to move to convert the case back to Chapter 7. The debtor may also elect to convert a Chapter 11 petition to Chapter 7 or 13; the creditors have the same right to attempt to convert it back.

If the debtor desires to contest the petition, the matter will be an adversary proceeding governed by the 7000 series of the Bankruptcy Rules. Each side will have the right to engage in discovery, and a trial will be held on any of the disputed

EXHIBIT 12.1 ✦ *Involuntary Petition*

FORM B5
(12/02)

United States Bankruptcy Court	INVOLUNTARY
Western District of California	PETITION

IN RE (Name of Debtor - If Individual: Last, First, Middle)	ALL OTHER NAMES used by debtor in the last 6 years (Include married, maiden, and trade names.)
Videos By Joe. Inc.	

SOC. SEC./TAX I.D. NO. (If more than one, state all.)
99-999899

STREET ADDRESS OF DEBTOR (No. and street, city, state, and zip code)	MAILING ADDRESS OF DEBTOR (If different from street address)
18 Hollywood Drive Los Angeles, California 90001	

COUNTY OF RESIDENCE OR PRINCIPAL PLACE OF BUSINESS
LOS ANGELES

LOCATION OF PRINCIPAL ASSETS OF BUSINESS DEBTOR   (If different from previously listed addresses)

CHAPTER OF BANKRUPTCY CODE UNDER WHICH PETITION IS FILED

[X] Chapter 7   [ ] Chapter 11

INFORMATION REGARDING DEBTOR (Check applicable boxes)

Petitioners believe:
[ ] Debts are primarily consumer debts
[X] Debts are primarily business debts (complete sections A and B)

TYPE OF DEBTOR
[ ] Individual   [ ] Corporation Publicly Held
[ ] Partnership   [X] Corporation Not Publicly Held
[ ] Other: _____

A.   TYPE OF BUSINESS (Check one)
[ ] Professional   [ ] Transportation   [ ] Commodity Broker
[ ] Retail/Wholesale   [ ] Manufacturing/   [ ] Construction
[ ] Railroad   [ ] Mining   [ ] Real Estate
                              [ ] Stockbroker   [X] Other Service.

B. BRIEFLY DESCRIBE NATURE OF BUSINESS
Provides video taping services to consumers.

VENUE

[X]   Debtor has been domiciled or has had a residence, principal place of business, or principal assets in the District for 180 days immediately preceding the date of this petition or for a longer part of such 180 days than in any other District.

[ ]   A bankruptcy case concerning debtor's affiliate, general partner or partnership is pending in this District.

PENDING BANKRUPTCY CASE FILED BY OR AGAINST ANY PARTNER
OR AFFILIATE OF THIS DEBTOR (Report information for any additional cases on attached sheets.)

Name of Debtor	Case Number	Date
Relationship	District	Judge

ALLEGATIONS
(Check applicable boxes)

COURT USE ONLY

1.   [X] Petitioner(s) are eligible to file this petition pursuant to 11 U.S.C. § 303(b).
2.   [X] The debtor is a person against whom an order for relief may be entered under title 11 of the United States Code.
3.a. [X] The debtor is generally not paying such debtor's debts as they become due, unless such debts are the subject of a bona fide dispute;
                              or
b.   [ ] Within 120 days preceding the filing of this petition, a custodian, other than a trustee, receiver, or agent appointed or authorized to take charge of less than substantially all of the property of the debtor for the purpose of enforcing a lien against such property, was appointed or took possession.

If a child support creditor or its representative is a petitioner, and if the petitioner files the form specified in § 304(g) of the Bankruptcy Reform Act of 1994, no fee is required.

—CONTINUED

EXHIBIT 12.1 ♦ *Involuntary Petition* (CONTINUED)

FORM 5 Involuntary Petition
(12/02)

Name of Debtor **Videos By Joe, Inc.** _____

Case No. _____
(court use only)

TRANSFER OF CLAIM

☐ Check this box if there has been a transfer of any claim against the debtor by or to any petitioner. Attach all documents evidencing the transfer and any statements that are required under Bankruptcy Rule 1003(a).

REQUEST FOR RELIEF

Petitioner(s) request that an order for relief be entered against the debtor under the chapter of title 11, United States Code, specified in this petition.

Petitioner(s) declare under penalty of perjury that the foregoing is true and correct according to the best of their knowledge, information, and belief.

X_____ Signature of Petitioner or Representative (State title) **Ace Trucking** Name of Petitioner Date Signed	X_____ Signature of Attorney **Iona Portia** Date **Portia & Carrera** Name of Attorney Firm (If any)

Name & Mailing
Address of Individual   **Jack Q. King**
Signing in Representative   **2309 Mack Street**
Capacity   **Los Angeles, CA 90001**
	Address **Two Lane Highway**
	     San Diego, CA 92123
	Telephone No.
	    (906) 891-5595

X_____ Signature of Petitioner or Representative (State title) **Imperial Processing** Name of Petitioner Date Signed	X_____ Signature of Attorney Date Name of Attorney Firm (If any)
Name & Mailing Address of Individual **Carl Douglas** Signing in Representative **84 Steel Road** Capacity **Industry, CA 90050**	Address Telephone No.
X_____ Signature of Petitioner or Representative (State title) **Abe's Office Supplies** Name of Petitioner Date Signed	X_____ Signature of Attorney Date Name of Attorney Firm (If any)
Name & Mailing Address of Individual **Abe Morrow** Signing in Representative **20 Hollywood Dr.** Capacity **Los Angeles, CA 90001**	Address Telephone No.

PETITIONING CREDITORS

Name and Address of Petitioner	Nature of Claim	Amount of Claim
Ace Trucking **2309 Mack St., L.A., CA 90001**	**Shipping sevices provided** **to debtor**	**$990.00**
Imperial Processing **84 Steel Rd., Industry, CA**	**Processing services provided** **to debtor**	**$11,000.00**
Abe's Office Supplies **20 Hollywood Dr., L.A., CA**	**Goods provided to debtor**	**$14.50**
Note: If there are more than three petitioners, attach additional sheets with the statement under penalty of perjury, each petitioner's signature under the statement and the name of attorney and petitioning creditor information in the format above.	Total Amount of Petitioners' Claims	**$12,004.50**

_0_ continuation sheets attached

EXHIBIT 12.2 ✦ *Sample Pleading*

BANKRUPT C. LAWYER
White Charger Legal Clinic
One Learned Way
Los Angeles, California 90001

Attorneys for Debtors

UNITED STATES BANKRUPTCY COURT
WESTERN DISTRICT OF CALIFORNIA

In re	)	Case No. 03-00001-JF
	)	
VIDEOS BY JOE, INC.,	)	Chapter 11
	)	
Debtor.	)	CONSENT TO ENTRY OF AN
	)	ORDER FOR RELIEF
Debtor's Address:	)	
18 Hollywood Drive	)	
Los Angeles, CA 90001	)	
	)	
Debtor's Tax Id. No. 99-999899	)	
	)	

TO THE HONORABLE JUSTIN FAIR, UNITED STATES BANKRUPTCY JUDGE:

Videos by Joe, Inc. hereby consents to the entry of an Order for Relief under Chapter 11, Title 11 of the United States Code in the case commenced by the Involuntary Case: Creditors' Petition filed against it, the Summons with respect to which was issued on October 1, 1995. Filed concurrently with this Consent as Exhibits A through D are those paper, pleadings, and documents required by Bankruptcy Rules 1007(a)(2), 1007(a)(3), 1007(d), and 2016(b).

DATED: October 20, 2003

VIDEOS BY JOE, INC.

_____
JOE BUSINESSMAN
President

issues. If the court finds that the petition is well founded, it will enter the order for relief. If it finds for the debtor, it will dismiss the petition and may award damages to the debtor against the petitioning creditors for the debtor's costs, including attorneys' fees, and any damages caused by the improper commencement of the involuntary case.

Dismissal   Once an involuntary petition is filed, it cannot be simply dismissed by the petitioning creditors. The debtor must be given a chance to request damages. Also, to prevent a debtor who properly should be in a bankruptcy case from buying the petitioning creditors' cooperation by paying their debts, the debtor and the petitioning creditors cannot just dismiss the case. Any request for a dismissal must be noticed to all creditors and a court hearing held.

Effect of Filing an Involuntary Petition   Unlike voluntary cases, the order for relief is not entered upon the filing of the involuntary petition. However, the bankruptcy case has officially been commenced. Whenever the Bankruptcy Code speaks of the commencement of the case, it will mean the filing of the involuntary petition.

If, instead, it speaks of the entry of the order for relief, it will not apply in involuntary cases as soon as the petition is filed. For example, Section 362(a) provides that the automatic stay takes effect upon the commencement of the case. Thus, the debtor that has just had an involuntary petition filed against it is protected by the automatic stay. On the other hand, the time limit by which executory contracts and unexpired leases must be assumed or rejected begins upon the entry of the order for relief. Therefore, a debtor subject to an involuntary case need not worry about losing valuable contracts or leases while fighting an involuntary petition.

There are a number of rules that govern the debtor's conduct pending the entry of the order for relief in an involuntary case. Section 303(f) of the Bankruptcy Code allows the debtor to operate its business and to use, acquire, and dispose of its property as if the case had not been commenced. Any debt incurred between the filing of the petition and the entry of the order for relief, which is called the "gap" period, is entitled to a priority in payment over any prepetition claim under Section 507(a)(2). In addition, Section 549 permits the trustee or the debtor in possession to recover any assets transferred during this time if an order for relief is ultimately entered. While that power provides certain protections, it is not as good as preventing the transfer from taking place. Pursuant to Section 303(g), if necessary to preserve or protect the debtor's property against loss, the court has the power to appoint an interim trustee to take possession of the debtor's business pending the hearing on the involuntary petition. The debtor can defeat the appointment of a trustee by posting a bond. If the appointment of a trustee would be too harsh, the court may otherwise restrict the debtor's operations, for example, by preventing it from making transfers out of the ordinary course of business. A simple motion seeking just such a restriction is found in Exhibit 12.3.

Compensation   Creditors who hire counsel to bring an involuntary petition may file a motion with the court to be reimbursed for the attorneys' fees and costs they incurred.

Proofs of Claim

In General   A *claim* is defined in Section 101(5) to be any right to payment, whether or not secured, liquidated, contingent, disputed, or matured. Payments or distributions in bankruptcy cases are made on allowed claims. There are several different ways in which a claim becomes allowed, but the most common is through the creditor filing a *proof of claim*.

A proof of claim is a relatively simple document that is usually filed with the court by a creditor. It is fairly simple because it is designed to be completed by creditors without the assistance of an attorney. Attorneys can file proofs of claim on behalf of their clients. Non-attorneys can also file proofs of claim on behalf of creditors, but if they do so, a power of attorney in the form of Official Form 11A should be used.

Official Form 10 is the proof of claim that can be used by all creditors whether they are unsecured, secured, prepetition, priority, or non-priority. Official Form 10 can also be used in cases under every chapter of the Bankruptcy Code. Official Form 10 should not be used, however, to make a claim for an administrative expense that arose after the bankruptcy case was begun. A request for the payment of an administrative expense may be filed pursuant to Section 503 of the Bankruptcy Code. Exhibit 12.4 is a blank Official Form 10 proof of claim. The discussion below explains each part of Exhibit 12.4.

Court, Name of Debtor, and Case Number   The top three boxes of Official Form 10 ask for case caption information. As in all other papers filed in a

EXHIBIT 12.3 ✦ *Sample Pleading*

SARAH PORTIA
Portia & Carrera
Two Lane Highway
San Diego, California 92123

Attorneys for Petitioning Creditors

UNITED STATES BANKRUPTCY COURT
WESTERN DISTRICT OF CALIFORNIA

In re	)	Case No. 03-00001-JF
	)	
VIDEOS BY JOE, INC.,	)	Chapter 11
	)	
Debtor.	)	MOTION FOR ORDER RESTRICTING
	)	OPERATIONS OF DEBTOR PENDING
Debtor's Address:	)	TRIAL ON INVOLUNTARY
18 Hollywood Drive	)	PETITION
Los Angeles, CA 90001	)	
	)	
Debtor's Tax Id. No. 99-999899	)	
	)	

TO THE HONORABLE JUSTIN FAIR, UNITED STATES BANKRUPTCY JUDGE:

Imperial Processing, Act Trucking, and Abe's Office Supply (the "Petitioning Creditors"), through their attorneys, hereby move the Court for its order restricting the operations of the debtor pending trial of the issue of whether an Order for Relief should be entered. In support of this Motion, the Petitioning Creditors respectfully represent as follows:

1. Videos by Joe, Inc. (the "Debtor") is the debtor in the above-captioned involuntary Chapter 11 case, which was commenced on October 1, 2003 by the filing of an Involuntary Case: Creditors' Petition against Debtor by Petitioning Creditors. Petitioning Creditors hold claims against Debtor in the aggregate amount of approximately 50,000.

2. Petitioning Creditors understand that on or about September 20, 2003, Debtor transferred to certain of its film vendors unrecorded video tape valued at approximately $10,000. This transfer was made in partial satisfaction to the indebtedness of Debtor to such vendors. Petitioning Creditors believe that additional transfers of film inventory are contemplated and suspect that similar transactions may be occurring with other vendors.

3. Such transfers are prejudicial to unsecured creditors. From the standpoint of creditors, Debtor receives no value for the inventory. The transfer may be avoidable as a preference, but creditors then bear the expense and risk of litigation, including the risk that the transferees will be unable to respond to a judgment. Furthermore, the depletion of inventory may impact negatively on Debtor's ability to make future sales.

4. Bankruptcy Code Section 303(f) provides that

   Notwithstanding Section 363 of this title, *except to the extent that the court orders otherwise,* and until an order for relief in the case, any business of the debtor may continue to operate, and the debtor may continue to use, acquire, or dispose of property as if an involuntary case concerning the debtor had not been commenced (emphasis added).

5. An order imposing upon Debtor the requirements of Section 363(b)(1) of the Bankruptcy Code and prohibiting the payment of prepetition debts should be entered. Such an order is only minimally burdensome on Debtor. Debtor will remain in control of its business and can operate in the ordinary course. Transactions that are outside the ordinary course of business are permissible, but only after notice to creditors and an opportunity for them to be heard.

—*CONTINUED*

EXHIBIT 12.3 ✦ *Sample Pleading* (CONTINUED)

6. Such an order will have important benefits to unsecured creditors. Transfers of inventory, with the resulting prejudice, will cease. The core business will be preserved for the benefit of all creditors, not just the preferred few.

WHEREFORE, Petitioning Creditors request that the Court enter its order imposing the requirements of Bankruptcy Code Section 363(b)(1) upon Debtor and prohibiting Debtor from making any transfers on account of any prepetition indebtedness.

DATED: October 3, 2003

PORTIA & CARRERA

SARAH PORTIA
Attorneys for Petitioning Creditors

---

bankruptcy case, Form 10 must indicate the particular bankruptcy court in which the case is pending (e.g., Central District of California), the name of the debtor in the bankruptcy case, and the case (docket) number as assigned by the court. All of this information is near the top of the notice of the case, if one has been received from the court.

Administrative Expense Note   Immediately following the top three boxes is a note explaining that Official Form 10 is not to be used for administrative expenses.

Information about the Creditor   The next five boxes request various information about the creditor. The first three of these boxes ask for the creditor's name, address, and telephone number, along with any account number by which the creditor identifies the debtor. If the creditor wants all communication to be handled through its attorneys, the second of these boxes, "Name and address where notices should be sent," may be filled in with the name and address of the attorney. (See Exhibit 12.9.) The fourth box (positioned to the right) has three check boxes asking the creditor to indicate: (1) if it is aware of anyone who has filed a proof of claim relating to this particular claim; (2) if it has never received notices from the bankruptcy court on this case; and (3) if its address differs from the one on the envelope sent to the creditor by the court. This last question allows the court to record the creditor's correct address from this proof of claim, in case the debtor provided incorrect information. The fifth, and final, box in this section asks the creditor to indicate whether the claim replaces or amends a previously filed claim. If it does, the creditor must indicate the date of the previously filed claim.
The rest of Form 10 is a set of nine numbered items described below.

Basis for Claim   Item 1 is a series of check boxes where the creditor indicates the type of debt for which the proof of claim is being filed (goods sold; services performed; money loaned; personal injury/wrongful death; taxes; other, which should be specified; retiree benefits; or wages, salaries, and compensation). The additional information required for "Wages, salaries, and compensation" (including social security number and dates of unpaid compensation) will assist the trustee or debtor to make the appropriate withholding calculations and reports, as well as help determine whether any priority amount is properly claimed.

Date Debt Was Incurred   Item 2 asks the creditor to provide the date the debt was first owed by the debtor.

EXHIBIT 12.4 ✦ *Proof of Claim*

FORM B10 (Official Form 10) (4/01)

UNITED STATES BANKRUPTCY COURT _____ DISTRICT OF _____		PROOF OF CLAIM
Name of Debtor	Case Number	

NOTE: This form should not be used to make a claim for an administrative expense arising after the commencement of the case. A "request" for payment of an administrative expense may be filed pursuant to 11 U.S.C. § 503.

Name of Creditor (The person or other entity to whom the debtor owes money or property):	☐ Check box if you are aware that anyone else has filed a proof of claim relating to your claim. Attach copy of statement giving particulars.	
Name and address where notices should be sent:	☐ Check box if you have never received any notices from the bankruptcy court in this case. ☐ Check box if the address differs from the address on the envelope sent to you by the court.	
Telephone number:		THIS SPACE IS FOR COURT USE ONLY

Account or other number by which creditor identifies debtor:

Check here
if this claim ☐ replaces   a previously filed claim, dated:_____
          ☐ amends

1. Basis for Claim

☐ Goods sold
☐ Services performed
☐ Money loaned
☐ Personal injury/wrongful death
☐ Taxes
☐ Other _____

☐ Retiree benefits as defined in 11 U.S.C. § 1114(a)
☐ Wages, salaries, and compensation (fill out below)
Your SS #: _____ _____ _____
Unpaid compensation for services performed
from _____ to_____
        (date)   (date)

2. Date debt was incurred:

3. If court judgment, date obtained:

4. Total Amount of Claim at Time Case Filed: $ _____

If all or part of your claim is secured or entitled to priority, also complete Item 5 or 6 below.
☐ Check this box if claim includes interest or other charges in addition to the principal amount of the claim. Attach itemized statement of all interest or additional charges.

5. Secured Claim.

☐ Check this box if your claim is secured by collateral (including a right of setoff).
Brief Description of Collateral:
☐ Real Estate   ☐ Motor Vehicle
☐ Other_____
Value of Collateral: $_____

Amount of arrearage and other charges <u>at time case filed</u> included in secured claim, if any: $_____

6. Unsecured Priority Claim.
☐ Check this box if you have an unsecured priority claim
Amount entitled to priority $_____
Specify the priority of the claim:
☐ Wages, salaries, or commissions (up to $4,650),* earned within 90 days before filing of the bankruptcy petition or cessation of the debtor's business, whichever is earlier - 11 U.S.C. § 507(a)(3).
☐ Contributions to an employee benefit plan - 11 U.S.C. § 507(a)(4).
☐ Up to $2,100* of deposits toward purchase, lease, or rental of property or services for personal, family, or household use - 11 U.S.C. § 507(a)(6).
☐ Alimony, maintenance, or support owed to a spouse, former spouse, or child - 11 U.S.C. § 507(a)(7).
☐ Taxes or penalties owed to governmental units - 11 U.S.C. § 507(a)(8).
☐ Other - Specify applicable paragraph of 11 U.S.C. § 507(a)(____).
*Amounts are subject to adjustment on 4/1/04 and every 3 years thereafter with respect to cases commenced on or after the date of adjustment.

7. Credits: The amount of all payments on this claim has been credited and deducted for the purpose of making this proof of claim.

8. Supporting Documents: *Attach copies of supporting documents,* such as promissory notes, purchase orders, invoices, itemized statements of running accounts, contracts, court judgments, mortgages, security agreements, and evidence of perfection of lien. DO NOT SEND ORIGINAL DOCUMENTS. If the documents are not available, explain. If the documents are voluminous, attach a summary.

9. Date-Stamped Copy: To receive an acknowledgment of the filing of your claim, enclose a stamped, self-addressed envelope and copy of this proof of claim.

THIS SPACE IS FOR COURT USE ONLY

Date	Sign and print the name and title, if any, of the creditor or other person authorized to file this claim (attach copy of power of attorney, if any):

Penalty for presenting fraudulent claim: Fine of up to $500,000 or imprisonment for up to 5 years, or both. 18 U.S.C. §§ 152 and 3571.

If Court Judgment, Date Obtained   Immediately to the right of item 2 on the form is item 3 asking for the date a court entered judgment, if a court judgment was obtained for the debt being claimed.

Total Amount of Claim at Time Case Filed   Item 4 requires the creditor to provide the total amount of the claim at the time the bankruptcy case was filed. In completing this section, the creditor must also note if the claim includes interest or any other charges in addition to the principal amount of the claim. If it does, the creditor must provide an itemized statement of all interest or additional charges.

Secured Claim and Unsecured Priority Claim   Items 5 and 6 need to be completed only if all or part of the claim is secured or entitled to priority. For secured creditors, the form requests a brief description of the collateral, the value of the collateral, and the amount of any past due amounts (arrearages) and other charges incurred *at the time the case was filed* that are included in the secured claim. A sample proof of claim for a secured creditor is shown in Exhibit 12.11.

Item 6 is used by unsecured priority creditors. These creditors must state the amount entitled to priority and specify both the priority of the claim and under which provision of Section 507(a) it is allowed. The form was revised after the 1994 amendments to include the renumbering caused by the addition of the new Section 507(a)(7) priority for alimony and support. A claim filed by a creditor with both a secured claim and unsecured priority claim is shown in Exhibit 12.9.

If a creditor has different types of claims, information may be put in more than one category. For example, a secured creditor whose collateral is worth less than the amount of the debt will have a secured claim up to the value of the collateral and an unsecured nonpriority claim for the deficiency.

Credits, Supporting Documents, and Date-Stamped Copy   Item 7, "Credits," is a statement—affirmed by the creditor's signature on the form—that any payments on the claim previously made by the debtor have been credited and deducted when making the proof of claim.

Item 8, "Supporting Documents," instructs the creditor to attach copies of supporting documents. Such documents include promissory notes, purchase orders, invoices, contracts, court judgments, and evidence of perfection of liens. The instructions specify that the creditor should not send original documents, and that if the documents are voluminous, summaries should be attached.

Item 9, "Date-Stamped Copy," instructs the creditor to enclose a stamped, self-addressed envelope along with a copy of the proof of claim if the creditor wants to receive an acknowledgment of the filing of the claim.

Date and Signature   The final boxes on the bottom of Official Form 10 call for the date and signature of the creditor or authorized representative.

Exhibit 12.5 shows a proof of claim filled out by a trade creditor with an unsecured, no priority claim.

Who Can File   Obviously, proofs of claim are usually filed by creditors. Sometimes they can be filed by other parties. If a creditor fails to file a proof of claim, Section 501(c) and Bankruptcy Rule 3004 allow the debtor or the trustee to do so in the name of the creditor. The debtor may want to file a claim on behalf of a creditor to ensure that the creditor is paid, especially if there is an affiliate of the debtor that is also obligated on the debt or the debt is not dischargeable and will survive the bankruptcy case. The trustee may file a claim on behalf of a creditor if, perhaps, the trustee believes the creditor should be paid but for some reason the creditor did not file the claim. For example, sometimes the trustee will file proofs of claim on behalf of unpaid employees who did not understand their right to file proofs of claim.

EXHIBIT 12.5 ✦ *Completed Proof of Claim*

FORM B10 (Official Form 10) (4/01)

UNITED STATES BANKRUPTCY COURT Western	DISTRICT OF California	PROOF OF CLAIM

Name of Debtor Videos By Joe, Inc.	Case Number 01-00001-JF	

NOTE: This form should not be used to make a claim for an administrative expense arising after the commencement of the case. A "request" for payment of an administrative expense may be filed pursuant to 11 U.S.C. § 503.

Name of Creditor (The person or other entity to whom the debtor owes money or property): Ace Trucking	☐ Check box if you are aware that anyone else has filed a proof of claim relating to your claim. Attach copy of statement giving particulars.	
Name and address where notices should be sent: Ace Trucking 2309 Mack St. Los Angeles, CA 90001 ATTN: Jack Q. King Telephone number: 213-891-0700	☐ Check box if you have never received any notices from the bankruptcy court in this case. ☐ Check box if the address differs from the address on the envelope sent to you by the court.	THIS SPACE IS FOR COURT USE ONLY

Account or other number by which creditor identifies debtor: X11144	Check here if this claim ☐ replaces a previously filed claim, dated:_____ ☐ amends

1. Basis for Claim
  ☐ Goods sold
  ☒ Services performed
  ☐ Money loaned
  ☐ Personal injury/wrongful death
  ☐ Taxes
  ☐ Other _____
	☐ Retiree benefits as defined in 11 U.S.C. § 1114(a)
	☐ Wages, salaries, and compensation (fill out below)
	Your SS #: _____ _____ _____
	Unpaid compensation for services performed
	from _____ to_____
	      (date) (date)

2. Date debt was incurred: Sept. 15, 2003	**3. If court judgment, date obtained:**

4. Total Amount of Claim at Time Case Filed: $ 990.00 _____

If all or part of your claim is secured or entitled to priority, also complete Item 5 or 6 below.

☐ Check this box if claim includes interest or other charges in addition to the principal amount of the claim. Attach itemized statement of all interest or additional charges.

5. Secured Claim. ☐ Check this box if your claim is secured by collateral (including a right of setoff). Brief Description of Collateral: ☐ Real Estate ☐ Motor Vehicle ☐ Other_____ Value of Collateral: $_____ Amount of arrearage and other charges <u>at time case filed</u> included in secured claim, if any: $_____	**6. Unsecured Priority Claim.** ☐ Check this box if you have an unsecured priority claim Amount entitled to priority $_____ Specify the priority of the claim: ☐ Wages, salaries, or commissions (up to $4,650),* earned within 90 days before filing of the bankruptcy petition or cessation of the debtor's business, whichever is earlier - 11 U.S.C. § 507(a)(3). ☐ Contributions to an employee benefit plan - 11 U.S.C. § 507(a)(4). ☐ Up to $2,100* of deposits toward purchase, lease, or rental of property or services for personal, family, or household use - 11 U.S.C. § 507(a)(6). ☐ Alimony, maintenance, or support owed to a spouse, former spouse, or child - 11 U.S.C. § 507(a)(7). ☐ Taxes or penalties owed to governmental units - 11 U.S.C. § 507(a)(8). ☐ Other - Specify applicable paragraph of 11 U.S.C. § 507(a)(___). *Amounts are subject to adjustment on 4/1/04 and every 3 years thereafter with respect to cases commenced on or after the date of adjustment.

7. Credits: The amount of all payments on this claim has been credited and deducted for the purpose of making this proof of claim. **8. Supporting Documents:** *Attach copies of supporting documents,* such as promissory notes, purchase orders, invoices, itemized statements of running accounts, contracts, court judgments, mortgages, security agreements, and evidence of perfection of lien. DO NOT SEND ORIGINAL DOCUMENTS. If the documents are not available, explain. If the documents are voluminous, attach a summary. **9. Date-Stamped Copy:** To receive an acknowledgment of the filing of your claim, enclose a stamped, self-addressed envelope and copy of this proof of claim.	THIS SPACE IS FOR COURT USE ONLY

Date Oct. 15, 2003	Sign and print the name and title, if any, of the creditor or other person authorized to file this claim (attach copy of power of attorney, if any): Jack Q. King, Owner	

Penalty for presenting fraudulent claim: Fine of up to $500,000 or imprisonment for up to 5 years, or both. 18 U.S.C. §§ 152 and 3571.

Bankruptcy Code Section 501 and Bankruptcy Rule 3005 allow any person who is liable with the debtor on a debt, such as a guarantor or co-borrower, or who has given security for the debt, to file a proof of claim for a creditor if the creditor has not filed one. If an entity other than the creditor files a claim on behalf of that creditor, the creditor may later file its own claim; this claim will supersede any claim filed for it.

Filing and Service   Proofs of claim are generally filed with the clerk of the court. In some jurisdictions they will be filed with the Chapter 13 trustee. In addition, in some very large cases, the court will order that they be sent directly to the debtor or the trustee. In those cases, usually an employee of the debtor or the trustee, or an employee of their attorney, will be made a special deputy clerk.

There is no requirement in the Bankruptcy Code or in the Bankruptcy Rules that proofs of claim be served on any party in interest. Some local rules may require that they be served on the debtor and the trustee, if any. Even if the local rules do not require any service, it is often customary to provide a copy to the debtor in possession or the trustee as a matter of courtesy.

Timing   Pursuant to Bankruptcy Rule 3002(c), in all cases except those under Chapter 11, proofs of claim must be filed within 90 days after the first date set for the meeting of creditors. Even if the first meeting of creditors is continued to another date, the claim filing deadline will be determined by reference to the date on which it was first set. This is a very important date to calendar when the paralegal first learns of the commencement of the case because if a claim is not filed in a timely manner, it is unlikely that the creditor will receive a distribution. It is always a good idea to prepare and file the proof of claim as soon as is possible in the case to ensure that the task does not fall between the cracks.

Some claims, although treated as prepetition claims, cannot be filed within the deadline provided in Bankruptcy Rule 3002(c). One example is claims arising from the rejection of an executory contract, which may not happen until after the claims filing deadline has passed. Bankruptcy Rule 3002(c)(4) provides that those claims must be filed within the time set by the court. Claims that arise because of the result of a judgment, such as claims of creditors who had to pay back a preference, must be filed within 30 days after the judgment becomes final. Bankruptcy Rule 3005 allows a codebtor to file a claim only within the 30-day period following expiration of the time for creditor filings. There is no deadline for claims filed by the debtor or the trustee.

Chapter 11 cases are very different from cases in other bankruptcy chapters when it comes to filing proofs of claim. Bankruptcy Rule 3003(c) and Bankruptcy Code Section 1111 provide that if a creditor or equity security holder is listed in the schedules and the debtor does not list the claim as disputed, contingent, or unliquidated, the claim is deemed filed and the creditor need not file a proof of claim if the amount scheduled is correct. If the claim is scheduled as disputed, contingent, or unliquidated, the creditor must file a proof of claim to participate in the distribution to creditors. If the amount is wrong, unless the creditor files a proof of claim, the wrong amount will be deemed correct. If a proof of claim is filed, it will supersede the scheduled amount.

Although a creditor need not file a claim if its claim has been deemed filed, there is no prohibition against it doing so. In fact, it is usually easier to simply file a proof of claim than to try to learn how a creditor is scheduled and in what amount.

There is no 90-day deadline for the filing of a proof of claim in a Chapter 11 case as there is in other cases. However, sometime before plan confirmation, the court will set a date by which required proofs of claim must be filed.

If a proof of claim is filed in a Chapter 11 case that is later converted to a Chapter 7 case, the creditor need not file another proof of claim. Although at least one case has held that a creditor whose claim was deemed filed in a Chapter 11 case need not file a claim in the converted case, the better practice is to file a proof of claim.

Amendments and Withdrawals   Once a claim is timely filed, regardless of the chapter in which the case is pending, it can be later amended to correct any mistakes in amount. The power to amend should not be relied on too heavily since not all courts will allow amendments if the debtor or the trustee has relied on the amount in the original claim or if the amendment is substantially different from the original claim.

The creditor may withdraw its claim simply by filing a notice of withdrawal at any time prior to an objection being filed. A creditor may want to withdraw a claim if it was contingent and the contingency never happened or it might agree to withdraw its claim as part of a settlement of any dispute with the debtor.

The No-Asset Case

In most consumer and many business Chapter 7 cases, there are no assets or there are insufficient assets for the trustee to administer. In a consumer case, usually all of the debtor's property is exempt. What other property there is may not be worth the cost of its liquidation, and it will be abandoned by the trustee. In a business case, there might be a secured creditor who has a lien on all the assets, which are worth less than the amount owed. In those very common scenarios, unsecured creditors will not receive a distribution from the estate in exchange for the discharge of the debt due them.

Often the trustee will examine the debtor's schedules, and if it appears that there is nothing to be administered, the trustee will issue what is commonly referred to as a **no-asset report.** There is no reason for proofs of claim to be filed since there will not be a distribution. The clerk will issue a notice informing creditors that they should not file proofs of claim. Later, the trustee may discover that there are assets to administer and will determine whether a distribution could be made. If the trustee decides a distribution could be made, creditors will be so informed and told to file their proofs of claim by the date set in the notice. This date, as provided in Bankruptcy Rule 3002(c)(5), will be 90 days after the mailing of the notice telling of the possible distribution.

If no assets are ever located, the case will be closed without creditors receiving a distribution.

♦ no-asset report
A report filed by a Chapter 7 trustee upon determining that there are no assets to be administered by the trustee and no likelihood of a distribution to creditors.

Case Monitoring

Bankruptcy cases have many players, some of whom have major roles (such as the debtor, the trustee, or the creditors' committee). Most of the players have very minor roles (such as small unsecured creditors). If the office in which a paralegal works is representing one of the major players, the status of the case and the events that are taking place in it will be easily known because of direct and frequent communication between the parties. The paralegal will not be called on to do much monitoring of the case as a whole, but may be asked to watch the progress of a particular adversary proceeding.

When the client has a minor role in a case, the paralegal will be most effectively used as a cost-efficient method of obtaining information. Depending on the client's desires and budget, the paralegal can take on the following tasks:

✦ Obtain copies of the schedules and provide the client with a list of the major liabilities and assets and any other information that may be of use to the client, such as whether the client's claim is scheduled.

✦ Early in the case, prepare and file a request for special notice (see Exhibit 12.6) so that all papers served by the parties in the case are received by the legal assistant's office. The request for special notice should be served on the debtor, the trustee, the committee, and any other known major players in the case.

✦ The paralegal can summarize the pleadings received in a weekly, monthly, or quarterly status letter for the client.

✦ Periodically call or write to the trustee or counsel for the debtor in possession for an update as to the status of the case and plan negotiations or distributions to creditors. A friendly relationship with the trustee's administrator or the debtor's counsel's paralegal will usually facilitate receipt of those answers.

✦ Obtain a docket of the papers filed and orders entered from the clerk's office in the case and in any adversary proceeding of interest. If information concerning the claims filed in the case is important to the client, a copy of the claim register should be ordered as well.

Priority Creditors

✦ priority claim
A type of claim that Congress has decided should receive special treatment. Priority claims must be paid in full before general unsecured creditors receive a distribution.

Sections 507(a)(2) through (a)(9) of the Bankruptcy Code list nine types of unsecured, prepetition claims that are entitled to be paid in full before any distribution is made to other unsecured prepetition creditors. These claims, which are fully detailed in the section on the schedules in Chapter 7 of this book, are known as **priority claims**, and the entity that holds one is known as a *priority creditor*.

If the client is a priority creditor, the proof of claim should be clearly marked that the claimant is entitled to priority in payment. If only part of the claim is entitled to be paid ahead of other creditors, the portion entitled to the priority should be clearly indicated. Exhibit 12.7 represents a proof of claim for a debt that is entitled to a partial priority in payment because a portion of it was incurred in the involuntary gap period.

In some cases, if it has sufficient assets to do so, the debtor or the trustee may move the court for permission to pay all or some of the priority creditors early so that they are not required to wait until plan confirmation or the closing of the case to be paid. This is certainly true if the debtor owes its employees for unpaid payroll and is attempting to reorganize. Since employee cooperation and high morale may be crucial to the success of that reorganization, the debtor is likely to want to see that there is no delay in payment to its workers. If the estate is prepared to pay priority creditors ahead of time, the procedure to be followed is to make a motion to the court for the necessary authority. A sample of such a motion was included in Chapter 11 of this book as Exhibit 11.4.

There is nothing in the Bankruptcy Code or the Bankruptcy Rules that allows a priority creditor to be paid early. The making of such a motion rests with the representative of the estate; however, the creditor certainly could and should ask the debtor in possession or the trustee to consider it.

Administrative Creditors

✦ administrative claim
A claim incurred after the commencement of the bankruptcy case that is a reasonable and necessary expense of the estate.

During the course of a bankruptcy case, the trustee and the debtor in possession will incur debts. The debts could range from professionals' fees, rent, wages, liquidation costs, or goods purchased. Debts incurred subsequent to the commencement of the case are typically called **administrative claims** because they were incurred during the administration of the case.

EXHIBIT 12.6 ✦ *Sample Pleading*

GEORGE G. SNOW
Snow & Porter
4 Wheel Drive
Los Angeles, California 90017

Attorneys for First City Bank

UNITED STATES BANKRUPTCY COURT
WESTERN DISTRICT OF CALIFORNIA

In re	)	Case No. 03-00001-JF
	)	
VIDEOS BY JOE, INC.,	)	Chapter 11
	)	
Debtor.	)	
	)	
Debtor's Address:	)	REQUEST FOR SPECIAL NOTICE
18 Hollywood Drive	)	AND INCLUSION IN MAILING LIST
Los Angeles, CA 90001	)	
	)	
Debtor's Tax Id. No. 99-999899	)	
	)	

TO THE CLERK OF THE BANKRUPTCY COURT AND PARTIES IN INTEREST:

PLEASE TAKE NOTICE that First City Bank, a creditor of the debtor in the above-captioned case, hereby requests special notice of all matters that must be noticed to creditors, or other parties in interest and further requests that for all notice purposes the following address be added:

SNOW & PORTER
4 Wheel Drive
Los Angeles, California 90017
Attention: George G. Snow

This request includes the type of notice referred to in Bankruptcy Rules 2002(i) and 3017(a) and also includes without limitation, all schedules, notices of any orders, applications, complaints, demands, hearings, motions, petitions, pleadings or requests, any other documents brought before the Court in this case, whether formal or informal, whether written or oral, and whether transmitted or conveyed by mail, delivery, telephone, telegraph, telex, or otherwise.

DATED: October 5, 2003

SNOW & PORTER

_____
GEORGE G. SNOW
Attorneys for First City Bank

Administrative claims of the type specified in Section 503(b) of the Bankruptcy Code are entitled to a first-in-line priority in payment under Section 507(a)(1). With the exception of payments to professionals, administrative claims are, or at least usually should be, paid when due in the ordinary course of the administration of the case. No court order is required. Sometimes they are not paid promptly, usually because the debtor in possession has no better ability to pay its bills after it filed its bankruptcy case than it did before. It may also be that the claim is disputed.

EXHIBIT 12.7 ✦ *Proof of Claim*

FORM B10 (Official Form 10) (4/01)

UNITED STATES BANKRUPTCY COURT **Western** DISTRICT OF **California**	**PROOF OF CLAIM**

Name of Debtor Videos By Joe, Inc.	Case Number 01-00001-JF	

NOTE: This form should not be used to make a claim for an administrative expense arising after the commencement of the case. A "request" for payment of an administrative expense may be filed pursuant to 11 U.S.C. § 503.

Name of Creditor (The person or other entity to whom the debtor owes money or property): Great Film, Inc.	☐ Check box if you are aware that anyone else has filed a proof of claim relating to your claim. Attach copy of statement giving particulars.	
Name and address where notices should be sent: Great Film, Inc. 84 Steele Plate Rd. City of Industry, CA 90050 ATTN: Manuel Perez Telephone number: 213-891-5595	☐ Check box if you have never received any notices from the bankruptcy court in this case. ☐ Check box if the address differs from the address on the envelope sent to you by the court.	THIS SPACE IS FOR COURT USE ONLY
Account or other number by which creditor identifies debtor:	Check here ☐ replaces a previously filed claim, dated:_____ if this claim ☐ amends	

1. Basis for Claim
- ☒ Goods sold
- ☐ Services performed
- ☐ Money loaned
- ☐ Personal injury/wrongful death
- ☐ Taxes
- ☐ Other _____

- ☐ Retiree benefits as defined in 11 U.S.C. § 1114(a)
- ☐ Wages, salaries, and compensation (fill out below)

Your SS #: _____ _____ _____

Unpaid compensation for services performed

from _____ to_____
        (date)   (date)

2. Date debt was incurred: August 1, 2001, Sept. 15, 2003

3. If court judgment, date obtained:

4. Total Amount of Claim at Time Case Filed: $ 700.00

If all or part of your claim is secured or entitled to priority, also complete Item 5 or 6 below.

☐ Check this box if claim includes interest or other charges in addition to the principal amount of the claim. Attach itemized statement of all interest or additional charges.

5. Secured Claim.

☐ Check this box if your claim is secured by collateral (including a right of setoff).

Brief Description of Collateral:
- ☐ Real Estate   ☐ Motor Vehicle
- ☐ Other_____

Value of Collateral: $_____

Amount of arrearage and other charges <u>at time case filed</u> included in secured claim, if any: $_____

6. Unsecured Priority Claim.

☑ Check this box if you have an unsecured priority claim

Amount entitled to priority $200.00

Specify the priority of the claim:
- ☐ Wages, salaries, or commissions (up to $4,650),* earned within 90 days before filing of the bankruptcy petition or cessation of the debtor's business, whichever is earlier - 11 U.S.C. § 507(a)(3).
- ☐ Contributions to an employee benefit plan - 11 U.S.C. § 507(a)(4).
- ☐ Up to $2,100* of deposits toward purchase, lease, or rental of property or services for personal, family, or household use - 11 U.S.C. § 507(a)(6).
- ☐ Alimony, maintenance, or support owed to a spouse, former spouse, or child - 11 U.S.C. § 507(a)(7).
- ☐ Taxes or penalties owed to governmental units - 11 U.S.C. § 507(a)(8).
- ☑ Other - Specify applicable paragraph of 11 U.S.C. § 507(a)(2).

Amounts are subject to adjustment on 4/1/04 and every 3 years thereafter with respect to cases commenced on or after the date of adjustment.

7. Credits: The amount of all payments on this claim has been credited and deducted for the purpose of making this proof of claim.

8. Supporting Documents: *Attach copies of supporting documents,* such as promissory notes, purchase orders, invoices, itemized statements of running accounts, contracts, court judgments, mortgages, security agreements, and evidence of perfection of lien. DO NOT SEND ORIGINAL DOCUMENTS. If the documents are not available, explain. If the documents are voluminous, attach a summary.

9. Date-Stamped Copy: To receive an acknowledgment of the filing of your claim, enclose a stamped, self-addressed envelope and copy of this proof of claim.

THIS SPACE IS FOR COURT USE ONLY

Date Oct. 15, 2003	Sign and print the name and title, if any, of the creditor or other person authorized to file this claim (attach copy of power of attorney, if any): Manuel Perez, President

Penalty for presenting fraudulent claim: Fine of up to $500,000 or imprisonment for up to 5 years, or both. 18 U.S.C. §§ 152 and 3571.

When the estate has failed to pay an administrative claim, the creditor has several alternatives. It may simply file a priority proof of claim, so long as the administrative claim did not arise after the commencement of the bankruptcy case. If the proof of claim is filed, the creditor must wait to be paid at the close of the case or plan confirmation or for a party in interest to file an objection to the proof of claim.

The creditor may also file suit in the appropriate state court. That lawsuit would not be subject to the automatic stay since it does not involve a claim that arose before the commencement of the case. Such a lawsuit would not be worthwhile since any judgment could not be enforced because all the property of the estate is also given the protection of the automatic stay. Any levy or attachment of a judgment lien by the administrative creditor would violate that stay.

The best alternative is for the administrative creditor to file an action in the bankruptcy court to compel payment. Section 503(a) specifically provides that an administrative creditor may do so. Since it would be an action to recover money, it would be an adversary proceeding commenced by the filing of a complaint as required by Bankruptcy Rule 7001.

Lessors

There are few bankruptcy cases in which the estate does not have real or personal leased property. In fact, it is very common for the debtor to have rented its business premises and all the equipment in it. The successful representation of lessors, for both real and personal property, is dependent in large measure on vigilance and on moving quickly. The paralegal's completion of a number of tasks that will need to be done shortly after the petition is filed can ensure successful representation of the lessor.

Expired Leases The only part of leased property that comes into the estate is the debtor's interest in it. If the lease has expired or has otherwise terminated prepetition, the debtor no longer has a legally recognized interest in the property and no right to use it. Not all terminations will be effective, and any termination based only on the debtor's financial condition or its commencing a bankruptcy case is never effective. But, if there has been a proper termination of the lease, the debtor or the trustee must surrender the property.

If the debtor refuses to surrender the property, the lessor's recourse is different depending on the type of property involved. For business real property, Section 362 provides that the automatic stay does not apply to attempts to regain possession if the term of the lease expired. In those situations, the landlord is free to pursue its unlawful detainer claims in the state courts. For residential real property, nonresidential real property with an unexpired term, and all personal property, there is no automatic stay exemption, and the lessor must either file a motion to obtain relief from the automatic stay (see Exhibit 12.8) before pursuing the rights and remedies granted by the lease and state law or file a complaint for the turnover of property in the bankruptcy court. The lessor should move quickly to regain possession because any delay may be deemed to be consent to the estate's continued use.

Administrative Claim If the estate continues to use leased property after the commencement of the bankruptcy case, it is only fair that the estate should have to pay for the use. The compensation must only be reasonable. It need not necessarily be the amount called for in the lease, although most courts will hold the contract rate to be strong evidence of a reasonable rate. The estate will be able to argue for a lower figure if, for example, it is using only a portion of the premises or the equipment or if what it formerly used for manufacturing operations is now being used for storage (which usually rents for a lower amount).

EXHIBIT 12.8 ✦ *Sample Pleading*

HAROLD SCHWARTZ
Schwartz & Schwartz
1800 Development Way
Thousand Oaks, California 92017

Attorneys for Leona Properties

UNITED STATES BANKRUPTCY COURT
WESTERN DISTRICT OF CALIFORNIA

In re	)	Case No. 03-00001-JF
	)	
VIDEOS BY JOE, INC.,	)	Chapter 11
	)	
Debtor.	)	
	)	
Debtor's Address:	)	
18 Hollywood Drive	)	
Los Angeles, CA 90001	)	
	)	
Debtor's Tax Id. No. 99-999899	)	
————————————————	)	
	)	
LEONA PROPERTIES,	)	MOTION FOR ORDER GRANTING
	)	RELIEF FROM THE AUTOMATIC
Movant,	)	STAY
	)	
v.	)	
	)	
VIDEOS BY JOE, INC.,	)	
	)	
Respondent.	)	
————————————————	)	

TO THE HONORABLE JUSTIN FAIR, UNITED STATES BANKRUPTCY JUDGE:

Leona Properties ("Lessor"), through its attorneys, in support of its Motion for Order Granting Relief from the Automatic Stay, respectfully represents as follows:

1. Lessor is the owner and lessor of real property commonly known as 19890 Santa Clara Avenue, Rancho Dominguez, County of Los Angeles, State of California (the "Property").

2. On or about September 16, 1998, Lessor and Videos by Joe, Inc., the debtor in possession in the above-captioned case ("Debtor"), entered into a written lease agreement (the "Lease"). The Lease provided that Debtor would lease the Property from Lessor for a period of ten (10) years commencing on October 15, 1998 and ending on October 15, 2008.

3. Under the terms of the Lease, Debtor was to make monthly payments to Lessor in the amount of $2,000.00 on or before the fifteenth of every month.

4. Debtor has refused and failed to pay the required monthly rent for the Property since August 1, 2003.

5. Pursuant to paragraph 10.1 of the Lease, Debtor was obligated to pay all real property taxes for the Property. Debtor has refused and failed to pay these taxes due for the period of July 12, 2002 through October 1, 2003.

6. As of September 1, 2003, Debtor was indebted to Lessor in the total amount of $6,700.00 for rent, late charges, and real property taxes.

—CONTINUED

EXHIBIT 12.8 ✦ *Sample Pleading* (CONTINUED)

7. On or about September 1, 2003, Lessor served upon Debtor a Three-Day Notice to Pay Rent or Quit (the "Notice"). The Notice demanded that Debtor pay the delinquent rent and real property taxes due within three days after service of the Notice or surrender possession of the Property. The Notice further provided that Lessor elected to declare the forfeiture of the Lease if all unpaid amounts were not paid within the required time period.

8. Debtor failed and refused to tender the unpaid rent and real property taxes within three days after service of the Notice, and the Lease was thereby terminated by Lessor pursuant to relevant state law.

9. On September 10, 2003, Lessor filed its Complaint for Unlawful Detainer in Superior Court of the State of California for the County of Los Angeles, entitled *Leona Properties v. Videos by Joe, Inc.* (the "Complaint").

10. On October 1, 2003, Debtor filed its voluntary petition under Chapter 11 of the Bankruptcy Code.

11. Pursuant to Section 362(a) of the Bankruptcy Code, Lessor is precluded from continuing its action on the Complaint. By this Motion, Lessor seeks relief from the automatic stay imposed in Debtor's bankruptcy case.

12. Lessor submits that relief from the automatic stay is mandated under Section 362(d) of the Bankruptcy Code for cause. Lessor effectively terminated the Lease prior to the commencement of Debtor's bankruptcy case. Therefore, Debtor has no legal interest in the Lease or the Property.

WHEREFORE, Lessor requests that this Court enter its Order as follows:

1. That the automatic stay arising under Section 362(a) of the Bankruptcy Code be vacated so that Lessor may continue with its unlawful detainer proceedings in the State Court and proceed to obtain possession of the Property;

2. That the Court order that the subsequent filing by Debtor of any case under the Bankruptcy Code or the conversion of Debtor's present case will not operate as an automatic stay against Lessor's rights and remedies with respect to the Property; and

3. For such other and further relief as this Court may deem to be just and proper.

DATED: October 5, 2003

SCHWARTZ & SCHWARTZ

_____

HAROLD SCHWARTZ
Attorneys for Leona Properties

For whatever the amount the estate is liable, the lessor will have an administrative claim in that amount. Again, the rules are very different as to how that amount gets paid between nonresidential real and other property.

With respect to business real property, Section 365 provides that the trustee or the debtor in possession must pay the amount due to the landlord on a timely basis. The estate may obtain an extension of time to comply with that requirement, but the court is prevented from granting any extension beyond 60 days after the entry of the order for relief. If the payments are not timely received and no motion to extend the time for performance is made, the landlord will be required to bring the matter to the court's attention by filing either a motion for relief from the automatic stay, so as to begin unlawful detainer proceedings, or an action to compel payment of the accruing administrative claim.

For residential real property, there is no statutory requirement that the estate make all lease payments timely. It is much more important in these situations for the lessor to be diligent in having the administrative claim paid by making demands and going to court to compel payment.

The 1994 Amendments added special rules for personal property leases other than leases for property used primarily for personal, family, or household uses. New Section 365(d)(10) provides that the trustee or debtor in possession must perform the debtor's obligations under a lease of business personal property beginning 60 days after the case is commenced and continuing until the lease is assumed or rejected unless the court, based on the equities of the case, orders otherwise. Lessors of property used primarily for personal, family, or household uses will need to move the court to compel payments if the debtor is not making timely payments.

Assumption and Rejection   In a Chapter 7 case for real and personal property, the trustee must decide to either assume or reject an unexpired lease within 60 days after the entry of the order for relief or obtain a court order extending the time to make the decision. A lessor is entitled to ask the court to have the trustee make its decision earlier than the 60 days if the landlord has a good reason. Since the trustee has a duty to investigate whether the lease has value to the estate, the court will not require the trustee to make rash judgments. As a result, motions to shorten the 60-day period are not usually granted.

In Chapter 11 cases, leases of business real property must also be assumed or rejected within the first 60 days unless an extension is granted. The only deadline for assumption or rejection of all other types of leases is upon plan confirmation. While the estate may reject leases as soon as it can determine they have little or no value, unless there is an intended assignment, the debtor in possession has no motivation to assume leases any sooner than is necessary. Because assumption will mean the curing of all defaults and rejection will mean the return of the property, the personal property lessor should move quickly to have a deadline sooner than plan confirmation set for the assumption or rejection of the lease. However, the lessor might not want to incur the expense of such a motion if the lease is not in default or if it has little chance of releasing the property.

Damages   If the estate ultimately assumes a lease, all defaults will be cured and lessor will have no remaining prepetition claim in the bankruptcy case. If a lease is assumed and then breached, the lessor will have an administrative claim for all of its damages. These must be paid in full before the prepetition creditors are paid. If a lease is assumed in a Chapter 11 case and then rejected in the superseding Chapter 7 case, the lessor's damage claim will be a Chapter 11 administrative claim paid ahead of prepetition claims but behind Chapter 7 administrative claims.

If a lease is rejected, the lessor may have three different types of claims. First, it may have a prepetition claim for any defaults that existed at the time of the commencement of the bankruptcy case. Second, it may have a claim for any rent that became due while the estate was still in possession of the leased property that has not been paid. Third, it will have a claim arising from the rejection of the lease; this is treated like a breach of the lease. Under Section 502(g), this last claim is deemed to be a prepetition claim. There is also a statutory limit as to its amount. Section 502(b)(6) states that it cannot exceed the greater of one year's future rent under the lease or, for long-term leases, 15 percent of the remaining term as long as 15 percent of the remaining term is not greater than three years. Proofs of claim for the damages caused by the rejection of the lease should be filed no later than 30 days after the rejection.

Security Deposits   In many leases, the lessor holds a deposit from the debtor to secure lease payments. Because the automatic stay prevents setoffs, if there are prepetition defaults, the lessor will need to obtain relief from the automatic stay in order to apply the deposit to the defaults. Some debtors would prefer that the landlord under a rejected lease apply the deposit to any postpetition amounts that are due and let the landlord have a claim for the prepetition defaults. If under the plan creditors will not be paid in full, the benefit to the debtor of such an application is obvious. However, courts have been disinclined to require the lessor to follow the debtor's preference.

Exhibit 12.9 is an example of a proof of claim filed by a landlord who had a $2,000 prepetition claim secured by a $2,000 security deposit, $2,000 administrative claim for the one month the trustee used the property, and a prepetition claim for one year's rent caused by the trustee's rejection.

Reclamation

Chapter 9 of this book discussed the right of a trustee to compel turnover of property of the estate in the hands of third persons. The opposite side of the coin is the right of a third party to recover its property in the hands of the bankruptcy estate. This is called **reclamation.** The grounds for reclamation can include any theory of ownership or title that is better than the title of the estate.

In addition to the grounds for reclamation just discussed, there is a statutory basis of reclamation that can be very significant to unsecured creditors. Uniform Commercial Code Section 2-702 provides a right of reclamation to a seller of goods on credit who discovers that its buyer is insolvent. Section 2-702 allows the seller to reclaim the goods simply by making a demand within 10 days of the buyer's receipt of the goods.

Section 546 of the Bankruptcy Code preserves the seller's right to reclaim when the buyer is in bankruptcy. Specifically, Section 546(c) provides that the rights of a trustee are subject to any statutory or common law right of a seller of goods who has sold goods to the debtor in the ordinary course of the seller's business if the buyer receives the goods while insolvent and the seller makes demand on the goods in writing within 10 days after receipt of the goods. Section 546(c) was amended in the 1994 Amendments to provide that if the 10-day reclamation period expires after the bankruptcy case is commenced, the writing need only be made before 20 days after receipt of the goods. For example, if the goods were delivered on September 23, and the bankruptcy case was filed on October 1, the seller would have until October 13 to make the reclamation demand. A sample of such a demand follows as Exhibit 12.10.

Under the Uniform Commercial Code, if the seller properly makes the demand, it is entitled to the goods. However, under Section 546's reclamation, the right to obtain the goods is not absolute. If the trustee or the debtor in possession wants to keep the goods, it may do so; however, it must either give the seller an administrative claim for the value of the goods subject to reclamation or a lien to secure the claim. Also, a new Section 546(g) was added in the 1994 Amendments that allows the court to permit a debtor to return goods to a seller and let the seller credit the purchase price of the goods to its prepetition claim.

Obviously, reclamation is an important right for suppliers who were unaware of the debtor's pending bankruptcy; it means the difference between being paid in full or receiving only what other prepetition unsecured creditors receive. For it to be effective, however, the supplier must act immediately because the 10- and 20-day periods pass quickly. Further, if the seller's goods have already been sold by the debtor in the ordinary course of its business before it receives the reclamation notice, the seller's exercise of its reclamation rights will be too late.

If the seller gives the required notice and the debtor in possession or trustee does not respond, the creditor will have to file a complaint to enforce its reclamation rights and recover the property.

✦ **reclamation**
The right of a person to seek to obtain possession of its property in the hands of the estate.

EXHIBIT 12.9 ✦ *Proof of Claim*

FORM B10 (Official Form 10) (4/01)

UNITED STATES BANKRUPTCY COURT <u>Western</u> DISTRICT OF <u>California</u>	**PROOF OF CLAIM**

Name of Debtor Videos By Joe, Inc.	Case Number 03-00001-JF	

NOTE: This form should not be used to make a claim for an administrative expense arising after the commencement of the case. A "request" for payment of an administrative expense may be filed pursuant to 11 U.S.C. § 503.

Name of Creditor (The person or other entity to whom the debtor owes money or property): Leona Properties Name and address where notices should be sent: Leona Properties c/o Harold Schwartz 1800 Development Way Thousand Oaks, CA 92017 Telephone number: 818-667-4300	☐ Check box if you are aware that anyone else has filed a proof of claim relating to your claim. Attach copy of statement giving particulars. ☐ Check box if you have never received any notices from the bankruptcy court in this case. ☑ Check box if the address differs from the address on the envelope sent to you by the court.	THIS SPACE IS FOR COURT USE ONLY

Account or other number by which creditor identifies debtor:	Check here if this claim ☐ replaces / ☑ amends a previously filed claim, dated: <u>Oct. 15, 2003</u>

1. Basis for Claim

☐ Goods sold
☐ Services performed
☐ Money loaned
☐ Personal injury/wrongful death
☐ Taxes
☑ Other <u>Rental of Real Property</u>

☐ Retiree benefits as defined in 11 U.S.C. § 1114(a)
☐ Wages, salaries, and compensation (fill out below)
Your SS #: _____ _____ _____
Unpaid compensation for services performed
from _____ to _____
    (date)   (date)

2. Date debt was incurred: Sept. 1, 2003 to Nov. 1, 2003 | **3. If court judgment, date obtained:**

4. Total Amount of Claim at Time Case Filed: $ <u>28,000</u>

If all or part of your claim is secured or entitled to priority, also complete Item 5 or 6 below.

☐ Check this box if claim includes interest or other charges in addition to the principal amount of the claim. Attach itemized statement of all interest or additional charges.

5. Secured Claim.

☑ Check this box if your claim is secured by collateral (including a right of setoff).

Brief Description of Collateral:

☐ Real Estate   ☐ Motor Vehicle
☑ Other <u>Cash Security</u> Deposit

Value of Collateral: $ <u>2,000</u>

Amount of arrearage and other charges <u>at time case filed</u> included in secured claim, if any: $_____

6. Unsecured Priority Claim.

☑ Check this box if you have an unsecured priority claim
Amount entitled to priority $ <u>2,000</u>
Specify the priority of the claim:

☐ Wages, salaries, or commissions (up to $4,650),* earned within 90 days before filing of the bankruptcy petition or cessation of the debtor's business, whichever is earlier - 11 U.S.C. § 507(a)(3).
☐ Contributions to an employee benefit plan - 11 U.S.C. § 507(a)(4).
☐ Up to $2,100* of deposits toward purchase, lease, or rental of property or services for personal, family, or household use - 11 U.S.C. § 507(a)(6).
☐ Alimony, maintenance, or support owed to a spouse, former spouse, or child - 11 U.S.C. § 507(a)(7).
☐ Taxes or penalties owed to governmental units - 11 U.S.C. § 507(a)(8).
☐ Other - Specify applicable paragraph of 11 U.S.C. § 507(a)(<u>1</u>).

*Amounts are subject to adjustment on 4/1/04 and every 3 years thereafter with respect to cases commenced on or after the date of adjustment.

7. Credits: The amount of all payments on this claim has been credited and deducted for the purpose of making this proof of claim.

8. Supporting Documents: *Attach copies of supporting documents,* such as promissory notes, purchase orders, invoices, itemized statements of running accounts, contracts, court judgments, mortgages, security agreements, and evidence of perfection of lien. DO NOT SEND ORIGINAL DOCUMENTS. If the documents are not available, explain. If the documents are voluminous, attach a summary.

9. Date-Stamped Copy: To receive an acknowledgment of the filing of your claim, enclose a stamped, self-addressed envelope and copy of this proof of claim.

THIS SPACE IS FOR COURT USE ONLY

Date Nov. 15, 2003	Sign and print the name and title, if any, of the creditor or other person authorized to file this claim (attach copy of power of attorney, if any): Harold Schwartz, Attorney

Penalty for presenting fraudulent claim: Fine of up to $500,000 or imprisonment for up to 5 years, or both. 18 U.S.C. §§ 152 and 3571.

EXHIBIT 12.10 ✦ *Sample Pleading*

October 3, 2003

DEMAND FOR RETURN OF GOODS

TO: VIDEOS BY JOE, INC.
        18 Hollywood Drive
        Los Angeles, California 90017

FROM: GREAT FILM, INC.
        84 Steel Plate Road
        City of Industry, California 91744

NOTICE IS HEREBY GIVEN THAT pursuant to California Uniform Commercial Code Section 2702 and Bankruptcy Code Section 546(c), and by reason of your insolvency, Great Film, Inc. hereby demands the return of all goods delivered to you on and after September 23, 2003.

GREAT FILM, INC.

MANUEL PEREZ
President

Seeking a Discharge or Dischargeability Determination

Perhaps the greatest result an attorney representing an unsecured creditor could obtain in a case in which creditors will not be paid in full is to obtain a judgment determining that the client's claim will not be discharged. Second best—but far more detrimental to the debtor—is a judgment determining that the debtor is not entitled to a discharge at all and all debts will be enforceable despite the bankruptcy case. The grounds for denying the debtor a discharge on a particular debt or on all debts were set out in Chapter 8 of this book (in the section on dischargeability). To review, the grounds for dischargeability that require a court determination are obtaining money or property by fraud, certain consumer debts incurred just before bankruptcy, fraud or defalcation while acting as a fiduciary, embezzlement, larceny, or willful and malicious injury. The debtor's improper and/or illegal acts that could prevent a discharge from any claim include transfers or concealment of assets, unjustifiable destruction or concealment of books and records, fraudulent false oaths or false claims, fraudulently attempting to obtain an advantage by acting or forebearing to act, failure to satisfactorily explain a loss of assets, willful refusal to obey an order of the court, and improper actions with respect to the bankruptcy case of an insider.

In a Chapter 7 case, if the creditor is entitled to have its claim declared nondischargeable or to deny the debtor a discharge, Bankruptcy Rules 4004 and 4007 require the creditor to file a complaint and commence an adversary proceeding within 60 days of the date first set for the Section 341(a) meeting of creditors. As is true with the deadline for filing proofs of claim, even if the meeting is continued to another date, the 60 days will be measured from the original date. The 60-day time limit is very strict, and the deadline should be calendared as soon as notice of the Section 341(a) meeting is received. The time period may be extended, but only if a motion to do so is brought before the end of the 60 days.

Sometimes the debtor's improper and/or illegal acts that give rise to a claim that the debtor should not receive a discharge do not occur until after the 60 days have passed or even until after the debtor has received the discharge. In those circumstances, the creditor's remedy is to attempt to revoke the discharge. Revocation is allowed in Section 727(d).

In a Chapter 11 case of an individual, an objection to discharge need not be filed until confirmation of the plan. A complaint to determine the dischargeability of a debt is the same as in Chapter 7 cases.

In order to discourage baseless dischargeability litigation that a debtor may not be able to afford to defend, Section 523(d) of the Bankruptcy Code states that if a creditor seeks to have a consumer debt allegedly incurred through fraud or certain consumer debts incurred on the eve of bankruptcy deemed nondischargeable, and the debt is discharged, the debtor may be entitled to costs and expenses of suit, including attorneys' fees, if the creditor did not have a good faith belief that the debt was not entitled to be discharged.

THE SECURED CREDITOR

Proofs of Claim

Unlike other creditors, a secured creditor is not required to file a proof of claim in order to retain its lien on the debtor's property. It would be prudent, however, for the secured creditor to file a proof of claim if it wants notices directed a particular way or to put the debtor or trustee on notice of its lien. Further, if there is a risk that the collateral is not worth the amount of the debt, the secured creditor will need to file a proof of claim in order to preserve the right to share as an unsecured creditor for its deficiency claim. A sample proof of claim for a secured creditor is given in Exhibit 12.11.

Cash Collateral Use

As mentioned in Chapters 9 and 11 of this book, Section 363 of the Bankruptcy Code defines *cash collateral* to mean property of the estate that is cash, negotiable instruments, deposit accounts, and other cash equivalents in which a creditor has a security interest. If a creditor has a security interest in the debtor's accounts receivable, as the accounts are collected, the checks and the cash will become the creditor's cash collateral.

As discussed in Chapters 9 and 11 in the sections on financing liquidations and operations, once the petition is filed, the trustee or the debtor in possession may not use a creditor's cash collateral without its consent or an order of the court authorizing the use. If the secured creditor consents to the use of cash collateral, whatever terms and conditions it has negotiated with the debtor or the trustee should be placed in writing. A sample of such a written agreement was found in Chapter 11, as Exhibit 11.9. Bankruptcy Rule 4001(d) contains the procedure for obtaining bankruptcy court approval of the agreement. Generally, with limited notice, the court may approve a stipulation to allow the use of cash collateral for a short period of time and only so much cash collateral as is necessary to avoid harm to the debtor's operations. To obtain an order approving continuing use, the parties must bring a motion that sets out the terms of the agreement and provide no less than 15 days notice of the motion to the creditors' committee or, if there is no committee, to the 20 largest unsecured creditors and such other parties as the court may direct. If any party with notice of the motion files an objection, the court will hold a hearing to determine the matters raised in the objection and to see if the motion should be granted. If no objection is made, there need not be a hearing, and the court can grant the motion without one.

If the secured creditor does not consent to the use of its cash collateral, then Section 363(c) obligates the trustee or the debtor in possession to segregate and

EXHIBIT 12.11 ✦ *Proof of Claim for Secured Creditor*

FORM B10 (Official Form 10) (4/01)

UNITED STATES BANKRUPTCY COURT __Western__	DISTRICT OF __California__	**PROOF OF CLAIM**

Name of Debtor Videos By Joe, Inc.	Case Number 03-00001-JF	

NOTE: This form should not be used to make a claim for an administrative expense arising after the commencement of the case. A "request" for payment of an administrative expense may be filed pursuant to 11 U.S.C. § 503.

Name of Creditor (The person or other entity to whom the debtor owes money or property): First City Bank Name and address where notices should be sent: First City Bank c/o George G. Snow, Esq. 4 Wheel Dr. Los Angeles, CA 90017 Telephone number: 213-891-5595	☐ Check box if you are aware that anyone else has filed a proof of claim relating to your claim. Attach copy of statement giving particulars. ☐ Check box if you have never received any notices from the bankruptcy court in this case. ☑ Check box if the address differs from the address on the envelope sent to you by the court.	THIS SPACE IS FOR COURT USE ONLY
Account or other number by which creditor identifies debtor:	Check here if this claim ☐ replaces a previously filed claim, dated:_____ ☐ amends	

1. Basis for Claim
- ☐ Goods sold
- ☐ Services performed
- ☑ Money loaned
- ☐ Personal injury/wrongful death
- ☐ Taxes
- ☐ Other _____

- ☐ Retiree benefits as defined in 11 U.S.C. § 1114(a)
- ☐ Wages, salaries, and compensation (fill out below)

Your SS #: _____ _____ _____

Unpaid compensation for services performed

from _____ to _____
   (date)   (date)

2. Date debt was incurred: Oct. 1, 1998

3. If court judgment, date obtained:

4. Total Amount of Claim at Time Case Filed: $ __50,000__

If all or part of your claim is secured or entitled to priority, also complete Item 5 or 6 below.

☐ Check this box if claim includes interest or other charges in addition to the principal amount of the claim. Attach itemized statement of all interest or additional charges.

5. Secured Claim.

☑ Check this box if your claim is secured by collateral (including a right of setoff).

Brief Description of Collateral:

☐ Real Estate ☐ Motor Vehicle
☑ Other __Video Equipment__

Value of Collateral: $ __50,000__

Amount of arrearage and other charges <u>at time case filed</u> included in secured claim, if any: $ __2,700__

6. Unsecured Priority Claim.

☐ Check this box if you have an unsecured priority claim

Amount entitled to priority $_____

Specify the priority of the claim:

- ☐ Wages, salaries, or commissions (up to $4,650),* earned within 90 days before filing of the bankruptcy petition or cessation of the debtor's business, whichever is earlier - 11 U.S.C. § 507(a)(3).
- ☐ Contributions to an employee benefit plan - 11 U.S.C. § 507(a)(4).
- ☐ Up to $2,100* of deposits toward purchase, lease, or rental of property or services for personal, family, or household use - 11 U.S.C. § 507(a)(6).
- ☐ Alimony, maintenance, or support owed to a spouse, former spouse, or child - 11 U.S.C. § 507(a)(7).
- ☐ Taxes or penalties owed to governmental units - 11 U.S.C. § 507(a)(8).
- ☐ Other - Specify applicable paragraph of 11 U.S.C. § 507(a)(___).

Amounts are subject to adjustment on 4/1/04 and every 3 years thereafter with respect to cases commenced on or after the date of adjustment.

7. Credits: The amount of all payments on this claim has been credited and deducted for the purpose of making this proof of claim.

8. Supporting Documents: *Attach copies of supporting documents,* such as promissory notes, purchase orders, invoices, itemized statements of running accounts, contracts, court judgments, mortgages, security agreements, and evidence of perfection of lien. DO NOT SEND ORIGINAL DOCUMENTS. If the documents are not available, explain. If the documents are voluminous, attach a summary.

9. Date-Stamped Copy: To receive an acknowledgment of the filing of your claim, enclose a stamped, self-addressed envelope and copy of this proof of claim.

THIS SPACE IS FOR COURT USE ONLY

Date Oct. 15, 2003	Sign and print the name and title, if any, of the creditor or other person authorized to file this claim (attach copy of power of attorney, if any): George G. Snow, Attorney

Penalty for presenting fraudulent claim: Fine of up to $500,000 or imprisonment for up to 5 years, or both. 18 U.S.C. §§ 152 and 3571.

account for all cash collateral coming within the possession or other control of the estate. It is common for the secured creditor's counsel to inform a Chapter 11 debtor's counsel in writing that the creditor has not consented and the cash collateral should be segregated. A sample of such a letter follows as Exhibit 12.12.

In real life, sometimes debtors in possession do use cash collateral without consent and without court authorization. In some cases debtors, usually guided by incompetent counsel, use cash collateral for days or even weeks before the secured creditor is even informed of the filing of the bankruptcy petition. In those situations, which bode very ill for a cooperative reorganization, the secured creditor must quickly file a motion that requests that the court prevent the use of cash collateral. Bankruptcy Rule 4001(a) provides the procedures. Courts are usually willing to hear these motions on an emergency basis.

If the secured creditor refuses to consent to the use of cash collateral, the proper procedure is to file a motion and notice a hearing for permission to use the cash collateral. Since very few debtors with secured creditors can operate without the use of cash collateral to buy inventory and pay payroll and other operating expenses, the hearing will usually be held on very short notice. If there is a sufficient showing of an emergency, the court may even authorize the use without a hearing. A sample motion seeking authority to use cash collateral is found in Chapter 11, as Exhibit 11.7.

At a hearing of a motion to use cash collateral, the trustee or the debtor in possession will be required to prove that the secured creditor will not be harmed by the estate's use of cash collateral. To do so, the estate must show that the creditor is or

Exhibit 12.12 ✦ *Sample Pleading*

SNOW & PORTER
Attorneys at Law
4 Wheel Drive
Los Angeles, California 90017
October 2, 2003

Bankrupt C. Lawyer, Esq.
White Charger Legal Clinic
One Learned Way
Los Angeles, California 90001

Re: In re Videos by Joe, Inc. ("VBJ")
    Case No. 03-00001-JF

Dear Mr. Lawyer:

As you know, this law firm represents First City Bank (the "Bank"), a secured creditor of VBJ with a duly perfected lien on its inventory, equipment, accounts receivable, and all proceeds of the foregoing. As a result, all funds coming into the possession of VBJ constitute the Bank's "cash collateral" as that term is defined in 11 U.S.C. § 363(a).

This letter will serve to inform you and VBJ that the Bank does not consent to the use of its cash collateral by VBJ. Further, the Bank will expect VBJ to strictly comply with the requirements of 11 U.S.C. § 363(c)(4). Please call me immediately with the location of the Bank's segregated cash collateral and when the Bank might expect an accounting of its cash collateral.

Very truly yours,

SNOW & PORTER

George G. Snow

can be adequately protected. There is no definition of **adequate protection** in the Bankruptcy Code, but examples are given in Section 361. They include periodic cash payments, replacement liens, and other actions that will ensure that a secured creditor receives what it is entitled to. Commonly, the debtor in possession or the trustee will attempt to make this showing by offering the secured creditor replacement liens on all assets acquired after the filing of the bankruptcy case and demonstrating through projections of sales and expenses that the creditor's pool of collateral will increase by virtue of continued operations. It may offer to turn over to the creditor all cash collateral received that is not necessary for operations. It may offer a lien on previously unencumbered property.

The court will make the ultimate determination as to whether the estate should be allowed to use cash collateral and on what terms. The secured creditor should keep in mind that the court is not likely to compel the debtor to terminate operations if the evidence is close on the issue of adequate protection. Often the creditor is better served by attempting to negotiate a stipulation that has protection rather than relying on the court to agree with its position. There is, however, at least one benefit of contesting cash collateral use. If the court determines that the creditor is adequately protected and at the end of the case it turns out that the creditor suffers a deficiency, Section 507(b) provides that the deficiency is entitled to a priority in payment ahead of all other administrative claims, including attorneys' fees.

Finally, faced with the debtor's use of cash collateral, the creditor, especially one that has been providing account receivable financing for the debtor prepetition, should investigate providing financing to the debtor under Section 364 rather than cash collateral use under Section 363. Financing can offer even greater protections for the secured creditor, including a priority lien even ahead of the creditors who suffer a deficiency after a court determination that they are adequately protected. Financing and the procedure for obtaining the required court approval were discussed in Chapters 9 and 11 of this book.

Relief from the Automatic Stay

In General   The scope of the automatic stay was covered in Chapter 4 of this book. With respect to secured creditors, the automatic stay prevents them from taking any action to foreclose or in any other way enforce their security interests in their collateral. Although the automatic stay usually remains in effect until the case is closed, the secured creditor may have the stay terminated earlier by requesting that the court grant it relief from the automatic stay.

The effect of an order granting a secured creditor relief from the automatic stay is that it may proceed to enforce its rights and remedies with respect to its collateral as if the bankruptcy case was over. The creditor could commence or renew foreclosure proceedings, demand turnover of collateral, and the like. The secured creditor also may ask the court to annul the automatic stay; this would have the same effect as if no bankruptcy case had ever been commenced. A creditor might want to seek annulment rather than termination when some act was performed in violation of the automatic stay prior to the creditor obtaining relief, and the creditor wants that act to be valid.

Grounds   Section 362(d) of the Bankruptcy Code sets out three grounds for relief from the automatic stay. If any of the grounds can be established, the Bankruptcy Code provides that the creditor must be given relief from the stay.

The first ground is for cause. Cause is not defined in Section 362(d) or anywhere else in the Bankruptcy Code. All Section 362(d) states is that it includes a lack of adequate protection of a secured creditor's interest in its collateral. Adequate protection is not defined in the Bankruptcy Code, but examples of it are

✦ adequate protection
Property, lien, conduct, or other asset or act that is sufficient to ensure that a creditor with an interest in property to be used, sold or leased by the estate will not be disadvantaged.

given in Section 361. The examples provided are periodic cash payments equal to at least the amount by which the collateral is depreciating, replacement liens in assets that are not encumbered or in which the existing liens are less than the property's worth, and any other method of providing the secured creditor with the equivalent of the property being used by the debtor. The list is not exhaustive, and the ways in which secured creditors can assert that they are not adequately protected is limited only by the extent of their creativity. Possible other reasons why the creditor is not adequately protected and cause exists for relief from the automatic stay are a lack of insurance on the property, unpaid taxes, a deteriorating condition with insufficient upkeep, and the like.

The second ground for relief is that the debtor has no equity in the property and the property is not necessary for an effective reorganization. Both elements of this second ground must exist for relief to be granted.

The third ground for relief, which is only applicable in single-asset real estate cases, as that phrase is defined in Section 101(51B) of the Bankruptcy Code, is that 90 days has passed since the case was commenced and the debtor has neither: (1) filed a plan of reorganization that has a reasonable possibility of being confirmed within a reasonable time; nor (2) begun making monthly interest payments to the secured creditor.

If they can, secured creditors will allege more than one ground as reasons why they should be granted relief from the automatic stay. This is usually not difficult because they overlap. For example, cause is commonly alleged because of the lack of equity in the property.

Defenses In response to a request for relief from the automatic stay for lack of adequate protection, the debtor will allege that the creditor is, in fact, adequately protected. The debtor may assert that the value of the property is more than enough to adequately protect the secured creditor. This method of adequate protection is usually referred to as the *equity cushion,* and the courts differ as to whether it alone is sufficient and, if it is, the size or percentage of the cushion necessary to provide adequate protection. Equity cushion is described further in Chapter 9 of this book.

If there is an insufficient equity cushion, the debtor may also offer a different method of adequate protection to defeat the creditor's relief from stay action, such as monthly payments to decrease the size of the debt. The debtor may also be willing to stipulate to a grant of relief from the automatic stay at a date in the future if the debtor has not restructured the debt through a plan or sold the collateral and paid the creditor off.

If the relief from stay request is based on the second ground, the debtor may assert that it does have equity in the collateral and that even if it does not, the property is necessary to an effective reorganization.

Burdens Pursuant to Section 362(g), in any hearing on a motion for relief from the stay, the burden is on the secured creditor to establish the debtor's equity in the property. The party opposing the relief (usually the debtor or the trustee) has the burden on all other issues, such as adequate protection. While this statement may seem to suggest that the debtor or the trustee has the more difficult burden, as a practical matter, it is just the opposite. Because adequate protection is so linked with value and equity, if the secured creditor has the burden on equity, it also has at least some of the burden on adequate protection.

Procedure Obtaining relief from stay is discussed in Bankruptcy Rule 4001; it in turn references Rule 9014; relief from the automatic stay is obtained by the filing of a motion (see Exhibit 12.13). Any additional procedures that need to be adhered to are left to local rule.

EXHIBIT 12.13 ✦ *Sample Pleading*

GEORGE G. SNOW
Snow & Porter
4 Wheel Drive
Los Angeles, California 90017

Attorneys for First City Bank

UNITED STATES BANKRUPTCY COURT
WESTERN DISTRICT OF CALIFORNIA

In re	)	Case No. 03-00001-JF
	)	
VIDEOS BY JOE, INC.,	)	Chapter 11
	)	
Debtor.	)	
	)	
Debtor's Address:	)	
18 Hollywood Drive	)	
Los Angeles, CA 90001	)	
	)	
Debtor's Tax Id. No. 99-999899	)	
	)	
	)	
FIRST CITY BANK,	)	MOTION FOR ORDER GRANTING
	)	RELIEF FROM AUTOMATIC
Movant,	)	
	)	
v.	)	
	)	
VIDEOS BY JOE, INC.,	)	
	)	
Respondent.	)	
	)	

TO THE HONORABLE JUSTIN FAIR, UNITED STATES BANKRUPTCY JUDGE:

First City Bank (the "Bank"), through its attorneys, in support of its Motion for Order Granting Relief from the Automatic Stay, respectfully represents as follows:

1. Videos by Joe, Inc. is the debtor in the within case, having filed a petition for relief under Chapter 11 of the Bankruptcy Code on October 1, 2003 ("Debtor").

2. Among the assets of Debtor's estate is that real property commonly known as 18 Hollywood Drive, situated in the City and County of Los Angeles, State of California, more particularly described as follows:

   Lot 18 of Parcel 64 recorded in the records of the County of Los Angeles, State of California on Page 59-10562;

3. On or about October 1, 2002, Debtor made, executed, and delivered a written promissory note to the Bank in the principal sum of $100,000 together with interest thereon at the rate of 10 percent per annum (the "Note"). The Note called for monthly installment payments of interest only in the sum of $835.00 to be paid on the first day of every month, commencing on November 1, 2002, and continuing on the first day of every month for 35 months thereafter at which time the principal and any unpaid interest was to be all due and payable. A complete and accurate copy of the Note is attached as Exhibit 1 of the concurrently filed Declaration of Horace Hardman.

—CONTINUED

EXHIBIT 12.13 ✦ *Sample Pleading* (CONTINUED)

4. As part of the same transaction described in the preceding paragraph, to secure payment and performance of the Note, Debtor made, executed, and delivered to the Bank a Deed of Trust and Assignment of Rents pertaining to the Property, a complete and accurate copy of which is attached to the Hardman Declaration as Exhibit 2 (the "Deed of Trust"). The Deed of Trust was duly recorded in the Official Records of the County of Los Angeles, State of California, on October 3, 2002, as instrument No. 88-64321.

5. Debtor has defaulted in the performance of its obligations under the Note and the Deed of Trust. The defaults include, but are not limited to, the following:
   (a) Debtor has failed to make the monthly payments required under the Note since March 1, 2003;
   (b) The Note is now all due and payable;
   (c) Debtor has not maintained insurance in an amount sufficient to protect the interest of the Bank under the Note and Deed of Trust; and
   (d) Debtor has failed to pay real property taxes pertaining to the Property for fiscal year 1994[en]1995, which taxes have become delinquent.

6. As of November 1, 2003, the following sums had become due and owing under the Note:
   (a) Principal balance $100,000
   (b) Interest $ 9,174
   (c) Late Charges $ 459
   Total $109,633

7. The Bank is informed and believes that the Property is additionally encumbered by a deed of trust in favor of Big Bank securing repayment of a promissory note, having a principal balance of approximately $50,000 recorded *prior* to the date of the recordation of the Deed of Trust.

8. Debtor has not offered to provide adequate protection to the Bank of its interest in the Property.

9. In addition to the foregoing, cause for relief from the automatic stay exists in that Debtor has not paid current real property taxes pertaining to the Property and has not adequately insured the Property. By virtue of the foregoing, the Bank is entitled to relief from the automatic stay to proceed with foreclosure as authorized by Section 362(d)(1) of the Bankruptcy Code.

10. The indebtedness owing to the Bank under the Note, and to the holders of senior deeds of trust, is in excess of $164,000. Filed concurrently with this Motion is the Declaration of O. Pinion, a certified real estate appraiser, declaring that the fair market value of the Property is less than $165,000. The Bank is, therefore, of the informed opinion that after payment of all amounts due, including attorneys' fees and costs, Debtor will not have any equity in the Property and the Property is not necessary to an effective reorganization. By virtue thereof, the Bank is entitled to relief from the automatic stay to proceed with foreclosure as authorized by Section 362(d)(2) of the Bankruptcy Code.

WHEREFORE, the Bank requests that this Court enter its Order:

1. Vacating the automatic stay arising under Section 362(a) of the Bankruptcy Code under either Section 362(d)(1) or 362(d)(2) of the Bankruptcy Code and authorizing the Bank to proceed according to law to foreclose upon its lien encumbering the Property;

2. Directing that no additional motion to this Court for any further relief from the automatic stay will be required in the event it becomes necessary to initiate unlawful detainer proceedings against Debtor after a foreclosure sale pertaining to the Property; and

3. Granting such other and further relief as the Court deems appropriate.

DATED: November 1, 2003

SNOW & PORTER

GEORGE G. SNOW
Attorneys for First City Bank

One of the returns Congress has provided to creditors in exchange for imposing the automatic stay is that relief from stay actions against property are to be
given expedited treatment by the courts. Section 362(e) provides that a stay against
property of the estate terminates 30 days after a motion for relief has been made
unless the court orders the stay to be continued at a hearing held before the end of
the 30-day period. This hearing need not be a final hearing on the motion, but if
it is a preliminary hearing, in order to continue the stay in effect, the court must
find that there is a reasonable likelihood that the party opposing the relief will
prevail at the final hearing. In addition, the final hearing must be completed
within 30 days after the preliminary hearing unless the parties consent to extend
the 30-day deadline or the court extends it for a specific time because of compelling circumstances.

Bankruptcy Rule 4001(b) provides that the stay against property expires 30 days
after the final hearing unless, within that time, the court denies the motion. In short,
at the longest, the entire matter must be heard and decided no later than 60 days after
the motion is filed unless there is an agreement or compelling circumstances.

Even given the expedited pace of relief from stay actions, there may be situations in which the creditor believes that it needs relief earlier. If the creditor can
establish that its collateral will be irreparably harmed before it can be heard on the
normal time schedule, Section 362(f) allows it to bring its motion on an *ex parte*
basis. Bankruptcy Rule 4001(c) provides that oral and written notice must be given
to the debtor or the trustee of the *ex parte* motion. They also have the right to seek
to reinstate the stay on two days notice.

Stipulations   Often the creditor and the debtor or the trustee will reach an
agreement as to the appropriate level of adequate protection for the creditor prior
to any hearing. Bankruptcy Rule 4001(d) provides the method for having such
an agreement approved by the court. In order to prevent collusion between the
creditor and a friendly debtor, one of the parties must file a motion that discloses the terms of the agreement. (See Exhibit 12.14.) The motion must be served
on the committee if there is one and, if not, on the debtor's 20 largest unsecured
creditors. A party in interest then has 15 days to file an objection to the motion.
If an objection is filed, there will be a hearing, and the court will determine
whether the stipulation should be approved or not. If there is no objection, the
court can enter its order granting the motion and approving the stipulation without a hearing.

Chapter 12 and 13 Cases   Unlike Chapter 7 and 11 bankruptcy cases, in
Chapter 12 and 13 cases, the automatic stay is extended to creditor actions to collect consumer debts from those individuals who are obligated on the debt with the
debtor. These individuals are called codebtors. To obtain relief from the stay in
order to proceed against a codebtor, the creditor follows the normal procedure.
The grounds are set out in Section 1201(c) and 1301(c), and are as follows:

- ✦ The codebtor is really the principal debtor because it received the consideration that gave rise to the claim.
- ✦ The debtor's plan does not propose to pay the claim. If it only proposes to
  pay a percentage of the debt, the creditor may obtain relief from the stay but
  only to collect the deficiency against the codebtor.
- ✦ Continuing the stay against the codebtor until the case is closed would
  cause irreparable harm to the creditor.

EXHIBIT 12.14 ✦ *Sample Pleading*

GEORGE G. SNOW
Snow & Porter
4 Wheel Drive
Los Angeles, California 90017

Attorneys for First City Bank

**UNITED STATES BANKRUPTCY COURT
WESTERN DISTRICT OF CALIFORNIA**

In re	)	Case No. 03-00001-JF
	)	
VIDEOS BY JOE, INC.,	)	Chapter 11
	)	
Debtor.	)	
	)	
Debtor's Address:	)	NOTICE OF MOTION AND MOTION
18 Hollywood Drive	)	FOR APPROVAL OF AGREEMENT
Los Angeles, CA 90001	)	FOR RELIEF FROM THE AUTOMATIC
	)	STAY
Debtor's Tax Id. No. 99-999899	)	
	)	

First City Bank (the "Bank") and Videos by Joe, Inc., the debtor in possession in the above-captioned case (the "Debtor"), in support of their Motion for Approval of Agreement for Relief from the Automatic Stay, state as follows:

1. The Bank and the Debtor have entered into a stipulation for relief from automatic stay (the "Stipulation"), a complete and accurate copy of which is attached to this Motion as Exhibit 1.

2. This Motion seeks approval of the Stipulation as required by Bankruptcy Rule 4001. Grounds for approval of the Stipulation are that the debtor has no equity in the Property as that term is defined in the Stipulation; the Property is not necessary to an effective reorganization; and the Bank is not adequately protected as that phrase is defined in Section 361 of the Bankruptcy Code since the value of the Property does not exceed the amount of the debt owing to the Bank and other secured creditors.

3. Objections to this Motion and the Stipulation must be filed within fifteen (15) days of the date on which the Motion was mailed. Objections must be in writing, filed with the Court, and served upon the attorneys identified in the left-hand corner of page 1 of the Motion and upon attorneys for the Debtor. Objections must be accompanied by a written request for a hearing thereon.

4. If no objection is filed, the Court may enter an Order approving or disapproving this Motion and the Stipulation without conducting a hearing. If an objection is filed or if the Court determines a hearing is appropriate, the Court will hold a hearing on no less than five (5) days notice to the objector, the Bank, the Debtor, and upon any other entities as the Court may direct.

DATED: November 15, 2003

SNOW & PORTER

_____
GEORGE G. SNOW
Attorneys for First City Bank

—CONTINUED

EXHIBIT 12.14 ✦ *Sample Pleading* (CONTINUED)

Exhibit 1

GEORGE G. SNOW
Snow & Porter
4 Wheel Drive
Los Angeles, California 90017

Attorneys for First City Bank

UNITED STATES BANKRUPTCY COURT
WESTERN DISTRICT OF CALIFORNIA

In re	)	Case No. 03-00001-JF
	)	
VIDEOS BY JOE, INC.,	)	Chapter 11
	)	
Debtor.	)	
	)	
Debtor's Address:	)	
18 Hollywood Drive	)	
Los Angeles, CA 90001	)	
	)	**STIPULATION FOR ORDER**
Debtor's Tax Id. No. 99-999899	)	**GRANTING RELIEF FROM THE**
	)	**AUTOMATIC STAY**

First City Bank (the "Bank") and Videos by Joe, Inc., the debtor in possession in the above-captioned case (the "Debtor"), through their attorneys, hereby stipulate and agree, subject to Court approval, as follows:

1. The Debtor is the owner of improved real property located at 18 Hollywood Drive, Los Angeles, California (the "Property").

2. The Property is encumbered by a first in priority deed of trust in favor of Big Bank securing repayment of a note with a balance due, as of November 1, 2003, of approximately $50,000. The Property is additionally encumbered by a second in priority deed of trust in favor of the Bank securing repayment of a note with a balance due, as of November 1, 2003, of approximately $110,000.

3. The fair market value of the Property does not exceed $170,000.

4. The Debtor uses the Property in order to operate its business. The Debtor will move to new premises to operate its business on March 1, 2004.

Based on the foregoing facts, the Bank and the Debtor agree as follows:

A. Except as provided in Paragraph B of this Stipulation, the Bank shall be entitled to relief from the automatic stay of Section 362(a) of the Bankruptcy Code effective upon the entry of the Order approving this Stipulation and shall thereafter be entitled to take such acts as may be necessary to foreclose its interest in the Property.

B. Provided the Debtor pays to the Bank the sum of $835.00 per month for each of the months of December 2003, January 2004, and February 2004, this Bank shall not conduct a foreclosure sale of its interest in the Property until on or after March 1, 2004. In the event that the Debtor fails to make any of the payments provided in this paragraph, the Bank shall be entitled to conduct its foreclosure sale at the earliest time provided by law.

DATED: November 15, 2003

SNOW & PORTER

_____
GEORGE G. SNOW
Attorneys for First City Bank

—CONTINUED

Exhibit 12.14 ✦ *Sample Pleading* (CONTINUED)

DATED: November 15, 2003

WHITE CHARGER LEGAL CLINIC

_____

BANKRUPT C. LAWYER
Attorneys for Debtor

Surcharge of Collateral

The general rule in bankruptcy cases is that a secured creditor is entitled to be paid an amount equal to the value of its interest in its collateral. One exception is if it agrees to receive less. Another exception discussed in Chapter 9 of this book is found in Section 506(c) of the Bankruptcy Code, which states that the costs of preserving, protecting, and disposing of the collateral may be assessed against the creditor to the extent the creditor is benefited. The exception is based on fairness. If the trustee incurs costs and expenses in performing some service that benefited the secured creditor, it is only fair that the secured creditor pay those costs and expenses. If, for example, the trustee incurred auctioneer fees and costs in liquidating equipment that secured the debt owed to a creditor, then the Bankruptcy Code provides a method in Section 506(c) for the trustee to recoup those fees and costs from the proceeds of the equipment sold. This is especially true if the secured creditor consented to the trustee's actions.

There are many open questions in the application of Section 506(c). One question is whether any entity other than the trustee or the debtor in possession can use Section 506(c) to collect claims from the secured creditor. A similar question is whether the estate is first required to pay the claim and then seek reimbursement from the creditor. Another issue that is being considered by the courts is whether a secured creditor should have to pay the debtor in possession's attorneys' fees if a Chapter 11 case is administratively insolvent and the secured creditor has a lien on all the assets. Because of these and other open questions, and a creditor's inherent dislike of giving up a part of the proceeds of its collateral, actions brought under Section 506(c) are usually very hotly contested.

Another section in the Bankruptcy Code provides an alternative method of surcharging secured creditors. Section 552(b) provides that if the debtor granted to the creditor a security interest in certain assets and the proceeds of those assets, then after the commencement of the bankruptcy case the creditor's security interest will continue in the proceeds unless the court, for a good reason, orders otherwise. More and more trustees and debtors in possession are arguing that if their time, effort, and expenses added value to collateral that created those proceeds, the creditor's security interest should not extend to all of the proceeds.

Whatever the theory used to try to force the secured creditor to fund at least some of the costs of administration of the case, if a party in interest wishes to surcharge a secured creditor's collateral, it must commence an adversary proceeding by the filing of a complaint. A sample complaint for surcharge of collateral was found in Chapter 9, as Exhibit 9.12.

ETHICAL CONSIDERATIONS

As a paralegal, you will be exposed to a lot of confidential information. For that reason, you may find yourself in what you may come to view as a rewarding, but lonely job—rewarding in the sense that the job is interesting, but lonely because you are precluded from talking about it, even with your family. You have to be able to say firmly, but politely, "I can't talk about work due to its confidential nature."

Even though you are not an attorney, you are bound by the same standards of attorney/client privilege as your supervising attorney. If you work for a firm that handles bankruptcy cases, it would be a clear violation of attorney/client privilege to casually mention to your neighbor that "We talked to the XYZ Widget Company today about their pending bankruptcy filing." You have no way of knowing whether or not your neighbor, or someone they know, may be in a creditor status with your client. If they are, your tipping them off to a possible bankruptcy would give them information other creditors would not have, and this would be a clear violation of your client's confidentiality.

SUMMARY

Bankruptcy cases can be commenced voluntarily by the debtor or involuntarily by creditors. An involuntary case cannot be filed against a farmer or a charitable institution; in addition, an involuntary case can only be brought under Chapters 7 and 11. If the debtor has more than 12 creditors, the petition can be filed by as few as three creditors so long as those creditors have unsecured claims that total at least $10,000. If the debtor has fewer than 12 creditors, an involuntary petition can be filed by only one creditor. If an involuntary petition is filed, the debtor may either consent or fight the petition on the ground that the creditors are ineligible or that the debtor is paying its debts. If the court finds that the petition was properly filed, it will enter an order for relief and the case will proceed in the same manner as a case filed by the debtor.

A creditor presents its claim in a bankruptcy case by filing a proof of claim. A proof of claim is a simple form designed to be completed and filed by a nonattorney. The same form can be used by secured, unsecured, and priority creditors. Unpaid administrative creditors should file a complaint for payment rather than a proof of claim. The deadline for filing a proof of claim varies among the chapters of the Bankruptcy Code.

Special rules apply to lessors of real and personal property. A lessor under an expired lease may need to bring a motion for relief from the automatic stay if the trustee or debtor will not surrender the leased property. When the lease must be assumed or rejected will vary based on the type of property, the type of lease, and the chapter of the case.

Other rights of unsecured creditors include reclamations—recovering property sold to a debtor on the eve of the filing of its bankruptcy case—and having a claim determined nondischargeable.

A secured creditor will face issues of cash collateral use, financing, and relief from the stay. There are three grounds for relief from the stay: cause; the debtor has no equity in the property and it is not necessary for an effective reorganization; and in a small real estate Chapter 11 case, 90 days has passed and the debtor has not filed a plan that has a reasonable possibility of confirmation and has not begun making payments to the secured creditor. On a hearing on a motion for relief from the stay, the debtor will have the burden on all issues other than the existence in equity in the property. Motions for relief from stay will be heard on an expedited basis. If the debtor and the secured creditor settle their dispute, notice of the settlement must be given to creditors.

✦ KEY TERMS

adequate protection   involuntary case   priority claim
administrative claim   no-asset report   reclamation

✦ IMPROVE YOUR UNDERSTANDING

1. Creditor A is owed $5.00 from the debtor. Creditor B is owed $9,995.00 from the debtor. Creditor C is owed $1,000.00 from the debtor, but that debt is secured by the debtor's real estate worth twice that amount. If the debtor has more than 12 creditors, can creditors A, B, and C alone be petitioning creditors?

2. In determining the number of creditors a debtor has, are governmental units included?

3. May an insider be a petitioning creditor?

4. May an involuntary Chapter 11 debtor convert its case to Chapter 7? If so, how could the petitioning creditors respond?

5. Create a table indicating the last date to file claims in Chapter 7, 11, 12, and 13 cases by the creditor, the debtor, the trustee, and a co-obligor.

6. If a priority creditor's claim is correctly described as such in the debtor's Schedule E, need the priority creditor file a proof of claim in order to participate in the estate?

7. What other types of priority claims might a debtor want to pay prior to the end of the case? Why?

8. Review Sections 503(b) and 507(a)(1) of the Bankruptcy Code. Are there any claims incurred in the administration of the case that are not entitled to a priority in payment?

In responding to Exercises 9 through 11, rely on the following information:
    A company has the following leases:

- A lease for its building premises. This lease expires in the year 2015 and calls for rent of $10,000 per month. Rent is now three months behind.
- A five-year lease for an automatic photograph development machine. This lease requires monthly payments of $1,000. All payments are current.
- A lease for six vans at $500 each per month. This lease is automatically renewed each month unless there is a 30-day notice of termination given. Such a notice has not been given, but three months of payments have been missed.

9. What are the debtor in possession's deadlines for assuming or rejecting each of these leases? If a Chapter 11 trustee is appointed, what are the trustee's deadlines for assuming or rejecting each of these leases?

10. How can each of the lessors most diligently guard their rights? In what situation would the most diligent solution be the most uneconomic?

11. The Chapter 11 case proceeds for three months, and the debtor in possession does not assume any of the leases. The case converts to Chapter 7, and 30 days later, the trustee rejects all leases. What is the measure of each lessor's claim, and what portion of it is prepetition, Chapter 11 administrative, and Chapter 7 administrative?

Uniform Commercial Code Section 2-702 requires the seller to have sold the goods to the buyer on credit. Bankruptcy Code Section 546(c) does not have this provision.

12. Can a seller of goods only use Section 546(c) if it sold the goods on credit?

13. Can you think of any set of circumstances where a right to reclaim would exist if the sale was not on credit terms?

14. Review the section in Chapter 8 on discharge and dischargeability. If you did not complete the Improve Your Understanding exercises and the Drafting Project then, do them now.

15. Give four examples of cash collateral.
16. A lender has a security interest in a debtor's inventory and its proceeds. Postpetition, the debtor obtains inventory on credit and sells it for a check. Is the check the lender's cash collateral? Consider Section 552(a) in your response.
17. If the secured creditor does not consent to the use of its cash collateral, pending a court hearing, must the trustee turn over the cash collateral to the secured creditor?
18. If the trustee is holding a secured creditor's cash collateral, must the trustee provide the creditor with adequate protection?
19. In order for there to be cash collateral, does the creditor need to have a consensual lien?
20. The debtor is the owner and developer of an 18-hole golf course scheduled to open in six months. Three of the holes are located on a parcel of real property the debtor purchased in 1994 for $1,000,000. The debtor borrowed the money to purchase the parcel from First City Bank; this financing required monthly payments of $5,000. Debtor had failed to make any of the payments when it filed its Chapter 11 case on October 1, 2003, the day before the Bank's scheduled foreclosure sale. The Bank is now owed $1,100,000 due to accrued interest and costs. The entire golf course recently has been appraised at $9,000,000 when completed. The parcel (of three holes) by itself has been appraised at only $900,000 since by itself it has a lesser value.

    Is this a "single-asset real estate" case? Construct arguments for the debtor and for the Bank in the relief from stay litigation the Bank brings.
21. Why do you think there is a codebtor stay in Chapter 12 and 13 cases but not in Chapter 7 cases of individuals?
22. A secured creditor files and serves its motion for relief from the stay and the debtor responds. At the hearing, the parties agree to a settlement. Does Bankruptcy Rule 4001(d) apply? Should it?
23. Think of three acts or omissions by a debtor not mentioned in this chapter that may constitute cause for the real property secured creditor to obtain relief from the automatic stay.
24. Are all relief from stay motions entitled to expedited treatment? Think of two examples that might not be entitled to such treatment.

✦ RESEARCH PROJECTS

1. Locate one case in which the court allowed a creditor to file an untimely claim that would be treated as timely. What was the basis for the court's decision?
2. The debtor in possession wants to assume a business real property lease and files a motion to do so on the 50th day after it commenced its case. The hearing is set for the 70th day after the case is commenced. On day 61, the landlord moves for relief from stay on the ground that the lease has been rejected because it was not assumed within the first 60 days. Find a reported decision that tells you who will win.
3. Locate two cases involving operating companies in which the court refused to authorize the use of cash collateral. To the extent you can tell from the opinion, what was the impact on operations?
4. Find two reported decisions discussing when annulment of the automatic stay is appropriate.
5. If you did not do the Research Project at the end of the section in Chapter 9 on financing the liquidation, do so now.

✦ DRAFTING PROJECT

1. In a Chapter 7 case, the Internal Revenue Service failed to file a proof of claim for debtor's $10,000.00 prepetition income tax liability. Prepare a proof of claim on behalf of the debtor for such a claim.

Taxes in Bankruptcy

DURING THE COURSE of any bankruptcy case, tax issues will arise. Although tax laws and regulations are beyond the scope of this book, this Chapter addresses some of the more common tax issues in bankruptcy cases, such as the priority and discharge of tax claims. It also summarizes some of the rules and procedural provisions relating to taxes owed by the debtor and the estate.

TAXES ON THE ESTATE

The trustee or debtor in possession is liable for all federal, state, and local taxes incurred in operating the debtor's business, subject to the limitations and the rules set forth in the Bankruptcy Code. For example, the debtor in possession must pay income taxes on profits earned after it filed its bankruptcy case. The trustee and the debtor in possession must also withhold from any payments made to creditors all taxes required to be withheld by nonbankruptcy law. Section 346(f) of the Bankruptcy Code states that the trustee must pay the withheld taxes to the appropriate taxing agency "at the time and in the manner required by such tax law."

DETERMINATION OF TAXES

Bankruptcy Court Jurisdiction Over Tax Claims

Section 157 of Title 28 of the United States Code authorizes bankruptcy judges to determine core proceedings. Core proceedings include "matters concerning the administration of the estate . . . allowance or disallowance of claims against the estate . . . determination as to the dischargeability of particular debts [and] other proceedings affecting . . . the adjustment of the debtor-creditor . . . relationship." Determination of tax claims against the debtor or the estate should be included within this list of core proceedings. Accordingly, tax disputes may properly be resolved by bankruptcy courts.

The Procedure for Determining the Estate's Liability

Postpetition Taxes Section 505 sets out the procedure to determine the amount of most taxes against the debtor and the estate. Briefly, it provides that the trustee can file a tax return and ask for an expedited determination of the estate's tax liability. Unless the trustee hears from the taxing agency within a relatively short period of time, the return will be deemed correct and there will be no future liability. Section 505 is discussed in more detail below.

Prepetition Taxes   The bankruptcy court may determine prepetition taxes in the same way it determines other claims unless they have been determined by a different court before the commencement of the bankruptcy case. If that has happened, the bankruptcy court cannot make a new determination. The one exception is where the taxes were determined without a contest before the bankruptcy case was commenced. In those circumstances, the bankruptcy court can make a new determination.

Chapter 11 and 12 Plans   Sections 1146(d) and 1231(d) provide that the court may authorize a plan proponent to seek a determination, limited to legal issues, from a state or local governmental income taxing agency of the effect of the plan. If there is a controversy, the bankruptcy court can resolve the controversy on the earlier of when the governmental unit has responded or 270 days after the determination request is made.

The Proper Forum for Determining the Estate's Liability

Just because the bankruptcy court can determine tax claims does not necessarily mean that it will want to or that it will be the best place for such determinations. What the bankruptcy court may do is direct traffic among the various courts and other tribunals that might have jurisdiction to determine taxes. This ability is implemented by granting relief from the automatic stay. Section 362(a)(6) stays the assessment of taxes after commencement of the case. Section 362(a)(8) stays the "commencement or continuation of a proceeding before the United States Tax Court concerning the debtor." In addition, Section 362(a)(1) stays "the commencement or continuation . . . of a judicial, administrative, or other action or proceeding against the debtor . . . to recover a claim against the debtor." Since only the bankruptcy court may grant relief from the automatic stay, any litigation in another court or administrative tribunal regarding taxes must first be approved by the bankruptcy court.

This is not to suggest that the taxing agencies cannot do anything without relief from the automatic stay. Since the 1994 Amendments, Section 362(b)(9) has provided that the following acts by a taxing agency are not covered by the automatic stay: (1) an audit by a governmental unit to determine tax liability; (2) the issuance to the debtor by a governmental unit of a notice of tax deficiency; (3) a demand for tax returns; and (4) the making of an assessment for any tax and issuance of a notice and demand for payment. This last exemption will allow a tax lien to be created unless the tax is a debt of the debtor that will not be discharged and the property or its proceeds are transferred out of the estate or otherwise revested in the debtor.

If the bankruptcy court grants relief from the automatic stay to permit postpetition tax litigation in other forums, it may not later redetermine the amount or legality of those taxes after the other court has ruled.

Prepetition Taxes

There are two issues in the postpetition determination of prepetition taxes: whether the tax is a claim against the estate or just against the debtor and whether the debtor is liable for a nondischargeable tax.

One reason the Bankruptcy Code makes the bankruptcy court the traffic director over tax claims is to permit the debtor the advantage in the choice of the forum for the determination of tax claims and to prevent the debtor from being bound on the issues of dischargeability and amount of the tax by a determination against the estate. The estate and the debtor have different interests in contesting tax claims, especially in a situation where the estate will not be able to pay the tax because it has insufficient assets and the taxing agency will look to the debtor for payment. If, however, a tax liability is determined against the debtor before bankruptcy, that determination will bind the estate, which is a successor to the debtor.

Allowability Against the Estate   If there is an administrative or judicial tax proceeding pending when the bankruptcy case commences, it will involve only the debtor and will be stayed by Section 362 except as noted above. The trustee may consent to a lifting of the stay and may intervene in the proceeding. In that event, the estate will be bound by any determination made.

The trustee may oppose relief from the automatic stay to prevent a determination of the debtor's tax liability by the nonbankruptcy forum or may seek to have the bankruptcy court limit the effect of the other court's determination as a condition for granting relief from the automatic stay. The trustee may also object to the tax claim in the bankruptcy court while the other proceeding is pending. If the bankruptcy court grants relief from the automatic stay to let the other proceeding continue but reaches a determination on the trustee's objection to the tax claim before the other forum makes its determination, then the trustee will not be bound by the ruling of the other forum. Conversely, the debtor will not be bound by the bankruptcy court's ruling because the debtor is not a party to the claim objection proceeding.

Debtor's Liability   As discussed in Chapter 8 of this book, many taxes are not dischargeable. Any question concerning whether the tax is nondischargeable may be determined in an action in the bankruptcy court brought by the taxing agency or by the debtor. If neither party acts, then the debtor's liability for the tax and the tax's nondischargeability will be determined after bankruptcy in the usual administrative or judicial forum.

Administrative Expense Taxes

Expedited Determination   The statute of limitations on tax issues may be as long as seven years. Pursuant to Section 505, the trustee may obtain an expedited determination of the estate's liability for administrative expense taxes by submitting the tax return to the appropriate taxing agency along with a request for a determination of liability. The trustee is discharged from liability upon payment of the tax shown on the return if the taxing agency does not select the return for examination within 60 days and complete such an examination within 180 days after the trustee's request. A sample request is shown in Exhibit 13.1. If the taxing agency completes its examination, the trustee will be discharged upon payment of the tax determined by the taxing agency or, if the trustee disputes the results of the taxing agency's examination, by the amount determined by the court. If the return is fraudulent or contains a material misrepresentation, however, the trustee will not be discharged.

Individuals   The bankruptcy estate of an individual debtor is a separate taxable entity. The debtor's tax year ceases on the entry of the order for relief, and the estate's tax year then commences. The estate will not be liable as an administrative expense for any tax on income earned by and paid to the debtor before the case was commenced.

Exhibit 13.1 ✦ *Sample Request of Tax Determination*

Mildred Pierce, Trustee
700 Flower Street
Los Angeles, California 90001

October 15, 2003

Internal Revenue Service
Special Procedures Department
Laguna Niguel, California 90003

Re: In re Videos by Joe, Inc.
     Case No. LA03-00001-JF
     United States Bankruptcy Court
     Western District of California

Ladies and Gentlemen:

The undersigned is the duly appointed, acting and qualified Chapter 7 trustee of the above-referenced bankruptcy estate. Enclosed is the final tax return in connection with the estate. Also enclosed is the estate's check in the amount of $1,200.00, representing the full tax liability shown in the return.

Pursuant to 11 U.S.C. § 505(b), I request a prompt determination by you of any unpaid liability of the estate for any tax incurred during its administration. Unless you notify me within 60 days that the return has been selected for examination, I will be discharged from any liability for such tax.

Very truly yours,

Mildred Pierce
Trustee

As shown in Exhibit 13.2, the trustee is required to file tax returns in a liquidation case of an individual only if during the entire period of administration of the case there is taxable gain. In a reorganization case, the trustee must file a tax return for each postpetition taxable period during the case.

Partnerships   In the case of a partnership debtor, there is no change in the taxpayer's status, and the trustee must file returns in the same form and same manner as the partnership. As shown in Exhibit 13.2, in liquidation as well as reorganization cases, a return is required for each taxable period, whether or not there is gain or loss during that time period.

Corporations   Like partnerships, there is no change in the status of a corporation for tax purposes upon the filing of the petition, and the trustee must file returns in the same form and manner as the corporation. (See Exhibit 13.2.) As in an individual case, however, the trustee must file an income tax return in a liquidation case only if there is taxable gain over the entire period of the administration of the case.

EXHIBIT 13.2 ✦ *Responsibility for Tax Return*

Must They File a Tax Return?

Chapter 7

Debtor	No, except for individual debtors with nonestate income.
Trustee	
Individual Debtor	Yes, but only if there is net taxable income during the Chapter 7 case.
Corporate Debtor	Yes, but only if there is net taxable income during the Chapter 7 case.
Partnership Debtor	Yes.

Chapter 11

Debtor in possession or trustee	Yes.
Debtor out of possession	No, except for individual debtor with nonestate income.

Chapter 12

Debtor in possession or trustee	Yes.
Debtor out of possession	No, except for individual debtor with nonestate income.

Chapter 13

Debtor	Yes.

PRIORITIES OF TAXES

In General

Unsecured claims for taxes may be entitled to a first priority in payment as an administrative expense under Section 503(b), an eighth priority under Section 507(a)(8), general unsecured status without priority, subordination in Chapter 7 under Section 726(a)(4), or any priority as a withholding tax, the same as the claim from which the tax is withheld. Secured tax claims are treated like other secured claims up to the value of the taxing agency's collateral. The chart in Exhibit 13.3 summarizes the following discussion.

Postpetition Income Taxes

Income taxes include any taxes on or measured by gross receipts. Pursuant to Section 503(b)(1)(B)(i), income taxes are entitled to a first-in priority payment as administrative expenses if the taxes are incurred by the estate.

✦ **income tax**
Any tax on or measured by gross receipts.

Unsecured Prepetition Income Taxes

An unsecured tax either on or measured by income or gross receipts is entitled to an eighth in priority payment under Section 507(a)(8)(A) if:

✦ The tax year ended on or before the date of bankruptcy and the tax return was last due within three years before the date of bankruptcy or was due after bankruptcy;

✦ The tax has not yet been assessed at the date of the bankruptcy but is still subject to being assessed under applicable tax law; or

✦ The tax was assessed within 240 days before bankruptcy.

EXHIBIT 13.3 ✦ *Tax Priority*

Priority Taxes

Common Types of Taxes		Priority?
Incurred Postpetition		Yes, Sections 503(b) and 507(a)(1).
Income Taxes	For a tax period more than three years prepetition	No, unless fits within one of the other categories.
	For a tax period less than three years prepetition	Yes, Section 507(a)(8)(A)(i).
	Assessed within 240 days prepetition	Yes, Section 507(a)(8)(A)(ii).
	Assessable postpetition by law or agreement	Yes, Section 507(a)(8)(A)(iii).
Property Taxes	Payable more than one year prepetition	No, but it may be a secured claim.
	Payable within one year prepetition	Yes, Section 507(a)(8)(B).
Taxes Debtor Is Required to Collect or Withhold		Yes, Section 507(a)(8)(C).
Employment Taxes Earned from the Debtor	For a tax period more than three years prepetition	No.
	For a tax period less than three years prepetition	Yes, Section 507(a)(8)(D).
Penalties		Only if related to a priority tax and in compensation for actual monetary loss.
Interest		Unclear. Some jurisdictions allow if on a priority tax claim; some do not allow.

If the tax does not fit within one of these categories, and is not an administrative expense or withholding tax, it will be treated the same as other nonpriority prepetition claims.

Property Taxes

✦ **property tax**
Tax imposed on the ownership or real or personal property based on the property's value, number, weight, or size.

Property taxes are taxes imposed on the ownership of real or personal property, and may be based on value or on number, weight, size, and so on. Section 507(a)(8)(B) grants priority status to a property tax claim assessed prepetition and payable in the year before the petition was filed. Any tax assessed for a postpetition period will be an administrative claim.

Excise Taxes

✦ **excise tax**
A tax on a transaction, event, or occurrence.

An **excise tax** is a tax on a transaction, event, or occurrence. Examples of excise taxes are sales taxes, estate and gift taxes, and gasoline and special fuel taxes. Except as discussed here, an excise tax is entitled to administrative expense status if the transaction, event, or occurrence on which the tax is based occurs after the commencement of the case and the tax is incurred by the estate. Thus, if the trustee is operating the retail sales business of the debtor, any sales tax imposed by the state will be entitled to administrative expense priority. A sales or use tax imposed directly on the trustee for goods that the trustee purchases will also be entitled to administrative expense status as an excise tax.

If the transaction, event, or occurrence happened before bankruptcy, then the related excise tax will be a prepetition claim, even though the return or the tax may not be due until after the commencement of the bankruptcy case. Under Section 507(a)(8)(E), the excise tax will be entitled to priority only if the return was due, including extensions, within three years before bankruptcy or after bankruptcy. If no return is required, then the tax is entitled to priority if the transaction on which the tax is imposed occurred within three years before bankruptcy.

Penalties

There are two kinds of penalties for nonpayment of taxes. One is strictly punitive in nature and is intended to penalize the taxpayer for failure to pay on time. The other is compensatory and is designed to help the taxing authority collect the tax from a different source. An example of the latter is the 100 percent penalty imposed on a responsible officer for failure to withhold and pay over to the taxing agency the employees' share of income and social security taxes.

A prepetition tax penalty will be entitled to eighth in priority treatment along with other taxes only if the penalty is a compensatory penalty. Punitive claims are subordinated and paid only after the claims of all general unsecured creditors in liquidation cases.

NONDISCHARGEABLE TAXES

The Bankruptcy Code generally implements the policy that all taxes that are nondischargeable in an individual's case should also be entitled to priority. This policy gives some relief to a debtor with nondischargeable taxes by increasing the probability that all or a portion of the taxes will be paid from the estate. If the priority nondischargeable tax claim is $100 and the trustee has enough assets to distribute $50 to the taxing agency, the debtor will have a remaining liability of only $50. If it was not entitled to a priority in payment, the debtor's remaining liability would probably be much greater.

There are some taxes that are not entitled to priority but are also excepted from discharge under Section 523(a)(1). If the debtor fails to file a required return or files the return so late that the taxing agency did not have a fair opportunity to collect the tax before bankruptcy, or if the debtor made a fraudulent return or willfully attempted in any manner to evade or defeat the tax, then the tax is excepted from discharge even though it may not be entitled to priority. Giving such taxes a priority in payment would penalize other creditors by reducing the amount of assets available to satisfy unsecured claims. That prejudice to other creditors is not fair when the action was the result of the debtor's wrongdoing.

Interest and penalties on nondischargeable taxes are also not dischargeable. In contrast, interest and penalties on dischargeable taxes are discharged.

PAYMENT OF TAXES

Most taxes are entitled to a priority in payment and therefore will be paid, assuming sufficient assets, in any case under the Bankruptcy Code. The rules for the timing of payment of priority taxes differ slightly for administrative expense taxes and prepetition priority taxes and differ among the various chapters of the Bankruptcy Code. Under all chapters, nonpriority unsecured taxes are treated the same as all other general unsecured claims and secured tax claims are treated just like other secured claims.

Chapter 7

In a Chapter 7 case, taxes entitled to administrative expense priority are paid first under Sections 726(a)(1) and 507(a)(1) with all other administrative expenses.

Prepetition taxes that are entitled to a priority in payment under Section 507(a)(8) will be satisfied after the Section 507(a)(1) through Section 507(a)(7) priority claims are paid and immediately before payment of Section 507(a)(9) and general unsecured claims.

Chapter 11

Administrative expense taxes must be paid in cash in full on confirmation of a Chapter 11 reorganization plan. Unsecured priority taxes must also be paid in full, but the cash payments may stretch over a period of six years beginning upon the date of the assessment of the tax. A fair market rate of interest must be paid on the principal amount to the taxing agency.

Chapters 12 and 13

A Chapter 12 or 13 plan must provide for the full payment of all priority tax claims. Payments can be deferred and paid in installments over the life of the plan. Interest on the tax claim is not required, except to the extent that Sections 1225(a)(4) and 1325(a)(4) require otherwise. Under those provisions, the debtor must pay interest under the plan on any unsecured claim if the creditor would be paid interest in a Chapter 7 liquidation case.

ETHICAL CONSIDERATIONS

While the Model Rules of Professional Responsibility do not specifically prohibit actions that create an appearance of impropriety, the ethical codes for attorneys of various states certainly do. As a paralegal, you would be held to the same standard as your supervising attorney.

Whether or not your state precludes actions that create an appearance of impropriety, you should avoid such actions at all costs. There is an expression, "perception is reality." If there is the perception of impropriety, many will assume there is actual impropriety.

If you or your firm develops a reputation for improper actions and/or behavior, it will negatively impact your ability to work with opposing counsel, the court, and other paralegals. "If it doesn't feel right, don't do it" is perhaps the best attitude to develop. It means that there may be times you need to be assertive with your supervising attorney. If he or she asks you to do something you feel uncomfortable doing, you should politely but firmly indicate that you have concerns. You can always get another job—rebuilding your reputation is not so easy.

SUMMARY

Being a debtor or a trustee in a bankruptcy case does not excuse the need to file tax returns or pay taxes incurred by the estate. The one general exception is that in a Chapter 7 case of an individual or a corporation, the trustee will not have to file a tax return if there is no taxable income during the case.

Bankruptcy courts have the ability to determine the estate's liability for pre- and postpetition taxes. The bankruptcy court can, however, lift the automatic stay and let any dispute over the taxes owed proceed in the tax courts. For prepetition taxes, a tax court may determine the debtor's liability, which would not be binding on the trustee unless he or she participated in the tax court proceedings. The Bankruptcy Code establishes procedures for a trustee or debtor in possession to obtain an expedited determination of the estate's tax liability so that the estate can be closed without the fear that the Internal Revenue Service will later claim that additional taxes are due.

Postpetition taxes will need to be paid as an administrative priority in the bankruptcy case. Most prepetition taxes, unless they were due at least three years before the bankruptcy case was commenced, are treated as eighth priority claims. Property taxes may be secured claims in addition to being priority taxes. Most priority taxes will also be nondischargeable.

In a Chapter 11, 12, or 13 plan, priority tax claims can be stretched out for up to as long as six years. Interest must be paid.

✦ KEY TERMS

excise tax   income tax   property tax

✦ IMPROVE YOUR UNDERSTANDING

1. What is the priority of the debtor in possession's portion of employment taxes incurred after the commencement of its bankruptcy case?
2. If the debtor in possession fails to pay income taxes accrued postpetition, will the automatic stay prevent the Internal Revenue Service from assessing the tax? Will it prevent the IRS from taking steps to collect the tax?
3. Just before it filed its Chapter 7 case, the debtor lost a hearing before the tax court that resulted in a judgment. Is the debtor bound by the tax court's determination? Is the trustee?
4. If the debtor was in the midst of trial at the tax court when it filed its Chapter 7 case, could it continue the trial? What would it have to do? How could the trustee react?
5. Are there any taxes entitled to a priority in payment under Section 507(a)(8) that are dischargeable?
6. Why do you think Congress gave trustees the right to an expedited determination of tax liability?
7. The debtor fails to file tax returns for the three years prior to the filing of its Chapter 7 case. The Internal Revenue Service discovers this fact one year later while the case is still open. What could the IRS do? If the IRS found liability in each of the three years, what priority would the taxes be entitled to under the Bankruptcy Code? Are they dischargeable?
8. Must interest be paid on priority taxes in a Chapter 7 case? In a Chapter 11 case? In a Chapter 12 or 13 case?
9. A taxing agency with a nondischargeable tax fails to timely file a proof of claim in an individual debtor's Chapter 7 case. Should the debtor be concerned on behalf of the taxing agency? If so, what can the debtor do?

✦ RESEARCH PROJECT

1. Are there any Bankruptcy Rules specifically concerning tax issues?

Electronic Filing

CHAPTER 5 DISCUSSED how computers and the internet have changed legal research. Similarly, new technology has brought changes in bankruptcy case management that were only dreamed of a decade ago. This chapter will examine how computer-based Case Management/Electronic Case Filing (**CM/ECF**) has revolutionized bankruptcy practice and developed from a three-court pilot project to a nationwide program, with more courts coming online every month. This chapter, while short, concerns a topic with long-range ramifications to paralegals.

    As of May 2003, 53 United States bankruptcy courts were using a component of CM/ECF, while 40 courts had adopted the electronic case filing option. Some courts, including Louisiana, accept *only* electronic case filing. It is anticipated that each of the 94 bankruptcy courts in America will be online and handling cases electronically by the end of 2004.

✦ **CM/EFC**
An acronym for Case Management/Electronic Case Filing. This is the federal judiciary's electronic case filing system.

WHAT IS CM/ECF?

CM/ECF (the System) is the federal judiciary's electronic case filing system. It allows trained and certified attorneys and paralegals to file new bankruptcy cases, adversary proceedings, or documents from their computers. While both attorneys and paralegals may access the system, only attorneys are given a password. For a firm's paralegal to access the system, he or she must obtain the password of the supervising attorney and use his or her password. To show how the System works, this chapter will look closely at how one district, the United States Bankruptcy Court, District of New Hampshire, has recently implemented the System, and will use its standards as an example of what is needed to participate in the program.

    The System requires the use of standard computer hardware, an internet connection and browser, plus software to format a document for electronic filing. Upon filing, the System user receives an electronic notice of filing, and the court processes a charge against the user's credit card if a fee payment is required. The user will also need a valid **PACER** account. PACER, an acronym for Public Access to Court Electronic Records, is an electronic public access service. This service allows users to obtain case and docket information from federal appellate, district, and bankruptcy courts, and from the U.S. Party/Case Index. PACER is available 24 hours a day, seven days a week. PACER used to require direct modem connection, but it is now also available as a web service for anyone with an internet connection. In accordance with policy set by the Judicial Conference of the United States courts, registered agencies and/or individuals will be charged a fee of 60 cents per minute for dial-up service, or an access fee of 7 cents a page for internet service, up to a

✦ **PACER**
An acronym for Public Access to Court Electronic Records, an eledtronic public access service for the federal courts.

maximum charge of $2.10 per document. Users are billed on a quarterly basis. Registration can be accomplished via mail or the internet. To help keep track of costs, users must enter the client's individual code at the start of each new PACER session.

There is a way, however, for firms and their paralegals to avoid having the fee imposed on them. Once a document is filed in a bankruptcy case, the system generates an e-mail. Attorneys representing the debtor, creditors, and other interested parties may provide an e-mail list of persons who should receive notice of any electronic filings. Upon receiving notice of the filing, the recipient has the opportunity for one "free look." The purpose of the "free look" is to allow the filing party to make certain that the document was transmitted correctly, and for interested parties to have the opportunity to read it without paying for the first view. Upon accessing the document, the attorney or paralegal can save it to disk or forward it to him- or herself as an e-mail with a PDF attachment. Charges will only accrue when the paralegal or attorney returns to the system a day or two later in order to review the document a second time. That is why it is important to save the document to disk, so that it can be reviewed again at the viewer's convenience, without charge.

While a user's login and password serve as a signature for the CM/ECF system, there are still a limited number of documents where an original signature is required. For these documents, the original must be filed with the court. New Hampshire, for example, requires that the original of its local bankruptcy form 5005-4A and 4B, Declaration Regarding Electronic Filing be signed and delivered to the court (See Exhibit 14.1 for form 4A). Form 4B is for Chapter 13 plans and certain affidavits.

TYPICAL HARDWARE AND SOFTWARE

The System supports either a PC running Windows 95 or higher, or a Macintosh. It also requires an internet browser (either Internet Explorer, Version 5.x or higher, or Netscape Navigator, Version 4.73 or higher) and software that supports the portable document format (PDF). Adobe Acrobat Reader™ can be used to read PDF files. To create PDF files for filing with the System, you will need a word processor that can convert documents to the PDF format. This can be done with Adobe Acrobat Writer, and with Macintosh or Windows-based versions of WordPerfect or Word. Adobe Acrobat Reader is used to read the PDF files. The Bankruptcy Court, District of New Hampshire has developed a one-page summary of CM/ECF hardware and software requirements. (See Exhibit 14.2.)

TRAINING ON THE SYSTEM

Each bankruptcy district using the System has developed its own training program. Training sessions vary in length, ranging from two hours in some districts to seven hours in others. New Hampshire has a four-hour training program consisting of hands-on training for the practicing attorney and one paralegal from his or her office. Training takes place in a training facility with computers to allow for direct interaction between the System and the person(s) being trained.

The PACER Online Service Center also provides general Computer-Based Training on its own website (http://www.pacer.psc.uscourts.gov/ecfcbt/).

SECURITY AND PRIVACY ISSUES

In any new computer-based technology, there are privacy and security concerns. This is especially true when dealing with the type of documents and data involved

EXHIBIT 14.1 ✦ *Local Declaration Regarding Electronic Filing*

LBF 5005–4A

UNITED STATES BANKRUPTCY COURT
DISTRICT OF NEW HAMPSHIRE

In re: Bk. No. *-JMD or -MWV

                                                                          Chapter*

*,

　　　　　Debtor(s)

DECLARATION REGARDING ELECTRONIC FILING

PART 1 - Declaration of Petitioner:

I [We] _____ and _____, the undersigned debtor(s), corporate officer or partnership member, hereby declare under penalty of perjury that the information I have given my attorney and the information contained in the electronically filed petition, statements and schedules, or amendments thereof (the "petition and schedules"), con-sisting of _____ pages, is true and correct, to the best of my knowledge and belief. I understand that this DECLARATION REGARDING ELECTRONIC FILING is to be filed with the Clerk after the petition and schedules have been filed electronically but, in no event, no later than 5 business days after the petition and schedules have been filed. I acknowledge receipt of a copy of the electronically filed petition and schedules.

- [If petitioner is an individual whose debts are primarily consumer debts and has chosen to file under chapter 7] I am aware that I may proceed under Chapter 7, 11, 12, or 13 of title 11 of the United States Code, understand the relief available under each such chapter, and choose to proceed under chapter 7. I request relief in accordance with the chapter specified in the peti-tion.

- [If petitioner is a corporation, partnership, or limited liability entity] I declare under penalty of perjury that the information provided in this petition is true and correct, and that I have been authorized to file this petition on behalf of the debtor. The debtor requests relief in accordance with the chapter specified in this petition.

I understand that failure to file the signed original of this DECLARATION is grounds for dismissal of my case pur-suant to 11 U.S.C.[sec]707(a)(3).

Dated: _____

                                                          _____
                                                          Authorized Corporate Officer/Partnership Member
Signed:_____
　　　　Debtor   _____
                                                          Joint Debtor (if joint case, both spouses must sign)

Part 2 - Declaration of Attorney:

I declare that, to the best of my knowledge, information, and belief, formed after an inquiry reasonable under the circumstances, that the petition and schedules are not being presented for any improper purpose; that the claims, defenses, and other legal con-tentions therein are warranted and are not frivolous; that the allegations and other factual contentions have, or will have, evidentiary support; and that the denials of factual contentions are warranted. I further certify that the debtor(s) signed this Declaration and authorized me to electronically file the petition and schedules, that I gave the debtor(s) a copy of the electronically filed petition and schedules, and that the petition and schedules identified in the attached Notice of Electronic Filing from the CM/ECF system fully and accurately reflect the information given to me by the debtor(s). I have complied with all other electronic filing requirements. I have informed the individual petitioner that [he and/or she] may proceed under chapter 7, 11, 12, or 13 of title 11 of the United States Code, and I have explained the relief available under each such chapter. This declaration is based upon all information of which I have knowledge.

Dated: _____

                                                          _____
                                                          Attorney for Debtor(s)

Attach the Notice of Electronic Filing as an Exhibit.

(FILE ORIGINAL WITH COURT. DO NOT FILE ELECTRONICALLY.)

EXHIBIT 14.2 ◆ *CM/ECF Requirements*

UNITED STATES BANKRUPTCY COURT
DISTRICT OF NEW HAMPSHIRE
Norris Cotton Federal Building
275 Chestnut Street
Manchester, NH 03101
(603) 222-2600

CM/ECF Hardware and Software Requirements

In order to use the Court's CM/ECF system, you will need the following computer hardware, software, and accounts:

- Personal computer running a standard platform (e.g., Windows 95, 98, 2000, NT, Macintosh)
- Word processing software for creating pleadings (e.g., Corel WordPerfect, Microsoft Word)
- Bankruptcy forms software for preparing petitions (optional but recommended)
- Adobe Acrobat 4.0 (or higher), which includes both the Acrobat Reader for reading documents in portable document format (pdf) and Acrobat PDF Writer/Distiller for converting documents into portable document format (pdf)
- Internet Service Provider for accessing the internet, using Netscape Navigator 4.7 (or higher) or Internet Explorer 5.x, and for sending and receiving e-mail
- PACER account with PACER login and password
- Document scanner and optical character reader (ocr) software that converts to portable document format (pdf)

You will also need the following skills:

- Ability to access the Internet, specifically the Court's CM/ECF system
- Ability to perform the following functions using an internet browser:
  - Use the Forward and Back buttons
  - Set up bookmarks
  - Click on check boxes using a mouse
  - Type in text boxes
  - Download files
  - Print documents
  - Set home page addresses
  - Use hyperlinks
  - Attach a file within a web browser
- Ability to read a document in portable document format (pdf) using Adobe Acrobat Reader
- Ability to convert a word processing document into portable document format (pdf) using Adobe Acrobat Writer (requires the full Adobe Acrobat program)
- Ability to scan a document into portable document format (pdf)
- Ability to utilize an internet e-mail system to send and receive messages from outside of your office
- Ability to attach files to an e-mail message

in a bankruptcy. In New Hampshire, the System is run from a secure web server, and every effort is made to ensure that all transactions are handled securely.

Identity theft is increasing on an almost daily basis. An identity thief may take out credit cards in someone else's name, often destroying that person's credit. The essential bit of information that an identity thief uses is the victim's social security number. Because social security numbers of numerous parties may be part of any bankruptcy filing, every possible step must be taken to eliminate, or at the least, reduce as much as possible, the chance of the System's being accessed by a computer hacker.

While no system is foolproof, all possible steps are taken to ensure the integrity of the System. Although New Hampshire has a secure site that uses effective firewalls, the paralegal should be proactive and do more than simply rely on the integrity of the System to protect his or her client's confidentiality. A law office without adequate security procedures compromises the security of the System and its own clients. The paralegal should make it his or her responsibility to check with the bankruptcy court to make sure that the law firm is taking every possible step at its end to ensure the integrity of the System.

FUTURE ROLE OF PARALEGALS

The advent of CM/ECF is good news for paralegals. While large firms may have information technology departments, in most small firms, it is the paralegal who is responsible for keeping the computer system up and running. The paralegal will usually have the greatest understanding of the office computer system and will often be the contact person between the firm and the bankruptcy court. Paralegals, therefore, find themselves playing an ever greater role in coordinating communications between their firm and the bankruptcy court to ensure that the electronic filing proceeds smoothly.

ETHICAL CONSIDERATIONS

Just as electronic filing opens up beneficial new horizons, this new procedure also creates its own ethical concerns. Paralegals must be very careful when dealing with e-mail communications from the court. Many of us have experienced a sense of panic when we realize that, with the click of a mouse, we have forwarded an e-mail to someone who should not have seen it. While it is critical that any document be directed to the right person, it is especially important when dealing with documents that contain social security numbers and other such information.

It is also important that e-mails from the court concerning the case cannot be read by those with occasional access to our computer system, such as computer repairpersons who may be called in to work on the system. Paralegals should get into the habit of printing out for the file all messages that pertain to a particular case, and then deleting these messages. However, this only deals with the risk of accidental viewing. A deleted file can be retrieved, and the only sure way of protecting the confidentiality of computer records is through a document encryption system.

Paralegals must also be alert to the issue of billing clients for time spent on the PACER system. If a paralegal accesses the system by entering a client's client code, and then, without thinking, proceeds to obtain necessary information on another client's case, the potential for inaccurate billing exists. Paralegals must remember that it is unethical to bill one client for work done for another client. Care must be taken to use the PACER system in such a way as to ensure accurate client billing. For example, Helen has accessed the PACER system using John Smith's client code. After two minutes, she is ready to log off. As she is about to, her supervising attorney sticks her head into Helen's office and requests information on client Mary Jones. Helen, while still on PACER using Smith's client code, immediately starts to research the information needed on Jones's case. When she exits the PACER system, Helen forgets to note the split time. John Smith, in this instance, will probably end up paying for the research done on Mary Jones' case. This is clearly unacceptable, and it must be avoided.

While the new world of electronic case filing does raise some ethical concerns involving privacy and client billing, it also opens up a new world of opportunity for the bankruptcy paralegal.

SUMMARY

With the advent of electronic filing, bankruptcy courts have moved into the 21st century. Supported by an ever-growing number of bankruptcy courts, CM/ECF—the computer-based electronic case management and filing system allows attorneys and/or paralegals who are trained and certified by the bankruptcy court to file new bankruptcy cases and selected other documents from their computer. CM/ECF supports both Windows PCs and the Mac. Many bankruptcy courts provide custom-designed training programs that include hands-on training. While security and privacy issues are a concern for all users, electronic filing opens up new opportunities for paralegals.

✦ KEY TERMS

CM/ECF   PACER

✦ IMPROVE YOUR UNDERSTANDING

1. What is the CM/ECF?
2. What is PACER?
3. What is required to file a bankruptcy claim electronically?
4. What training is required by the bankruptcy court prior to an attorney or paralegal using the system?
5. What computer hardware and software is required for electronic filing?
6. What ethical problems must be considered when filing electronically?
7. How does electronic case filing potentially expand the role of paralegals?

✦ RESEARCH PROJECT

1. What requirements has your local district bankruptcy court set regarding electronic filing, and training on the CM/ECF system?
2. How many bankruptcy courts are currently accepting cases electronically?

Glossary

abandonment The release by the bankruptcy trustee or debtor in possession of the estate's rights in property.

abstention The refusal of a court to hear and rule with respect to a particular case or proceeding despite the fact that it has jurisdiction to do so.

adequate information Information in sufficient detail that would enable a hypothetical reasonable investor to make an informed decision whether to vote for or against a plan of reorganization.

adequate protection Property, lien, conduct, or other asset or act that is sufficient to ensure that a creditor with an interest in property to be used, sold, or leased by the estate will not be disadvantaged.

administrative claim A claim incurred after the commencement of the bankruptcy case that is a reasonable and necessary expense of the estate.

adversary proceeding Litigation in the bankruptcy court that is commenced by the filing of a complaint.

affiliate An entity that owns 20 percent or more of the debtor's stock, a corporation 20 percent or more of whose stock is owned by the debtor, a person whose business or property is operated by the debtor, or an entity that operates the debtor's business or property.

affirmative defenses Procedural or substantive claims that a defendant may use to defeat the claims made by the plaintiff in a complaint.

answer The pleading filed by a defendant that admits or denies the allegations in a complaint and asserts any affirmative defenses.

antideficiency laws Legislation that prevents a secured creditor from recovering its deficiency (the difference between what is owed and what is received in the liquidation of its collateral) from the debtor.

assignee for the benefit of creditors The person who acts like a bankruptcy trustee in an assignment for the benefit of creditors.

assignment The transfer of property, rights in property, or money to another person.

assignment for the benefit of creditors A nonbankruptcy proceeding that is similar to a Chapter 7 case, in which the debtor turns over all of its nonexempt property to a third party for liquidation and distribution of the proceeds to creditors.

assignment of rents An agreement between a lender and a borrower that provides that the rental proceeds from property will be paid to the lender.

assumption The means for the estate to bind itself to an executory contract or unexpired lease of the debtor.

attachment The process of making a security interest enforceable. Unless explicit agreement postpones the time of attachment, it occurs when: (a) secured party pursuant to agreement possesses collateral, or debtor has signed a security agreement describing collateral; (b) value has been given; (c) debtor has rights in the collateral.

automatic stay The injunction that becomes effective upon the filing of a bankruptcy petition (whether voluntarily or involuntarily) and that prevents virtually all actions by creditors to collect their claims, enforce their liens, or exercise control over the debtor's property.

balance sheet insolvency When the amount of liabilities on an entity's balance sheet exceeds the value of the assets on the balance sheet.

ballot The document submitted by holders of impaired claims or interests accepting or rejecting a Chapter 11 plan of reorganization.

bankruptcy An organized system for creditor payment from a debtor's nonexempt assets.

Bankruptcy Act The bankruptcy law enacted by Congress in 1898 that was substantially amended in 1938 and repealed in 1978.

Bankruptcy Code The bankruptcy law enacted by Congress that became effective on October 1, 1978, as it has been subsequently amended, and that is found in Title 11 of the United States Code.

bankruptcy courts The branch of the federal judicial system that presides over bankruptcy cases and proceedings. Bankruptcy courts are units of the district court.

Bankruptcy Petition Preparer A person regulated and defined by Section 110 as a person, other than an attorney or an employee of an attorney, who prepares a petition or other document filed by a debtor in bankruptcy case for money.

Bankruptcy Rules The rules of practice and procedure governing bankruptcy cases and proceedings drafted by the Judicial Conference of the United States and adopted by the Supreme Court.

Bluebook The common name for *A Uniform System of Citation,* the standard most often used for proper citation format.

book value The value of an asset as carried in the owner's books and records. Typically, cost less accumulated depreciation.

bulk transfer   Any transfer of a major part of the transferor's materials, supplies, merchandise, or other inventory not made in the ordinary course of the transferor's business.

buyer in the ordinary course of business   A buyer in good faith who buys goods from a person in the business of selling goods of that kind and without knowledge that the sale is in violation of the security interests of others.

cash collateral   Property of the estate that is cash, negotiable instruments, deposit accounts, and other cash equivalents in which a creditor has an interest.

chain of title   A list of successive transfers of real property arranged consecutively, from the government or original source of title down to the present holder.

chattel paper   A document that shows both a debt and the fact that the debt is secured by specific personal property.

cite checking   The process of reviewing legal writing to ensure that all cases have not been reversed or modified, are correctly cited, and that all quotations are accurate.

claim   A right to payment from the debtor, whether or not such right is liquidated, contingent, disputed, or secured.

claims register   A list prepared by the clerk of the bankruptcy court of all proofs of claim filed in the bankruptcy case.

CM/ECF   An acronym for Case Management/Electronic Case Filing. This is the federal judiciary's electronic case filing system.

collateral   Property subject to a security interest.

comity   A willingness to do something official, not as a matter of right, but out of goodwill and tradition.

commercial transaction   A phrase used to designate dealings of persons engaged in business.

complaint   The first main pleading filed in a civil lawsuit. It includes, among other things, a request for specific help from the court and an explanation as to why the court has the power to do what the plaintiff wants.

conclusions of law   Arguments or answers arrived at not only by drawing a conclusion from facts, but also by applying the law to the facts.

consequential damages   Damages that do not flow directly and immediately from the wrongful act of the party but only from the consequences or results of such act.

contested matter   An action in the bankruptcy court seeking relief that is commenced by the filing of a motion.

contingent claim   A debt for which liability is dependent on a future event that may or may not occur.

conversion   The voluntary or involuntary transfer of a bankruptcy case from one chapter of the Bankruptcy Code to a different chapter.

core matters   Those matters directly tied to a bankruptcy case and arising under the Bankruptcy Code.

core proceeding   Those matters directly concerning the bankruptcy case and arising under the Bankruptcy Code.

cram down   The approval of a plan of reorganization over the objection or negative votes of creditors.

creditors' committee   A committee composed of two or more of the debtor's creditors appointed in a Chapter 11 case by the United States trustee for the purpose of representing the creditors' interests in the case.

cross-collateralization   The securing of prepetition claims with assets acquired postpetition or the securing of postpetition claims with prepetition assets.

debtor in possession   A debtor in a case under Chapters 9 and 13, a debtor in a case under Chapter 11 in which no trustee has been appointed, and a debtor in a case under Chapter 12 unless the standing trustee has been directed to take control of the debtor's farming operations.

deed   A document conveying an interest in real property other than a leasehold estate.

deed of trust   A document used in many states that takes the place of a mortgage and by which legal title is placed in a trustee to secure repayment of a loan or performance of an obligation.

discharge   The release given to an individual debtor of the difference between the amount of a creditor's unsecured claims and the assets distributed to creditors in a bankruptcy case.

disclosure statement   The document containing adequate information that is distributed with a Chapter 11 plan of reorganization.

disposable income   A debtor's income that is not necessary for the payment of the reasonable living expenses of the debtor and his or her dependents, or if the debtor is engaged in business, the income that is not necessary for the payment of the expenses necessary for the continuation, preservation, and operation of the business.

disputed claim   A debt of which the debtor objects to the amount or allowability.

documents of title   A piece of paper normally accepted in business as proof of a right to hold goods.

domicile   The principal place of residence in which the debtor intends to remain.

earn-out   A plan of reorganization that provides for distributions to creditors to be made from the debtor's future income.

enabling loans   A loan made for the purpose of paying the purchase price of property.

entity   A person, estate, trust, governmental unit, or the United States trustee.

equity committee   A committee of equity security holders (e.g., stockholders, warrant holders, general or limited partnership interests) appointed in a Chapter 11 case by the United States trustee.

equity cushion   The excess of the value of property over the claims secured by that property.

examiner   A court-appointed investigator authorized to delve into the financial and business affairs of a debtor in possession in a Chapter 11 case.

excise tax   A tax on a transaction, event, or occurrence.

exclusivity period   In a Chapter 11 case, the period of time in which only the debtor may propose a plan of reorganization.

executory contract   An agreement between two parties in which sufficient performance remains on each side such that failure of one party to perform will excuse performance by the other.

exempt property   The property that a debtor is allowed to keep and not make subject to creditors' claims.

exemptions   Those interests in property that a debtor is allowed to keep and not make subject to creditors' claims.

ex parte   A Latin term used to describe an act done without notice to other parties.

face sheet filings   The commencement of a bankruptcy case by filing only the minimal amount of papers required, usually just the petition, and nothing more to obtain an automatic stay.

family farmer   An individual receiving more than 50 percent of income, and incurring debts not exceeding $1,500,000 from farming. Alternatively, a corporation or partnership where the majority of stock is held by one family and more than 80 percent of the corporation's assets relate to farming, and debts, arising from farming, do not exceed $1,500,000.

family farmer with regular income   A family farmer whose annual income is sufficiently stable and regular to allow it to make payments under a Chapter 12 plan.

fee simple absolute   An estate in property held by a person and his or her heirs and assigns forever and without limitation.

final report and account   The document filed by the trustee at the end of a Chapter 7 case that sets out the receipts, distributions, and allowed claims of the estate as well as any other relevant information.

financing statement   The document typically filed with the secretary of state that contains the name of the debtor, the name of the secured creditor, and a description of the collateral. It is used to perfect a secured interest for most types of collateral.

findings of fact   A decision by a fact finder (e.g., judge, jury, hearings officer) about a question of fact.

fixtures   Goods that are so related to a particular parcel of real estate that an interest in them arises under real estate law.

foreclosure   The enforcement of a security interest, mortgage, or deed of trust in which the secured creditor takes the collateral in partial or full satisfaction of the debt.

fraudulent conveyances   The transfer of the debtor's property with an actual intent to defraud creditors or for less than reasonably equivalent value while the debtor was insolvent or became insolvent as a result.

goods   All things that are movable or are fixtures, but not money, documents, instruments, accounts, chattel paper, general intangibles or minerals, or the like before extraction.

hardship discharge   The discharge granted to a Chapter 12 or 13 debtor who did not complete all plan payments but whose failure to do so was due to circumstances for which the debtor should not justly be held accountable.

headnotes   Summaries of points of law made in a judicial opinion. They generally precede the text of the opinion.

incidental damages   Damages incurred as a direct result of the breach of contract.

income tax   Any tax on or measured by gross receipts.

indenture trustee   A trustee appointed under a mortgage, deed or trust, or other document under which there is a debt against or interest in the debtor.

indispensable party   One who, in an adversary proceeding, must be a defendant in order for complete relief to be granted, or who has a significant interest in the subject of the action.

insider   For individual debtors, a relative, partnership in which the debtor is the general partner, or corporation in which the debtor is an officer, director, or otherwise in control. For partnership debtors, a general partner or its relative or person in control. For corporate debtors, a director, officer, or person in control, or a relative of an insider.

instruments   Items such as promissory notes, stocks, and bonds that evidence a right to the payment of money.

intangibles   Assets that are owned by an ongoing business such as goodwill, trademarks, copyrights, franchises, and the like.

interim compensation   Postpetition payments made to professionals employed at the expense of the estate prior to the end of the bankruptcy case.

interim fee application   The document filed with the court by which professionals seek interim compensation.

involuntary case   A bankruptcy case commenced by one or more creditors against a debtor.

***ipso facto* clauses**   Latin for "by the fact itself" or "by the mere fact that." A provision in a contract or lease that provides that the contract or lease is breached or terminated if one of the parties becomes insolvent or the subject of a bankruptcy case.

joint administration or administrative consolidation   The merger of two or more bankruptcy cases for the limited purpose of making their administration more convenient.

judicial foreclosure   An action to obtain a court order requiring the sheriff to hold an auction sale of collateral.

judicial lien   A lien obtained by judgment, levy, or another legal or equitable process or proceeding.

jurisdiction   The power of a court to preside over and decide a dispute between people or property.

land sale contract   An agreement whereby the seller of real property retains title to the property until the full purchase price is paid by the buyer.

lease   A contract for the use of land or buildings, but not for their ownership.

leasehold   An estate in real property held under a lease; an estate for a fixed term.

levy   The physical or constructive seizure of property in order to enforce a judgment.

life estate   An estate whose duration is limited to the life of the person or of some other person.

liquidating or pot plan   A plan of reorganization that provides for the sale or other disposition of all of the assets of the estate or distributes the proceeds of a previous sale or other disposition in the plan.

liquidation   A form of bankruptcy in which the debtor's nonexempt property is sold or otherwise disposed of and the proceeds are distributed to creditors.

mortgage   An agreement that creates or provides for a security interest in real property.

motion   A request that a judge make a ruling or take a particular action.

municipality   A political subdivision, public agency, or instrumentality of a state.

nondischargeable claims   Claims that will be enforceable against the debtor despite the discharge.

no-asset case   A bankruptcy case in which there are no assets to sell by the trustee. As a result, creditors do not receive a distribution.

no-asset report   A report filed by a Chapter 7 trustee upon determining that there are no assets to be administered by the trustee and no likelihood of a distribution to creditors.

opting-out   An option granted to the states allowing them to require their residents to use the state statutory exemptions rather than those in the Bankruptcy Code.

ordinary course of business   Transactions made by a business in its day-to-day operations.

PACER   An acronym for Public Access to Court Electronic Records, an electronic, public access service for the Federal courts.

perfection   The steps necessary under the Uniform Commercial Code or other law to make a lien effective against a third party and a bankruptcy trustee.

person   An individual, partnership, or corporation, but not a governmental unit unless it is acting as a receiver or liquidating agent of a person.

personal property   Property that consists of temporary or movable items.

petition   The paper filed with the bankruptcy court that commences a bankruptcy case.

petitioner   Another name for the debtor in a voluntary case.

plan exclusivity   The fact that for a period of time, only the debtor may propose a plan of reorganization.

plan of reorganization   A document filed in a reorganization case that divides the claims of creditors into classes and provides for their payment or other treatment.

plan proponent   The entity that proposes a plan of reorganization.

pocket parts   The method of updating bound compilations of decisions, statutes, or digests consisting of periodically issued paperback editions that are usually attached to the inside back cover of a bound volume.

postpetition transfers   A transfer made after the commencement of a bankruptcy case that may be avoidable.

precedent   A case or decision considered as authority for an identical or similar case or question of law arising later.

preferences   A transfer of the debtor's property to a creditor in satisfaction of an existing debt made during the 90 days (or one year if the transfer was made to an insider) before the bankruptcy case was commenced and which enables the creditor to receive more than other creditors.

priming lien   A new lien that is made senior in priority to existing liens.

priority claim   A type of claim that Congress has decided should receive special treatment. Priority claims must be paid in full before general unsecured creditors receive a distribution.

proof of claim   The form completed and filed by a creditor in order to protect its right to payment or performance in a bankruptcy case.

property tax   Tax imposed on the ownership or real or personal property based on the property's value, number, weight, or size.

purchase money security interest   A security interest to the extent that it is taken or retained by the seller of the collateral to secure all or part of its price, or taken by a person who gives value in order to enable the debtor to acquire the collateral if such value is in fact so used.

reaffirm   The act of agreeing to remain liable on a claim despite a discharge.

receiver   A person usually appointed by a state court in a nonbankruptcy case whose duties are similar to those of a bankruptcy trustee.

reclamation   The right of a person to seek to obtain possession of its property in the hands of the estate.

redemption   The payment to a secured party of the value of its collateral in exchange for the release of the security interest.

regular income   A source of income that is fairly stable whether earnings, pension or other retirement benefits, public assistance benefits, or dividends.

rejection   The means for the estate to rid itself of any ongoing obligations under an executory contract or unexpired lease of the debtor.

related matters   Disputes that would have existed between parties even if one of them was not in a bankruptcy case.

related proceeding Those matters concerning a bankruptcy case only because one of the parties to the dispute is a debtor in a bankruptcy case.

remand The return of a removed proceeding to the court in which it was originally commenced.

removal The transfer of an adversary proceeding from the court in which it was commenced to a different type of court.

reorganization A form of bankruptcy in which the debtor's business is preserved and its creditors are paid from the business' earnings.

revested debtor A debtor after confirmation of a plan of reorganization if the plan provides that title to the estate's assets will be vested in the debtor upon confirmation.

right of redemption The right to free property from a foreclosure or other judicial sale or recover the title that passed in a foreclosure by paying what is due.

rights evidenced by a writing Instruments, documents of title, and chattel paper.

schedules The document filed by a debtor that discloses all of its property and debts and other pertinent information.

secret liens A lien, usually created by statute, the existence of which cannot be discovered through a search of the applicable public records.

Section 341(a) meeting Meeting called by United States Trustee that debtor is required to attend in order to address any creditor questions.

secured creditor A person whose money is protected by a mortgage, lien, pledge, or other security interest.

secured party A lender, seller, or other person in whose favor there is a security interest.

secured transactions A phrase used to describe dealings involving the granting or taking of a security interest.

security agreement An agreement that creates or provides for a security interest.

security interest A lien created by an agreement.

setoff The application of a debt owed to a person against a debt owed from that same person.

shepardizing Determining the subsequent history of a case by use of *Shepard's Citations.*

stare decisis The policy of courts to abide by or adhere to precedent.

statement of financial affairs The document filed by a debtor that discloses all information not found in the schedules that a trustee would need to effectively administer the estate.

statutory liens A lien arising under a state or federal statute solely due to specified circumstances or conditions.

substantial abuse A Chapter 7 bankruptcy case of a debtor with primarily consumer debts that offends notions of the proper use of bankruptcy. Typically used to refer to a case in which the debtor could fund a Chapter 13 plan.

substantially contemporaneous exchange for new value A preference defense that destroys the creditor's liability if the antecedent debt was intentionally created at or about the same time as the otherwise preferential transfer was made.

substantive consolidation The merger of two or more entities, at least one of which is a debtor, into a single entity under a plan of reorganization or by motion.

summons A document issued by the clerk of the court when a complaint is filed that informs the defendant when it must answer or otherwise respond to the complaint.

surcharge The payment of administrative expenses from the proceeds of collateral because the expenses benefited the secured party.

trustee A person appointed to administer the bankruptcy estate. The nature and extent of a trustee's duties differ among Chapters 7, 11, 12, and 13 of the Bankruptcy Code.

turnover The act of delivering possession or control of property of the estate to the trustee.

unexpired lease A lease whose term has not been reached prior to its rejection or assumption.

Uniform Commercial Code A comprehensive set of laws adopted in whole or in part by every state on every major type of business law, including contract law as it applies to the sale of goods, banking law, and negotiable instruments law.

unliquidated claim A debt that has not been fixed as to amount.

venue Where, either geographically or among different types of courts, a case or proceeding is or may be pending.

wage earner reorganization Chapter 13 cases so designated under the misconception that only employed persons qualify for relief. The statute requires only a regular income that may come from a variety of sources.

Table of Statutes

Table of Rules and Forms

Bankruptcy Websites

General Bankruptcy Websites

AMERICAN BANKRUPTCY INSTITUTE
Provides a Bankruptcy Code FAQ, legislative news, and ABI publications relating to bankruptcy matters. Requires membership.
www.abiworld.org/

BANKRUPTCYDATA.COM - BANKRUPTCY COURT DIRECTORY
Directory of U.S. bankruptcy courts is organized by state and includes addresses and phone numbers.
www.bankruptcydata.com/Courts/Courts.htm

BANKRUPTCY LAW
A unique guide to world bankruptcy law with access to the United Nations website, the European Union website, and governments and laws worldwide.
www.hg.org/bankrpt.html

BANKRUPTCY LAWFINDER
View a directory of bankruptcy case law, statutes, regulations, and government resources.
www.agin.com/lawfind

BANKRUPTCY LAWYER - LAWINFO.COM
Search for a bankruptcy attorney in your area from this directory of lawyers, expert witnesses, and private investigators.
www.bankruptcylawyerdirectory.com/
lawinfo.com/

BANKRUPTCY LAW RESOURCE
Commercial site with overviews of Chapter 7, 11, and 13 bankruptcy laws. Link to download official bankruptcy court forms.
www.bankruptcy-software.com/

BANKRUPTCY STATISTICS
Bankruptcy filings in a variety of formats, from 1980 to the present. Includes business and nonbusiness filings, from ABI World.
www.abiworld.org/stats/newstatsfront.html

COLLAPSE OF ENRON: A BIBLIOGRAPHY OF ONLINE LEGAL, GOVERNMENT AND LEGISLATIVE RESOURCES
A bibliography of official documents relating to the bankruptcy and federal investigations of Enron.
www.llrx.com/features/enron.htm

FEDERAL RULES OF EVIDENCE
Rules governing proceedings in the courts of the United States and before United States bankruptcy judges and United States magistrate judges.
www.law.cornell.edu/rules/fre/overview.html

INSTITUTE STATE SURVEY OF IRA PROTECTION IN BANKRUPTCY
Provides a state-by-state summary of the tax treatment of IRAs in bankruptcy under state law.
www.ici.org/issues/ret/arc-leg/99_state_bankrupt_surv.html

LAWDOG - BANKRUPTCY CENTER

Explains bankruptcy laws, furnishes a dictionary, and offers links to bankruptcy courts organized by state.

www.lawdog.com/bankruptcy.htm

LEGAL INFORMATION INSTITUTE - BANKRUPTCY: AN OVERVIEW

Learn about bankruptcy law and procedures, including recent court decisions and extracts of the US Bankruptcy Code.

www.law.cornell.edu/topics/bankruptcy.html

NATIONAL BANKRUPTCY REVIEW COMMISSION

Independent commission established pursuant to the Bankruptcy Reform Act. Access fact sheets, news, reports, an archive, and links.

www.abiworld.org/legis/review/

NOLO PRESS - DEBT, CREDIT AND BANKRUPTCY

Read articles on using credit, debt-repaying strategies, student loans, debt collection, bankruptcy, and credit repair.

www.nolo.com/ChunkDC/DC.index.html

STEEL INDUSTRY BANKRUPTCIES, 1998-2002

Trace the history of the North American steel crisis with links to information on each major domestic steel producer filing for bankruptcy between 1998 and 2002.

www.steelnews.org/companies/steel_bankruptcies.htm

USALAW - BANKRUPTCY LAW

Get brief answers to questions about bankruptcy, including the types of bankruptcy and the procedures involved in declaring bankruptcy.

www.usalaw.com/bankrlaw.html

Bankruptcy Law Websites by State

Generally providing an overview of the process, filing procedure, list of exemptions, court directories, answers to frequently asked questions, and lists of attorneys. These sites are easy to find using any search engine.

Bankruptcy Court Websites

Individual bankruptcy courts may be found by accessing pacer.psc.uscourts.gov/lookup.html.

Index